Attention and Performance XVI

Attention and Performance

Attention and Performance XVI

Information Integration in Perception and Communication

edited by Toshio Inui and James L. McClelland

This book is based on the papers that were presented at the Sixteenth International Symposium on Attention and Performance held at Kyoto Research Park, Kyoto, Japan, July 11–15, 1994

A Bradford Book
The MIT Press
Cambridge, Massachusetts
London, England

This book was set in Palatino by Asco Trade Typesetting Ltd., Hong Kong and was printed and bound in the United States of America.

ISSN: 1047
ISBN: 0-262-09033-3

Contents

Preface

The Sixteenth Symposium of the International Association for the Study of Attention and Performance was held at Kyoto Research Park (Japan) on 11–15 July 1994. This is the first time the symposium has been held outside of the United States or Europe since it was inaugurated in the Netherlands in 1966. The general theme of this symposium was "information integration in perception and communication."

During the 1980s many higher brain functions were studied in detail. One important framing concept at that time was modularity—the idea that many functions are independently realized in specialized, autonomous modules. In Attention and Performance XVI we revisited this issue. While there is considerable evidence of specialization of function in the brain, there is at the same time ample reason to suppose that the outcome of processing across domains depends on the synthesis of a wide range of constraining influences. This symposium considered the process of integrating these influences in perception, attention, language comprehension, and motor control. We considered the mechanisms of information integration in the brain; we examined the status of the modularity hypothesis in light of efforts to understand how information integration can be successfully achieved; and we discussed information integration from the viewpoints of psychophysics, physiology, and computational theory.

The symposium grew out of our own interests in issues of information integration. The initial seed of the idea was sown in 1989, when the two editors made a weeklong lecture tour of various Japanese universities, institutes, and conferences on the occasion of the Japanese publication of *Parallel Distributed Processing*. During this week we exchanged ideas and established our common interests and perspectives. The detailed planning for the Kyoto meeting took place through later discussions with the executive committee of the Attention and Performance Association, with the benefit of input solicited from the advisory council of the association, which consists of approximately ninety-one experts in the field of attention and performance from over nineteen countries.

We were gratified by the quality of the papers presented at the symposium and by the enthusiastic reaction of the participants to the themes and questions addressed. The contributors represented a wide range of scientific disciplines and nationalities, but they all shared a deep interest in the issue of information integration. Each paper touched upon issues addressed by several other papers, both in the same topic area and in other areas. This supports our view that the issues and mechanisms of information integration are quite general, so that insights into information integration in, say, the domain of language may arise from studies of integration in other domains such as visual perception. In view of this, it should not be surprising that there was a very free flow of commentary and discussion between the participants in the different sessions of the symposium.

We hope this book captures the integrated nature of the conference itself; it contains all the papers presented at the symposium, together with an introduction by one of us and a retrospective summary by the other. Toshio Inui's introduction (chap. 1) reviews some of the background leading to the central issues of the conference and lays out five questions we hoped the speakers in the symposium would address. James McClelland's summary (chap. 24) provides an integrative overview of the conference, discussing the implications of the papers in terms of Inui's five questions plus a sixth posed by McClelland.

The chapters from the symposium itself begin with Anne Triesman's Association Lecture (coauthored with Brett DeSchepper), which summarizes several experiments that relate to the question of the limits of information integration in object perception outside of the focus of attention. This chapter is followed by those of section III, which address integration in perception of visual structure. These chapters challenge the modularist paradigm through theoretical and experimental analyses. Chapter 3, by Heinrich Bülthoff and Alan Yuille, offers a framework for information integration based on a Bayesian analysis of the optimal ways of combining information and a comparison of their Bayesian approach to other, more modular approaches. John Frisby, David Buckley, and Jonathan Freeman (chap. 4) provide compelling experimental evidence of interactions between sources of information in perception of visual structure, and John Hummel and Brian Stankiewicz (chap. 5) provide a detailed model for the integration of information about the global shape of an object and its various parts into a structural description.

Section IV considers the integration of information over successive fixations in vision, presenting evidence from psychophysics (David Irwin and Rachel Andrews, chap. 6) and neurophysiology (Carol Colby, chap. 7) on integration of object identity and spatial location information, respectively. The theme of information integration in the representation of space is continued in the chapters of section V. Michael Graziano and Charles Gross (chap. 8) consider physiological evidence that the brain maintains multiple spatial representations in several different frames of reference, including frames centered on particular body parts. Jon Driver and Peter Grossenbacher (chap. 9), Okihide Hikosaka and colleagues (chap. 10), and Lawrence Marks and Laura Armstrong (chap. 11) consider evidence of integration of information from vision, touch, and audition in the construction of representations of space.

Section VI ("Integration for Motor Control") begins with a chapter by Jean Roll and colleagues demonstrating how we combine proprioceptive information from joints to construct motor images (chap. 12). Their chapter also touches on the role this proprioceptive feedback plays in maintaining a representation of the location of objects in extrapersonal space. Chapter 13, by David Rosenbaum and colleagues, and chapter 14, by Mitsuo Kawato, both provide integrative computational models of aspects of information integration for motor control, complemented by detailed experimental investigations. Melvyn Goodale (chap. 15) considers neuropsychological evidence for a specialized system in the brain that represents actions in relation to objects in space. He points out how this system depends in certain cases on information from other systems specialized for representing what the objects are instead of how to act upon them.

Many of the themes and issues surrounding the idea of modularity were explored initially within the area of language knowledge and language processing. The five chapters on this topic in section VII ("Integration in Language") revisit these issues from the viewpoint of contemporary theoretical and experimental developments. Dominic Massaro (chap. 16) presents his overall framework for information integration, stressing how language perception exploits multiple sources of constraint both within and across modalities. Maryellen MacDonald (chap. 17) directly addresses the extent to which initial parsing decisions are encapulated products of an autonomous syntax module, rejecting this view in favor of an interactive perspective inspired by interactive, activation-based connectionist approaches. Chapter 18, by Michael Tanenhaus and colleagues, and chapter 19, by Gerry Altmann, present empirical and theoretical arguments in favor of the inseparability of language from the real-world context of objects and events. Tanenhaus and colleagues stress the joint influence of linguistic and external spatial information in lexical access, while Altmann considers how correlations between the structure of language, on the one hand, and the structure of objects and events in the world, on the other, influence language acquisition. Marta Kutas and Jonathan King (chap. 20) present evidence from evoked potential studies concerning the integration of information in lexical and syntactic processes in language comprehension.

Section VIII ("attention") begins with John Duncan's broad theoretical synthesis of computational, behavioral, and neurophysiological perspectives on the nature and allocation of attention (chap. 21). Duncan argues that attention is itself the product of a cooperative and competitive information integration process that takes place via bidirectional influences among systems of interconnected brain regions. Chapter 22 by Asher Cohen and Richard Ivry considers preattentive processing of motion and orientation, raising again the important themes touched on in the Association Lecture (chap. 2) concerning the extent of information processing outside of attention. Chapter 23, by Shinsuke Shimojo and colleagues, nicely completes the set of papers presented at the symposium by touching on the multiple determinants of spatial attention and on the interplay of attention, perception, and action.

Acknowledgments

We would like to thank, first of all, the contributors to this symposium and the other scientists around the world who have contributed to the study of integration of information over a span of many years. More than anything else, their contributions made the symposium possible.

We also thank the executive committee of the International Association for the Study of Attention and Performance (Max Coltheart, then president) and the members of the advisory council of the association for their assistance in planning the symposium. The members of the executive committee and the attendees of the symposium served as referees of the papers, and their thoughtful comments enhanced the quality and integration of the final product.

Special thanks are due to Sylvan Kornblum, secretary/treasurer of the executive committee, for his unflagging efforts on behalf of the association, his contributions to fund-raising and organization for this symposium, and his role in negotiations with MIT Press.

We gratefully acknowledge the following cosponsors of the symposium:

Toyobo Biotechnology Foundation

International Media Research Foundation

U.S. National Institutes of Health

Finally, we acknowledge the support and efforts of Dr. Yoichi Tohkura, president of ATR Human Information Processing Research Laboratories, without whom this symposium would not have been successful, and the many private Japanese electronics and medical companies that supported Attention and Performance XVI.

Participants

Alan Allport
Department of Experimental
Psychology
University of Oxford

Gerry T. M. Altmann
Laboratory of Experimental
Psychology
Sussex University

Heinrich H. Bülthoff
Max-Planck Institut für Biologische
Kybernetik

Asher Cohen
Department of Psychology
The Hebrew University

Carol L. Colby
Laboratory of Sensorimotor
Research
National Eye Institute
National Institutes of Health

Max Coltheart
Department of Psychology
School of Behavioural Sciences
Macquarie University

Jon Driver
Department of Experimental
Psychology
University of Cambridge

John Duncan
MRC–Applied Psychology Unit

John P. Frisby
AI Vision Research Unit
University of Sheffield

Jiro Giyoba
Department of Psychology
Kyushu University

Melvyn A. Goodale
Department of Psychology
Graduate Program in Neuroscience
University of Western Ontario

Daniel Gopher
Department of Psychology
Technion—Israel Institute of
Technology
Faculty of Medicine Sleep Lab

Michael S. A. Graziano
Department of Psychology
Princeton University

Okihide Hikosaka
Department of Physiology
Juntendo University School of
Medicine

Hitoshi Honda
Faculty of Humanities
Niigata University

John E. Hummel
Department of Psychology
University of California, Los
Angeles

Toshio Inui
Department of Psychology
Kyoto University

David E. Irwin
Department of Psychology
University of Illinois,
Urbana-Champaign

Mitsuo Kawato
ATR Human Information Processing
Research Laboratories

Steven W. Keele
Department of Psychology
University of Oregon

Sylvan Kornblum
Mental Health Research Institute
University of Michigan

Marta Kutas
Department of Cognitive
Neuroscience
University of California, San Diego

Maryellen C. MacDonald
Program in Neural, Informational,
and Behavioral Sciences
University of Southern California

Lawrence E. Marks
John B. Pierce Laboratory
Yale University

Dominic W. Massaro
Department of Psychology
University of California, Santa Cruz

Hiroshi Matsushima
Central Research Laboratories
Matsushita Electric Industrial Co., Ltd.

James L. McClelland
Department of Psychology
Carnegie Mellon University

Osamu Mimura
Department of Opthalmology
Hyogo College of Medicine

Toshiaki Miura
Faculty of Human Sciences
Osaka University

Nobuji Miyasaka
Fundamental Research Laboratories
Osaka Gas Co., Ltd.

Stephen Monsell
Department of Experimental
Psychology
University of Cambridge

Kazunari Nakane
NTT Project Inter Communication
Center

Ryohei Nakatsu
Information Science Research
Laboratory
NTT Basic Research Laboratories

Wolfgang Prinz
Max-Planck-Institute für
Psychologische Forschung

Jean P. Roll
Laboratoire de Neurobiologie
Humaine
Université de Provence

David A. Rosenbaum
Department of Psychology
Pennsylvania State University

Hirofumi Saito
Cognitive Informatics Unit
Graduate School of Human
Informatics
Nagoya University

Mark Seidenberg
Program in Neural, Informational,
and Behavioral Sciences
University of Southern California

Shinsuke Shimojo
Department of Psychology
University of Tokyo

Tadashi Shiomi
Communications Research
Laboratory
Ministry of Posts and
Telecommunications

Michael K. Tanenhaus
Department of Psychology
University of Rochester

Yoh'ichi Tohkura
ATR Human Information Processing
Research Laboratories

Anne Treisman
Department of Psychology
Princeton University

Carlo Umiltà
Dipartimento di Psicologia Generale
Università di Padova

Kazuhiko Yokosawa
Information Science Research
Laboratory
NTT Basic Research Laboratories

Group Photo

I Introduction

1 Mechanisms of Information Integration in the Brain

Toshio Inui

In the 1980s we saw rapid progress in studies of higher functions of the brain in many research fields, most notably in psychology and neurophysiology. The functions of different brain areas have been elucidated to a great extent. Now it has become important to ask, How is information integrated? As Marr (1982) suggested, it may be fruitful to examine the brain as an information-processing system at three distinct levels, namely, (1) computational theory, (2) representation and algorithm, and (3) implementation (as a neural network). At Attention and Performance XVI we discussed the issue of information integration at these three levels.

1.1 MODULARITY AND INFORMATION INTEGRATION

Marr's philosophy played a significant role in studies of the brain, especially in the study of vision during the 1980s (Marr 1982; Pentland 1986; Richards 1988). Here I will summarize some of the important points of his theory. First, he proposed that the major function of vision is to estimate the three-dimensional structure of the world from the two-dimensional image projected on the retina. Mathematically this is an ill-posed problem, and a general solution cannot be given in most cases. Marr suggested that a unique solution to this ill-posed problem could be given if physical laws were taken into consideration as constraints. It was later pointed out that this was conceptually equivalent to Tikhonov's method of standard regularization, a common method in solving inverse problems in mathematics (Poggio et al. 1985). With this realization, various computations in vision have been formulated in precise mathematical terms.

Second, Marr suggested that in early vision there were many modules and that estimation of surfaces from the retinal image was computed independently in each module. Bela Julesz's (1971, 1995) demonstrations with random-dot stereograms clearly implied the existence of the disparity module and the broader prospect that certain functions (and the modules that implement them) could be studied by psychological methods. Now generally called "shape-from-X" theory (where "X" represents binocular disparity, shading, texture, motion, or some other source of information relevant to shape determination), the computational theory of modules has generated a large body of research. Marr himself regarded the proposal of the $2\frac{1}{2}$-D sketch" as his most significant contribution (Marr 1982, 269). The $2\frac{1}{2}$-D sketch refers to the viewer-centered structural description of the surfaces visible to the viewer. Concerning the $2\frac{1}{2}$-D sketch, two problems arise:

1. How are the outputs from multiple modules integrated to yield a unique representation?

2. How is the retinocentric representation at lower levels transformed into the viewer-centered representation, that is, a representation in head coordinates or body coordinates?

If one retains Marr's general framework, these problems remain major issues for a thorough understanding of vision, and similar problems arise in other domains as well. Alternative approaches challenging the notion that the contributions of different information sources can be treated separately have also arisen in reaction to Marr's highly modular perspective; these must be considered in the context of efforts to understand the nature and process of information integration.

1.2 FEATURE INTEGRATION AND PSYCHOLOGICAL CONSIDERATIONS

Feature Integration and the Binding Problem

Another major development in a field of research separate from Marr's, the study of attention, was Treisman's "feature integration" (Treisman and Gelade 1980; Treisman and Schmidt 1982). Starting from Neisser's (1967) framework of preattentive and attentive processes, Treisman gave a novel answer to the old question, What is attention for? She suggested that attention was necessary in binding the different kinds of features processed in parallel in different visual modules. Combinatorial explosion, which would arise if individual neurons were tuned to combinations of features, could be avoided by using attention to integrate different kinds of features. With her experimental paradigm, Treisman has shown us how information integration in the brain can be studied by psychological methods; her work has inspired many studies elucidating dynamic aspects of information integration (e.g., Humphreys and Bruce 1989).

Ambiguity Resolution in Perception and Sentence Comprehension

Are there other types of information integration? Let us return to the problem of vision. A retinal image, $I(x, y)$, is determined by many factors. In a formal fashion, we may write:

$$I(x, y) = R \text{ (depth of surface, orientation of surface, vantage point,}$$
$$\text{position of light source, configuration of objects, } \dots)$$

Here R stands for the mapping function from three-dimensional structure to retinal image, and could be called "generalized optics" (Kawato, Hayakawa, and Inui 1993). We can decide on the values of all the variables on the right side of the equation from $I(x, y)$. For example, we perceive the structure of a surface from the variation of the light reflecting from the surface, which is what the perception of a monochromatic photograph is about. In this situation, if we know the position of the light source and the surface reflectance, we should be able to compute the structure of the surface. This is a problem of shape-from-shading. The structure of the surface, the position of the light source, and the reflectance of the surface are closely interrelated. If the shading of a part of the surface is very different from that of another part, how should it be interpreted? We may attribute it to variation in the structure of the surface, or in the reflectance of the surface, or in the light source itself.

As you can see from this example, it is necessary to determine the conditions of many factors in order to perceive the structure of a surface correctly. In a real situation, however, none of the factors is given beforehand, and it seems that a solution that satisfies all the factors at the same time without contradiction is required. In other words, if we take a different hypothesis about the position of the light source, perception of the structure will be altered (Ramachandran 1988). Furthermore, by changing the interpretation about the configuration around the surface, perception, that is, lightness, color, structure of the surface, and so on, changes even when we keep looking at the same surface (Gilchrist 1977, 1980). To put it differently, perception of the lightness and the color of a surface is affected by the context comprising various aspects of the environment of the surface. Different interpretations of the context give different computational solutions, and hence lead to different perceptions. In modeling the visual process, we have to consider it as a dynamic system of optimal inference based on information from various modules that process different aspects in the input. From the discussion so far, we can conclude the following. Information integration of multiple modules is required because a single module cannot give a unique solution without ambiguity. In other words, information integration is necessary for ambiguity resolution.

The same kind of problem may arise in sentence comprehension. Modular approaches have received a great deal of attention in the language-processing literature, both for syntax processing and for lexical access. However, it remains the case that most words have several meanings, and the meaning of a word in a particular sentence is determined by its context. Syntactic knowledge and semantic knowledge work together for correct understanding of sentences (St. John and McClelland 1990). Whether the initial computations are modular or not, an explicit understanding of how the different sources of information are ultimately combined remains an important open issue. The process of how the brain determines of word meaning has been studied experimentally by the method of "priming." Experiments have shown that facilitatory and inhibitory processes are at work in the determination of word meaning. Many of the experimental findings can be understood from the viewpoint of spreading activation processes as implemented in some connectionist models (Collins and Loftus 1975). On the other hand, relatively long-range effects of context have not been successfully modeled, although the effects have been demonstrated since the earliest research on word perception (e.g., Tulving, Mandler, and Baumal 1964). Waltz and Pollack's model (1985) based on microfeature appears very attractive, but its validity as a model of the brain is yet to be evaluated.

In sentence comprehension, just as in perception, information integration is necessary for ambiguity resolution. To better understand the process, it is necessary to elucidate the microstructure of the mechanisms of context effects. Is the process essentially modular at least in its early stages—with integration coming only through combining the outputs of separate, independent computations—or is it instead truly interactive?

Representation for Motor Control and Object Recognition

The $2\frac{1}{2}$-D sketch is a precise representation of a surface in terms of the depth and orientation. We may not need such a detailed representation in recognizing an object. The $2\frac{1}{2}$-D sketch can be considered as a representation of an object for motor control, such as manipulation and navigation while avoiding obstacles. Physiological studies have shown that the space relatively close to the body is represented in relation to the body itself, with the information from different modalities (e.g., from visual motion and tactile sensation; Leinonen, Hyvarinen, and Linnankoski 1979). As to the representation of such a space, how the information from different modalities is integrated becomes a problem.

On the other hand, Marr (1982) proposed a "3-D model representation" as the representation for recognition. A 3-D representation, by definition, includes the representation of invisible surfaces as well visible ones. In addition, this representation is not viewer-centered but object-centered and thus independent of vantage point. However, the hypothesis that this kind of representation is employed in the brain has been challenged by the results of recent psychological studies (Tarr and Pinker 1989). The most important observation is the existence of "mental rotation," which would appear to be unnecessary if 3-D model representation were employed. The discovery of neurons in the temporal lobe that respond to images of a face viewed from a specific direction (Perrett, Mistlin, and Chitty 1989) is also in conflict with the hypothesis. The results of these studies gave rise to a question of how a unique representation of an object is formed by integrating information from different views (multiview representation). In exploring the integration of multiple views, we should consider both approaches—3-D model representation and multiple-view representation—and evaluate their validity. The interaction between the representation for recognition and the representation for motor control is also an important question to be considered.

1.3   RESEARCH IN COMPUTATIONAL THEORY

Just around the time computations in visual processes were being formulated by way of standard regularization theory, other researchers were studying the problem of image restoration within the framework of stochastic theory. They showed that with weak assumptions it was possible to solve mathematically the problems of noise reduction in images and estimation of the original three-dimensional structure, using the method of Bayesian estimation (Geman and Geman 1984). In this framework the estimation is done by minimizing an appropriate cost function. Interestingly, the cost function in this approach is homologous to the one suggested by the standard regularization theory. Following this line of research, integration of output information of modules has been discussed in terms of Bayesian estimation (Clark and Yuille 1990; Inui 1994).

Workers in the field of artificial intelligence have adopted the Bayesian approach, and have applied it to consider how information from different modules might be combined. This actually raises challenges for more modular approaches. For one thing, true Bayesian estimation (to choose the most probable interpretation, given the outputs of all of the modules taken together) requires that each module output a probability for each of the possible interpretations of the input; it will not work if each module simply averages the best of its interpretations considered separately, or even if it selects the one with the highest independent likelihood. In any case, Bayes's estimation has become a normative theory of information integration, and ongoing explorations of the integration of information often exploit this approach.

1.4   SUGGESTIONS FOR IMPLEMENTATION OF INFORMATION INTEGRATION

Since the 1980s, with the rapid progress in the study of anatomy and physiology of higher visual areas, the structure and function of the brain have been clarified to a great extent (Zeki 1993). The visual area is divided into about thirty subareas. Many of the connections between those areas are also being identified. Some of the important characteristics of this system are as follows:

1. The mechanism of information processing is neither completely parallel nor simply hierarchical. It may be called a "parallel-hierarchical structure."

2. There are different modules for different aspects of visual input. Along a single pathway the information is processed in a hierarchical fashion. For example, information about color is processed through the pathway; blob in V1 → thin stripe of V2 → V4 (e.g., Van Essen et al., 1990).

3. Connections between cortical areas are bidirectional. If there is a pathway from area A to area B, there is almost always a pathway going directly from area B to area A (Zeki and Shipp 1988).

Several computational theories have exploited bidirectional connections in models of information integration. Interactive models in perception and language processing (as discussed in the Attention and Performance papers of Rumelhart 1977 and McClelland 1987) use such connections to allow information from multiple sources to be combined in a mutual constraint satisfaction process. Taking a slightly different approach, Kawato, Hayakawa, and Inui (1993) demonstrated that, theoretically, fast and accurate visual computation can be realized by utilizing the bidirectional connections. According to their theory, forward connections perform approximate inverse optics, while backward connections perform optics. In other words, hypothesis generation is carried out bottom-up and hypothesis verification top-down, and by repeating this interactive process, the accurate solution is attained in a very short time. Inui (1992) also suggested the following as possible functions of the bidirectional connections: (1) optics and approximate inverse optics, (2) consistency maintenance between modules, (3) selective attention through backward connections, and (4) image acquisition and recall.

By noting that some backward connections are made to areas from which no forward connections are made, Zeki and Shipp (1989a,b) suggested that these backward connections support information integration, and proposed the "reentry hypothesis." For example, in the forward connections from V2, the signals are clearly separated in two pathways: V2-thin stripe (color and form) → V4; and V2-thick stripe (stereo and motion) → V5 (also called "MT"). But the backward connections, V5 → V2, not only project to thick stripe but also to thin stripe of V2 (reentry). Zeki and Shipp (1989a,b) suggested that the information of shape and movement is integrated through these connections.

Information integration is not likely to be separate from other aspects of vision. In particular, it seems that information integration should be accompanied by coordinate transformation. On this topic, an interesting result has been reported about the characteristics of the receptive fields of the neurons in the parietal association cortex. The receptive field of a neuron in the parietal association cortex is fixed in the retinal coordinates, but the response to stimuli presented within the receptive field is modulated by gaze direction at the moment (Andersen et al. 1985; Galletti and Battaglini 1989). From their neural network simulation, Zipser and Andersen (1988) suggested that these neuron populations transform the representation from the retinotopic coordinates to head coordinates.

1.5 FIVE QUESTIONS FOR INFORMATION INTEGRATION IN PERCEPTION AND COMMUNICATIONS

With these developments as background, James McClelland and I posed the following questions to the speakers of the Attention and Performance XVI symposium and asked that they organize their talks in terms of them.

General Questions

1. Are there supramodel representations for integration across modalities, or is integration merely mutual constraint between modality or dimension-specific representation?

2. Are there dimensions that provide a strong organizing frame for integration? Are time and space examples of such dimensions?

3. Are there common principles of integration that span domains in which integration is necessary?

4. How do constraints propagate efficiently for integration of information?

5. What are the limitations on the integration of information? Are there impenetrable modules in the cognitive system, and if so, what are their boundaries?

More Specific Questions

Integration within Modality   There are several modules in the sensory system. How are their outputs integrated into one percept within modality? In vision how are the results of computation from different cues integrated into one representation? In auditory perception how is the information extracted serially (in time) integrated into one percept? Does integration occur at abstract representational levels, or at lower levels, or both? Is there feedback from higher levels to lower levels, or are there direct integrations between representations of different attributes?

How are the attributes for one individual object integrated, and how are false integrations across objects avoided? Every object has attributes (shape, color, texture, depth, motion, spatial location); some researchers claim that attention is needed to bind these different attributes. Are there phenomena of binding without attention? How are binding processes implemented in the brain? How are the activities of each area or module related to each other? Essentially, the image of the object is multimodal. Is there any abstract representation of the object or not?

Integration for Representing Space   Is there an abstract representation for space? Or are there different representations for each modality? How do the outputs from different modalities interact each other?

Integration for Motor Control   We can operate tools and manipulate various things; we can walk, avoiding obstacles. How is this accomplished? How are visual information and motor commands integrated in the brain? One proposals is that the representation used for motor control is something like Marr's $2\frac{1}{2}$-D sketch. If so, how is the $2\frac{1}{2}$-D sketch related to motor commands? Motor control and sensory processing must be tightly related to each other. The results of motor control are fed back to the sensory system through proprioceptive, haptic, and visual channels. How is the image of the object constructed through these cycles? How does the motor system constrain motion in real time?

Neuropsychological Approaches   Neuropsychological evidence relevant to issues of integration comes from neuropsychological studies in which various forms of failure of integration occur. All the questions posed earlier can arise, depending on the details of the cases considered. General issues of the interpretation of apparent failures of integration will be considered as well. Do these necessarily reflect a disconnection of modular parts of the cognitive system, or might they have other explanations?

Integration in Language Processing   How are different sources of information combined in recognizing units at different levels of information combined in recognizing units at different levels of language analysis? Does integration occur via a feedforward process or are mutual constraints propagated bidirectionally? Does the cognitive system actually compute several different representations (phonological, orthographic, semantic/word; syntactic, schematic/concept), or are some of these representations merely embedded parts of others? Do multiple representations maintain each other via resonance and mutual support? How do "right context effects" (i.e., influences of subsequent information on integration of prior information) get handled in a sequential processing system?

REFERENCES

Andersen, R. A., Essick, G. K., and Siegel, R. M. (1985). Encoding of spatial location by posterior parietal neurons. *Science, 230,* 456–458.

Clark, J. J., and Yuille, A. L. (1990). *Data fusion for sensory information processing systems.* Norwell, MA: Kluwer.

Collins, A. M., and Loftus, E. F. (1975). A spreading activation theory of semantic processing. *Psychological Review, 82,* 407–428.

Galletti, C., and Battaglini, P. P. (1989). Gaze-dependent visual neurons in area V3A of monkey prestriate cortex. *Journal of Neuroscience, 9,* 1112–1125.

Geman, S., and Geman, D. (1984). Stochastic relaxation, Gibbs distributions, and the Bayesian restoration of images. *IEEE Transactions on Pattern Analysis and Machine Intelligence, 6,* 721–741.

Gilchrist, A. (1977). Perceived lightness depends on perceived spatial arrangement. *Science, 195,* 185–187.

Gilchrist, A. (1980). When does perceived lightness depend on perceived spatial arrangement? *Perception and Psychophysics, 28,* 527–538.

Humphreys, G. W., and Bruce, V. (1989). *Visual cognition: Computational, experimental, and neuropsychological perspectives.* Hillsdale, NJ: Erlbaum.

Inui, T. (1992). Computational considerations on the possible functions of the backward connections between brain modules. In *Proceedings of the 1st Asian Conference in Psychology,* 181–182.

Inui, T. (1994). Visual reconstruction in the human modular systems. In T. Ishiguro (Ed.), *Cognitive processing for vision and voice,* 27–33. Philadelphia: Society for Industrial and Applied Mathematics.

Julesz, B. (1971). *Foundations of cyclopean perception.* Chicago: University of Chicago Press.

Julesz, B. (1995). *Dialogues on perception.* Cambridge, MA: MIT Press.

Kawato, M., Hayakawa, H., and Inui, T. (1993). A forward-inverse optics model of reciprocal connections between visual cortical areas. *Network, 4,* 415–422.

Leinonen, L., Hyvarinen, G., and Linnankoski, I. (1979). Functional properties of neurons in lateral part of associative area 7 in awake monkeys. *Experimental Brain Research, 34,* 299–320.

Marr, D. (1982). *VISION: A computational investigation into the human representation and processing of visual information.* New York: W. H. Freeman.

McClelland, J. L. (1987). The case for interactionism in language processing. In M. Coltheart (Ed.), *Attention and performance XII,* 1–36. London: Erlbaum.

Neisser, U. (1967). *Cognitive psychology.* Englewood Cliffs, NJ: Prentice-Hall.

Pentland, A. P. (1986). Local Shading Analysis. In *A. P. Pentland (Ed.), From pixels to predicates,* 40–77. Norwood, NJ: Ablex Publishing Corporation.

Perrett, D. I., Mistlin, A. J., and Chitty, A. J. (1989) Visual neurons responsive to faces. *Trends in Neuroscience, 10,* 358–364.

Poggio, T., Torre, V., and Koch, C. (1985). Computational vision and regularization theory. *Nature, 317,* 314–319.

Ramachandran, V. S. (1988). Perceiving shape from shading. *Scientific American, 269,* 76–83.

Richards, W. (1988). *Natural computation.* Cambridge, MA: MIT Press.

Rumelhart, D. E. (1977). Toward an interactive model of reading. In S. Dornic (Ed.), *Attention and performance VI,* 573–603. Hillsdale, NJ: Erbaum.

St. John, M. F., and McClelland, J. L. (1990). Learning and applying contextual constraints in sentence comprehension. *Artificial Intelligence, 46,* 217–257.

Tarr, M., and Pinker, S. (1989). Mental rotation and orientation-dependence in shape recognition. *Cognitive Psychology, 21,* 233–282.

Treisman, A., and Schmidt, H. (1982). Illusory conjunctions in the perception of objects. *Cognitive Psychology, 14,* 107–141.

Treisman, A., and Gelade, G. (1980). A feature integration theory of attention. *Cognitive Psychology, 12,* 97–136.

Tulving, E., Mandler, G., and Baumal, R. (1964). Interaction of two sources of information in tachistoscopic word recognition. *Canadian Journal of Psychology, 18,* 62–71.

Van Essen, D. C., Felleman, D. J., DeYoe, E. A., Olavarria, J. and Knierim, J. (1990). Modular and hierarchical organization of extrastriate visual cortex in the macaque monkey. *Cold Spring Harbor Symposia on Quantitative Biology, 55*, 679–696.

Waltz, D. L., and Pollack, J. B. (1985). Massively parallel parsing: A strongly interactive model of natural language interpretation. *Cognitive Science, 9*, 51–74.

Zeki, S. (1993). *A vision of the brain.* Oxford: Blackwell Scientific.

Zeki, S., and Shipp, S. (1988). The functional logic of cortical connections. *Nature, 335*, 311–317.

Zeki, S., and Shipp, S. (1989a). The organization of connection between areas V5 and V2 in macaque monkey visual cortex. *European Journal of Neuroscience, 1*, 333–354.

Zeki, S., and Shipp, S. (1989b). Modular connections between areas V2 and V4 of macaque monkey visual cortex. *European Journal of Neuroscience, 1*, 494–506.

Zipser, D., and Andersen, R. (1988). A backpropagation-programmed network that simulates response properties of a subset of posterior parietal neurons. *Nature, 331*, 679–684.

II Association Lecture

2 Object Tokens, Attention, and Visual Memory

Anne Treisman and Brett DeSchepper

ABSTRACT

Attention is normally required to form representations of objects that can be consciously identified and remembered. In this chapter we explore the implicit memory representations that are formed for novel objects and events, seen without attention, without conscious processing, and without any contribution from prior knowledge. Using a negative priming paradigm, we found evidence for long-lasting memory traces formed in a single trial, independently of attention, of conscious recognition, and of repetition. These memory traces of novel unattended stimuli appear to last at full strength and specificity for delays of several days or weeks. For a majority of subjects, the traces interfere with subsequent attention to the same shape when it later becomes relevant, but for some subjects, they facilitate performance. The traces are stored at a level that precedes the allocation of a shared contour to the figure rather than the ground, and the interpretation of occlusion. The results suggest a surprising combination of plasticity and permanence in the visual system.

Research on selective attention has generally explored conscious perception and explicit memory in complex scenes with multiple objects. In this context, the feature integration or binding problem is important, and there is evidence suggesting that attention plays an important role in solving the problem (Treisman and Gelade 1980; Treisman 1988, 1993). More recently, however, researchers have also begun to explore perception and memory as measured *indirectly*, by priming tasks in much simpler displays with only two or three objects present. The data here suggest much fuller processing of unattended stimuli. In this chapter we report some new research using negative priming to explore the nature of the representations that are formed implicitly without attention in displays containing just two or three shapes. Although the data from the two different approaches seem initially to conflict, we think they can be reconciled, and we will end with a possible resolution.

The research we will describe is designed to probe the early, bottom-up registration of objects in conditions where conscious recognition and identification are ruled out. We do this (1) by using objects that are unfamiliar and thus have no preexisting representations; (2) by presenting them in conditions where attention and conscious processing are preempted by other objects. What kind of encoding does a novel object get under these conditions and what kind of memory trace, if any, does it lay down? Probably a great deal of vision takes this form, although we are aware only of the attended and actively constructed portion of the scenes we encounter. It should therefore be important to find out more about the fate of the information that "seeps in" around the consciously experienced segment. This should tell us something about what attention and conscious, active, top-down processing contribute to perception when they are available. Having established what representations are formed with neither kind of top-down contribution, we can explore the changes that result when we either allow attention and conscious processing, or use familiar objects with preexisting identities, or both.

2.1 OBJECT PERCEPTION: TYPES AND TOKENS

Object perception is usually assumed to be a process of reactivating stored structural descriptions through a matching process of some kind. We see a current stimulus as one of a known category—say an umbrella or a giraffe. But what happens the first time we perceive a new object? The perceptual matching models have difficulty accounting for our ability to see an unfamiliar stimulus and are therefore probably incomplete. In studying the perception of novel objects, we find it helpful to distinguish between visual types and visual tokens. By types, we mean the stored representations of familiar objects that are used in their identification and classification, as in the standard models of object recognition by perceptual matching. Tokens, on the other hand, represent particular instances, experienced on particular occasions and with specific, possibly arbitrary properties. The research we will describe is about tokens because the objects we used for the most part had no preexisting types.

The type-token distinction is also important in a number of other contexts. (1) We need some kind of temporary episodic representations to explain how we see even a familiar object in its current instantiation, its particular size, distance, angle of viewing, and with its current, possibly atypical properties —for example, a purple-spotted, three-legged giraffe. Temporary tokens are needed to bind the current set of properties together. (2) We need tokens to account for the ability to see more than one identical object at a time. (When we face a flock of sheep, we don't see one very big, or one intensely sheepish sheep.) (3) We also need tokens to maintain the perceptual unity and continuity of moving, changing objects in a dynamic display, as they move and change (Kahneman, Treisman, and Gibbs 1992), and to link different retinal images of the same object across saccades (see Irwin and Andrews, chap. 6, this volume). (4) The distinction between types and tokens helps to account for the phenomenon of repetition blindness, studied by Kanwisher (1987). Her subjects were asked to report a series of stimuli (words, pictures, or letters) presented rapidly in the same location. They did quite well on unrepeated items, up to rates of about 10 per second. However, if the series contained a repeated item, they were much less likely to see and report it (about 40 percent correct compared to 70 percent for unrepeated items). Kanwisher (1991) attributes repetition blindness to a difficulty in binding a single type to two different tokens at fast rates of presentation; she relates it to the converse difficulty in accurately binding two (feature) types to the same token, where failures may result in illusory conjunctions (Treisman and Schmidt 1982). (5) Finally, there is evidence from patients with associative agnosia that the ability to *identify* a familiar object can be lost independently of the ability to see it, draw it, and recognize different views as representing the same object (Warrington 1982). Conversely, amnesiac patients may lose the ability to recognize specific examplars while retaining the ability to classify them as members of a category (Knowlton and Squire 1993). Knowlton and Squire suggest that abstracted types and specific tokens may be stored in separate memory systems.

With this type-token distinction in mind, we can describe object perception, under normal conditions, as a process of setting up a token for a particular present stimulus and matching it to one or more stored types in order to identify it. If the object has never been seen before, the second step will fail, but the object does not thereby remain invisible. Our current interest is in exploring how a new token is set up, how later tokens of the same object are related to the first, and what role, if any, attention plays in the process.

Rock and Gutman (1981) showed their subjects pairs of overlapped nonsense shapes. They asked them to attend, for example, to the green ones, and to rate them for artistic merit. At the end of the series, they gave the subjects an unexpected recognition test for both the attended and the unattended shapes. Recognition was at chance for the unattended shapes, both on this delayed test and on a catch trial introduced immediately after the last pair in the series. There is no evidence here for the existence of either types or tokens of the unattended shapes. Rock and Gutman concluded (very sensibly) that attention is needed to set up representations of shape. Their conclusion also fits well with the evidence from search tasks and from studies of illusory conjunctions (Treisman, 1988, 1993), suggesting that attention is needed to form new token representations of individuated objects.

2.2 NEGATIVE PRIMING WITH NOVEL OBJECTS

Meanwhile, evidence was accumulating that some perceptual processing can occur and some memory representations can be formed implicitly, without attention or conscious awareness (e.g., Roediger 1990; Schacter 1987). Certain kinds of learning can be revealed by indirect measures, independently of whether the subjects can explicitly recall the relevant items. It seemed worth testing whether any perceptual traces of novel unattended objects would be revealed if we used an indirect means of probing for them.

We picked a negative priming paradigm to test this possibility, using novel shapes like those of Rock and Gutman (1981). Negative priming is shown when a stimulus that was irrelevant on one trial becomes the relevant stimulus on the next trial. The switch often results in a slower response than is made to a control stimulus not previously presented. It is as if the irrelevant stimulus had been suppressed to reduce any potential interference and the inhibition had lingered on into the next trial, making it harder to attend when it became the relevant object (Neill 1977).

Tipper (1985; Tipper and Cranston 1985) asked subjects to name one of two superimposed pictures as quickly as they could. For example, they might name the green picture of a kite and ignore the red picture of a trumpet presented with it. When the irrelevant red picture on one trial became the relevant green picture on the next, the naming latency was longer than for a new picture. This delay reveals an implicit memory trace for the picture shown on the preceding trial, even though subjects had no conscious recollection of having seen it. Tipper and Driver (1988) also showed that negative priming could be attached to a representation that carried only the generalized meaning or category of the object. For example, they found that inhibition in a classification task generalized from an unattended word naming one member of a category (e.g., the word "dog") to a subsequent attended picture of another member of the same category (e.g., a picture of a cat).

The results of Tipper and his colleagues are consistent with the view that attention acts late, on fully identified stimuli, to determine which will control the response; they appear to conflict with the conclusion by Rock and Gutman that attention is needed for any representation of shape to be formed. The tasks differed in two ways, however. Tipper and Driver used a small and highly familiar set of pictures or words, each presented repeatedly, in their experiment. These would therefore require relatively little perceptual analysis to activate the relevant nodes in the recognition network; a few disjunctive features might suffice. The two sets of experiments also differed in the measure of perceptual processing that was used. Whereas Rock and Gutman required explicit recognition of unattended shapes, Tipper used an implicit measure of processing—the negative priming effect of having previously ignored the currently relevant stimulus. A plausible account for Tipper's findings is that an unattended letter or picture automatically activates its type node in some kind of recognition network, whether symbolic or connectionist. These nodes are then inhibited, and the inhibition spreads to the other nodes to which they are linked by shared semantic category, making them harder to reactivate on the next trial. But if no such representations exist prior to the test presentation, would negative priming still be found? If so, would it be found on the very first presentation, reflecting the on-line establishment, without attention, of new tokens with no preexisting types?

Experiment 1

Our stimuli were overlapping outline nonsense shapes, subtending 3 or 4 degrees (see fig. 2.1) very similar to those used by Rock and Gutman (1981). They were hand-drawn by two research assistants, who tried to make them as

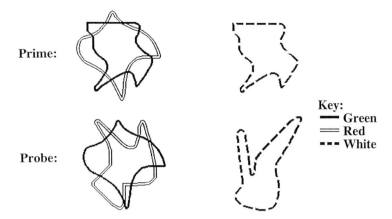

Prime:

Probe:

Key:
— Green
═ Red
••• White

Figure 2.1 Example of negative priming pair. Unattended red shape in prime trial becomes attended green shape in probe trial. Four combinations of "same" and "different" trials in prime and in probe ("same-same," "same-different," "different-same," and "different-different") were counterbalanced across trials in each condition.

distinctive as possible. Because nonsense shapes have no names, we used a same-different matching task instead of a naming task. Subjects decided as quickly as possible whether the green shape matched a separate white shape presented together with it, about 6.5 degrees to the right. The display remained present until the subject responded (a mean of around 700 ms). On trials testing negative priming, the unattended red shape on one trial would become the attended green one on the next. We call these "UA" trials. On control trials, two different shapes would appear. Figure 2.1 shows examples of a UA pair—a prime followed by a probe for negative priming. We used a set of 130 of these shapes. Figure 2.2 shows examples, ranging from the simplest to the most complex shapes we used.

The first question was whether we would get negative priming with these meaningless nonsense shapes. If so, would we get it only after subjects had had a chance to familiarize themselves with the shapes and to form types to represent them? In the first experiment, we compared negative priming for old familiarized shapes and for new shapes. We ran two blocks using only ten shapes repeatedly in both the attended and the unattended role, to familiarize subjects with them. These are the shapes we call "old." The "new" shapes were the other 120 shapes, each of which was tested once only for any given subject, or once as a prime and once as a probe. The particular shapes used in the different roles were counterbalanced across subjects in this and all the other experiments we will describe. In the third block we mixed in trials with new shapes paired with old shapes. Each new shape in a UA pair would be unattended in the first trial on which it appeared, and then switch to attended in the second trial. We compared response times on probe trials in UA pairs to control trials with an attended new shape that the subject had never seen before.

Figure 2.2 Examples of novel shapes used in experiments, to show range from simple to complex. Shapes we used were hand-drawn by two research assistants.

We found mean negative priming delays of 31 ms for the old shapes $(t(17) = 2.24; p < .05)$ and 55 ms for the new ones $(t(17) = 4.39; p < .001)$, which is significantly more, $(t(17) = 2.18; p < .05)$. Clearly the effect was at least as strong on trials where the shape had never been seen before. That it was actually stronger is an intriguing result, to which we will return later. These first results show that negative priming is not restricted to meaningful or namable stimuli, or even to previously familiarized nonsense shapes. In this experiment, negative priming cannot be due to inhibition of preexisting types in a recognition network. Even when novel unattended shapes are irrelevant to the task and compete for a response with the relevant shapes, subjects appear to form new and detailed traces of them, either as completed tokens or as fragments sufficiently detailed to differentiate one shape from the others in the set.

2.3 DELAY AND IMPLICIT MEMORY FOR NOVEL OBJECTS

Experiment 2

The next question we asked was, How long do the memory traces of new object tokens last? Are they temporary and evanescent traces of sensory activity that last until the next trial, but then either decay or are erased by a new display, or do they leave a more lasting record? We ran two experiments testing for negative priming after different numbers of intervening trials, still using new shapes, seen once only before being switched to the attended role. We increased the set of shapes used in these experiments to 270. Both experiments included lags of 1, 100, and 200 trials. To our surprise, we found no systematic loss in the size of the effect. There was at least as much negative priming after 200 intervening trials with a large set of 270 novel shapes as there was on the immediately succeeding trial at lag 1. The means for 37 subjects from two different experiments were 31, 28, and 32 ms for lags 1, 100, and 200, respectively (all significant at least at $p < .001$). Is this due to subjects remembering just a few highly distinctive shapes? We looked at the median reaction times and found almost as much effect as on the means. The means of the individual medians for the same subjects were 27, 20, and 31 ms, (all significant at least at $p < .01$). This rules out the possibility that the mean priming delay reflects selective memory for just a few of the most memorable shapes. The inhibition must be attached to at least half of the 270 shapes we tested.

We should mention, because it will be important later in the chapter, that there was considerable variability between subjects. The mean amount of priming (reaction times on probe trials minus reaction times on control trials) ranged in this experiment from $+185$ ms to -95 ms for particular subjects at particular lags. It was greater than zero at each lag in these two experiments for 30 or 31 out of 37 subjects and less than zero for 6 or 7 (depending on the lag). The variability increased in later experiments because we used only new and inexperienced subjects, most of whom had never taken part in any perceptual or reaction time experiment. We could not reuse our more experienced panel after they had seen the novel shapes in one experiment because we wanted to ensure that each shape was seen for the first time ever.

2.4 EXPLICIT MEMORY

Because our results differed so strikingly from those of Rock and Gutman (1981), who used an explicit recognition test, it seemed likely that we were measuring *implicit* memory—memory without awareness. To check on this assumption, at the end of each experiment, we gave subjects a catch trial in which they were shown a prime pair immediately followed by a recognition test with five shapes presented together on the same screen. Subjects were asked to pick which two they had seen in the immediately preceding display. They at chance for the unattended shape and slightly above chance for the attended shape. However, we worried that the surprise of this unexpected request might have obliterated an explicit memory that would otherwise have been present.

Experiment 3

We therefore ran an experiment in which we randomly mixed UA trials to test negative priming with explicit recognition trials. The lags in both cases averaged 88 trials (with a range from 72 to 104). On recognition trials, four shapes appeared and subjects had to pick which one they had seen before. Three were foils that had not been seen before and one had previously been presented, either in the attended or unattended role, or as one of the frequently presented old shapes. Negative priming at these lags averaged 54 ms and was again highly significant, but recognition was at chance (26 percent) for the unattended shapes. It was slightly but significantly better than chance (34 percent) for the attended ones that had been seen once only, and substantially better for the small set of old shapes that were seen several times each (70 percent). There seems, then, to be a clear dissociation between negative priming and recognition memory. Subjects have no consciously retrievable memory for the multitude of unattended shapes that apparently linger in their heads to prime or interfere with performance over these long periods of time.

Experiment 4

So when does this implicit memory disappear? Our brains could get very cluttered if they register everything, whether we attend to it or not. In the next experiment, we tested subjects after a delay of 24 hours, as well as at lag 1 on both days, using different counterbalanced sets of shapes at each delay. We did find negative priming after 24 hours—a mean of 20 ms, which was significant ($t(23) = 2.83, p < .01$). In fact, it did not differ from the 22 ms the same subjects showed in session 2 for negative priming from the immediately preceding trial.

This encouraged us to try testing another group of subjects, this time after a lag of one week as well as at lag 1 on both the first and final days. Here the negative priming was not significant after a week for the group as a whole, but it was not significant at lag 1 either. However, in this experiment the individual differences in priming seemed highly salient, and fairly consistent across conditions. A minority of subjects showed facilitation rather than inhibition at both lags and on both days. We therefore divided all the subjects into two groups on the basis of their priming in session 1 at lag 1; we then compared the results on different sets of shapes in session 2, separately for subjects who had shown facilitation in session 1 and for those who had shown inhibition. The results were now more impressive. The 18 people who showed negative priming in session 1 at lag 1 showed a mean delay of 14 ms ($t(17) = 2.45; p < .05$) on a different set of shapes one week later, and the 12 subjects who showed facilitation in session 1, lag 1, showed a much larger facilitation of −39 ms one week later ($t(11) = 4.45; p < .001$), which is significantly more than the −18 ms they showed on the same day for shapes tested at lag 1.

When we reanalyzed the results in the same way for the subjects tested after a day's delay, we found a similar separation, although fewer subjects in this group showed facilitation. The 18 subjects who showed negative priming above zero in session 1 at lag 1 showed negative priming of 35 ms after 24 hours ($t(17) = 6.39; p < .001$), and the 6 subjects who had shown facilitation in session 1 at lag 1 also showed -25 ms facilitation after 24 hours ($t(5) = 2.72; p < .05$). Finally, we tested another group of subjects a month after they had first seen the shapes. The results looked very similar to those we obtained after a week's delay. Again there was no significant negative priming for the group as a whole, but when we divided the subjects by their results in session 1, both the 14 ms inhibition and the -25 ms facilitation on different shapes a month later were significant ($t(18) = 2.67; p < .02$ and $t(12) = 2.29; p < .05$, respectively). To check on the consistency of the individual differences, we measured the correlation between priming on one set of shapes in UA trials at lag 1 in session 1 and priming on a different set of shapes in UA trials a day, a week or a month later. For the 86 subjects tested in these three versions of the experiment, $r = .508$ ($p < .001$).

Figure 2.3 summarizes the results on these long delays. It separates the subjects showing inhibition in session 1 from those showing facilitation. These results are for session 2 after a day, a week, or a month's delay. They show, for each group of subjects, the mean negative priming effects (a) for new shapes at lag 1, and (b) for shapes previously presented in the unattended role in session 1. The further the points are from the zero line in either direction, the more memory can be inferred. It is clear that many points differ significantly from zero after these long delays, showing surviving traces of a substantial number of novel shapes seen without attention, once only for about 700 ms (the mean reaction time). Overall, there is a shift toward more facilitation and less inhibition at the longer intervals, a shift that is significant over the groups as a whole ($F(2, 82) = 3.32; p < .05$).[1] There was no interaction between lag and the subgroups showing facilitation versus inhibition in session 1, lag 1.

The decreasing inhibition and increasing facilitation across the period of a month suggests that the inhibition may disappear independently of the memory for the shape, which stays intact across delays as long as a month; exposure to a novel object leaves in memory both a token representing its shape and (in conditions of potential response conflict) an "action tag" attached to the irrelevant token indicating that it is to be ignored. The trend in our data suggests that the tag disappears sooner than the shape itself.

What might account for the individual differences we found in negative priming? Tipper and Baylis (1987) found a negative correlation with the cognitive failures questionnaire (Broadbent et al. 1982). Some subjects might simply be better than others at suppressing unwanted stimuli. These subjects should show less interference when we compare performance on competing

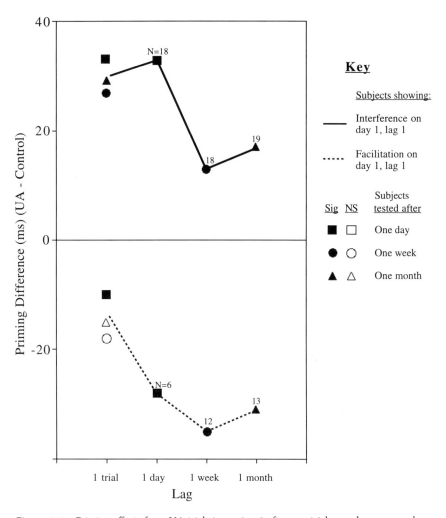

Figure 2.3 Priming effects from UA trials in session 2 after one trial, one day, one week, or one month, shown separately for subjects who had shown interference or facilitation in session 1 at lag 1. Baseline is given by latencies on control trials with new shapes not previously presented.

shapes with performance on a single shape. Another possibility is that there might be strategy differences in the way the task is performed. Some subjects may look first at the standard white shape and then compare that to the red and green composite to see if anything matches, without trying to suppress the irrelevant red shape; others may look first at the composite stimulus, suppressing the red and attending to the green shape, and then compare that to the white standard shape. This possibility could be tested by presenting the white shape either before or after the red and green ones. We are currently trying out these hypotheses to see if either can account for the different response patterns we found.

2.5 REPETITION EFFECTS

Memory is typically made more retrievable by multiple presentations. The substantially better recognition for old shapes than for new attended shapes in the preceding experiment shows that this holds for our stimuli as well, in the explicit recognition test. Can we also strengthen the implicit memory traces for unattended shapes, or the inhibition attached to them, by presenting them several times on the first day? In experiment 4, with lags of a day, a week and a month, we also gave subjects one set of unattended shapes four times each on successive trials on the first day, paired each time with a different attended shape. By looking at the reaction times to the different *attended* shapes on those four successive trials with the same unattended shape, we can see that the repetition of their unattended companion shapes did register—they became progressively easier to ignore. The reductions in latency relative to the mean on the first presentation were 3 ms (not significant), 14 ms ($t(85) = 3.82; p < .001$) and 22 ms ($t(85) = 6.76; p < .001$) for two, three, and four presentations of the same unattended shape. Note that repetition priming is further evidence that the unattended shape leaves a specific memory trace. There were no significant differences in the amount of repetition priming between the subjects showing negative and those showing positive priming when the unattended shape subsequently became the attended one.

Next we looked at whether repetition affected the amount of negative priming after a day, a week, or a month. The answer is "no, not at all." There was an average difference of only 2 ms, comparing shapes seen once and those seen four times in session 1, in the negative priming measured a day, a week, or a month later. This dissociation is puzzling. On the one hand, when the shape is repeated in the unattended role, it does get easier and easier to ignore. On the other hand, the negative priming measure suggests no change in the amount of inhibition attached to the repeated shapes. The reason may be that in negative priming two effects are canceling out: the repetition of a matching token facilitates its reperception, but the repetition of the conflicting action tag further slows the response on the probe trial.

If each trial sets up new tokens for the attended and the unattended shapes, a single act of attention might wipe out the negative priming associated with a previously unattended shape. In experiment 4, we retested the same groups of subjects on the same shapes in an identical block repeated immediately after the test at a day, week, or month's delay. The inhibition we saw in the first block of session 2 had indeed disappeared by the second. In the same experiments, we tested a set of shapes that were presented once unattended and once attended on two successive trials in session 1, and then attended again a day, a week, or a month later. The negative priming shown by the inhibition subjects in session 1 at lag 1 was absent when tested after a day, presumably cleared by the immediate probe in session 1. Surprisingly, however, it seems to return gradually and was significant again for the group who

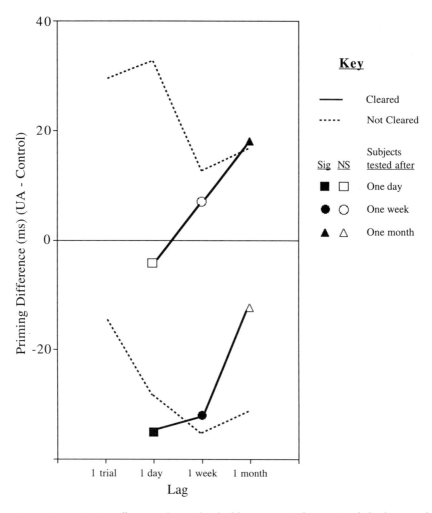

Figure 2.4 Priming effects on shapes that had been presented in unattended role, immediately followed by attended role in session 1 at lag 1. As in figure 2.3, data are shown separately for subjects who had shown interference or facilitation in session 1 at lag 1. Dotted line shows UA trials from figure 2.3, to compare shapes that had not previously been shown in attended role.

were tested after a month (fig. 2.4), although the between-group data were too noisy for the lag differences to reach significance. If the return of inhibition is real, we might explain it by the assumption that the initial token from the unattended presentation retains its original tag but is overshadowed by the new token while that is present. In subsequent trials, the two compete, each winning on some trials and canceling out the negative priming when the trials are averaged together. The apparent return of negative priming after a month may reflect a long-term advantage in memorability or retrievability for the first token ever formed for any given object.

2.6   PRIMING OF ATTENDED SHAPES

Early on, we pointed out that our paradigm eliminates two forms of top-down modulation that normally play a role in perception—focused attention and prior knowledge. We have preliminary data exploring the role of each separately. First we ask what happens to memory for the same shapes when they were originally seen *with* attention? Common sense might suggest that the memory traces should be stronger and more long-lasting. This is certainly the case for our nonsense shapes when we test explicit memory, as shown in the recognition test; it is also the case for immediate repetition priming. In a pilot experiment, we repeated the attended shape once, one trial later (an AA pair), and found facilitation of -35 ms ($t(19) = 3.68; p < .01$), whereas repeating the unattended shape once, one trial later (a UU pair), gave only -8 ms facilitation (not significant).

The difference might be due to a contribution from conscious recognition of the attended shape when it is immediately repeated. Would priming of attended shapes also be stronger and more lasting than priming of unattended shapes a day, a week, or a month later? In experiment 4, we also tested a set of shapes that were originally seen as the attended shapes in session 1 and then presented again as the attended shapes a day, a week, or a month later. Figure 2.5 shows the repetition priming for these AA pairs (with subjects sorted, as before, by the presence or absence of negative priming in session 1 at lag 1), together with those previously reported for the unattended shapes when they were switched to the attended role (UA pairs). In fact, the priming effects with attended shapes look very similar to those with the unattended shapes. Subjects who showed inhibition in session 1 on UA pairs show no facilitation on AA pairs when the attended shape is repeated a month later, even a little inhibition (although this is not significant). Subjects who showed facilitation in session 1 on UA pairs show facilitation in session 2 on AA pairs, of about the same magnitude as on session 2 UA pairs, certainly no more. Attention apparently makes no difference whatever to the persistence of the memory traces when we measure it by the priming effect an initial presentation has on reperception of the same shapes after a day, a week, or a month. Jacoby, Toth, and Yonelinas (1993) found a similar independence of attention in an implicit memory task, using Jacoby's process dissociation framework. Note that, like Jacoby's measure, the negative priming task separates intended from unintended effects because it generally takes the form of interference, opposing the efficient performance of the attended task.

2.7   MEANINGFUL STIMULI: WORDS

Experiment 5

Another way in which we normally invoke top-down processing is to use familiar, meaningful stimuli. We picked 270 random four-letter words (all

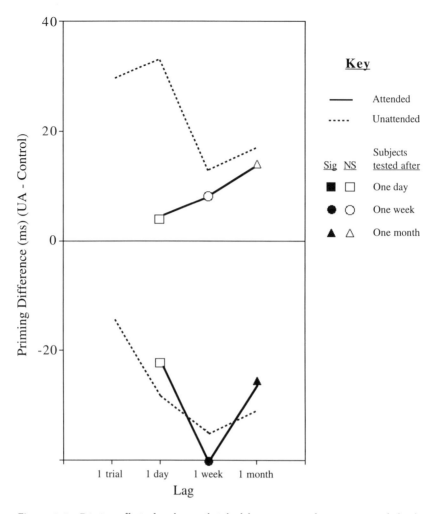

Figure 2.5 Priming effects for shapes that had been presented once in attended role in session 1. Again, data are shown separately for subjects who had shown interference or facilitation in session 1 at lag 1. Dotted line shows means on UA trials from figure 2.3, to compare priming from shapes that were presented in unattended role.

common nouns) and ran them after the novel shapes in experiment 2 with lags of 1, 100, and 200 trials.[2] The procedure was identical to the procedure we used with the novel shapes, except that, to ensure legibility, the words were not spatially overlapped. One was placed above the other at a center-to-center separation of 0.9 degree, with the attended green word equally often above or below the red one. The comparison word for the same-different judgment was presented in white, to the right of the pair, at a center-to-center separation of 6.3 degrees. As with the shapes, each of the new words was used once only, and they were paired with a small set of old words used as fillers. Table 2.1 shows the results. At lag 1 the negative priming seems to be the same for words and for novel shapes, although at

Table 2.1 Negative Priming with Words and Shapes: Lag Effects

	Lag 1	Lag 100	Lag 200
Shapes	31**	28**	32**
Words	30*	0	9

Note: Significance levels: $^*p < .05$; $^{**}p < .001$.

longer lags the results look different; the words lose their negative priming for most of the subjects.[3] It seems that priming disappears sooner for these familiar stimuli than it does for completely novel ones. We will come back to this after describing one more contrast between familiar and novel items.

2.8   FIGURE-GROUND STIMULI

In all the experiments so far, the attended and the unattended shapes have competed while remaining independent entities, with potentially equal perceptual status, except that one was selected to control the response. A different kind of competition might arise when one of two shapes has the status of figure and the other is seen only as the background. The "shape" of a background is typically not consciously represented in perceptual experience, not just because it is unattended but because its contour is allocated to the figure and given a different interpretation. For example, a curve must be seen as either convex or concave, and if it is convex in the figure, it will be concave in the background (or vice versa). This results in a completely different segmentation into parts, as shown by Hoffman and Richards (1985).

We thought that inhibition might be unnecessary, that the shape of the background would simply not be represented; it would not exist as such for the perceptual system. In the next experiment (in which we were joined by an undergraduate student, Anne Pugh), we tested this possibility.

Experiment 6

We used 120 different figure-ground pairs; figure 2.6 shows some examples. Again, 12 were used repeatedly and the others were used once only in a UA pair or as a control. Trials were organized in pairs, alternating a prime display and a probe display, or two equivalent but unrelated control pairs. The primes were figure-ground stimuli, and the probes were two separate figures (see fig. 2.7). Subjects attended and responded to the black figure in the figure-ground prime pair and the white one in the separated probe pair. The side on which the black figure was presented was randomized across pairs of trials but kept consistent within prime-probe pairs. Half the trials were UA trials in which the white probe was the same as the white background of an earlier prime pair, either one trial back or three trials back; the remaining half were control trials in which the white probe was a new shape. As in the previous experiments, subjects were asked to match the relevant shape to the

Figure 2.6 Examples of figure-ground stimuli used in negative priming experiment.

Prime   **Probe**

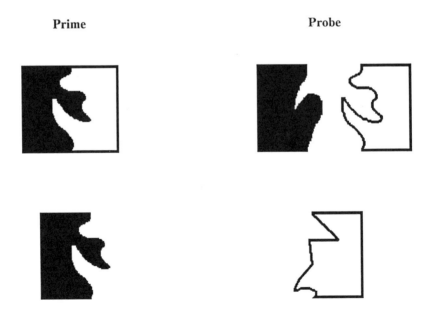

Figure 2.7 Example of prime-probe pair. Subjects matched black figure in prime to single black shape below, and white shape in probe to single white shape below. Shapes were presented on gray background, and there was no outline around white shapes.

single shape below (which always matched its color); the displays remained present until the subject responded. We also tested 15 of the subjects with a final catch trial of recognition and found that their performance on the background shape was at chance (3/15 correct = chance). Memory for the figure was slightly better than chance (6/15). Again, there seems to be no explicit memory whatever for the "shape" of the background.

With the new figures (those that were seen once only) we found significant negative priming when the background shape from the prime display became the attended figure in the UA probe. The negative priming averaged 26 ms at lag 1 ($t(29) = 2.97; p < .01$) and 34 ms at lag 3 ($t(29) = 2.22; p < .05$). It seems that negative priming in this paradigm is attached to representations formed at an early level, before the contour is interpreted as the boundary of the figure rather than of the ground. At this early level, the shared contour is attached both to a representation of the shape consciously seen as the figure, and also to a representation of the shape not seen at all because it is interpreted as the ground that continues behind the figure. Peterson and Gibson (1991) also found evidence that both interpretations of a shared contour are checked before one is selected to become the consciously perceived figure; in a task requiring report of the first interpretation made of a reversible figure-ground pair, their subjects reported meaningful figures earlier than meaningless figures. Thus selection for conscious access appears to follow a top-down match to stored representations of familiar objects. In our experiment, this match would fail, but both shapes seem nevertheless to be stored as new object tokens in memory.

2.9 ADVANTAGE FOR NOVEL ITEMS

An interesting result again appeared in this figure-ground experiment with the old stimuli—those that were used repeatedly. Negative priming at lag 1 was less for the old figures than for the new ones (a mean of 14 ms, which is significant only on a one-tailed test), and by lag 3 it had completely disappeared (a mean of −13 ms, not significant). Other researchers, also using small sets of familiar stimuli, have found that negative priming is typically quite evanescent, lasting at most a few seconds (e.g., Neill and Valdes, 1992; Tipper et al. 1991). Like the words in the previous experiment, a new presentation of a familiar pattern seems to leave only a very temporary trace, whereas a brand-new pattern leaves a lasting imprint.

Why this difference? We think it fits the account we have proposed, in terms of implicit memory tokens with action tags attached to them. Each time an object is presented, it sets up a new token. Familiar objects have already set up multiple tokens in memory, some that received attention and some that were ignored. When a familiar object is presented again and attended, it automatically retrieves one of its matching token traces (Logan 1990). If the object had just been presented in the unattended role (at lag 1), that token is the one that will most likely be retrieved, together with its attached "ignore" tag. However, the recency advantage in retrieval disappears almost immediately. If the object was seen two or more trials earlier, the new presentation is as likely to retrieve a token from an "attend" trial as one from an "ignore" trial. On the other hand, if an object has only ever been seen once, there will be no competition for retrieval when a matching object is presented again. Its unique token will be retrieved with whatever tag was attached on that one trial, however long ago it was presented. Words, of course, already have large numbers of tokens from the past, so a new token set up in the experiment would be unlikely to win out at retrieval after 100 or 200 intervening trials. Nor would the old shapes or the old figure-ground patterns that have already been seen repeatedly within the experimental session.

2.10 OCCLUSION IN NEGATIVE PRIMING

Experiment 7

The figure-ground experiment suggests that object tokens in negative priming are formed at quite an early stage, before the shared contour is allocated to the figure at the expense of the ground. In a related experiment, we looked for more evidence about the level of processing reached by the unattended shapes in negative priming. We showed pairs of shapes in which a red shape appeared to occlude a green shape (fig. 2.8). The question that interested us was whether the representation differs when subjects attend and when they do not attend to the occluded shape. Nakayama, Shimojo, and Silverman (1989) have suggested that occlusion is registered quite early in the visual system, on the basis of bottom-up cues like the presence of t-junctions. If this is the case, then even without attention subjects might store the completed version of the occluded shape, as if it continued behind the occluder. But if the representation of the unattended shape is confined to an earlier level of processing than the attended one, subjects might store simply the two-dimensional jigsaw pattern.

On prime trials in experiment 7A, the subject attended to the occluding red shape. On probe trials, as in the figure-ground experiment, the two shapes were separated, and the subject attended to the green. On half the UA trials the green shape in the probe was the jigsaw version of the apparently occluded green shape from the preceding trial, and on half it was the completed version (using a simple curve to join the points where the occluder interrupted the contour of the apparently occluded shape). Prime and probe trials alternated, as in the figure-ground experiment. We found negative priming only with the jigsaw version (12 ms, $t(30) = 2.21; p < .05$) There was none at all with the completed version (-2 ms). In contrast, in experiment 7B, another group of subjects attended to the occluded green shape instead of the occluding red shape in the prime trials, and again to the green shape in the probe trials (see fig. 2.9). These subjects showed facilitation (repetition priming) for the completed version (-17 ms, $t(23) = 2.53; p < .02$), but none

Prime

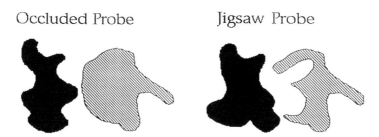

Occluded Probe   Jigsaw Probe

Figure 2.8 Examples of prime consisting of occluder and occluded shape, followed by two different probes. On prime trial subject decides whether green occluder matches white shape to right of display. On probe trial, previously occluded red shape is presented in green, either as completed shape or as jigsaw pattern made by previous occluding shape. Subject again decides whether green shape matches white shape presented to right.

for the jigsaw version. There was a negative correlation across subjects in both experiments between priming for the jigsaw and priming for the completed shape ($r(29) = -.334$, approaching significance, for the unattended shape, and $r(18) = -.604$; $p < .01$ for the attended shape). It seems that the stored token represents only one of the two interpretations of the occluded shape, and only this one has a priming effect. For the attended shape, the jigsaw probe actually showed some interference rather than facilitation ($+19$ ms), as if that interpretation had been suppressed when the shape was previously attended (although this interference did not reach significance). The dissociation between attended and unattended shapes again suggests that the unattended shapes are stored at an earlier level than the attended ones, perhaps in a fairly raw sensory form, and that they are interpreted in depth only when they receive attention.

It is interesting to relate these results to some reported by Sekuler and Palmer (1992), showing priming in a same-different matching task from an apparently occluded circle or square. In their experiment, subjects attended to both priming shapes—the occluder and the occluded. The results suggested that priming from the completed form of the occluded shape takes time to develop. Within the first 100 ms after presentation, the jigsaw form showed as much priming as the completed form. Our result with negative priming suggests that, without attention, the representation of the occluded shape is

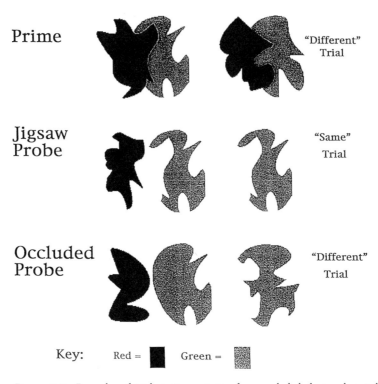

Comparison Figure   Standard

Prime   "Different"
                   Trial

**Jigsaw
Probe**   "Same"
                   Trial

**Occluded
Probe**   "Different"
                   Trial

Key: Red = ■   Green = ▨

Figure 2.9 Examples of trials testing priming from occluded shape when it has been attended. On prime trial, subject decides whether green occluded shape in comparison figure matches green occluded figure in standard pair to right. On some probe trials, green shape is previously attended jigsaw pattern and, on others, it is completed version of same shape. Half of trials of each type require response "same" and half require response "different."

arrested in its initial jigsaw or mosaic form. In another study of implicit memory for visual objects seen with attention, Schacter, Cooper, and Delaney (1990) also found evidence for three-dimensional representations; their subjects showed priming only for the three-dimensionally possible and not for the impossible figures. Schacter, Cooper, and Delaney suggest that the memory system responsible for perceptual priming stores structural descriptions of objects. If no consistent structural description can be generated, as with the impossible figures, no trace is stored. Our results, however, suggest that when the objects are unattended, priming may depend on less structurally developed representations. (Note also that Ratcliffe and McKoon 1995 offers an alternative interpretation of Schacter, Cooper, and Delaney's results).

Our results with occlusion are consistent with the hypothesis that implicit memory traces can be formed at different levels of processing and that they contain whatever information has been extracted up to that point (cf. Moscovitch, Vriezen, and Goshen-Gottstein 1993). With attention, the traces are more fully interpreted than without. Although our earlier results, and those of

Jacoby, Toth, and Yonelinas (1993), suggest no effect of attention on the *duration* of implicit memory, attention may nevertheless affect the level at which the representation is formed.

2.11 PRIMING AND VISUAL MEMORY FOR EVENTS

Kundera (1990) claims that memory consists of snapshots rather than moving pictures. When he tried to recall past amatory adventures, he found, to his regret, that he was limited to a few static images. He was of course describing his explicit, conscious memory. Using a partial report task, Treisman, Russell, and Green (1975) demonstrated iconic memory for the direction of motion of circling dots, that was as accurate as iconic memory for static shapes (that had been equated in difficulty when total report was required). At least an evanescent memory trace does seem to be laid down, directly representing motion as well as static stimuli

Experiment 8

We have recently begun using the negative priming paradigm to explore implicit visual memory for dynamic events as well as for static objects. Instead of pairs of static shapes, we present pairs of moving dots. In one experiment, a green dot and a red dot appeared superimposed (as a red and green striped dot) in the same location and then moved on separate, randomly generated, 8-segment journeys in an imaginary square grid, away from the initial location and back to it, taking 2,800 ms for the complete trajectory (fig. 2.10). At the start of the first segment there were 8 possible directions each dot could move (vertically up or down, horizontally left or right, or along any of the four diagonals), and the choice of direction was random. At the start of each subsequent segment, there were 7 possible directions, excluding an immediate return in the direction opposite to that just taken. The choice was random, with the constraint that the dots must end up where they began. The segments subtended 1.2 degrees for the vertical and horizontal segments and 1.7 degrees for the diagonal segments. The time for each segment was constant, so the velocity was higher for diagonal than for vertical or horizontal segments. The motion was too slow for visual persistence to give any direct impression of the figure as a whole; the appearance was of two single dots moving. The task was to track the green dot and to decide whether a static white shape, presented to the right of the display immediately after the motion was completed, exactly matched the trajectory that the green dot followed.

This is a difficult task and only about half the subjects could keep their errors below 30 percent in all conditions. For these 18 subjects, we found facilitation in reaction times, averaging 42 ms (significant $p < .001$) when the path that the green dot followed exactly matched the path that the red dot had followed on the immediately preceding trial, relative to the control

Time 1

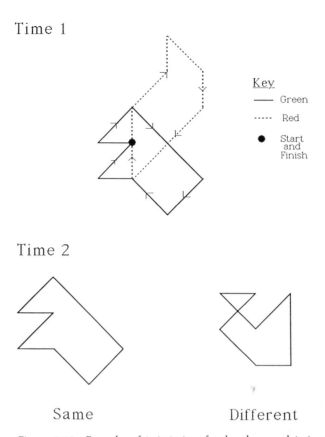

Key
—— Green
..... Red
● Start
and
Finish

Time 2

Same   Different

Figure 2.10 Examples of trajectories of red and green dots in moving dots experiment. Subjects attended to green dot and decided whether its path exactly matched white shape presented to right immediately after motion was completed. Path traced by unattended red dot in prime trial was retraced by attended green dot on probe trial.

condition in which a new, randomly generated path was shown. The 19 subjects who had more than 30 percent errors in one or more conditions showed interference, averaging 38 ms (significant, $p < .05$). The priming did not differ on "same" and on "different" trials, so it did not depend on a match to the static white shape presented on "same" trials. Perhaps we can interpret the group differences as differences in how much interference the red dot caused. The group with high errors may have suffered more interference and therefore may have tried to inhibit the irrelevant path, while the group with lower errors may have found it easy to ignore the irrelevant path without actively suppressing it. These subjects therefore registered the motion path without attaching any inhibition to it, and showed facilitation when it reappeared in the attended role in the next trial. We are testing this interference hypothesis by seeing whether subjects who show negative priming show more benefit than subjects who show facilitation when the irrelevant dot is removed. (The same account could, of course apply to the individual differences reported earlier with static stimuli.)

The significant priming effects, both positive and negative, suggest that memory traces are laid down for unattended events as well as for unattended objects. The motion trajectories were apparently stored after a single presentation and retrieved when they were re-presented, again with no awareness on the part of the subjects.

2.12 SUMMARY OF FINDINGS

This research is still in progress. We can, however, summarize our findings so far. With static overlapped stimuli, about two-thirds of subjects show negative priming and one-third show facilitation from an unattended novel nonsense shape, presented in the same location as the attended shape. These priming effects last across at least 200 intervening trials and for temporal durations of at least a month, although there is a trend for the negative priming to decrease and for the facilitation to increase with time. The priming is stronger for shapes that have never been seen before than for shapes presented repeatedly in the course of the experiment; moreover, priming for familiarized stimuli disappears almost immediately. Repetition increases the ability of subjects to ignore an unattended shape, but has no effect on negative priming. Priming at delays longer than a few trials seems to be about the same for attended and for unattended novel stimuli. Negative priming for novel shapes is removed by a single trial in which the previously unattended shape is attended. Explicit memory is nonexistent for unattended shapes, but above chance after a single presentation for attended ones. Unlike implicit memory for the same shapes, memory for attended shapes does increase substantially with repetition.

Negative priming also occurs for the unattended background in a figure-ground combination, and for a partly occluded shape in an overlapped pair. The occluded shape is stored as a jigsaw or mosaic shape when it is not attended, but as the amodally completed version of the shape when it receives attention during the prime trial. Finally, preliminary results suggest that priming can occur for events (patterns of motion) as well as for objects (novel shapes). Subjects who have high error rates show negative priming for motion patterns and subjects with low error rates show facilitation when the previously ignored motion path becomes the attended one.

2.13 CONCLUSIONS AND SPECULATIONS

The main conclusions we draw from these findings, and the interpretations we propose, are as follows:

1. Attention is not needed to establish a detailed representation of a novel shape. New object tokens are established automatically and on the fly during performance of a matching task on a different set of stimuli (at least for displays containing only two or three objects; see below for a discussion of

Object Tokens, Attention, and Visual Memory

load effects in implicit memory). On the other hand, attention *is* needed to form explicitly retrievable traces.[4]

2. Memory tokens of novel unattended shapes last at full strength and specificity across 200 intervening trials using very similar shapes, and persist for delays of several days or weeks. The unique shapes are preserved without loss for at least half the set of 270. This one-trial learning of novel shapes suggests a surprising combination of plasticity and permanence in the visual system. To achieve this degree of speed and specificity of learning within a neural network model, one would need to use sparse, distributed representations with fast-changing weights (McClelland and Rumelhart 1985).

3. The traces of unattended shapes are stored in a relatively uninterpreted form, at a level that precedes the choice for conscious awareness of which will be figure and which ground, and that also precedes the interpretation of occlusion. It seems that the tokens of unattended shapes represent 2-D patterns, rather than interpreted objects. It should be interesting, in future research, to compare the content of memory traces mediating negative priming with those underlying transsaccadic integration (Irwin and Andrews, chap. 6 this volume).

4. Patterns of motion also appear to be stored in implicit memory. Movies as well as stills can apparently be revived by re-presentations, even though we may share Kundera's intuition that we have voluntary access only to stills. Future research is planned to show whether the motion patterns are stored as such, or whether they are converted to static representations of the paths that the dots traced. The latter would predict priming from moving dots to the static shapes of their trajectories and vice versa, or from a dot moving in one direction to one moving in the opposite direction on the same path.

5. A minority of subjects show facilitation rather than negative priming when a previously unattended shape requires attention. The individual differences may reflect greater or lesser interference from unattended stimuli (shown, for example, by differences in error rates in the motion task) or differences in the strategy used in the matching task (active tagging and suppression of the unattended shape versus parallel processing of the composite stimulus). These individual differences suggest that the inhibition attached to the memory trace may be separable from the shape to which it is attached. Earlier results have shown a reversal from negative to positive priming when a single item is presented on the probe trials (Lowe 1979; Tipper and Cranston 1985), consistent with the idea that both components are present in the negative priming paradigm. We have found the same with our shapes.

6. Explicit memory is at chance for unattended objects, better than chance for attended objects seen once only, and much better than chance for repeated attended objects. The vagueness and confusion of explicit memory for both attended and unattended stimuli seen only once contrasts strikingly with the very specific traces revealed by the implicit measures. In some

exemplar models of concept formation (e.g., Hintzman 1986), traces of particular instances are merged and cannot be individually accessed; a representation of the prototype evolves from the superposition of multiple individual tokens. Our explicit memory results are consistent with this view. Subjects failed to recognize individual shapes, perhaps because, after a single presentation, explicit retrieval gets only the merged or superimposed effects of the multiple shapes. The specificity shown in the implicit measure could reflect a different way of accessing the same memory traces. The negative priming task may tap directly into the individual traces rather than reflecting only the merged effects proposed in Hintzman's model. The incoming attended shape on a UA trial would take a direct route through the perceptual system from the sensory receptors to the matching memory trace laid down by the earlier perceptual experience of the same stimulus, whereas explicit recognition depends on other, initially less selective pathways for retrieval.

7. Repetition apparently has no effect on the strength or persistence of negative priming, although it greatly increases explicit memory, and it does make the repeated shapes progressively easier to ignore. A possible explanation may be that in negative priming two effects of repetition are canceling each other out. Repetition makes it easier to retrieve a matching token, which in turn produces earlier conflict from the inappropriate action tag, but also earlier perceptual facilitation from the matching shape. The net effect is no difference in the negative priming measure between one stored token and four. In fact, the contrast between increasing facilitation with trials that repeat the same token in the same role and no change on trials that then reverse its role can be taken as further support for the distinction we make between facilitation from the stored token and interference from its attached action tag.

2.14 THEORETICAL FRAMEWORK

The theoretical framework that seems best to fit these findings is one in which each object or event (at least up to two or three), whether attended or not, forms a perceptual token representing its shape with considerable detail and specificity (cf. Logan 1988, 1990; Treisman 1992). Attention results in tokens that are perceptually more developed, including, for example, amodal completion of occluded shapes and a commitment to which is figure and which is ground. The tokens of both attended and unattended objects, formed in a single presentation, persist unchanged in visual memory for periods of at least several weeks. In tasks where two or more objects compete to determine the response, an action tag may be associated with each token, specifying whether it should be attended or ignored. The action tags are somewhat less long-lived than the objects to which they are attached, or may become detached from them.

When a matching stimulus is presented, it directly and automatically reactivates one of the earlier tokens, together with its action tag, if any remains.

The matching shape facilitates perception, producing positive priming. The action tag also facilitates performance if it is appropriate to the current task, but interferes when it conflicts, producing negative priming. Individual subjects may differ in their attention strategies, resulting in differences in the salience or even the existence of the action tags. Repetition of the same object lays down a new token as well as retrieving the old one. This facilitates performance when the action tag is consistent but has no net effect when the action tag must be changed, because the facilitation and interference cancel out.

We have no evidence of decay of the memory trace over the intervals we tested, for either old or new shapes. For a new shape, seen only once, there is no competition for retrieval when a matching shape is presented again. Its unique token is retrieved, with whatever tag was attached on the one earlier presentation, however long ago it occurred (at least up to a month). For familiar stimuli, whether old shapes or words, many tokens have been stored, but recency gives the last one an advantage in the perceptual matching process, so at lag 1 we do get negative priming. However, by lag 3, the new presentation of a familiar object is just as likely to retrieve a token from an earlier "attend" trial as one from an earlier "ignore" trial. Thus with familiar stimuli used repeatedly in both attended and unattended roles, negative priming disappears after even quite brief delays.

Explicit memory may reflect the same stored tokens as negative priming but depend on different retrieval routes. Initially, it accesses only the merged effects of all the tokens; attention and repetition are needed to establish individuated retrieval routes to each different object, so that they can be consciously differentiated and explicitly recalled or recognized.

2.15 POSSIBLE PHYSIOLOGICAL BASIS

What might be the neural substrate for the visual memory revealed by our negative priming results? Perceptual memory for objects is generally thought to depend on area IT. However, the tests leading to this conclusion mostly used tasks like delayed matching to sample, which are more like explicit memory tasks than the kind of implicit memory that we are studying. Priming may depend also on perceptual traces in earlier extrastriate areas such as V4, or MT (for the motion stimuli). The most relevant physiological study is one by Miller and Desimone (1994), dealing with the response of IT cells to repeated and to novel stimuli in a delayed matching to sample task. When the repeated object was a target for the behavioral response, the activation increased, whereas when it was irrelevant to the task, the neural response was reduced. The former parallels an explicit memory task for human subjects, whereas the latter is closer to automatic, implicit memory. Both effects were recorded in the same area of IT. The passive habituation lasted across as many as 35 intervening trials, although the effect was much larger at the short delays, unlike the perfect retention we found, extending to days or weeks. Miller and Desimone explain the rapid recovery from habituation in their results by the suggestion that the IT neurons act "as adaptive mnemonic filters that seek to preferentially pass information about new, unexpected, or not recently seen stimuli" (p. 521). Information about task relevance (the action tags in our negative priming studies) may last longer than the habituation reflecting recency of presentation.

Amnesiac patients show normal priming for novel attended shapes (Musen and Squire 1992) but no explicit memory for them—just as our subjects do for the unattended stimuli. This suggests that the memory revealed by priming is independent of the hippocampus and adjacent structures. The shapes themselves, together with their relevant action tags, may be stored automatically, passively, and relatively permanently as an aftereffect of a single perceptual registration, in area IT or other extrastriate visual areas. But their voluntary, conscious retrieval depends on attention to index the memory traces and to establish access routes to each individually, perhaps through activity in the hippocampus and adjoining areas. Many repetitions of each shape are required to consolidate these hippocampal connections, providing individuated access routes for voluntary retrieval. Implicit measures of memory typically show much less decay with time than explicit memory. What fades with time may again be voluntary access rather than the traces themselves.

2.16 ATTENTION LIMITS AND IMPLICIT MEMORY

Finally, we return to the issue of perceptual limits to attention and the binding or feature integration problem. What have we learned that is new? Can our present results be reconciled with the conclusions reached in the earlier research on search and conjunctions? When we measure subjects' ability to report or respond *explicitly* to unattended objects, they often appear to be limited to reporting simple features. Identification of more complex shapes or conjunctions of features seems to need either attention (or top-down constraints) or special grouping strategies (Treisman 1988). Yet in this chapter we have outlined evidence that fairly complex shapes and events are registered and stored *implicitly* without attention.

We have a choice of two possible accounts—the full perceptual processing hypothesis that sees attention limits simply as constraints on conscious awareness (provided that performance is not restricted by sensory acuity, masking, and other peripheral factors) or a modified perceptual limits hypothesis. Both start with the empirical finding that more information is implicitly registered, stored, and retrieved than we can consciously and explicitly access. Both agree that implicit perception and memory reflect access to information that is more detailed than and perhaps different in kind from, the limited information available for conscious processing and voluntary action. Both agree that attention is needed to make information explicitly accessible, probably involving neural structures beyond the visual areas V4, MT, and IT.

The perceptual limits hypothesis retains the idea that there are capacity limits for implicit as well as for explicit perceptual processing, although the constraints on explicit access are clearly more stringent than those revealed by implicit tests. This hypothesis starts with the observation that the tasks suggesting attentional limits in perception typically use high load displays, with brief exposures or multiple objects to be processed under high time pressure, whereas the implicit measures typically probe displays with only two or three objects which elicit potentially conflicting responses. When we tested negative priming for our novel shapes with exposures of only 200 ms, we found none; it may take longer than 200 ms to set up tokens for two novel shapes. Allport, Tipper, and Chmiel (1985) did find negative priming with brief exposures, but they used a small set of highly familiar pictures presented repeatedly, where little time would be needed to extract the information necessary to identify which pictures were present on any given trial. Neumann and DeSchepper (1992) found a steep reduction in negative priming as one to three unattended letters were added to the display although they attributed this to a limited pool of inhibition being spread too thin as the number of irrelevant letters increased.

Treisman (1969) suggested that whenever the perceptual load is low, perception is automatic and early selection impossible; her hypothesis was that we *have to* see or hear whatever we *can* see or hear. Please turn your eyes to figure 2.11a, but don't see the rabbit! On the other hand, if the rabbit is presented among ten other animals (fig. 2.11b) and you glance only briefly, it is much easier to miss the rabbit. At the perceptual level, attentional control may be indirect—we may be able to shut out one set of stimuli only by attending to another that fully occupies the relevant perceptual analyzers. We are free to choose *which* stimuli provided that the relevant and irrelevant stimuli are sufficiently discriminable from one another, but unless our capacity is fully occupied with other stimuli (or thoughts or tasks), we are forced to identify whatever stimuli are present. So early selection may be simply a choice of routing—of which stimuli to send through a bottleneck when the capacity would otherwise be exceeded. This idea may be similar to that proposed by Duncan (chap. 21, this volume) describing within-level inhibition between multiple objects.

When the load is *low*, on the other hand, the potential problem we face is not perceptual interference but possible conflicts of action. The way we avoid them is through late, (i.e., postperceptual) selection between stimuli to determine which will control our response. (See Lavie and Tsal 1994 for a review of relevant evidence, and Lavie 1995 for some ingenious experiments supporting the hypothesis.)

How then would perceptual load affect implicit memory? One idea is that traces of unattended stimuli are laid down at whatever level they have reached in the perceptual processing sequence. When the load is low, unattended stimuli are stored in sufficient detail to distinguish between our 270 nonsense shapes. Familiar objects automatically activate their identity and

A.

B.

Figure 2.11 *A.* It is difficult not to see single rabbit when one looks at it, even with brief presentation. *B.* One rabbit among many other animals will often be missed when display is briefly presented.

category nodes. When the load is high and perceptual limits are taxed, implicit memory may also be reduced or nonexistent, consistent with the finding by Neumann and DeSchepper (1992).

Whether future research favors the full-analysis hypothesis or confirms the existence of perceptual limits, our findings have clearly added to the growing evidence that explicit conscious experience may be a misleading guide to how much information is registered. More than we know of what reaches the eye also reaches and remains in some invisible corners of the brain and mind.

ACKNOWLEDGMENTS

This research was partly supported by the Air Force Office of Scientific Research and the Office of Naval Research grant 90-0370. The manuscript is submitted for publication with the understanding that the U.S. government is authorized to reproduce and distribute reprints for governmental purposes.

Figures 2.1, 2.2, and 2.3 appear in DeSchepper and Treisman 1996. Copyright 1996 by the American Psychological Association. Reprinted by permission.

NOTES

1. Although the inhibition subjects show reduced interference at the longer lags of a week and a month, this is not a simple case of regression to the mean (a) because the facilitation *increases* rather than decreases for the subjects with facilitation in session 1 at lag 1; and (b) because whatever regression there is will be present in the test at lag 1 in session 2 as well as at the longer delays.

2. We also ran a different group of subjects in the reverse order, with words before shapes, and got very different results. This group showed a mean facilitation of 22 ms (not significant) at lag 1, rather than negative priming. Because the words were familiar and spatially separated rather than overlapped, some of the subjects may have noticed the repetition on the early trials and used it explicitly to help their performance. On the other hand, subjects who were tested on the shapes before the words may have developed the strategy of actively inhibiting the unattended items, because this was more necessary with those overlapped and unfamiliar stimuli. This resulted in negative priming on the words as well as the shapes.

3. Three of the 36 subjects showed a large reversal, with strong facilitation at lag 1, resembling that shown by the subjects tested with words first. They may also have noticed the repetition. The interaction between lag and words versus forms was not significant for the group as a whole, but if the three subjects showing facilitation greater than 100 ms at lag 1 (two on words and one on forms) are omitted, the interaction is significant ($p < .05$) for the remaining 33 subjects.

4. An alternative account, suggested by John Duncan, John Dunn, and Max Coltheart (personal communication), is that attention may be needed to integrate the fragments of a shape into an organized whole. Negative priming arises, in this view, because the integration has been prevented for the previously unattended shape and this impairs the formation of a token from the same fragments of outline on a subsequent attended trial. This account is possible only if the unintegrated fragments are sufficiently specific to differentiate at least half the shapes in the set of 270 we used. Given the similarity between closest neighbors in the set, the fragments would need to contain a large part of the same information that is contained in the wholes. Nevertheless, the hypothesis is an interesting one, which could be tested by comparing priming from recombined fragments of previously presented shapes with priming from the original wholes.

REFERENCES

Allport, C. A., Tipper, S. P., and Chmiel, N. (1985). Perceptual integration and postcategorical filtering. In M. I. Posner and O. S. Marin (Eds.), *Attention and Performance XI*, 107–132. Hillsdale, NJ: Erlbaum.

Broadbent, D. E., Cooper, P. F., Fitzgerald, P., and Parkes, K. R. (1982). The cognitive failures questionnaire (CFQ) and its correlates. *British Journal of Clinical Psychology, 21*, 1–16.

DeSchepper, B., and Treisman A. (1996). Visual memory for novel shapes: Implicit coding without attention. *Journal of Experimental Psychology: Learning, Memory, and Cognition, 22*, 27–47.

Hintzman, D. L. (1986). Schema abstraction in a multiple-trace model. *Psychological Review, 93*, 411–428.

Hoffman, D. D., and Richards, W. A. (1985). Parts of recognition. In S. Pinker (Ed.), *Visual cognition*, 65–96. Cambridge, MA: MIT Press.

Jacoby, L. L., Toth, J. P., and Yonelinas, A. P. (1993). Separating conscious and unconscious influences of memory: Measuring recollection. *Journal of Experimental Psychology: General, 122,* 139–154.

Kahneman, D., Treisman, A., and Gibbs, B. (1992). The reviewing of object files: Object-specific integration of information. *Cognitive Psychology, 24,* 175–219.

Kanwisher, N. G. (1987). Repetition blindness: Type recognition without token individuation. *Cognition, 27,* 117–143.

Kanwisher, N. G. (1991). Repetition blindness and illusory conjunctions: Errors in binding visual types with visual tokens. *Journal of Experimental Psychology: Human Perception and Performance, 17,* 404–421.

Knowlton, B. J., and Squire, L. R. (1993). The learning of categories: Parallel brain systems for item memory and category knowledge. *Science, 262,* 1747–1749.

Kundera, M. (1990). *Immortalité.* Paris: Gallimard.

Lavie, N. (1995). Perceptual load as a necessary condition for selective attention. *Journal of Experimental Psychology: Human Perception and Performance, 21,* 451–468.

Lavie, N., and Tsal, Y. (1994). Perceptual load as a major determinant of the locus of selection in visual attention. *Perception and Psychophysics, 56,* 183–197.

Logan, G. D. (1988). Toward an instance theory of automatization. *Psychological Review, 95,* 492–527.

Logan, G. D. (1990). Repetition priming and automaticity: Common underlying mechanisms? *Cognitive Psychology, 22,* 1–35.

Lowe, D. G. (1979). Strategies, context, and the mechanism of response inhibition. *Memory and Cognition, 7,* 382–389.

McClelland, J. L., and Rumelhart, D. E. (1985). Distributed memory and the representation of general and specific information. *Journal of Experimental Psychology: General, 114,* 159–188.

Miller, E. K., and Desimone, R. (1994). Parallel neuronal mechanisms for short-term memory. *Science, 263,* 520–522.

Moscovitch, M., Vriezen, E., and Goshen-Gottstein, Y. (1993). Implicit tests of memory in patients with focal lesions or degenerative brain disorders. In F. Boller and J. Grafman, (Eds.), *Handbook of neuropsychology,* vol. 8, 133–173.

Musen, G., and Squire, L. R. (1992). Nonverbal priming in amnesia. *Memory and Cognition, 20,* 441–448.

Nakayama, K., Shimojo, S., and Silverman, G. H. (1989). Stereoscopic depth: Its relation to recognition of occluded objects. *Perception, 18,* 55–68.

Neill, W. T. (1977). Inhibitory and facilitatory processes in selective attention. *Journal of Experimental Psychology: Human Perception and Performance, 3,* 444–450.

Neill, W. T., and Valdes, L. A. (1992). The persistence of negative priming: Steady state or decay? *Journal of Experimental Psychology: Learning, Memory, and Cognition, 18,* 565–576.

Neumann, E., and DeSchepper, B. G. (1992). An inhibition-based fan effect: Evidence for an active suppression mechanism in selective attention. *Canadian Journal of Psychology, 46,* 1–40.

Peterson, M. A., and Gibson, B. (1991). The initial identification of figure-ground relationships: Contributions from shape recognition processes. *Bulletin of the Psychonomic Society, 29,* 199–202.

Ratcliffe, R., and McKoon, G. (1995). Bias in the priming of object decisions. *Journal of Experimental Psychology: Learning, Memory, and Cognition, 21,* 752–767.

Rock, I., and Gutman, D. (1981). The effect of inattention and form perception. *Journal of Experimental Psychology: Human Perception and Performance, 7,* 275–285.

Roediger, H. L. I. (1990). Implicit memory: Retention without remembering. *American Psychologist, 45,* 1043–1056.

Schacter, D. L. (1987). Implicit memory: History and current status. *Journal of Experimental Psychology: Learning, Memory, and Cognition, 13,* 501–518.

Schacter, D. L., Cooper, L. A., and Delaney, S. M. (1990). Implicit memory for novel objects depends on access to structural descriptions. *Journal of Experimental Psychology: General, 119,* 5–24.

Sekuler, A. B., and Palmer, S. (1992). Perception of partly occluded objects: A microgenetic analysis. *Journal of Experimental Psychology: General, 121,* 95–111.

Tipper, S. P. (1985). The negative priming effect: Inhibitory effects of ignored primes. *Quarterly Journal of Experimental Psychology, 37A,* 571–590.

Tipper, S. P., and Baylis, G. C. (1987). Individual differences in selective attention: The relation of priming and interference to cognitive failure. *Personality and Individual Differences, 8,* 667–675.

Tipper, S. P., and Cranston, M. (1985). Selective attention and priming: Inhibitory and facilitatory effects of ignored primes. *Quarterly Journal of Experimental Psychology, 37A,* 591–611.

Tipper, S. P., and Driver, J. (1988). Negative priming between pictures and words: Evidence for semantic analysis of ignored stimuli. *Memory and Cognition, 16,* 64–70.

Tipper, S. P., Weaver, B., Cameron, S., Brehaut, J. C., and Bastedo, J. (1991). Inhibitory mechanisms of attention in identification and localization tasks: Time course and disruption. *Journal of Experimental Psychology: Learning, Memory, and Cognition, 17,* 681–692.

Treisman, A. (1969). Strategies and models of selective attention. *Psychological Review, 76,* 282–299.

Treisman, A. (1988). Features and objects: The fourteenth Bartlett Memorial Lecture. *Quarterly Journal of Experimental Psychology, 40A,* 201–237.

Treisman, A. (1992). Perceiving and re-perceiving objects. *American Psychologist, 47,* 862–875.

Treisman, A. (1993). The perception of features and objects. In A. Baddeley and L. Weiskrantz (Eds.), *Attention: Selection, awareness and control: A tribute to Donald Broadbent,* 5–35. Oxford: Clarendon Press.

Treisman, A. and Gelade, G. (1980). A feature integration theory of attention. *Cognitive Psychology, 12,* 97–136.

Treisman, A., Russell, R., and Green, J. (1975). Brief visual storage of shape and movement. In P. M. A. Rabbitt and S. Dornic (Eds.), *Attention and Performance V,* 699–721. London: Academic Press.

Treisman, A., and Schmidt, H. (1982). Illusory conjunctions in the perception of objects. *Cognitive Psychology, 14,* 107–141.

Warrington, E. K. (1982). Neuropsychological studies of object recognition. *Philosophical Transactions of the Royal Society, London, B, 289,* 15–33.

III Integration in Perception of Visual Structure

3 A Bayesian Framework for the Integration of Visual Modules

Heinrich H. Bülthoff and Alan L. Yuille

ABSTRACT

The Bayesian approach to vision provides a fruitful theoretical framework both for modeling individual cues, such as stereo, shading, texture, and occlusion, and for integrating their information. In this formalism we represent the viewed scene by one, or more, surfaces using prior assumptions about the surface shapes and material properties. On theoretical grounds, the less information available to the cues (and the less accurate it is), the more important these assumptions become. This suggests that visual illusions, and biased perceptions, will arise for scenes for which the prior assumptions are not appropriate. We describe psychophysical experiments which are consistent with these ideas. Our Bayesian approach also has two important implications for coupling different visual cues. First, different cues cannot in general be treated independently and then simply combined together at the end. There are dependencies between them that have to be incorporated into the models. Second, a single generic prior assumption is not sufficient even if it does incorporate cue interactions because there are many different types of visual scenes and different models are appropriate for each. This leads to the concept of competitive priors where the visual system must choose the correct model depending on the stimulus.

3.1 INTRODUCTION

We define vision as perceptual inference, the estimation of scene properties from an image or a sequence of images.[1] Vision is ill posed in the sense that the retinal image is potentially an arbitrarily complicated function of the visual scene and so there is insufficient information in the image to uniquely determine the scene. The brain, or any artificial vision system, must make assumptions about the real world in order to overcome this problem. These assumptions must be sufficiently powerful to ensure that vision is well posed for those properties in the scene that the visual system needs to estimate. In this chapter we argue that Bayes (1783) provides a natural framework for modeling perceptual inference. We emphasize that we are describing a framework and *not* a theory. The usefulness of such a framework is that it is powerful enough to *compactly* describe most, ideally all, visual phenomena and that it leads to specific theories (by choosing priors and likelihoods) that can be tested experimentally.

How are these assumptions imposed in vision systems? The Bayesian formulation gives us an elegant way to impose constraints in terms of prior probabilistic assumptions about the world, based on Bayes formula (Bayes 1783):

$$P(S|I) = \frac{P(I|S)P(S)}{P(I)}. \tag{3.1}$$

Here S represents the visual scene, the shape and location of the viewed objects, and I represents the retinal image. $P(I|S)$ is the *likelihood function* for the scene and specifies the probability of obtaining an image I from a given scene S; it incorporates a model of image formation and of noise and hence is the subject of computer graphics. $P(S)$ is the *prior* distribution and specifies the relative probability of different scenes occurring in the world. The probabilistic model, specified by $P(I|S)$ and $P(S)$, contains the prior assumptions about the scene structure, including the geometry, the lighting, and the material properties. $P(I)$ can be thought of as a normalization constant and can be derived from $P(I|S)$ and $P(S)$ by elementary probability theory, $P(I) = \int P(I|S)P(S)[dS]$. Finally, the *posterior distribution* $P(S|I)$ is a function giving the probability of the scene being S if the observed image is I.

In words (3.1) states that the probability of the scene S, given the image I, is the product of the probability of the image, given the scene $P(I|S)$, times the a priori probability $P(S)$ of the scene, divided by a normalization constant $P(I)$.

To specify a unique interpretation of the image I, we must make a decision based on our probability distribution, $P(S|I)$, and determine an estimate, $S^*(I)$, of the scene. In Bayesian decision theory (Berger 1985) this estimate is derived by choosing a loss function that specifies the penalty paid by the system for producing an incorrect estimate. Standard estimators like the *maximum a posteriori* (MAP) estimator, $S^* = \arg\max_S P(S|I)$ (i.e., S^* is the most probable value of S given the posterior distribution $P(S|I)$) correspond to specific choices of loss function. In this chapter we will, for simplicity and reasons of space, assume that the MAP estimator is used though other estimators are often preferable (see Yuille and Bülthoff 1996).

Although the Bayesian framework is sufficiently general to encompass many aspects of visual perception including depth estimation, object recognition, and scene understanding, to specify a complete Bayesian theory of visual perception is, at present, completely impractical. Instead, we will restrict ourselves to model individual visual cues for estimating the depth and material properties of objects and the ways these cues can be combined. It has become standard practice for computational theories of vision to separate such cues into modules (Marr 1982) that only weakly interact with each other. From the Bayesian perspective, weak coupling between modules is often inappropriate, due to the interdependence between visual cues. Hence we argue in section 3.3 that the visual cues should often be more strongly coupled. In some cases weak coupling between modules is appropriate (see Landy, et al. 1995).

In the Bayesian framework the choice of prior assumptions used to model each visual cue is very important. Each visual cue is subject to built-in prior assumptions that will inevitably bias the visual system, particularly for the impoverished stimuli favored by psychophysicists. The human visual system is very good at performing the visual tasks necessary for us to interact effectively with the world. Thus the prior assumptions used must be fairly accurate, at least for those scenes that we need to perceive and interpret correctly. The prior assumptions used to interpret one visual cue may conflict with those used to interpret another, and consistency must be imposed when cues are combined. Moreover, the prior assumptions may be context-dependent and correspond to the categorical structure of the world. A single "generic" prior is not sufficient because there are many types of visual scenes and different models are appropriate for each. Each visual module, or coupled groups of modules, will have to determine automatically which prior assumption, or model, should be used; this can lead to a system of competitive prior assumptions (see section 3.4).

In section 3.2 we first describe Bayesian theories for individual cues and argue that several psychophysical experiments can be interpreted in terms of biases toward prior assumptions. Next, in section 3.3, we describe ways of combining different depth cues and argue that strong coupling between different modules is often desirable. Then in section 3.4 we argue that it is preferable to use competing, often context-dependent, priors rather than the single generic priors commonly used. Implications of this approach are described in section 3.5.

3.2 BAYESIAN THEORIES OF INDIVIDUAL VISUAL MODULES

We now briefly describe some Bayesian theories of individual visual cues and argue that psychophysical experiments can be interpreted as perceptual biases toward prior assumptions. From (3.1) we see that the influence of the prior is determined by the specificity of the likelihood function $P(I|S)$. In principle, according to standard Bayesian statistics, the likelihood function should make no prior assumptions about the scene, yet the likelihood functions used in most visual theories often make strong context-dependent assumptions. This fact will be briefly illustrated in this section and we will describe its implications in sections 3.3 and 3.4.

We will specifically discuss theories of shape from shading and shape from texture. All these modules require prior assumptions about the scene geometry, the material properties of the objects being viewed, and, in some cases, the light source direction(s). We will concentrate on the assumptions used by the theories rather than the specific algorithms. Although a number of theories described here were originally formulated in terms of energy functions (Horn 1986) or regularization theory (Poggio, Torre, and Koch 1985), the Bayesian approach incorporates, by use of the Gibbs distribution (Parisi 1988), these previous approaches (see Yuille and Bülthoff 1996).

Shape from Shading

Let us now look at one specific example. Standard models of image formation assume that the observed intensity depends on the tendency of the viewed surface to reflect light, its albedo, and a geometric reflectance factor that depends on the orientation of the surface, the viewing direction, and the light source(s) direction. Shape from shading models (Horn 1986) typically assume that the scene consists of a single surface with constant albedo, a single light source direction $\vec{s}$ that can be estimated, and a *Lambertian* reflectance function. This leads to an image formation model $I = \vec{s} \cdot \vec{n} + N$, where $\vec{n}$ denotes the surface normals and N is additive Gaussian noise. In this case the likelihood function can be written as $P(I|S) = (1/Z)e^{-(1/2\sigma^2)(I-\vec{s}\cdot\vec{n})^2}$, where σ^2 is the variance of the noise and Z is a normalization factor.[2] The prior model for the surface geometry $P(S)$ typically assumes that the surface is piecewise smooth and biases toward a thin plate or membrane. These theories also assume that the occluding boundaries of the object are known, which is helpful for giving boundary conditions.

This likelihood function contains the prior assumption that the reflectance function is Lambertian with constant albedo. Moreover, it ignores effects such as mutual illumination and self-shadowing. The model is therefore only applicable for a certain limited class of scenes and only works within a certain *context* (see fig. 3.1). A visual system using this module would require a

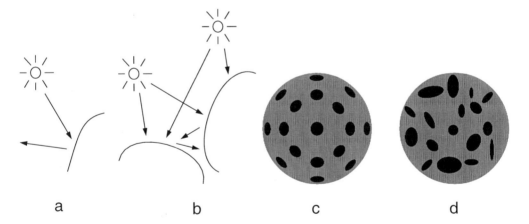

a   b   c   d

Figure 3.1 Cues are valid only in certain contexts. In (a) we sketch a Lambertian object illuminated by single light source and no mutual illumination; thus standard shape from shading algorithms will work. However, in (b) mutual illumination will prevent shape from shading from working. Similarly, shape from texture is possible for (c) but not for (d), where homogeneity assumption for texture elements is violated. Thus both shading and texture shape cues are only valid in certain contexts.

method for automatically checking whether the context was correct. We will return to this issue in section 3.4 on competitive priors.

What predictions would models of this type make for psychophysical experiments? Clearly, they would predict that the perception of geometry for shape from shading would be biased by the prior assumption of piecewise smoothness (see fig. 3.2). If we use the models of piecewise smoothness typically used in computer vision, then we would find a bias toward fronto-parallel surfaces. Such a bias is found for example in the psychophysical shape from shading experiments by Bülthoff and Mallot (1988), Mamassian and Kersten (1994), and Koenderink, van Doorn, and Kappers (1992). Of course, not all smoothness priors cause such a bias (see, for example, Pollard, Mayhew, and Frisby 1985); nevertheless, the bias appears to be there experimentally. The more impoverished the stimuli, the greater the bias; thus we might expect this effect to be larger for psychophysical experiments than for realistic stimuli (realistic stimuli, i.e., natural images, are typically less impoverished).

Shape from Texture

Existing shape from texture models also make similar, though incompatible, assumptions about the scenes they are viewing. They assume that texture variations can be modeled by spatial changes in the albedo and that the geometric reflectance factor can be neglected, or filtered out in some way.

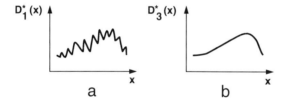

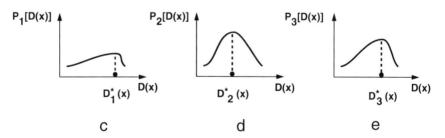

Figure 3.2 Prior assumption bias perception. Graph (a) shows true depth $D_1^*(x)$ and graph (b) shows biased depth percept $D_3^*(x)$ after smoothing. In (c) we assume that likelihood function $P_1[D(x)]$ is weakly peaked at true depth $D_1^*(x)$. Prior in (d), however, is peaked at $D_2^*(x)$. Resulting posterior distribution $P_3[D(x)]$ is shown in (e) and yields biased percept $D_3^*(x)$.

Texture elements are assumed to be "painted" onto piecewise smooth surfaces in a spatially statistically homogeneous manner. A specific example is given by Blake, Bülthoff, and Sheinberg (1993). Therefore the imaging model, or likelihood function, will assume that these texture elements are generated from a homogeneous distribution on the surface and then projected onto the image plane. Assumptions about the geometry, such as piecewise smoothness, are then placed in the prior.

Once again, the nature of the likelihood term means that the models will only be appropriate in certain contexts (see fig. 3.1). To become well posed, shape from texture must make strong assumptions about the world that are only valid for a limited class of scenes. If standard piecewise smoothness priors are used, then texture models will also predict biases toward the frontoparallel plane, as observed experimentally (Bülthoff and Mallot 1988). Stronger predictions can be made by testing the predictions of a specific model (see Blake, Bülthoff, and Sheinberg 1993).

What we have seen in this section are examples of individual visual modules. Although it is possible to interpret some psychophysical experiments as biases toward "reasonable" prior assumptions, we have stressed that the less constraint the likelihood function places on the scene, the stronger the bias. All these theories make strong contextual assumptions, and the visual system must be able to automatically verify whether the context is correct before believing the output of the model. In the next section we will look at how several different visual modules can be integrated to achieve a more robust interpretation of the visual world.

3.3 BAYESIAN THEORIES OF MULTIPLE VISUAL MODULES

It has become standard practice for computational theorists and psychophysicists to assume that different visual cues are computed in separate modules (Marr 1982) and thereafter only weakly interact with each other. Marr's theory did not fully specify this weak interaction but seemed to suggest that each module separately estimated scene properties, such as depth and surface orientation, and then combined the results in some way.[3] A more quantitative theory, which has experimental support (Bruno and Cutting 1988; Dosher, Sperling, and Wurst 1986; Maloney and Landy 1989), involves taking weighted averages for mutually consistent cues and using a vetoing mechanism for inconsistent cues. A further approach by Poggio and collaborators (Poggio, Gamble, and Little 1988) based on Markov random fields has been implemented on real data.

Coupling of Modules

The Bayesian approach suggests an alternative viewpoint for the fusion of visual information (Clark and Yuille 1990). This approach stresses the necessity of taking into account the prior assumptions used by the individual cues.

These assumptions may conflict or be redundant. In either case, it seems that better results can often be achieved by strongly coupling the modules in contrast to the weak methods proposed by Marr or the weighted averages theories, though weak coupling may indeed be appropriate in some situations (Landy et al. 1995).

To see the distinction between weak and strong coupling, suppose we have two sources of depth information, f and g. Marr's theory would involve specifying two posterior distributions, $P_1(S|f)$ and $P_2(S|g)$, for the individual modules. Two MAP estimates of the scene, S_1^* and S_2^*, would be determined by each module and the results combined in some unspecified fashion. See figure 3.3 for an overview of weak and strong coupling.

Weak Coupling

Although the weighted averages theories are not specified in a Bayesian framework, one way to obtain them would be to multiply the models together to obtain $P(S|f,g) = P_1(S|f)P_2(S|g)$. If the MAP estimates, S_1^* and S_2^*, from the two theories are similar, then it is possible to use perturbation theory and find, to first order, that the resulting combined MAP estimate $S_{1,2}^*$ is a weighted average of S_1^* and S_2^* (see Yuille and Bülthoff 1996).

Both Marr's and the weighted averages approach would be characterized as weak (Clark and Yuille 1990) because they assume that the information conveyed by the a posteriori distributions of the two modules is independent. But, as we have argued, the forms of the prior assumptions may cause the information to be dependent or even contradictory.

By contrast, the Bayesian approach would require us to specify a combined likelihood function $P(f,g|S)$ for the two cues and a single prior assumption $P(S)$ for the combined system. This will give rise to a distribution $P(S|f,g)$ given by

$$P(S|f,g) = \frac{P(f,g|S)P(S)}{P(f,g)} \tag{3.2}$$

and in general will not reduce to $P_1(S|f)P_2(S|g)$. A model like (3.2) that cannot be factorized is considered a form of strong coupling (Clark and Yuille 1990).

We now discuss an important intermediate case between weak and strong coupling. Consider two modules $P_1(f|S)$, $P_1(S)$ and $P_2(g|S)$, $P_2(S)$. Now suppose that the likelihood function for the combined cues can be factored as $P(f,g|S) = P_1(f|S)P_2(g|S)$. Then we get correct Bayesian integration of cues by using model (fig. 3.3c) provided the priors for the two modules are identical (i.e., $P_1(S) = P_2(S)$) and the prior for the coupled modules is unchanged (i.e., $P(S) = P_1(S) = P_2(S)$). For historical reasons, we refer to this as "weak" coupling. It is not unusual, however, for existing vision modules to use different priors (for example, binocular stereo modules typically use piecewise surface smoothness assumptions, while structure-from-motion algorithms

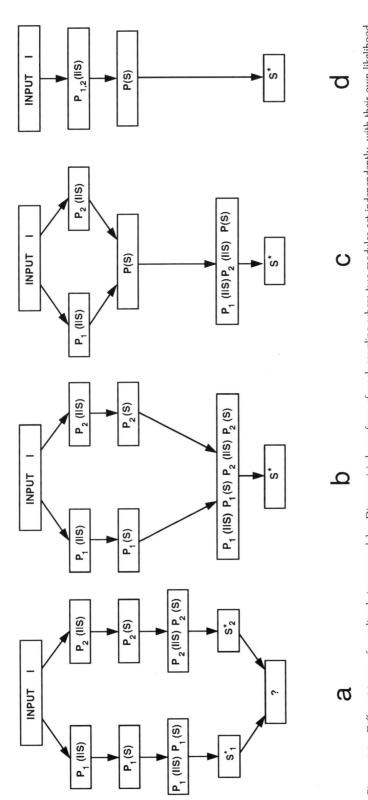

Figure 3.3 Different types of coupling between modules. Diagram (a) shows form of weak coupling where two modules act independently, with their own likelihood functions $P(I|S)$ and priors $P(S)$, producing MAP estimators $P(S)$. Diagram (a) shows form of weak coupling where two modules act independently, with their own likelihood functions $P(I|S)$ and priors $P(S)$, producing MAP estimators, $S^* = \arg\max_S P(I|S)P(S)$, as outputs, which are then combined in unspecified manner. Observe that this method provides no information at all about uncertainty of each estimate. Diagram (b) shows weak coupling where likelihood functions and priors of two modules are multiplied together and then MAP estimator is calculated. Such coupling would yield weighted combination of cues in some circumstances (see Yuille and Bülthoff 1995). In (c) likelihood functions of modules are combined with single prior for combined modules and then MAP estimator is found. This case is on borderline between weak and strong coupling. It is weak if prior $P(S)$ is same as that used for individual modules, and it is strong otherwise. Diagram (d) shows strong coupling where it is impossible to factor the likelihood function of the combined modules into the likelihood functions for the individual modules.

often assume rigidity). In this case, the prior for the coupled modules is different from the priors for the individual modules and we say the modules are "strongly" coupled.

The need for formulating cue combination by (3.2) may seem obvious to statisticians. Indeed, some might argue that the need for strong coupling is only an artifact of incorrect modularization of early vision. We have sympathy for such a viewpoint.

Observe also that there is no need for a veto mechanism between cues in our framework. Such a mechanism is only needed when two cues appear to conflict. But this conflict is merely due to using mutually inconsistent models for the two cues; if we combine the cues using (3.2), this conflict vanishes.

In the next subsection we will give one example of cue integration. We will demonstrate that for shading and texture the likelihood function usually cannot be factored, and thus strong coupling is required.

Strong Coupling of Shading and Texture

We now consider coupling shading with texture. First, we argue that in this case the likelihood functions are not independent and that strong coupling is usually required. Second, we describe an experiment from Bülthoff and Mallot (1990), which shows how the integration of shading and texture information gives a significantly more accurate depth perception than that attained by shading and texture independently.

As we discussed in the previous section, standard theories of shape from shading and texture, in particular their likelihood functions, are only valid in certain contexts; moreover, these contexts are mutually exclusive. Shape from shading assumes that the image intensity is due purely to shading effects (no albedo variations), while shape from texture assumes that it is due only to the presence of texture.

To couple shading with texture, we must consider a context where the image intensity is generated both by shading and textural processes. Such a context may be modeled by a simple reflectance model

$$I(x) = a(x)R(\vec{n}(x)), \tag{3.3}$$

where the texture information is conveyed by the albedo term $a(x)$ and the shading information is captured by $R(\vec{n}(x))$. It is typically assumed that the reflectance function is Lambertian $\vec{s} \cdot \vec{n}$ and that there are a class of elementary texture elements painted onto the surface in a statistically uniform distribution. This will induce a distribution on the albedo, $a(x)$, that depends on the geometry of the surface in space.

Typically, texture modules assume that $R(\vec{n}(x)) = 1$, $\forall x$, while shading modules set $a(x) = 1$, $\forall x$. For the coupled system, these assumptions are invalid (see fig. 3.4). The shading module has to filter out the albedo $a(x)$, or texture, while the texture information must ignore the shading information $R(\vec{n}(x))$. For some images, it may be possible to do this filtering independently

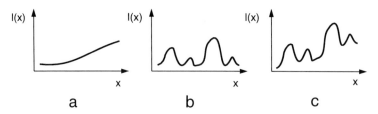

Figure 3.4 Difficulty of decoupling shading and texture cues. Graph (a) shows typical intensity profile for Lambertian surface with constant albedo, context in which shape from shading can be computed. Graph (b) shows intensity profile for surface with strong albedo variation, context for shape from texture. Graph (c) shows intensity profile when both cues are present. Separating this profile into its shading in (a), and textural components in (b), is hard in general. In Bayesian terms this is because likelihood function for combined shading and texture cannot, in general, be factored into likelihood functions for two individual cues.

(i.e., the texture model can filter out $R(\vec{n}(x))$ without any input from the shading module, and vice versa). In general, however, distinguishing between $R(\vec{n}(x))$ and $a(x)$ is not at all straightforward. Consider an object made up of many surface patches with Lambertian reflectance functions and differing albedos. For such a stimulus, it seems impossible to separate the intensity into albedo and shading components *before* computing the surface geometry. Thus we argue that the likelihood functions for the combined shading and texture module usually cannot be factored as the product of the likelihood functions for the individual modules, and hence strong coupling is required (a similar point is made by Adelson and Pentland 1991).

Other examples of "unfactorizable cues" include the phenomena of *cooperative processes*, where the perception of shape from shading depends very strongly on contour cues (Knill and Kersten 1991) or on stereo curvature cues (Buckley, Frisby, and Freeman 1993).

In addition we argue that, because more information is available in the likelihood term of the combined module, the prior assumption on the surface geometry can be weakened. Hence there is both less bias towards the fronto-parallel plane from the priors and more bias toward the correct perception from the shading and texture cues.

In the experiment reported below (fig. 3.5), shape from shading and shape from texture alone gave strong underestimations of orientation, yet the combined cues gave almost perfect orientation. Such a result seems inconsistent with Marr's (1982) theory or with coupling by weighted averages. Instead, it seems plausible that this is an example of strong coupling between texture and shading, with a weak prior toward piecewise smooth surfaces. The only way that these results might be consistent with weak coupling would be if simple filters could decompose the image into texture and shading parts, hence factorizing the likelihood function, and then combine the cues using the same prior used by both modules. This prior would have to be so weak that the likelihood functions of the two modules would dominate it.

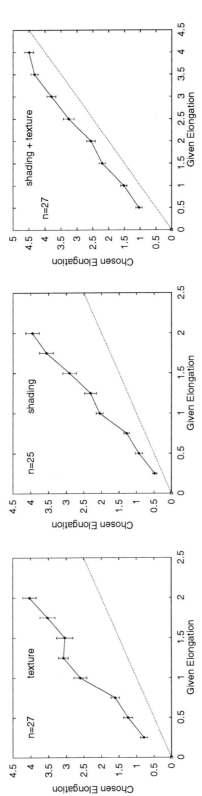

Figure 3.5 Psychophysical experiments on integration of shading and texture. In adjustment task subjects interactively adjusted shading or texture of simulated ellipsoid of rotation (seen by one eye) in order to match form of given ellipsoid seen with both eyes (in stereo). Ellipsoids were seen end-on so that outline was same for both surfaces. Shape from shading and shape from texture individually lead to strong underestimation of shape, that is, shading or texture of ellipsoid with much larger elongation had to be simulated in order to match given ellipsoid (slope ≫ 1). If shading and texture are presented simultaneously, shape is adjusted almost correctly (slope = 1). Redrawn from Bülthoff and Mallot (1990).

3.4 CONTEXTS AND COMPETITIVE PRIORS

As we have seen, the current models for visual cues make prior assumptions about the scene. In particular, the likelihood function often assumes a particular context—for example, Lambertian surfaces. The choices of priors and contexts is very important; they correspond to the "knowledge" about the world used by the visual system. In particular, the visual system will only function well if the priors and the contexts are correct.

What types of priors or contexts should be used? The influential work of Marr (1982) proposed that vision should proceed in a feedforward way. Low-level vision was performed by vision modules that each used a single general purpose prior such as rigidity for structure from motion or surface smoothness for stereo. Such priors were called "natural constraints" by Marr (1982). Low-level vision culminated in the $2\frac{1}{2}$-D sketch, a representation of the world in terms of surfaces. Finally, object specific knowledge was used to act on the $2\frac{1}{2}$-D sketch to perform object recognition and scene interpretation. Because the types of priors suggested for low-level vision are general-purpose we will refer to them as generic priors.

The question naturally arises whether models of early vision should have one generic prior. It is clear that when designing a visual system for performing a specific visual task, the prior assumptions should be geared toward achieving the task. Hence it can be argued (Clark and Yuille 1990; Yuille and Clark 1993) that a set of different systems geared toward different tasks and competing with each other is preferable to a single generic prior.

These competitive priors should apply both to the material properties of the objects and their surface geometries. We will sketch how the idea applies to competing models for prior geometries and then give a general mathematical formulation. An example of competing priors for material properties is described in Yuille and Bülthoff (1996).

To make this more precise, consider the specific example of shape from shading. Methods based on an energy function, such as Horn and Brooks (1986), assume a specific form of smoothness for the surface. The algorithm is therefore biased toward the class of surfaces defined by the exact form of the smoothness constraint, which prevents it from correctly finding the shape of surfaces such as spheres, cylinders, or cones.

On the other hand, there already exist algorithms that are guaranteed to work for specific types of surfaces. Pentland (1989) designed a local shape from shading algorithm that, by the nature of its prior assumptions, is guaranteed to work for spherical surfaces. Similarly, Woodham (1981) has designed a set of algorithms guaranteed to work on developable surfaces, a class of surfaces that includes cones and cylinders.

Thus, instead of a single generic prior, it would seem more sensible to use different theories; in this case, Horn and Brooks's, Pentland's, and Woodham's, in parallel. A fitness criterion is required for each theory to determine how well it fits the data; these criteria can then be used to determine which theory should be applied.

More formally, let $P_1(f)$, $P_2(f)$, ..., $P_N(f)$ be the prior assumptions of a set of competing models with corresponding imaging models $P_1(I|f)$, ..., $P_N(I|f)$. We assume prior probabilities $P_p(a)$ that the ath model is the correct choice, so $\sum_{a=1}^{N} P_p(a) = 1$. This leads to a set of different modules, each trying to find the solution that maximizes their associated conditional probability:

$$P_1(f|I) = \frac{P_1(I|f)P_1(f)}{P_1(I)},$$

$$P_N(f|I) = \frac{P_N(I|f)P_N(f)}{P_N(I)}.$$

(3.4)

Let our space of decisions be $D = \{d, i\}$, where d specifies the scene and i labels the model we choose to describe it. We must specify a loss function $L(d, i : f, a)$, the loss for using model i to obtain scene d when the true model should be a and the scene is f, and define a risk

$$R(d, i) = \sum_a \int L(d, i : f, a) P_a(f|I) P_p(a) [df],$$

(3.5)

where, for example, we might set $L(d, i : f, a) = -\delta(f - d)\delta_{ia}$ (i.e., we are penalized by δ_{ia} for not finding the right model and by $-\delta(f - d)$ for not finding the right surface). Here $\delta(f - d)$ denotes the Dirac delta function and δ_{ia} is the Kronecker delta, where $\delta_{ia} = 1$ if $i = a$ and 0 otherwise. The Bayes decision corresponds to picking the model i and the scene d that minimizes the risk.

A number of psychophysical experiments seem to require explanations in terms of competitive priors. In all cases the perception of the stimuli can be made to change greatly by small changes in the stimuli; some of these experiments would also seem to require strong coupling.

Transparency

Kersten et al. (1991) describe a transparency experiment in which the scene can be interpreted either as a pair of rectangles rotating rigidly around a common axis or as two independent rigid rectangles rotating around their own axis (fig. 3.6). The competitive priors correspond to assuming that the rectangles are coupled together to form a rigid object or that the rectangles are uncoupled and move independently; by adjusting the transparency cues, either perception can be achieved. Interestingly, the perception of the uncoupled motion is only temporary and seems to be replaced by the perception of the coupled motion. We conjecture that this is due to the buildup of support for the coupled hypothesis over time. The uncoupled interpretation is initially supported because it agrees with the transparency cue. Over a long period of time, however, the uncoupled motion is judged less likely than coupled

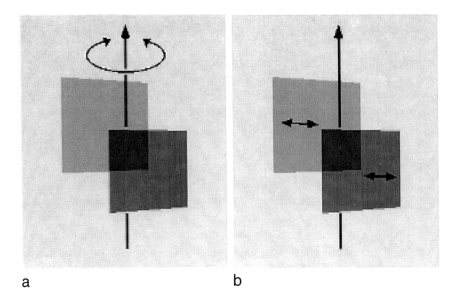

a   b

Figure 3.6 In order to study how structure from motion interacts with transparency cues, two rigidly coupled planar surfaces rocking back and forth about common vertical axis midway between them were simulated. Intensity relationships of various regions of overlapping faces bias apparent transparency faces and therefore depth ordering of faces. a. If simulated depth ordering was consistent with depth ordering suggested by transparency cue rigid motion around common axis was perceived. b. If motion parallax and transparency cue were contradictory, nonrigid motion of two faces slipping and sliding over one another was perceived. Redrawn from Kersten et al. (1991).

motion, although this hypothesis does require a relative ordering of competing explanations, which could be implemented by prior probabilities. It is not hard to persuade oneself that coupled motion is more natural, and hence should have higher prior probability, than uncoupled motion.

Specular Stereo

Blake and Bülthoff's (1990, 1991) work on specular stereo shows how small changes in the stimuli can dramatically change the perception. In these experiments a sphere is given a Lambertian reflectance function and is viewed binocularly. A specular component is simulated and is adjusted so that it can lie in front of the sphere, between the center and the surface of the sphere or at the center of the sphere (fig. 3.7). If the specularity is at the center, it is seen as a lightbulb and the sphere appears transparent. If the specularity lies in the physically correct position within the sphere (halfway between the center and the surface), the sphere is perceived as being a glossy, metallic object. It is interesting that, before doing the experiment, most people think that the specularity should lie on the convex surface and not behind. If the specularity lies in front of the sphere, it is seen as a cloud floating in front of a matte sphere. We can say that there are three competing assumptions for the

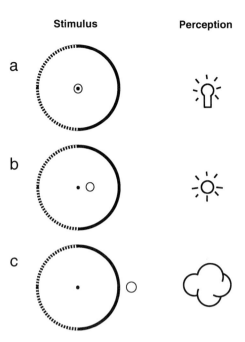

Stimulus **Perception**

a

b

c

Figure 3.7 Specular stereo where hemisphere is viewed binocularly. In (a) specularity (the white ellipsoid) is adjusted to lie behind center of sphere; it is perceived as lightbulb lying behind transparent sphere. In (b) specularity lies in approximately the correct position; the hemisphere is perceived to be metallic, with specularity appearing as image of light source. If specularity lies in front of hemisphere, as in (c), it is perceived as cloud floating in front of hemisphere.

material of the sphere: (1) transparent, (2) glossy, and (3) matte; the choice of model depends on the data. In addition, if the sphere is arranged so that its Lambertian part has no disparity, the stereo cue for the specularity resolves the concave/convex ambiguity from the shading cues (see Blake and Bülthoff 1990, 1991) for details.

Amodal Completion

Nakayama and Shimojo (1992) describe an impressive set of stereo experiments that suggest the visual system can interpret the world in terms of surfaces that may partially occlude each other. The visual system often performs significant interpolation in regions that are partially hidden. For example, one can obtain a strong perception of a Japanese flag (see fig. 3.8) even when the stimulus contains very little information, provided that the missing parts of the flag are occluded by another surface.

Nakayama and Shimojo (1992) themselves argue that their experiments can be described by having a set of competing hypotheses, $i = 1, \ldots, N$, about the possible scene and corresponding image formation models, $P_i(I|S_i)$.

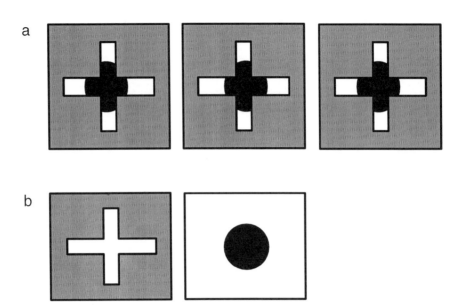

Figure 3.8 Binocular stereo cues for surfaces occluding each other. Observers of stereo pair (left pair for uncrossed fusion and right pair for crossed fusion) usually see planar surface, with cross-shaped hole in its central region, floating above surface with circle at its center (see decomposition below).

They suggest picking the interpretation j that maximizes $P_j(S_j|I) = P_j(I|S_j)/\{\sum_k P(I|S_k)\}$—which can be seen as a special case of our competitive prior formulation. They also argue that this is related to the generic viewpoint hypothesis (Freeman 1993)—if a regularity appears in an image, then the regularity is due to a regularity in the scene rather than an accidental result of the viewpoint. Recently, Bülthoff, Kersten, and Bülthoff (1994) showed that the presumption of a generic viewpoint can be extended also to the domain of illumination and the resulting shadow and lighting effects. Given an accidental view or a sequence of views of an object, the human visual system can make use of global information from the illumination (shadows) to determine the object's shape and properties. For example, shadow information strongly biases the perception of the horizontal bar in Nakayama and Shimojo's stereogram of a cross to appear nonplanar (fig. 3.9).

3.5 DISCUSSION

The competitive prior approach assumes that there is a large set of possible hypotheses about scenes in the world and that these scenes must be interpreted by the set of hypotheses, or competing priors, that best fit the data. We envision a far larger and richer set of competing priors than the natural constraints proposed in Marr (1982) or the regularizers occurring in regularization theory (Poggio, Torre, and Koch 1985).[4] These priors arise from the categorical structure of the world (see also Knill, Kersten, and Yuille, 1996).

Figure 3.9 Upper stereogram (left pair for uncrossed fusion and right pair for crossed fusion) shows "stereocross" by Nakayma and Shimojo (1992), which can be seen either as cross with frontoparallel horizontal bar or as cross with wings (horizontal bar bent toward the observer). Lower stereogram shows same three-dimensional layout but with added shadows. Shadow information can disambiguate many interpretations of upper stereogram and most observers will see horizontal bar bent toward the observer (Bülthoff, Kersten, and Bülthoff 1994).

How sophisticated must these contextural priors be? In this chapter we have only considered priors for low-level tasks such as surface estimation, but we see no reason why they should not reach up to object recognition and scene interpretation. At an intermediate stage we should mention the interesting results of Kersten, Mamassian, and Knill (1994), which showed that humans make use of shadow information for depth perception. In these experiments the perceived motion of a ball in a box was strongly affected by the motion of its shadow. But for this shadow information to be meaningful, the visual system must have decided that the geometry of the scene was a box—in other words, that the shadow was projected from a ball onto the planar surface at the bottom of the box.

It is clear that the most effective computer vision systems strongly exploit contextual knowledge and are geared to achieving specific tasks. To what extent should the competing priors be geared toward specific tasks? Ideally, one would like to have priors that accurately model all aspects of the visual scene, but this may be unrealistic. Instead, it would be simpler to have priors that accurately model the aspects of the world the visual system needs to know about, although the decision rules must be sophisticated enough to prevent the system from constantly hallucinating the things it desires to see. It is tempting to consider the hallucinations induced by sensory deprivation as an example of the prior imposing nonexistent structure on the data. Building up priors in this task-dependent way seems a sensible strategy for designing a visual system, but is there any evidence that biological systems are designed like this? It may be hard to test for humans because our visual system appears very general-purpose, but we believe that many lower animals behavior can be interpreted this way already. This emphasis on task dependence is at the heart of recent work on active vision (Blake and Yuille 1992). By making very specific prior assumptions about certain structures in the scene, and ignoring everything else, it has proven possible to design autonomous vehicles capable of driving at high speeds on the autobahn (Dickmanns, Mysliwetz, and Christians 1990).

Clearly the range of visual tasks that we can achieve is determined by the information, $P(S|I)$, we have about the scene. Thus the issue of what visual tasks we can achieve, or what scene parameters we can estimate, is determined by the form of $P(S|I)$, assuming we have exploited all our prior knowledge. It may well be that $P(S|I)$ contains enough information for us to make a reliable decision about whether one object is in front of another, but not enough to decide on the absolute depth values of the objects themselves.

In its current formulation the competitive prior approach leaves many questions unanswered. In particular, how many priors should there be, and how can one search efficiently through them? We believe that the answer to the first question is largely empirical and that, by building increasingly sophisticated artificial vision systems and performing more psychophysical experiments, it will be possible to determine the priors required. To search efficiently between competing priors seems to require a sophisticated mixed bottom-up and top-down strategy of the type described by Mumford (1992). In such an approach, low-level vision is constantly generating possible interpretations while, simultaneously, high-level vision is hypothesizing them and attempting to verify them.

In this Bayesian framework we have said nothing about the algorithms that might be used to make the decisions. In this we are following Marr's (1982) levels of explanation, where a distinction is made between the high-level information processing description of a visual system and the detailed algorithms for computing it.[5] Thus we may hypothesize that a specific visual ability can be modeled by a Bayesian theory without having to specify the algorithm. In a similar style, Bialek (1987) describes various experiments showing that the human visual system approaches optimal performance for certain tasks, such as estimating the number of photons arriving at the retina (Sakitt 1972), even though precise models for how these computational tasks are achieved are currently lacking. Certainly the algorithms used to compute a decision may be complex and require intermediate levels of representation. For example, a shape from texture algorithm might require first extracting textural features, which are then used to determined surface shape. Thus Bayesian theories certainly do not imply "direct perception" (Gibson 1979) in any meaningful sense. The issues of when to introduce intermediate levels of representations and of finding algorithms to implement Bayesian theories are important unsolved problems.

Finally, we have used a broad brush and not given specific details of many theories. Though much progress has been made, existing vision theories are still not as successful as one would like when implemented on real images. Bayesian decision theory gives a framework, but there are many details that need to be filled in. For example, the Bayesian approach emphasizes the importance of priors but does not give any prescription for finding them. Although workers in computational vision have developed a number of promising priors for modeling the world, it is an open research task to try to refine and extend these models in order to build systems of the type outlined here. Fortunately, the Bayesian framework is able to incorporate learning (see Kersten et al. 1987), and the success of (Bayesian) hidden Markov models for speech recognition (Paul 1990) suggests that it may be practical to learn Bayesian theories. It is particularly interesting to ask whether priors can be learned for new task.

3.6 CONCLUSION

In this chapter we have argued for a framework for vision based on Bayesian theory. Such a theory will inevitably cause biases toward the prior assumptions of the theory, particularly for the impoverished stimuli used by psychophysicists.

This approach suggests that, when coupling visual cues, one must keep in mind the interdependence between the cues and, in particular, the prior assumptions they might be subject to. In many cases, this will lead to strong coupling between visual cues rather than the weak coupling proposed by other theorists.

We also argue that the prior assumptions used by the visual system must be considerably more complex than the natural constraints and generic priors commonly used. Instead, there seems to be evidence for a competing set of prior assumptions or contexts, which also seems to be a pragmatic way to design a visual system to perform visual tasks. It may be better to design visual systems in terms of modules that are geared toward specific visual tasks in restricted contexts than modules based on the traditional concepts of visual cues.

ACKNOWLEDGMENTS

We would like to thank Andrew Blake, Stuart Geman, Dan Kersten, David Knill, Larry Maloney, David Mumford, Ken Nakayama, Whitman Richards, and Pawan Sinha for helpful discussions. Some of the material in this chapter appears also in the book *Perception as Bayesian Inference*, ed. D. Knill and W. Richards (Cambridge University Press, 1995). We would like to thank our reviewers for their very helpful comments.

NOTES

1. This is somewhat similar to the idea of "unconscious inference" developed by von Helmholtz (1910) and Gregory (1970).

2. That is, we assume the observed intensity at each point in the image is modeled by a Gaussian distribution with a mean given by the $\vec{n} \cdot \vec{s}$, where $\vec{n}$ is the normal of the corresponding point in space, and variance σ^2.

3. "The principle of modular design does not forbid weak interactions between different modules in a task, but it does insist that the overall organization must, to a first approximation, be modular" (Marr 1982, 102.).

4. The Bayesian approach to vision, and to statistics in general, emphasizes the importance of specifying precisely which prior assumptions are being used. Thus it intrinsically leads to the search and identification of priors/constraints.

5. Note that we treat the choice of modules and their coupling as being high-level descriptions rather than algorithmic ones.

REFERENCES

Adelson, E., and Pentland, A. (1991). The perception of shading and reflectance. In Blum, B. (Ed.), *Channels in the visual nervous system*. London: Freud.

Bayes, T. (1783). An essay towards solving a problem in the doctrine of chances. *Philosophical Transactions of the Royal Society, London, 53*, 370–418.

Berger, J. (1985). *Statistical decision theory and Bayesian analysis*. 2d ed. New York: Springer.

Bialek, W. (1987). Physical limits to sensation and perception. *Annual Review of Biophysics and Biophysical Chemistry, 16*, 455–478.

Blake, A., and Bülthoff, H. (1990). Does the brain know the physics of specular reflection? *Nature, 343*, 165–168.

Blake, A., and Bülthoff, H. (1991). Shape from specularities: Computation and psychophysics. *Philosophical Transactions of the Royal Society, London, B331*, 237–252.

Blake, A., Bülthoff, H., and Sheinberg, D. (1993). An ideal observer model for inference of shape from texture. *Vision Research, 33*, 1723–1737.

Blake, A., and Yuille, A. (Eds.). (1992). *Active vision*. Cambridge, MA: MIT Press.

Bruno, N., and Cutting, J. (1988). Minimodularity and the perception of layout. *Journal of Experimental Psychology: General, 117*, 161–170.

Buckley, D., Frisby, J., and Freeman, J. (1993). Lightness perception can be affected by surface curvature from stereopsis. Artificial intelligence vision research unit preprint, Department of Psychology, University of Sheffield.

Bülthoff, I., Kersten, D., and Bülthoff, H. (1994). General lighting can overcome accidental viewing. *Investigative Ophthalmology and Visual Science, 35*(4), 1741.

Bülthoff, H., and Mallot, H. (1988). Interaction of different modules in depth perception. *Journal of the Optical Society of America, A5*, 1749–1758.

Bülthoff, H., and Mallot, H. (1990). Integration of stereo, shading and texture. In A. Blake and T. Troscianko (Eds.), *AI and the eye*, 119–146. Chichester: Wiley.

Clark, J., and Yuille, A. (1990) *Data fusion for sensory information processing systems*. Boston: Kluwer Academic Press.

Dickmanns, E., Mysliwetz, B., and Christians, T. (1990). An integrated spatiotemporal approach to automated visual guidance of autonomous vehicles. *IEEE Transactions on Systems, Man, and Cybernetics, 20*, 1273–1284.

Dosher, B., Sperling, G., and Wurst, S. (1986). Trade-offs between stereopsis and proximity luminance covariance as determinants of perceived 3-D structure. *Vision Research, 26*, 973–990.

Freeman, W. (1993). Exploiting the generic view assumption to estimate scene parameters. In *Proceedings of the Fourth International Conference on Computer Vision, 347–356*. IEEE Computer Society Press. Los Alamitos, CA: Berlin.

Gibson, J. (1979). *The ecological approach to visual perception.* Boston: Houghton Mifflin.

Gregory, R. (1970). *The intelligent eye.* New York: McGraw-Hill.

Horn, B. (1986). *Robot vision.* Cambridge, MA: MIT Press.

Horn, B., and Brooks, M. (1986). The variational approach to shape from shading. *Computer Vision, Graphics, and Image Processing, 2*, 174–208.

Kersten, D., Bülthoff, H., Schwartz, B., and Kurtz, K. (1991). Interaction between transparency and structure from motion. *Neural Computation, 4*, 573–589.

Kersten, D., Mamassian, P., and Knill, D. (1994). Moving cast shadows and the perception of relative depth. Technical report no. 6, Max Planck Institute for Biological Cybernetics, Tübingen, Germany.

Kersten, D., O'Toole, A., Sereno, M., Knill, D., and Anderson, J. (1987). Associative learning of scene parameters from images. *Journal of the Optical Society of America, A26*(23), 4999–5006.

Knill, D., and Kersten, D. (1991). Apparent surface curvature affects lightness perception. *Nature, 351*, 228–230.

Knill, K., Kersten, D., and Yuille, A. (1996). A Bayesian formulation of visual perception. In Knill, D. and Richards, W., (Eds.), *Perception as Bayesian inference.* Cambridge: Cambridge University Press.

Koenderink, J., van Doorn, A., and Kappers, A. (1992). Surface perception in pictures. *Perception and Psychophysics, 52*, 487–496.

Landy, M., Maloney, L., Johnston, E., and Young, M. (1995). Measurement and modeling of depth cue combination: In defense of weak fusion. *Vision Research, 35*, 389–412.

Maloney, L., and Landy, M. (1989). A statistical framework for robust fusion of depth information. *Proceedings of the SPIE: Visual Communications and Image Processing*, Part 2, 1154–1163. Boston.

Mamassian, P., and Kersten, D. (1994). Perception of local orientation on shaded smooth surfaces. *Vision Research* Submitted.

Marr, D. (1982). *Vision.* San Francisco: W.H. Freeman.

Mumford, D. (1992). On the computational architecture of the neocortex. II. The role of cortico-cortical loops. *Biological Cybernetics, 66*, 241–251.

Nakayama, K., and Shimojo, S. (1992). Experiencing and perceiving visual surfaces. *Science, 257*, 1357–1363.

Parisi, G. (1988). *Statistical field theory.* Reading, MA: Addison-Wesley.

Paul, D. (1990). Speech recognition using hidden Markov models. *Lincoln Laboratory Journal, 3*, (1).

Pentland, A. (1989). Local shading analysis. In B. Horn, B. and M. Brooks (Eds.), *Shape from shading, 443–487*. Cambridge, MA: MIT Press.

Poggio, T., Gamble, E., and Little, J. (1988). Parallel integration of vision modules. *Science, 242*, 436–440.

Poggio, T., Torre, V., and Koch, C. (1985). Computational vision and regularization theory. *Nature, 317,* 314–319.

Pollard, S., Mayhew, J., and Frisby, J. (1985). A stereo correspondence algorithm using a disparity gradient limit. *Perception, 14,* 449–470.

Sakitt, B. (1972). Counting every quantum. *Journal of Physiology, 284,* 261.

von Helmholtz, H. (1910). *Treatise on physiological optics.* Trans. from 3d German ed. Vol. 3, ed. J. P. C. Southall. Reprint, New York: Dover, 1962.

Woodham, R. (1981). Analyzing images of curved surfaces. *AI Journal, 17,* 117–140.

Yuille, A., and Bülthoff, H. (1996). Bayesian decision theory and psychophysics. In D. Knill and W. Richards (Eds.), *Perception as Bayesian inference,* Cambridge: Cambridge University Press.

Yuille, A., and Clark, J. (1993). Bayesian models, deformable templates, and competitive priors. In L. Harris and M. Jenkin (Eds.), *Spatial vision in humans and robots.* Cambridge: Cambridge University Press.

4

Stereo and Texture Cue Integration in the Perception of Planar and Curved Large Real Surfaces

John P. Frisby, David Buckley, and
Jonathan Freeman

ABSTRACT

Studies of how stereo and texture depth cues are integrated have often used stereograms to present binocular disparity information about surface shape. However, we have found that quite different patterns of stereo and texture cue integration can be observed for surfaces portrayed by stereograms and by real 3-D objects of putatively identical shape. To avoid that problem, we have conducted a series of studies in which large real planar or curved surfaces are seen with carefully controlled texture cues projected onto them from above. In all experiments the physical nature of the surface determined the nature of the stereo cue, and small cue conflicts were created by manipulating the nature of the projected textures. The observer's task was to judge surface orientation at certain points using either a haptic paddle matching task or a visual stick probe set into the surface whose orientation had to be set to appear as a surface normal. The general finding was that perceived surface shape was determined by a roughly equally weighted combination of the stereo and texture cues. When textures were used with conflicting components, compression proved dominant for surface orientation judgments from curved surfaces, whereas perspective proved dominant for planar surfaces. This finding goes against theoretical expectations from cue variance power indices of the information portrayed by each component, which predict that compression should have been dominant in both cases. It is suggested that the special role observed for perspective in the case of planar surfaces may reflect the use of linear perspective cues in surface orientation recovery by human vision.

4.1 BACKGROUND

Although cue integration has been a topic of long-standing interest in human vision research, recent years have seen greatly increased efforts to elucidate its nature. There are a number of reasons why this should be so. Despite real progress in computer vision in developing so-called shape-from- algorithms (e.g., shape from stereo, texture, contour, shading, motion), shortcomings in existing methods for dealing with cues in isolation have awakened interest in the potential benefits of processing cues in combination, and guidance has been sought from how biological vision combines cues. Also, computer graphics techniques for stimulus generation have become widely available, allowing richer stimuli to be created on affordable computers, thus opening up new opportunities for psychophysical research. In this chapter, we do not review theoretical developments in the field. Interested readers should consult Bülthoff and Yuille's review of how problems in cue integration can be posed within a Bayesian framework (chap. 3, this volume) and Massaro's use of ideas from fuzzy logic theory (chap. 16, this volume). Also, a recent paper by Landy et al. (1995) provides a good review of weighted cue averaging theories, including their own "modified weak fusion" theory. Here we concentrate on describing some of our experiments that have adopted the distinctive empirical approach of examining stereo and texture cue integration in human vision using quasi-natural viewing of real objects. One general theme underlying this work is to determine whether conclusions concerning stereo and texture integration derived from the artificial world of laboratory computer displays extend to natural viewing of real-world objects. Another is to examine the power of texture to influence percepts of 3-D surface structure in conjunction with stereo, not only treating texture as a single cue but also as a multifaceted source of information in which different components, such as compression (c) and perspective (p), may be used by the human visual system for recovering different aspects of 3-D surface structure. Our starting point for the latter theme has been the seminal paper by Cutting and Millard (1984).

Stereograms are the standard psychophysical tool for presenting stereo cues in studies of cue integration. We have found, however, that quite different patterns of stereo/texture cue integration can be observed for certain real objects and stereograms of putatively the same objects (Buckley and Frisby 1993). We will not discuss in detail here why different patterns of results emerged for the two sorts of stimuli, simply noting that we believe it relates to the important role played by oculomotor factors (vergence and accommodation) in stereo vision (Frisby, Buckley, and Horsman 1995). In natural viewing of real scenes, there is a strong synkinesis between vergence eye movements and accommodation in response to disparity cues. For our real objects the disparity cues were, by virtue of the means used to create them (they were 3-D ridges made of white card), everywhere in synchrony with the oculomotor cues. In contrast, in the stereograms disparity was everywhere in conflict with accommodation, except at the mast distant edges of the stereogram ridges that lay in the plane of the monitor screen. This conflict possibly led to disruption in the operation of the normal vergence/accommodation synkinesis, particularly in view of the near viewing distance used (57 cm), with adverse effects on the strength of the stereo cues overall. But whatever the explanation, the realization that stereograms may produce quite different cue integration results from those found using real stimuli raises a daunting prospect. Many psychophysical laboratory findings on how stereo is integrated with other cues could be phenomena only of the impoverished visual environment that generated them, in which, typically, disparity cues are out of synchrony with oculomotor cues. Our general goal has been to study how human vision operates in a natural environment, and this is why we have concentrated our investigations on stereo/texture cue integration using real surfaces.

Another point concerning the general framework for our research is that we have investigated only small cue conflicts. We have avoided pitting one cue strongly against another because we wish to study how the visual system integrates different cues when it might reasonably consider the data arriving from any given cue module as giving information on the same scene surface, with cue conflicts interpreted as lying within "reasonable" error variation due to inevitable noise in each module. Of course, defining what is "reasonable" would require knowledge of the accuracy of any one cue considered on its own, from which could be computed a principled definition of "small cue conflict." Such knowledge is not available; instead, we adopted the strategy of studying only cue conflicts that did not appear to lead to perceptual flipping between cues, as one vetoed the other (see Bülthoff and Mallot 1987). Landy et al. (1995) provide a recent review of theoretical issues related to this question.

4.2 GENERAL METHODOLOGY AND APPARATUS

The apparatus we have developed to tackle our research questions is illustrated in figure 4.1. An observer standing at the edge of a table looks down on it through a tilted headrest that occludes the table's edges and provides a field of view of about $20° \times 20°$. The table surface can be arranged to be either planar or curved, the latter by fixing to it a large Gaussian-shaped ridge. We have used two viewing positions for the observer, labeled A and B in figure 4.1. Point A is positioned so that the observer's median plane is orthogonal to a pivot that allows the table to be slanted in the "uphill/downhill" direction from position A to angles $+/-10$ degrees from "horizontal" (itself defined as parallel to the ground plane on which the observers stood). Point B is positioned to one side of the table. We have used a variety of tasks for measuring 3-D surface orientation perceptions of planar and curved table surfaces, in particular: (1) subjectively estimating planar surfaces seen from position A following training with feedback (Frisby and Buckley, 1992); (2) setting the orientation of a haptically sensed paddle to match perceived surface orientation at various points on a Gaussian ridge; and (3) setting the orientation of a self-luminous perspex stick probe protruding from the surface so that it appeared to be a surface normal. This chapter deals only with the latter two methods and viewing position B, which created a viewing distance of 163 cm to the base of the stick probe. (See also Frisby et al. 1995 for a report of experiments in which steps of various sizes were placed on the table, with the observer's task being to judge step size, and the independent texture variable being the size of the texture cue to the slants of the step's.)

The advantage of this simple apparatus is that, because stereo cues to 3-D shape are created by natural viewing of a real surface, disparity, accommodation, and vergence are in synchrony wherever the observer looks, which is

Stereo and Texture Cue Integration in Perception of Surfaces

(a)

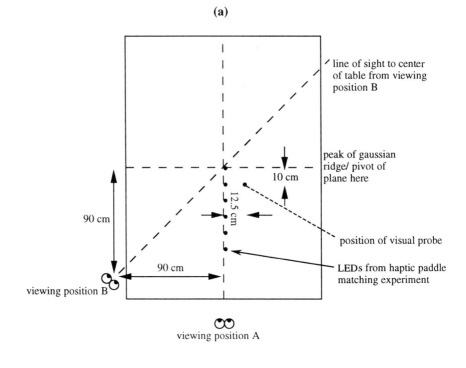

line of sight to center of table from viewing position B

peak of gaussian ridge/ pivot of plane here

10 cm

12.5 cm

90 cm

90 cm

position of visual probe

LEDs from haptic paddle matching experiment

viewing position B

viewing position A

(b)

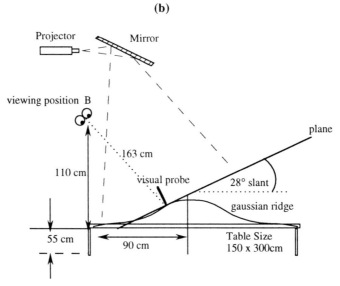

Projector

Mirror

viewing position B

plane

163 cm

110 cm

visual probe

28° slant

gaussian ridge

55 cm

90 cm

Table Size 150 x 300cm

Figure 4.1 Ground plane table apparatus. a. Plan view. b. Cross section. Details in text.

not the case in stereograms. The texture cues seen on the table surface are provided by slides projected from an overhead projector. Computer graphics were used to create laser-printed textures, which were then photographed to create the slides. The textures were seen as white elements lying on a dark ground provided by a sheet of black cloth laid over the table surface. Texture cues could be made consistent with the natural stereo cues or to conflict with them by signaling a plane with a different surface orientation or a Gaussian ridge with a different standard deviation. Textures projected on to the table always made due allowance for the viewpoint of the observer and for the effect of the physical characteristics of the table (its physical surface orientation or curvature), so that the required texture cues were seen from the observer's viewpoint irrespective of the structure of the table surface itself (and hence independently of the stereo cues).

4.3   METHODOLOGY FOR MEASURING PERCEIVED SURFACE ORIENTATION AND CURVATURE

Koenderink, van Doorn, and Kappers (1992) have used a technique in which a small outline picture of an "upturned drawing pin" is projected as a probe onto a sequence of locations distributed over a picture of an object (cf. the earlier usage by Stevens 1983 of a similar probe). The observer's task was to manipulate the orientation of the probe until it seemed to depict the surface normal at the location in question. Koenderink and colleagues showed how integration of the local gradient measures so obtained could then be carried out to estimate the observer's overall perception of the 3-D structure of the scene surface as implied by the local gradient measures.

The difficulty with the upturned drawing pin technique for our purposes, however, is that the orientation of the elliptical base of the pin can be set to be in synchrony with the orientation of local texture elements, as a local pattern match, to the exclusion of any influence from the stereo cue. That would be a particularly likely hazard given the elliptical surface texture elements of the kind we often use, as then a local pattern match would be particularly straightforward. We developed two methods for getting around this problem. The first did not use a visual probe at all but instead a haptic matching task. This proved only partly successful because the data were relatively noisy; hence we also developed a "visual stick probe," data from which constitute the major part of the present chapter. As its name suggests, this probe was simply a slick (12 cm long) protruding from the table surface (figs. 4.1b and 4.2a,b), so that it was unlikely to suffer from the problem just described for the upturned drawing pin probe. This indeed seemed to be the case because stick settings were by no means always in synchrony with the texture cue. Similar results were obtained from the haptic and visual probes to identical stimulus conditions, although with the advantage that the visual

(a) Circles SD 67cm

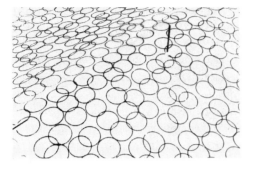

(b) Squares SD 17cm

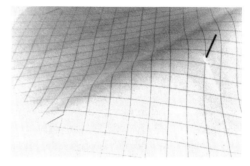

(c) Circles & Dots SD 17cm

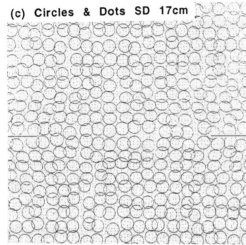

(d) Circles & Dots SD 67cm

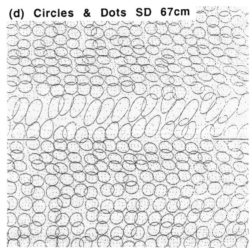

Figure 4.2 Photograph taken from observer's viewpoint when random circles texture signaling a Gaussian ridge with SD 67 cm was projected onto physical ridge with SD 17 cm. b. Same as (a) but for regular squares texture and for texture SD of 17 cm. c. Random circles plus dots texture that was projected onto rig from above for SD 17 cm. d. Same as (c) but for SD 67 cm. Note that distortions in (c) and (d) were not seen as such by observers, as can be judged from (a). Also, in experiments contrast was reversed (bright lines on dark ground), and shading was not present, being an artifact of printing photographs for this chapter.

probe matches were less noisy. Each methodology is described in this section, before proceeding to the results obtained with each one.

In experiment 1 the observer's task was to set a felt (and unseen) paddle, positioned comfortably within reach just below the headrest, so that its orientation matched that of the Gaussian ridge surface at the series of six points shown in figure 4.1a. An oblique viewpoint of the ridge was chosen (position B in fig. 4.1a) because, pilot studies indicated, that position produced more reliable gradient judgments at the required locations on the ridge profile than did position A. Paddle settings were logged as readings from a calibrated potentiometer whose shaft formed the paddle's pivot. This pivot was oriented parallel to the ridge axis to facilitate the observer's task. That arrangement of the paddle's orientation meant observers were required to set the paddle to what would be the surface slant angle seen from position A. This is mentioned for purposes of exposition only: slant and tilt angles are view-dependent quantities, and the actual slant and tilt angles seen from position B would be quite different. To avoid confusion, throughout this chapter, when we refer to measuring surface orientation, we do not separately specify slant and tilt angles, and we provide data plots that are oriented orthogonally to the table's pivot axis (which in the case of the ridges defined ridge orientation). Only when calculating the power in different texture components do we explicitly take into account viewing position (see later comments in connection with figure 4.3).

In experiment 1 each point for which a haptic paddle setting was required was marked by an LED inserted into the surface in a row on a line across the ridge, at 5 cm spacings measured along the base of the ridge. Each of the LEDs could be seen only when illuminated, which they were sequentially from peak to trough to mark the spot for which a gradient judgment was required. Pilot work showed that sequential illumination did not produce different results from a random order of illumination but that it had the considerable advantage of reducing the duration of the experiment. Training was given in the use of the paddle prior to the experiment proper in an attempt to achieve reliable data. During training, observers were shown pieces of wood cut to the shape of two Gaussian ridge profiles (neither used in the experiment proper), and they were asked to make paddle settings to gradients at various points on them, with feedback given. This training took about 10 minutes. In the experiment the observers required about 1.5 minutes to make the series of six local gradient measurements. Observers were instructed to keep their head still while viewing the textures; a tightly fitting headrest helped achieve that requirement. A shutter prevented sight of the tabletop when the projected texture was being changed. Two readings were taken for each condition, spread over two experimental sessions separated by a rest period of at least half an hour. The local gradient measures were integrated to give an overall description of the observer's surface perception using the technique described by Koenderink, van Doorn, and Kappers (1992).

In experiments 2, 3, and 4, the observer's task was to adjust, also from viewpoint B and using the same paddle, the 3-D orientation of the visual stick probe mounted in the ridge surface. The stick was made of transparent perspex with a roughened surface. It was rendered visible by a red LED mounted at its base so that it was seen as a self-luminous red stick protruding out above the white-on-black texture elements of the ridge. The location of the base of the stick was a point in the upper right-hand quadrant of the observer's view of the ridge or plane (details in fig. 4.1a). An impression of what the observer saw is given in figures 4.2a,b. The orientation of the stick had to be set so that it appeared to be the surface normal at this point; its angle had one degree of freedom by virtue of being mounted on the shaft of a servo-controlled motor whose set position signal was provided by a potentiometer fixed to the paddle under the observer's control. As for the paddle settings, the stick data also measured the slant angle that would have been seen from position A.

So far we have used this real stick probe to measure a gradient at only a single point on the surface, thereby keeping the apparatus simple. For the purposes of comparing data obtained from the two measuring techniques, a picture of the overall surface perception implied by this single gradient measure was obtained by finding the Gaussian whose shape fitted that gradient at the point where the probe was located. However, all statistical analyses for the visual probe data were conducted on just the single measured point, although exactly where the probe should be located in 3-D for the purpose of surface reconstruction is debatable. We report here analyses of the data in which a "perceived Gaussian" was found by transporting the gradient measure on a gravitationally vertical line above the base of the probe until a suitably fitting Gaussian was found. We have also tried transporting the gradient measure along a line of sight from the observer to the base of the probe; this gives a similar overall qualitative picture of the nature of stereo/texture that occurred, although obviously it changes the details of the inferred perceived ridge shapes.

The stereo and texture cues incorporated in the various experiments were as follows:

1. The stereo cue: This was determined by the physical structure of the tabletop. So far we have used either a single physical Gaussian real ridge fixed to the tabletop, with amplitude 15 cm and standard deviation (SD) 17 cm, or a single physical plane whose surface orientation matched the tangent plane on the ridge at the position where the base of the probe was located. For simplicity of notation, this plane will be termed the "28° planar condition" because that was the angle of the tangent plane to the physical ridge of SD 17 cm in the direction orthogonal to the ridge's axis (fig. 4.1b). Care was taken to ensure that the probe-setting task was similar for the planar and curved stimuli by creating a planar surface in experiment 4 with an identical surface orientation at the point in 3-space where the base of the probe was located on the ridge in experiment 3. This was achieved by elevating the table pivot and choosing a rotation angle of the table around that pivot such that the surface orientation of the planar surface was tangent to the point on the ridge where the probe was located (fig. 4.1b). This ensured that observers had to judge identical surface normals in the planar and curved surface stimuli when all cues were in synchrony. The observers were not aware that only one physical ridge or plane was present throughout because they only saw the tabletop through the viewing hood, which obscured all details of the apparatus. They were invariably surprised when told during debriefing that only one physical surface had been present all along.

2. The texture cue: For experiments 1, 2, and 3, textures of either the "random circles" or "regular squares" type were used to depict ridges with amplitudes of 15 cm and with SDs of either 17, 34, or 67 cm (see examples in fig. 4.2a,b). Experiment 4 used textures of the "regular squares" type for generating planes, although more accurately this texture should perhaps be called a "regular diamonds" condition. This is because, in order to manipulate the c texture component as we required, the lines conveying the c cue were set to be horizontal in the image plane, and because the table surface was slanted, this meant that the markings on the table surface were in the shape of diamonds. The planes conveyed by the texture cues were labeled either "9°" or "28°" because these were the equivalent tangent angles for the ridges at the probe position in the sense defined above. For the random circles texture used for experiments 1 and 2, the circles were always combined with a field of pseudorandom dots. The texture cues provided by these dots were arranged to be in synchrony with the texture cue depicted by the circles. The dots were included because they seemed to us to link the circle elements perceptually, and thereby increase the impression of a carpet of texture creating the ridge. In fact, however, certain conditions included in experiment 2 but not reported here showed that the dots on their own created only a weak texture effect (cf. Stevens 1981; Frisby and Buckley 1992), and other conditions showed that texture effects from circles alone were not in fact significantly different from those created when the circles and dots were combined. The dots were therefore eliminated from the stimuli used for experiments 3 and 4.

3. Monocular and binocular judgments: Monocular data were collected to give a measure of the strength of each texture cue considered on its own. The binocular data for the Gaussian ridge carrying a texture of SD 17 cm, in which condition the stereo and texture cues were signaling the same object, served as the baseline for what observers saw when both cues were consistent; likewise, mutatis mutandis, for the planar stimuli. The main experimental question was, How would perceptions of these baseline stereo/texture consistent-cues stimuli be shifted toward those shown for monocular viewing (in which of course just the texture cue was present unopposed by the stereo cue) when a stereo/texture cue conflict was present? Stereo/texture cue conflicts were created by the texture cues being set either to SDs of 34 and 67 cm (for the ridges used in experiments 1, 2, and 3), or to angles of 17° and 28° (for the planes of experiment 4). However, for brevity we omit reporting here data from the 34 cm/17° conditions, although they were included in the statistical analyses.

Screening ensured that each of the four (different) observers used in each experiment had a stereoacuity acuity of 20 sec arc or better. Instructions were given to them initially in writing and then expanded upon orally.

4.4 POTENTIAL ROLE OF PERSPECTIVE AND COMPRESSION TEXTURE COMPONENTS IN DETECTING SURFACE ORIENTATION IN PLANAR AND CURVED SURFACES

Recent reviews of computational analyses of the information contained in various components of texture are provided by Blake and Marinos (1991) and Gårding (1992). Almost all psychophysical work has manipulated texture components in stimuli generated on computer monitors, with the observer's task being to judge surface attributes such as flatness or curvature (Cutting and Millard 1984), surface slant (Attneave and Olson 1966; Braunstein 1968; Braunstein and Payne 1969; Phillips 1970), the shape of cylindrical or parabolic ridges (e.g., Blake, Bülthoff, and Sheinberg 1993; Cumming, Johnston, and Parker 1991; Young, Landy, and Maloney 1993), or the shape of ellipsoids (e.g., Todd and Akerstrom 1987; Curran and Johnston 1994). The apparatus described above has allowed us to explore the effects of manipulating p and c components of textures on real large planar and curved surfaces viewed both binocularly and monocularly.

Following the lead set by Cutting and Millard (1984), whose study was in several ways the starting point for the present experiments, we have analyzed the information provided by p and c components of texture for the planar and curved surfaces shown in our rig. We follow Gårding (1992) in using the projected heights and widths of texels in the image plane as measures of the c and p components of texture, respectively. We do not show here analyses of information in the texture density cue because, being a measure derived from projected texel areas, density is not normally independent of p and c texel components (although artificial textures can be created that do manipulate density separately from p and c; see, for example, Cutting and Millard 1984). Figure 4.3 shows the variation in measures of p and c along a line on the table surface lying in the observer's median plane from viewing position B through the center of the table (fig. 4.1). Each pair of graphs deals with a different pair of planar and curved table surfaces, with each pair linked by having the same surface orientation (either 9° or 28° in the sense defined above and illustrated in figure 4.1b) at the point where the visual stick probe was located. We use the labels "9°" and "SD67" interchangeably to refer to the same Gaussian rig surface, one with SD 67 cm and with surface orientation of 9° at the probe position. The same is true for the pair of labels "SD17" and "28°".

The first two columns of table 4.1 show the relative percentage strengths of the p and c components in curved and planar conditions in which the texture cue comprised conflicting texture components. These strengths were computed using the following simple indices of component cue "power":

$$\text{Power}_c = \sigma_c^2/(\sigma_c^2 + \sigma_p^2) \tag{4.1}$$

$$\text{Power}_p = \sigma_p^2/(\sigma_c^2 + \sigma_p^2) \tag{4.2}$$

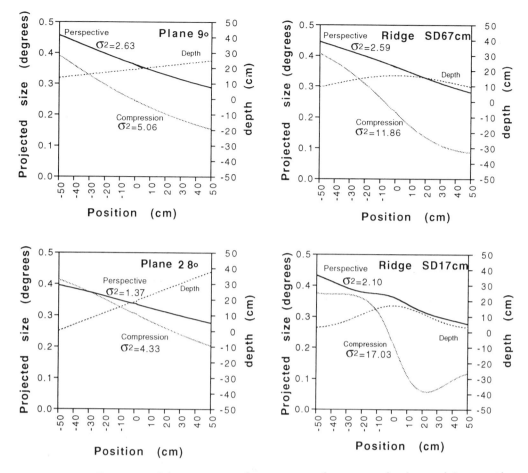

Figure 4.3 Information in p and c components of texture cues for planar and Gaussian ridge surfaces. Abscissas plot position on table surface along dashed diagonal line extending from position B in figure 4.1b. Dotted lines labeled "Depth" show depth profiles of table surface, with depth values plotted on right-hand ordinates. Cue component values are plotted on left-hand ordinates as image sizes (in degrees) of 1 cm radius texel on the table surface, with sizes for c derived from texel heights in the image plane and those for p from texel widths. Variances of image sizes of various p and c components are shown (each × 1,000 for clarity). Further details in text.

The variances for each component (σ_c^2 and σ_p^2) were computed as the mean of the squared deviations of the separate component measures shown in figure 4.3 from their mean value over approximately the visible range of the table surface. This was appropriate because these were the components used to make the conflicting p and c textures. The justification for using variances in measures of relative cue power relies on the assumption that the strength of a cue will be proportionate to the variation in the cue signal generated by the surface. Thus the power indices express the relative sizes of the variation in each cue across the surface; each index would be zero if the cue varied not at all and large if the cue varied a great deal while the other varied little. We

Stereo and Texture Cue Integration in Perception of Surfaces

Table 4.1 Power of Compression and Perspective Components of Texture Arising from Planar and Curved Surfaces Shown in Figure 4.3, Compared with Data Observed in Experiment 4.

		Component power (%)		Data (%)	
		P	C	P	C
Curved surfaces	P9C28	13	87	31	69
	P28C9	15	85	15	85
	Means	14	86	23	77
Planar surfaces	P9C28	38	62	81	19
	P28C9	21	79	50	50
	Means	29	71	65	35

use these indices to supply predictions about the extent to which p and c components can be expected to determine percepts if they are used in proportion to their strengths in the images.

The separate roles of p and c were explored in experiments 3 and 4. For experiments 1 and 2, texture was treated as a single cue for all stimuli (i.e., p and c components always in accord).

4.5   EXPERIMENT 1: HAPTIC MATCHING TASK

Random circles with dots were the textures used in this experiment; figure 4.4a shows the group means. For simplicity, data are shown only for stereo/texture cue conflicts for the texture cue of a ridge of SD 67 cm. The equivalent data for SD 34 cm showed qualitatively similar effects and were included in the statistical analyses. The curves in each case were obtained by finding a smoothly fitting line for the local gradient measures at the six sampled points using the integration technique described by Koenderink, van Doorn, and Kappers (1992). These surface profile curves were anchored to the 15 cm peak amplitude of the ridges at the zero point on the abscissas, the latter axis giving the positions of the sampled points on the physical ridge. The $+/-1$ s.e. bars shown as insets are the means of the s.e.s for all the data points shown, that is, they were computed from the inferred depths at the measured points, not from the paddle settings directly, and they reflect individual differences between observers.

The upper dotted lines show the profile signaled by the texture cue of SD 67 cm, hence the label "T67"; the data arising from this texture on its own (monocular viewing) are labeled "MONO T67." The lower dotted lines show the profile of the physical ridge that generated the stereo cue of SD 17 cm; this line also shows the profile of the texture cue for SD 17 cm cue and hence its label is "S17" or "T17." The data plot for this cues-consistent condition is labeled "S17T17." The label "S17T67" shows the cue conflict combination in which stereo was signaling SD 17 cm and texture SD 67 cm. Individual plots

Frisby, Buckley, and Freeman

were inspected for each of the four observers separately. These revealed that all showed the same qualitative cue combination effects, although there were substantial variations in perceived ridge curvature according to the haptic paddle judgments.

The group means for monocular viewing of the three SDs (17 cm, 34 cm and 67 cm) were significantly different ($p < .01$), from which we conclude that the apparatus was successful in achieving a method of signaling different levels of the texture cue for Gaussian ridges of different SDs. This conclusion is supported by the fact that the curves recovered by integration from the individual gradient measures were roughly Gaussian in shape, suggesting both that the textures were correctly portrayed and that observers could do the haptic task required of them at least qualitatively. The plot in figure 4.4a for MONO T67 shows that the group mean settings were shifted downward from expectations provided by the dotted lines, and the same tendency was present for the monocular T17 and T34 cases (data not reported here), but this was an attribute on which individual observers differed considerably.

The group means for the three texture SDs under binocular viewing were different but not significantly so, an outcome we interpret as being due to the haptic settings being relatively noisy. The introspections of observers on what they actually saw described clear differences in perceived curvature between the conditions. The general character of these descriptions fitted well the picture shown in figure 4.4a. These introspections accorded with our own and can be summarized as follows: the S17T67 condition fell roughly midway between the S17T17 and MONO T67 conditions, which is a pattern of roughly equally weighted cue stereo/texture cue integration.

It was because we regarded the failure of this observation to reach statistical significance as due to relatively noisy haptic paddle settings that we devised the visual stick probe technique used in subsequent experiments. We felt that a more sensitive technique would be necessary to examine the separate roles of p and c.

4.6   EXPERIMENT 2: VISUAL STICK PROBE MATCHING TASK

The textures used in the experiment were mainly random circles plus dots; figure 4.4b provides the group means they produced, thereby plotting equivalent data to those shown in figure 4.4a for the haptic paddle settings. Some conditions were repeated with random circles on their own, but these did not differ significantly from those with dots present, and so dots were excluded in later experiments. To facilitate comparison between experiments 1 and 2, the visual probe graphs are inferred from just the single gradient measure taken at the probe's position, whereas the haptic graphs are derived from six gradient measures. However, all tests of significance of the visual data used solely the points measured at the probe position.

It can be seen that the visual probe data provide a very similar overall picture to the haptic data. In particular, the S17T67 plot falls roughly midway

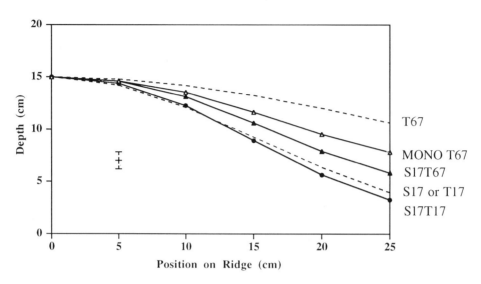

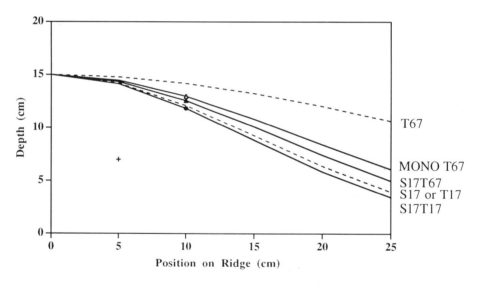

Figure 4.4   Results from experiments 1 and 2. Labels for each plot are explained in text.

between the MONO T67 and S17T17 plots, although now all relevant effects are statistically significant ($p < .01$ or better). Moreover, the (new) observers said they found setting the visual probe to be an easy and natural task (cf. similar remarks from the observers in Koenderink, van Doorn, and Kappers 1992, 1994). This ease is reflected in the inset $+/-1$ s.e. bars, which are so small that they almost fall within the size of the plotted symbols.

The main result from experiment 2 is therefore clear and statistically significant evidence for a roughly equally weighted pattern of stereo and texture cue combination in the perception of curved surfaces set into a large real ground plane. It should be noted, however, that the texture cue on its own (i.e., in monocular viewing) did not create the full expected effect, perhaps because of a role played by other cues to the shape of the physical ridge even under monocular viewing, such as accommodation.

The methodological improvements achieved with the visual stick probe were thus significant. There seemed no reason to suppose that the probe favored either stereo or texture, and hence we proceeded to use this technique to examine the role of p and c texture components in the perception of surface orientation in curved and planar surfaces, within the framework of our stereo/texture cue integration setting.

4.7 EXPERIMENTS 3 AND 4: THE RELATIVE EFFECTIVENESS OF PERSPECTIVE AND COMPRESSION TEXTURE COMPONENTS

Experiment 3 used Gaussian ridges, while experiment 4 used a planar tabletop. Regularly ruled grids were used in both studies because this facilitated the computer graphics computations that had to take into account the oblique viewpoint in manipulating p and c components. Lines running from top to bottom of the grids were oriented parallel to the observer's median plane. Because of the observer's oblique viewpoint, it can be seen in figure 4.2b that the lines crossed the Gaussian ridges in experiment 3 at an angle to the ridge axis, and the same was true for the horizontal lines. Experiment 3 also included random circle textures for conditions that did not manipulate p and c. This was done to check whether the regular grids produced different results when both p and c operated in synchrony; in fact, no significant differences emerged for the two texture types. Data were collected using the visual probe methodology described for experiment 2. The SDs of the Gaussian ridges in experiment 3 were either 17 cm, 34 cm, or 67 cm, although as before we do not report the SD 34 cm data. The surface orientation at the probe position on the 67 cm ridge was 9°, and on the (physical) 17 cm ridge it was 28°.

Figure 4.5 provides the group means from the two experiments (each derived from four different observers in each experiment). To facilitate comparisons between the data collected from the ridges and the planes, the labels "9°" and "28°" are used instead of the labels "67" and "17" hitherto used for

(a) Experiment 3 - Visual stick probe, ridges

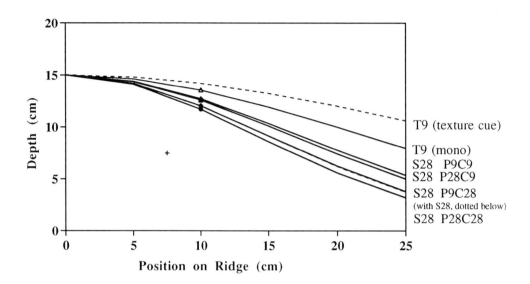

T9 (texture cue)

T9 (mono)
S28 P9C9
S28 P28C9

S28 P9C28
(with S28, dotted below)
S28 P28C28

(b) Experiment 4 - Visual stick probe, planes

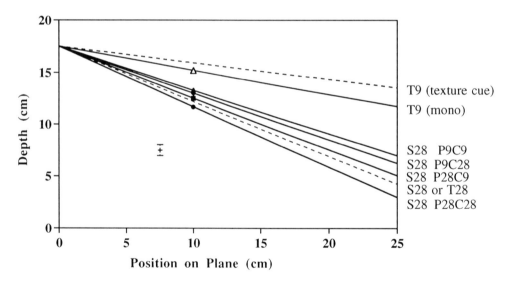

T9 (texture cue)

T9 (mono)

S28 P9C9
S28 P9C28
S28 P28C9
S28 or T28
S28 P28C28

Figure 4.5   Results from experiments 3 and 4. Labels for each plot are explained in text.

the ridge data. Otherwise, similar labeling conventions are used to those in figure 4.4. Thus in figure 4.5a, the label "T9" refers to the Gaussian profile with an SD of 67 cm created by a texture cue with a surface orientation of 9° at the probe point for a ridge. In figure 4.5b, the label "T9" refers to a planar texture cue with a surface orientation of 9° at the probe point. The label "S28 P9C28" means that the stereo cue (physical stimulus) provided a cue for surface orientation of 28°, p signaled a surface orientation of 9°, and c signaled an orientation of 28°, with these values arising from either ridges or planes as the case may be.

The first point to be noticed for the ridge data shown in figure 4.5a is that the S28 P9C9 condition fell roughly midway between the MONOC T9 data and the consistent cues condition of S28 P28C28 (differences between conditions were significant at $p < .01$). This is a replication of the approximately equal weighting of stereo and texture observed for the ridges in experiment 2 when both p and c were in synchrony.

The second point to be noted from the ridge data in figure 4.5a is that most of this effect derives from the C9 component, as shown by the very similar graphs for S28 P9C9 and S28 P28C9, and for S28 P28C28 and S28 P9C28. The power of each cue is expressed in last two columns of table 4.1 as percentages obtained as follows:

$$\text{Power}_c = 100 \frac{(\text{S28 P28C9} - \text{S28 P9C9})}{(\text{S28 P28C28} - \text{S28 P9C9})} \tag{4.3}$$

$$\text{Power}_p = 100 \frac{(\text{S28 P9C28} - \text{S28 P9C9})}{(\text{S28 P28C28} - \text{S28 P9C9})} \tag{4.4}$$

Equations (4.3) and (4.4) express the proportion of the difference produced when p and c are both different from stereo (denominators) that can be accounted for by either p or c considered on their own (numerators). Table 4.1 sets out the percentages observed for each condition. It shows that, taking the mean of the two p and c conflicting conditions (P9C28 and P28C9) for the ridges, 77 percent of the texture effect of S28 P9C9 was achieved by c, and only 23 percent by p. This is in quite good accord with theoretical expectations for the ridges (obtained using the power indices based on variances described earlier and also shown in table 4.1), for which the equivalent figures are 86 percent and 14 percent.

Data for the planar stimuli (figure 4.5b) were also significantly different ($p < .05$) and also showed a roughly equally balanced weighting for stereo and texture. Thus, as for the ridges, the S28 P9C9 condition fell roughly midway between the MONOC T9 data and the consistent cues condition (S28 P28C28). However, the picture for the relative powers of p and c for judging planar surface orientation is almost the exact opposite of that found for the ridges. As table 4.1 shows, for the planes the mean power of p was 65 percent as against 35 percent for c. This is the reverse of theoretical expectations for the planar surface which were 29 percent for p and 71 percent for c.

This pattern of c being dominant for curvature and p dominant for planarity is similar to the pattern we found in earlier work with the table rig using viewing position A, a similar viewing distance, a method of subjective estimation of slant, and regular grid textures (Frisby and Buckley 1992). In that study p and c contributed 73 percent and 27 percent, respectively, for regular grids on a planar surface. That study was also similar to the present one in showing roughly equally weighted stereo/texture cue integration when both p and c components were combined against stereo.

The present data are also qualitatively very similar to those observed by Cutting and Millard (1984) for their experiments on judgments of flatness and curvature. Observers were shown a pair of textures on a computer monitor and asked to judge which one looked more like a flat (or curved) surface receding into the distance. They then had to indicate the degree (1 to 9) to which the preferred stimulus revealed flatness (or curvature) over the non-preferred stimulus. For their curved surfaces, 96 percent of the variance in the data was accounted for by c and less than 2 percent by p. For their flat surfaces, in contrast, only 6 percent of the variance was attributable to c, whereas 65 percent related to p (the remainder was accounted for by density). Although it not a factor we manipulated in the present experiments, Buckley, Frisby, and Blake (1995) found density to be a weak cue in the context of our table rig. Cutting and Millard's (1984) data thus show more extreme differences between the curved and planar stimuli than ours; nevertheless, the two sets of data are qualitatively very alike. This is a matter of considerable interest to us because it suggests that Cutting and Millard's conclusions from artificial computer monitor displays were in keeping with our data from real surfaces. However, it needs to be borne in mind, as Cutting and Millard (1984) themselves emphasized, that judging flatness is a very different task from judging surface orientation. Clearly, flat surfaces can have any orientation; this makes it not at all obvious why we should find the same pattern of p dominance for planar surface orientation judgements, as they did for flatness judgments. Cutting and Millard explained their own findings on the importance of p for flatness in terms of an invariant expression incorporating eye height, an invariant that, as far as we can see, does not help to explain our own finding that p is especially important for surface orientation also.

Perhaps a clue as to why we found p to be dominant for planar surface orientation comes from our previous work with the table rig (Frisby and Buckley 1992), which found that square texels arranged in a randomly jittered layout produced more equally balanced contributions of p and c (52 percent and 48 percent, respectively, although we report in that paper only mean data pooled from six different textures). Jittering texels sharply reduces linear perspective effects. Thus the finding here of dominance of p for the planes when linear perspective is strongly present suggests that it may be utilized as

Frisby, Buckley, and Freeman

a special cue by the human visual system in the recovery of planar surface orientation. There is the potential for it to do so; Gårding (1991) has shown how linear perspective provides an opportunity to exploit information about vanishing points in the recovery of planar but not curved surface orientation. Linear perspective is unlikely to have been an appreciable factor contributing to Cutting and Millard's (1984) data because they used jittered textures specifically to minimize its role.

4.8 SUMMARY

The two main points we draw from these studies are as follows:

1. Texture cues can have substantial effects on the perceived shape of 3-D surfaces even when pitted against wholly natural stereo cues generated by large real curved and planar surfaces. In the particular circumstances of the present experiments, a pattern of roughly equally weighted stereo/texture cue integration was observed. Of course, if we had chosen a smaller viewing distance, the stereo cue might well have been relatively stronger, as found by Frisby and Buckley (1992).

2. Both p and c texture components seem to play a role in judgments of surface orientation for both planes and curved surfaces. However, the c component is dominant for judgments from curved surfaces, whereas p is the most important component for planes. The latter departs from theoretical expectations derived from an analysis of information in the p cue based on variance indices of cue power, but it might be explained in terms of a special role for linear perspective in the recovery of planar surface orientation. Although the importance of p for planar surface orientation observed here appears at first sight to be an outcome similar to that observed by Cutting and Millard (1984) for flatness versus curved judgments, this may be misleading because the latter task does not require judgments of surface orientation.

ACKNOWLEDGMENTS

This work was funded by an Esprit BRA grant within the INSIGHT consortium. We thank Jonas Gårding, John Mayhew, John Porrill, and Andrew Blake for many useful discussions. Michael Port helped build the apparatus and Len Hetherington made the slides. We are especially indebted to Stephen Hippisley-Cox for writing the computer program that inferred perceived surfaces from the gradient measures and for mathematical advice used in creating the computer graphics texture program.

REFERENCES

Attneave, F., Olson, R. K. (1966). Inferences about visual mechanisms from depth effects, *Psychonomic Science*, 4, 133–134.

Blake, A., Bülthoff, H., and Sheinberg, D. (1993). Shape from texture: Ideal observers and human psychophysics. *Vision Research, 33,* 1723–1737.

Blake, A., Marinos, C. (1991). Shape from texture: estimation, isotropy and moments. *Artificial Intelligence, 45,* 323–380.

Braunstein, M. (1968) Motion and texture as sources of slant information. *Journal of Experimental Psychology, 78,* 247–253.

Braunstein, M., and Payne, J. W. (1969). Perspective and form ratio as determinants of relative slant judgments, *Journal of Experimental Psychology, 81,* 584–590.

Buckley, D., and Frisby, J. P. (1993). Interaction of stereo, texture and outline cues in the shape perception of three-dimensional ridges. *Vision Research, 33,* 919–934.

Buckley, D., Frisby, J. P., and Blake, A. (1995). Does the human visual system implement an ideal observer theory of slant-from-texture? *Vision Research* (in press).

Bülthoff, H. H., and Mallot, H. A. (1987). Interaction of different modules in depth perception. In *Proceedings of First International Conference on Computer Vision,* 295–305.

Cumming, B. G., Johnston, E. B., and Parker, A. J. (1991). Effects of different texture cues on curved surfaces viewed stereoscopically. *Vision Research, 33,* 827–838.

Curran, W., and Johnston, A. (1994). Integration of shading and texture cues: Testing the linear model. *Vision Research, 34,* 1863–1874.

Cutting, J. E., and Millard, R. T. (1984). Three gradients and the perception of flat and curved surfaces. *Journal of Experimental Psychology, 113,* 198–224.

Frisby, J. P., and Buckley, D. (1992). Experiments on stereo and texture cue combination in human vision using quasi-natural viewing. In G. Orban and H. Nagel (Eds.), *Artificial and biological vision systems into vision,* 267–297. Berlin: Springer.

Frisby, J. P., Buckley, D., and Horsman, J. M. (1995). Integration of stereo, texture, and outline cues during pinhole of real ridge-shaped objects and stereograms of ridges, *Perception, 24,* 181–198.

Frisby, J. P., Buckley, D., Wishart, K. A., Porrill, J., Gårding. J., and Mayhew. J. E. W. (1995). Interaction of stereo and texture cues in the perception of three-dimensional steps. *Vision Research, 35,* 1463–1472.

Gårding, J. (1991). Shape from surface markings. Ph.D. diss. Royal Institute of Technology, University of Stockholm.

Gårding, J. (1992). Shape from texture for smooth curved surfaces in perspective projection. *Journal of Mathematical Imaging and Vision, 2,* 327–350.

Koenderink, J. J., van Doorn, A. J., and Kappers, A. M. L. (1992). Surface perception in pictures. *Perception and Psychophysics, 52,* 487–496.

Koenderink, J. J., van Doorn, A. J., and Kappers, A. M. L. (1994). On so-called paradoxical monocular stereoscopy. *Perception, 23,* 583–594.

Landy, M. S., Maloney, L. T., Johnston, E. B., and Young, M. (1995). Measurement and modeling of depth cue combination: In defense of weak fusion. *Vision Research, 35(3),* 389–412.

Phillips, R. J., (1970). Stationary visual texture and the estimation of slant angle. *Quarterly Journal of Experimental Psychology, 22,* 389–397.

Stevens, K. A. (1981). The information content of texture gradients. *Biological Cybernetics, 42,* 95–105.

Stevens, K. A. (1983). Surface tilt (the direction of slant): A neglected psychophysical variable. *Perception and Psychophysics, 33,* 241–250.

Todd, J. T., and Akerstrom, R. A. (1987). Perception of three-dimensional form from patterns of optical texture. *Journal of Experimental Psychology: Human Perception and Performance, 13,* 242–255.

Young, M. J., Landy, M. S., and Maloney, L. T. (1993). A perturbation analysis of depth perception from combinations of texture and motion cues. *Vision Research, 33,* 2685–2696.

5 An Architecture for Rapid, Hierarchical Structural Description

John E. Hummel and Brian J. Stankiewicz

ABSTRACT

Dynamic binding is a necessary prerequisite to structural description, but it is not straightforward to represent structural descriptions suitable for object recognition, given the limitations of dynamic binding (specifically, limitations of speed and reliability). This chapter presents a model of object recognition addressed to this problem. The model generates hierarchical representations that function as structural descriptions in the event of correct dynamic binding but that still support object recognition in the event of dynamic binding errors. The model can recognize objects rapidly (i.e., before dynamic binding is established) but has the properties of a structural description when dynamic binding is established correctly (e.g., it can recognize objects from novel viewpoints). The model provides an account of several phenomena in human object recognition, including the time course of recognition and viewpoint invariance and the role of attention in object recognition.

5.1 INTRODUCTION

One of the great problems in the study of human object recognition is to understand how we recognize objects despite variations in the image presented to the retina. This problem takes two forms. The most commonly studied is generalization over viewpoint: We can recognize objects in a wide variety of views despite the fact that different views can present radically different images to the retina. This capacity is particularly challenging to understand because human object recognition is robust to some *but not all* variations in viewpoint. Recognition is robust to translation (the position of the image on the retina), left-right reflection (Biederman and Cooper 1991a), scale (Biederman and Cooper 1992), and some rotations in depth (Biederman and Gerhardstein 1993). However, recognition is sensitive to rotation in the picture plane (as when an object is upside-down; Jolicoeur 1985; Tarr and Pinker, 1989, 1990). A related problem concerns how we recognize objects as members of a class, such as "car" or "chair," rather than just as specific instances, such as "Mazda 626" or "my office chair." That is, how do we recognize objects at the *basic level* (Rosch et al. 1976) or *entry level* (Biederman 1987)? Here, the problem is to understand how we generalize over variations in an object's actual 3-D shape, such as changes in the length of a chair's legs, or the distance between a car's front and rear wheels.

Together, our limited robustness to viewpoint and our capacity to ignore irrelevant variations in shape make human object recognition challenging to understand because they defy explanation in terms of simple geometric laws. The mathematics of projective geometry are well understood; if human recognition performance were predictable in terms of them, then models based on geometric laws would provide an adequate account of human object recognition. But these laws do not explain our capacity for object recognition. A system based strictly on the laws of projective geometry (e.g., that somehow mapped images into object-centered representations of 3-D shape) would be equally able to accommodate all changes in viewpoint (which the human is not) but would not tolerate changes in an object's 3-D shape (which the human does).

Structural Descriptions in Human Object Recognition

These and other properties of human object recognition have led many researchers to postulate that we recognize objects on the basis of *structural descriptions*—representations specifying an object's parts (or features) and their interrelations (Biederman 1987; Clowes 1967; Hummel and Biederman 1992; Marr and Nishihara 1978; Palmer 1977; Sutherland 1968; Winston 1975). The most explicit such theory to date is Biederman's (1987) "recognition by components" and its variants (Bergevin and Levine 1993; Dickenson, Pentland, and Rosenfeld 1992; Hummel and Biederman 1990, 1992). According to this theory, objects are recognized as configurations of simple volumes, called "geons," in particular relations. For example, a coffee mug would be represented as an elongated curved cylinder (the handle) side-attached to a straight vertical cylinder (the body). The relations are critical; if the curved cylinder were attached to the top of the straight cylinder, the object would be a bucket rather than a mug (Biederman 1987). This type of representation provides a natural account of many properties of human object recognition. Note that the above description will not change as the mug is translated across the visual field, moved closer to or farther from the viewer, or rotated in depth (provided the handle does not disappear behind the body). But rotating the mug 90° about the line of sight, so that the body is horizontal and the handle is on top, will change the description. Like human object recognition, this description is sensitive to rotations about the line of sight, but insensitive to translation, scale, left-right reflection, and some rotations in depth. It is also insensitive to things such as the exact length of the handle or the exact width of the body, so it is suitable as a basis for class recognition (Biederman 1987).

There is empirical support for the use of parts-based structural descriptions in human object recognition. For example, Biederman and Cooper (1991b) have shown that one object image will visually prime another to the extent that they depict the same parts in the same relations (see also Cooper 1994). And Hummel and Stankiewicz (1995) have shown that subjects are much more sensitive to the pairwise relations between an object's parts, that is, relations of the type posited by structural description theories, than to their parts' positions relative to *any* single reference point, that is, coordinates of the type proposed in view-based accounts of object recognition (Poggio and Edelman 1990; Ullman 1989; Ullman and Basri 1991; and many others). These and other findings suggest that objects are represented in memory as structural descriptions specifying their parts and their parts' interrelations (see Quinlan 1991 for a review). Of course, this is not to say that objects are represented exclusively as structural descriptions (see, for example, Farah 1992; Tarr and Pinker 1990), a point to which we shall return shortly.

Generating Structural Descriptions from Object Images

Inasmuch as structural descriptions play a role in human object recognition, it is important to understand how the visual system generates them from object images. Generating a structural description entails solving a number of difficult problems (see Hummel and Biederman 1992). Consider generating the description "curved cylinder side-attached to straight cylinder" from the image of a coffee mug. First, the parts' local features (e.g., contours and vertices) must be segmented into groups so that the features of one part do not interfere with the interpretation of the other. Likewise, any interpretations of the parts' attributes (e.g., the shapes of their cross sections and axes, their orientation and aspect ratio, etc.) must also be bound into sets. Next, the representation of "curved cylinder" must be bound to the agent role of "side-attached," and "straight cylinder" to the patient role.

An important problem for structural description concerns the manner in which these attributes are bound together. Bindings can be either dynamic or static. A *dynamic* binding is one in which a single representational unit can be used in many different combinations without sacrificing its independence. For example, one unit might represent cylinders and another might represent the side-attached relation; a cylinder side-attached to another part would be represented by explicitly tagging these units as bound together. Because tags are assigned to units dynamically (i.e., on the fly), the same units can enter into different conjunctions at different times. A *static* binding is one in which a separate unit is predicated for each conjunction. For example, one unit might respond to cylinders side-attached to other parts, another might respond to cylinders above other parts, and so forth. Structural description requires dynamic binding (Hummel and Biederman 1992). The number of units required to precode all possible part-relation conjunctions would be enormous (growing exponentially with the number of relations). More importantly, static binding sacrifices the independence—and therefore the similarity structure—of the bound attributes. That a cylinder side-attached to something is more similar to a cylinder above something than to slab above something is completely lost in a representation where each part-relation binding is coded by a separate unit (von der Malsburg 1981). This loss of similarity structure is a fundamental property of static binding that cannot be overcome even with sophisticated static codes, such as Smolensky's (1990) tensor products (see Hummel and Biederman 1992; Hummel and Holyoak 1993). Dynamic binding is thus a prerequisite to structural description.

The dynamic binding problem poses a substantial challenge to understanding how the visual system generates structural descriptions from object images. In contrast to static binding, dynamic binding requires a *mechanism* to actively tag independent units as bound. This need for an active binding mechanism imposes strong constraints on the use of structural descriptions for object recognition. These constraints—and the question of how the visual system might satisfy them—are the motivation for the modeling effort reported here.

Dynamic Binding in Structural Description

Dynamic binding imposes a computational bottleneck on structural description because the tag assignment process is necessarily time-consuming and error-prone, and structural description can be no faster or more reliable than the dynamic binding process. We elaborate these issues using synchrony of firing—one proposed mechanism for dynamic binding—as an example. The basic idea is that neurons fire in synchrony when they represent elements of the same group, and out of synchrony when they represent elements of different groups. There is some evidence, albeit controversial, that synchrony is used for dynamic binding in biological nervous systems (see, for example, Eckhorn et al. 1988; Gray et al. 1989; Gray and Singer 1989), and it is straightforward to establish synchrony in artificial neural networks. Synchrony has been used to model sensory segmentation (e.g., Eckhorn et al. 1990; von der Malsburg and Buhmann 1992), and dynamic binding for structural description (Hummel and Biederman 1992). Although we illustrate the limitations of dynamic binding using synchrony, these limitations are very general, and apply regardless of the particular mechanism used. Synchrony is a plausible and convenient means for dynamic binding, but we do not claim that it is the only (or necessarily even one) means to this end in real nervous systems. Rather, our claims are that (1) dynamic binding is necessary for structural description, and (2) dynamic binding, in whatever form, is time-consuming and error-prone.

Dynamic binding is time-consuming because it is a process, and processes takes time. In the case of synchrony, units must actively synchronize and desynchronize their outputs. Moreover, the time required to establish synchrony (or any other binding tag) can be substantial because it will likely require iterative constraint satisfaction (see, for example, von der Malsburg and Buhmann 1992). Note that the time required for dynamic binding is separate from (i.e., in addition to) the time required to map one representation onto another (e.g., in the way that units in one layer of a feedforward neural network activate units in the next layer). While static binding can be accomplished simply as a function of mapping (and is therefore "free")[1], dynamic binding requires additional processing and time (and is therefore "expensive").

Dynamic binding is error-prone for two reasons. First, if the processes that establish synchrony and asynchrony are at all stochastic, then units belonging to separate groups may occasionally fire in synchrony "accidentally," and units belonging to the same group may occasionally fire out of synchrony. Binding errors become progressively more likely as the number of groups approaches the number of available tags (e.g., the number of "slices" in the temporal window limits the number of separate groups than can fire out of synchrony; Hummel and Biederman 1992). Second, given that synchrony takes time to establish, it is virtually guaranteed to be incorrect until enough time has elapsed to establish it.

This is problematic because binding errors can have catastrophic effects on structural description. As observed by Ullman (1989), structural description is exquisitely sensitive to the manner in which an object is segmented into parts. The same image, segmented in different ways, will give rise to radically different structural descriptions. Moreover, if independent attributes are represented by independent units, then the binding of attributes into groups will be completely lost when two or more separate groups fire in synchrony. For example, imagine that a cone is represented by units for "curved cross section," and "nonparallel sides," and a brick is represented by "straight cross section" and "parallel sides." Accidentally synchronizing a cone with a brick will superimpose these attributes into the pattern "curved cross section, straight cross section, parallel sides, and nonparallel sides." Such a pattern cannot distinguish cone-and-brick from cylinder- ("curved cross section; parallel sides") and-wedge ("straight cross section; nonparallel sides"). This kind of "superposition catastrophe" (von der Malsburg 1981) is an intrinsic limitation of any distributed representation.

The limitations of dynamic binding are problematic for structural description theories of object recognition. Structural description cannot be faster than dynamic binding, but object recognition apparently is. Face recognition in the macaque is accomplished to a high degree of certainty based on the *first* set of spikes to reach inferotemporal cortex (Oram and Perrett 1992; Tovee et al. 1992). Clearly, the macaque visual system recognizes faces without waiting around for several sets of desynchronized spikes. Inasmuch as face recognition differs from the recognition of nonface objects (see Farah 1992), the implications of these findings for structural description are indirect. But common (nonface) objects are also recognized very rapidly. Intraub (1981) showed that human subjects can recognize common objects presented at the rate of ten per second (see also Potter 1976). These findings suggest that object recognition is much too fast to depend on dynamic binding for structural description.

5.2   ARCHITECTURE FOR ENTRY-LEVEL OBJECT RECOGNITION

Many behavioral data suggest that human object recognition is mediated by structural description, but object recognition is apparently too fast to rely on dynamic binding (or any other time-consuming process). We present a model to account for these apparently contradictory properties of human entry-level object recognition. Our thesis is that object recognition is mediated by a hybrid representation in which fully independent units representing shape attributes and relations are integrated with a viewlike representation (à la Lowe, 1987; Poggio and Edelman 1990; Ullman and Basri 1991) in which shape attributes are represented separately at each of several positions in a coordinate space. The independent shape and relation units are bound dynamically into structural descriptions by synchrony of firing (see Hummel and Biederman 1992). This representation is robust to variations in viewpoint, but dependent on dynamic binding. In the coordinate representation, shape attributes are bound statically to positions (i.e., each unit codes a particular attribute at a particular position in the space), maintaining the separation of an object's parts even when they fire in synchrony. This representation can be generated rapidly (i.e., even before features are dynamically bound into parts), but it is sensitive to changes in viewpoint.

These representations are integrated to permit structural description once dynamic binding is established but to preserve the separation of an object's parts—thereby permitting reliable recognition—even when separate parts fire in synchrony. Over time, the result is a hierarchical description of an object's shape, in which groups of features are represented in terms of their shape attributes and relations to other groups (on the independent units), and their substructure (on the coordinate representation). Behaviorally, the result is cascaded recognition (McClelland 1979). Object recognition is fast but initially viewpoint-sensitive (by virtue of the coordinate representation); once the image is segmented into parts, recognition is robust to changes in viewpoint (by virtue of the independent representation). There is empirical support for this type of cascaded performance in human object recognition (e.g., Ellis and Allport 1986), and this approach to representing object structure has implications for a wide variety of other findings in human shape perception. These issues are elaborated in the discussion (section 5.4). For now, the question of primary concern is, How might the visual system generate such a representation from an object's image?

This chapter presents a model of object recognition addressed to this question. As input, the model takes the local features (contours, vertices, and axes) in an object's image; it segments them into groups corresponding to geons by synchronizing the outputs of feature units responding to the same geon, and desynchronizing units responding to separate geons. However, segmentation takes time; initially, all an object's features tend to fire together, even if they belong to separate geons. The heart of the model is an architecture that maps the outputs of local features into the independent and coordinate representations in an integrated fashion. Based on the instantaneous outputs of local feature units, the architecture generates an interpretation of the shape attributes of an object's geons, and maps that interpretation into the independent and coordinate representations.

Mapping local features into a representation of shape is relatively straightforward: Given the appropriate set of inference rules (e.g., "a curved L vertex is evidence for a geon with a curved cross section"), it is only necessary to let each local feature unit, regardless of its position in the image, send its output to every shape attribute to which it is relevant (Hummel and Biederman 1992). Mapping features into the coordinate representation and integrating the coordinate and independent representations are more challenging. The architecture described here is motivated by three constraints on this problem. First, behavioral data (e.g., Ellis et al. 1989) suggest that the coordinate representation should be invariant with translation and scale. Second, the mapping must be rapid—preferably, feedforward. The 100 ms figure on face recognition in the macaque leaves little or no time for recurrent (i.e., feedback or lateral) interactions between neurons prior to initial recognition. And third, the mapping should integrate the independent and coordinate representations such that whatever group is represented on the independent units at time t should also be represented on the coordinate space at time t.

Model

The model consists of six layers of units (fig. 5.1). As input, it takes the contours in a line drawing, and as output, it activates a single unit corresponding to the object's identity. Units in the first layer (L1) represent image contours; L2 units represent vertices and axes of symmetry. Contours and vertices interact to synchronize their outputs given evidence that they belong to the same geon, and desynchronize their outputs given evidence that they belong to different geons. L3 consists of *modules* of units that map the output of L2 into the independent and coordinate representations (in layer 4). L4 has two parts. The *independent geon array* (IGA) consists of units that represent a group's shape attributes and relations to other groups independently; these units are bound into parts-based sets by the synchrony established in L1 and L2. The *substructure matrix* (SSM) is the coordinate representation; here, each unit responds to a particular shape attribute (the same attributes coded in the IGA) at one of 17 positions relative to the group as a whole (a static binding of attributes to coordinates). Layers 5 and 6 use the hybrid representation in L4 as the basis for object recognition. Units in L5 respond to specific patterns of activation in L4; roughly, each L5 unit responds to a particular set of geon attributes in a particular set of relations, with a particular substructure. Each unit in L6 takes its input from a collection of L5 units, and responds to a complete object.

The theoretical focus of this work is the architecture of layers 3 and 4. The remainder of the model is simplified and is intended only to serve the

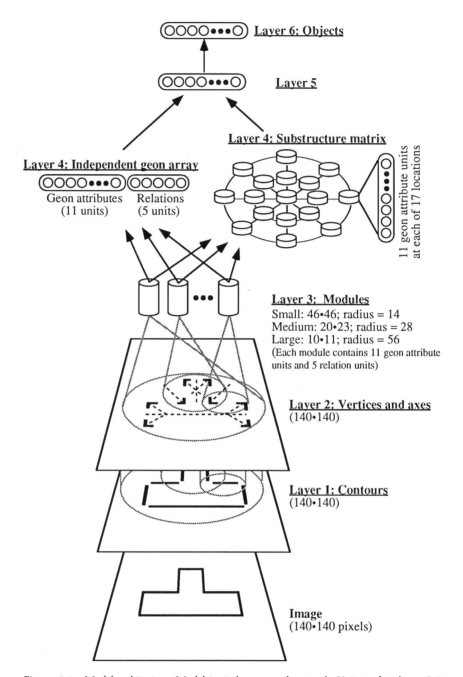

Figure 5.1 Model architecture. Model is six-layer neural network. Units in first layer (L1) represent contours in object's image. Units in L2 respond to vertices (heavy solid lines) and axes of parallel and nonparallel symmetry (dashed lines). L3 consists of modules of units (cylinders) with finite circular receptive fields (light ellipses over L1 and L2). Receptive fields of three sizes are distributed in hexagonal lattice over visual field. L4 consists of two parts: (1) independent geon array (IGA) contains 11 units that code shape attributes of geons and 5 units that code one part's categorical relations to other parts; (2) substructure matrix (SSM) contains 11 shape attribute units at each of 17 positions in circular coordinate space. Units in L5 respond to specific patterns of activation in L4, and units in L6 sum the outputs of L5 units over time to respond to complete objects.

practical functions necessary for exploring the properties of the hybrid representation (L4) and the architecture that generates it (L3). Layers 1 and 2 provide the architecture with local features from which to generate a structural description, and layers 5 and 6 use the output of L4 as a basis for object classification, but the details of these layers are not intended as theoretical claims.

Layers 1 and 2: Contours, Vertices, and Axes

Units in the first two layers represent the contours, vertices, and axes in an object's image, and group themselves into geons by synchronizing their outputs. The operation of L1 and L2 is detailed in Hummel (1994), and is described here only briefly. Each unit in L1 represents a single contour in terms of its location, orientation, and curvature. Vertices are defined where the endpoints of separate contours meet, and axes of symmetry are defined between all pairs of contours. Units update their states in discrete time steps, t. Contour, vertex, and axis units interact to synchronize their outputs if they belong to the same geon and to desynchronize their outputs if they belong to different geons. The most notable property of the algorithm is that it segments objects into parts at matched concavities, exploiting Hoffman and Richards's (1985) "transversality regularity," without having to be "told" where the object's interior lies.

Figure 5.2 shows the output of the algorithm on a representative run. As input, it was given the eight contours in the key. Broken curves in the graph show the outputs of contour units depicted as broken lines in the key, and solid curves show the outputs of contours depicted as solid lines. The desired pattern is to have the broken contours fire in synchrony with one another and out of synchrony with the solid contours. Figure 5.2 illustrates two important properties of the grouping algorithm. First, all units initially fire in synchrony with one another (i.e., at $t = 1$), but eventually group themselves as desired (by $t = 37$). There is a stochastic component to the algorithm, so the number of iterations it takes to establish the correct groupings varies. On this run, it took about 40, which is representative of the model's average performance. Second, the synchrony produced is somewhat noisy. Even when units fire in synchrony, they rarely fire in perfect synchrony. One property of the algorithm not apparent in the figure is that, even after groups get properly desynchronized, separate groups may temporarily drift back into synchrony with one another. The likelihood that two or more parts will drift into accidental synchrony grows with the number of parts.

Layers 3 and 4: Modules, Geons, Relations, and Substructures

The model's third layer characterizes the instantaneous outputs of local feature units in terms of their shape attributes and maps that characterization to layer 4. Units in L3 are organized into *modules* with finite, circular receptive

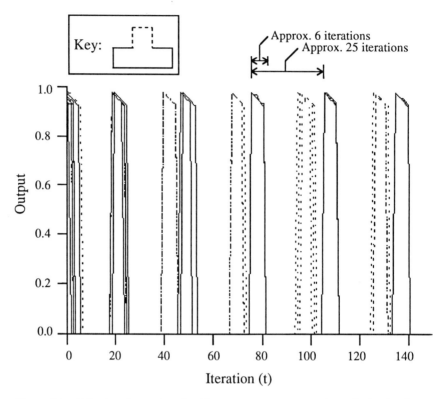

Figure 5.2 Behavior of grouping algorithm on one run given contours depicted in key as input. Broken lines in figure show output of contour units depicted as broken lines in key; solid lines in figure correspond to solid contours in key.

fields. There are three receptive field sizes distributed in a hexagonal lattice over the model's visual field (figure 5.1). Each module uses the outputs of vertices and axes in its receptive field to generate a representation of the geon(s) in the corresponding part of the image. Modules interact to map their interpretations to the appropriate parts of L4, imposing an interpretation of the entire group on the IGA, and interpretations of its local components on the appropriate parts of the SSM.

Geon Attributes   Each module contains eleven units that respond to various attributes of a geon's shape. Two units code the shape of a geon's cross section (one for *straight* and one for *curved*); two code the shape of its axis (*straight* or *curved*); three code whether its sides are *parallel* (as in a brick), *nonparallel* (e.g., a cone), or *mixed* (e.g., a wedge), and four code its *aspect ratio* (a measure of elongation, coarsely coded). The same eleven attributes are represented in the IGA, and at each location in the SSM. The manner in which geon attributes are inferred from vertices and axes is borrowed largely from Hummel and Biederman (1992) and is not elaborated here. Each module also contains five units that code its categorical relations to other active modules (described below).

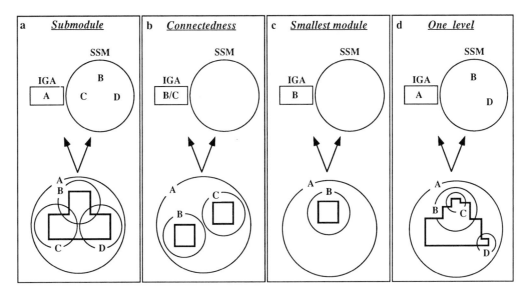

Figure 5.3 Constraints governing the mapping of module outputs to L4: (a) submodule constraint (also connectedness); (b) connectedness; (c) smallest module, and (d) one level. See text for details.

Mapping from Modules to Layer 4   For any pattern of output from L2, each module will have an interpretation of some subset of that pattern on its geon attribute units. Given that our goal is to map an interpretation of the entire group to the IGA, and to map interpretations of its local elements to the SSM, the next problem is to determine where (i.e., to which part of L4) each module should send its interpretation of the features in its receptive field. Any module with the whole group in its receptive field (as defined below) sends its output to the IGA, and any module with a subset of the group sends its output to the corresponding part of the SSM. This mapping is performed by gating the connections from the modules to L4. There is one gate associated with each module. When a module has a whole group in its receptive field, its gate will open. A module with an open gate (an *open module*) directs its own output to the IGA, and directs the outputs of other modules to the SSM. For example, consider the contours and module receptive fields in the bottom of figure 5.3a. When module A is open, it will send its own output to the IGA, and the outputs of B, C, and D to the SSM. Mapping from layer 3 to layer 4 is thus a problem of deciding (a) which gates to open, and (b) how each gate should control the mapping from modules to L4. Four constraints govern this mapping. These constraints are described in general terms here and in detail in the appendix.

Connectedness   The first problem is to determine whether a given module has a whole group—more specifically, a whole object part—in its receptive field. Features occupying two or more disconnected regions in the image (e.g., fig. 5.3b), are unlikely to belong to the same part. Therefore, a module will open its gate whenever it has a *complete* set of *connected* features in its receptive field. For example, there is one group of connected features (one part) in figure 5.3a, and only module A has the whole group in its receptive field; therefore, A will open, but B–D will not. By contrast, the image in figure 5.3b consists of two distinct groups of connected features, so two modules (B and C) satisfy connectedness with respect to this image. The connectedness constraint is implemented via the contours in or near a module's receptive field. Any contour contained wholly inside a module's receptive field is consistent with that module's having a complete, connected group in its receptive field (such a contour's firing constitutes evidence that the module contains a complete connected group). Contours tend to open the gates of modules with which they are consistent (i.e., when the contour fires, it drives the module's gate toward 1.0). Contours partly inside and partly outside a module's receptive field (*inconsistent* contours) tend to keep the module closed. Their firing suggests that the module does not have a complete group in its receptive field; they drive its gate toward 0.0. Modules ignore contours completely outside their receptive fields. Together, these interactions implement connectedness, ensuring that a module will remain closed unless it has a complete, connected part in its receptive field.

Submodules   A submodule constraint governs the mapping from modules to the SSM. Module j is a *submodule* of i if and only if all points in j's receptive field are in i's receptive field and $j \neq i$. For example, B, C, and D in figure 5.3a are all submodules of A. When i has a whole group in its receptive field, its active submodules (i.e., submodules with features in their receptive fields) will have the subsets of that group in their receptive fields. Moreover, the position of any given submodule relative to i corresponds to the subset's position relative to the group as a whole. For example, the subset in B's receptive field (fig. 5.3a) is in the upper center of the group as a whole, just as B is in the upper center of A. A's gate controls the connection from each of A's submodules to the corresponding region of the SSM (e.g., A's gate controls the connection from B to the upper center of the matrix, and from C to the middle left of the matrix). Therefore, when a module opens, its submodules send their outputs to the corresponding regions of the SSM.

Smallest module   Consider the contours and module receptive fields depicted at the bottom of figure 5.3c. A and B have the same features in their receptive fields, so they will generate the same representation on their geon attribute units; moreover, both satisfy connectedness. If A opens, it will send its output to the IGA and B's output to the SSM. As a result, the group would be represented on both the IGA, and the SSM—as a subset of itself. The *smallest module* constraint serves to prevent this; by this constraint, only the smallest module(s) satisfying connectedness can open. For example, B would open rather than A, so that B would send its output to the IGA and nothing would go to the SSM (B has no active submodules). The smallest module constraint also prevents a module with two or more disconnected groups (two or more parts) in its receptive field from opening. For example, in figure 5.3b, A will not open because B and C satisfy connectedness with respect to each group individually.

One level of hierarchy   The *one level* constraint operates to ensure that only one level of modules below an open module send their outputs to the SSM. In figure 5.4d, B, C, and D are submodules of A, and C is a submodule of B. When A opens, it will send its output to the IGA, and the outputs of B and D to the SSM. However, by the one level constraint, C's output will not go to the SSM. This constraint prevents superposition of different geons on the SSM. B and C are in similar positions relative to A; if both their outputs went to the SSM, they would be superimposed on the same part of the matrix. This superposition would defeat the purpose of the SSM, which is to preserve the separation of an object's parts in the event of binding errors.

Relations   Relations in this model are highly simplified. Each module contains five units that code its categorical relations to other active modules. These are *above* (active when a module is above another module), *below*, *beside* (active when a module is either left or right of another module), *larger*, and *smaller*. When a module sends its output to the SSM, the SSM activates the module's relation units. For instance, when A in figure 5.3a is open, B's output will go to the upper center of the SSM and C's will go to the left of the SSM, so that the SSM will activate B's *above* unit, and C's *beside* unit. Relative position is thus coded in terms of each module's categorical position relative to the module(s) of which it was most recently a subset; relative size is computed in a similar fashion. The SSM activates a module's *smaller* unit (to send output to the matrix, a module must be a submodule of another module), and when a module opens, any activation in the SSM activates its *larger* unit. A module's relations go to the IGA only when the module is open.

Illustration   Figure 5.4 illustrates the modules' operation. Consider first what will happen when all contours in the image fire together (figure 5.4a). The contours of the cone are consistent with module B so they will push its gate (G_B) toward 1 (open), but the contours of the brick, also firing, will keep G_B at zero (closed). G_C and G_D will similarly remain closed (neither is consistent with the brick's longest edges). All the contours are consistent with A, thus G_A will open; A will send its output to the IGA, and the outputs of B, C, and D to the SSM. Next consider how the modules will behave once the cone and brick come to fire out of synchrony. When the cone fires (figure 5.4b), B will receive input from consistent contours and no input from inconsistent contours, thus it will open. By the smallest module constraint, A will remain closed. B will send its output to the IGA, but because it has no submodules, nothing will go to the SSM. When the brick fires (fig. 5.4c), A will again open and send its output to the IGA; and C and D will continue to go to the SSM.

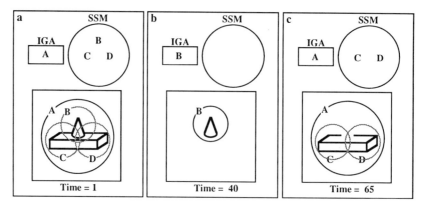

Figure 5.4 Illustration of behavior of layers 3 and 4 over time. See text for details.

C and D still cannot open because they are both are inconsistent with brick's long contours. Modules B and A will alternate in this fashion as long as their respective contours continue to fire out of synchrony. The resulting patterns of activation in L4 will be a structural description specifying the shapes of the cone and the brick, the cone's position relative to the brick, and the brick's substructure.

Layers 5 and 6: Object Classification

The model's fifth and sixth layers use the series of representations produced on L4 as a basis for object recognition. Each unit in L5 responds selectively to an instantaneous pattern of activation on L4. Each unit in L6 sums the outputs of L5 units over time to activate a local representation of a complete object. Layers 5 and 6 are detailed in the appendix.

5.3 SIMULATIONS

The purpose of this modeling effort was to determine whether the architecture of layers 3 and 4 can generate structural descriptions but still support rapid recognition and tolerate errors of dynamic binding. The model's capacity for rapid (indeed, strictly feedforward) recognition can be assessed by examining its response on the first iteration after an image is presented (i.e., at $t = 1$). All an object's features will tend to fire all together at first (whether they belong to the same geon or not; recall fig. 5.2); thus the model's immediate response to an image also provides an index of its capacity to tolerate errors of dynamic binding. However, the SSM, which will play the dominant role in the model's early performance, is not by itself a structural description. It is equally important to test whether, given time to segment an object into parts, the model actually *uses* the structural descriptions it generates. To this end, we tested the model's ability to recognize objects under left-right reflection. The IGA encodes both *left-of* and *right-of* as *beside*, so the structural

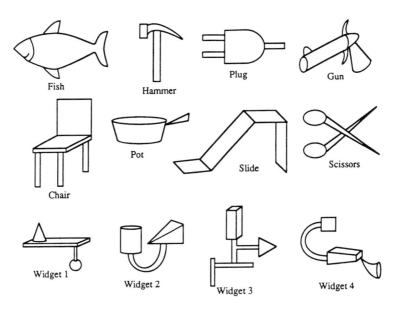

Figure 5.5 Trained object views.

description of an object facing to the left will be the same as the structural description of that object facing to the right. By contrast, left-right reflection changes an object's representation in the SSM; it moves the object's parts in the coordinate space, changing which units respond to each part. Recognition based on the SSM alone will be left-right sensitive. If the model can exploit its hybrid representations for object recognition, then the following pattern should obtain. Trained on an object facing left, the model should rapidly recognize that object facing to the left; given time to segment the object into parts, it should also recognize it from a right-facing image (but, trained only on a left-facing image, recognition of a right-facing image should be relatively slow).

Stimuli

The model was trained to recognize the twelve objects depicted in figure 5.5 (as described in the appendix). Most of the objects are composed of several parts, increasing the likelihood that two or more parts will fire in synchrony accidentally. Moreover, some (e.g., "slide," "gun," and "fish") are difficult to segment based on the local cues used by the model's grouping algorithm. This difficulty produces variability in the way they are segmented (e.g., sometimes the head of the fish is grouped as part of the body, and sometimes it is separated as a distinct part). The objects' complexity makes it possible to observe the model's robustness to nontrivial segmentation errors. The most important objects are the four widgets. They were designed to yield similar patterns on the IGA when their parts fired in synchrony with one another (e.g., the Hummel and Biederman model could not distinguish these objects under accidental synchrony). The model's ability to recognize them before their parts are desynchronized thus constitutes an important test of its ability to tolerate binding errors. The widgets were also designed to be left-right asymmetrical, so that the model's ability to recognize them under left-right reflection is a meaningful test of its capacity for left-right invariance. Importantly, the model was trained on only one view of each object (the view depicted in fig. 5.5).

Simulation Procedure

All simulations were run under exactly the same procedure, varying only the images presented. On each run, an image was presented to L1, and the model was allowed to run for 180 iterations. We recorded two measures of performance. *Initial activation* is the activation of an object unit on the first iteration after the presentation of an image (i.e., at $t = 1$). *Mean activation* is the mean activation of an object unit over an entire 180-iteration run. Initial activation indicates the model's immediate (rapid) estimate of an object's identity (before it is segmented into parts), and mean activation indicates its ability to recognize an object from its structural description. All simulations were run ten times, and we report the means of these response measures over the ten runs. The responses of the object units (L6) to each image are depicted as matrices (see fig. 5.6), with initial activations in one matrix and mean activations in the other. Each cell of a matrix shows the mean value (over the ten runs) of the response metric for one object unit (columns) given one image (rows). The diagonals of a matrix correspond to the correct response to each image. Data are depicted as circles whose area is proportional to the mean value of the response metric over the ten runs (rounded to the nearest 0.1).

The numbers in the rightmost column and bottommost row of each matrix indicate, respectively, the degree to which the corresponding image selectively activated the correct object unit (*image selectivity*), and the degree to which each object unit selectively responded to the correct image (*object selectivity*). Selectivity was calculated as the response of the correct cell (i.e., the value on the diagonal) divided by the sum of all values in the same row or column, respectively. Image selectivity indicates the overall accuracy of the model's response to the corresponding image. Object selectivity indicates the degree to which the object unit responded selectively to the object on which it was trained. The mean object and image selectivities (bottom right corner of each matrix) are indices of overall performance.

Simulation 1: Trained Images

The most basic index of the model's performance is its ability to recognize each object in the view that was used for training. This test was performed as described above, where the images presented far testing were those used for training. The results are shown in figure 5.6.

Mean responses of object units to the trained images (10 runs):

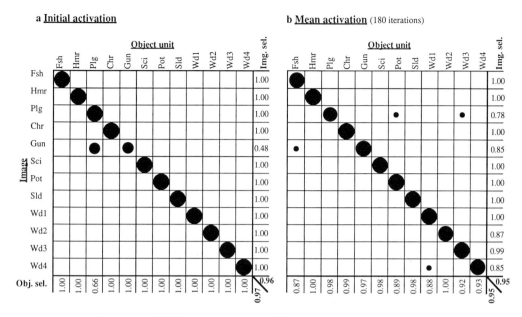

Figure 5.6 Model responses to trained object views.

The model's immediate recognition performance is quite good (fig. 5.6a). Given the image of "gun," the initial activation of the object unit for "plug" was higher than the initial activation of the unit for "gun" (0.52 vs. 0.48, respectively; the model initially mistook the image of "gun" for an image of "plug") but all other image selectivities are 1.00, indicating that initial recognition of all other images was flawless. In fact, this level of performance is *too* high. Although biological visual systems recognize faces to a high degree of certainty based on the first spikes to reach IT, recognition is not perfect (see Tovee et al. 1993). The model's overestimate of initial performance likely reflects a few factors, including (a) its small vocabulary (only 12 objects), and (b) the fact that each image was presented for testing exactly as it was trained.

Performance over the full 180 iterations (fig. 5.6b) is interesting in comparison to initial performance. As measured by mean object selectivity, performance over 180 iterations was slightly *worse* than initial performance (0.95 vs. 0.96, respectively). This noisier responding is also visible as the four off-diagonal circles in figure 5.6b (compared with only one in fig. 5.6a). However, none of the off-diagonal *mean activations* is greater than any on the diagonal. Given time to generate a structural description, the model made no catastrophic errors of the initial "gun"-for-"plug" variety. The greater noise observed over the full 180 iterations is actually expected given the nature of the model's structural descriptions. Recall that representing attributes independently preserves their similarity across different bindings. This preservation of attribute similarity manifested itself as a tendency for the geons of one object to activate L5 units for similar geons in other objects, resulting in noise once an object was segmented into parts. By contrast, when all an object's geons fire together (as on the first iteration), each geon is represented on different units in the SSM, so that geons with similar shapes can wind up represented on completely different units. This loss of attribute similarity manifests itself cleaner initial performance.

Overall, the results of this simulation show that the model can recognize objects before they are segmented into their parts. Moreover, the model's ability to correct the initial "plug"-for-"gun" error suggests that the structural descriptions it generates aid object classification.

Simulation 2: Left-Right Reflection

The second simulation was designed as a stronger test of the model's capacity to use the structural descriptions it generates. Recall that one property of the model's structural descriptions is robustness to left-right reflection. This robustness is not a property of the SSM. If the model can use its structural descriptions for object recognition, then recognition of a left-right reflection of a trained image should be poor initially and improve once the image has been segmented into parts. (Note that complete left-right invariance is not expected even after an object is decomposed into parts because the SSM continues to play a role, representing the substructure of each part). This simulation was conducted as described above, with left-right reflections of the trained images as stimuli. The results are shown in figure 5.7.

As expected, immediate recognition under left-right reflection was poorer than immediate recognition of the trained images. The mean image and object selectivities on the first iteration of this simulation were 0.70 and 0.69, respectively, as compared to 0.96 and 0.95 with the trained images. Immediate recognition of the reflected images was better than expected (revealing only three catastrophic errors), but recognition nonetheless improved over time. The mean activations (figure 5.7b) reveal no catastrophic errors (but some tendency to confuse *slide* for *chair*). This improvement relative to initial performance shows that the model can use its structural descriptions to recognize left-right reflections of trained images.

These preliminary simulations suggest that the model satisfies its basic goals. Given a familiar object view, recognition is fast and accurate; and given time to segment an object into its parts and compute their interrelations, recognition is robust to left-right reflection.

5.4 DISCUSSION

An important problem confronting structural description theories of object recognition is to explain why recognition is both fast, given the temporal requirements of dynamic binding, and reliable, given that dynamic binding is

Mean responses of object units to left-right reflections of the trained images (10 runs):

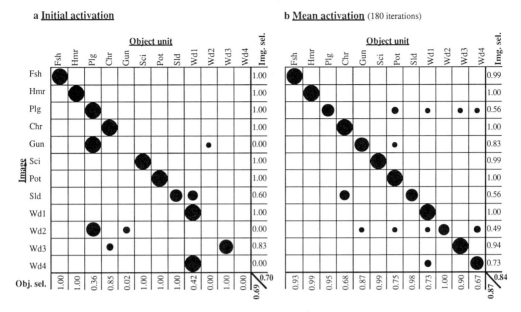

Figure 5.7 Model responses to left-right reflections of trained views.

likely to be error-prone. We have proposed a model of object recognition addressed to this problem. The model represents shape in a hybrid fashion, coding shape attributes both independently (the IGA) and statically bound to specific positions in a coordinate space (the SSM). These representations are integrated by means of an architecture that maps the instantaneous outputs of local feature detectors simultaneously to both, representing each group's shape attributes and relations both independently, and in terms of their sub-components' positions in a group-centered coordinate space. The model integrates an object's shape attributes both by space (common location in the SSM) and by time (synchrony of firing). This approach exploits dynamic binding for structural description, but generates a viewpoint-sensitive estimate of object identity before dynamic binding is correctly established. The model is currently in an early stage of development, but preliminary simulation results are encouraging. Moreover, the general approach suggests an account of several properties of human object recognition.

Behavioral Implications

As a theory of human object recognition, a fundamental tenet underlying this work is that dynamic binding plays a central role in object representation but is a computational bottleneck. Inasmuch as the resources necessary for dynamic binding are available, recognition should evidence the properties of a structural description; but inasmuch as those resources are unavailable, recognition should evidence the properties of the SSM. This account has implications for several issues in object recognition, including the time course of recognition, and the role of attention in object recognition.

Time Course of Recognition   One of the most straightforward predictions of our account is that recognition should initially be viewpoint-sensitive, and later be robust to viewpoint. Ellis and Allport (1986) report some findings consistent with this prediction. They had subjects view two pictures in succession and report whether the objects in the pictures had the same name. Subjects were faster to respond "yes" if the pictures depicted physically identical objects (e.g., two pictures of the same car) than if they depicted different objects with the same name (two different cars). Moreover, at ISIs under two seconds, Ellis and Allport found that response times were faster still if the pictures depicted the object at the same orientation in depth. That is, at brief ISIs, subjects were faster to decide that two pictures depicted the same object if the pictures were identical: recognition was sensitive to viewpoint. But at longer ISIs, this same-view benefit disappeared: recognition was robust to viewpoint. As Ellis and Allport observed, these data suggest that recognition is mediated by two representations, one fast but viewpoint-sensitive, the other slow but viewpoint-robust. Using a similar paradigm, Ellis et al. (1989) showed that the same-view benefit is insensitive to translation and, under some circumstances, scale. That is, even the fast representation, albeit view-sensitive, is not strictly retinotopic (Ellis et al. 1989). These data are strikingly consistent with the model described here. The SSM supports rapid recognition that is robust to translation and scale, but sensitive to orientation in depth (and left-right reflection). By contrast, a useful representation on the IGA is slow to develop (due to the need for dynamic binding) but robust to viewpoint.

Irwin and his colleagues (Carlson-Radvansky and Irwin 1994; Irwin 1992; Irwin and Andrews, chap. 6, this volume) have shown that the information preserved across saccadic eye movements has the properties of a structural description rather than a literal representation of the positions of local features in the image (e.g., among other things, it is capacity-limited in the manner consistent with the capacity limits of binding by synchrony). Interestingly, it takes approximately 300 ms to initiate a saccade. It is tempting to speculate that part of this time reflects the visual system's generating a structural description prior to the saccade. The description—which will be used to integrate information from the prior fixation with information from the subsequent fixation—takes time to generate, so that the visual system postpones making the saccade until it has been generated. Other factors undoubtedly contribute to the delay as well, and our associating it with the time required for structural description is admittedly speculative. But the relationship is suggestive.

The earliest representations to develop on the SSM depict an entire object. As such, the model may speak to the role of "global" information early in processing (e.g., Kimchi 1992; Navon 1977; Paquet 1992; Sanocki 1993). The time it requires to establish dynamic binding for structural description is also consistent with findings showing that the detection of structure is time-consuming (e.g., Ichikawa 1985).

Attention in Object Recognition   There is substantial reason to believe that attention is required to bind independent representations of an object's attributes (see, for example, Treisman 1993; Treisman and Gelade 1980). Visual attention is also required to detect search targets defined by part-relation conjunctions (Enns 1992; Logan 1994). These findings strongly suggest that attention is necessary for structural description (see also Hummel and Biederman 1992). However, attention is *not* necessary for object recognition, as shown by findings of negative priming for ignored objects (e.g., Tipper 1985). What kind of representation might mediate object recognition in the absence of visual attention? If attention is necessary for dynamic binding, then whatever representation mediates the recognition of unattended objects must be based on static binding (or no binding at all, but this seems extremely unlikely). We hypothesize that something like the SSM may serve this function.

Treisman and DeSchepper (chap. 2, this volume) report a finding consistent with this hypothesis. They used a negative priming paradigm with pairs of overlapping nonsense figures to examine the visual representation of ignored objects. In their prime displays, one figure occluded the other, and subjects attended to either the occluding figure or the occluded figure. When subjects selected against the occluded figure, they were slower to respond (on a subsequent trial) to the portion of the figure that was visible in the prime trial, but they were not slower to respond to what the figure would have looked like had they completed it behind the occluder. That is, only the visible portion of an occluded shape was negatively primed by inattention. From this and similar findings with figure-ground displays, Treisman and DeSchepper concluded that negative priming operates on "relatively uninterpreted 2-D patterns." However, it is unlikely that negative priming operates on very early visual representations (e.g., in visual areas V1 or V2) because it is insensitive to an object's absolute position in the visual field. Rather, it is more likely that it operates on a representation akin to the SSM, a relatively literal coordinate-like representation of an object's local elements (features or parts), but not one specified in strictly retinotopic coordinates.

More direct support for the role of the SSM in the recognition of unattended objects comes from some recent experiments in our laboratory (Stankiewicz, Hummel, and Cooper 1995). We used a naming paradigm to examine the role of attention in visual priming for left-right reflections of object images. We found that when subjects attended to an object on one trial, both the same view and its reflection were visually primed on the next trial, but ignored objects were primed only in the same view. Moreover, the effects of view (same vs. reflected) and attention (attended vs. unattended) were strictly additive. Attended objects in the same view enjoyed the same advantage in priming over attended objects in a reflected view that ignored objects in the same view enjoyed over ignored objects in a reflected view. If the same-view advantage reflects priming in the SSM, then on the hypothesis that the SSM mediates the recognition of ignored objects, same-view priming is expected in both the attended and ignored conditions; and if the advantage for left-right reflections reflects priming in the IGA, then priming for reflected views is expected only in the attended condition.

Relation to Other Models

We have discussed the problem addressed by this model in the context of the time required for dynamic binding in structural description. However, the problem of time is not unique to structural description models. Most models of object recognition posit various transformations (e.g., alignment) to bring images into correspondence with stored representations (e.g., Lowe 1987; Poggio and Edelman 1990; Olshausen, Anderson, and Van Essen 1993; Poggio and Vetter 1992; Siebert and Waxman 1992; Ullman 1989; Ullman and Basri 1991). Importantly, these transformations take time. Just as a structural description requires dynamic binding prior to recognition, these models require the transformations to occur prior to recognition. The question of how recognition can be accomplished rapidly is thus a very general one. Our model suggests a specific answer to this question. Recognition operates in cascade, generating an initial estimate of object identity very rapidly (via the SSM) and refining its estimate as additional information is gathered (via dynamic binding). This capacity is important because it is not trivial to specify how object recognition could operate in cascade. Most models—both structural description and transformation-based—cannot estimate an object's identity at all until the necessary operations have taken place.

Although the SSM is a viewlike representation similar to those proposed in transformation-based models of object recognition, it differs from other view-based representations in several important respects. First, all the view-based models with which we are familiar are based on very simple features (such as line junctions), represented at precise coordinates. By contrast, the SSM represents complex features (geon shape attributes) in a very coarse coordinate space (only 17 positions, rather than thousands). Second, in contrast to some coordinate representations (e.g., Poggio and Edelman 1990), the SSM is invariant with translation and scale. Olshausen, Anderson, and Van Essen (1993) have also proposed a model that maps images into a translation- and scale-invariant coordinate space, but their model requires iterative constraint satisfaction to perform this mapping, predicting that even translation and scale invariance should be time-consuming. Their model also predicts that translation and scale invariance (indeed, recognition *at all*) should require attention. The findings of Ellis et al. (1989), Tipper (1985), and Stankiewicz, Hummel, and Cooper (1995) suggest that both these predictions are incorrect.

By contrast, the model described here performs the image-to-SSM mapping in a strictly feedforward fashion, predicting that translation and scale invariance should be fast and should not require attention.

The idea that the visual system exploits both viewlike representations and structural descriptions for object recognition is not unique to this proposal (see, for example, Bülthoff and Edelman 1992; Ellis et al. 1989; Farah 1992; Tarr and Pinker 1990). However, the architecture presented here constitutes the first explicit proposal for how these two types of representation might work together. Interestingly, the factors that led us to propose the hybrid are entirely different from those that have led others to propose it. For instance, Bülthoff and Edelman note that view-based representations may provide a better account of our ability to identify particular objects, while structural descriptions may provide a better account of class recognition. Tarr and Pinker proposed the hybrid to account for the strengths and limitations of our ability to recognize objects misoriented in the picture plane (see also Jolicoeur 1990). By contrast, we propose the hybrid as a solution to a specific computational problem: coping with binding errors in a system for structural description. We suggest that the visual system must solve the same problem, and that the solution it has adopted gives rise to these other hybridlike properties as a consequence.

APPENDIX

Mapping Constraints Every module has connections to the IGA and to every part of the SSM. The state of module i's gate, G_i, is determined by two factors. The contours in or near its receptive field enforce connectedness. With respect to the receptive field of module i (r_i), any contour, j, is *consistent* if all points on j are in r_i, and *inconsistent* if a subset of points are inside r_i and a subset are outside. The set of all G_l, where l are submodules of i, drive G_i toward zero, enforcing *smallest module*. The value of a module's gate is

$$G_i^t = \begin{cases} 1 \text{ if } \left[\sum_j c_j^t - 2 - \kappa \sum_k c_k^t - \kappa \sum_l G_l^t \right] > 0 \\ 0 \text{ otherwise,} \end{cases} \tag{5.1}$$

where c_j^t is the output of any consistent contour, j, c_k^t is the output of any inconsistent contour, k, and G_l^t the gate of any module l that is a submodule of i. $\kappa = 10$. By (5.1), G_i will be 1 at time t if and only if: (a) more than two consistent contours are firing, (b) no inconsistent contours are firing, and (c) no submodules of i have nonzero gates. Modules are updated from smallest to largest on the assumption that smaller modules receive their inputs before larger modules. Thus, although modules are discussed as belonging to a single layer (L3), L3 actually consists of three layers of units, one per module size.

The net input to the IGA is the vector sum of all open modules' geon and relation units:

$$n_{IGA}^t = \sum_i G_i^t \mathbf{g}_i^t, \tag{5.2}$$

where $\mathbf{g}_i^t$ is the activation vector on both the geon and relation units of module i. The activation of each unit in the IGA is computed as a Weber fraction of its input:

$$a_i^t = \frac{n_i^t}{1 + n_i^t}, \tag{5.3}$$

where n_i^t is the ith element of the IGA's input vector. Each submodule of an open module sends its output to the part of the SSM corresponding to its position relative to that open module. The input, $\mathbf{n}_k^t$, to the kth array in the SSM is given by the vector sum of geon arrays, $\mathbf{g}_j$, over all j that are submodules of an open module (subject to the one-level constraint). Each term of the vector sum (i.e., each $\mathbf{g}_j$) is weighted by the difference between k's position in the matrix ($\mathbf{p}_k$) and j's position relative to the mean positions of all open modules ($\mathbf{p}_j^t$):

$$\mathbf{n}_k^t = \sum_i \sum_j G_i^t S(j, i) H(i, j, m) \mathbf{g}_j^t \left[1 - \frac{\mathbf{p}_k - \mathbf{p}_j}{w_k} \right]^+, \tag{5.4}$$

where S returns 1 if j is a subset of i and zero otherwise, and where w_k is the width of k's receptive field in the SSM. The receptive fields of the arrays in the matrix are defined so that adjacent arrays have overlapping receptive fields, and w_k increases with k's distance from the center of the matrix. The position of each subpart relative to the whole part is coded coarsely over the 17 arrays in the matrix. H implements the one level constraint, returning zero if there is any active module m such that j is a subset of m, and m is a subset of i (otherwise, H returns 1). Activation in the SSM is given by (5.3).

Relations   Relative size units take binary activations, but relative position units take real valued activations. For each module i:

$$Above_i = [2(y_j - y_i)/rad_j]^+, \tag{5.5}$$

$$Below_i = [2(y_i - y_j)/rad_j]^+, \tag{5.6}$$

$$Beside_i = [2|x_i - x_j|/rad_j]^+, \tag{5.7}$$

where x_i and y_i are the coordinates of the center of i's receptive field, x_j and y_j are the mean coordinates of all open modules' receptive fields, and rad_j is the radius of the largest open receptive field.

Layers 5 and 6   Bottom-up input to layers 5 and 6 is strictly excitatory. The excitatory input to each L5 unit is the sum of dot products:

$$e_i^t = \mathbf{g}^t \cdot \mathbf{w}_{gi} + \mathbf{s}^t \cdot \mathbf{w}_{si}, \tag{5.8}$$

where $\mathbf{g}^t$ is the activation vector on the IGA, $\mathbf{s}^t$ is the activation vector on the SSM, and $\mathbf{w}_{gi}$, and $\mathbf{w}_{si}$ are the corresponding weight vectors to unit i. During training, the weights to a L5 unit are determined by setting each vector equal to the corresponding vector in the to-be-learned pattern and by normalizing its length ($\mathbf{w}_{gi}$ is normalized to length 4, and $\mathbf{w}_{si}$ to length 1). Initially, each unit's activation is set to its excitatory input. Units compete via shunting inhibition:

$$a_i^t = \frac{(a_i^t)^3}{\sum\limits_j (a_j^t)^3}, \quad \sum_j (a_j^t)^3 > 0. \tag{5.9}$$

For L5 units, this equation is iterated three times per t. Unit i's output is taken as the greater of its current activation and its previous output multiplied by a decay:

$$o_i^t = \max(a_i^t, 0.95 o_i^{t-1}). \tag{5.10}$$

L5 units' outputs decay gradually, so that L6 units effectively sum their inputs over time.

The excitatory input to L6 unit i is the sum of the outputs of L5 units to which it is connected, weighted as a Weber function of the number its connections:

$$e_i^t = \left[\sum_{j=1}^{n_i} o_j^t \right] / (1 + n_i), \tag{5.11}$$

where L5 unit j is connected to object unit i and n_i is the number of L5 units connected to i. Equation 5.11, derived from a function by Marshall (1990), allows L6 with few connections from L5 units to compete with L6 units that have many. The initial activation of each L6 unit is set to its excitatory input, and L6 units compete via shunting inhibition (eq. 5.9). Equation 5.9 is applied once per t.

Training   The model was trained on one view of each object as follows. One unit in L6 was designated to represent the object as a whole. The contours in the view were presented to L1, and the model was allowed to run. Each time at least one module opened. a pattern of activation was produced in L4. A unit was created in L5 for each part into which the object was segmented during the run. The unit's excitatory weights were set as described above. The new L5 unit was then connected to the current L6 unit. This procedure resulted in one L5 unit for the object as a whole (before it could be segmented), and one for each of the smaller parts into which it was segmented during the run.

NOTES

This research was supported by a research grant from the UCLA Academic Senate to JEH. We are grateful to Lisa Travis, Irv Biederman, Jun Saiki, and Nancy Kanwisher for useful discussions about this work, and to Lisa Travis, Jay McClelland, and two anonymous reviewers for their extremely helpful comments on an earlier draft of this manuscript.

1. For example, a unit that responds preferentially to vertical edges at a particular location in the visual field statically binds the attribute "vertical" to the location. Such a unit can be activated in a strictly feedforward fashion from, say, local contrast detectors.

REFERENCES

Bergevin, R., and Levine, M. D. (1993). Generic object recognition: Building and matching course descriptions from line drawings. *IEEE Transactions on Pattern Analysis and Machine Intelligence, 15,* 19–36.

Biederman, I. (1987). Recognition-by-components: A theory of human image understanding. *Psychological Review, 94*(2), 115–147.

Biederman, I., and Cooper, E. E. (1991a). Evidence for complete translational and reflectional invariance in visual object priming. *Perception, 20,* 595–593.

Biederman, I., and Cooper, E. E. (1991b). Priming contour deleted images: Evidence for intermediate representations in visual object recognition. *Cognitive Psychology, 23,* 393–419.

Biederman, I., and Cooper, E. E. (1992). Size invariance in visual object priming. *Journal of Experimental Psychology: Human Perception and Performance, 18,* 121–133.

Biederman, I., and Gerhardstein, P. C. (1993). Recognizing depth-rotated objects: Evidence and conditions for 3-dimensional viewpoint invariance. *Journal of Experimental Psychology: Human Perception and Performance, 19,* 1162–1182.

Bülthoff, H. H., and Edelman, S. (1992). Psychophysical support for a two-dimensional view interpolation theory of object recognition. *Proceedings of the National Academy of Science, 89,* 60–64.

Carlson-Radvanski, L., and Irwin, D. E. (1994). Memory for structural descriptions across eye movements. Submitted.

Clowes, M. B. (1967). Perception, picture processing and computers. In N. L. Collins & D. Michie (Eds.), *Machine intelligence,* vol. 1, 181–197. Edinburgh: Oliver and Boyd.

Cooper, E. E. (1994). Does global shape play a role in visual object priming? *Journal of Experimental Psychology: Human Perception and Performance.* Submitted.

Dickinson, S. J., Pentland, A. P., and Rosenfeld, A. (1992). 3-D shape recovery using distributed aspect matching. *IEEE Transactions on Pattern Analysis and Machine Intelligence, 14,* 174–198.

Eckhorn, R., Bauer, R., Jordan, W., Brish, M., Kruse, W., Munk, M., and Reitboeck, H. J. (1988). Coherent oscillations: A mechanism of feature linking in the visual cortex? Multiple electrode and correlation analysis in the cat. *Biological Cybernetics. 60,* 121–130.

Eckhorn, R., Reitboeck, H., Arndt, M., and Dicke, P. (1990). Feature linking via synchronization among distributed assemblies: Simulations of results from cat visual cortex. *Neural Computation, 2,* 293–307.

Ellis, R., and Allport, D. A. (1986). Multiple levels of representation for visual objects: A behavioral study. In A. G. Cohen and J. R. Thomas (Eds.), *Artificial intelligence and its applications,* 245–257. New York: Wiley.

Ellis, R., Allport, D. A., Humphreys, G. W., and Collis, J. (1989). Varieties of object constancy. *Quarterly Journal of Experimental Psychology, 4,* 775–796.

Enns, J. T. (1992). Sensitivity of early human vision to 3-D orientation in line-drawings. *Canadian Journal of Psychology, 46,* 143–169.

Farah, M. (1992). Is an object an object an object? Cognitive and neuropsychological investigations of domain-specificity in visual object recognition. *Current Directions in Psychological Science, 1*, 164–169.

Gray, C. M., König, P., Engel, A. E., and Singer, W. (1989). Oscillatory responses in cat visual cortex exhibit intercolumn synchronization which reflects global stimulus properties. *Nature, 338*, 334–337.

Gray, C. M., and Singer, W. (1989). Stimulus specific neuronal oscillations in orientation columns of cat visual cortex. *Proceedings of the National Academy of Sciences, 86*, 1698–1702.

Hoffman, D. D., and Richards, W. A. (1985). Parts of recognition. *Cognition, 18*, 65–96.

Hummel, J. E. (1994). Segmenting images at matched concavities with synchrony for binding. Technical report 94-1. Shape Perception Laboratory, University of California, Los Angeles.

Hummel, J. E., and Biederman, I. (1990). Dynamic binding: A basis for the representation of shape by neural networks. In *Proceedings of the 12th Annual Conference of the Cognitive Science Society*, 614–621.

Hummel, J. E., and Biederman, I. (1992). Dynamic binding in a neural network for shape recognition. *Psychological Review, 99*, 480–517.

Hummel, J. E., and Holyoak, K. J. (1993). Distributing structure over time. Review of L. Shastri and V. Ajjenegadde, From simple associations to systematic reasoning: A connectionist representation of rules, variables and dynamic bindings. *Behavioral and Brain Sciences*, 464.

Hummel, J. E., and Stankiewicz, B, J. (1995). Representing spatial relations in object memory. *Cognitive Psychology*. Submitted.

Ichikawa, S. (1985). Quantitative and structural factors in the judgment of pattern complexity. *Perception and Psychophysics, 38*, 101–109.

Intraub, H. (1981). Identification and processing of briefly glimpsed visual scenes. In D. Fisher, R. A. Monty, and J. W. Sender (Eds.), *Eye movements: Cognition and visual perception*, 181–190. Hillside, NJ: Erlbaum.

Irwin, D. E. (1992). Perceiving an integrated visual world. In D. E. Meyer and S. Kornblum (Eds.), *Attention and performance XIV: Synergies in experimental psychology, artificial intelligence, and cognitive neuroscience—A silver jubilee*, 121–142. Cambridge, MA: MIT Press.

Jolicoeur, P. (1985). The time to name disoriented natural objects. *Memory and Cognition, 13*, 289–303.

Jolicoeur, P. (1990). Identification of disoriented objects: A dual systems theory. *Mind and Language, 5*, 387–410.

Kimchi, R. (1992). Primacy of wholistic processing and global/local paradigm: A critical review. *Psychological Bulletin, 112*, 24–38.

Logan, G. D. (1994). Spatial attention and the apprehension of spatial relations. *Journal of Experimental Psychology: Human Perception and Performance*. In press.

Lowe, D. G. (1987). The viewpoint consistency constraint. *International Journal of Computer Vision, 1*, 57–72.

Marr, D., and Nishihara, H. K. (1978). Representation and recognition of three-dimensional shapes. *Proceeding of the Royal Society, London, B200*, 269–294.

Marshall, J. A. (1990). A self-organizing scale-sensitive neural network. In *Proceedings of the International Joint Conference on Neural Networks*, San Diego, CA, June, vol. 3, 649–654.

McClelland, J. L. (1979). On the time relations of mental processes: An examination of systems of processes in cascade. *Psychological Review, 86*, 287–330.

Navon, D. (1977). Forest before trees: The precedence of global features in visual perception. *Cognitive Psychology, 9*, 353–383.

Olshausen, B. A., Anderson, C. H., and Van Essen, D. C. (1993). A neurobiological model of visual attention and invariant pattern recognition based on dynamic routing of information. *Journal of Neuroscience, 13*, 4700–4719.

Oram, M. W., Perrett, D. I. (1992). *Journal of Neurophysiology, 68*, 70–84.

Palmer, S. E. (1977). Hierarchical structure in perceptual representation. *Cognitive Psychology, 9*, 441–474.

Paquet, L. (1992). Global and local processing in nonattended objects: A failure to induce local processing dominance. *Journal of Experimental Psychology: Human Perception and Performance, 18*, 512–529.

Poggio, T., and Edelman, S. (1990). A neural network that learns to recognize three-dimensional objects. *Nature, 317*, 314–319.

Poggio, T., and Vetter, T. (1992). Recognition and structure and from one 2-D model view: observations on prototypes, object classes, and symmetries. MIT AI memo 1347, Massachussetts Institute of Technology, Cambridge, MA.

Potter, M. C. (1976). Short-term conceptual memory for pictures. *Journal of Experimental Psychology: Human Learning and Memory, 2*, 509–522.

Quinlan, P. T. (1991). Differing approaches to two-dimensional shape recognition. *Psychological Bulletin, 109*(2), 224–241.

Rosch, E., Mervis, C. B., Gray, W. D., Johnson, D. M., and Boyes-Braem, P. (1976). Basic objects in natural categories. *Cognitive Psychology, 8*, 382–439.

Sanocki, T. (1993). Time course of object recognition: Evidence for a global-to-local contingency. *Journal of Experimental Psychology: Human Perception and Performance, 19*, 878–898.

Siebert, M., and Waxman, A. M. (1992). Learning and recognizing 3-D objects from multiple views in a neural system. In H. Wechsler (Ed.), *Neural networks for perception. Vol. 1, Human and machine perception*, 427–444. New York: Academic Press.

Smolensky, P. (1990). Tensor product variable binding and the representation of symbolic structures in connectionist systems. *Artificial Intelligence, 46*, 159–216.

Stankiewicz, B. J., Hummel, J. E., and Cooper, E. E. (1995). The role of attention in priming for left-right reflections of object images. In preparation.

Sutherland, N. S. (1968). Outlines of a theory of visual pattern recognition in animals and man. *Proceedings of the Royal Society, London, B171*, 95–103.

Tarr, M. J., and Pinker, S. (1989). Mental rotation and orientation dependence in shape recognition. *Cognitive Psychology, 21*, 233–283.

Tarr, M. J., and Pinker, S. (1990). When does human object recognition use a viewer-centered reference frame? *Psychological Science, 1*(4), 253–256.

Tipper, S. P. (1985). The negative priming effect: Inhibitory effects of ignored primes. *Quarterly Journal of Experimental Psychology, 37A*, 571–590.

Tovee, M. J., Rolls, E. T., Treves, A., and Bellis, R. P. (1992). Information encoding and the responses of single neurons in the primate inferior temporal cortex. Preprint.

Treisman, A. (1993). The perception of features and objects. In A. Baddeley and L. Weiskrantz (Eds.), *Attention: Selection, awareness, and control: A tribute to Donald Broadbent*, 5–35. Oxford: Clarendon Press.

Treisman, A., and Gelade, G. (1980). A feature integration theory of attention. *Cognitive Psychology, 12*, 97–136.

Ullman, S. (1989). Aligning pictoral descriptions: An approach to object recognition. *Cognition, 32*, 193–254.

Ullman, S., and Basri, R. (1991). Recognition by liner combinations of models. *IEEE Transactions on Pattern Analysis and Machine Intelligence, 13*, 992–1006.

von der Malsburg, C. (1981). The correlation theory of brain function. Internal report 81-2. Department of Neurobiology, Max-Planck-Institute for Biophysical Chemistry. Göttingen, Germany.

von der Malsburg, C., and Buhmann. J. (1992). Sensory segmentation with coupled neural oscillators. *Biological Cybernetics, 67*, 233–242.

Winston, P. (1975). Learning structural descriptions from examples. In P. Winston, *The psychology of computer vision*, 157–209. New York: McGraw-Hill.

IV   Integration over Fixations in Vision

6 Integration and Accumulation of Information across Saccadic Eye Movements

David E. Irwin and Rachel V. Andrews

ABSTRACT

Two experiments investigated the nature of information integration and accumulation across saccadic eye movements. In experiment 1, subjects viewed an array of colored letters while they fixated a central point; this array was erased upon initiation of a saccade to a target. Some time after the saccade, a cue was presented above or below one of the array locations and each subject attempted to report the color and the identity of the letter that had occupied the probed position. Subjects remembered 3–4 color + identity + position units across the saccade; information near the saccade target was remembered better than information appearing in other array locations. Probe delay had little effect on performance. Most errors were mislocations rather than misidentifications. Experiment 2 showed that memory for position and identity information was improved only slightly when subjects made two as opposed to one fixation on the letter array, suggesting that limited information accumulation occurs across multiple eye movements. The results are discussed in terms of a new theory of transsaccadic memory conceived within the theoretical framework for object perception proposed by Treisman (1988).

6.1 INTRODUCTION

Because the visual world contains more information than can be perceived in a single glance, our eyes make rapid saccadic movements from point to point in space several times each second. Between movements, brief fixations are made on objects of interest in the world; it is generally assumed that somehow the contents of individual eye fixations are integrated or accumulated across saccades to produce the unified and continuous perception of the visual world that we ordinarily experience. There is no feeling of "starting anew" with each fixation; rather, we remember some objects and their spatial relationships and the overall gist of a scene, even if we close our eyes. Some information from successive fixations must be maintained across eye movements (in what we will call "transsaccadic memory") in order for this percept to be achieved. How this is accomplished has puzzled psychologists and vision researchers for over a century.

Until fairly recently, it was often assumed that something like an *integrative visual buffer* (McConkie and Rayner 1976) was responsible for the perception of a stable and continuous visual world across eye movements (e.g., Banks

1983; Breitmeyer 1984; Jonides, Irwin, and Yantis 1982; Trehub 1977). According to this view, the visible contents of successive eye fixations are aligned and superimposed in the buffer on the basis of their environmental or spatiotopic coordinates to produce an integrated, composite representation of the visual environment. Irwin (1992b) referred to this assumption as the "spatiotopic fusion hypothesis."

Although the notion of spatiotopic fusion within an integrative visual buffer is intuitively appealing, it appears to be incorrect. Irwin, Yantis, and Jonides (1983) showed that subjects are unable to integrate two different visual patterns presented in the same spatial location but separated by an eye movement, that is, they are unable to perceive some composite pattern. Specifically, four dots from a 3 × 3 matrix of dots were presented while a subject fixated one part of a display, and then four different dots from the matrix were presented in the same spatial location after the subject made an eye movement; together, eight of the nine dots in the matrix were presented, and the subject's task was to identify the location of the missing dot. Accuracy was very low, even though this task is very easy to perform if subjects do not move their eyes and the two frames of dots are presented to the same retinal and spatial locations. This inability to combine visual patterns across saccades has been replicated several times (e.g., Bridgeman and Mayer 1983; Irwin, Brown, and Sun 1988; O'Regan and Levy-Schoen 1983; Rayner and Pollatsek 1983). Other experiments have shown that both visual masking and visual integration across saccadic eye movements (Irwin, Brown, and Sun 1988) and pursuit eye movements (Sun and Irwin 1987) occur on the basis of retinotopic, and not spatiotopic coordinates. Furthermore, Irwin, Zacks, and Brown (1990) showed that spatiotopic summation does not occur across saccades; namely, one's ability to detect a sine wave grating presented after a saccade is unaffected by presenting a sine wave grating with the same spatial frequency in the same spatial location before the saccade. Taken together, these findings indicate that the perception of a stable and continuous visual world across eye movements is not accomplished through the spatiotopic superposition and fusion of the visible contents of successive eye fixations.

This conclusion receives further support from the results of other studies showing that changes in the visual characteristics of words and pictures (such as letter case and object size) and changes in spatial position across eye movements frequently are not detected and have little or no disruptive effect on reading, word naming, or picture naming (e.g., Bridgeman, Hendry, and Stark 1975; McConkie 1991; McConkie and Zola 1979; Pollatsek, Rayner, and Collins 1984; Pollatsek, Rayner, and Henderson 1990). Such changes should be quite disruptive if spatiotopic fusion occurs across saccades. In sum, many empirical findings demonstrate that a literal representation of the entire visual scene does not survive a saccadic eye movement, as the spatiotopic fusion hypothesis suggests. Furthermore, recent neurophysiological evidence indicates that stimulus locations are coded in terms of oculocentric rather than spatiotopic coordinates across saccades (Colby, chap. 7, this volume; Duhamel, Colby, and Goldberg 1992). Thus it appears that there is no internal, spatiotopically integrated stimulus representation that can explain the continuity and stability of visual perception (see also O'Regan 1992). Some other answer must be sought.

Given the demise of the spatiotopic fusion hypothesis, recent research has begun to examine what and how information is accumulated across eye movements. Even though detailed, literal images of successive fixations are not integrated across saccades, several studies have shown that at least some visual information is remembered from one fixation to the next. For example, Palmer and Ames (1992) found that subjects could make precise discriminations between lines of different lengths and shapes of slightly different sizes even when the stimuli were viewed in separate fixations. Irwin, Zacks, and Brown (1990) found that subjects could determine accurately whether two dot-patterns viewed in successive fixations were identical or different, even when the two patterns appeared in different spatial positions across the saccade. This result indicates that some visual information is maintained across eye movements in a location-independent format. However, Hayhoe, Lachter, and Feldman (1991) found that subjects could judge precisely whether or not three points viewed in successive fixations (one point per fixation) formed a right triangle, indicating that, when the task requires it, precise spatial information about several points can be held in a maplike representation across multiple eye movements.

Several other studies have shown that higher-order structural aspects of the stimulus information influence memory across eye movements. For example, Carlson-Radvansky and Irwin (1995) found that structural descriptions, rather than edge-based representations, are retained across eye movements. A structural description is a hierarchical representation whose top level corresponds to a figure as a whole, and whose lower levels represent specific parts of the figure and connections that specify the relations of the parts to each other (e.g., Hummel and Stankiewicz, chap. 5, this volume; Marr 1982; S. E. Palmer 1977; Sutherland 1968). Subjects in this study performed three different tasks. In one, they had to determine whether a part viewed in one fixation was present in a whole viewed in a second fixation; in another, they had to determine whether a whole viewed in one fixation was identical to a whole viewed in a second fixation; in the third, they were required to integrate a part viewed in one fixation with a part viewed in a second fixation and then compare this integrated representation with a presented whole figure. In all three tasks the structural characteristics of the parts and wholes affected performance in a manner consistent with the use of structural descriptions. Additional evidence for the maintenance of higher-order structural information across eye movements was reported by Verfaillie, De Troy, and Van Rensbergen (1994), who found that violations of biological motion in a point-light display were detected better than other kinds of motion violations when they occurred during a saccade.

Priming of long-term memory representations also occurs across saccades. For example, Rayner, McConkie, and Zola (1980) found that a word presented in the parafovea of one fixation facilitated naming latency for a word viewed foveally in a subsequent fixation if the two words shared the same beginning letters, regardless of letter case. Pollatsek et al. (1992) found that shared phonemic codes also provided a preview benefit. Pollatsek, Rayner, and Collins (1984) and Pollatsek, Rayner, and Henderson (1990) also found evidence for visual feature and abstract conceptual priming of pictures viewed during successive fixations. In addition, Henderson (1992) found that a parafoveal preview of an object facilitated its identification in a subsequent fixation, while Boyce and Pollatsek (1992) found that scene context facilitated object identification across saccades.

While these studies have provided important insights into the kinds of information that are maintained across eye movements, other studies have examined the capacity and time course of transsaccadic memory. Irwin (1991) found that accuracy in the pattern discrimination task used by Irwin, Zacks, and Brown (1990) was highly dependent on pattern complexity, such that simple dot-patterns were recognized more accurately than complex dot-patterns. Varying the temporal interval separating the two patterns from 0 to 5 seconds, however, had very little effect on performance. As in Irwin, Zacks, and Brown (1990), spatially displacing one pattern relative to the other had no effect on recognition accuracy. These results indicate that transsaccadic memory is, at least in part, a limited-capacity, location-independent, long-lasting memory like visual short-term memory.

Additional support for this conclusion was provided by Irwin (1992a), whose subjects were presented with an array of letters in one fixation and a partial-report cue (e.g., an arrow) in a second fixation, after an eye movement had occurred. Subjects were required to report the letter that had occupied the spatial location indicated by the report cue; in order to respond correctly, they had to remember the position and the identity of the cued letter across the eye movement. Irwin (1992a) found that memory was rather poor; subjects could remember only 3–4 letters (i.e., position + identity units) across an eye movement, regardless of the number of letters (6 or 10) presented in the letter array. Report of the letters spatially near the saccade target was much more accurate than report of other letters in the array, however, suggesting that attention, which precedes the eyes to a saccade target (Shepherd, Findlay, and Hockey 1986), determined which information was stored in transsaccadic memory. Delaying the partial report cue from 40 to 750 ms after the eye movement had only a slight effect on report accuracy, suggesting little loss of information over time. Intra-array errors (erroneous report of a noncued letter from the array) were much more frequent than extra-array errors (erroneous report of a letter not contained in the array), suggesting that identity information may be retained better than location information when the eyes move. To account for these results, Irwin (1992a) proposed that a small number (3–4) of integrated position + identity codes were held in short-term memory across the saccade, while priming of "unlocated" identity codes in long-term memory also occurred, producing the preponderance of intra-array errors over extra-array errors. That is, if subjects were unsure what the probed letter was, unprobed items in the array would be more available in memory than unpresented items, leading to location (intra-array) errors rather than intrusion (extra-array) errors.

Based on these results, and following up on a suggestion by Kahneman, Treisman, and Gibbs (1992), Irwin (1992a) proposed a new theory of transsaccadic memory within the conceptual framework for object perception proposed by Treisman (1988) and Kahneman and Treisman (1984). This framework contains four levels of representation: (1) feature maps, which register independently the presence of different sensory features in the display, such as color and shape; (2) a master map of locations, which registers where in the display features are located; (3) temporary object representations or object files, (episodic descriptions of what objects are where in the display), which are formed when attention conjoins features into unitary wholes (e.g., colored shapes); and (4) an abstract, long-term recognition network, which stores descriptions of objects along with their names. This theory accounts for the results of Irwin (1992a) as follows. When a letter array is presented, the letter identities in the array automatically activate their corresponding entries in the recognition network, generating "unlocated" identity codes; at the same time, the shapes of the letters are represented in a feature map. Attention is directed from one array location to the next to produce an object file (i.e., an integrated identity + position code) in short-term memory for each letter. Because attention ordinarily precedes eye movements, object files for letters near the saccade target are more likely to be created than object files for letters at other positions in the array. Given the limited capacity of short-term memory, only a small number (3–4) of object files (integrated position + identity codes) can be retained across the saccade; priming of the unlocated identity codes in long-term memory makes it more likely that subjects will erroneously report an item from the array rather than an unpresented item when the subject is unsure of the correct response. In sum, according to Irwin (1992a), transsaccadic memory consists of the object files that are produced before a saccade and of residual activation in long-term memory.

The conception of transsaccadic memory proposed by Irwin (1992a), which we will call the "object file theory of transsaccadic memory," is undetailed in many respects; nonetheless, it provides a useful framework for investigating how and what information is maintained across saccadic eye movements. In particular, it makes several specific predictions that can be tested experimentally (it should be emphasized that these predictions are based on Irwin's 1992a instantiation of the ideas of Kahneman and Treisman, who might not agree with all of the predictions). First, objects (rather than spatial locations, say) should be the fundamental organizing units for representing and maintaining information across saccades. Second, attention should play a critically important role in determining what information is stored in transsaccadic memory because it controls which object files are created. Third, only a limited number of object files should be created and maintained across a saccade because of short-term memory limitations. Fourth, because object files are held in (relatively) slow-decaying short-term memory, there should be little loss of information from transsaccadic memory over short (<5 sec) retention intervals. Fifth, surface characteristics (e.g., color, form) of at least some of the elements in a display (specifically, the attended ones) should be maintained in transsaccadic memory because object files are formed when attention conjoins the features present at a display location into a unitary whole, containing both pre- and postcategorical information (Kahneman, Treisman, and Gibbs 1992). Note that, according to the object file theory, relatively little information actually *accumulates* across saccades; rather, one's mental representation of a scene consists of mental schemata and identity codes activated in long-term memory and of a small number of detailed object files in short-term memory.

The experiments reported below used the transsaccadic partial report technique of Irwin (1992a) to investigate further the nature of information retained across eye movements and to test some of the predictions of the object file theory of transsaccadic memory. The first experiment examined whether surface characteristics of the elements in the presaccadic fixation (e.g., color) are maintained across a saccade; whether these characteristics remain bound together over time; and the role of attention in memory for such information. The second experiment examined transsaccadic memory for multiple fixations, to determine whether information accumulates across saccades.

6.2   EXPERIMENT 1

This experiment investigated whether color information is retained with item identity information across a saccade. On each trial the subject fixated a central point on an empty screen, then a saccade target appeared in the left or right periphery. Simultaneous with saccade target onset, two rows of three letters each were presented, as in Irwin (1992a). Each letter appeared in a different color. The letters were presented until a saccade was initiated to the saccade target (approximately 340 ms). After a delay of either 50, 150, or 750 ms, during which the saccade was completed and fixation was established and maintained on the saccade target, a bar marker was presented above or below one of the positions previously occupied by a letter. The subjects' task was to report the identity and the color of the letter indicated by the marker. Accuracy of letter report and of color report was measured as a function of probe delay, and the accuracy of color report conditionalized on correct letter report was calculated for each delay in order to determine whether, and for how long, color information is retained with identity information in transsaccadic memory. To allow a comparison of memory within and between fixations, data from a no-saccade control condition were also collected.

The object file theory of transsaccadic memory predicts that subjects should remember 3–4 identity + position + color units across the saccade; that is, letter report and color report should be nonindependent because all of the information at a given spatial location in the array should be conjoined via attention into a unitary object file. Accuracy for items near the saccade target should be higher than for items at other array locations because of attention preceding the eyes to the saccade target. There should be little effect of interstimulus interval on performance because the object files are held in short-term memory. The contingency between letter report and color report should also remain relatively constant over interstimulus interval because information in the object files should remain bound together over time. When an incorrect response is made, intra-array errors (report of a noncued item present in the array) should be more common than extra-array errors (report of an unpresented item) because of identity code activation in long-term memory; however, there should be no contingency between letter identity and letter color on intra-array error responses because these responses reflect priming of long-term memory representations rather than specific, episodic properties of the stimulus display.

Method

Subjects   Ten subjects, including the authors, participated in this experiment. Except for Irwin, the subjects were undergraduate and graduate students at the University of Illinois. Most of them had participated in previous eye movement experiments. Except for the authors, the subjects were naive about the experimental hypotheses. The subjects were paid $5 per hour for their participation and received a 1-cent bonus for each correct response.

Stimuli   The stimuli consisted of letter arrays containing six colored letters arranged in two rows and three columns. The letters were drawn randomly without replacement on each trial from the set: D, F, J, L, N, S, T, Z. The colors were drawn randomly without replacement on each trial from the set: light cyan, red, blue, magenta, brown, green, yellow, and white. An asterisk (*) appearing above (top row) or below (bottom row) one of the array locations was used as the partial-report cue.

Apparatus   Stimuli were presented on a NEC MultiSync 3FGx color monitor equipped with a monitor lens that reduced screen reflectance. A Gateway2000 486 50 MHz microcomputer controlled stimulus presentation with a SVGA graphics adaptor and collected subjects' keyboard responses. The computer also recorded the output from an Applied Science Laboratories Model 210 scleral reflectance eye tracker by means of an analog-to-digital converter. The eye tracker was mounted on eyeglass frames that were held in place on the subject's head by a headband. The eye tracker was configured to record horizontal movements of the left eye only. Eye position was sampled once each ms. A bite bar with dental impression compound was used to keep the subject's head steady during the experiment. Subjects completed a calibration sequence (described later) before every experimental trial. The accuracy of the eye tracker under these conditions was +/−0.3 degree.

During the experiment, subjects were seated 57 cm from the display monitor. At this viewing distance, the total display area subtended 26 degrees of visual angle horizontally and 19.7 degrees vertically. The letter arrays were presented in the center of the display area. The letter arrays subtended 4.3 degrees horizontally and 2.2 degrees vertically. Each letter was 0.3 degrees wide and 0.7 degrees high; the spaces between letters were 1.7 degrees horizontally and 0.8 degrees vertically. The asterisk used as the bar probe was 0.3 degree wide and 0.4 degree high; it was presented 0.2 degree above or below the target letter position. Calibration, saccade target, and fixation points used during the experiment subtended 0.2 degree horizontally and 0.4 degree vertically.

Characters were presented in graphics mode (640 × 200), using the default font which presents characters in an 8 × 8 grid. Colors were chosen from the standard PC color palette to be maximally discriminable from each other. The display background was light gray, while the calibration, saccade target, and fixation points were dark gray.

Procedure   Each subject completed several preliminary procedures before participating in the eye movement experiment proper. The purpose of these was to familiarize the subjects with the stimuli and with the partial report task. First the subjects were shown the letter and color sets that would be used in the experiment. They were instructed to use the following color names to refer to the colors; "sky" for light cyan, "red" for red, "blue" for blue, "purple" for magenta, "orange" for brown, "green" for green, "yellow" for yellow, and "white" for white. These names were chosen so that each color could be referred to by a unique beginning initial, S, R, B, P, O, G, Y, and W, respectively, when subjects typed their color responses into the computer keyboard. Subjects were given several minutes to study these materials, and then they completed 50 trials in which a single colored letter was flashed for 100 ms on the display monitor. After each presentation, subjects entered the letter they had seen and the beginning initial of the letter's color name into the computer keyboard. Half of the subjects responded letter first, color second, while the other half responded color first, letter second. Order of response was constant for an individual subject throughout all practice and experimental sessions. A chart listing the letter set and the color set (including names and initials) was present throughout all sessions. Accuracy on letter and color naming was greater than 90 percent for all subjects in this familiarization task, indicating that they were able to use the response coding scheme accurately and that they had no serious color vision deficiencies.

Next each subject completed 50 partial report trials while maintaining fixation on a central point. During these trials a 2 × 3 array of colored letters was presented for 250 ms; then the bar probe was presented for 33 ms immediately after stimulus offset. Probe position varied randomly from trial to trial. Each subject completed 180 more partial report trials while maintaining fixation, but on these trials the probe delay was either 50, 150, or 750 ms. Probe position and probe delay varied randomly from trial to trial. By the end of these practice blocks, subjects had become very familiar with the basic partial report task, the experimental stimuli, and the response scheme. Following this exposure they were introduced to the eye movement (transsaccadic) version of the partial report task; the procedure for these trials is described next.

The sequence of events for a typical trial in the transsaccadic partial report task is depicted in figure 6.1; note that the letters appeared in color. Each trial began with a calibration routine during which a calibration point (+) stepped across the display at three locations separated by 2.0 degrees. Each point was presented for 1.5 sec, and the subject was instructed to fixate each carefully. Eye position at each location was sampled (at a rate of 1,000 Hz) for 100 ms

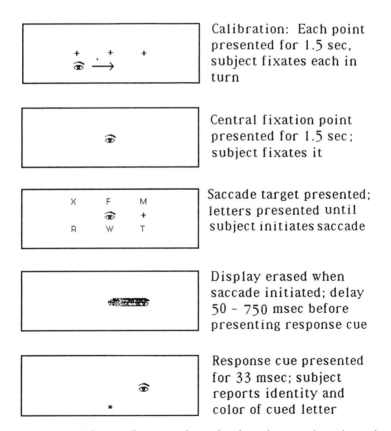

Calibration: Each point presented for 1.5 sec, subject fixates each in turn

Central fixation point presented for 1.5 sec; subject fixates it

Saccade target presented; letters presented until subject initiates saccade

Display erased when saccade initiated; delay 50 – 750 msec before presenting response cue

Response cue presented for 33 msec; subject reports identity and color of cued letter

Figure 6.1 Schematic illustration of procedure for trials in saccade condition of experiment 1.

near the middle of this interval. These recordings served to calibrate the output of the eye tracker against spatial position.

After calibration, the first fixation point was presented, always where the second (central) calibration point had appeared. The subject was instructed to fixate this point carefully. After 1.5 sec, this central fixation point disappeared and the saccade target (another +) appeared in the parafovea. On rightward-movement trials, the saccade target appeared at the location of the rightmost calibration location; on leftward-movement trials, it appeared at the location of the leftmost calibration location. The subject was instructed to saccade to this target when it was presented. Sampling of eye position began with the presentation of the saccade target.

The letter array was presented simultaneously with the onset of the saccade target. As described earlier, the six letters were chosen without replacement from a set of 8 consonants, and they were displayed in six different colors, also chosen from a pool of 8 alternatives. Two rows of three uppercase letters each were presented, with one letter situated 0.2 degree above and another letter situated 0.2 degree below each of the three calibration locations. The letters were presented until a saccade was initiated to the saccade target (mean = 339 ms). Saccade onset was defined as a change in eye position in the same direction with a velocity greater than 50 deg/sec for three consecutive ms. After the offset of the letter array, a delay of either 50, 150, or 750 ms elapsed before the bar probe was presented for 33 ms. Subjects were instructed to maintain fixation on the saccade target during the probe delay and during probe presentation. After presentation of the probe, the subject attempted to report the identity and the color of the letter that had occupied the probed position; these responses were typed into the computer keyboard, using the coding scheme described earlier.

In order for a trial to be acceptable, the subject's eye movement had to have a latency between 100 and 700 ms. This criterion eliminated anticipatory eye movements that might not have allowed for adequate processing of the letter array and delayed eye movements potentially indicative of attention lapses. Trials in which the eyes were not within 1.0 degree of the central fixation point when the letter array was presented and trials in which a saccade was made in the wrong direction (away from the saccade target) were also discarded. In total, 19 percent of the trials were discarded for one or more of these reasons.

Each subject completed six blocks of 36 trials each in the transsaccadic partial report task. Saccade direction (left and right), probe delay (50, 150, and 750 ms), and probe position were sequenced randomly across trials but were balanced within each block for each subject. Each subject completed several practice blocks of eye movement trials before completing the six experimental blocks. Data collection was spread over two experimental sessions, with three blocks per session.

Following the completion of these eye movement trials, each subject completed a no-saccade control session during which the letter arrays and bar probes were viewed while the subject maintained fixation on the central fixation point. The exposure duration for each subject was set equal to the mean saccade latency (hence exposure duration) that the subject produced during the eye movement trials. Each subject completed 180 trials in this session, balanced for probe delay and probe position.

Results

Preliminary analysis of the eye movement data showed that mean saccade latency (hence stimulus exposure duration) and mean saccade duration did not vary significantly with saccade direction or across probe delays. Mean saccade latency was 339 ms (s.e. = 14 ms) and mean saccade duration was 27 ms (s.e. = 1 ms).

On each trial, subjects attempted to report the identity and the color of the item that had appeared in the probed position. Order of report (identity first, color second vs. color first, identity second) was included as a factor in all of the analyses reported below, but it had no significant effect on performance in any analysis and so will not be discussed further.

Table 6.1 shows the percentage of response outcomes as a function of probe delay for both the saccade condition and the no-saccade control condition. A separate analysis of variance (ANOVA) was conducted on each response outcome, with probe delay as the single factor. The most common response outcome was for both the identity and the color of the probed item to be recalled correctly (mean = 60.7 percent); this outcome declined as probe delay increased, $F(2,16) = 22.8$, $p < .001$. Correct identity report with incorrect color report (mean = 11.2 percent) increased with probe delay, $F(2,16) = 17.8$, $p < .001$, as did the percentage of trials in which both the identity and the color of the probed item (mean = 14.3 percent) were reported incorrectly, $F(2,16) = 16.3$, $p < .001$. The percentage of trials in which the identity of the probed item was reported incorrectly but its color

Table 6.1 Percentage of Response Outcomes as Function of Probe Delay in Experiment 1

Response outcome	Probe delay (ms)		
	50	150	750
	Saccade condition		
Identity correct, color correct	66.3	66.0	49.8
Identity correct, color incorrect	9.0	8.0	16.5
Identity incorrect, color correct	13.8	14.9	12.8
Identity incorrect, color incorrect	10.6	11.3	21.0
	No-saccade condition		
Identity correct, color correct	87.9	84.4	66.8
Identity correct, color incorrect	4.1	6.2	12.7
Identity incorrect, color correct	6.1	5.8	12.2
Identity incorrect, color incorrect	2.0	3.2	8.3

was reported correctly (mean = 13.8 percent) was constant ($F(2,16) < 1$) across probe delays. All of the probe delay effects occurred between delays of 150 and 750 ms; there were no significant performance differences between the two shortest probe delays. As is apparent in table 6.1, there was a high degree of contingency between identity report and color report, especially at the two shortest probe delays; the probability of correctly recalling the color of the probed item, conditionalized on correct recall of the identity of the probed item, was 0.87, 0.89, and 0.75 for probe delays of 50, 150, and 750 ms. The pattern of results was similar in the no-saccade control condition, except that fewer incorrect responses were made.

It is of interest to examine in more detail the kinds of errors that subjects made because this might reveal whether some kinds of information are remembered better than others across eye movements. One way to examine the errors is to consider the identity and color responses separately, classifying the errors for each response class as either intra-array or extra-array in character. Incorrect responses were classified as intra-array errors if the reported items had not appeared at the probed positions but had appeared elsewhere in the letter array, or as extra-array errors if the reported items had not appeared anywhere in the letter array. These two categories account for all errors because response omissions were not allowed. In partial report research, intra-array errors are generally assumed to reflect loss of location information from memory, whereas extra-array errors are assumed to reflect loss of identity information (e.g., Irwin and Yeomans 1986; Mewhort et al. 1981; Townsend 1973). Table 6.2 shows the percentage of correct responses,

Table 6.2 Percentage Correct and Percentage of Intra-array and Extra-array Errors for Identity Responses (Ignoring Color) and Color Responses (Ignoring Identity) as Function of Probe Delay in Experiment 1

Response outcome	Probe delay (ms)		
	50	150	750
	Saccade condition		
Identity correct	75.6	73.9	66.1
Identity intra-array error	21.5	22.8	28.1
Identity extra-array error	2.7	3.5	5.6
Color correct	80.2	80.8	62.8
Color intra-array error	17.5	15.7	33.3
Color extra-array error	2.1	3.6	4.0
	No-saccade condition		
Identity correct	91.9	90.8	79.4
Identity intra-array error	6.3	7.2	16.1
Identity extra-array error	2.1	2.0	4.8
Color correct	94.1	90.3	79.0
Color intra-array error	4.4	7.6	16.8
Color extra-array erorr	1.8	2.4	4.5

intra-array errors, and extra-array errors for the identity responses (ignoring color) and the color responses (ignoring identity). Each of these response outcomes was analyzed separately in an ANOVA, with probe delay as the single factor.

In the saccade condition, there were significantly more correct identity responses at the two shortest probe delays than at the longest probe delay, $F(2, 16) = 10.7$, $p < .001$. This was true for correct color responses, as well, $F(2, 16) = 37.2$, $p < .001$. There were significantly more identity intra-array errors ($F(2, 16) = 8.0, p < .005$), identity extra-array errors ($F(2, 16)) = 4.0$, $p < .05$), and color intra-array errors ($F(2, 16) = 39.6, p < .001$) at the longest probe delay than at the two shortest probe delays. The slight increase in color extra-array errors as probe delay increased was not significant, $F(2, 16) = 2.6$, $p > .10$. There were many more intra-array errors (mean = 24.1 percent for identity and 22.2 percent for color) than extra-array errors (mean = 3.9 percent for identity and 3.2 percent for color) for both identity and color responses. There was very little contingency between identity and color reports when an intra-array error occurred: The probability of reporting the color of the erroneously reported identity when an identity intra-array error occurred was 0.18, and the probability of reporting the identity of the erroneously reported color when a color intra-array error occurred was 0.19. These values are not much different from chance (0.13). In contrast, recall that there was a high contingency (0.84) between identity and color reports when a correct response was made. The pattern of results was similar in the no-saccade control condition, except that fewer errors occurred.

The data in tables 6.1 and 6.2 are averaged across letter position in the array and eye movement direction (in the saccade condition). The object file theory of transsaccadic memory predicts that accuracy should be higher for items near the saccade target than for items at other display locations because of attention preceding the eyes to the saccade target. Table 6.3 shows the percentage of identity-correct, color-correct trials as a function of probe position under both saccade and no-saccade conditions, averaged across probe delay. An ANOVA was conducted on the saccade condition data with factors of saccade direction (left vs. right) and probe position (1–6, where 1 refers to the leftmost letter in the top row and 6 refers to the rightmost letter in the bottom row). There was a significant main effect of position, $F(5, 40) = 24.9$, $p < .001$, and a significant interaction between saccade direction and position, $F(5, 40) = 18.2$, $p < .001$. The first two rows of table 6.3 show the means for this interaction. Report of the leftmost item in the top row (position 1) and report of the leftmost item in the bottom row (position 4) were significantly more accurate when the eyes moved to the left than when the eyes moved to the right. Similarly, report of the rightmost item in the top row (position 3) and report of the rightmost item in the bottom row (position 6) were significantly more accurate when the eyes moved to the right than when the eyes moved to the left. In sum, subjects were most

Table 6.3 Percentage of Identity-Correct, Color-Correct Trials as Function of Probe Position in Experiment 1

Condition	Probe position					
	1	2	3	4	5	6
Saccade to left	93.0	54.2	60.3	68.5	35.0	59.5
Saccade to right	70.3	35.6	90.6	48.7	20.7	84.3
No saccade	85.7	82.1	83.7	78.7	69.2	79.0

accurate at reporting the letter + color units that appeared spatially near the location to which they moved their eyes, even though these items fell on the parafovea during display presentation. Report of the items in the center of the display (positions 2 and 5) was significantly worse than report of the other items, even though the central items fell on the fovea during the presentation of the letter array.

For comparison, the last row of table 6.3 shows the percentage of identity-correct, color-correct trials as a function of probe position in the no-saccade control condition. Items in the top row (positions 1–3) were reported more accurately (83.8 percent vs. 75.6 percent) than items in the bottom row, probably reflecting an attentional bias induced by reading experience. A similar top-row advantage was found in the saccade condition as well.

Discussion

The results of the first experiment show that identity information and color information are remembered about equally well across an eye movement (table 6.2). Furthermore, they are remembered as integral units (e.g., colored letters), rather than as separate pieces of information (e.g., colors and letters). Thus transsaccadic memory appears to retain surface characteristics of items, such as their color, in addition to abstract identity information. Of course, it is possible that the colors were translated into abstract color names and held in that form in transsaccadic memory. If that were the case, however, one might expect that the number of identities and colors that could be maintained across a saccade would be much lower than what was observed, given the limited capacity of transsaccadic memory. To elaborate, the accuracy results can be expressed as *items remembered* by multiplying the percentage correct by the number of items in the array (Sperling 1960); this calculation shows that subjects remembered 4.0 integrated identity + position + color units at the two shortest probe delays, and 3.0 units at the longest probe delay. This is very similar to what Irwin (1992a) observed (3.9–3.2 identity + position units) when subjects had to report only letter identity. Thus it appears that there is little cost in remembering color information in addition to remembering identity information across an eye movement. Subjects appear to store integrated wholes (e.g., "red T, blue D, purple N, white J") rather than separate features (e.g., "red, blue, T, D") in transsaccadic memory. This result is consistent with the hypothesis that subjects remember a limited number of integrated object files (identity + position + color units) in transsaccadic memory, as predicted by the object file theory. The high degree of contingency between identity reports and color reports on correct trials also supports this conclusion. The results show that the number of object files held in transsaccadic memory is not constant over all probe delays, however, no loss occurred during the first 150 ms after saccade onset, but one object file was lost 150–750 ms after the eyes moved.

When errors occurred, they were much more likely to involve the report of an item from the array, rather than an unpresented item. Of course, chance guessing favors intra-array over extra-array errors, because the six items presented on each trial were chosen from a pool of only eight alternatives. Thus, given that an error occurred, the likelihood of an intra-array error is 5/7, while the likelihood of an extra-array error is only 2/7. In other words, chance guessing predicts that there should be about 2.5 times as many intra-array as extra-array errors. Table 6.2 shows that, on average, there were about 6.5 times as many intra-array as extra-array errors, considerably higher than the 2.5 times expected by chance guessing. Thus it appears that location information is more likely to be lost than identity information when the eyes move. However, an analysis of the distribution of location errors showed that approximately 65 percent of them involved report of the identity or of the color of the item adjacent to the probed position, indicating that some coarse coding of location apparently survives the saccade. This was true for both the identity and the color responses. As predicted by the object file theory, there was very little contingency between identity and color reports when an intra-array error occurred. Integrated identity + color units did not "migrate" together to cause an error; rather, identity and color were independent.

Analysis of the relationship between eye movement direction and probe position on performance showed that presentation of the saccade target led subjects to shift their attention toward the items that appeared near it, increasing the likelihood that those items would be encoded into transsaccadic memory at the expense of the other items in the array. These results are consistent with the object file theory of transsaccadic memory. The inferior recall of the central items relative to the terminal items on the side opposite the saccade target is somewhat mysterious; perhaps the central items were encoded first, then bumped out of memory as the other array items were encoded.

A no-saccade control condition was included in this study so that comparisons could be made between memory within and across fixations. Accuracy in the no-saccade control condition was considerably higher than in the saccade condition; for example, averaged across probe delays, the identity and the color of the probed item were reported correctly on 79.7 percent of the trials, compared to 60.7 percent in the saccade condition. Subjects remembered 5.3–4.0 identity + position + color units across probe delays in the no-saccade control condition, compared to 4.0–3.0 in the saccade condition. The superior performance in the no-saccade control condition occurred because subjects can make use of two kinds of memory when they do not move their eyes: "iconic" memory (a brief, retinotopic, high-capacity, veridical representation) and visual short-term memory. Because iconic memory is largely eliminated when the eyes move (Irwin 1992a; Irwin, Brown, and Sun 1988), subjects can use only visual short-term memory in the saccade condition. That accuracy at the shortest probe delay in the saccade condition was equal to accuracy at the longest probe delay in the no-saccade condition is consistent with this conclusion because iconic memory typically decays away within 500 ms of stimulus offset (e.g., Sperling 1960). Error patterns in the no-saccade control condition were quite similar to those of the saccade condition, both in terms of the predominance of intra-array errors over extra-array errors and the spatial distribution of intra-array errors near the probed position.

In summary, the predictions of the object file theory of transsaccadic memory were supported quite well by the results of the first experiment. Subjects remembered 3–4 identity + position + color units across the saccade, and letter report and color report were nonindependent on correct trials. This supports the hypothesis that all of the information at a given spatial location in the array was conjoined via attention into a unitary object file for storage in transsaccadic memory. Accuracy for items near the saccade target was higher than for items at other array locations because of attention preceding the eyes to the saccade target. Intra-array errors were much more common than extra-array errors, perhaps because of identity code activation in long-term memory; there was no contingency between letter identity and letter color on intra-array error responses, consistent with the idea that these responses reflect priming of long-term memory representations rather than specific, episodic properties of the stimulus display. That intra-array errors were distributed close to the spatial location of the probed item seems inconsistent with the conclusion that these errors are due to priming in long-term memory, however, because there is no reason to believe that coarse episodic location information should be maintained in long term memory. The implications of this finding are discussed further in the general discussion (section 6.4). Probe delay had a somewhat larger effect on memory than expected, as information loss occurred between 150 and 750 ms after saccade onset. If object files are held in short-term memory, one might expect little decay over the range of times we explored. It is known that information decays in short-term memory, however (e.g., Reitman 1974), so perhaps this result is not completely surprising.

Experiment 2 investigated a different aspect of the object file theory, the idea that information accumulation across multiple eye fixations is limited by the capacity of transsaccadic memory.

6.3 EXPERIMENT 2

This experiment examined transsaccadic memory for multiple fixations. In the first experiment the letter array was present for only one fixation, disappearing as soon as the subject initiated a saccade to the saccade target. In Experiment 2 the letter array remained visible for either 1 or 2 fixations before it disappeared and the partial report cue was presented. In the two-fixation case, the subject saccaded from the central fixation point to a saccade target on one side of the letter array (as in fig. 6.1), but then saccaded back to the central fixation point. The letter array remained visible during the first saccade and during fixation of the saccade target location, and it was not extinguished until a saccade was initiated back to the central fixation point. After some probe delay, the partial report cue was presented, and the subject attempted to report the identity of the cued letter. An array of 10 letters (2 rows of 5), rather than 6, was used to avoid potential ceiling effects. To simplify the subjects' task, the color of the letters in this experiment was not varied, so this experiment measured memory for letter identity + position information only.

Irwin's (1992a) object file theory of transsaccadic memory makes the following (perhaps counterintuitive) predictions about memory performance in this task. First, subjects should remember only 3–4 letters (i.e., position + identity units) from the array, regardless of the number of fixations they make. Second, report of the letters spatially near the *final* saccade target should be more accurate than report of other letters in the array, even if those letters were foveated in a prior fixation. These predictions follow from the theory's claims that only a limited number of object files can be held in short-term memory and that object file creation is determined by attentional allocation to items near the saccade target. In the absence of rehearsal, forgetting in short-term memory is first-in, first-out, so that only the final set of object files should be remembered. The bias for errors due to mislocalization rather than to misidentification should be stronger in the two-fixation condition than in the one-fixation condition because subjects have more time to identify the letters in the array and to activate their long-term memory representations.

It seemed possible that some of these predictions might be violated. Intuitively, more fixations on a display should lead to superior memory performance, and, given unlimited viewing time and an unlimited number of fixations, this would no doubt occur because the contents of the letter array could be transferred to long-term memory. Given only 1–2 fixations, however, we expected little transfer of information to long-term memory to occur. Furthermore, there is actually very little empirical support for the intuition that memory should improve with increasing number of fixations. Loftus (1972) found that long-term recognition memory for a series of pictures improved as the number of fixations per picture increased, but using line drawings as stimuli, Tversky (1974) found the opposite result. In addition, several investigators have found that increasing exposure duration over a range that included several fixations has very little effect on whole-report performance in within-fixation studies of memory for letter arrays (e.g., Irwin and Brown 1987; Sperling 1960), which is also thought to rely on short-term memory. In fact, inverse duration effects (i.e., worse performance with increasing exposure duration) have been found in some partial-report studies (Di Lollo and Dixon 1992). Thus, even though the prediction is counterintuitive, it is not completely unreasonable.

Method

Subjects   Seven subjects, including Andrews, participated in this experiment. The subjects were undergraduate and graduate students at the University of Illinois. All but two of them had participated in the first experiment. Except for Andrews, the subjects were naive about the experimental hypotheses. The subjects were paid $5 per hour for their participation and received a 1-cent bonus for each correct response.

Stimuli   The stimuli consisted of letter arrays containing ten letters arranged in two rows and five columns. The letters were drawn randomly without replacement on each trial from the set of all consonants, excluding y. An asterisk (*) appearing above (top row) or below (bottom row) one of the array locations was used as the partial-report cue.

Apparatus   The apparatus was the same as in experiment 1. The letter arrays subtended 4.3 degrees horizontally and 2.2 degrees vertically. Each letter was 0.3 degree wide and 0.7 degree high; the spaces between letters were 0.7 degree horizontally and 0.8 degree vertically. The asterisk used as the bar probe was 0.3 degree wide and 0.4 degree high; it was presented 0.2 degree above or below the target letter position. Calibration, saccade target, and fixation points used during the experiment subtended 0.2 degree horizontally and 0.4 degree vertically.

Characters were presented in graphics mode (640 × 200), using the default font which presents characters in an 8 × 8 grid. The display background was light gray, while the calibration, saccade target, fixation points, and letters were dark gray.

Procedure   To gain familiarity with the 10-letter version of the partial-report task, each subject completed 50 partial report trials while maintaining fixation on a central point. During these trials a 2 × 5 array of letters was presented for 250 ms, then the bar probe was presented for 33 ms immediately after stimulus offset. Probe position varied randomly from trial to trial. Each subject completed 180 more partial report trials while maintaining fixation, but on these trials the probe delay was either 50, 150, or 750 ms. Probe position and probe delay varied randomly from trial to trial. On each trial, subjects attempted to report the letter that had appeared in the probed position, as well as the position of the probe (i.e., array location 1–10). They used the numbers 1–9 and 0 to report probe position, with 1 referring to the leftmost letter in the top row and 0 (for 10) to the rightmost letter in the bottom row. By the end of these practice blocks, the subjects had become very familiar with the 10-letter partial-report task and with the response scheme. Following this exposure they were introduced to the transsaccadic version of the 10-letter partial-report task; the procedure for these trials is described next.

The sequence of events for a one-fixation trial in the transsaccadic partial-report task was very similar to that depicted in figure 6.1, except that ten letters were displayed instead of six. After a calibration sequence, the first fixation point was presented where the second (central) calibration point had appeared. After 1.5 sec, the saccade target (another +) appeared in the parafovea, 2 degrees to the left or right of the central fixation point, which remained visible. Simultaneous with the onset of the saccade target, the letter array was presented. Two rows of five uppercase letters each were presented until the subject initiated a saccade toward the target. After the offset of the letter array, an interval of 50, 150, or 750 ms elapsed before the bar probe was presented for 33 ms. Only the saccade target was visible during the probe delay and during probe presentation. After presentation of the probe, the subject attempted to report the letter that had occupied the position indicated by the probe as well as the probe's spatial position; these responses were typed into the computer terminal keyboard, using the coding scheme described earlier.

The sequence of events on two-fixation trials was very similar, except that the letter array remained visible during the first saccade and while the subject fixated the saccade target. The letter array was extinguished when the subject initiated a saccade back from the saccade target to the central fixation point. An interval of 50, 150, or 750 ms then elapsed before the bar probe was presented for 33 ms. Only the central fixation point was visible during the probe delay and during probe presentation. The subject then attempted to report the letter that had occupied the probed position and the position of the probe, as in the one-fixation condition.

In order for a trial to be acceptable, the subject must have fixated the letter array between 100 and 1,000 ms in the one-fixation condition and between 100 and 2,000 ms in the two-fixation condition. Trials in which the eyes were not within 1.0 degree of the central fixation point when the letter array was initially presented and trials in which a saccade was made in the wrong, direction (away from the saccade target) were also discarded. In total, 7 percent of the trials in the one-fixation condition and 11 percent of the trials in the two-fixation condition were discarded for one or more of these reasons.

Each subject also completed two no-saccade control sessions during which the letter arrays and bar probes were viewed while the subject maintained fixation on the central fixation point. In one session (short-duration condition) the exposure duration for each subject was set equal to the approximate mean saccade latency (hence exposure duration) that the subject had produced during the one-fixation eye-movement trials (mean = 391 ms); in the other session (long-duration condition) the exposure duration for each subject was set equal to the approximate mean exposure duration (the sum of the two fixations plus the duration of the intervening saccade) that the subject had experienced during the two-fixation eye movement trials (mean = 760 ms). Eye position was monitored to ensure that subjects maintained fixation at the center fixation point throughout the presentation of the letter array and the probe. Less than 1 percent of the trials had to be deleted in each control condition for failure to maintain fixation.

In total, each subject completed six blocks of 40 trials each in the one-fixation and two-fixation transsaccadic partial-report tasks, and six blocks of 40 trials each in the short-duration and long-duration no-saccade control conditions. Probe delay (50, 150, and 750 ms), probe position, and saccade direction (in the eye movement blocks) were sequenced randomly across trials, but were balanced throughout the course of the experiment for each subject. Three subjects completed all of the one-fixation saccade trials and short-duration no-saccade trials before completing the two-fixation saccade trials and long-duration no-saccade trials, while four subjects completed all of the two-fixation saccade trials and long-duration no-saccade trials before completing the one-fixation saccade trials and short-duration no-saccade trials. Each subject completed several practice blocks of eye movement trials before completing the six experimental blocks. Data collection was spread over 9–10 experimental sessions, typically with three blocks per session.

Results

Mean saccade latency (hence mean exposure duration) was 389 ms (s.e. = 4 ms) in the one-fixation saccade condition. Mean exposure duration in the two-fixation saccade condition was 773 ms (s.e. = 8 ms), approximately twice that of the one-fixation saccade condition Mean saccade duration was 26 ms (s.e. < 1 ms). Mean saccade latency and mean saccade duration did not vary significantly across probe delays. Because preliminary analyses showed that order of task completion (one-fixation vs. two-fixation) had no significant effect on performance, this factor was not included in any of the analyses reported below.

On each trial subjects attempted to report the letter that had occupied the probed position, and the position of the probe (array location 1–10). Accuracy for the probe position responses was examined first. A two-way ANOVA was conducted on the data from the saccade conditions with factors of number of fixations (one vs. two) and probe delay (50, 150, 750 ms). There was a significant effect of probe delay, $F(2, 12) = 10.2$, $p < .005$, and a significant interaction between number of fixations and probe delay, $F(2, 12) = 4.4$,

$p < .05$. Accuracy of probe position report in the one-fixation condition was 72 percent, 80 percent, and 88 percent for probe delays of 50, 150, and 750 ms, whereas it was 87 percent, 91 percent, and 92 percent in the two-fixation condition. It is clear that subjects had some difficulty in localizing the probe in the one-fixation case, especially at the shortest probe delay. The effect of probe delay on probe localization accuracy is reminiscent of findings from the literature on visual direction constancy showing that people's ability to locate a stimulus briefly flashed just before, during, or shortly after a saccade is rather poor (see Matin 1986 for a review). The accuracy of spatial coding appears to be disrupted at least momentarily when the eyes change position. The difference between the one-fixation and two-fixation conditions is probably due to the fact that subjects were fixating the edge of the letter display when the probe was presented in the one-fixation condition, whereas they were fixating the center of the display when the probe was presented in the two-fixation condition. In support of this hypothesis, when the probe was presented at an "internal" array location (locations 2, 3, 4, 7, 8, 9), it was localized much more accurately in the two-fixation condition (91 percent) than in the one-fixation condition (70 percent), whereas number of fixations mattered little when "terminal" locations (locations 1, 5, 6, 10) were probed (88 percent vs. 94 percent for two vs. one fixations). For reasons of visual acuity and perceptual organization, it is probably easier to locate the position of a stimulus in space when it is presented to symmetric locations around a central fixation point (as in the two-fixation condition) than when it is presented to peripheral locations that vary in eccentricity in one direction from the fixation point (as in the one-fixation condition).

In contrast, a two-way ANOVA conducted on the data from the no-saccade conditions found that probe localization accuracy decreased from 98 percent to 96 percent as probe delay increased, $F(2,12) = 3.9$, $p < .05$. There was no significant effect of exposure duration (mean = 96.8 percent) in the short-exposure condition and 97.2 percent in the long-duration condition) in the no-saccade conditions.

Because it seemed possible that subjects might be able to use the probe to access the appropriate location in their memory of the letter display without being able to accurately report the position of the probe (i.e., they might know that the probe appeared above the letter R, but be unsure whether R had appeared at location 2 or 3), subjects' letter responses were classified as correct if the reported letter had appeared at the probed position, regardless of whether subjects reported the position of the probe correctly. Table 6.4 shows accuracy of letter report as a function of probe delay for the one-fixation and two-fixation saccade conditions, the corresponding results for the no-saccade control conditions, and error breakdowns for each condition.

Separate ANOVAs were conducted on the saccade and no-saccade conditions on the percentage of correct letter reports. Letter report was slightly, but not significantly, more accurate in the two-fixation saccade condition (mean = 46 percent) than in the one-fixation saccade condition (mean = 43

Table 6.4 Percentage Correct and Percentage of Intra-array and Extra-array Errors as Function of Probe Delay in Experiment 2

	Probe delay (ms)		
Condition	50	150	750
	Correct letter reports		
One-fixation saccade	45.9	43.3	39.9
Two-fixation saccade	46.1	48.9	41.4
Short-duration no-saccade	67.4	66.1	52.6
Long-duration no-saccade	66.9	63.7	54.3
	Intra-array errors		
One-fixation saccade	46.1	50.4	49.3
Two-fixation saccade	45.7	42.0	46.3
Short-duration no-saccade	25.0	27.7	38.0
Long-duration no-saccade	25.6	27.0	37.4
	Extra-array errors		
One-fixation saccade	7.7	6.3	11.1
Two-fixation saccade	8.3	8.9	12.0
Short-duration no-saccade	7.9	6.6	9.7
Long-duration no-saccade	8.1	9.3	8.7

percent), $F(1,6) = 1.5$; $p > .25$. Accuracy of letter report declined as probe delay increased, $F(2,12) = 3.9$; $p < .05$; accuracy was lower at the longest probe delay (40 percent) than at the two shorter probe delays (46 percent). Similar results were obtained in the no-saccade conditions. Letter report accuracy was 62 percent in both the short- and long-exposure conditions ($F < 1$), but declined from 66 percent at the two shortest probe delays to 53 percent at the longest probe delay, $F(2,12) = 23.8$; $p < .001$. Thus memory during maintained fixation was superior to memory across fixations, as in experiment 1, but neither making an additional fixation on the letter array nor viewing the letter array for a longer duration during a single fixation increased the number of letters that subjects could remember from the display.

Errors were classified as intra-array or extra-array, as in experiment 1, and each error class was analyzed in a separate ANOVA. There were significantly more intra-array errors in the one-fixation saccade condition (48 percent) than in the two-fixation saccade condition (45 percent), $F(1,6) = 9.7$, $p < .025$. There was no effect of probe delay. Number of fixations had no effect on the percentage of extra-array errors (8 percent vs. 10 percent), $F < 1$, but there were significantly more extra-array errors at the longest probe delay (12 percent) than at the two shortest probe delays (8 percent), $F(2,12) = 4.7$, $p < 05$. In the no-saccade conditions, there was no effect of exposure duration on the percentage of intra-array or extra-array errors, but there were more intra-array errors at the longest probe delay than at the two shortest probe delays, $F(2,12) = 9.4$, $p < .005$. As in experiment 1, most of the intra-array errors (55 percent) in the saccade conditions and 61 percent in the

Table 6.5 Percentage of Correct Letter Reports as Function of Probe Position in Experiment 2

Condition	Probe position				
	1	2	3	4	5
One-fixation saccade	78.5	16.3	41.1	17.9	59.5
Two-fixation saccade	87.3	21.2	50.6	22.7	46.4
Short-duration no-saccade	66.6	38.9	86.1	61.9	55.9
Long-duration no-saccade	64.0	37.0	82.8	67.5	53.9

Note: Results are averaged across top and bottom rows of the array. Probe position in the saccade conditions refers to position relative to the initial saccade target (1 = saccade target location, 5 = side opposite the saccade target location). Probe position in the no-saccade conditions refers to columns 1–5 in the letter array (1 = leftmost, 5 = rightmost).

no-saccade conditions) involved report of a letter adjacent to the probed position, suggesting some coarse coding of location information in memory.

The effect of saccade direction and probe position on accuracy of letter report was also examined. Because of the large number of positions and conditions involved, the results were averaged across rows (top and bottom) in the letter array. The positions were then coded as being either in the direction of the initial saccade or in the direction opposite the initial saccade and the data collated, based on that classification; the results are shown in table 6.5. For the saccade conditions, position 1 reports the average percentage correct for the positions above and below the initial saccade target, averaged over saccade direction. Position 3 reports the average percentage correct for the position in the center of the letter display, averaged across rows and saccade direction. Recall that this position corresponds to the location of the second saccade target in the two-fixation condition. Position 5 reports the average percentage correct for the array location furthest removed from the initial saccade target, averaged across rows and saccade direction. Positions 2 and 4 refer to the intermediate positions. For comparison, the results of the no-saccade condition, averaged across rows only, are also shown. For the no-saccade conditions, "position" refers to columns 1–5 of the letter array (1 = leftmost, 5 = rightmost), averaged across rows.

Table 6.5 shows that letter report was more accurate when the position above or below the initial saccade target (position 1) was probed than when other array locations were probed, $F(4,24) = 34.6$, $p < .001$. This was true for both the one-fixation and two-fixation saccade conditions. Accuracy was next highest for the letter position furthest removed from the saccade target in the one-fixation condition, but in the two-fixation condition it was next highest for the middle position (the target of the return saccade). Accuracy of letter report was better for every probe position except for the one furthest removed from the initial saccade target (which dropped dramatically) in the two-fixation condition than in the one-fixation condition, $F(4,24) = 6.5$, $p < .001$. Thus, even though there was little improvement in overall letter report accuracy as number of fixations increased in the saccade condition, there was a big difference in which letter positions were available in memory. In contrast, report of the middle position was always most accurate in the no-saccade conditions, and there were no effects of exposure duration.

Discussion

As predicted, the accumulation of information across multiple eye fixations was limited by the capacity of transsaccadic memory. Even though subjects identified the position of the probe more accurately in the two-fixation condition than in the one-fixation condition, letter report was only slightly more accurate when two fixations were made on the letter display (46 percent) than when only one fixation was made (43 percent). Subjects remembered 4.6 to 4.0 position + identity units across probe delays in the one-fixation condition and 4.6 to 4.1 units in the two-fixation condition. This is more than they remembered in experiment 1 (4.0 to 3.0), but not much more. These results provide good support for the object file theory of transsaccadic memory. It is important to note that the theory does not predict that information accumulation across multiple fixations will never occur, but only that it will be limited to approximately four items. If subjects were presented with a sparsely populated display containing widely separated items, such that only one item could be identified within a single fixation (as in the study of Hayhoe, Lachter, and Feldman 1991 described in the introduction), then accumulation across multiple eye fixations should occur, up to the capacity limit of transsaccadic memory. Because four items could be identified within a single fixation in the present experiment, no additional accumulation occurred in subsequent fixations (although which items were remembered did change, as the position analyses showed).

Other results provide mixed support for the theory. We predicted that report of the letters spatially near the final saccade target would be more accurate than report of other letters in the array, because of attentional allocation and the limited-capacity nature of transsaccadic memory. In support of the theory, even though the total number of position + identity units remembered across eye movements was constant, the array positions that were remembered changed if two fixations rather than one were made on the letter display. Memory for every position except for the position furthest removed from the initial saccade target improved in the two-fixation condition; memory for that position dropped precipitously. It was not the case that letters near the final saccade target location were recalled best in the two-fixation condition; rather, letters near the initial saccade target location retained their advantage. One problem with this analysis is that there is no independent measure of where attention was allocated in the letter display; we merely assumed that it always preceded the eyes to the saccade target. The question of attentional allocation and how it affects the encoding of information into transsaccadic memory is a complex one that requires further investigation.

We also predicted that extra-array errors would decrease when two fixations rather than one were made on the letter array, because subjects would have more time to identify the letters in the array and to activate their long-term memory representations. This did not occur. Rather, the percentage of intra-array errors decreased in the two-fixation condition relative to the one-fixation condition; there was actually a slight increase in extra-array errors in the two-fixation case. This is inconsistent with the object file theory of transsaccadic memory. As in experiment 1, most of the intra-array errors involved report of a letter spatially near the probed position. This, too, is awkward for the theory in its present form.

The no-saccade control conditions were included in this study to measure any differences that might arise merely as a result of longer processing time in the two-fixation as opposed to the one-fixation saccade condition; they also allow comparisons to be made between memory within and across fixations. As in experiment 1, accuracy in the no-saccade control conditions was considerably higher than in the saccade conditions, but it did not vary with exposure duration. This replicates other studies that have examined the effects of exposure duration on partial report (e.g., Irwin and Brown 1987; Irwin and Yeomans 1986). Interestingly, the performance advantage in the no-saccade conditions seems to be due to more accurate position coding in memory. Table 6.5 shows that there is essentially no difference in the percentage of extra-array errors made within and across eye fixations, but there is a large difference in the percentage of intra-array errors. What "iconic" memory appears to do is maintain high-fidelity position information; when it decays, or when it is eliminated by an eye movement, this precise spatial information is lost.

6.4 GENERAL DISCUSSION

The goal of the present research was to investigate the nature of information integration and accumulation across saccadic eye movements by testing some of the predictions of Irwin's (1992a) object file theory of transsaccadic memory. This theory claims that only a limited number of feature-integrated, episodic descriptions of objects are retained across a saccade in short-term memory, with residual activation of unlocated identity codes for other objects in long-term memory. The theory predicts that 3–4 integral objects should be remembered across a saccade; objects near the saccade target should be remembered better than objects at other locations because of attention; little loss of information should occur over time; mislocation errors should be more prevalent than misidentification errors; and information accumulation over multiple fixations should be limited by the capacity of transsaccadic memory.

In experiment 1, subjects viewed an array of colored letters while they fixated a central point. This array was erased upon initiation of a saccade to a saccade target. Some time after the saccade, a bar probe was presented above or below one of the array locations and subjects attempted to report the color and the identity of the letters that had occupied the probed positions. To do this accurately, subjects had to integrate the probe with some representation of the positions, identities, and colors of the letters in the display. Subjects remembered 3–4 color + identity + position units across the saccade. Information near the saccade target was remembered better than information appearing in other array locations. Probe delay had little effect on performance. Most errors were due to mislocations rather than to misidentifications.

Experiment 2 investigated the accumulation of position and identity information across saccades. In the "one fixation" condition, procedure was similar to experiment 1. Subjects viewed an array of letters until they initiated a saccade to a target; some time after the saccade, they were probed to report the contents of one of the letter positions. In a second condition ("two fixation") the array of letters remained visible during the saccade and during a second fixation on the letter display, and disappeared only when a saccade was initiated back to the central fixation point. Some time after this second saccade, subjects were probed to report the contents of one of the letter positions. Memory for position and identity information was improved only slightly in the two-fixation condition, relative to the one-fixation condition, suggesting that information accumulation across multiple eye movements is limited by the capacity of transsaccadic memory (approximately four items).

In sum, the predictions of the object file theory of transsaccadic memory were largely supported by the results of the present research. Two results were unexpected, however. First, we expected the number of misidentifications to decrease as the number of fixations increased in experiment 2 because of greater activation of identity codes in long-term memory. This did not occur. Second, analysis of the spatial distribution of mislocation errors showed that the vast majority of the errors involved report of an item spatially near the probed item. If mislocation errors are due to residual activation of unlocated identity codes in long-term memory, as Irwin (1992a) proposed, there is no reason to expect this to occur; rather, the errors should have been randomly distributed over array locations. Both of the unexpected results call into question the idea that mislocation errors occur because of the presence of unlocated identity codes in long-term memory.

To account for these results, we propose the following revision to Irwin's (1992a) model. Most of the elements of the model remain intact, but mislocation errors are attributed to a different source. According to the revised model, when a display is presented, the features in the display are represented in the visual system in feature maps that register the presence of different sensory features (e.g., color, shape) in the display; in addition, a master map of locations registers the precise spatial location of each feature in the display (e.g., Treisman 1988). However, unlike Treisman's model, our revised model assumes that coarse or partial location information is registered with each feature as well. Cohen and Ivry (1989, 1991) proposed this modification to Treisman's model based on several visual search and illusory conjunction experiments, and we adopt it here. As before, we assume that attention must be directed from one array location to the next to conjoin features and to obtain precise spatial location information from the master map of locations to produce an integrated object file (e.g., for displays like those used in experiment 1, an identity + color + position unit). Note that letter shape, rather than letter parts, are assumed to be features in this account. We propose, as before, that a limited number of these object files can be maintained in short-term memory. According to our revised model, when the eyes move, the links between the feature maps and the master map of locations are disrupted (e.g., retinal positions change), so that precise spatial information about the locations of the features is lost. The coarse location information registered with each feature in the feature maps is still available, however, as long as the feature itself is available (presumably feature maps also decay with time after stimulus offset). In sum, according to the revised model, performance in the transsaccadic partial-report task is based on the object files that are produced before the saccade and of residual activation in the *feature maps*, rather than in long-term memory. The revised model accounts for the same phenomena that the original model did, but in addition it now accounts for the two unexpected results as well. Persistence of shape information in the feature maps explains why mislocations are more prevalent than misidentifications, and coarse coding of spatial location in the feature maps explains why mislocation errors are distributed spatially near the correct item.

Note that although the revised model proposes that performance in the transsaccadic partial report task is based on a limited number of object files and on residual activation in coarsely coded feature maps, we still believe that a complete account of transsaccadic memory must include activation of long-term memory representations as well. This seems necessary to account for the results of Rayner, Pollatsek, Henderson, and colleagues discussed in the introduction, and for recent results reported by Henderson and Anes (1994). The relationship between these representations and object files requires further investigation.

One final comment concerns the relationship between the object file theory of transsaccadic memory and the perception of a stable visual world across eye movements. If transsaccadic memory consists of a few object files and of residual activation in feature maps and in long-term memory, why does the world appear stable and continuous across eye movements? Intuitively, this perception would seem to require a detailed memory for the contents of successive fixations. Irwin (1992a,b) argued that this intuition may be exactly backward; the world may appear stable and continuous across saccades not because a detailed memory exists but because very little is remembered from one fixation to the next. According to this account, instability across saccades would be detected only if one of the few objects encoded in transsaccadic memory were involved; otherwise, stability would be assumed by the perceptual system (cf. MacKay 1973). Very recent research provides support for this argument (Currie et al. 1994; see also Irwin et al. 1994; McConkie and Currie 1993). In this research we have found that the perception of stability across eye movements depends critically on whether the object to which the eyes are sent maintains its spatial position. If this object changes its position during a saccade, instability is usually perceived; if this object maintains its position, then stability is usually perceived—even if everything else in the scene changes position! Thus the perception of stability across saccades seems to depend on a very local evaluation process centered on the saccade target object, which is the object most likely to be stored in transsaccadic memory. In sum, the object file theory of transsaccadic memory may provide a unified account for the nature of information integration across saccades and for the perception of a stable visual world across eye movements. It would be interesting to know whether the spatial representation in parietal cortex investigated by Colby (chap. 7, this volume) codes only a few stimulus locations (as opposed to an entire display), with a bias to code the saccade target location. Such a finding would provide a satisfying neurophysiological corollary to the behavioral data reported above.

NOTE

This research was supported by National Science Foundation Grant SBR 93-09564 to David E. Irwin. We thank Carol Colby, Jon Driver, John Duncan, Mel Goodale, John Hummel, Art Kramer, Gordon Logan, and Jay McClelland for helpful comments on the research, and Natalie Lambajian and Corey Medders for assistance with data collection. Correspondence concerning the chapter should be addressed to David E. Irwin, Department of Psychology, University of Illinois at Urbana-Champaign, 603 East Daniel Street, Champaign, Illinois 61820 (E-mail: dirwin@s.psych.uiuc.edu).

REFERENCES

Banks, W. (1983). On the decay of the icon. *Behavioral and Brain Sciences, 6,* 14.

Boyce, S., and Pollatsek, A. (1992). Identification of objects in scenes: The role of scene background in object naming. *Journal of Experimental Psychology: Learning, Memory, and Cognition, 18,* 531–543.

Breitmeyer, B. G. (1984). *Visual masking: An integrative approach.* New York: Oxford University Press.

Bridgeman, B., Hendry, D., and Stark, L. (1975). Failure to detect displacement of the visual world during saccadic eye movements. *Vision Research, 15,* 719–722.

Bridgeman, B., and Mayer, M. (1983). Failure to integrate visual information from successive fixations. *Bulletin of the Psychonomic Society, 21,* 285–286.

Carlson-Radvansky, L., and Irwin, D. E. (1995). Memory for structural information across eye movements. *Journal of Experimental Psychology: Learning, Memory, and Cognition.* In press.

Cohen, A., and Ivry, R. (1989). Illusory conjunction inside and outside the focus of attention. *Journal of Experimental Psychology: Human Perception and Performance, 15,* 650–663.

Cohen, A., and Ivry, R. (1991). Density effects in conjunction search: Evidence for a coarse location mechanism of feature integration. *Journal of Experimental Psychology: Human Perception and Performance, 17,* 891–901.

Currie, C., McConkie, G. W., Carlson-Radvansky, L. A., and Irwin, D. E. (1994). Maintaining visual stability across saccades: Role of the saccade target object. Paper presented at the 35th annual meeting of the Psychonomic Society, St. Louis, MO.

Di Lollo, V., and Dixon, P. (1992). Inverse duration effects in partial report. *Journal of Experimental Psychology: Human Perception and Performance, 18,* 1089–1100.

Duhamel, J.-R., Colby, C. L., and Goldberg, M. E. (1992). The updating of the representation of visual space in parietal cortex by intended eye movements. *Science, 255,* 90–92.

Hayhoe, M., Lachter, J., and Feldman, J. (1991). Integration of form across saccadic eye movements. *Perception, 20,* 393–402.

Henderson, J. (1992). Identifying objects across saccades: Effects of extrafoveal preview and flanker object context. *Journal of Experimental Psychology: Human Perception and Performance, 18,* 521–530.

Henderson, J., and Anes, M. (1994). Roles of object-file review and type priming in visual identification within and across eye fixations. *Journal of Experimental Psychology: Human Perception and Performance, 20,* 826–839.

Irwin, D. E. (1991). Information integration across saccadic eye movements. *Cognitive Psychology, 23,* 420–456.

Irwin, D. E. (1992a). Memory for position and identity across eye movements. *Journal of Experimental Psychology: Learning, Memory, and Cognition, 18,* 307–317.

Irwin, D. E. (1992b). Perceiving an integrated visual world. In D. E. Meyer and S. Kornblum (Eds.), *Attention and performance XIV: Synergies in experimental psychology, artificial intelligence, and cognitive neuroscience—A silver jubilee,* 121–142. Cambridge, MA: MIT Press.

Irwin, D. E., and Brown, J. (1987). Tests of a model of informational persistence. *Canadian Journal of Psychology, 41,* 317–338.

Irwin, D. E., Brown, J. S., and Sun, J.-S. (1988). Visual masking and visual integration across saccadic eye movements. *Journal of Experimental Psychology: General, 117,* 274–285.

Irwin, D. E., McConkie, G. W., Carlson-Radvansky, L. A., and Currie, C. (1994). A localist evaluation solution for visual stability across saccades. *Behavioral and Brain Sciences, 17,* 265–266.

Irwin, D. E., Yantis, S., and Jonides, J. (1983). Evidence against visual integration across saccadic eye movements. *Perception and Psychophysics, 34,* 49–57.

Irwin, D. E., and Yeomans, J. M. (1986). Sensory registration and informational persistence. *Journal of Experimental Psychology: Human Perception and Performance, 12,* 343–360.

Irwin, D. E., Zacks, J. L., and Brown, J. S. (1990). Visual memory and the perception of a stable visual environment. *Perception and Psychophysics, 47,* 35–46.

Jonides, J., Irwin, D. E., and Yantis, S. (1982). Integrating visual information from successive fixations. *Science, 215,* 192–194.

Kahneman, D., and Treisman, A. (1984). Changing views of attention and automaticity. In R. Parasuraman and D. Davies (Eds.), *Varieties of attention,* 29–61. New York: Academic Press.

Kahneman, D., Treisman, A., and Gibbs, B. J. (1992). The reviewing of object files: Object-specific integration of information. *Cognitive Psychology, 24,* 175–219.

Loftus, G. R. (1972). Eye fixations and recognition memory for pictures. *Cognitive Psychology, 3,* 525–551.

MacKay, D. (1973). Visual stability and voluntary eye movements. In R. Jung (Ed.), *Handbook of sensory physiology*, vol. 7, no. 3, 307–332. Berlin: Springer.

Marr, D. (1982). *Vision*. San Francisco: Freeman.

Matin, L. (1986). Visual localization and eye movements. In K. R. Boff, L. Kaufman, and J. P. Thomas (Eds.), *Handbook of perception and human performance*, vol. 1, 20.1–20.45. New York: Wiley.

McConkie, G. W. (1991). Perceiving a stable visual world. Paper presented at the Sixth European Conference on Eye Movements, Leuven, Belgium.

McConkie, G. W., and Currie, C. (1993). Perceiving an unstable visual world. Paper presented at the 34th annual meeting of the Psychonomic Society, Washington, DC.

McConkie, G. W., and Rayner, K. (1976). Identifying the span of the effective stimulus in reading: Literature review and theories of reading. In H. Singer and R. B. Ruddell (Eds.), *Theoretical models and processes of reading*, 137–162. Newark, DE: International Reading Association.

McConkie, G. W., and Zola, D. (1979). Is visual information integrated across successive fixations in reading? *Perception and Psychophysics, 25*, 221–224.

Mewhort, D. J. K., Campbell, A., Marchetti, F., and Campbell, J. (1981). Identification, localization, and "iconic" memory: An evaluation of the bar-probe task. *Memory and Cognition, 9*, 50–67.

O'Regan, J. K. (1992). Solving the "real" mysteries of visual perception: The world as an outside memory. *Canadian Journal of Psychology, 46*, 461–488.

O'Regan, J. K., and Levy-Schoen, A. (1983). Integrating visual information from successive fixations: Does transsaccadic fusion exist? *Vision Research, 23*, 765–768.

Palmer, J., and Ames, C. (1992). Measuring the effect of multiple eye fixations on memory for visual attributes. *Perception and Psychophysics, 52*, 295–306.

Palmer, S. E. (1977). Hierarchical structure in perceptual representation. *Cognitive Psychology, 9*, 441–474.

Pollatsek, A., Lesch, M., Morris, R., and Rayner, K. (1992). Phonological codes are used in integrating information across saccades in word identification and reading. *Journal of Experimental Psychology: Human Perception and Performance, 18*, 148–162.

Pollatsek, A., Rayner, K., and Collins, W. (1984). Integrating pictorial information across eye movements. *Journal of Experimental Psychology: General, 113*, 426–442.

Pollatsek, A., Rayner, K., and Henderson, J. (1990). The role of spatial location in the integration of pictorial information across saccades. *Journal of Experimental Psychology: Human Perception and Performance, 16*, 199–210.

Rayner, K., McConkie, G., and Zola, D. (1980). Integrating information across eye movements. *Cognitive Psychology, 12*, 206–226.

Rayner, K., and Pollatsek, A. (1983). Is visual information integrated across saccades? *Perception and Psychophysics, 34*, 39–48.

Reitman, J. (1974). Without surreptitious rehearsal, information in short-term memory decays. *Journal of Verbal Learning and Verbal Behavior, 13*, 365–377.

Shepherd, M., Findlay, J., and Hockey, R. (1986). The relationship between eye movements and spatial attention. *Quarterly Journal of Experimental Psychology, 38A*, 475–491.

Sperling, G. (1960). The information available in brief visual presentations. *Psychological Monographs, 74*(11, Whole no. 498).

Sun, J. S., and Irwin, D. E. (1987). Retinal masking during pursuit eye movements: Implications for spatiotopic visual persistence. *Journal of Experimental Psychology: Human Perception and Performance, 13*, 140–145.

Sutherland, N. S. (1968). Outlines of a theory of visual pattern recognition in animals and man. *Proceedings of the Royal Society, London, 171*, 297–317.

Townsend, V. M. (1973). Loss of spatial and identity information following a tachistoscopic exposure. *Journal of Experimental Psychology, 98*, 113–118.

Trehub, A. (1977). Neuronal models for cognitive processes: Networks for learning, perception, and imagination. *Journal of Theoretical Biology, 65*, 141–169.

Treisman, A. (1988). Features and objects: The fourteenth Bartlett memorial lecture. *Quarterly Journal of Experimental Psychology, 40A*, 201–237.

Tversky, B. (1974). Eye fixations in prediction of recognition and recall. *Memory and Cognition, 2*, 275–278.

Verfaillie, K., De Troy, A., and Van Rensbergen, J. (1994). Transsaccadic integration of biological motion. *Journal of Experimental Psychology: Learning, Memory, and Cognition, 20*, 649–670.

7 A Neurophysiological Distinction between Attention and Intention

Carol L. Colby

ABSTRACT

The activity of single neurons in monkey parietal cortex is separately modulated by attention and by intention. The amplitude of the neural response to stimulus onset increases when the animal must attend to a visual stimulus. Significantly, this response enhancement is independent of the kind of action the monkey will perform in response to the stimulus. In contrast, when the monkey intends to make an eye movement, there is a change in the location of the receptive field. Further, visual information being processed in parietal cortex is remapped at the time of an eye movement so that the contents of visual memory match the new eye position following a saccade. Spatial integration of visual information across saccades is achieved both by shifting the location of the receptive field and by remapping stored visual information. In a direct test of the neural effects of attention versus intention, a covert shift of attention could not produce a change in the location of the receptive field. Only the intention to move the eyes could produce such a change. Parietal neurons thus show differential modulation by attention and intention. Attention produces amplitude modulation of sensory responses, independent of the behavioral response, while intention produces a spatial modulation that depends crucially on the next intended action.

7.1 INTRODUCTION

When we attend to an object, we also select it as a potential target for action. Since the pioneering studies of Hyvärinen and Poranen (1974) and Mountcastle et al. (1975), it has been known that neurons in monkey parietal cortex are modulated by the intention to act on a stimulus. More recent work on parietal cortex has emphasized the sensory nature of these neurons and their modulation by attention (Robinson, Goldberg, and Stanton 1978; Bushnell, Goldberg, and Robinson 1981; Goldberg, Colby, and Duhamel 1990). Attention can be studied in animals by using tasks that require the animal to use a visual stimulus as the target for a cognitive or motor act (see Colby 1991 for review). This chapter contrasts the effects of attending to a stimulus with the effects produced by intending to perform a particular motor act.

In order to study neural mechanisms of attention, we compare the neural response to a behaviorally irrelevant stimulus with the response to the same stimulus when it is made behaviorally significant. As will be shown, the amplitude of the neural response to stimulus onset increases when the stimulus becomes a target for action. Significantly, this response enhancement is independent of the kind of action the monkey will perform. The same enhancement is seen regardless of whether the monkey must look at the target or perform some other response while refraining from looking at it; all that matters is that the animal must attend to the target.

In contrast to the change in amplitude of response produced by attention, the intention to perform a specific act can change the location to which a neuron responds. Neurons in parietal cortex have retinotopic receptive fields, as do neurons throughout visual cortex. When the monkey is about to make an eye movement, the receptive field of a parietal neuron can shift even before the eye movement begins (Duhamel, Colby, and Goldberg 1992). Thus the intention to look at a new fixation point can change the location of the receptive field, which allows the neuron to anticipate the sensory consequences of the impending saccade. This may contribute to the integration of visual information across saccades and help maintain spatial constancy; it could also provide the neural basis for a continuously updated motor representation of visual space. Without such a predictive mechanism, the animal would have to wait for new visual signals to arrive in parietal cortex following a saccade in order to know the locations of objects.

This finding on the effects of intention has led to a new conception of spatial representation in parietal cortex. The traditional view of spatial perception, strongly supported by subjective experience, is that we "know where things are" in some absolute, world-based frame of reference and that we use this spatial information to guide our movements. In this standard and intuitively plausible view, spatial perception is a monolithic process: the brain forms a single, world-based spatial representation of each object regardless of what action is going to be performed in relation to that object.

A new and somewhat counterintuitive view is that the spatial location of an object is represented many times over in different cortical areas (Colby and Duhamel 1991, Fogassi et al. 1992; Gentilucci et al. 1988; Goodale and Milner 1992; Gross and Graziano 1995; Rizzolatti, Riggo, and Sheliga 1994). These multiple spatial representations are action-centered; they code stimulus location in terms of the action necessary to acquire or avoid the object. For example, in areas responsible for visual guidance of head movements and mouth movements, visually sensitive neurons encode the location of an object relative to the head (Rizzolatti et al. 1987; Colby and Duhamel 1991; Colby, Duhamel, and Goldberg 1993b; Duhamel, Colby, and Goldberg 1991). In contrast, areas involved in limb movement have neurons that encode object location relative to limb position (Rizzolatti et al. 1981; Gentilucci et al. 1983; 1988; 1989; Fogassi et al. 1992; Graziano and Gross 1993; Graziano, Yap, and Gross 1994) (see also Graziano and Gross, chap. 8, this volume). In areas guiding eye movements, visually sensitive neurons encode the location of an object relative to the fovea (Goldberg and Colby 1989; Goldberg, Colby, and Duhamel 1990). These observations suggest that spatial perception is modular and action-based. These multiple representations are not tied to body parts per se but rather to the actions that can be performed in relation to an object. One representation describes how an object can be reached by the hand while another describes how the object can be foveated. Multiple internal representations are used to guide behavior (Rizzolatti et al. 1987; 1988), and these can be selectively modulated by attention (Tipper, Lortie, and Baylis 1992; Tipper, Weaver, and Houghton 1994; Rizzolatti, Riggio, and Sheliga 1994). This segregation of different kinds of spatial processing in sensorimotor cortex is analogous to the separate analysis of form, color, and stimulus motion that occurs at earlier stages of the visual system (Desimone and Ungerleider 1989). When we see a bouncing red ball we perceive a single object, even though different visual neurons signal its shape, color, and trajectory of motion. Likewise, beneath the apparent unity of subjective spatial experience lies a diversity of spatial representations, each with specific knowledge of how to act on the stimulus.

The following sections describe response properties of parietal neurons and how these responses are independently modulated by attention and intention. We then discuss the implications of intentional modulation for spatial integration in parietal cortex. Finally, we consider whether moving attention is functionally equivalent to intending to move the eyes.

7.2 ATTENTIONAL MODULATION OF NEURAL ACTIVITY IN PARIETAL CORTEX

Parietal cortex in the monkey is divided into a number of functionally and anatomically distinct areas (Andersen, Asanuma, et al. 1990; Colby and Duhamel 1991; Colby, Duhamel, and Goldberg 1993b). Several of these areas are contained within the intraparietal sulcus (Andersen, Asanuma, and Cowan 1985; Colby et al. 1988). Neurons in one of these, the lateral intraparietal area (LIP), are active in relation to both visual and oculomotor events (Andersen, Bracewell, et al. 1990; Goldberg, Colby, and Duhamel 1990; Barash et al. 1991a,b; Colby, Duhamel, and Goldberg 1993a). In order to characterize neurons in such a high-order area, it is essential to record neural activity while the monkey performs a large number of different tasks (fig. 7.1).

The monkey is initially trained simply to look at a fixation point on a screen while seated in a primate chair with its head fixed. Eye position is monitored continuously by means of a magnetic search coil, and the monkey is rewarded with a drop of water for maintaining fixation for a certain period of time. An eye movement during the fixation period automatically stops the trial and the monkey must wait for the next trial to begin. All the experimental tasks described below are built from this basic fixation control paradigm. Tasks are usually run in blocks of several dozen trials. There is no explicit signal to the monkey when the experimenter changes tasks. A well-trained monkey will run through its repertoire of behavioral responses to discover which is currently the correct response and will begin responding appropriately in a new task within a few trials.

Fixation

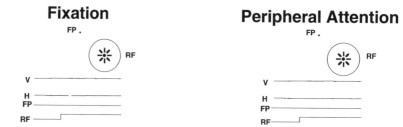

Peripheral Attention

Remembered Saccade

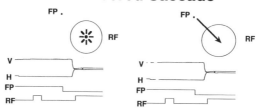

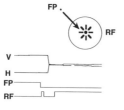

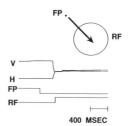

Visually triggered Saccade   **Learned Saccade**

400 MSEC

Figure 7.1 Tasks used to analyze activity in LIP neurons. Each panel shows cartoon of tangent screen, with fixation point (FP), receptive field (RF), and visual stimulus (star). Saccade is indicated by arrow, with saccade destination at arrowhead. Beneath each cartoon are time lines showing vertical (V) and horizontal (H) eye position, and status of lights at FP and RF (up is on, down is off). Adapted from Goldberg, Colby, and Duhamel 1990.

To examine the relationship of neural activity to visually guided behavior, we studied LIP neurons in five tasks designed to characterize different aspects of the neurons' activity. Each neuron was studied in as many of these tasks as possible. Once a single neuron was isolated, the location of its receptive field was established using the fixation task (see fig. 7.1; Wurtz 1969). In this task, the monkey initiates a trial by placing its hand on a contact bar, causing a spot of light to appear on a tangent screen. The monkey is required to look only at this fixation point, and does not respond to a second visual stimulus, which can be presented anywhere on the screen. The monkey is rewarded for maintaining fixation until the fixation point dims, at which time it must release the bar. The second visual stimulus can then be used to analyze visual properties of the neuron, such as the location of its receptive field and its discharge intensity. The neuron illustrated in figure 7.2 gave a brisk response

Fixation　　　　　　　　　**Peripheral Attention**

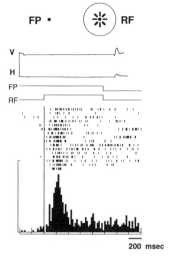
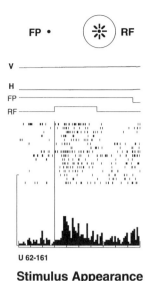

Stimulus Appearance　　　　**Stimulus Appearance**

Figure 7.2　Activity of LIP neuron in fixation and peripheral attention tasks. Cartoon above each diagram shows relative locations of fixation point (FP) and receptive field stimulus (RF). Vertical (V) and horizontal (H) eye position are plotted against time. FP and RF lines show times of appearance and disappearance of stimuli. Each tic mark in the raster diagram signifies single action potential. Successive trials are shown in successive lines, synchronized on given event that occurs at vertical line. Both rasters here are synchronized on stimulus appearance. Histogram at the bottom sums activity in raster above. Calibration line at left signifies response rate of 100 spikes per second. Adapted from Goldberg, Colby, and Duhamel 1990.

to the appearance of the stimulus in the fixation task (left panel). This task is run in blocks of trials, and the monkey was never required to respond to the stimulus. The stimulus is not behaviorally significant, and we infer that the monkey did not actively attend to it.

The neuron's visual response may be contrasted with its response in a task where the stimulus is made behaviorally significant. In the peripheral attention task, the monkey is required to look at the fixation point but must release the bar when a peripheral stimulus in the receptive field dims (Wurtz and Mohler 1976). Note that although the visual events are identical to those in the fixation task, the behavioral situation is very different: the monkey must use information about the stimulus in the receptive field rather than being free to ignore it. Because the monkey responds to the stimulus, it is reasonable to infer that the animal has attended to it. The visual response to the onset of the stimulus is enhanced in this task, which can be seen by comparing the amplitude of the response in the fixation task (fig. 7.2, left) to that in the peripheral attention task (fig. 7.2, right). An analysis of response strength for a population of LIP neurons indicated that an enhancement of the visual response was common when the stimulus was made behaviorally significant

Remembered Saccade

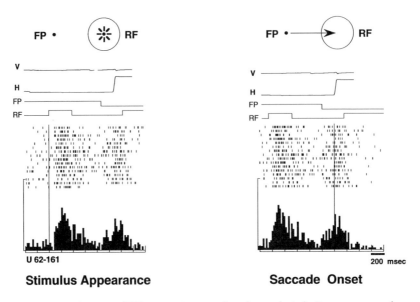

Figure 7.3 Activity of LIP neuron in remembered saccade task. Same neuron and conventions as in Figure 7.2. Separate visual and motor bursts can be seen in each raster. On left, rasters and histogram are synchronized on stimulus appearance, as shown in cartoon. On right, rasters are aligned on beginning of saccade. Note that activity returns to baseline levels during delay period. Adapted from Goldberg, Colby, and Duhamel 1990.

by requiring the monkey to attend to it (Colby, Duhamel, and Goldberg 1993a).

An easier way to make a stimulus behaviorally significant is to require the monkey to make a saccade to it. When a stimulus becomes the target for a saccade, the visual response is enhanced. This enhancement was demonstrated in the remembered saccade task (fig. 7.3), in which the monkey looks at a fixation point while a stimulus appears in the receptive field and then disappears (Hikosaka and Wurtz 1983). After a variable delay, the fixation point is extinguished and the monkey makes a saccade in total darkness to the location where the stimulus was flashed. If the saccade is accurate, the stimulus reappears and the monkey is rewarded for releasing the bar when the stimulus subsequently dims. This task has a visual component, a memory component (the monkey must remember the location of the target), an attentional component (the monkey must attend both to the fixation point, waiting for it to disappear, and to the target location), and a motor component.

The data from this task are analyzed with respect to two different time points. In order to measure the visual response, neural responses for each trial are aligned with respect to stimulus onset (fig. 7.3, left). In order to measure saccade-related activity, the same responses are aligned according to when

Visually triggered Saccade   Learned Saccade

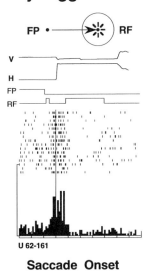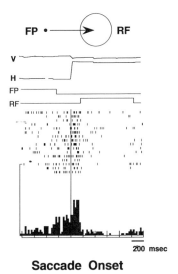

Saccade Onset   **Saccade Onset**

Figure 7.4 Activity of LIP neuron in visually triggered and learned saccade trials. Same neuron and conventions as in Figure 7.2. Two trial types are randomly interleaved. On left, monkey saccades to visual stimulus as soon as it appears. On right, monkey makes same saccade when fixation point is extinguished. Both histograms are synchronized on beginning of saccade. Adapted from Goldberg, Colby, and Duhamel 1990.

the monkey initiated the saccade (fig. 7.3, right). This neuron gives an enhanced visual response to the appearance of the stimulus but also discharges again immediately before the saccade, as was originally described by Gnadt and Andersen (1988). It is important to note that the size and direction of the saccade that gives rise to this motor activation brings the fovea to the location where the stimulus appeared. In other words, there is a correspondence between the location of the visual receptive field and the location of the motor field for a given neuron. As in the peripheral attention task, there is an enhancement of the visual response: the amplitude of the response to saccade target onset is larger than the visual response to the same stimulus in the fixation task. Because both the peripheral attention task and the remembered saccade task produce enhancement of the visual response, we conclude that enhancement reflects attention to the stimulated location and not motor preparation for a specific action.

Activity that occurs immediately before the saccade in a remembered saccade task could reflect motor encoding of the saccade itself, or it could be a reactivation of the visual response to the recently vanished target (Boch and Goldberg 1989; Fischer and Boch 1981). The learned saccade task was used to distinguish between these alternatives (fig. 7.4). Two different types of trials are interleaved in this task. In the visually triggered saccade trials, the monkey begins by looking at the fixation point. A target appears briefly in the receptive field at the same time the fixation point goes out. The monkey must then make a saccade to the location where the stimulus appeared. If the monkey makes a saccade of the proper amplitude and direction, the stimulus reappears and the monkey must fixate it and release a lever when it dims. In learned saccade trials, the fixation point disappears, just as in the visually triggered saccade trials, but no saccade target appears. Instead, the monkey must make a saccade in total darkness to the same spatial location where the target appeared in the visually triggered trials. During learned saccade trials, no visual target is presented; thus firing at the time of the saccade cannot be construed as a simple reactivation of a visual response.

The same single neuron that had a brisk visual response (in the fixation task) and an enhanced visual response (in the peripheral attention and remembered saccade tasks) also showed a presaccadic activation in the learned saccade task where no stimulus had appeared for several seconds (fig. 7.4). Analysis of the responses in a population of LIP neurons showed no consistent difference between the amplitude of the presaccadic burst in the learned saccade task, where there was no recent visual stimulus, and that in the remembered saccade task, where there was a recent visual stimulus (Colby, Duhamel, and Goldberg 1993a). This confirms that saccade-related activation is independent of visual stimulation.

In addition to visual and motor signals, many LIP neurons also carry a memory signal (Gnadt and Andersen 1988; Colby and Duhamel 1991). These neurons continue to respond to a visual stimulus in the remembered saccade task during the interval between the disappearance of the stimulus (fig. 7.5, left) and the onset of the saccade (fig. 7.5, right). Because there is no visual stimulus present in the receptive field, the monkey must retain an image of the stimulus location during the delay interval. Tonic activity during the delay period reflects a memory trace of stimulus location.

Finally, LIP neurons are activated by anticipation of significant sensory events. When the monkey is performing a fixation task, the stimulus in the receptive field is irrelevant for its behavior and there is relatively little activity during the interval between achievement of fixation and the appearance of the target (fig. 7.6, left). But when the monkey performs a series of remembered saccade trials, the level of activity increases even before the target appears (fig. 7.6, right). The neuron is more active before the expected appearance of a saccade target than before the expected appearance of the same stimulus when it is irrelevant to the animal's behavior. Thus LIP neuron activity reflects not just that the stimulus is expected but also that it is behaviorally significant.

In summary, visual signals predominate in LIP, despite the presence of presaccadic activity. LIP neurons almost invariably give stronger visual than presaccadic responses. Visual input is not the sole source of activation, however, because a significant number of neurons exhibit presaccadic activity independent of recent visual stimulation. These results underline the impor-

Remembered Saccade

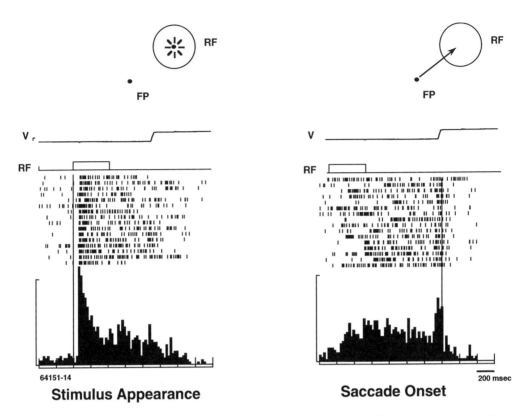

Figure 7.5 Activity of tonic LIP neuron in remembered saccade task. Left raster is synchronized on stimulus appearance; right raster, on beginning of saccade. Note that activity remains above baseline during memory period.

tance of studying single neurons in different behavioral tasks. If these neurons had been studied only in the learned saccade task, we might have thought that they were driving eye movements. But the neurons cannot be involved just in motor preparation because they are active in circumstances where movement is irrelevant (fixation task) or forbidden (peripheral attention task). Conversely, if we had used only a fixation task, we might have thought that LIP neurons were purely visual. But they cannot be performing only a visual analysis because they consistently respond in a task in which there is no stimulus (learned saccade task). The results observed in multiple tasks indicate that the responses of LIP neurons do not depend exclusively on either vision or movement. The single point of intersection of the various activations observed is the spatial location of the receptive field. We conclude that LIP neurons encode the current locus of attention as determined by recent sensory events or impending motor actions. The neurons' activity is modulated

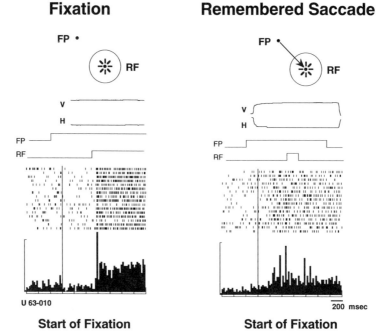

Figure 7.6 Anticipatory activity in LIP. Each raster is synchronized on start of fixation. Stimulus appearance occurs at least 600 ms after fixation is achieved. In both tasks, monkey can predict where stimulus will appear. Anticipatory activity during fixation is higher in eye movement task where monkey must use information provided by stimulus (right) than in fixation task where stimulus can be ignored (left). Adapted from Goldberg, Colby, and Duhamel 1990.

by attention to a spatial locus that is defined not by a stimulus or by a movement but by the spatial vector that could describe either. In essence, the activity of an LIP neuron encodes an attended spatial location.

7.3 INTENTIONAL MODULATION OF NEURAL ACTIVITY IN PARIETAL CORTEX

If LIP is encoding the spatial locus of attention, rather than specific visual or motor events, it is important to understand the coordinate system in which it operates. The most introspectively satisfying coordinate system is one in which objects are coded relative to some inertial center independent of both receptor surfaces and potential motor output. But evidence for such a representation is scant (see Stein 1992 and Rizzolatti, Riggio, and Sheliga 1994 for discussion). For parietal area LIP, there are two plausible coordinate frames for representing stimulus position. If LIP were operating in retinal coordinates, then neural activity would signal where the stimulus is on the retina. In head-centered coordinates, neural activity signals where the stimulus is relative to the head, regardless of gaze direction. These coordinate frames remain in momentary alignment only so long as the eyes do not move. In order to discern which coordinate frame is used in LIP, we designed two tasks in which an eye movement disrupts the alignment.

The first of these tasks looks specifically at what happens to visual information currently being processed in parietal cortex at the time of a saccade. Every time an eye movement occurs, the projection of the visual world changes on the retina and, by implication, in all the retinotopically mapped areas of the brain. As shown above, some LIP neurons have memory-related activity that persists after a stimulus is extinguished. We were curious about what happens to such memory-related activity when the monkey makes a saccade such that the receptive field of the neuron is moved to a previously stimulated location. Is the memory trace simply erased in conjunction with the saccade, or is its representation updated to take the eye movement into account?

In the memory trace task, the monkey fixates a central point while a stimulus is briefly presented (50 ms) at a location well outside of the receptive field of the neuron (fig. 7.7B). A new fixation point then appears, and the monkey makes a saccade to it. The stimulus is no longer present at the time of the saccade. The effect of the saccade is to bring the receptive field onto the external location that was previously stimulated. Strikingly, we find that LIP neurons respond when the receptive field is moved to a previously stimulated location (fig. 7.7B). There is no stimulus present on the screen, so the neuron can only be responding to a memory trace of the stimulus. Control experiments confirm that neither the stimulus alone (fig. 7.7C) nor the saccade alone (fig. 7.7D) can drive the neuron. This remapping of the memory trace occurs in LIP neurons even when the stimulus is presented a full second before the new fixation point appears (Duhamel, Colby, and Goldberg 1992).

We have seen above that LIP neurons carry memory signals. The present result shows that memory signals can be remapped in conjunction with saccades. We define remapping as a shift in the internal representation of a stimulus. In the example shown, the stimulus is flashed outside of the receptive field of the neuron from which we are recording, although the stimulus is in the receptive field of some other parietal neuron. This other neuron, which initially responds to stimulus onset and represents the location of the stimulus before the saccade, must pass off its information to the cell under study at the time of the eye movement. Remapping the representation of the stimulus location serves to maintain an alignment between the external world and the internal representation of it. By remapping memory traces, parietal cortex constructs a spatial representation that encodes stimulus location in terms of distance and direction from the current center of gaze. We conclude that neurons encode the memory trace of a stimulus not in head-centered coordinates but in dynamically updated retinotopic coordinates.

Psychophysical evidence for remapping has been presented by Hikosaka and his coworkers (Hikosaka, Miyauchi, and Shimojo 1993a,b) (see Hikosaka

A. Stimulus In Receptive Field
No Saccade

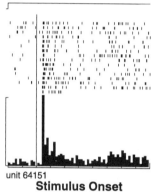

unit 64151

Stimulus Onset

B. Saccade to FP 2
Stim flashed for 50 msec

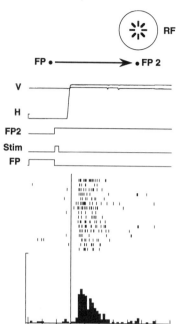

200ms

Beginning of Saccade

C. Stimulus Outside Receptive Field
No Saccade

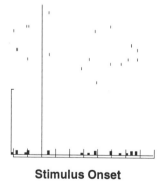

Stimulus Onset

D. Saccade to FP 2
No Stimulus

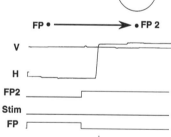
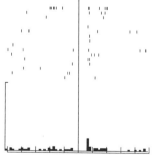

Saccade to FP 2

et al., chap. 10, this volume). They show that the locus of attention can remain stationary with respect to the environment even when the eyes move. They suggest that "some mechanism must be at work that would compensate for the saccade." Remapping could be that mechanism. In their experiment, a flash of light draws attention to a particular location. When a stationary bar is subsequently presented adjacent to the flashed location, the observer perceives a line moving out from the spot. The illusion is unchanged by an intervening saccade, indicating that attention remains at the original location in space. Remapping of a memory trace of the flashed stimulus would have exactly this effect. The flash is perceived as remaining at the original location despite the eye movement because the memory trace of the flashed stimulus is remapped. In other words, remapping produces the functional equivalent of environmental coordinates for stimulus representation without requiring that single neurons have head-centered receptive fields.

An open question is how much stored visual information is remapped. The work of Irwin and his colleagues suggests that representations of only a few items are carried over from one fixation to the next (Irwin 1991; see Irwin and Andrews, chap. 6, this volume). The experiments described here involve only a single object, which is always remapped. Another open question concerns the spatial precision of remapped memory traces. Many psychophysical studies (Matin, Matin, and Pola 1970; Honda 1989; Dassonville, Schlag, and Schlag-Rey 1992; 1995; Honda 1993) and recent physiological studies (Kusunoki, Colby, and Goldberg 1994) suggest that the accuracy of localization is diminished immediately around the time of a saccade. Nonetheless, both humans and monkeys perform accurate eye movements in the double-step task, which requires an updated representation of stimulus location (Hallett and Lightstone 1976; Mays and Sparks 1980). Patients with damage to parietal cortex are unable to perform the double-step task correctly, suggesting that the remapping mechanism is critical for spatial integration (Duhamel et al. 1992; Heide, Zimmerman, and Kompf 1993).

In a second set of remapping experiments, we found that the intention to make a saccade is itself sufficient to shift the receptive field of an LIP neuron. An example of predictive remapping is shown in figure 7.8. In the fixation task (fig. 7.8A), this LIP neuron responds to the appearance of stimulus in its receptive field with a latency of 70 ms. In the predictive remapping experiment, a stationary stimulus is presented outside of the receptive field, and the monkey is required to make the specific saccade that will bring the stimulus

Figure 7.7 LIP neuron response to memory trace of a stimulus. A. Fixation condition: Neuron responds to stimulus in receptive field. B. Memory trace condition: Stimulus is flashed outside of receptive field for 50 ms, as indicated on time line. Stimulus is gone before saccade to FP 2. LIP neuron responds following saccade that moves receptive field to previously stimulated location. C. Control condition 1: Presentation of stimulus outside receptive field does not drive neuron in absence of saccade. D. Control condition 2: Saccade alone does not drive neuron in absence of stimulus. Adapted from Duhamel, Colby, and Goldberg 1992.

A. Stimulus in Receptive Field No Saccade

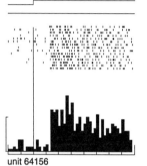

unit 64156

Stimulus Appearance

B. Saccade to FP 2 Brings Stimulus into RF

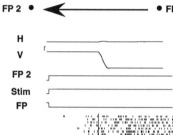

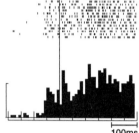

100ms

Saccade Onset

C. Stimulus Outside Receptive Field No Saccade

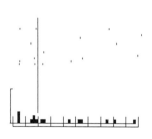

Stimulus Appearance

D. Saccade to FP 2 No Stimulus

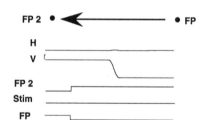

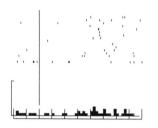

Onset of FP 2

into the receptive field. Surprisingly, the neuron begins to respond even before the saccade is initiated (fig. 7.8B). Control experiments confirm that this activity is a predictive visual response. The first control condition shows that the stimulus is in fact outside the receptive field when the monkey looks at the original fixation point (fig. 7.8C). The second control condition shows that the saccade to the new fixation point is not associated with neural activity by itself (fig. 7.8D).

This experiment demonstrates that when the monkey intends to make a saccade, the receptive field transiently shifts. The neuron responds in advance to a stimulus that will be in its retinal receptive field after the saccade. LIP neurons can thus predict the sensory consequences of an impending saccade; they respond to a stimulus that will be brought into the receptive field as if the stimulus were already present in it. This sensory remapping occurs with every saccade, whether or not the stimulus will be the target of a later saccade. An alternative interpretation is that the monkey plans to look at the stimulus and the neural activity reflects this motor planning. However, about half the population of LIP neurons, including the neuron illustrated here, have visual responses and do not have presaccadic bursts. Even these purely sensory neurons have predictive responses, indicating that the predictive response is a visual one, rather than a manifestation of motor planning.

More than a century ago, Helmholtz (1866) proposed that the world stays still when we move our eyes because the effort of will involved in generating a saccade simultaneously adjusts perception to take that eye movement into account. The present experiment indicates that this adjustment is based on the intention to move the eyes. Because remapping occurs even before the eyes begin to move, it must be generated by a corollary discharge of the eye movement command. It cannot be based on static eye position signals or even on an efference copy of the signal sent to the eye muscles because these signals occur only in conjunction with the actual eye movement.

The advantage of predictive remapping is that it enables localization of visual objects without the processing delay inherent in relying on reafferent visual information following a saccade. Remapping provides the oculomotor system with updated information about the vector of the saccadic eye movement necessary to acquire the stimulated location. It is the means by which a coordinate transformation is effected from retinotopic to oculomotor coordinates. This transformation obviates the need for neurons to operate in

Figure 7.8 Predictive remapping preceding a saccade that will bring stimulus into receptive field. A. Fixation condition: LIP neuron responds to stimulus in receptive field. B. Saccade condition: While monkey fixates, stimulus appears outside of receptive field and new fixation point appears (FP 2). At end of saccade, stimulus will be in receptive field. Neuron begins to respond to the stimulus even before saccade has been initiated, indicating that RF has shifted. C. Control condition 1: Presentation of stimulus outside receptive field does not drive neuron in absence of saccade. D. Control condition 2: Saccade alone does not drive neuron in absence of stimulus. Adapted from Duhamel, Colby, and Goldberg 1992.

head-centered or absolute spatial coordinates. Instead, parietal cortex creates an action-centered representation for generating eye movements.

In summary, neurons in LIP encode events at specific spatial locations. Their activity is not uniquely related to either sensory or motor events; rather, they signal the location of an event. The coordinate frame used by LIP neurons is a constantly updated retinotopic frame: locations are specified in terms of their distance and direction from the current or anticipated location of the fovea. This representation is of prime usefulness for the oculomotor system, which must program movements not to a target in absolute space but relative to the current center of gaze.

7.4   ATTENTION VERSUS INTENTION

A final question of relevance to psychology concerns whether attention is equivalent to intention (see Klein 1980 for discussion). Is a covert shift of attention alone sufficient to remap the internal representation of a stimulus? We have shown above that the intention to make a particular eye movement can transiently shift the receptive field of an LIP neuron and can remap the internal representation of a previous stimulus. Can a movement of attention alone accomplish the same thing? We tested this, using a variant of the peripheral attention task in which the monkey attends to a peripheral "fixation point" without looking at it (fig. 7.9). A stimulus is then presented on the screen in a location that would be in the receptive field if the monkey were permitted to look at the new fixation point. If shifting attention to the new fixation point is equivalent to intending to move the eyes there, then the neuron should respond to the onset of the stimulus. Because the neuron does not respond, we conclude that a shift of attention alone does not induce a shift in the parietal representation the way that an intended eye movement does.

This failure to shift the parietal representation in conjunction with an attentional shift suggests that the function of remapping is to maintain an accurate alignment between the visual world and its internal representation. With an attentional shift alone, nothing moves on the retina and there is no need to remap the internal representation. Indeed, it would be counterproductive to do so because it would introduce a mismatch between the external world and the internal parietal image of it. When a saccade is about to occur, however, parietal cortex can make use of information about the intended eye movement to anticipate the retinal consequences of that saccade and update the stored representation of object locations.

In parietal cortex, a distinction is made between attention and intention. The relevance for psychology is foremost in studies on covert shifts of attention (Posner 1980). The above results suggest that we cannot equate tasks where the response is an eye movement with those where the response is some other kind of a movement, such as a key release. The programming of eye movements has consequences for information processing in parietal cor-

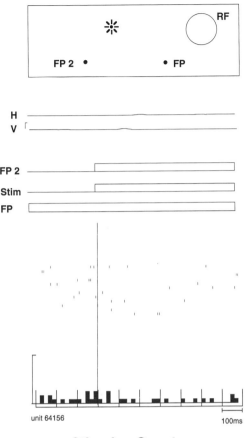

**Attention at FP2
Stimulus Outside Receptive Field,
No Saccade**

unit 64156

100ms

Stimulus Onset

Figure 7.9 Attention shift alone does not produce receptive field shift. Monkey looks at fixation point (FP) while attending to peripheral target (FP 2). Neuron has no visual response to onset of stimulus.

tex that may make apparently similar tasks very different in execution. The separate effects of attention and intention on neuronal activity in parietal cortex suggest that these are distinct neural as well as cognitive processes.

7.5 CONCLUSIONS

Visual responses of neurons in posterior parietal cortex are modulated both by overt movements of the eyes and by covert shifts of attention. Quite different purposes are served by sensitivity to intended eye movements and to attentional shifts. Response modulation by attentional state permits enhanced processing of images within the focus of attention. In contrast, response modulation by intended eye movements makes it possible to maintain perceived spatial constancy of the visual world as images are displaced on the retina. Two mechanisms contribute to spatial integration. First, parietal neurons respond to the memory trace of a visual stimulus when an eye movement brings the spatial location of that stimulus into the receptive field. This memory trace response indicates that the parietal representation of the visual world is shifted in conjunction with eye movements. Second, some parietal neurons accomplish this shift in anticipation of the actual eye movement. This anticipatory shift may reflect the attentional shift that normally precedes eye movements, although an attentional shift alone cannot produce a shift in the stored representation. Only when an intended eye movement is about to occur do we see evidence for a remapped representation. These results suggest that while eye movements and attention normally coincide, the underlying neural mechanisms are distinct and subserve different cognitive functions. Further, the neurophysiological distinction between attention and intention indicates that these are separate cognitive processes.

ACKNOWLEDGMENT

I thank Jean-René Duhamel and Michael E. Goldberg, with whom these experiments were done and these concepts developed.

REFERENCES

Andersen, R. A., Asanuma, C., and Cowan, M. (1985). Callosal and prefrontal associational projecting cell populations in area 7a of the macaque monkey: A study using retrogradely transported fluorescent dyes. *Journal of Comparative Neurology, 232,* 443–455.

Andersen, R. A., Asanuma, C., Essick, G., and Siegel. R. M. (1990). Cortico-cortical connections of anatomically and physiologically defined subdivisions within the inferior parietal lobule. *Journal of Comparative Neurology, 296,* 65–113.

Andersen, R. A., Bracewell, R. M., Barash, S., Gnadt, J. W., and Fogassi, L. (1990). Eye position effects on visual, memory, and saccade-related activity in areas LIP and 7a of macaque. *Journal of Neuroscience, 10,* 1176–1196.

Barash, S., Bracewell, R. M., Fogassi, L., Gnadt, J. W., and Andersen, R. A. (1991a). Saccade-related activity in the lateral intraparietal area. I. Temporal properties. *Journal of Neurophysiology, 66,* 1095–1108.

Barash, S., Bracewell, R. M., Fogassi, L., Gnadt, J. W., and Andersen, R. A. (1991b). Saccade-related activity in the lateral intraparietal area. II. Spatial properties. *Journal Neurophysiology, 66,* 1109–1124.

Boch, R. A., Goldberg, M. E. (1989). Participation of prefrontal neurons in the preparation of visually guided eye movements in the rhesus monkey. *Journal of Neurophysiology, 61,* 1064–1084.

Bushnell, M. C., Goldberg, M. E., Robinson, D. L. (1981). Behavioral enhancement of visual responses in monkey cerebral cortex. I. Modulation in posterior parietal cortex related to selective visual attention. *Journal of Neurophysiology, 46,* 755–772.

Colby, C. L. (1991). The neuroanatomy and neurophysiology of attention. *Journal of Child Neurology, 6,* S88–S118.

Colby, C. L., and Duhamel, J.-R. (1991). Heterogeneity of extrastriate visual areas and multiple parietal areas in the macaque monkey. *Neuropsychologia, 29,* 497–515.

Colby, C. L., Duhamel, J.-R., and Goldberg, M. E. (1993a). The analysis of visual space by the lateral intraparietal area of the monkey: The role of extraretinal signals. In T. P. Hicks, S. Molotchnikoff, and T. Ono (Eds.), *Progress in brain research,* vol. 95, 307–316.

Colby, C. L., Duhamel, J.-R., and Goldberg, M. E. (1993b). Ventral intraparietal area of the macaque: Anatomic location and visual response properties. *Journal of Neurophysiology, 69,* 902–914.

Colby, C. L., Gattass, R., Olson, C. R., and Gross, C. G. (1988). Topographic organization of cortical afferents to extrastriate visual area PO in the macaque: A dual tracer study. *Journal of Comparative Neurology, 238,* 1257–1299.

Dassonville, P., Schlag, J., and Schlag-Rey, M. (1992). Oculomotor localization relies on a damped representation of saccadic eye displacement in human and nonhuman primates. *Visual Neuroscience, 9,* 261–269.

Dassonville, P., Schlag, J., and Schlag-Rey, M. (1995). The use of egocentric and exocentric location cues in saccadic programming. *Vision Research, 35,* 2191–2199.

Desimone, R., and Ungerleider, L. G. (1989). Neural mechanisms of visual processing in monkeys. In F. Boller and J. Grafman (Eds.), *Handbook of neuropsychology,* 267–299. Amsterdam: Elsevier.

Duhamel, J.-R., Colby, C. L., and Goldberg, M. E. (1991). Congruent representations of visual and somatosensory space in single neurons of monkey ventral intraparietal cortex (area VIP). In J. Paillard (Ed.), *Brain and space,* 223–236. Oxford: Oxford University Press.

Duhamel, J.-R., Colby, C. L., and Goldberg, M. E. (1992). The updating of the representation of visual space in parietal cortex by intended eye movements. *Science, 255,* 90–92.

Duhamel, J.-R., Goldberg, M. E., FitzGibbon, E. J., Sirigu A., and Grafman, J. (1992). Saccadic dysmetria in a patient with a right frontoparietal lesion: The importance of corollary discharge for accurate spatial behavior. *Brain, 115,* 1387–1402.

Fischer, B., and Boch, R. (1981). Selection of visual targets activates prelunate cortical cells in trained rhesus monkey. *Experimental Brain Research, 41,* 431–433.

Fogassi, L., Gallese, V., Di Pellegrino. G., Fadiga, L., Gentilucci, M., Luppino, G., Matelli, M., Pedotti, A., and Rizzolatti, G. (1992). Space coding by premotor cortex. *Experimental Brain Research, 89,* 686–690.

Gentilucci, M., Fogassi, L., Luppino, G., Matelli, M., Camarda, R., and Rizzolatti, G. (1988). Functional organization of inferior area 6 in the macaque monkey. I. Somatotopy and the control of proximal movements. *Experimental Brain Research, 71,* 475–490.

Gentilucci, M., Fogassi, L., Luppino, G., Matelli, M., Camarda, R., and Rizzolatti, G. (1989). Somatotopic representation in inferior area 6 of the macaque monkey. *Brain Behavior and Evolution, 33,* 118–121.

Gentilucci, M., Scandolara, C., Pigarev, I. N., and Rizzolatti, G. (1983). Visual responses in the postarcuate cortex (area 6) of the monkey that are independent of eye position. *Experimental Brain Research, 50,* 464–468.

Gnadt, J. W., and Andersen, R. A. (1988). Memory-related motor planning activity in posterior parietal cortex of macaque. *Experimental Brain Research, 70,* 216–220.

Goldberg, M. E., Colby, C. L. (1989). The neurophysiology of spatial vision. In F. Boller and J. Grafman (Eds.), *Handbook of neuropsychology*, vol. 2, 301–315. Amsterdam: Elsevier.

Goldberg, M. E., Colby, C. L., and Duhamel, J.-R. (1990). The representation of visuomotor space in the parietal lobe of the monkey. *Cold Spring Harbor Symposia on Quantitative Biology*, 55, 729–739.

Goodale, M. A., and Milner, A. D. (1992). Separate visual pathways for perception and action. *Trends in Neuroscience*, 15, 20–25.

Graziano, M. S., Yap, G. S., and Gross, C. G. (1994). Coding of visual space by premotor areas. *Science*, 266, 1054–1057.

Graziano, M. S. A., and Gross C. G. (1993). A bimodal map of space: Somatosensory receptive fields in the macaque putamen with corresponding visual receptive fields. *Experimental Brain Research*, 97, 96–109.

Gross, C., and Graziano, M. (1995). Multiple representations of space in the brain. *The Neuroscientist*, 1, 43–50.

Hallett, P. E., and Lightstone, A. D. (1976). Saccadic eye movements to flashed targets. *Vision Research*, 16, 107–114.

Heide, W, Zimmermann, E., and Kompf, D. (1993). Double-step saccades in patients with frontal or parietal lesions. *Society for Neuroscience Abstracts*, 19, 427.

Helmholtz, H. (1866). *Treatise on physiological optics*. New York: Dover, 1924.

Hikosaka, O., Miyauchi, S., and Shimojo, S. (1993a). Visual attention revealed by an illusion of motion. *Neuroscience Research*, 18, 11–18.

Hikosaka, O., Miyauchi, S., and Shimojo, S. (1993b). Voluntary and stimulus-induced attention detected as motion sensation. *Perception*, 22, 517–526.

Hikosaka, O., and Wurtz, R. H. (1983). Visual and oculomotor functions of monkey substantia nigra pars reticulata. III. Memory-contingent visual and saccade responses. *Journal of Neurophysiology*, 49, 1268–1284.

Honda, H. (1989). Perceptual localization of visual stimuli flashed during saccades. *Perception and Psychophysics*, 45, 162–174.

Honda, H. (1993). Saccade-contingent displacement of the apparent position of visual stimuli flashed on a dimly illuminated structured background. *Vision Research*, 33, 709–716.

Hyvärinen, J., and Poranen, A. (1974). Function of the parietal associative area 7 as revealed from cellular discharges in alert monkeys. *Brain*, 97, 673–692.

Irwin, D. E. (1991). Information integration across saccadic eye movements. *Cognitive Psychology*, 23, 420–456.

Klein, R. (1980). Does oculomotor readiness mediate cognitive control of visual attention? In R. S. Nickerson (Ed.), *Attention and performance VIII*, 259–276. Hillsdale, NJ: Erlbaum.

Kusunoki, M., Colby, C. L., and Goldberg, M. E. (1994). Perisaccadic changes in the excitability of visual neurons in monkey parietal cortex. *Society for Neuroscience Abstracts*, 20, 773.

Matin, L., Matin, E., and Pola, J. (1970). Visual perception of direction when voluntary saccades occur. II. Relation of visual direction of a fixation target extingished before a saccade to a subsequent test flash presented before the saccade. *Perception and Psychophysics*, 8, 9–14.

Mays, L. E., and Sparks, D. L. (1980). Saccades are spatially, not retinocentrically, coded. *Science*, 208, 1163–1165.

Mountcastle, V. B., Lynch, J. C., Georgopoulos, A., Sakata, H., and Acuna, C. (1975). Posterior parietal association cortex of the monkey: Command functions for operations within extra-personal space. *Journal of Neurophysiology, 38*, 871–908.

Posner, M. I. (1980). Orienting of attention. *Quarterly Journal of Experimental Psychology, 32*, 3–25.

Rizzolatti, G., Camarda, R., Fogassi, L., Gentilucci, M., Luppino, G., and Matelli, M. (1988). Functional organization of inferior area 6 in the macaque monkey. II. Area F5 and the control of distal movements. *Experimental Brain Research, 71*, 491–507.

Rizzolatti, G., Scandolara, C., Matelli, M., and Gentilucci, M. (1981). Afferent properties of periarcuate neurons in macaque monkeys: II. Visual responses. *Behavioral Brain Research, 2*, 147–163.

Rizzolatti, G., Gentilucci, M., Luppino, L., Matelli, M., and Ponzoni-Maggi, S. (1987). Neurons related to goal-directed motor acts in inferior area 6 of the macaque monkey. *Experimental Brain Research, 67*, 220–224.

Rizzolatti, G., Riggio, L., and Sheliga, B. M. (1994). Space and selective attention. In S. Kornblum (Ed.), *Attention and performance XV*, 231–265.

Robinson, D. L., Goldberg, M. E., and Stanton, G. B. (1978). Parietal association cortex in the primate: Sensory mechanisms and behavioral modulations. *Journal of Neurophysiology, 41*, 910–932.

Stein, J. F. (1992). Posterior parietal cortex and egocentric space. *Behavioral and Brain Science, 15*, 3–30.

Tipper, S. P., Lortie, C., and Baylis, G. C. (1992). Selective reaching: Evidence for action-centred attention. *Journal of Experimental Psychology: Human Perception and Performance, 18*, 891–905.

Tipper, S. P., Weaver, B., and Houghton, G. (1994). Behavioral goals determine inhibitory mechanisms of selective attention. *Quarterly Journal of Experimental Psychology, 47A*, 809–840.

Wurtz, R. H. (1969). Visual receptive fields of striate cortex neurons in awake monkeys. *Journal of Neurophysiology, 32*, 727–742.

Wurtz, R. H., and Mohler, C. W. (1976). Organization of monkey superior colliculus: Enhanced visual response of superficial layer cells. *Journal of Neurophysiology, 39*, 745–765.

V   Multimodal Integration for Representation of Space

8 Multiple Pathways for Processing Visual Space

Michael S. A. Graziano and Charles G. Gross

ABSTRACT

In the macaque, neurons in ventral premotor cortex and in the putamen have tactile receptive fields on the face or arms, and corresponding visual receptive fields that extend outward from the tactile fields into the space near the body. For cells with tactile receptive fields on the arm, when the arm is moved, the corresponding visual receptive fields move with it. However, when the eyes move, the visual receptive fields remain stationary, "attached" to the arm. We suggest that these "arm-centered" visual responses play a role in visuomotor guidance. We predict that other portions of the somatotopic map in premotor cortex and in the putamen contain similar receptive fields, centered on the corresponding body parts. This "body-part-centered" representation of space is only one of several ways in which space is represented in the brain.

8.1 INTRODUCTION

Where is space represented in the brain? A variety of sites have been implicated, including the inferior parietal lobe, the hippocampus, the superior colliculus, the frontal eye fields, and dorsolateral prefrontal cortex (Andersen 1987; Bruce 1990; Goldman-Rakic 1987; Stein and Meredith 1993; O'Keefe and Nadel 1978). Many of these areas appear to represent a specific kind of space for a specific purpose. We propose that the space near the body is represented by neurons in two interconnected brain structures: (1) ventral area 6 in the premotor region of the frontal lobes; and (2) the putamen, part of the basal ganglia.

Area 6 and the putamen have been studied extensively in monkeys (for review, see Alexander, DeLong, and Strick 1986; Wise 1985). Both areas receive topographic projections from somatosensory and motor cortex, and project back to motor cortex, directly in the case of area 6 and indirectly via the globus pallidus and the ventrolateral thalamus in the case of the putamen. Area 6 and the putamen are also directly interconnected (Kunzle 1978; Parthasarathy, Schall, and Graybiel 1992). Both areas are somatotopically organized; their neurons respond to somatosensory stimuli and have receptive fields that are arranged to form a map of the body (Crutcher and Delong 1984a; Gentilucci et al. 1988). Many cells respond during voluntary movement, and electrical stimulation in a part of the map will cause muscle contractions in the corresponding part of the body (Alexander and DeLong 1985a,b; Crutcher and DeLong 1984b; Rizzolatti et al. 1988; Weinrich and Wise 1982; Weinrich, Wise, and Mauritz 1984).

The putamen and area 6 also receive input from visual areas in the posterior parietal lobe (Cavada and Goldman-Rakic 1989, 1991; Kunzle 1978, Matelli et al. 1986; Mesulam et al. 1977; Weber and Yin 1984). About a third of the neurons in the putamen and area 6 are visually responsive, and some are bimodal, responding to both visual and somesthetic stimuli (Gentilucci et al. 1988; Graziano and Gross 1993, 1994a; Graziano, Yap, and Gross 1994; Rizzolatti et al. 1981). For these bimodal cells, the visual receptive field usually matches the location of the somatosensory field and is confined in depth to a region near the body. Thus each of the two areas contains a somatotopically organized map of the visual space that immediately surrounds the body.

In this chapter we describe the properties of bimodal, visual-tactile neurons in the putamen and area 6. We then discuss how these response properties might encode the locations of nearby objects in body-part-centered coordinates. We suggest that the function of these somatotopic visual maps is to faciliate movement within the space near the body (Graziano and Gross 1992, 1994b), that is, they are sensorimotor mechanisms. Finally, we discuss the relationship between these areas and other areas of the brain thought to be involved in the processing of visual space.

8.2 BIMODAL, VISUAL-TACTILE RESPONSE PROPERTIES IN THE PUTAMEN

We recorded from single neurons in the putamen of both anesthetized and awake macaque monkeys (Graziano and Gross, 1993, 1994a). Somatosensory receptive fields were plotted by stroking the skin with cotton swabs and manipulating the joints. Visual receptive fields were plotted with small objects mounted on the end of a wand and were tested quantitatively with stimuli presented by a robot. To distinguish a visual response from a tactile response, the cells were also tested with the animal's eyes covered.

Anesthetized Recording

Of the 354 neurons studied in the putamen of anesthetized, paralyzed monkeys, 40 percent responded only to somatosensory stimuli, 12 percent responded only to visual stimuli, and 24 percent were bimodal, responding to both types of stimuli. The remaining cells did not respond under our test conditions. (See fig. 8.1).

Figure 8.2 shows a representative electrode penetration, passing vertically through the putamen. Cells in the dorsal part of the putamen had somatosensory receptive fields on the tail or legs. As the electrode moved ventrally, we encountered cells with receptive fields on the trunk, then the shoulders

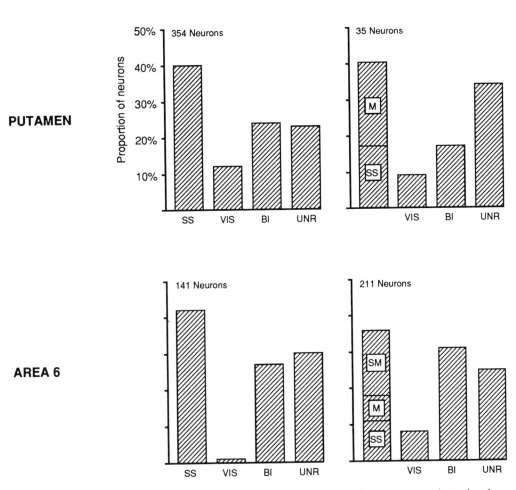

Figure 8.1 Proportions of cell types in the putamen and area 6, in anesthetized and unanesthetized monkeys. (SS: somatosensory cells; M: motor cells; SM: somatosensory-motor cells; VIS: visual cells; BI; bimodal, visual-somatosensory cells; UNR: unresponsive cells.)

and arms, the face, and finally inside the mouth. A similar somatotopic progression was previously reported by Crutcher and Delong (1984a). However, in our experiments, we found visual and bimodal, visual-somesthetic neurons in the face and arm portions of this somatotopic map (see, for example, fig. 8.2, cells 6, 7, and 8).

The responses of a bimodal cell are shown in figure 8.3. The tactile receptive field was plotted while the animal's eyes were covered. The cell was activated by lightly touching the facial hair, and the responsive region covered most of the contralateral cheek and the area around the mouth (fig. 8.3A and B). When the animal's eyes were uncovered, the cell responded

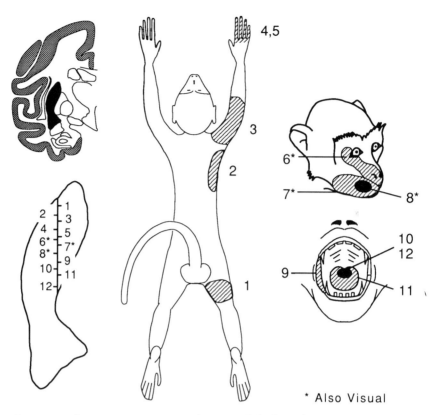

Figure 8.2 Somatotopic organization of putamen. Left: Coronal section at anterior-posterior level 14, and enlarged view of putamen, showing location of representative electrode penetration. Receptive field locations for neurons are shown to right. Cells indicated with asterisks responded to visual as well as tactile stimuli. (Adapted from Graziano and Gross 1993).

as the stimulus approached the face without touching (fig. 8.3C). This response was not caused by inadvertent tactile stimulation, such as by air movement, since the response was eliminated by covering the eyes (fig. 8.3D). By moving the stimulus toward the tactile receptive field from various angles, we measured the extent of the visual receptive field. This responsive region differed from a classical visual receptive field because it was not only restricted in visual angle but was also limited in depth to within about 10 cm of the face.

Figure 8.4 shows several more examples of bimodal receptive fields on the face. For the cells in figure 8.4A and B, the visual receptive field extended outward about 10 cm from the face. For the cell in figure 8.4C, the visual receptive field extended out about one meter from the monkey.

Figure 8.5 shows several examples of bimodal receptive fields on the arm. The cells shown in figure 8.5A and B had tactile receptive fields on the contralateral arm and visual receptive fields in the contralateral periphery. Both cells responded to visual stimuli as far away as 1.5 m. The cell shown in

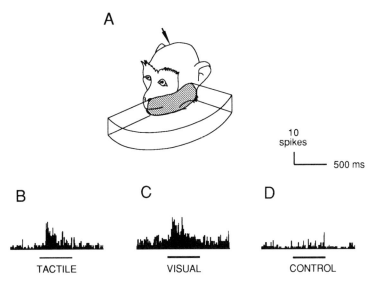

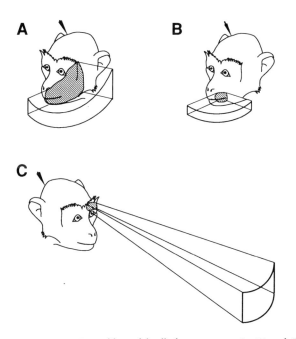

Figure 8.3 Poststimulus time histograms, summed over 10 trials, for typical bimodal putamen cell. A. Tactile receptive field (stippled) and visual receptive field (boxed) are in register. Arrow indicates hemisphere recorded from. B. Response to cotton swab touching face while eyes are covered. C. Response to cotton swab approaching face within 10 cm while eyes are open. D. Same as C, with eyes covered. (Graziano and Gross 1993).

Figure 8.4 Typical bimodal cells from putamen. In (A) and (B), visual receptive field extends about 10 cm from tactile receptive field. In (C), visual receptive field extends about 1 m from tactile receptive field. (Adapted from Graziano and Gross 1993).

Multiple Pathways for Processing Visual Space

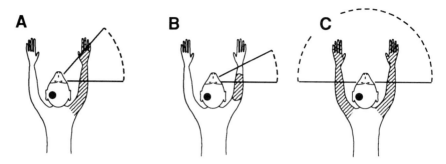

Figure 8.5 Bimodal cells from putamen with tactile receptive fields on arm. Lines indicate angle subtended by visual receptive fields in horizontal plane. Dashed lines indicate that receptive fields extend farther than 1 m. Stippling shows tactile fields, and black dots on head show hemisphere recorded from. (Adapted from Graziano and Gross 1993).

figure 8.5C responded to touching both arms, and the visual receptive field was bilateral. Again, the cell responded to stimuli as far away as 1.5 m.

How would the cell behave if the arm were moved to a new location? Would the tactile and visual receptive fields become dissociated, or would one receptive field shift in order to remain in register with the other? Figure 8.6 shows the result for two cells. The cell shown in figure 8.6A responded to visual stimuli only when the arm was propped forward in the monkey's field of view. When the arm was tucked back, thus placing the tactile receptive field out of sight, the cell no longer responded to visual stimuli presented anywhere in the visual field. The tactile response, however, was equally good for both arm positions. The cell shown in figure 8.6B had a particularly close match between the tactile and visual receptive field; when the arm was moved to different locations within the animal's sight, the visual receptive field also moved to follow the location of the hand. Of 25 bimodal cells with tactile receptive fields on the arm or hand, 5 had visual responses that depended on the position of the arm.

Unanesthetized Recording

Previous studies of single neuron activity in the putamen used awake monkeys sitting in a chair (e.g., Alexander 1987; Crutcher and Delong, 1984a,b, Kimura et al. 1992; Liles 1985; Schultz and Romo 1988). Under these conditions, bimodal cells with visual receptive fields near the body were not observed. One possible reason for this oversight is that stimuli moving close to the head or arms would have made the monkey flinch, and any associated neuronal discharge might have been interpreted as motor or somatosensory in nature, rather than visual.

In order to clarify this discrepancy between our results and the previous ones, we recorded in the putamen of an awake monkey whose head was fixed by a head bolt and whose arms were restrained in padded arm rests. Eye position was measured with a scleral search coil, and EMG was measured

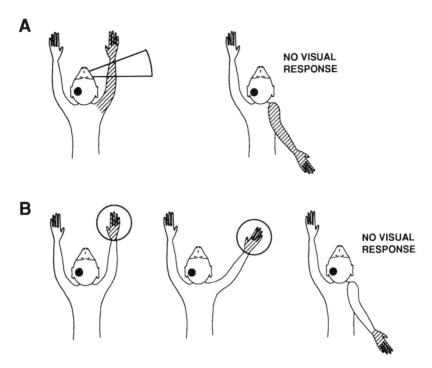

Figure 8.6 Effects of arm movement on some bimodal arm cells in putamen. These cells responded visually only when arm was within the monkey's field of view (left), but did not respond when arm was moved out of view (right). For cell shown in B, visual receptive field moved as hand moved. (Graziano and Gross 1993).

through surface electrodes pasted over various muscles of the upper and lower arm. The animal was trained to fixate a spot of light during presentation of visual stimuli, which consisted of small objects mounted on the end of a wand and brought near the face, shoulders, arms, or hands at various speeds. After several weeks, the animal became habituated to the presentation of these stimuli and sat quietly, fixating the light.

Although our sample size in this control animal was small (35 neurons), we were able to demonstrate that bimodal neurons with corresponding visual and tactile receptive fields do exist in the awake preparation. For example, the neuron shown in figure 8.7 had a tactile receptive field on the contralateral arm and responded to visual stimuli within about 10 cm of the arm. The rasters and histogram in figure 8.7B show the response as the visual stimulus was moved toward the tactile receptive field. A record of the EMG during one trial is also shown. There was no change in EMG activity during the presentation of the stimulus, that is, this particular cell had a pure sensory response, not associated with voluntary movement.

Figure 8.1 shows the relative proportions of somatosensory, visual, and bimodal cells that we found in the awake animal. These proportions are similar to those found in the anesthetized preparation, except that in the

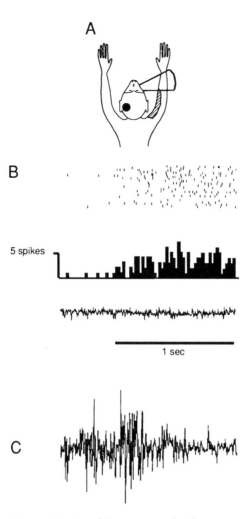

Figure 8.7 Bimodal neuron recorded from putamen of awake, fixating monkey. A. Visual receptive field was confined within 10 cm of tactile receptive field. B. Neuronal response, based on 20 trials, as visual stimulus approached tactile receptive field. Time bar indicates stimulus duration. EMG trace (palmaris longus muscle), taken from one of 20 trials, shows that arm was stationary during stimulus presentation. C. EMG trace while animal touched grape presented near its fingers. (Graziano and Gross 1994a).

awake animal 23 percent of the neurons fired in relation to active reaching movements of the arm. The relevance of this motor-related activity will be discussed in a later section.

8.3 BIMODAL, VISUAL-TACTILE RESPONSE PROPERTIES IN VENTRAL AREA 6

The bimodal, visual-tactile cells we discovered in the putamen are similar to neurons described by Rizzolatti and colleagues in ventral area 6 (Gentilucci

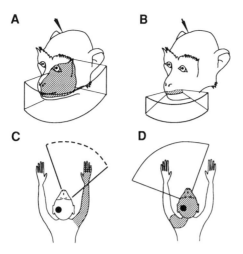

Figure 8.8 Typical bimodal cells from ventral area 6. Visual and tactile receptive fields correspond spatially, just as for neurons in putamen (see fig. 8.4).

et al. 1988; Rizzolatti et al. 1981). In order to compare the two areas directly, we recorded from area 6 in both anesthetized and awake monkeys, using the same procedures that we used to study the putamen (Graziano and Gross 1994a; Graziano, Yap, and Gross 1994).

Anesthetized Recording

We found somatosensory cells (42 percent), visual cells (27 percent), and bimodal cells (30 percent) in ventral area 6 of anesthetized, paralyzed monkeys. These proportions are similar to those found in the putamen (see fig. 8.1). The somatosensory receptive fields were somatotopically organized in a manner consistent with previous reports (Gentilucci et al. 1988). When electrode penetrations were made in the lateral part of ventral area 6, the tactile receptive fields were located on the face, and when electrode penetrations were made in the medial part, the tactile receptive fields were located on the arm. We found bimodal, visual-somesthetic neurons throughout the entire region, also in agreement with previous reports (Gentilucci et al. 1988; Rizzolatti et al. 1981).

Figure 8.8 shows the receptive fields of several representative bimodal neurons. The response properties are strikingly similar to those in the putamen. The cells shown in figure 8.8A–B had tactile receptive fields on the contralateral side of the face and matching visual receptive fields within about 10 cm of the face. For the cell in figure 8.8C, the tactile receptive field covered the contralateral arm and the visual receptive field extended outward beyond one meter. For the cell in figure 8.8D, the tactile receptive field covered both the face and a portion of the shoulder. This cell was unusual in that it responded to stimulation of the ipsilateral but not the contralateral

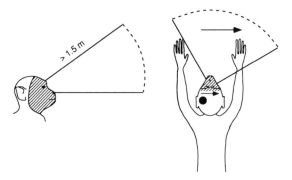

Figure 8.9 Example of bimodal cell from area 6. Both visual and tactile response preferred rightward motion. (Adapted from Graziano and Gross 1994a).

shoulder. The visual receptive field also extended farther into the ipsilateral periphery.

Figure 8.9 shows the results from a cell with a directionally selective tactile response; it preferred stimuli that moved across the skin from left to right. The visual response matched the location of the tactile response and was also directionally selective, again from left to right.

For bimodal neurons with tactile responses on the arm, we tested the effect of placing the arm in different locations. Figure 8.10 shows the result for one neuron. When the arm was bent backward (fig. 8.10A), the visual response began 45° in the contralateral field and extended to the edge of the monkey's sight. When the arm was positioned out to the side (fig. 8.10B), the visual response began closer to the midline, at 30°. When the arm was bent forward (fig. 8.10C), the visual response began 20° in the ipsilateral field and no longer extended to the edge of the contralateral field. Finally, with the hand roughly centered at the nose (fig. 8.10D), the visual response extended 70° into the ipsilateral field.

In total, 12 bimodal neurons with tactile receptive fields on the arm were tested by placing the arm in different positions, and for 8 of these the visual receptive field moved with the arm. A related phenomenon was noted earlier by Rizzolatti and colleagues (Fogassi et al. 1992; Gentilucci et al. 1983), who studied ventral area 6 in awake monkeys trained to fixate. They found that for many cells, the visual receptive field remained stationary in space, even when the monkey's eyes moved; they interpreted their results as indicating that the visual receptive fields were anchored to the head, encoding the locations of visual stimuli in "head-centered" space. In fact, their data show only that the receptive fields were not anchored to the eye. By contrast, our results indicate that at least some visual receptive fields are anchored to the arm, encoding the locations of stimuli in "arm-centered" space. As described in the next section, we recorded from awake behaving monkeys in order to test the effect of both eye and arm position in the same neurons.

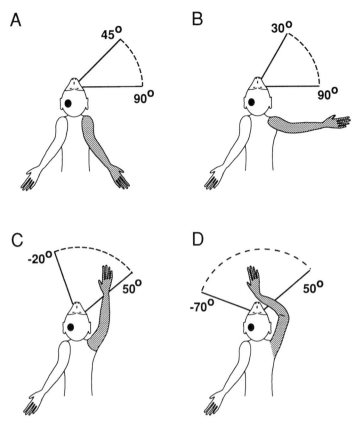

Figure 8.10 Example of bimodal cell from ventral area 6 for which visual receptive field moved as arm moved. (Adapted from Graziano and Gross 1994a).

Unanesthetized Recording

The proportions of cell types that we found in area 6 of awake, behaving monkeys were similar to the proportions found in the anesthetized animal (see fig. 8.1): 39 percent of the neurons were somatosensory, motor, both; 10 percent were visual; and 25 percent were bimodal.

Figure 8.11 (left) shows the experimental paradigm that we used to test the effect of eye and arm position on the visual response. Each trial began with illumination of one of three lights, A, B, or C, spaced 20° apart along the horizontal meridian. The monkey was required to fixate the light and maintain fixation throughout the trial for a juice reward. During fixation, a 10 cm diameter white ball mounted on a robot was advanced toward the monkey at 14.5 cm/sec along one of the four trajectories shown. The 3 eye positions and 4 stimulus positions yielded 12 conditions, which were presented in an interleaved fashion. The effect of arm position was studied by running a block of trials while the arm was in one position, and then strapping the arm into to a new position and running a second block.

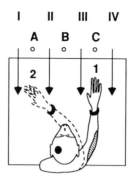

Stimulus Trajectory

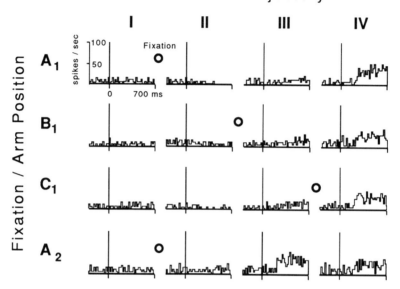

Figure 8.11 Upper: Experimental paradigm for studying area 6 in awake preparation. On each trial animal fixated one of three lights 20° apart (A, B, or C), and stimulus was advanced along one of four trajectories (I–IV). Arm was fixed in one of two positions (1 or 2). Stippling shows tactile receptive field of cell illustrated beneath. Lower: Histograms of neuronal activity, summed over 10 trials, as function of eye position (A, B, C), stimulus position (I–IV), and arm position (on right in A_1, and B_1, and C_1, on left in A_2). Vertical lines indicate stimulus onset. Circles indicate location of fixation light. When arm was fixed in position 1, neuron responded best to stimulus trajectory IV, whether eye looked to left (A_1), to center (B_1), or to right (C_1). However, when arm was fixed in position 2 (A_2), neuron responded best to stimulus trajectory III, that is, visual receptive field moved toward left with tactile receptive field. (Graziano, Yap, and Gross 1994).

Stimulus Trajectory

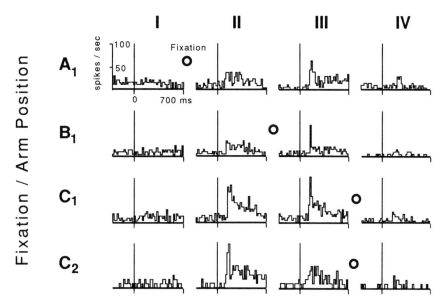

Figure 8.12 Response of bimodal neuron from area 6 with tactile receptive field on eyebrows. Visual response was best when stimulus was near midline (trajectories II and III), matching location of tactile receptive field. Visual receptive field remained at same location in space, whether eyes looked to left (A_1), center (B_1), or right (C_1). However, magnitude of the response varied with eye position. When arm was moved toward left (C_2), visual receptive field still did not move, presumably because it was anchored to tactile field on head. (See also caption to fig. 8.11). (Graziano, Yap, and Gross 1994).

Figure 8.11 (right) shows the result for one neuron. This cell had a tactile receptive field on the contralateral arm. A_1, B_1, and C_1 show the visual response when the arm was held to the right. The cell gave a significant visual response only when the stimulus was presented on the far right, near the arm. The visual response remained at the same location in the right-hand periphery, whether the eyes were fixating light A, light B, or light C, that is, even a 40° shift in eye position failed to change the location of the visual receptive field. The arm was then bent toward the left, and the cell was retested. As shown in A_2, the visual response moved with the arm. (B_2 and C_2, not shown, were similar to A_2).

Responses from a second neuron are shown in figure 8.12. This cell had a bilateral tactile receptive field on the eyebrow. The corresponding visual receptive field did not move when the eyes moved. This spatial invariance is particularly striking because the fovea fell to the left of the receptive field when the monkey fixated light A, and fell to the right of the receptive field when the monkey fixated light C. Although the location of the response was independent of eye position, the magnitude of the response was greatest when the eyes were fixating to the right. Similar modulation by gaze has

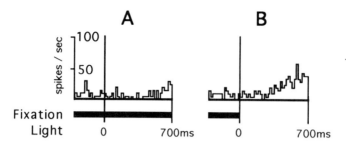

Figure 8.13 Response of bimodal area 6 neuron to stimulus at position III (see fig. 8.11) while monkey fixated central light. A. When fixation light was on continuously through trial, there was little or no response. B. When fixation light was extinguished at stimulus onset but monkey was still required to fixate until the end of trial, cell responded vigorously.

been reported for neurons in several regions of the parietal lobe, including area 7a (Andersen, Essick, and Siegel 1985) area LIP (Andersen et al. 1990), area PO (Galletti, Battaglini, and Fattori 1993), and area V3a (Galletti and Battaglini 1989).

Condition C_2 (fig. 8.12) shows the result for the same neuron when the arm was bent toward the left. The visual receptive field still did not move, that is, as expected, when the tactile receptive field is not on the arm, the visual receptive field does not move with the arm.

Many cells gave a more robust visual response when the animal was not fixating on a light. An example is shown in figure 8.13. When the monkey was required to fixate continuously on a spot of light throughout the entire trial, there was no significant response to the visual stimulus (fig. 8.13A). However, when the fixation light was extinguished at stimulus onset but the monkey was still required to fixate until the end of the trial, the cell gave a significant visual response (fig. 8.13B). Richmond, Wurtz, and Sato (1983) described a similar "blink" effect for visual neurons in IT cortex; they suggested that the fixation light modifies the attentional state of the animal, which in turn modulates the responses of the neurons. Perhaps a similar attentional modulation occurs for area 6 neurons.

The act of fixation itself also contributes to the suppression the response, as illustrated in figure 8.14 for one neuron. In this experiment, the fixation light was never illuminated during stimulus presentation. In conditions A–C, the fixation light was briefly flashed at the beginning of the trial, and the animal was required to fixate throughout the trial. In A_1, when the eyes looked to the left, the visual response was best at stimulus position III, near the arm. This peak response remained at the same location even when the eyes looked to the center (B_1) and to the right (C_1), that is, the visual receptive field did not move with the eyes. The cell had a tactile receptive field on the arm, and when the arm was bent toward the left, the visual response moved with it (C2).

Because the visual receptive field for this cell was independent of the position of the eyes, it was not necessary for the animal to fixate in order for

Stimulus Trajectory

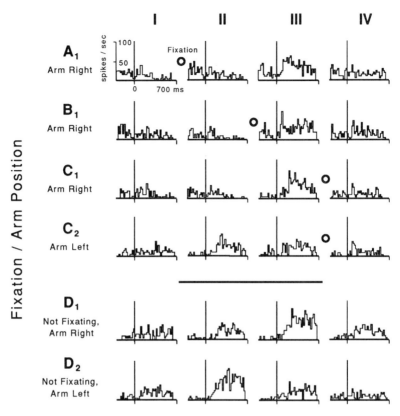

Figure 8.14 Response of bimodal neuron from area 6 with tactile receptive field on arm. In A–C, fixation light was extinguished at stimulus onset but monkey was still required to fixate until end of trial. Visual receptive field remained at same location in space, whether eyes looked to left (A_1), center (B_1), or right (C_1). However, when arm was bent toward left (C_2), visual response also moved toward left. In D_1 and D_2, fixation light was never illuminated and monkey was not required to fixate; response improved.

us to plot the receptive field. In D_1 and D_2, the fixation light was never illuminated and the animal was not required to fixate at all; the stimuli were presented automatically, regardless of the monkey's behavior. The cell gave a much stronger visual response, and the movement of the visual receptive field with the arm became more clear; the peak response moved leftward, from position III to position II. Perhaps the highly artificial situation of a long, continuous fixation interferes with the animal's allocation of attention and thus obscures the response properties of these neurons.

In total, 33 cells were tested by varying the position of the eye (fig. 8.15). For 32 cells (97 percent), the visual receptive field remained at the same location in space, despite the 40° shift in eye position. Only one cell, with a tactile response on the chin, had a visual receptive field that was not anchored

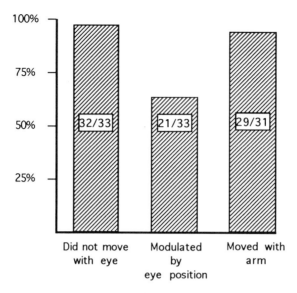

Figure 8.15 Proportions of cell types in area 6, studied in awake preparation. For 32 of 33 cells, visual receptive field did not move with eye. For 21 of 33 cells, visual response magnitude was significantly modulated by eye position. For 29 of 31 cells with tactile receptive fields on arm, visual receptive field moved with arm.

to its tactile receptive field and that moved with the eye. For 21 cells (64 percent), the magnitude of the response was significantly modulated by eye position.

Thirty-one "arm" bimodal cells were tested by varying the position of the arm. For 29 cells (94 percent), the visual receptive field moved with the arm. Twenty-two of the 29 were tested with multiple eye positions, and in all cases the visual receptive field remained near the arm, independent of the position of the eyes.

8.4 REPRESENTATION OF VISUAL SPACE IN BODY-PART-CENTERED COORDINATES

In most visual areas of the brain, the receptive fields are "retinocentric," that is, when the eyes move, the visual receptive fields also move. Although cells of this type can measure the coordinates of a stimulus on the retina, some investigators have suggested that a retinocentric coordinate system is too unstable for representing visual space because it shifts every time the eyes move (Fogassi et al. 1992; Galletti, Battaglini, and Fattori 1993; Schlag et al. 1980; Andersen, Essick, and Siegel 1985). Instead, a slightly more stable coordinate frame attached to the head or trunk might better serve visuospatial function. Accordingly, various groups have looked for nonretinocentric visual receptive fields, that is, receptive fields which do not move with the eye. Such cells have been found by Wiersma (1966) in the crayfish, by

Schlag et al. (1980) in the thalamus of the cat, by Pigarev and Rodionova (1988) in parietal cortex of the cat, by Galletti, Battaglini, and Fattori (1993) in area PO of the monkey parietal cortex, and by Fogassi et al. (1992) in monkey area 6. In some cases these nonretinocentric visual receptive fields were interpreted as forming the long-sought head- or trunk-centered coordinate system, providing a "stable" map of space. However, the results do not support such a conclusion because the head and trunk were not rotated during the experiments; instead, these results show only that the visual receptive fields were not fixed to the retina.

Our results in the putamen and area 6 suggest an entirely different interpretation. For many bimodal cells with tactile receptive fields on the arm or hand, the visual receptive fields remain anchored to the arm, moving as the arm moves. These visual receptive fields are not retinocentric, head-centered, or trunk-centered. They are "arm-centered," that is, they encode the location of the stimulus with respect to the arm. We predict that bimodal cells associated with other body parts will behave in a similar fashion. For example, if the tactile receptive field is on the face, then the visual receptive field will be head-centered, moving as the head is rotated.[1] Area 6 and the putamen, according to this view, represent visual space by means of multiple coordinate frames attached to multiple parts of the body.

What function might such a "body-part-centered" representation of space serve? Arm-centered neurons would be useful for hand-eye coordination, such as guiding the arm toward or away from visual targets. Indeed, a high proportion of the neurons in both the putamen and area 6 are active during voluntary movement (e.g., Alexander 1987; Crutcher and DeLong 1984b; Gentilucci et al. 1988; Rizzolatti et al. 1988; Weinrich, Wise, and Mauritz 1984). In area 6, cells that are active during movements of the arm are spatially tuned, responding best when the arm reaches into a particular region of space. When the arm is shifted to a different location, this motor field also shifts, rotating by the same angle that the shoulder has rotated (Caminiti, Johnson, and Urbano 1990); that is, just as for the visual receptive fields, the motor response fields are arm-centered. These neurons would appear to form a sensory-motor interface, encoding the location of the target in the same coordinate system used to control the arm.

Head-centered visual receptive fields would also be useful for visuomotor coordination, such as for reaching with the mouth toward food or enemies, flinching from approaching objects, heading soccer balls, or kissing accurately. Indeed, it would be useful to have a visual coordinate frame fixed to each part of the body surface for the purpose of hitting, grasping, or avoiding visual stimuli in the space near that body part. We hypothesize that area 6 and the putamen provide exactly this type of visual map. In support of this view, lesions to area 6 impair the ability to localize visual stimuli that are within reaching distance but leave intact the ability to localize more distant stimuli (Rizzolatti, Matelli, and Pavesi 1983).

8.5 MULTIPLE MAPS OF SPACE BEYOND PARIETAL CORTEX

On the basis of anatomical and lesion studies in monkeys and humans, Ungerleider and Mishkin (1982) proposed that visual space is processed by a sequence of cortical areas, beginning with striate cortex, continuing through areas in the dorsal part of the occipital lobe, and culminating in posterior parietal cortex (see fig. 8.16). The general idea of this "dorsal stream" has been confirmed in many subsequent anatomical, physiological, and neuro-psychological experiments (for review, see Desimone and Ungerleider 1989; Merigan and Maunsell 1993).

Nevertheless, exactly how space is represented in the parietal cortex remains obscure. Most posterior parietal areas (e.g., 7a, 7b, LIP, and VIP; see fig. 8.16) have little or no topographic organization. Because visual receptive fields in parietal cortex move with the eye, Duhamel, Colby, and Goldberg (1992) speculate that parietal neurons represent space in retinocentric coordinates. However, Andersen and colleagues have shown that for neurons in LIP and 7a, the magnitude of the visual response is modulated by proprioceptive input about the position of the eye and the rotation of the head (Andersen, Essick, and Siegel 1985; Andersen et al. 1990; Brotchie and Andersen 1991).

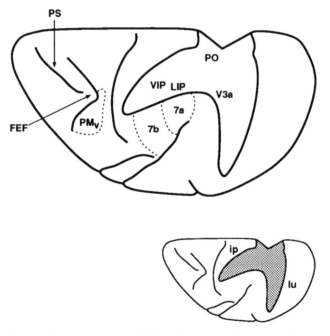

Figure 8.16 Dorsal view of left cerebral cortex of macaque with lunate and intraparietal sulci opened, showing some of the cortical areas involved in processing of space: FEF, frontal eye fields (area 8); LIP, lateral intraparietal area; PMv, ventral premotor area (ventral area 6); PO, parieto-occipital area; PS, principal sulcus; VIP, ventral intraparietal area. In small brain, shaded area shows extent of buried cortex in lunate (lu) and intraparietal (ip) sulci revealed in main figure.

They suggest that a population of these neurons forms a distributed code for a coordinate system centered on the head or maybe the trunk (Zipser and Andersen 1988). Some authors have even concluded that there is no coordinate frame and no map of space anywhere in the brain but instead a "distributed system of rules" to represent space in a way that is not explicit (Stein 1992).

One reason for this confusion is the persistent belief that the posterior parietal cortex is the end point of spatial processing. This is unlikely, since posterior parietal cortex projects to a variety of other brain structures also known to process visual space (see fig. 8.17). In our view, parietal cortex is an

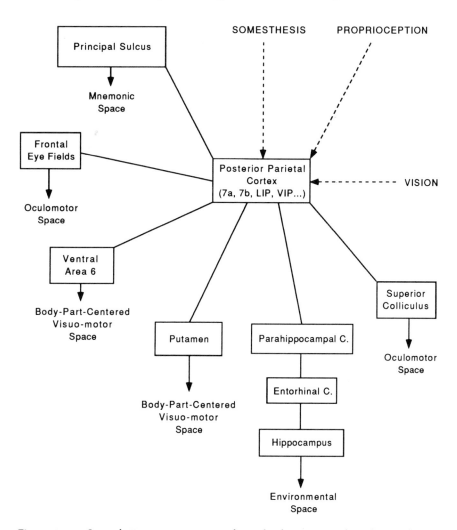

Figure 8.17 Somesthetic, proprioceptive, and visual information are brought together in various areas of posterior parietal cortex, which project to extraparietal structures for further, more specialized, processing of spatial information. All connections shown are monosynaptic. Not shown are interconnections among different targets of parietal cortex such as between ventral area 6 and putamen and between frontal eye fields and superior colliculus.

early stage of spatial processing; it is where vision, touch, and proprioception come together for the first time. Projections from parietal cortex then distribute this implicit, partially processed spatial information to other areas, which construct their own, special purpose maps, variously head-centered, eye-centered, arm-centered, or allocentric. Some of these areas are shown in figure 8.17, and discussed below.

Area 6 and Putamen

As described above, the putamen and area 6 contain maps of the space near the body. At least in the arm area, the visual receptive fields are body-part-centered, and could contribute to sensorimotor coordination. The somesthetic and visual information required to construct these maps is presumably provided to area 6 and the putamen through the monosynaptic projections from the parietal lobe, specifically from area 7b (Cavada and Goldman-Rakic 1989, 1991; Kunzle 1978; Matelli et al. 1986; Mesulam et al. 1977; Weber and Yin 1984). Area 7b itself contains bimodal, visual-tactile neurons (Hyvarinen 1981; Robinson and Burton 1980a,b), but the response properties are different from in the putamen and area 6, and consistent with it being an earlier processing stage in this hierarchy of bimodal areas. Specifically, the somato-topic organization in area 7b is much more crude, if indeed it exists at all, and the visual receptive fields near the arm do not appear to move when the arm is moved (Graziano and Gross 1994a).

Bimodal, visual-tactile responses have also been found in parietal area VIP (Colby, Duhamel, and Goldberg 1993; Duhamel, Colby, and Goldberg 1991), which projects to area 7b and possibly directly to area 6 and the putamen (Jones and Powell 1970; Mesulam et al. 1977; Cavada and Goldman-Rakic 1989, 1991). Therefore, VIP may be another source for the properties we have seen in the putamen and area 6.

Frontal Eye Fields and Superior Colliculus

Saccadic eye movements are controlled by several interconnected brain areas including the frontal eye fields, the deep layers of the superior colliculus and parietal area LIP (Andersen et al. 1990; Bruce 1990; Sparks 1991). These three areas appear to be arranged hierarchically, with LIP as an earlier processing stage, supplying information to the other two areas (Andersen, Asanuma, and Cowan 1985; Cavada and Goldman-Rakic 1989; Felleman and Van Essen 1991; Lynch, Graybiel, and Lobeck 1985). The superior colliculus and the frontal eye fields each contain a topographic map of space, but area LIP apparently does not.

In all three areas, the movements of the eye are guided by receptive fields that are fixed to the eyeball, just as movements of the arm may be guided by receptive fields in area 6 and the putamen that are fixed to the arm. In LIP and the frontal eye fields, this correspondence between the position of the receptive fields and of the eye is unusually close; for many neurons, the visual receptive field actively follows the eye, instead of lagging behind by the expected visual latency of approximately 70 ms (Duhamel, Colby, and Goldberg 1992).

In addition to their visual responses, neurons in all three areas also respond to auditory stimuli, presumably to guide saccadic eye movements to sound sources. Just as for the visual receptive fields, these auditory receptive fields are also anchored to the eyeball, shifting as the animal looks in different locations (Jay and Sparks 1984; Mazzoni et al. 1993; Russo and Bruce 1989; Stricanne et al. 1994).

All three eye movement areas also contain cells that continue to fire after a visual stimulus is extinguished, especially if the monkey is required to remember the location of the stimulus (Bruce and Goldberg 1985; Gnadt and Andersen 1988; Mays and Sparks 1980a,b). These cells could help to guide the eyes toward remembered targets. In one memory paradigm, the visual stimulus is flashed briefly outside the receptive field of the cell, and therefore does not elicit a response. The monkey is then required to fixate a new location, and consequently the receptive field of the cell moves with the eye. In its new location the receptive field encompasses the remembered location of the stimulus, and therefore the neuron responds. No visual stimulus has actually entered the receptive field of the cell; rather, the cell is activated when a remembered stimulus falls within its "memory" field.

In summary, neurons involved in programming saccadic eye movements have receptive fields that are anchored to the eye. Not just visual, but even auditory and memory fields are eye-centered. Therefore, these brain areas, like the putamen and area 6, use body-part-centered coordinate systems; the body part in this case is the eyeball. We suggest that a general principle of sensorimotor control is that the sensory stimulus is located by means of a coordinate system that is anchored to the relevant body part.

Hippocampus

Numerous functions have been ascribed to the hippocampus (e.g., Eichenbaum and Otto 1992; O'Keefe and Nadel 1978; Zola-Morgan and Squire 1993). At least in rats, the hippocampus is critical for learning to navigate through a complex spatial environment (O'Keefe and Nadel 1978; Nadel 1991). Lesions to the hippocampus impair the rat's ability to learn mazes (e.g., Morris, Garrud, and Rawlins 1982; Olton, Walker, and Gage 1978). Furthermore, hippocampal neurons have remarkable spatial properties; each neuron responds only when the animal is in a particular small region of his environment, the "place field" of the cell (O'Keefe and Nadel 1978). These neurons encode the allocentric or external location of the animal. In the monkey, hippocampal neurons appear to encode the allocentric locations of visual stimuli (Feigenbaum and Rolls 1991; Ono et al. 1991; Rolls et al. 1989).

Parietal areas 7a and LIP project to the parahippocampal cortex, which projects to the entorhinal cortex, which in turn projects to the hippocampus (Jones and Powell 1970; Seltzer and Pandya 1976; Suzuki and Amaral 1994). Presumably, the allocentric spatial properties in the hippocampus are generated at least in part from information supplied by the parietal cortex along this pathway.

Principal Sulcus

Ever since the lesion studies of Jacobsen (1936), the dorsolateral prefrontal cortex, area 46, has been known to play a role in short-term spatial memory. Recently, Funahashi, Bruce, and Goldman-Rakic (1989, 1990, 1993) have shown that the region around the principal sulcus, within area 46, contains a map of mnemonic space. Neurons in this region respond when the monkey holds the location of a visual target in working memory. Each neuron is sensitive to a particular region of space, its "memory field." Furthermore, these memory fields are organized topographically, such that lesions to the principal sulcus will produce selective scotomas—holes in the monkey's spatial working memory. The principal sulcus receives a dense projection from parietal area 7a (Andersen, Asanuma, and Cowan 1985; Cavada and Goldman-Rakic 1989), from which it presumably gets the spatial information necessary to construct its mnemonic map (Goldman-Rakic 1987).

Parietal Cortex

In summary, the parietal lobe is the hub and information source for several areas that are specialized for a variety of visuospatial functions. Each area contains its own, specially tailored map of space. This scheme of how spatial processing is organized in the brain suggests an answer to one of the long-standing questions about parietal function. Lesions to parietal cortex produce a vast array of spatial deficits, many of which are not dissociable by smaller lesions (for review, see Critchley 1953; DeRenzi 1982; Ratcliff 1991). Humans with parietal damage have difficulty reaching and saccading accurately, estimating distances, remembering routes, reading maps, and navigating through a room full of obstacles. They sometimes show neglect of an entire half of space; they may even confuse the locations of tactile stimuli, such as in finger agnosia, the inability to know which finger has been touched. Perhaps the reason for this diversity of dysfunction is that parietal lesions deafferent a large number of spatial maps located in different brain areas and serving different purposes.

ACKNOWLEDGMENTS

We thank G. Yap, H. Biola, H. Rodman, and N. Rebmann for their help in all phases of the experiment, which was supported by N.I.H. grant MH 19420 and NASA grant U94-089.

NOTE

1. We have recently confirmed our hypothesis and found that about 95 percent of bimodal cells with a tactile response on the face have head-centered visual receptive fields that move when the head is rotated but do not move with the eye or the arm.

REFERENCES

Alexander, G. E. (1987). Selective neuronal discharge in monkey putamen reflects intended direction of planned limb movements. *Experimental Brain Research, 67,* 623–634.

Alexander, G. E., and DeLong, M. R. (1985a). Microstimulation of the primate neostriatum. I. Physiological properties of striatal microexcitable zones. *Journal of Neurophysiology, 53,* 1401–1416.

Alexander, G. E., and DeLong, M. R. (1985b). Microstimulation of the primate neostriatum. II. Somatotopic organization of striatal microexcitable zones and their relation to neuronal response properties. *Journal of Neurophysiology, 53,* 1417–1430.

Alexander, G. E., DeLong, M. R., and Strick, P. L. (1986). Parallel organization of functionally segregated circuits linking basal ganglia and cortex. *Annual Review of Neuroscience, 9,* 357–381.

Andersen, R. A. (1987). Inferior parietal lobule function in spatial perception and visuomotor integration. In F. Plum, (Ed.), *Handbook of physiology,* 483–518. Bethesda, MD: American Physiological Society.

Andersen, R. A., Asanuma, C., and Cowan, W. M. (1985). Callosal and prefrontal associational projecting cell populations in area 7a of the macaque monkey: A study using retrogradely transported fluorescent dyes. *Journal of Comparative Neurology, 232,* 443–455.

Andersen, R. A., Essick, G. K., and Siegel, R. M. (1985). Encoding of spatial location by posterior parietal neurons. *Science, 230,* 456–458.

Andersen, R. A., Bracewell, R. M., Barash, S., Gnadt, J. W., and Fogassi, L. (1990). Eye-position effects on visual, memory, and saccade-related activity in areas LIP and 7a of macaque. *Journal of Neuroscience, 10,* 1176–1196.

Brotchie, P. R., and Andersen, R. A. (1991). A body-centered coordinate system in posterior parietal cortex. *Society for Neuroscience Abstracts, 17,* 1281.

Bruce, C. J. (1990). Integration of sensory and motor signals in primate frontal eye fields. In G. M. Edelman, W. E. Gall, and W. M. Cowan (Eds.), *From signal and sense: Local and global order in perceptual maps,* 261–314. New York: Wiley-Liss.

Bruce, C. J., and Goldberg, M. E. (1985). Primate frontal eye fields. I. Single neurons discharging before saccades. *Journal of Neurophysiology, 53,* 606–635.

Caminiti, R., Johnson, P. B., and Urbano, A. (1990). Making arm movements within different parts of space: Dynamic aspects in the primate motor cortex. *Journal of Neuroscience, 10,* 2039–2058.

Cavada, C., and Goldman-Rakic, P. S. (1989). Posterior parietal cortex in rhesus monkey. II. Evidence for segregated corticocortical networks linking sensory and limbic areas with the frontal lobe. *Journal of Comparative Neurology, 287,* 422–445.

Cavada, C., and Goldman-Rakic, P. S. (1991). Topographic segregation of corticostriatal projections from posterior parietal subdivisions in the macaque monkey. *Neuroscience, 42,* 683–696.

Colby, C. L., Duhamel, J., and Goldberg, M. E. (1993). Ventral intraparietal area of the macaque: Anatomic location and visual response properties. *Journal of Neurophysiology, 69,* 902–914.

Critchley, M. (1953). *The parietal lobes.* Now York: Hafner Press.

Crutcher, M. D., and DeLong, M. R. (1984a). Single cell studies of the primate putamen. I. Functional organization. *Experimental Brain Research, 53,* 233–243.

Crutcher, M. D., and DeLong, M. R. (1984b). Single-cell studies of the primate putamen. II. Relations to direction of movement and pattern of muscular activity. *Experimental Brain Research, 53,* 244–258.

De Renzi, E. (1982). *Disorders of space exploration and cognition.* New York: Wiley.

Desimone, R., and Ungerleider, L. G. (1989). Neural mechanisms of visual processing in monkeys. In F. Boller and J. Grafman (Eds.), *Handbook of neuropsychology,* vol. 2, 267–299. New York: Elsevier.

Duhamel, J., Colby, C. L., and Goldberg, M. E. (1991). Congruent representations of visual and somatosensory space in single neurons of monkey ventral intraparietal cortex (area VIP). In J. Paillard (Ed.), *Brain and space,* 223–236. New York: Oxford University Press.

Duhamel, J., Colby, C. L., and Goldberg, M. E. (1992). The updating of the representation of visual space in parietal cortex by intended eye movements. *Science, 255,* 90–92.

Eichenbaum, H., and Otto, T. (1992). The hippocampus: What does it do? *Behavioral and Neural Biology, 57,* 2–36.

Feigenbaum, J. D., and Rolls, E. T. (1991). Allocentric and egocentric spatial information processing in the hippocampal formation of the behaving primate. *Psychobiology, 19,* 21–40.

Felleman, D. J., and Van Essen, D. C. (1991). Distributed hierarchical processing in the primate cerebral cortex. *Cerebral Cortex, 1,* 1–47.

Fogassi, L., Gallese, V., di Pellegrino, G., Fadiga, L., Gentilucci, M., Luppino, G., Matelli, M., Pedotti, A., and Rizzolatti, G. (1992). Space coding by premotor cortex. *Experimental Brain Research, 89,* 686–690.

Funahashi, S., Bruce, C. J., and Goldman-Rakic, P. S. (1989). Mnemonic coding of visual space in the monkey's dorsolateral prefrontal cortex. *Journal of Neurophysiology, 61,* 331–349.

Funahashi, S., Bruce, C. J., and Goldman-Rakic. P. S. (1990). Visuospatial coding in primate prefrontal neurons revealed by oculomotor paradigms. *Journal of Neurophysiology, 63,* 814–831.

Funahashi, S., Bruce, C. J., and Goldman-Rakic, P. S. (1993). Dorsolateral prefrontal lesions and oculomotor delayed-response performance: Evidence for mnemonic "scotomas." *Journal of Neuroscience, 13,* 1479–1497.

Galletti, C., and Battaglini, P. P. (1989). Gaze-dependent visual neurons in area V3a of monkey prestriate cortex. *Journal of Neuroscience, 9,* 1112–1125.

Galletti, C., Battaglini, P. P., and Fattori, P. (1993). Parietal neurons encoding spatial locations in craniotopic coordinates. *Experimental Brain Research, 96,* 221–230.

Gentilucci, M., Fogassi, L., Luppino, G., Matelli, M., Camarda, R., and Rizzolatti, G. (1988). Functional organization of inferior area 6 in the macaque monkey. I. Somatotopy and the control of proximal movements. *Experimental Brain Research, 71,* 475–490.

Gentilucci, M., Scandolara, C., Pigarev, I. N., and Rizzolatti, G. (1983). Visual responses in the postarcuate cortex (area 6) of the monkey that are independent of eye position. *Experimental Brain Research, 50,* 464–468.

Gnadt, J. W., and Andersen, R. A. (1988). Memory related motor planning activity in posterior parietal cortex of macaque. *Experimental Brain Research, 70,* 216–220.

Goldman-Rakic, P. S. (1987). Circuitry of primate prefrontal cortex and regulation of behavior by representational memory. In F. Plum (Ed.), *Handbook of physiology: The nervous system,* vol. 5, 373–417. Bethesda, MD: American Physiological Society.

Graziano, M. S. A., and Gross, C. G. (1992). Somatotopically organized maps of near-visual space exist. *Behavioral and Brain Sciences, 15,* 750.

Graziano, M. S. A., and Gross, C. G. (1993). A bimodal map of space: Somatosensory receptive fields in the macaque putamen with corresponding visual receptive fields. *Experimental Brain Research, 97,* 96–109.

Graziano, M. S. A., and Gross, C. G. (1994a). The representation of extrapersonal space: A possible role for bimodal, visual-tactile neurons. In M. S. Gazzaniga (Ed.), *The cognitive neurosciences,* 1021–1034. Cambridge, MA: MIT Press.

Graziano, M. S. A., and Gross, C. G. (1994b). Mapping space with neurons. *Current Directions in Psychological Science, 3,* 164–167.

Graziano. M. S. A., Yap, G. S., and Gross, C. G. (1994). Neuronal coding of near extrapersonal visual space. *Science, 266,* 1054–1057.

Hyvärinen, J. (1981). Regional distribution of functions in parietal association area 7 of the monkey. *Brain Research, 206,* 287–303.

Jacobsen, C. F. (1936). Studies of cerebral function in primates. *Comparative Psychological Monographs, 13,* 1–68.

Jay, M. F., and Sparks, D. L. (1984). Auditory receptive fields in the primate superior colliculus that shift with changes in eye position. *Nature, 309,* 345–347.

Jones, E. G., and Powell, T. P. S. (1970). An anatomical study of converging sensory pathways within the cerebral cortex of the monkey. *Brain, 93,* 793–820.

Kimura, M., Aosaki, T., Hu, Y., Ishida, A., and Watanabe, K. (1992). Activity of primate putamen neurons is selective to the mode of voluntary movement: Visually guided, self-initiated, or memory-guided. *Experimental Brain Research, 89,* 473–477.

Kunzle, H. (1978). An autoradiographic analysis of the efferent connections from premotor and adjacent prefrontal regions (areas 6 and 9) in *Macaca fasicularis. Brain Behavior and Evolution, 15,* 185–234.

Liles, S. L. (1985). Activity of neurons in putamen during active and passive movement of wrist. *Journal of Neurophysiology, 53,* 217–236.

Lynch, L. C., Graybiel, A. M., and Lobeck, L. J. (1985). The differential projection of two cytoarchitectonic subregions of the inferior parietal lobule of macaque upon the deep layers of the superior colliculus. *Journal of Comparative Neurology, 235,* 241–254.

Matelli, M., Camarda, R., Glickstein, M., and Rizzolatti, G. (1986). Afferent and efferent projections of the inferior area 6 in the macaque monkey. *Journal of Comparative Neurology, 251,* 281–298.

Mays, L. E., and Sparks, D. L. (1980a). Saccades are spatially, not retinocentrically, coded. *Science, 208,* 1163–1165.

Mays, L. E., and Sparks, D. L. (1980b). Dissociation of visual and saccade-related responses in superior colliculus neurons. *Journal of Neurophysiology, 43,* 207–232.

Mazzoni, P., Bracewell, R. M., Barash, S., and Andersen, R. A. (1993). Spatially tuned auditory responses in area LIP of macaques performing memory saccades to acoustic targets. *Society for Neuroscience Abstracts, 19*, 26.

Merigan, W. H., and Maunsell, J. H. R. (1993). How parallel are the primate visual pathways? *Annual Review of Neuroscience, 16*, 369–402.

Mesulam, M., Van Hoesen, G. W., Pandya, D. N., and Geschwind, N. (1977). Limbic and sensory connections of the inferior parietal lobule (area PG) in the rhesus monkey: A study with a new method for horseradish peroxidase histochemistry. *Brain Research, 136*, 393–414.

Morris, R. G. M., Garrud, P., and Rawlins, J. N. P. (1982). Place navigation impaired in rats with hippocampal lesions. *Nature, 297*, 681–683.

Nadel, L. (1991). The hippocampus and space revisited. *Hippocampus, 1*, 221–229.

O'Keefe J., and Nadel L. (1978). *The hippocampus as a cognitive map.* Oxford: Clarendon Press.

Olton, D. S., Walker, J. A., and Gage, F. H. (1978). Hippocampal connections and spatial discrimination. *Brain Research, 139*, 295–308.

Ono, T., Nakamura, K., Fukuda, M., and Tamura, R. (1991). Place recognition responses of neurons in monkey hippocampus. *Neuroscience Letters, 121*, 194–198.

Parthasarathy, H. B., Schall, J. D., and Graybiel, A. M. (1992). Distributed but convergent ordering of corticostriatal projections: Analysis of the frontal eye field and the supplementary eye field in the macaque monkey. *Journal of Neuroscience, 12*, 4468–4488.

Pigarev, I. N., and Rodionova, E. I. (1988). Neurons with visual receptive fields independent of the position of the eyes in cat parietal cortex. *Sensornie Sistemi, 2*, 245–254.

Ratcliff, G. (1991). Brain and space: Some deductions from the clinical evidence. In J. Paillard (Ed.), *Brain and space*, 237–250. New York: Oxford University Press.

Richmond, B. J., Wurtz, R. H., and Sato, T. (1983). Visual responses of inferior temporal neurons in awake rhesus monkey. *Journal of Neurophysiology, 50*, 1415–1432.

Rizzolatti, G., Camarda, R., Fogossi, L., Gentilucci, M., Luppino, G., and Matelli, M. (1988). Functional organization of inferior area 6 in the macaque monkey. II. Area F5 and the control of distal movements. *Experimental Brain Research, 71*, 491–507.

Rizzolatti, G., Matelli, M., and Pavesi, G. (1983). Deficits in attention and movement following the removal of postarcuate (area 6) and prearcuate (area 8) cortex in macaque monkeys. *Brain, 106*, 655–673.

Rizzolatti, G., Scandolara, C., Matelli, M., and Gentilucci, M. (1981). Afferent properties of periarcuate neurons in macaque monkeys. II. Visual responses. *Behavioural Brain Research, 2*, 147–163.

Robinson, C. J., and Burton, H. (1980a). Organization of somatosensory receptive fields in cortical areas 7b, retroinsular, postauditory, and granular insula of *M. fascicularis. Journal of Comparative Neurology, 192*, 69–92.

Robinson, C. J., and Burton, H (1980b). Somatic submodality distribution within the second somatosensory area (SII), 7b, retroinsular, postauditory, and granular insular cortical areas of *M. fascicularis. Journal of Comparative Neurology, 192*, 93–108.

Rolls, E. T., Miyashita, Y., Cahusac, P. M. B., Kesner, R. P., Niki, H., Feigenbaum, J., and Bach, L. (1989). Hippocampal neurons in the monkey with activity related to the place in which a stimulus is shown. *Journal of Neuroscience, 9*, 1835–1845.

Russo, G. S., and Bruce, C. J. (1989). Auditory receptive fields of neurons in frontal cortex of rhesus monkey shift with direction of gaze. *Society of Neuroscience Abstracts, 15,* 1204.

Schlag, J., Schlag-Rey, M., Peck, C. K., and Joseph, J. P. (1980). Visual responses of thalamic neurons depending on the direction of gaze and the position of targets in space. *Experimental Brain Research, 40,* 170–184.

Schultz, W., and Romo, R. (1988). Neuronal activity in the monkey striatum during the initiation of movements. *Experimental Brain Research, 71,* 431–436.

Seltzer, B. and Pandya, D. N. (1976). Some cortical projections to the parahippocampal area in the rhesus monkey. *Experimental Neurology, 50,* 146–160.

Sparks, D. L (1991). The neural encoding of the location of targets for saccadic eye movements. In J. Paillard (Ed.), *Brain and space,* 3–19. New York: Oxford, University Press.

Stein, B. E., and Meredith, M. A. (1993). *The merging of the senses.* Cambridge, MA: MIT Press.

Stein, J. F. (1992). The representation of egocentric space in posterior parietal cortex. *Behavioral and Brain Sciences, 15,* 691–700.

Stricanne, B., Xing, J., Mazzoni, P., and Andersen, R. A. (1994). Response of LIP neurons to auditory targets for saccadic eye movements: A distributed coding for sensorimotor transformation. *Society for Neuroscience Abstracts, 20,* 143.

Suzuki, W. A., and Amaral, D. G. (1994). The perirhinal and parahippocampal cortices of the monkey: Cortical afferents. *Journal of Comparative Neurology, 350,* 497–533.

Ungerleider, L. G., and Mishkin, M. (1982). Two cortical visual systems. In D. J. Ingle, M. A. Goodale, and R. J. W. Mansfield (Eds.), *Analysis of visual behavior,* 549–586. Cambridge, MA: MIT Press.

Weber, J. T., and Yin, T. C. T. (1984). Subcortical projections of the inferior parietal cortex (area 7) in the stump-tailed monkey. *Journal of Comparative Neurology, 224,* 206–230.

Weinrich, M., and Wise, S. P. (1982). The premotor cortex of the monkey. *Journal of Neuroscience, 2,* 1329–1345.

Weinrich, M., Wise, S. P., and Mauritz, K. H. (1984). A neurophysiological study of the premotor cortex in the rhesus monkey. *Brain, 107,* 385–414.

Wiersma, C. A. G. (1966). Integration in the visual pathway of crustacea. *Symposium for the Society for Experimental Biology, 20,* 151–177.

Wise, S. P. (1985). The primate premotor cortex: Past, present, and preparatory. *Annual Review of Neuroscience, 8,* 1–19.

Zipser, D., and Andersen, R. A. (1988). A backpropagation-programmed network that simulates response properties of a subset of posterior parietal neurons. *Nature, 311,* 679–684.

Zola-Morgan, S., and Squire, L. R. (1993). Neuroanatomy of memory. *Annual Review of Neuroscience, 16,* 547–564.

9 Multimodal Spatial Constraints on Tactile Selective Attention

Jon Driver and Peter G. Grossenbacher

ABSTRACT

Five experiments examined whether tactile selective attention is purely somatotopic, or operates within a more abstract spatial frame of reference that is influenced by visual or proprioceptive inputs. The task throughout was speeded discrimination of fingertip vibrations. Target and distractor vibrations were presented simultaneously to a homologous finger on each hand. The distractor vibrations could be congruent or incongruent with the target. We manipulated the spatial separation of the relevant and irrelevant finger within subjects by positioning their hands close together or far apart. This manipulation does not affect the somatotopic separation of the stimulated tactile receptors. Between studies, we manipulated whether subjects consistently faced the relevant hand, the irrelevant hand, or neither hand, and also whether they were blindfolded. Incongruent distractors impaired performance in every experiment; this interference declined when the hands were spatially separated for subjects facing the relevant hand, or neither hand, whether they were blindfolded or not. These results demonstrate contributions from upper-limb proprioception to spatially selective tactile attention. For subjects facing the irrelevant hand, interference did not vary with hand separation, whether blindfolded or not. This suggests a role for head or eye orientation in the spatial selection of even unseen tactile stimuli.

9.1 INTRODUCTION

Anatomy, physiology, psychophysics, and even phenomenology provide abundant evidence for the conventional distinctions between sensory modalities. One can readily distinguish receptor sheets for vision, hearing, and touch (the retina, cochlea, and skin, respectively), each transducing different aspects of the physical world. The separation between these sensory modalities can apparently be maintained at higher levels of representation as well. For example, there is now considerable physiological and anatomical evidence for numerous spatially organized "maps" in primate cortex, many of them coding aspects of just a single sensory modality (e.g., Cowey 1985; Woolsey 1981).

As noted by Driver and Spence (1994) at the Attention and Performance XV meeting, the majority of prior research on attention has adhered to these conventional distinctions between modalities; as a result, it has typically considered attention within each sense taken in isolation. Thus there have been abundant studies of visual attention, and of auditory attention (see Kahneman and Treisman 1984; Johnston and Dark 1986; Allport 1993 for overviews) and more recently a few investigations of tactile attention (e.g., Evans and Craig 1991; Whang, Burton, and Shulman 1991). On the other hand, previous experiments on possible attentional *interactions* across these sensory modalities have been extremely scarce (though see Buchtel and Butter 1988; Butter, Buchtel, and Santucci 1989; Driver and Spence 1994; Grossenbacher 1992; Hikosaka et al., chap. 10, this volume; Spence and Driver 1995a,b; Ward 1994).

Of course, it could be that such intermodal attentional interactions are relatively scarce themselves in the nervous system and that the emphasis on unimodal attention in prior studies is therefore appropriate. Given the abundance of modality-specific cortical maps, there is certainly no shortage of candidate substrates for the operation of modality-specific spatial attention. However, several considerations suggest that interactions between modalities may in fact be widespread, with far-reaching consequences for the operation of spatial attention.

First, neuroscience has identified a number of areas with spatiotopic organization that have sensory inputs from multiple modalities, including the superior colliculus (Stein and Meredith 1993), areas in posterior parietal cortex (Stein 1992; Duffy and Burchfiel 1971) and the putamen (Graziano and Gross 1993 and chap. 8, this volume). The superior colliculus and posterior parietal cortex in particular have long been thought to play important roles in spatial attention (see Rafal and Robertson 1995). The correspondences in spatiotopic organization across different modalities within these areas (e.g., the closely aligned auditory and visual "maps" in the colliculus; see King 1993) raise the possibility that spatial attention may operate in an amodal manner (Farah et al. 1989; Posner 1990); at the very least, they provide a potential substrate for interactions between the modalities during spatial selection (Stein 1992).

A second reason to question the strictly unimodal approach of prior attention research was raised by Driver and Spence (1994) from a functional perspective. They noted that many real-world tasks provide stimulation in many modalities, and require attention to be *coordinated* across these to select multimodal information from the same relevant object or spatial area, despite its different representation within the various modalities. Given that the senses have very contrasting spatial organizations at input (i.e., retinotopic in vision, somatotopic in touch, and tonotopic rather than spatial in hearing), a solution to this coordination problem provides a considerable computational challenge even for the case of purely spatial selection (see Hikosaka et al., chap. 10, this volume).

A third reason to question the unimodal approach of most prior research is that detailed psychological analyses of many ostensibly "unimodal" tasks reveal that several modalities may in fact contribute to performance even in such situations. The role of proprioception in particular is often overlooked (see Roll et al., chap. 12, this volume). For example, Biguer et al. (1988)

illustrated that afferent proprioceptive information can affect visual localization, a task that may seem unimodal until considered in detail. Biguer et al. applied vibration to neck muscles, thus stimulating the nerves that usually signal muscle stretch during head turning, and hence producing the impression of head turning even while the head remained still. More importantly, the neck vibration also induced illusions concerning the location of purely *visual* targets; for example, stationary points of light appeared to move during the vibration.

This example raises the possibility that the representational space in which "visual" attention is directed may well derive from proprioceptive inputs in addition to visual inputs (and perhaps also vestibular inputs; see Làdavas 1987). Such complexities arise because the alignment of our various receptors (relative to each other and relative to environmental factors such as gravity) can change in many different ways as we adopt different postures (likewise for our various effectors). To achieve accurate spatial coding, these various realignments must be compensated for by integrating information from several distinct sources (see Jeannerod 1991; Hikosaka et al., chap. 10, this volume; Karnath, Schenkel, and Fischer 1991).

Touch provides a particularly interesting case of this integration problem and is the focus for the rest of this chapter. Tactile receptors can adopt innumerable spatial configurations relative to each other (Hikosaka et al., chap. 10, this volume; Lederman, Browse, and Klatzky 1988), and relative to the receptor sheets for other senses. For example, the fingertips on different hands are a considerable distance apart in the somatotopic coordinates of body surface, but they can be placed arbitrarily far apart or close together in external space, within the limits of arm length. Thus an individual may tactually explore two widely separated objects simultaneously, one with each hand. By contrast, when touching a single object with both hands, the fingertips on different hands may now contact adjacent regions of a single object. These contrasting examples illustrate a fundamental point. Perceiving the spatial characteristics of external objects via touch requires that the *somatotopic* separation of receptors in the sensory array (e.g., those on different hands, which are somatotopically far apart) be corrected by some measure of their current *spatial* separation in the real world (which may be very close for receptors on different hands in some circumstances, as in our example of exploring a single object bimanually). This correction presumably requires coordination of tactile information with proprioceptive or visual inputs that specify the current relative locations of the two hands in external space.

Our experiments examine the extent to which tactile selective attention operates on a purely somatotopic representation (i.e., in terms of the separation between receptors on the body surface, such as on the same versus different hand), as opposed to a representation employing some higher-order spatial frame of reference (e.g., in terms of the separation between the hands in external space) that results from the integration of tactile information with visual and/or proprioceptive information. The empirical papers reviewed below provide some precedents for this question.

As noted earlier, there have been rather few studies of tactile attention in comparison with the abundance of visual or auditory studies. Detection masking between simultaneous tactile stimuli (e.g., threshold elevation under double stimulation with von Frey hairs) is known to be a function of the separation of the two stimuli on the skin surface (e.g., Gilson 1969; Meyer, Gross, and Teuber 1963; Sherrick 1964; Sherrick and Cholewiak 1986; Uttal 1960). In general, the disruption of detection performance relative to single stimulation falls off as the somatotopic distance between the two stimuli increases (e.g., the disruption is greater for double stimulation of thumb and index finger on one hand than for thumb and middle finger). Such results are found even when subjects are instructed to attend only a single prespecified target location (Craig 1974, Gilson 1969; Sherrick and Cholewiak 1986). It remains unknown whether somatotopic separation alone is the critical factor in such detection masking, rather than the separation in external space between the two stimuli, because this has invariably been confounded with somatotopic distance in prior studies.

A similar problem of interpretation applies to more recent studies that have examined tactile pattern identification, rather than mere detection, in the presence of distractors. Weisenberger (1981; cited in Evans and Craig 1991) presented tactile patterns to the upper region of an index finger pad. The presence of distractor patterns in the lower region of the same finger pad disrupted identification. Such interference can be reduced by presenting targets and distractors to different fingers (Craig 1985), but this manipulation again confounds somatotopic separation with separation in external space.

Evans and Craig (1991) recently showed that tactile discrimination for the direction of movement (in a pattern swept across a target finger pad) can be disrupted by stimulation of another finger; in particular, direction discriminations were less accurate when the irrelevant finger pad was stimulated with motion in the opposite direction to the relevant finger pad. This study demonstrates that the *nature* of the tactile distractor can be coded, rather than its mere presence alone. Importantly, the interference from opposite motion was reduced when the distractor was applied to the irrelevant hand rather than to an adjacent finger on the same hand as the relevant finger. Because the separation between target and distractor information in external space was held constant across this manipulation, this result demonstrates that somatotopic distance per se can affect the efficiency of spatial tactile attention.

A recent neuropsychological study by Moscovitch and Behrmann (1994) suggests that more abstract frames of reference can also affect tactile spatial attention. They examined eleven patients with tactile extinction after unilateral parietal injury. Extinction patients can detect both contralesional and ipsilesional stimuli when either is presented individually but typically detect only ipsilesional events when stimulated on both sides simultaneously. This deficit is increasingly regarded as an attentional problem (e.g., Baylis, Driver, and Rafal 1993). Moscovitch and Behrmann examined the coordinates in which tactile extinction arose for their patients. They tapped the patients simultaneously on the left and right side of the wrist on the ipsilesional hand, which was tested in both a palm-up and a palm-down posture. Note that the wrist rotation that differentiates these two postures has the effect of reversing which tactile receptors face left or right in space (relative to the patient's trunk, head, etc.). The patients missed the stimulus on the contralesional side as defined in these *spatial* coordinates under double stimulation. In other words, they did not miss stimuli on a fixed region of the skin regardless of wrist rotation, as would be predicted by a purely *somatotopic* deficit. Our experiments examine whether tactile attention in normal subjects can similarly be sensitive to nonsomatotopic spatial factors.

We required our normal subjects to perform a speeded discrimination for vibrotactile stimuli applied to a fingertip. The relevant fingertip for target vibrations was specified in advance, but simultaneous distractor vibrations could be applied to the homologous finger on the irrelevant hand, and these vibrations could be congruent or incongruent with the target. Our critical manipulation was whether the two hands were placed close together or far apart. Note that hand separation varies the distance between target and distractor in *external* space, while holding constant the anatomical separation of the stimulated tactile receptors in *somatotopic* space. In the visual and auditory modalities, it is well established that increasing the spatial separation of target and distractor reduces interference effects (e.g., Eriksen and Eriksen 1974; Moray 1969). If increasing just the separation of tactile target and distractor in external space can similarly reduce interference, the implication would be that tactile attention can operate within a more abstract spatial frame of reference than a purely somatotopic representation. Such an abstract representation, sensitive to the current separation between tactile receptors in external space, would entail integration of proprioceptive and/or visual signals together with tactile information.

Axelrod, Thompson, and Cohen (1968) previously carried out a similar manipulation of relative hand position. They examined temporal thresholds for discriminating whether electrocutaneous stimulation of the two hands was simultaneous or successive. The critical temporal separation for accurate perceptions of successive stimuli was greater when the hands were held far apart (thumbs separated by 115 cm.) rather than adjacent (separated by 15 cm). As Axelrod, Thompson, and Cohen noted (p. 194), "the dependence of threshold on position is puzzling, in view of the invariant anatomical positions of the stimulated loci.... A decision on whether the dependence is to be explained on postural or attentional grounds must await further experimental analysis...." The attentional hypothesis they had in mind was that it may take longer to shift attention between information at tactile receptors with a given somatotopic separation when they have a greater separation in external space. This is similar to our own hypothesis concerning the possibility of an abstract spatial frame of reference for tactile spatial attention. The postural hypothesis they had in mind was that the different limb contortions required at the different hand separations may have had a peripheral effect on tactile sensitivity (e.g., by affecting blood circulation). To examine any role for such factors, our studies included unimanual trials. These provided a measure of tactile discrimination in the absence of any tactile distractor, but with subjects adopting the same hands-together and hands-apart postures (and thus the same limb contortions) as in our bimanual trials.

9.2 GENERAL METHOD

The apparatus, stimuli, design, and procedure were very similar across our five experiments. The task was always a speeded two-choice discrimination (long and continuous versus two short bursts) for vibrotactile stimuli applied to the little (i.e., fourth) finger on one or the other hand. Target vibrations were presented to just one, relevant hand, which was constant throughout a block but varied across blocks. In unimanual blocks the target vibration was presented in isolation; these unimanual blocks served as a control for any effects that the required arm contortions might have on tactile perception. During bimanual blocks a distractor vibration was presented simultaneously with the target vibration, but on the little finger of the other, irrelevant hand. This distractor could be congruent (i.e., same as the target) or incongruent (i.e., different from the target). Any congruency effect from the distractor vibration on response to the target vibration provides a measure of the efficiency in focusing attention on just the relevant hand.

Our question was whether this efficiency would depend on the separation of the two hands in external space, even though the location of the stimulated cutaneous receptors in anatomical (i.e., somatotopic) terms remains constant across such a manipulation. The separation of the two hands was manipulated between blocks, with the hands being placed either very close together in the same hemispace or as far apart as possible (given the subject's arm length) within separate hemispaces. Across experiments we also manipulated whether subjects faced the relevant hand, the irrelevant hand, or straight ahead (i.e. directly between the two hands when these were separated), and whether the hands were visible or not (by means of a blindfold). In this way we could determine the possible contributions of overt orienting, and of proprioceptive versus visual inputs, to any effects of hand separation in external space upon the efficiency of spatially selective tactile attention.

Apparatus

Two desks were positioned adjacently along one wall of a windowless room, separated by 7 cm. Each subject sat at one of these desks ("sitting" desk) such that one of their arms could be directed forwards and to either side while still falling above this desk. Two flat wooden boards attached to the top of this sitting desk provided armrests on either side of the chair (see, fig. 9.1). The chair was positioned so that the subject found it comfortable to rest both arms palm-upward on foam blocks that were 7.5 cm high. A chin rest attached to the sitting desk kept the subject's head at a fixed location throughout the experiment.

The second, "side" desk provided a mechanically independent foam support on a single wooden board. Subjects directed the arm closer to this side desk toward it, resting their hand palm-up on the foam so that the little finger was at a fixed location, marked by a fixed vertical wooden peg on the side desk. Subjects placed their arm so that this peg was between the little finger and the adjacent finger on the hand in question (see fig. 9.1). On the sitting desk there were two such wooden pegs, and thus two possible hand positions for the other arm. This second arm was directed toward one of these positions, either crossing the subject's midline to place the little fingers of the two hands about 4 cm apart, or extending away from the body such that the two hands were far apart (65–74 cm, depending on the subject's arm length) and equidistant from the body midline (see figs. 9.1a and 9.1b for illustrations of the far and near conditions, respectively). Thus we manipulated the separation between the two hands by varying only the position of the hand on the sitting desk.

A fan located on the sitting desk, directly in front of the subject, produced noise that completely masked the very weak auditory cues from the vibrators. Two foot pedals were placed beneath the sitting desk, one under the toes and one under the heel of the right foot. Subjects kept both these pedals depressed at the beginning of each trial and made their tactile discrimination by releasing one or other pedal. Closed-circuit video monitoring provided a means to ensure fixation of the appropriate hand in experiments 1a and 3a, while an infrared eye movement monitor (Eye-Trac 210, Applied Science Laboratories) was used to ensure that fixation was straight ahead in experiment 2. A Macintosh IIsi microcomputer, with National Instruments NB-MIO-16X input/output board and a switching amplifier, provided control and interface circuitry. Skin vibration was achieved using two force transducers (model V1220 standard, Audiological Engineering), each resting on the pad of one little finger. Each transducer rested a flat contact surface of 1.75 cm^2 on top of the finger pad and was gravitationally held by a 50 g lead weight suspended from a small leather loop (see figure 9.1). Vibrations were driven by sine wave twelve-bit signals (maximum amplitude ± 3.0 V) digitized at 10 kHz. Experiments 1a and 3a both used two red light-emitting diodes (LEDs), one attached to each leather loop so as to face the subject.

Stimuli

Fingertip vibrations were produced by mechanical oscillations driven at 300 Hz with ± 1.7 V under one of two amplitude modulations. The single/ long stimulus was designed to induce a perception of constant intensity; its

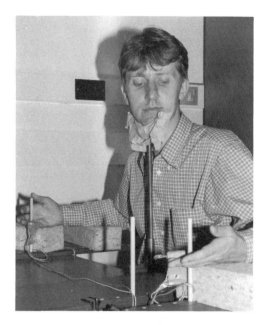

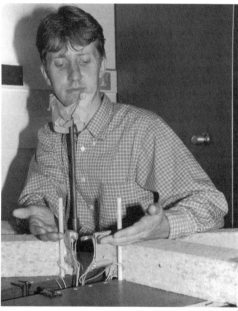

Figure 9.1 Photographs depicting apparatus and manipulation of hand separation that was used throughout. A. Hands are placed far apart in distinct hemispaces. Subject has head and eyes turned toward left hand in this example. In experiments 1a and 1b, target vibration was delivered to faced and fixated hand, and the distractor vibration to the other, irrelevant hand. In experiments 3a and 3b, hand that was faced and fixated received distractor vibration, while other hand received target. In experiment 2, subject faced and fixated directly ahead, between two separated hands. Vibrators were held on the pad of the little (fourth) finger on each hand by lead weight at bottom of leather loop placed over this finger. Vibrations were neither visible nor audible to subject. Note three wooden pegs (white and vertical), two of which are

amplitude linearly increased from ± 0.85 to ± 1.7 V during the initial 255 ms, followed by a linear decrease to ± 0.85 V for the remaining 45 ms. The double/short stimulus was designed to induce the perception of two discrete bursts. This 300 ms stimulus was driven by a 75 ms, ± 1.7 V square wave burst, and then 150 ms of zero voltage, followed by another identical square wave burst. The single/long and double/short stimuli were informally judged to have comparable subjective duration and intensity during piloting.

Procedure

Familiarization with the vibrotactile stimuli was followed by the subject labeling them and then practicing discrimination with these verbal labels, prior to the speeded discrimination trials on which nonverbal choice reaction time (RT) data were collected. Familiarization involved mere exposure to a random sequence of twenty vibrotactile stimuli, ten applied unimanually to the little finger on one hand and then ten to the little finger of the other hand, with the two kinds of vibration equally likely in both cases. No response was required at this stage; subjects were simply instructed to discern how the two possible vibrations were different. They then described to the experimenter how the two vibrations differed, designating each with a nonarbitrary label of their own choosing (typically "short" versus "long," or "double" versus "single"). During the subsequent discrimination practice, five stimuli were presented to one hand, then five to the other hand. Subjects named each stimulus with one of their chosen labels and received immediate verbal feedback on accuracy. This discrimination practice was iterated as necessary until there were zero errors in ten successive trials. Throughout the familiarization stage and the discrimination practice, the hands were positioned as for the initial block of RT data collection (see below).

There were eight blocks of RT data collection, and the entire experiment lasted about one hour for each subject. The first four RT blocks each comprised 70 trials of unimanual stimulation, with the relevant hand constant throughout a block. These trials gave a measure of any effects of limb contortion (due to the different arm positions we required) on tactile discrimination at the fingertip. Subjects made a speeded discrimination of the single vibrotactile stimulus applied to just one little finger, responding via the pedals under the right foot. They released the toe pedal to indicate the single/long

attached to sitting desk (leftmost in pictured example) and one to side desk (rightmost in picture, where subject's left hand is located). Each hand is arranged palm-up on foam blocks that rest upon boards attached to desks, such that there is a wooden peg between little and ring finger to fix that hand's position. Hands are placed far apart or near together by varying which of two pegs on sitting desk is used. B. Hands are placed near together within same hemispace by positioning right hand at other peg on sitting desk. In this illustration, subject is now facing and fixating right hand. Hand separation and direction of head and eyes were orthogonal factors in experiments 1 and 3.

vibration, and the heel pedal for the double/short vibration. The two kinds of vibration were equally likely and appeared in random sequence.

The subjects rested briefly after the four unimanual blocks and then commenced the four bimanual blocks. The speeded tactile discrimination required for the relevant hand was as before, but the target vibration was now accompanied by a simultaneous distractor vibration on the irrelevant hand. The target and distractor vibrations were equally likely to be single/long or double/short and were just as likely to be the same as each other (congruent) or different (incongruent). There were 120 trials in each of these bimanual blocks.

Although the unimanual and bimanual trials were analyzed separately, a common factor across these trials was the manipulation of separation in external space between the stimulated fingers. This was varied between blocks by positioning the hands close together on the same side of the body midline, or far apart on opposite sides. In the far condition, the arms were outstretched symmetrically, each within its own uncrossed hemispace (see fig. 9.1a). In the near condition, the arm on the sitting desk crossed over the body midline toward the side desk, with its hand placed near the hand that was permanently on the side desk. The little fingers of the two hands were then as close as possible without either them or the transducers touching each other (see fig. 9.1b).

For half the subjects, data collection began with the hands positioned near together, while the remaining subjects positioned their hands far apart during the first block. Arm position was changed after the first block, and then changed every two blocks for each subject throughout the session. The relevant hand was similarly counterbalanced across subjects; half began attending to the right hand, while the remainder attended to the left hand during the first two blocks. Starting with the third block, the attended hand alternated every two blocks for each subject throughout the session. The sequence of attended hand and of hand separation was thus counterbalanced across subjects, with only one of these factors changing its level every block. Whether the side desk was located to the left or right of the sitting desk was partially counterbalanced across subjects (four subjects had one configuration and eight had the other in the studies with twelve subjects, while the counterbalancing of desk side was complete in experiment 2).

The red LEDs attached to the leather loops that held the force transducers onto the fingertip served as multipurpose visual stimuli. Their primary role was to provide a fixation light in experiments 1a and 3a on just the relevant hand (i.e., the LED was not illuminated on the irrelevant hand for any block). They also provided feedback in those studies by flickering at a slow rate if the subject failed to depress both foot pedals (in the ready position) at the beginning of a trial, and by flickering at a rapid rate immediately after an erroneous response. On each trial in experiments 1a and 3a the fixation LED was illuminated 300 ms prior to onset of the 300 ms vibrotactile stimulation. It remained on until the subject responded by lifting heel or toe, or until

2,500 ms had elapsed (which was considered a miss response and discarded). Responses with latencies of 150 ms or less were likewise discarded as anticipations; these discarded trials were replaced at random positions later within the trial sequence of the same block. The intertrial interval was 300 ms.

9.3 EXPERIMENTS 1A AND 1B

In our first study, subjects were instructed both to face (orient the head toward) and fixate (direct the eyes toward) the relevant hand throughout all experimental trials. To confirm compliance, the experimenter monitored output from a video camera that faced subjects from beyond their relevant hand. Subjects turned their head and eyes toward the relevant hand while remaining in the chin rest, with their trunk facing forward. In order to examine any effect of visual input, two separate groups of subjects were run. These were given the same instructions (i.e., to turn the head and eyes towards the relevant hand), but one group could always see (experiment 1a), while the other group were blindfolded throughout the session (experiment 1b). For the blindfolded group, we could only monitor the direction of the head on video, but the gaze instructions were given nevertheless. The blindfolded subjects received auditory feedback instead of visual feedback via the LEDs, which broadcast the digitized word "Incorrect" from 3 m behind the subject when an error was made. In all other respects, the experiment followed the general method given above, for both groups of subjects.

Subjects

The twelve right-handed subjects in experiment 1a (no blindfold) were seven men and five women, who ranged in age from 19 to 33 years (with a mean of 24.6 years) and who were paid £3.60 for participation. The twelve different right-handed subjects in experiment 1b (blindfolded) were five men and seven women, who ranged in age from 19 to 29 years (with a mean of 22.0 years) and who were paid as for the other group.

Results

The intersubject means of subjects' median RTs for correct responses, together with the associated mean error rates, are given for each condition of interest in figure 9.2, shown separately for the two groups of subjects (i.e., those with and without blindfolds). Separate analyses of variance (ANOVAs) were conducted on the unimanual trials and the bimanual trials. For the unimanual trials, the two-way mixed-design ANOVA had the between-subject factor of group (with versus without blindfold, i.e., experiment 1b versus experiment 1a) and the within-subject factor of hand separation (near or far). In the RT data, neither factor had any main effect, and there was no interaction (all Fs < 1.4). For the bimanual trials, the three-way mixed ANOVA had

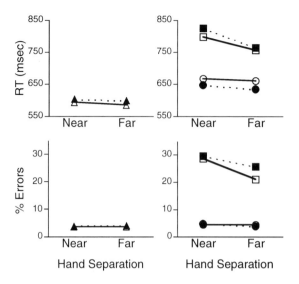

Figure 9.2 Intersubject means of median correct reaction times (RT, in upper graphs) and mean error percentages (lower graphs) for various conditions in experiments 1a and 1b. Data from unimanual trials appear in left graphs (triangle symbols), while bimanual trials appear in right graphs. Results for seeing subjects (experiment 1a) are shown with open symbols and solid lines, while those for blindfolded subjects (experiment 1b) are shown with filled symbols and dotted lines. Circles represent congruent bimanual trials (where concurrent target and distractor were same type of vibration), while squares represent incongruent bimanual trials (where concurrent target and distractor vibrations were of different types). Abscissa distinguishes two hand separations.

the same between-subject factor of group, and the two within-subject factors of congruence (congruent versus incongruent distractors) and hand separation (near versus far). There was a main effect of congruence ($F(1, 22) = 84.1$, $p < .001$) in the RT data, with slower responses in the incongruent conditions, and a main effect of hand separation ($F(1, 22) = 5.6$, $p < .03$) with slower responses in the near condition. There was no main effect or interaction involving subject group (all $Fs < 1.9$), but there was an interaction between congruence and hand separation ($F(1, 22) = 13.4$, $p < .001$), with a larger effect of congruence at the near separation. Planned contrasts revealed that incongruent trials were slower at the near hand separation than the far ($F(1, 22) = 40.4$, $p < .0001$), while hand separation had no such effect for the congruent trials ($F(1, 22) = 1.4$, n.s.).

Corresponding ANOVAs on the error data found for unimanual trials that neither group nor hand separation had a main effect, and there was no interaction (all $Fs < 0.2$). For the bimanual trials, there was a main effect. of congruence ($F(1, 22) = 100.8$, $p < .0001$) with more errors in the incongruent conditions, and a main effect of hand separation ($F(1, 22) = 11.2$, $p < .005$) with more errors in the near condition. There was no main effect or interaction involving subject group (all $Fs < 1.9$), but there was an interaction between congruence and hand separation ($F(1, 22) = 9.4$, $p < .006$), with a larger congruence effect at the near separation. Planned contrasts revealed that incongruent trials were less accurate at the near hand separation than the far ($F(1, 22) = 22.1$, $p = .0001$), while hand separation had no such effect for the congruent trials ($F(1, 22) < 0.2$, n.s.). These error results mirror the pattern of the RT data, and thus rule out speed-accuracy trade-offs as an explanation for the observed effects.

Discussion

The distractor vibrations produced a clear congruence effect, delaying response and increasing errors substantially when they were incongruent with the simultaneous target. Thus, in our short/double versus long/single vibrotactile discrimination task, tactile attention cannot be perfectly restricted to one hand, to the complete exclusion of vibrotactile information on the other hand. Selection was imperfect even though the relevant hand was known in advance and remained constant throughout a block (cf. Evans and Craig 1991).

More importantly, the congruence effect from distractors was significantly reduced, in both RTs and errors, when the hands were placed far apart rather than near together (see figure 9.2, bimanual trials). As discussed earlier, the somatotopic separation of the receptors stimulated by the target and distractor remains constant across this manipulation. The implication is that the efficiency of spatial-tactile attention depends in part on the current separation of the stimulated tactile receptors in external space, rather than solely on their somatotopic separation. This external separation must be coded by vision and/or proprioception (provided it has no effect on the peripheral tactile receptors themselves, as we consider below). The effect of external separation on distractor interference therefore implies that multiple modalities contribute to the control of spatial-tactile attention.

The equivalence in results for the blindfolded group and the seeing group suggest that proprioception was primarily responsible for the modulation of interference by hand separation in external space. Indeed, proprioceptive inputs seem the only possible explanation for this aspect of the results in the blindfolded subjects because no other source of information was available to them for distinguishing the two hand separations that had a differential effect on their performance. The comparable results in the seeing group suggest that visual information about the hand separation played no significant role. On the other hand, we may simply have lacked the power to detect a small contribution from vision in the context of a more substantial effect from proprioception.

The effect of hand separation in external space on distractor interference is particularly compelling when one considers that the tactile stimuli to be discriminated were *identical* across the postural manipulation, which was quite irrelevant to the specified "unimodal" task of discriminating just the tactile input to the relevant hand. The manipulation of spatial separation between the relevant and irrelevant hands did not affect the somatotopic separation of the relevant and irrelevant vibrotactile stimuli, and presumably introduced no new tactile stimulation of the hands either (see below). Thus our results seem to provide another case in which an apparently unimodal task actually involves more than one modality on closer inspection (see earlier discussion of Biguer et al. 1988). In such contexts, Gibson's (1966) perspective on the senses as functional systems making use of information from a *variety* of receptor surfaces may be more appropriate than the conventional distinctions between senses as defined by receptor sheets.

Of course, one might argue that the different hand positions actually had a direct peripheral effect on processing within the tactile modality itself. Some factor such as blood circulation in the arms might have varied with the different limb contortions required by the designated hand positions (as originally discussed by Axelrod, Thompson, and Cohen 1968). Alternatively, the different limb contortions may have produced different pressure points on the skin, thus in themselves varying tactile stimulation and so affecting the target discrimination. Fortunately, the unimanual trials allow us to rule out such possibilities; the same hand positions (and thus limb contortions) were required in these unimanual trials as for the bimanual trials, and yet there was no effect of hand separation in the unimanual trials. Likewise, hand separation had no effect on *congruent* bimanual trials. If some peripheral effect of limb contortion were impairing tactile target discrimination under the near hand separation, this should presumably have arisen in both the incongruent *and* congruent bimanual trials.

Can our results be explained in terms of overt orienting? Recall that both groups of subjects turned their head toward the relevant hand and that both were instructed to direct eyes toward it. As a result their head (and probably their eyes, although this could only be confirmed for the seeing subjects in experiment 1a) pointed in the general direction of both the target *and* the distractor in the near condition, but pointed towards the target and *away* from the distractor in the far condition. Could this differential directing of the head and eyes (i.e., toward versus away from the distractor) explain the effect of spatial separation on distractor interference in the bimanual trials? Such an explanation would certainly be consistent with the absence of any separation effect in the unimanual trials because there was no distractor to face toward or away from on these trials.

Morais (1978) has previously reported that the direction of eyes, head, and trunk can affect the efficiency of spatial selection in a listening task. Moreover, Honoré, Bourdeaud'hui, and Sparrow (1989) and Pierson et al. (1991) have observed that the direction of gaze can affect response to tactile stimuli, reducing cutaneous reaction times for stimuli in the fixated direction. Larmande and Cambier (1981) have similarly shown an effect of gaze on tactile detection in extinction patients with right parietal injury, reporting that tactile extinction of the contralesional event on double stimulation was reduced when the patients fixated toward the contralesional side. Thus there are several precedents for suggesting that the direction of gaze (and perhaps of the head also) might affect tactile processing in our task. Of course, any such effect could not be visually mediated for our blindfolded subjects. However, Honoré, Bourdeaud'hui, and Sparrow (1989) found effects of gaze direction on cutaneous judgments even in the dark.

It is therefore possible that our effect of spatial separation on distractor interference arose because subjects fixated and faced in the general direction of the distractor under the near hand separation, but away from the distractor under the far hand separation, thus producing a relative benefit for the target in the latter condition. To test this explanation, our next experiment repeated the manipulation of hand separation within the same tactile task, but now the seeing subjects always faced and fixated straight ahead. Thus the direction of eyes and head now had exactly the same relation to the distractor location under the near hand separation as under the far separation.

9.4   EXPERIMENT 2

Subjects

The sixteen new right-handed subjects were six men and ten women, who ranged in age from 18 to 31 years (with a mean of 24.0 years) and who were paid as before.

Apparatus

The apparatus was as before with the addition of an infrared eye monitor (Eye-Trac model 210, Applied Science Laboratories) used to measure the horizontal direction of the left eye. The LEDs on the leather loops were no longer employed; instead, three red LEDs were mounted on a white card at 114 cm directly in front of the subject, in a centered row with 11 cm between adjacent LEDs. The central LED was used as the fixation light and feedback signal; the two peripheral LEDs were used to calibrate the eye monitor. No blindfold was ever employed.

Procedure

This experiment differed from the previous (and subsequent) studies in that subjects always had their head and eyes facing straight ahead, in addition to their trunk. They fixated a central red LED that was always remote from either hand (by at least 25°). Eye position was monitored using the infrared system, and trials could proceed only if the subject fixated within 1.5° of the fixation light at the beginning of the trial. If they failed this fixation criterion during a trial, it was eliminated from analysis. Error feedback after an erroneous tactile discrimination was delivered auditorily (as in experiment 1b). All other aspects of the method were as before.

Results

The intersubject means of subjects' median RTs for correct responses are given in figure 9.3 for the conditions of interest, together with the associated mean error rates. A one-way ANOVA on the RT data from the unimanual trials examined any effect of hand separation, which was nonsignificant ($F(1, 15) = 1.8$, n.s.). A two-way ANOVA on the bimanual RTs had the within-subject factors of hand separation and congruence. This found a main effect of congruence ($F(1, 15) = 198.9$, $p < .0001$) with slower RTs on the incongruent trials as in experiment 1; there was also a main effect of hand separation ($F(1, 15) = 9.4$, $p < .01$) with slower RTs at the near separation. Most importantly, the critical interaction between congruence and hand separation was significant ($F(1, 15) = 5.4$, $p < .05$), with a larger congruence effect at the near separation (see fig. 9.3). The effect of hand separation was now significant for both types of trials in planned contrasts: $F(1, 15) = 456.6$, $p < .0001$ for the incongruent trials; $F(1, 15) = 11.9$, $p = .004$ for the congruent trials).

A one-way ANOVA on the error data from unimanual trials found no effect of hand separation ($F(1, 15) = 0.1$, n.s.). A two-way ANOVA on the bimanual error rates found a main effect of congruence ($F(1, 15) = 40.3$, $p < .0001$) with more errors in the incongruent conditions. There was also a main effect of hand separation ($F(1, 15) = 6.9$, $p < .02$) with more errors at the

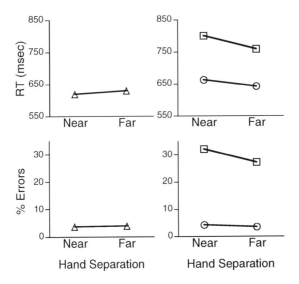

Figure 9.3 Intersubject means of median correct reaction times (RT, in upper graphs) and mean error percentages (lower graphs) for various conditions in experiment 2. Data from unimanual trials appear in left graphs (triangle symbols), while bimanual trials appear in right graphs. Circles represent congruent bimanual trials (where target and distractor were same type of vibration), while squares represent incongruent bimanual trials (where target and distractor vibrations were of different types). Abscissa distinguishes two hand separations.

near separation, and the critical interaction between hand separation and congruence was again significant ($F(1, 15) = 6.5$, $p = .02$). This interaction reflects the larger congruence effect at the near separation compared to the far. Planned contrasts revealed that incongruent trials were less accurate at the near hand separation ($F(1, 15) = 13.6$, $p = .002$), while hand separation had no effect for congruent trials ($F(1, 15) = .01$, n.s.).

Discussion

This experiment replicated the important results from the previous study, even though subjects always fixated and faced straight ahead, so that the direction of head and eyes toward versus away from the distractor no longer covaried with the separation between the hands. As before, there was a substantial effect of the congruence between simultaneous target and distractor vibrations on the two hands, with slower responses and more errors on incongruent trials. Moreover, this interference from incongruent distractors was again reduced when the hands were placed further apart, demonstrating a role for the separation in external space between the tactile stimuli, even when their somatotopic separation was held constant. Because there were no blindfolds in the present experiment, this effect of separation in external space might be attributed either to proprioceptive inputs, visual inputs, or both. As before, the null effect of hand separation on unimanual trials rules out any explanation of the reduced interference for the far condition in terms of any peripheral effect of limb contortion on tactile perception.

These results demonstrate that the direction of head and eyes is not the *sole* factor responsible for the modulation of interference by spatial separation between the hands. This modulation was still observed with head and eyes directed straight ahead toward a "neutral" location. However, the modulation was numerically smaller than in experiment 1 (compare figs. 9.2 and 9.3 for the bimanual trials), where head and eyes were directed in the direction of the distractor with the near separation but away from it with the far separation. This numerical trend is at least consistent with an enhancement of tactile processing in the direction of head and gaze (Honoré, Bourdeaud'hui, and Sparrow 1989; Larmande and Cambier 1981), which would give the target an additional advantage over the distractor in the far conditions of experiment 1, as compared with experiment 2.

To examine this possibility further, our final experiment set the direction of head and eyes *against* any hand separation effect. The method was as for experiment 1, except that seeing or blindfolded subjects now faced and fixated the *irrelevant* hand throughout. If the direction of head and eyes plays no role, the results should be as before, with a clear modulation of distractor interference by hand separation. A different prediction follows, however, if tactile processing is indeed boosted for stimuli that are faced or fixated. Our studies so far have identified a greater efficiency in ignoring tactile distractors when they are remote from the target in external space (i.e., under the far hand separation). However, with the new requirement to face and fixate the distractor, this benefit in selection would be opposed by a boosted representation of the distractor under the far hand separation. Under the new instructions, subjects face and fixate in the general direction of both the distractor and target for the near condition. However, they face and fixate toward the distractor but *away* from the target under the far condition. Thus distractor processing may now be boosted relative to the target in the far condition; any effects of the direction of eye and head would oppose the benefit for the far condition (in terms of reduced interference) that we found in the previous studies and should therefore reduce, negate, or even reverse this benefit.

9.5 EXPERIMENTS 3A AND 3B

Subjects

None of the subjects had taken part in the previous experiments. The twelve right-handed subjects in the seeing group (experiment 3a) were two men and ten women, ranging in age from 17 to 27 years (with a mean of 22.3 years). The twelve right-handed subjects in the blindfolded group (experiment 3b) were seven men and five women, who ranged in age from 17 to 29 years (with a mean of 22.2 years). Both groups of subjects were paid for participation as before. All subjects had to face and fixate the irrelevant hand throughout. In all other respects, the method followed experiment 1 exactly.

Results

The intersubject means of subjects' median RTs for correct responses, together with the associated mean error rates, are given for each condition of interest in figure 9.4, shown separately for the two groups of subjects (i.e., those with and without blindfolds). Separate mixed-design ANOVAs were conducted on the unimanual trials (two-way) and the bimanual trials (three-way) just as for experiment 1, with the between-subject factor of group (with or without blindfold). For the unimanual trials, the RT data showed no main effect of hand separation or of group, and there was no interaction (all $Fs < 0.5$). For the bimanual trials, the ANOVA on RTs found a main effect of congruence ($F(1, 22) = 71.5$, $p < .0001$) with slower responses in the incongruent conditions as before, but no main effect of hand separation ($F(1, 22) = 0.1$). As in experiment 1, there was no main effect or interaction involving subject group (all $Fs < 1.8$). In contrast to experiment 1, there was no interaction involving hand separation ($F(1, 22) = 0.6$, for the critical interaction of congruence with hand separation; all other $Fs < 1.8$).

Corresponding ANOVAs on the error data for unimanual trials found that there was no main effect of group ($F(1, 22) = 0.2$) but that the effect of hand separation ($F(1, 22) = 3.6$, $p = .07$) and its interaction with group ($F(1, 22) = 4.2$, $p = .053$) were both marginal. Inspection of the unimanual data in figure

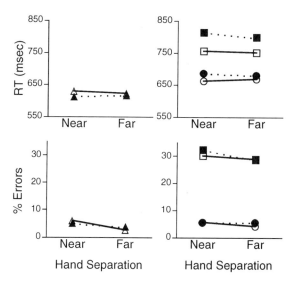

Figure 9.4 Intersubject means of median correct reaction times (RT, in upper graphs) and mean error percentages (lower graphs) for various conditions in experiments 3a and 3b. Data from unimanual trials appear in left graphs (triangle symbols), while bimanual trials appear in right graphs. Results for seeing subjects (experiment 3a) are shown with open symbols and solid lines, while those for blindfolded subjects (experiment 3b) are shown with filled symbols and dotted lines. Circles represent congruent bimanual trials (where target and distractor were same type of vibration), while squares represent incongruent bimanual trials (where target and distractor vibrations were of different types). Abscissa distinguishes two hand separations.

9.4 reveals a trend for more errors at the near hand separation for subjects without the blindfold (who were fixating the irrelevant hand) but no such trend for blindfolded subjects (who faced the irrelevant hand but could not see it). For the bimanual trials, the mixed-design ANOVA on the error data found a main effect of congruence ($F(1, 22) = 96.7$, $p < .00001$) with more errors in the incongruent conditions, and a trend for an effect of hand separation ($F(1, 22) = 3.1$, $p = .09$) with numerically more errors in the near condition. There was no main effect or interaction involving subject group (all $Fs < 1.5$), and the critical interaction between congruence and hand separation did not approach significance ($F(1, 22) = 1.0$).

Discussion

As in our previous experiments, vibrotactile distractors on the irrelevant hand impaired vibrotactile discrimination on the relevant hand, delaying responses and increasing errors when they were incongruent. However, with the new requirement to face and fixate the irrelevant hand, this interference was no longer modulated by the separation of the hands in external space. In our three previous experiments, the interference had been reduced when the hands were placed further apart, which we have taken as evidence that spatial-tactile attention does not operate on a purely somatotopic representation but is affected by the current separation of relevant and irrelevant tactile receptors in external space. However, there was no such modulation by spatial separation in experiments 3a and 3b.

One explanation for this outcome is that, on bimanual trials, the direction of head and eyes toward the distractor boosts tactile processing of this stimulus relative to the target, for the far hand separation only. This would negate any benefit to the target from the more efficient spatial selection in the far condition that we have documented in the prior experiments. Certainly, any such effects of the direction of head and gaze would apply differentially to the near and far conditions. Under the near hand separation, head and eyes were directed in the general direction of both the distractor *and* the target; they were therefore unlikely to boost the processing of one relative to the other. Under the far hand separation, however, head and eyes were directed toward the distractor but *away* from the target and so might favor the former relative to the latter.

Thus, while experiment 2 demonstrated that the direction of head and gaze is not the *sole* factor behind the hand separation effect, the null result for experiment 3 suggests that head turning and gaze may nevertheless influence the efficiency of spatial tactile attention to some extent. Of course, this conclusion rests on a between-experiment comparison, namely, the contrast between the positive results of hand separation in experiments 1 and 2 and the null result for this manipulation in experiment 3. It would be worthwhile to corroborate the apparent effect of overt orienting in future studies using a within-subject manipulation, varying whether a given subject faces the relevant or irrelevant hand within one session.

Because the bimanual results of experiment 3 were equivalent for the blindfolded and seeing subjects, the suggested influence of the direction of head and/or eyes is presumably not visually mediated (consistent with Honoré, Bourdeaud'hui, and Sparrow's 1989 previous findings that the direction of gaze can affect tactile perception even in the dark). On the other hand, the unimanual results for experiment 3 did reveal some evidence for a difference between the two groups of subjects in the error data (see fig. 9.4). The seeing subjects made marginally more errors in the near condition than the far condition for these unimanual trials, whereas there was no such trend for the blindfolded subjects. We can only offer post hoc speculations concerning this unpredicted trend. It may be that subjects found it particularly hard to maintain fixation on the distracting hand when the relevant hand also fell into their field of view. (This would only apply for seeing subjects, and only in the near condition; the hand that the subjects were instructed *not* to fixate was always outside the field of view in the far condition in experiments 1 and 3.) Indeed, several of the nonblindfolded subjects spontaneously reported a difficulty in preventing fixation of the relevant hand in the near condition. Although this difficulty may have impaired performance for near unimanual trials, note that the apparent difficulty of the near condition for seeing subjects was not apparent in the bimanual trials. We can only conjecture that at this later point in the experiment, practice had reduced the difficulty of divorcing the direction of fixation from the direction of tactile attention within the field of view. We will not discuss these unimanual results further because the effect of hand separation in them for seeing subjects was both marginal and unpredicted.

9.6 GENERAL DISCUSSION

We began by noting that there have been very few studies of intermodal interactions in the control of attention (although see Hikosaka et al., chap. 10, this volume, for some recent exceptions). This dearth of multimodal research may be a considerable oversight because (1) many tasks require attention to be coordinated across the modalities, and this is a nontrivial computational problem; (2) many of the neural substrates traditionally associated with spatial attention (e.g., areas in parietal cortex or the superior colliculus) receive inputs from multiple senses, which appear to be closely interwoven and represented in spatiotopic register in at least some cases; and (3) fine-grained analysis of many ostensibly "unimodal" tasks reveals that several modalities may in fact be involved (e.g., proprioceptive and vestibular inputs can contribute to the representation of "visual" space).

From this perspective, we derived a new question concerning touch, a sense modality that poses particular integration problems because some of its most sensitive receptor organs (e.g., the fingertips) can adopt an indefinite number of different relative positions (Lederman, Browse, and Klatzky 1988). For this reason, coding the spatial properties of external objects by touch will often require integration of tactile information on the skin surface with other sources of information (e.g., proprioceptive or visual) about the current arrangement of the tactile receptors in external space. Such considerations led to our specific question of whether spatially selective tactile attention operates within a purely somatotopic representation (mirroring the anatomical organization of its input) or within a more abstract spatial frame of reference, as appropriate for the coding of external space. Our experiments clearly demonstrate that tactile attention is sensitive to some nonsomatotopic spatial factors.

In all five of our experiments, a congruence effect from vibrotactile distractors on a finger of one hand was found upon discrimination responses to a vibrotactile target on the homologous finger of the other hand. Responses were slower and less accurate when target and distractor were incongruent rather than congruent. This interference from incongruent distractors demonstrates that subjects could not completely exclude information on the irrelevant hand from processing. Because the distractors in all five experiments were always either congruent or incongruent, the interference effect does not entail that the distractors were identified in detail. Subjects may simply have been sensitive to whether the distractors were the same as the target, or differed from it, not to precisely how they differed. This could be examined in future experiments by including "neutral" distractors, which like incongruent distractors would differ from the target, but unlike them would have no association with the alternative response.

The critical issue in the present experiments, however, was the *modulation* of the distractor interference that we observed, rather than the level of distractor identification that it implied. In three of our experiments (1a, 1b, and 2), the interference from incongruent distractors was substantially reduced when the two hands were placed farther apart in external space, even though this manipulation did not alter the separation between target and distractor in somatotopic coordinates and did not affect the discriminability of tactile targets presented in isolation or with congruent distractors.

The observation of this nonsomatotopic distance effect in blindfolded subjects (experiment 1b) demonstrates a proprioceptive contribution to tactile-spatial attention. Proprioceptive information from the two arms is known to converge in area 5 of primate parietal cortex along with tactile information (Duffy and Burchfiel 1971), providing one possible substrate for the modulation of tactile attention by hand separation that we have observed. Representation of the body's disposition in space (the so-called body image) has long been considered to involve parietal networks, based on human lesion studies (Roth 1949). Our task and modifications thereof might be used to assess neurological abnormalities in body image quantitatively.

Experiment 2 showed that the modulation of tactile attention by hand separation is not solely caused by the direction of head and gaze toward the tactile target and away from the distractor. However, experiments 3a and 3b suggest that the direction of head and gaze can have an influence on tactile spatial attention (consistent with Honoré, Bourdeaud'hui, and Sparrow 1989; Larmande and Cambier 1981) because the reduction in interference when relevant and irrelevant hands were placed farther apart was eliminated if subjects faced and gazed toward the distractor and away from the target under this condition.

The effect of spatial separation between the hands in our first three experiments seems somewhat paradoxical when one considers that the imperative tactile stimuli were identical, in composition and placement on the skin, across the manipulation of hand separation. However, it makes more sense from a functional perspective (e.g., Gibson's 1966 approach to the senses), given that a primary purpose of tactile perception is presumably to code the real-world properties of external objects sensed through the skin. From this perspective, it seems essential that tactile stimulation, which arises in somatotopic coordinates, should ultimately get transformed into a representation of the external object producing that stimulation, in a more abstract spatial frame of reference. This will require integration of somatotopic tactile information with other sources of information about the current disposition of the tactile receptors in external space, such as the proprioceptive inputs implicated for the blindfolded subjects in experiment 1.

In chapter 12 of this volume, Jean Roll and colleagues suggest that proprioception provides a crucial link between personal and extrapersonal space; they base this argument primarily on visual performance. Our results and considerations suggest that the same may apply for tactile performance. While tactile input must by its nature arise in personal space (i.e., across the skin surface), it can be used to judge the properties of stimuli in external space. Representing external space through touch, however, must involve integration of somatotopic input with proprioceptive information about the current locus of the tactile receptors in external space.

Our results demonstrate that some aspects of tactile-spatial selectivity operate in a relatively abstract spatial frame of reference, which is sensitive to the current disposition of the hands in external space. Moscovitch and Behrmann (1994) have made a similar point on the basis of their tactile extinction study with unilateral parietal patients, as discussed earlier. Finally, a similar conclusion has recently been reached in a study of normal tactile attention by Rinker and Craig (1994). Their subjects had to judge the direction of motion for pins moved across one of their thumbs, while ignoring moving pins on the index finger of the same hand. Subjects were less accurate when the two concurrent motions were in different directions. By altering the posture of the hands, Rinker and Craig were able to show that the critical factor behind this interference effect from distractors was the direction of movement in *external* space, rather than the local somatotopic direction of movement across the finger pad.

The issue of the level of representation at which spatial tactile attention operates is reminiscent of similar questions that have recently arisen about the frame of reference(s) in which *visual*-spatial attention operates. Recent results for the visual case points to contributions from a number of coordinate systems (e.g. retinal, gravitational, trunk-centered, and even object-centered; see Driver and Halligan 1991; Driver, Baylis, and Rafal 1992; Karnath, Schenkel, and Fischer 1991; Làdavas 1987). In the light of such evidence for multiple coordinates in the visual case, the present findings of non-somatotopic contributions to tactile attention should certainly not be taken to imply that somatotopic factors *never* play any role in the control of tactile attention. Just as for vision, several coordinate systems may be involved, depending perhaps on the task and the level of representation required. Indeed, Evans and Craig (1991) have already demonstrated that somatotopic separation alone can modulate distractor interference for tactile stimuli under some circumstances.

The dearth of previous studies on intermodal interactions in attention is mirrored by a corresponding paucity of theories about any such interactions (although see Hikosaka et al., chap. 10, this volume). Perhaps the most influential recent theory of attention has been Treisman's feature integration theory, developed specifically for the visual case (e.g., Treisman 1988). The basic tenet of this well-known theory (at least in its original form) is that

Tactile Attention and the Representation of Space

spatial attention is required to combine correctly those visual features (e.g., color, orientation, etc.) that are coded separately in distinct feature maps. Each map has a spatiotopic organization that allows it to communicate with other maps via attention within a common spatial medium. One might be tempted to extend this theory from distinct features within a modality to the case of distinct modalities. After all, neuroscience has identified a number of modality-specific maps (as discussed in our introduction), which one might perhaps think of as analogous to the visual feature maps posited in Treisman's theory. The main prediction from such an adaptation of feature integration theory to the multimodal case would presumably be as follows. The coding of distinct features within a modality might proceed without attention, but integration between the modalities should only take place correctly for attended locations or objects.

We think our present findings warn against any such multimodal extension of feature integration theory, at least in the naive form presented above. We have found that tactile spatial attention can be sensitive to proprioceptive (and perhaps visual) inputs as well as to tactile inputs. It is difficult to see how the efficiency of spatial selection could be influenced by intermodal integration in this way if such integration were only to take place *after* the operation of spatial selection. A similar argument was made by Driver and Spence (1994) at the Attention and Performance XV meeting, but for the audiovisual case. As they discussed, Driver (1994) has observed that the ventriloquism effect, resulting from audiovisual integration of lip movements and speech, can affect the efficiency of selective shadowing. Once again, it is difficult to see how such intermodal integration could influence the efficiency of spatial attention if it were only to take place *after* the operation of spatial attention. The implication seems to be that at least some forms of audiovisual and proprioceptive-tactile integration can take place prior to attentional selection.

Although it remains to be established how pervasive such effects of intermodal integration on attention may be, at this juncture it seems that we may just be glimpsing the tip of a veritable iceberg.

NOTE

This research was supported by a Medical Research Council (U.K.) project grant (G9123295). Requests for reprints may be addressed to Dr. J. S. Driver, Department of Experimental Psychology, University of Cambridge, Downing Street, Cambridge, CB2 3EB, U.K. Our thanks to Charles Spence for helpful discussions, to Ian Cannell for taking the mug shots, and to the referees for their helpful comments.

REFERENCES

Allport, A. (1993). Attention and control: Have we been asking the wrong questions? A critical review of twenty-five years. In D. E. Meyer and S. Kornblum (Eds.), *Attention and Performance XIV*, 183–218. Cambridge, MA: MIT Press.

Axelrod, S., Thompson, L. W., and Cohen, L. D. (1968). Effects of senescence on the temporal resolution of somesthetic stimuli presented to one hand or both. *Journal of Gerontology, 23*, 191–195.

Baylis, G. C., Driver, J., and Rafal, R. (1993). Visual extinction and stimulus repetition. *Journal of Cognitive Neuroscience, 5*, 453–466.

Biguer, B., Donaldson, I. M. L., Hein, A., and Jeannerod, M. (1988). Neck muscle vibration modifies the representation of visual motion and detection in man. *Brain, 111*, 1405–1424.

Buchtel, H. A., and Butter, C. M. (1988). Spatial attention shifts: Implications for the role of polysensory mechanisms. *Neuropsychologia, 26*, 499–509.

Butter, C. M., Buchtel, H. A., and Santucci, R. (1989). Spatial attentional shifts: Further evidence for the role of polysensory mechanisms using visual and tactile stimuli. *Neuropsychologia, 27*, 1231–1240.

Cowey, A. (1985). Aspects of cortical organization related to selective attention and selective impairments of visual perception: A tutorial review. In M. I. Posner and O. S. M. Marin (Eds.), *Attention and Performance XI*, 41–62. Hillsdale, NJ: Erlbaum.

Craig, J. C. (1974). Vibrotactile difference thresholds for intensity and the effect of a masking stimulus. *Perception and Psychophysics, 15*, 123–127.

Craig, J. C. (1985). Tactile pattern perception and its perturbations, *Journal of the Acoustical Society of America, 77*, 238–246.

Driver, J. (1994). Crossmodal integration can affect the efficiency of selective listening and lip reading. Submitted.

Driver, J., Baylis, G. C., and Rafal, R. D. (1992). Preserved figure-ground segregation and symmetry perception in visual neglect. *Nature, 360*, 73–75.

Driver, J., and Halligan, P. W. (1991). Can visual neglect operate in object-centered coordinates? An affirmative single-case study. *Cognitive Neuropsychology, 8*, 475–496.

Driver, J., and Spence, C. J. (1994). Spatial synergies between auditory and visual attention. In C. Umlità and M. Moscovitch (Eds.), *Attention and Performance XV*, 311–331. Cambridge, MA: MIT Press.

Duffy, F. H., and Burchfiel, J. L. (1971). Somatosensory system: Organizational hierarchy from single units in monkey area 5. *Science, 172*, 273–275.

Eriksen, B. A., and Eriksen, C. W. (1974). Effects of noise-letters on identification of a target letter in a nonsearch task. *Perception and Psychophysics, 16*, 143–149.

Evans, P. M., and Craig, J. C. (1991). Tactile attention and the perception of moving stimuli. *Perception and Psychophysics, 49*, 355–364.

Farah, M. J., Wong, A. B., Monheit, M. A., and Morrow, L. A. (1989). Parietal lobe mechanisms of spatial attention: Modality-specific or supramodal? *Neuropsychologia, 27*, 461–470.

Gibson, J. J. (1966). *The senses considered as perceptual systems*. Boston: Houghton Mifflin.

Gilson, R. D. (1969). Vibrotactile masking: Some spatial and temporal aspects. *Perception and Psychophysics, 5*, 176–180.

Graziano, M. S. A., and Gross, C. G. (1993). A bimodal map of space: Somatosensory receptive-fields in the macaque putamen with corresponding visual receptive fields. *Experimental Brain Research, 97*, 96–109.

Grossenbacher, P. G. (1992). Interaction between vision and touch: Correspondence between frequency dimensions. Ph.D. diss., University of Oregon, Eugene.

Honoré, J., Bourdeaud'hui, M., Sparrow, L. (1989). Reduction of cutaneous reaction time by directing eyes towards the source of stimulation. *Neuropsychologia, 27*, 367–371.

Jeannerod, M. (1991). A neurophysiological model for the directional coding of reaching movements. In J. Paillard (Ed.), *Brain and space*, 49–69. Oxford: Oxford University Press.

Johnston, W. A., and Dark, V. J. (1986). Selective attention. *Annual Review of Psychology, 37*, 43–75.

Kahneman, D., and Treisman, A. (1984). Changing views of attention and automaticity. In R. Parasuraman and D. R. Davies (Eds.), *Varieties of attention*, 29–61. New York: Academic Press.

Karnath, H. O., Schenkel, P., and Fischer, B, (1991). Trunk orientation as the determining factor of the "contralateral" deficit in the neglect syndrome and as the physical anchor of the internal representation of body orientation in space. *Brain, 114*, 1997–2014.

King, A. J. (1993). A map of auditory space in the mammalian brain: Neural computation and development. *Experimental Physiology, 78*, 559–590.

Làdavas, E. (1987). Is the hemispatial deficit produced by right parietal lobe damage associated with retinal or gravitational coordinates? *Brain, 110*, 167–180.

Larmande, P., and Cambier, J. (1981). Influence de l'état d'activation hémisphérique sur le phénomène d'extinction sensitive chez 10 patients atteints de lésions hémisphériques droites. *Revue Neurologique, 137*, 285–290.

Lederman, S. J., Browse, R. A., and Klatzky, R. L. (1988). Haptic processing of spatially distributed information. *Perception and Psychophysics, 44*, 222–232.

Meyer, V., Gross, C. G., and Teuber, H. L. (1963). Effect of knowledge of site of stimulation on the threshold for pressure sensitivity. *Perceptual and Motor Skills, 16*, 637–640.

Morais, J. (1978) Spatial constraints on attention to speech. In J. Requin (Ed.), *Attention and Performance VII*, 245–260. Hillsdale, NJ: Erlbaum.

Moray, N. (1969). *Attention: Selective processes in vision and hearing*. London: Hutchinson.

Moscovitch, M., and Behrmann, M. (1994). Coding of spatial information in the somatosensory system: Evidence from patients with neglect following parietal lobe damage. *Journal of Cognitive Neuroscience, 6*, 151–155.

Pierson, J. M., Bradshaw, J. L., Meyer, T. F., Howard, M. J., and Bradshaw, J. A. (1991). Direction of gaze during vibrotactile choice reaction time tasks. *Neuropsychologia, 29*, 925–928.

Posner, M. I. (1990). Hierarchical distributed networks in the neuropsychology of selective attention. In A. Caramazza (Ed.), *Cognitive neuropsychology and neurolinguistics: Advances in models of cognitive function and impairment*, 187–210. Hillsdale, NJ: Erlbaum.

Rafal, R., and Robertson, L. (1995). The neurology of visual attention. In M. Gazzaniga (Ed.), *The cognitive neurosciences*, 625–648. Cambridge, MA: MIT Press.

Rinker, M. A., and Craig, J. C. (1994). The effect of spatial orientation on the perception of moving tactile stimuli. *Perception and Psychophysics, 56*, 356–362.

Roth, M. (1949). Disorders of the body image caused by lesions of the right parietal lobe. *Brain, 72*, 89–111.

Sherrick, C. E. (1964). Effects of double simultaneous stimulation of the skin. *American Journal of Physiology, 77*, 42–53.

Sherrick, C. E., and Cholewiak, R. W. (1986). Cutaneous sensitivity. In K. R. Boff, L. Kaufman, and J. P. Thomas (Eds.), *Handbook of perception and human Performance: Sensory processes and perception*, vol. 12, 1–58. New York: Wiley.

Spence, C. M., and Driver, J. (1995a). Audiovisual links in exogenous covert orienting. *Perception and Psychophysics*, in press.

Spence, C. M., and Driver, J. (1995b). Audiovisual links in endogenous covert orienting. *Journal of Experimental Psychology: Human Perception and Performance*.

Stein, B. E., and Meredith, M. A. (1993). *The merging of the senses.* Cambridge, MA: MIT Press.

Stein, J. (1992). The representation of egocentric space in the posterior parietal cortex. *Behavioral and Brain Sciences, 15*, 691–700.

Treisman, A. (1988). Features and objects: The fourteenth Bartlett memorial lecture. *Quarterly Journal of Experimental Psychology, 40A*, 201–237.

Uttal, W. R. (1960). Inhibitory interaction of responses to electrical stimuli in the fingers. *Journal of Comparative and Physiological Psychology, 53*, 47–51.

Ward, L. M. (1994). Supramodal and modality-specific mechanisms for stimulus-driven shifts of auditory and visual attention. *Canadian Journal of Psychology, 48*, 242–259.

Weisenberger, J. M. (1981). Tactile pattern similarity. Ph.D. diss., Indiana University, Bloomington.

Whang, K. C., Burton, H., and Shulman, G. L. (1991). Selective attention in vibrotactile tasks: Detecting the presence and absence of amplitude change. *Perception and Psychophysics, 50*, 157–165.

Woolsey, C. N. (Ed.). (1981). *Cortical sensory organization.* Vol. 1, *Multiple somatic areas.* Clifton, NJ: Humana Press.

10 Multimodal Spatial Attention Visualized by Motion Illusion

Okihide Hikosaka, Satoru Miyauchi,
Hiroshige Takeichi, and Shinsuke Shimojo

ABSTRACT

We previously found that the gradient of attention can express itself visually in an illusory motion perceived in a line. The motion illusion was produced by both stimulus-induced (bottom-up) and voluntary (top-down) attention, which suggested that the two kinds of attention act on relatively early stages of visual processing. The objective of our study was to examine how various modes of spatial attention might be represented and reorganized in the brain. Using the induction of illusory line motion as a measure we found that (1) once attention is captured by a moving object, it follows the object as it moves; and (2) attention moves with a saccade in the retinal coordinates such that its focus remains fixed in space. We then asked whether attention acts across different sensory modalities. We found that both auditory and somatosensory cues induced focal visual attention at the location in space where the cue was presented. Based on these findings, we propose a model that would allow (1) matching of visual spatial information obtained across saccades; and (2) matching of spatial information obtained in different sensory modalities.

10.1 INTRODUCTION

Our studies on attention have relied on a simple illusion of visual motion that, we believe, can be used to express the strength of attention and its gradient. This measure, which we call "line motion effect," is appealing because it is simple and direct.

In this chapter we will examine how space or spatial attention might be represented in the brain. We have examined this issue from different aspects by using the line motion effect. There are two behavioral situations that were especially relevant to this problem. First, we ask whether attention moves when the eye moves. If so, does attention move with respect to the eye or space? Second, we ask whether attention acts across different sensory modalities. If so, how is somatosensory or auditory position translated into visual position, and vice versa? These questions are crucial because both movements and coordinate systems are relative.

We will first summarize our previous findings on the nature of spatial attention and then show some new data that are particularly relevant to the representation of space in the brain. Finally, we will present some models to account for the results and raise further questions.

10.2 ATTENTION VISUALIZED BY MOTION ILLUSION

We have indicated previously that the gradient of attention can be visualized by a motion illusion in a probe line (Hikosaka, Miyauchi, and Shimojo 1993a). A typical example is schematized in figure 10.1, where a small spot of light, which we called a "cue stimulus" (C), was used to attract attention of the subject. While the subject kept fixating a center spot (F), the cue stimulus was presented either to the right or to the left. After a random time interval (cue lead time) a probe line was presented, connecting the two possible cue locations. A striking motion illusion was perceived such that the line appeared to grow in length over time, emanating from the cue stimulus, even though the line was presented physically all at once. The line motion effect was strongest when the cue lead time was between 50 and 150 ms, weaker with longer or shorter cue lead times, and virtually absent with zero lead time.

This finding was correlated with a well-known effect of attention—local acceleration of sensory information processing (Sternberg and Knoll 1973; Maylor 1985; Stelmach and Herdman 1991): when two visual stimuli are presented simultaneously at different locations and the subject has attended to one of the two locations, the attended stimulus appears to precede the other. For the two stimuli to appear simultaneous, the unattended stimulus must precede the attended stimulus by up to 100 ms.

On the other hand, the judgment of temporal order is often difficult and requires many trials to reach a conclusion. The ambiguity virtually disappeared when we used an array of spots or bars or a single line. The line

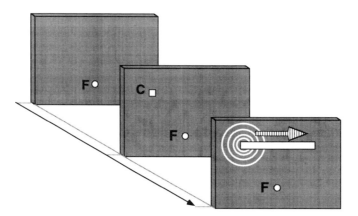

Figure 10.1 Gradient of attention is visualized by illusory motion in line. *Method*: While subject was fixating (frame 1), cue stimulus (C) was presented on right or left (frame 2). After random time interval, line was presented between two cue locations (frame 3). *Result*: Line appeared to stick out from cue stimulus. *Interpretation*: Onset of cue stimulus produces focus of attention (as illustrated by concentric white lines around cued location) that accelerates visual information processing in its neighborhood. Visual signals derived from then-presented line reach central motion detector sequentially from cued location outward, thus producing sensation of motion.

motion effect is a sensitive measure to detect the strength of attention and its gradient.

Let us consider the process by which the visual information from the probe line in figure 10.1 might be fed into a motion detector. A line can be regarded as a linear aggregate of spots of light. If the spots come on sequentially from left to right, the corresponding visual signals reach the motion detector sequentially, which will activate the motion detector. If the spots come on simultaneously, the visual signals reach the motion detector simultaneously, so that no motion will be detected. This is the case, however, only when the visual signals are processed at the same speed among the different spots. What happens if attention is directed selectively to one end of the line? As shown in the temporal order judgment task, attention will increase the speed of visual processing locally, that is, the attended signal will reach the motion detector earlier. In the experiment in figure 10.1, attention was attracted passively by the cue stimulus. If we assume that the effect of attention decays outward from its locus (as shown schematically by concentric white rings at the location of the cue stimulus in fig. 10.1), the visual signals will reach the motion detector sequentially from the attended side (e.g., from left in fig. 10.1) to the unattended side (e.g., right). The motion detector will be deceived and hence indicate that motion has occurred (e.g., from left).

A motion detector can be regarded as a sensitive detector of sequence (Biederman-Thorson, Thorson, and Lange 1971; Nakayama 1985). But it works only when the sequential events occur in close proximity. Thanks to the high sensitivity of the motion detector, the experimental paradigm in figure 10.1 allowed us to detect subtle differences in the speed of visual processing. The illusory motion in the line thus represents the spatial gradient of attention.

Using the line motion method, we and other investigators (von Grünau and Faubert 1994) have shown that almost all kinds of visual transients produce a focus of attention at the site of the transients. This includes onset and offset of a luminant stimulus, onset of an equiluminant color stimulus, a change in color, a change in shape, a change in depth, and so forth.

Quantitative data were obtained using a cancellation method (Miyauchi, Hikosaka, and Shimojo 1991, 1992). Consider the situation shown in figure 10.1. If the spots constituting the line are presented sequentially from right to left with appropriate time intervals, the attention-induced asynchrony of visual processing should be canceled. Our results indeed showed that this is the case. The physical asynchrony required for the cancellation can thus be defined as "the differential of the magnitude of attention" between the endpoints of the line.

With the cancellation method we can see the distribution of an attentional field. First, for example, we presented two spots of light and asked the subject to attend to the right spot, followed by a short probe line at a random position, to the right or left of the attended or unattended spot. If the subject perceived motion in the line, he adjusted the asynchrony of line drawing until he perceived no motion. The degree of asynchrony required for the cancellation would indicate the differential of the function representing the attentional field; the attentional field was thus obtained by integrating the differential values across space. Our results showed that both onset and offset of a spot of light produced a strong focus of attention that decayed outward quasi-exponentially. A similar result was obtained by Steinman, Steinman, and Lehmkuhle (1995).

We have shown so far that attention locally accelerates visual information processing. Where in the central visual areas does the acceleration occur? Our line motion measure gives some clue to answering this question. For a motion to be perceived, attention must act at a level (or levels) *before* the motion detector. If we assume that the motion detector is in area MT, the site of the attentional effect should precede MT.

How much earlier is the site of the attentional effect? Does it occur before or after visual signals reach the visual cortex? Before or after binocular convergence? We designed a dichoptic viewing experiment to answer this question (Hikosaka, Miyauchi, and Shimojo 1993a). In the experiment as shown in figure 10.1, we presented the cue stimulus and the probe line to different eyes (e.g., cue to right eye, line to left eye). We found that the same magnitude of motion sensation was perceived in this condition. This suggests that the effect of attention acts after binocular convergence—perhaps in or after the primary visual cortex (V1) (Hubel and Wiesel 1962).

These results led to the hypothesis that attention acts on some visual cortical areas between V1 and MT. But there are multiple routes from V1 to MT, including a direct connection from V1 to MT, a route via V2 and V3, and a pathway via V4 (Ungerleider and Desimone 1986). Subcortical areas such as the superior colliculus and pulvinar may well contribute to this process (Robinson and McClurkin 1989). In addition, we cannot exclude the possibility that motion sensation may occur at stages later than MT (Colby, Duhamel, and Goldberg 1993).

10.3 BOTH BOTTOM-UP ATTENTION AND TOP-DOWN ATTENTION ACT ON EARLY VISUAL PROCESSING

Attention has two aspects—passive (bottom-up or stimulus-induced) and active (top-down or voluntary). Does active attention act on cognitive processes that occur after sensory processes? Or does it act on the early levels of visual processing, as does passive attention? If the latter is true, we would expect that illusory motion can be induced by active attention.

The latter hypothesis was confirmed by the experiment shown in figure 10.2 (Hikosaka, Miyauchi, and Shimojo 1993b). While the subject was fixating a center-lower spot, red and green squares came on; their lateral positions were randomized. The subject was required to attend to either one of the squares (e.g., green square) as quickly as possible after its onset. Eye

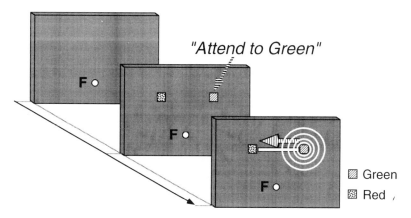

"Attend to Green"

■ Green
▨ Red

Figure 10.2 Voluntary attention is similarly detected by illusory line motion. *Method*: Green and red squares were presented simultaneously, their lateral positions randomized (frame 2). Subject was instructed to attend, say, to green square throughout block of trials. Probe line was presented between two squares (frame 3). *Result*: Motion was perceived in line if time interval between onset of squares and line was sufficiently long (>300 ms). *Interpretation*: As in case of passive attention (fig. 10.1), focus of attention is generated around the attended object (green square).

movements were not allowed. After a random period of time (cue lead time), a probe line was presented between the two squares, and the subject reported the side from which the line was perceived to be drawn. When the cue lead time was long enough (>300 ms), the subject clearly perceived motion that was directed from the attended square (e.g., green square). In the next block of experiment, we changed the square to be attended (e.g., red square) and the direction of the illusory motion reversed (e.g., from red to green).

To summarize these results, active attention produces an illusory sensation of motion, as does passive attention, and its direction is from the attended object to the unattended object. This suggests that active (top-down) attention, as well as passive (bottom-up) attention, locally accelerates early visual processing. This, of course, does not preclude the possibility that attentional effects are exerted at stages later than perception (e.g., motor program or memory storage).

What happens if these two types of attention occur simultaneously? To answer this question, we modified the experiment shown in figure 10.2 (Hikosaka, Miyauchi, and Shimojo 1993b). While the subject was attending to, say, the green square, the red square was flashed. If the probe line was presented just after the flash of the red square, robust motion was perceived from the side of the red square, opposite to the direction that would have been perceived had it not been for the flash. This reversal of illusory motion indicates that the flash-induced passive attention overcame and nullified the preexisting active attention. The reversal occurred immediately after (<50 ms) the flash and continued at least for 400 ms. The subject had to exert strong effort in order to re-reverse the direction of attention to the green square.

The result leads to the following suggestion. Active attention can easily and quickly be distracted by a local change in the visual field. But passive attention is generally short-lasting, and thus could be followed by active attention. Thanks to this type of interaction, we can concentrate on a task and yet can respond quickly to an external event.

The information producing active attention probably originates in non-sensory areas, especially frontal and parietal cortical areas (Posner and Petersen 1990). If our hypothesis is correct, the information must reach the early stages of visual processing. Are there such routes?

It is known that connections between different cortical areas are almost always mutual. There are polysynaptic connections from V1 via area MT and parietal association cortex to the frontal association cortex. This suggests that there are reverse connections from the frontal association cortex to V1 (Van Essen and Maunsell 1983). Such reverse connections may play an important role in active attention. It may take a considerable amount of time before such polysynaptic, transcortical connections become fully activated. In fact, in the experiment shown in figure 10.2, active attention developed gradually, reaching its peak after 300 ms. This contrasted with passive attention (fig. 10.1), which developed within 100 ms.

10.4   SHIFT OF ATTENTION WITH OBJECT MOVEMENT: ATTENTION FOLLOWS A MOVING OBJECT

We have shown that a local change in the visual field produces a focus of attention at the location where the change occurred. What happens if the object that produced the local transient moves? Consider the experiment in figure 10.1. The onset of the cue stimulus (spot of light) draws our attention. Is attention directed to the location of the spot? Or is it directed to the spot itself? In this experiment the location and the object were not differentiated.

We therefore carried out the following experiment (fig. 10.3; Hikosaka, Miyauchi, and Shimojo 1993b). While the subject was fixating a central spot, four blue spots appeared and rotated around the fixation point. One of the four spots was brightened briefly, and then all the four spots continued to rotate. After a random amount of rotation (90, 180, 270, or 360 degrees) a probe line came on, connecting two of the four spots. Consider the situation in which the line came on after a 90° rotation (fig. 10.3). The right end of the line marks the flashed location, while the left end marks the flashed spot, not its location. Our results showed that motion was perceived always to emanate from the flashed spot, but not its location. To summarize, once attention is drawn to a moving object, the attention does not stay at the initial location but follows the object as it moves.

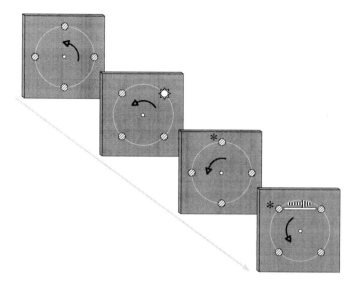

Figure 10.3 Object, once attended, carries attention as it moves. *Method*: Four blue spots appeared and rotated around fixation point (frame 1). One of them was flashed (frame 2) and four spots continued to rotate (frame 3). Probe line was presented between location where spot had been flashed (right-up) and current location of the flashed spot (left-up) (frame 4). *Result*: Motion was perceived from flashed spot (from left to right). *Interpretation*: Attention is bound to moving object, not to location where stimulus is presented.

10.5 SHIFT OF ATTENTION WITH EYE MOVEMENT: ATTENTION REMAINS IN SPACE, NOT IN THE RETINA

We have shown that attention moves with a moving object. Now what happens to attention if the eye moves? Does attention remain stationary, at the same position in the retinal coordinates? If so, then the attentional focus should shift in space with the saccade. Or does the attentional focus remain stationary in space? If so, then the focus should shift in the retinal coordinate, but in the direction opposite to the saccade.

Consider the situation shown in figure 10.4. Suppose a cue stimulus is briefly flashed to the left of your line of sight and you make a saccade to the left across the stimulus. Now where is the focus of attention?

To answer these questions, we performed the following three experiments.

Experiment 1: Is Attention Locked in Space or in the Retina?

Methods

Subjects Four subjects participated in this experiment: two experienced (authors) and two naive.

Apparatus and stimuli A microcomputer (NEC PC9821Ap2) was used for stimulus presentation and the control of experiments. The visual stimuli

Is attention directed to a point in space or in retina?

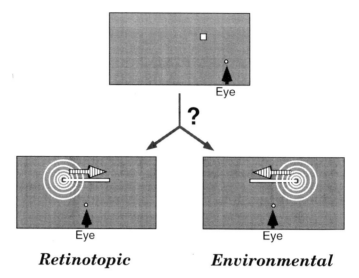

Figure 10.4 Does attention move with saccadic eye movement? Suppose spot of light is presented in left visual field and then saccade occurs to left across location of cue stimulus. Is focus of attention induced by light spot bound to retinal location of cue stimulus (left) or to its location in space (right)? This can be tested by presenting probe line between two locations, as shown in figure 10.5.

(fixation point, cue stimulus, and probe line) were displayed on a color CRT display; the frame rate was 56 Hz. The fixation point was a green cross and the cue stimulus was a green rectangle ($0.35° \times 0.35°$); the probe line was white, 0.1 degree in width and 6.5 degrees in length. The luminance of these stimuli was 60 cd/m². The stimuli were presented on a dark background (< 0.2 cd/m²).

Procedure The subject sat in front of the CRT display in a dark room. The observation distance was 57 cm. The subject's head was restrained by a chin rest. The subject initiated each trial by pressing a key. The fixation point then appeared in the center of the screen on which the subject had to fixate (fig. 10.5). After 0.7–1.4 seconds, the fixation point stepped to the right or left by 6.5 degrees, and the subject had to follow the step by making a saccade. The direction of the step was randomized. After 50 ms following the step of the fixation point (before the saccade started), the cue stimulus was presented briefly (17 ms) at one of two positions, which fell at the midpoints horizontally between the center and the two peripheral locations of the fixation point and 5.5 degrees above them. After the saccade, the probe line was presented directly above the new location of the fixation point. The line was presented physically at once. The interval between the end of the saccade and

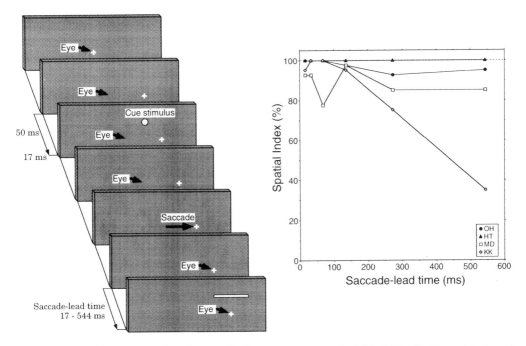

Figure 10.5 Attention remains in space across saccade. *Method* (left): Fixation point stepped from center to right or left (frame 1 to frame 2), and 50 ms later cue stimulus was briefly presented (17 ms) on right or left, halfway to location of peripheral fixation point (frame 3). Saccade then occurred to new fixation point (frame 5). At random interval after the end of the saccade (saccade lead time, 17–544 ms), probe line was presented directly above new fixation point (frame 7). *Result* (right): Spatial index (see text) was calculated for each cue lead time and was plotted against the saccade lead time for each subject. Subjects perceived motion in line from environmental location, not retinal location, of cue stimulus in most of trials.

the onset of the probe line (saccade lead time) was randomized between 17 and 544 ms in 6 steps.

There are four conditions of stimulus arrangement: right saccade and right cue (RS-RC), right saccade and left cue (RS-LC), left saccade and left cue (LS-LC), and left saccade and right cue (LS-RC). In the RS-RC and LS-LC conditions, the probe line was presented such that its medial end was aligned at the *spatial* location of the cue stimulus that was now absent, while its lateral end was at the *retinal* location of the cue stimulus (see fig. 10.5 for RS-RC condition). In the RS-LC and LS-RC conditions, the medial end of the probe line corresponded to the retinal location of the cue stimulus, while the lateral end was at neither the spatial nor retinal position of the cue stimulus.

The subject's task was to report in which direction the line appeared to be drawn by pressing one of three keys that were assigned to (1) answers from left, (2) answers from right, and (3) no motion. The experiment was carried out as a single block, with the direction of the saccade (× 2), the side of the cue stimulus (× 2), and the saccade lead time (× 6) all randomized. Ten trials were tested for each condition, so that each block contained a total of 240 trials ($2 \times 2 \times 6 \times 10$).

Eye movement recording Horizontal and vertical eye positions were recorded with electro-oculography (EOG) and were digitized at 500 Hz. The start and end of a targeting saccade were determined by a velocity threshold criterion: a saccade was judged to start and end when the instantaneous velocity became greater or smaller, respectively, than 100 deg/sec. Presentation of the probe line was timed from the end the saccade (see "Procedure").

Analysis Among the four conditions described above, we analyzed two conditions, RS-RC and LS-LC, in which the probe line was presented between the environmental position and the retinal position of the cue stimulus. Such a conflict situation allowed us to examine which of the two cue positions was more effective in inducing attention. The other two conditions were invalid in this sense because the environmental position fell outside the probe line.

To quantify how selectively the attention was directed at the environmental position compared with the nonenvironmental position, we defined a spatial index, which was calculated as follows. A trial with the answer indicating the environmental position of attention (e.g., "from left" in case of the RS-RC condition; see fig. 10.5) was assigned 2 points; a trial with the answer indicating no motion was assigned 1 point; and a trial with the answer indicating the nonenvironmental position of attention was assigned 0 points. We then calculated the total points for the 20 trials (excluding the trials in which the environmental position of the cue was outside the line) for each saccade lead time. This value (e.g., 30) was normalized as a percentage of the complete environmental focusing of attention which was 40 (2×20) (e.g., 75 percent).

Results and Comments In figure 10.5 we plotted the spatial index against the saccade lead time for each subject. The index was close to 100 percent at short saccade lead times, indicating that motion sensation was clearly perceived in the line and that its direction was almost always from the environmental position of the cue stimulus, not from the retinal position.

The index tended to decrease at longer saccade lead times. This is not surprising; we had previously shown that the focal attention produced by a light flash was initially strong (at about 100 ms) and then became gradually weaker (Hikosaka, Miyauchi, and Shimojo 1993a). Because in this experiment the interval between the cue stimulus and the end of the saccade was 165, 143, 170, 192 ms for the subjects HT, OH, KK, MD, respectively, the probe line was presented about 687–736 ms after the cue stimulus when the saccade lead time was 544 ms, the period at which focal attention is expected to be fading away.

Experiment 2: Control—Relation to Saccade Direction

In experiment 1, the direction of the perceived motion turned out to be the same as the direction of saccade. One might therefore argue that the perceived motion was causally related the direction of the saccade, not attention. To exclude the possibility, we modified the experiment such that the motion sensation was expected to occur in the direction same or opposite to the saccade direction.

Methods The same four subjects participated in this experiment and the same apparatus was used.

Procedure Unlike in experiment 1, the fixation point first appeared at a peripheral position (right or left) and then shifted to the center. The probe line was presented directly above the central fixation point. The cue stimulus was presented at one of the two positions between which the probe line would appear.

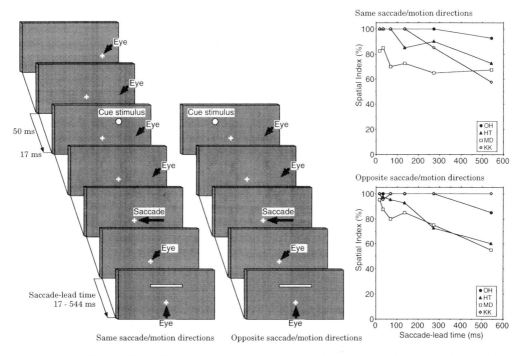

Figure 10.6 Direction of motion of line does not depend on saccade direction. *Method* (left): Same as experiment shown in figure 10.5, except that fixation point stepped from peripheral location (right or left) to center. Environmental location of cue stimulus was on right (left column) or left (right column) of line. *Result* (right): Spatial index is shown separately for two conditions shown on left. Subjects perceived motion in line from environmental location of cue stimulus, regardless of saccade direction.

Results and Comments Robust motion sensation was perceived again from the environmental position of the previously flashed cue stimulus. In the LS-RC condition (leftward saccade and right cue stimulus, as shown in fig. 10.6, left), the illusory motion was perceived from the right, in the same direction as the saccade, while in the LS-LC condition (leftward saccade and left cue stimulus, as shown in fig. 10.6, right), the motion was from the left, opposite to the saccade direction.

The spatial index was plotted separately for these conditions: for the conditions in which the line motion was expected to be in the same direction as the saccade (LS-RC, RS-LC) (fig. 10.6, left top) and for the conditions in which the line motion was expected to be the opposite to the saccade (LS-LC, RS-RC) (fig. 10.6, left bottom). The results indicate again that the focus of attention depended on the environmental position of the cue stimulus and that the line motion effect was unrelated to the direction of the saccade.

This experiment would further refute a possible retinal effect. A light flash by the cue stimulus might produce a negative aftereffect, namely, suppression of subsequent visual processing at the stimulated site. The suppressed retinal locus would, after the saccade, be aligned at the left end of the probe line so that the visual information from this region might reach the motion detector after the other regions of the line, thus producing a motion illusion from the right side. However, this explanation cannot be applied to the LS-LC condition because the stimulated retinal locus was further left to the probe line, yet the motion was perceived from the left, inconsistent with the possibility described above.

Experiment 3: Control—Phosphor on the Screen

We considered another possible artifact: phosphor remaining on the CRT screen after the brief presentation of the cue stimulus might act to induce attention. To examine this possibility, we used a decrease in luminance for the cue stimulus (fig. 10.7).

Methods The two experienced subjects performed these experiments and the same apparatus was used.

Procedure The procedure was the same as for experiment 2, except that a gray background was used and the cue stimulus was a black rectangle (0.65° × 0.65°). Before the experiment, we confirmed that the black cue stimulus was effective in inducing attention when no eye movement was allowed.

Results and Comments The results were qualitatively the same as those in experiment 2: the two subjects perceived the sensation of motion to emanate from the environmental position of the black cue stimulus.

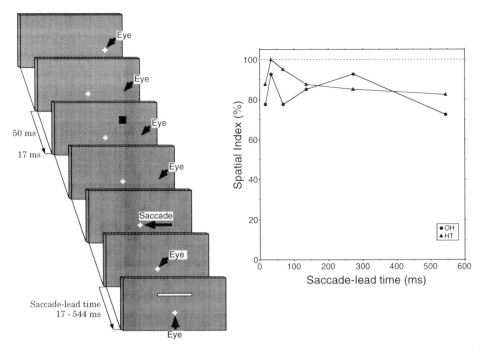

Figure 10.7 Motion illusion is not produced by physical artifact. *Method* (left): Same as experiment shown in figure 10.6, except that gray background was used on which black cue stimulus was presented (frame 3). *Result* (right): Subjects perceived motion in line from environmental location of cue stimulus in most trials.

Discussion for Experiments 1–3

Experiments 1–3 showed that the focus of attention remains stationary in space even when the visual field shifts by a saccadic eye movement. The behavioral significance of this result is twofold. First, an attentional focus (or attentional foci) may be present outside the goal of the saccade. This is not to say that there is no attentional focus at the goal of the saccade. In fact, it has been indicated that attention moves with a saccade toward the same location and that the movement of attention precedes the movement of the eye. Our experiments, in agreement with Posner and Cohen (1984), indicated that attention is not always localized at the saccade goal but may be present at a separate location. This conclusion seems reasonable when we consider behavioral situations such as visual search. Say you are a man talking with a woman friend of yours. When you talk with your friend, you may look at her mouth or nose while your attention may well be directed to her eyes. The result seems also consistent with the physiology of saccadic eye movements. We make saccades incessantly, even in total darkness, though we may not be aware of them. Such saccades, often called "spontaneous saccades", would not require activation of higher-order neurons in the central nervous system, such as the cerebral cortex (e.g., frontal eye field) or the basal ganglia (e.g., caudate nucleus or substantia nigra) (Goldberg and Segraves 1989; Hikosaka and Wurtz 1989).

The second behavioral significance is the robustness of attention in terms of location. This is desirable but not trivial because attention was induced by a visual input through the eyes, which then rotated by a saccade (see model of neural mechanisms below). To examine how desirable this feature is, let us consider the visual search again with the same example. If your friend winks, it may well be very attractive and your attention would be drawn to her eye. Now if she winks just before you make a saccade from her nose to her ear, you would not want to have your attention directed to a location somewhere outside her face as would be expected if attention were retinotopic.

Posner and Cohen (1984), using a cued reaction time task, reached a different conclusion: the focus of attention moved in the environment (or remained stationary with respect to the eyes). In their experiment, a cue stimulus (to induce attention) came on simultaneously with or prior to a saccade target and a probe stimulus (to which the subject responded) was presented after the saccade. In this study the reaction time was shortest when the probe stimulus was presented at the retinal location, not at the environmental location. The time interval between the cue stimulus and the probe stimulus was probably more than 250 ms, given the saccade latency and duration, although the authors did not mention the actual values. We think that this interval was too long: they have repeatedly shown that visual cueing shortens reaction time only during a very short period following the cuing (about 200 ms); beyond this point, lengthening of the reaction time was consistently observed (which Posner and Cohen called "inhibition of return").

10.6 MODEL TO EXPLAIN THE SPACE-BOUND NATURE OF ATTENTION

Our experiments have shown that attention is kept stationary in the environment. This is remarkable because most central neurons encode the position of an object by the retinal coordinates (i.e., they tell where the object is with respect to the line of sight) and because our previous line motion experiments suggested that attention acts on early stages of visual information processing. Because attention is induced by a visual input and should act on central visual neurons, both constrained by the retinal coordinates and ignorant of space in general, some mechanism must be at work that would compensate for the saccade. We therefore present the following model of the underlying mechanisms (see fig. 10.8).

In this model we assume that all visual information is encoded in retinal coordinates (with respect to the direction of gaze). Let us examine the behavioral situation shown at the bottom of figure 10.8. The cue stimulus is presented before the saccade in the left visual field. The visual information would be fed into the visual areas in the right hemisphere, first into the sim-

Shift of Attention with Saccade

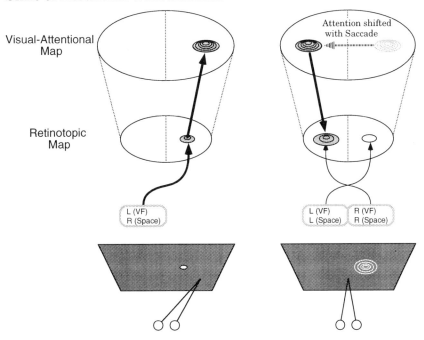

Figure 10.8 Model to explain how focus of attention might be kept stationary in space across saccade.

ple retinotopic map and then into another map, which we call the "visual-attentional map," where a focus of attention is generated.

A unique feature of this map is that the focus of attention shifts simultaneously with every saccade. Here the saccade occurs to the left across the location of the cue stimulus, and the focus of attention also shifts to the left perhaps across hemispheres. The shifted focus of attention would now enhance visual inputs from the right visual field, corresponding to the previous location of the cue stimulus.

What is striking here is that the shift operation is performed in such a short period of saccade. This would probably require that the visual-attentional map be retinotopically organized and that local neural activity move nearly linearly across the map.[1]

Let us consider how neurons might behave in the visual-attentional map. Suppose the attentional shift occurs simultaneously with the saccade in the situation as shown in figure 10.8, bottom. A transient visual input would come from the left visual field, and a locus in the visual-attentional map on the right side would initially be activated (fig. 10.8, left), which then would be replaced by a new locus in the left visual-attentional map because of the attentional shift (fig. 10.8, right). Neurons at the initial attentional focus would stop discharging; instead, neurons at the new (shifted) focus would start discharging even though the visual stimulus, now absent, had never been presented inside the neurons' receptive field. Indeed, Duhamel, Colby, and Goldberg (1992) and Colby (chap. 7, this volume) found that neurons in the monkey parietal cortex (LIP) behave exactly in this manner.

Although our data suggest that the attentional shift should be completed by the end of a saccade, it is possible that the shift starts before the saccade. If so (and assuming the visual stimulus remains on), neurons in the newly activated locus would start responding to the visual stimulus, which currently fell outside its receptive field but will fall inside the receptive field after the upcoming saccade. Such predictive behavior was indeed observed in some (not all) neurons in the LIP (Colby, chap. 7, this volume). These comparisons suggest that the visual-attentional map is either in the parietal cortex or intimately connected with it.

Another important question is, Is the shift of an activity focus really feasible and likely to occur? Physiological data relevant to this idea have been obtained by Munoz and Wurtz (1995). It has been well known that neurons in the intermediate layer of the superior colliculus determine the vector of a saccade by sending phasic burst signals to the saccadic generators in the brainstem. Just beneath the burst layer, but still in the intermediate layer, Munoz and Wurtz found a sublayer in which a focus of neural activity moves during the saccade from a retinotopic site corresponding to the saccade vector toward the central foveal region. This phenomenon, as they argued, would represent a key mechanism for the control of a saccade and in addition might be related to the shift of attentional focus, as discussed above.

We do not claim that the physiological substrate of the visual-attentional map is the superior colliculus. We would expect that similar traveling wave mechanisms are present in other visual areas, perhaps provided that they consist of precise retinotopic maps. It should be noted, however, that our model cannot describe space in general because position information is encoded with respect to the direction of gaze. This might be a serious drawback if we consider space from the viewpoint of the somatosensory or auditory modalities.

10.7 CROSS-MODAL SPATIAL ATTENTION DEPENDS ON SPACE, NOT ON HEMISPHERE

Although we have examined spatial attention using visual stimuli as both attentional cue and probe, the concept of space is also constructed from somatosensory and auditory information and from body movements. Spatial attention should thus extend to the nonvisual sensory modalities. To test this hypothesis, we performed a line motion experiment using nonvisual stimuli as cues (Shimojo et al., chap. 23, this volume). Auditory cues (beeps) were elicited from speakers located beside the CRT screen on which the probe line was presented. Somatosensory cues (electric pulses) were applied to the tips of the index fingers of both hands, which were placed beneath the ends of the probe line (fig. 10.9, left).

Cross-modal Spatial Attention (somatosensory to visual)

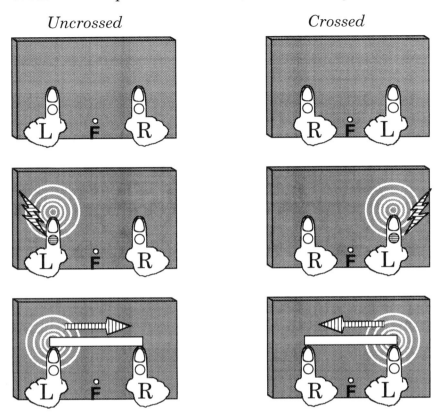

Figure 10.9 Cross-modal spatial attention: somatosensory-to-visual effect is bound to space, not to hemisphere. *Method*: Stimulating electrodes were attached to tips of right and left index fingers, which were placed at locations between which probe line would appear. Somatosensory cue (short train of electric pulses) was applied to one of index fingers, and then line was presented. Experiments were performed in two conditions: when subjects did not cross (left) and crossed (right) their hands. *Result*: Subjects perceived motion in line from location where cue stimulus was applied, regardless of side of hand stimulated.

We found that a similar illusory motion was evoked by these nonvisual cues: the line motion was perceived to emanate from the side on which the auditory or somatosensory cues were applied. Its time course was similar to the one obtained when a brief visual stimulation was used as the cue: the sensation of motion was most robust immediately (0–100 ms) after the onset of the cues and diminished thereafter.

A peculiar feature was that the nonvisual cues were often effective even when they were presented up to 100 ms *after* the probe line.[2] Such a paradoxical reversal of temporal order may be explained by the difference in the central processing times between different sensory modalities. The simple reaction time, for example, was longest to the visual stimulus, followed by somatosensory and auditory stimuli in this order, the difference ranging between 30 and 87 ms.[3]

Obviously, the spatial information derived from sensory information depends on the direction or position of the sensory organ, as we have noted for the effect of saccades on the attentional focus. The hand is also quite mobile and therefore the spatial information from the hand should critically depend on its position. We therefore examined the effect of hand position on the line motion effect. The subjects, by crossing their hands, placed the right index finger on the left side and the left index finger on the right side (fig. 10.9, right). When electrical stimulation was applied, say, to the left hand (which was placed on the right side), the line motion sensation was perceived from the right side most of the time. The onset of the line motion effect, however, appeared delayed compared with the uncrossed condition.

This result suggested that cross-modal attention exerts its effects on sensory signals that are aligned in space to the position of the attentional cue; it excludes the possibility of intrahemispheric facilitation, in which sensory signals may facilitate other sensory processing that occurs within the same hemisphere. Although the feature of cross-modal attention is purposeful (or obligatory), it would require some mechanisms of remapping (see the model below).

We confirmed this result by an event-related potential study (Miyauchi et al. 1993). We recorded visual evoked potentials (VEPs) from the occipital areas. The stimulus arrangement was the same as that in the line motion experiment, except that a probe spot of light (instead of a probe line) was presented just above the right or left index finger. The VEP components including a prominent positive peak at 170 ms were greater when the cue stimulus (finger electrical stimulation) matched spatially with the probe spot than when the cue and the probe were on opposite sides. This was so even when the hands were crossed. Thus alignment in space was critical, rather than sides of the body, confirming the line motion experiment.

Using reaction time measures, Driver and Grossenbacher (chap. 9, this volume) have reached similar conclusions. For example, a sound cue was presented at one of four positions (right/left and upper/lower) and the subject had to judge whether the sound came from the upper or lower position; the sound cue was followed by a light stimulus on the right or left, to which the subject had to respond as quickly as possible. The reaction time for responding to the light stimulus was shorter when it was presented on the same side, compared with the opposite side, as the sound cue. A similar result was obtained by using a tactile stimulus as a cue instead of a sound stimulus.

Driver and Grossenbacher (chap. 9, this volume) further showed that, when a target tactile stimulus was applied to one hand while a distractor stimulus was applied to the other hand, the perception of the target stimulus was more strongly interfered by the distractor when the two hands were positioned more closely.

These results, taken all together, indicate that sensory (visual, auditory, and somatosensory) stimulation evokes attention at the location in space where the stimulus is applied and its effect is transferred to the other sensory modalities.

10.8 SPACE AND ATTENTIONAL FOCUS MAY BE REMAPPED IN THE BRAIN

It is now clear that somatosensory information must somehow reach the visual areas while preserving its positional information, finally enhancing local visual processing. In figure 10.10 we postulate a brain region that acts as an interface for positional information between different sensory modalities, a region that we call the "cross-modal spatial map." We assume that position is encoded in this map in the coordinates that are *relatively* free from the directions or positions of sensory organs (e.g., eye, hand, ear). The framework could be head-centered, body-centered, or object-centered, or it could be

Cross-modal Spatial Attention (Somatosensory to Visual)

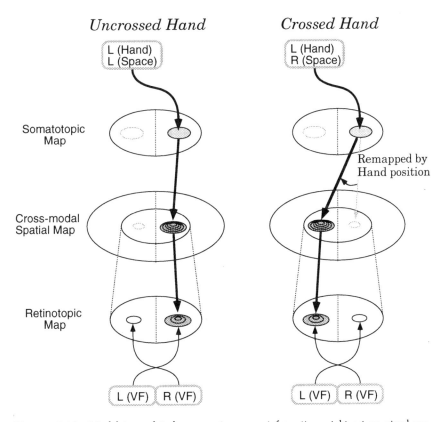

Figure 10.10 Model to explain how somatosensory information might act on visual processing to produce focal visual attention while maintaining its spatial information.

based on, say, cross-correlation between snapshots of visual information obtained at recent eye fixations. In any case, what the cross-modal spatial map encodes would roughly correspond to our concept of the stable world.

An inevitable feature of the cross-modal spatial map is that sensory information coming into this area will be redirected or remapped each time the hand or eye moves. When the left hand is placed on the left side, for example, its somatosensory information would be sent to the right somatosensory cortical areas and then to the cross-modal spatial map on the same (right) side. When the left hand is now placed on the right side, the neural process would be the same until the somatotopic map, but the information would be redirected to the cross-modal map on the opposite (left) side.[4] That the line motion effect was slightly delayed in the crossed-hand condition might indicate that the redirected contralateral projection involves more interneurons than the ipsilateral one, which probably is the default pathway.

The above result does not necessarily indicate that every bit of somatosensory information is remapped in a point-to-point fashion; this would require too heavy a demand for the brain. Because somatosensory information is heavily biased to the hand-and-finger region, the projection from the somatotopic map to the cross-modal spatial map may largely be reduced to two vectors that correspond to the positions of both hands.

10.9   REPRESENTATION OF SPACE IN THE BRAIN

This feature of the cross-modal spatial map in turn requires that visual information coming into this map also be remapped depending on eye position (fig. 10.11). Suppose a visual stimulus is presented on the right side in space when the gaze is directed farther right to the stimulus and then a saccade occurs to the center. The representation of stimulus in the retinotopic map would shift from the right hemisphere to the left, but the representation of stimulus in the spatial map should remain in the left hemisphere. Consequently, the connection from the visual-attentional map to the cross-modal spatial map must be remapped.

The remapping of all visual information, if faithfully performed in every detail, would be highly demanding because point-to-point connections between maps must be canceled and reestablished for every saccade. Our model instead proposes that the amount of visual information is first reduced at the level of the visual-attentional map owing to the attentional selection mechanism and then the visual information is remapped when it is sent to the cross-modal spatial map so as to be matched spatially with somatosensory or auditory information.

Neurons in the cross-modal spatial map would thus respond to visual objects at a particular location in space irrespective of the direction of gaze. Although expected for a long time, there had been no indication for the existence of such neurons, until Galletti, Battaglin, and Fattori (1994) discovered neurons that encode visual space in craniotopic (not retinotopic)

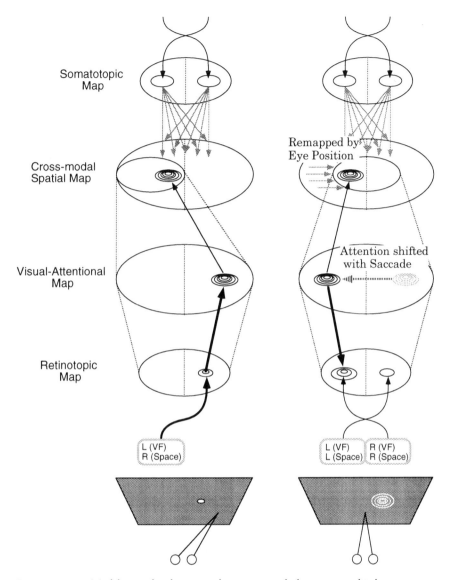

Figure 10.11   Model to explain how spatial attention might be represented in brain.

coordinates in a parieto-occipital region that they called area V6. Similar spatiotopic cells have been discovered in the parietal cortex (Colby, Duhamel, and Goldberg 1993), premotor cortex (Fogassi et al. 1992), and putamen (Graziano and Gross 1993).

We would similarly expect the existence of spatiotopic somatosensory neurons, neurons that respond to somatosensory stimulation only when the stimulation is applied at a particular location in space (see fig. 10.10). There has been no report, to the best of our knowledge, to support this prediction.

Figure 10.10 shows how somatosensory information reaches the visual map. If the trace of information is reversed, visual information would reach the somatosensory map and modulate its information processing. We confirmed this prediction by an event-related potential study (Miyauchi et al. 1993). We used a visual stimulus as a cue to induce attention and a somatosensory stimulus (electric pulse) as a probe. The response to the probe (somatosensory evoked potentials or SEPs) was enhanced when the cue and probe were spatially aligned—a pattern symmetric to the data obtained in the somatosensory-to-visual modulation (see above).

By further exploring the predictions, we came across the striking finding by Graziano and Gross (1993 and chap. 8, this volume). They found that a group of neurons in the premotor cortex and putamen (not in the parietal cortex) respond to visual stimuli when and only when the stimuli are presented at locations close to the hand, irrespective of its position. This seemingly peculiar result may be explained by the model in figure 10.10. Suppose the visual information sent to the somatotopic map were strong enough to produce neural responses, not just by modulating them. When the left hand is in the left hemispace, the neurons should respond to visual stimuli in the left visual field (fig. 10.10, left); when the left hand is in the right hemispace, the neurons should respond to visual stimuli in the right visual field (fig. 10.10, right).

Finally, we think it useful to list some of the questions that remain unanswered. Is the visual-attentional map necessary? Why should it be separate from the retinotopic map? Doesn't the cross-modal spatial map suffice to account for all of our experimental data? Can't the information from different sensory modalities talk with each other without such an interface as the cross-modal spatial map? What are the coordinates of the cross-modal spatial map? Is it centered on the head or body? Or is it maintained by comparison of visual information obtained at successive eye fixations? What is the mechanism underlying remapping? Although we have no data to answer any of these questions, they should be helpful for designing experiments to resolve the issues they raise.

10.10 CONCLUSION

In summary, our model proposes that space is represented in the brain by a strategy of reduction-then-matching. Because signals for spatial position in different sensory modalities are encoded by different coordinates based on different body parts (e.g., eye, hand), they must be compared and matched each time the body parts move. This would require a large amount of reorganization in neural connections for every movement if every positional information were to be compared. According to our model, the amount of position information in a given sensory modality is first reduced by a selection process—attention—and then is used for matching with position information derived from other sensory modalities or information within the same modality obtained previously. Thanks to the reduction, the reorganization would be much less demanding and thus more feasible.

NOTES

1. We have left out an alternative possibility that the focus of attention is encoded in the coordinates that are bound to space, rather than to the retina. This would correspond to the "cross-modal spatial map" that we postulate to account for the cross-modal nature of spatial attention (see fig. 10.11). Without the attentional filtering mechanism in the visual-attentional map, all visual information would be mapped directly onto the cross-modal spatial map at every saccade, which is highly demanding (see section 10.8, "Representation of Space in the Brain"). The data presented by Irwin and Andrews (chap. 6, this volume) would also argue that such one-to-one remapping for every saccade is unlikely.

Still another possibility is that the focus of attention is encoded in an object-centered coordinate. At the time of a saccade the frame of display, for example, moves with respect to the retina. Given the object-bound nature of attention (fig. 10.3), the object here being the frame of display, the focus of attention would move in the direction opposite to the saccade, which may appear consistent with our results. However, our results (figs. 10.5–10.7) indicated that the attentional shift was completed by the end of a saccade, which makes it more likely that the attentional shift is a central phenomenon time-locked with a saccade, rather than a sensory phenomenon induced by the motion of an object. This question, however, should be answered by repeating the experiments in complete darkness.

2. One might argue that the subject judged the direction of the line motion based on the side of the cue that the subject was aware of. This cannot be the reason because the precue effect of line motion showed a distinct time course such that the direction judgment approached the chance level when the cue appeared more than 200 ms after the probe line.

3. Another possibility would be that a visual signal (e.g., onset of a line) is processed in a parallel fashion at different pathways at different speeds (e.g., magno- and parvocellular systems) before reaching the putative motion detector (e.g., MT) so that somatosensory or auditory signal, even though coming later, can create a spatial gradient of processing speed in the slower visual pathways.

4. Here we assume that there is a single cross-modal spatial map lying over the both hemispheres such that each hemispheric part deals with a contralateral hemispace, by the analogy of the retinotopic map. This need not be the case, however. The cross-modal map might reside exclusively in one hemisphere (e.g., right hemisphere), in view of the functional asymmetry of the human brain.

REFERENCES

Biederman-Thorson, M., Thorson, J., and Lange, G. D. (1971). Apparent movement due to closely spaced sequentially flashed dots in the human peripheral field of vision. *Vision Research, 11*, 889–903.

Colby, C. L., Duhamel, J.-R., and Goldberg, M. E. (1993). Ventral intraparietal area of the macaque: Anatomic location and visual response properties. *Journal of Neurophysiology, 69*, 902–914.

Duhamel, J.-R., Colby, C. L., and Goldberg, M. E. (1992). The updating of the representation of visual space in parietal cortex by intended eye movements. *Science, 255*, 90–92.

Fogassi, L., Gallese, V., Di Pellegrino, G., Fadiga, L., Gentilucci, M., Luppino, G., Matelli, M., Pedotti, A., and Rizzolatti, G. (1992). Space coding by premotor cortex. *Experimental Brain Research, 89*, 686–690.

Galletti, C., Battaglini, P. P., and Fattori, P. (1994). Cortical mechanisms of visual space representation. *Biomedical Research, 14*, 47–54.

Goldberg, M. E., and Segraves, M. A. (1989). The visual and frontal cortices. In R. H. Wurtz and M. E. Goldberg, (Eds.), *The neurobiology of saccadic eye movements*, 283–313. Amsterdam: Elsevier.

Graziano, M. S. A., and Gross, C. G. (1993). A bimodal map of space: somatosensory receptive fields in the macaque putamen with corresponding visual receptive fields. *Experimental Brain Research, 97*, 96–109.

Hikosaka, O., Miyauchi, S., and Shimojo, S. (1993a). Focal visual attention produces illusory temporal order and motion sensation. *Vision Research, 33*, 1219–1240.

Hikosaka, O., Miyauchi, S., and Shimojo, S. (1993b). Voluntary and stimulus-induced attention detected as motion sensation. *Perception, 22*, 517–526.

Hikosaka, O., and Wurtz, R. H. (1989). The basal ganglia. In R. H. Wurtz and M. E. Goldberg (Eds.), *The neurobiology of saccadic eye movements*, 257–281. Amsterdam: Elsevier.

Hubel, D. H., and Wiesel, T. N. (1962). Receptive fields, binocular interaction and functional architecture in the cat's visual cortex. *Journal of Physiology, London, 160*, 106–154.

Maylor, E. A. (1985). Facilitatory and inhibitory components of orienting in visual space. In M. I. Posner and O. S. A. Marin (Eds.), *Attention and performance XI*, 189–204. Hillsdale, NJ: Erlbaum.

Miyauchi, S., Hikosaka, O., and Shimojo, S. (1991). Spatiotemporal dynamics of stimulus-induced visual attention. *Society for Neuroscience Abstracts, 17*, 1210.

Miyauchi, S., Hikosaka, O., and Shimojo, S. (1992). Visual attention field can be assessed by illusory line motion sensation. *Investigative Ophthalmology and Visual Science, 33*, 1262.

Miyauchi, S., Hikosaka, O., Shimojo, S., and Okamura, H. (1993). Spatial attention is cross-modal: An evoked potential study. *Investigative Ophthalmology and Visual Science, 34*, 1234.

Munoz, D. P., and Wurtz, R. H. (1995). Saccade-related activity in monkey superior colliculus. II. Spread of activity during saccades. *Journal of Neurophysiology, 73*, 2334–2348.

Nakayama, K. (1985). Biological image motion processing: a review. *Vision Research, 25*, 625–660.

Posner, M. I., and Cohen, Y. (1984). Components of visual orienting. In H. Bouma and D. Bouwhuis (Eds.), *Attention and performance X*, 531–556. London: Erlbaum.

Posner, M. I., and Petersen, S. E. (1990). The attention system of the human brain. *Annual Review of Neuroscience, 13*, 25–42.

Robinson, D. L., and McClurkin, J. W. (1989). The visual superior colliculus and pulvinar. In R. H. Wurtz and M. E. Goldberg (Eds.), *The neurobiology of saccadic eye movements*, 337–360. Amsterdam: Elsevier.

Steinman, B. A., Steinman, S. B., and Lehmkuhle, S. (1995). Visual attention mechanisms show a center-surround organization. *Vision Research, 35*, 1859–1869.

Stelmach, L. B., and Herdman, C. M. (1991). Directed attention and perception of temporal order. *Journal of Experimental Psychology: Human Perception and Performance, 17*, 539–550.

Sternberg, S., and Knoll, R. L. (1973). The perception of temporal order: Fundamental issues and a general model. In S. Kornblum (Ed.), *Attention and performance IV*, 629–685. New York: Academic Press.

Ungerleider, L. G., and Desimone, R. (1986). Cortical connections of visual area MT in the macaque. *Journal of Comparative Neurology, 248*, 190–222.

Van Essen, D. C., and Maunsell, J. H. R. (1983). Hierarchical organization and functional streams in the visual cortex. *Trends in Neuroscience, 6*, 370–375.

von Grünau, M., and Faubert, J. (1994). Intraattribute and interattribute motion induction. *Perception, 23*, 913–928.

11 Haptic and Visual Representations of Space

Lawrence E. Marks and Laura Armstrong

ABSTRACT

The scale of perceptual space is neither homogeneous nor constant. Not homogeneous because both visual and haptic space show anisotropies—variations in scale that depend on stimulus orientation or direction; vertical extents are generally perceived to be spatially greater than horizontals by both senses. And not constant because visual space shows "recalibration," or adaptation-like changes in scale; presenting short horizontals and long verticals (or the reverse) increases the perceived extent of verticals relative to horizontals (or the reverse), and thus modulates the orientational anisotropy. Two experiments (a) confirmed the presence of this orientation-sensitive recalibration in vision and demonstrated its analogue in haptic touch (where tangential and radial arm movements correspond to horizontal and vertical visual orientations), and (b) showed recalibration to be specific to each modality, with no evidence of transfer to the other modality. A third experiment found no evidence of orientation-based recalibration in the perception of visual duration, consistent with the hypothesis that recalibration requires differential adaptation across attribute-sensitive channels. Recalibrations in vision and in haptic touch appear to be independent, and presumably arise prior to the site of intermodal integration of spatial information.

Information provided by various sense modalities eventually links up to represent space in the external world and to guide behavior. Although, in some simple situations, humans process signals arising from different modalities as if all of the information converged in a psychologically "common space" (e.g., Auerbach and Sperling 1974), nevertheless, each modality can maintain considerable independence. When, or in what ways, do the senses reveal communality in processing spatial information, and when or in what ways do they reveal independence?

This chapter seeks to help answer this question within the framework of two phenomena that have undergone new, or renewed, scrutiny in recent years. One of these phenomena, the class of spatial *anisotropies*, refers to orientation-based nonhomogeneities in perceptual space; the other, *recalibration*, refers to adaptation-like changes in relative perceived magnitudes of stimuli processed through different channels, for instance, changes in the relative perceived extent of stimuli presented in different spatial orientations.

First, consider anisotropy. How many of us have with trepidation approached a mirror, our tongue having warned us that a tooth has suffered a cavernous gouge, only for our eyes to dispel this anxiety by showing the defect to be considerably more modest? Perceptual space is not isotropic or uniform, either when considered across modalities or within them; and anisotropies set limits on intermodal integration, or constrain the capacity of perceptual systems to detect common, amodal information. More than a century ago, Jastrow (1886) showed that linear spatial extents given to the eye are perceived as greater in magnitude than those given proprioceptively; furthermore, anisotropy is evident within a single sense modality. Thus James (1890) noted that a square does not look "square," its vertical dimension being perceptually greater than its horizontal. To appear equally wide and high, the horizontal dimension must be stretched by about 6 percent, according to results of Potts (1991).

Second, and central to this study, is recalibration. Recalibration, as already noted, refers to adaptation-like shifts in responsiveness to stimuli that are processed within particular sensory channels (Marks 1994). In general, recalibration is observed only with extensive and intensive dimensions of perception, such as spatial extent, duration, and intensity, but not in qualitative dimensions, such as auditory pitch (Marks 1992b). Listening to several brief, relatively loud tones of a fixed signal frequency reduces loudness at that frequency relative to loudness at other frequencies, and viewing several brief, relatively long lines in one orientation reduces the perceived lengths of lines in that orientation relative to other orientations. Thus auditory recalibration of loudness reveals itself within frequency-specific channels or critical bands (Marks 1993, 1994; Marks and Warner 1991), and visual recalibration of spatial extent reveals itself in orientation-specific channels (Potts 1991). Evidence has mounted over the last several years suggesting that many cases of perceptual "context effects," often attributed to shifts in semantic labeling or more generally to changes in decision processes, may actually involve channel-specific perceptual adaptation.

We report here the results of two main experiments that used paradigms of cross-modal transfer in order to determine, first, whether stimulus conditions conducive to producing spatial recalibration in vision also produce recalibration in haptic touch and, second, whether recalibration in vision and touch show intermodal communality. With both vision and touch, we focus on recalibration of stimuli presented in different spatial orientations. Note that our approach ties recalibration to spatial anisotropy. The existence of recalibration implies that the scales of perceptual space within a modality are not fixed. Given that a linear object oriented vertically appears longer than the identical object oriented horizontally, presenting relatively long horizontals recalibrates visual space by increasing the degree of anisotropy, whereas presenting relatively long verticals decreases the anisotropy.

11.1 ANISOTROPY IN VISUAL AND HAPTIC PERCEPTION

Examples of anisotropy abound. Already in 1834, for example, Ernst H. Weber discovered that spatially separated or extended objects, when impressed on the skin, feel greater in spatial magnitude when their main axis is oriented transversely than when it is oriented longitudinally. Set the two points of a compass to a fixed displacement and place them so they fall on a line between the wrist and elbow, or between the elbow and shoulder, and the gap between the points feels smaller than it does when the compass is rotated 90° (cf. Green 1982). A similar anisotropy is revealed when the two points are stimulated electrically (Marks et al. 1982); because electrocutaneous stimuli probably bypass cutaneous receptors and act directly on peripheral fibers (Rollman 1974), the skin's anisotropy most likely resides in post-receptor, spationeural organization of information.

Both visual perception and haptic perception display anisotropies that are in some way analogous to the tactile anisotropy found by Weber, a visual analogue being evident in the well-known vertical-horizontal illusion and a haptic analogue in the less familiar radial-tangential illusion. In many circumstances, vertical extents appear greater than horizontal ones of the same physical magnitude (e.g., Finger and Spelt 1947; Künnapas 1955): the vertical-horizontal illusion, or VHI. The VHI appears in single lines, unencumbered by any configuration (Potts 1991), in line segments incorporated into two-dimensional figures—either open figures, such as *L*s (Finger and Spelt 1947; Künnapas 1955), or enclosed figures, such as rectangles (Potts 1991)—and in visual angles (Higashiyama 1992). The VHI is smaller in two-dimensional than one-dimensional configurations (Potts 1991) and is evident even when the normally "trapezoidally" shaped visual field is spatially distorted (Künnapas 1959) or suppressed by viewing stimuli in the dark (Künnapas 1957; Potts 1991). Potts (1991), working in Marks's laboratory, found a robust VHI in the perception of individual line segments, measured by asking subjects to give quantitative judgments (magnitude estimates) of the extent of each stimulus. Armstrong and Marks (1995a) confirmed this result, using a sequential method of paired comparison, and noted that the VHI with line segments is substantial in size—a horizontal had to be roughly 8–12 percent greater than an equivalent vertical to be perceived by eye as equally long.

A haptic analogue, evident in what Lederman, et al. (1987) call the "arm's manipulatory space," is the radial-tangential illusion, or RTI. Radial and tangential stimuli (more precisely, the arm movements that the stimuli elicit) may be treated as analogous to visual verticals and horizontals. Consider a person's torso as an idealized cylinder, about whose central axis project an infinitude of concentric circles. We may classify the directions of arm movements in terms of this ensemble of circles, identifying a given movement as either radial to them (as, for example, in throwing a bowling ball) or tangential (as, for example, in writing on a chalkboard). By and large, radial movements appear perceptually greater than tangential movements of equal physical extent (Cheng 1968; Davidon and Cheng 1964; Deregowski and Ellis 1972). Recently, using the sequential method of paired comparison, we found the RTI, like the VHI in vision, to be substantial in size—a tangential excursion of the arm had to be 10–15 percent greater than a radial excursion in order to be perceived as equal in extent (Armstrong and Marks 1995b).

It seems likely that the RTI and VHI derive from different sources, that is, each probably depends on processes that are unique to its own modality (e.g., Marchetti and Lederman 1983; Wong 1977). Nevertheless, the RTI and VHI could reside at least partly in a common process. The VHI, for instance, is notably sensitive to the visual frame (Künnapas 1957; Prinzmetal and Gettleman 1993), and there is evidence that haptic percepts are sometimes referred to a visual frame (e.g., O'Connor and Hermelin 1981); consequently, the two illusions (or the anisotropies implicit in them) might interact. Are the corresponding visual and haptic percepts wholly independent? Or do they interact in a way that suggests a common representation of space?

11.2 RECALIBRATION

Both Potts (1991) and Armstrong and Marks (1995a) found the perception of visual extent—and hence the magnitude of the VHI—to show recalibration. Presenting subjects with a sequence of stimuli in which the verticals are relatively long and the horizontals are relatively short acts to decrease, relatively speaking, apparent extent in the vertical, and thus decreases the magnitude of the VHI, whereas presenting a sequence containing short verticals and long horizontals acts to increase relative extent in the vertical, and thus increases the size of the VHI. It is as if the unit psychological magnitudes along the axes of perceptual space were elastic. Although recalibration was first thought to reflect decisional processes, and perhaps differential labeling (e.g., Marks 1988), evidence continues to point to a mechanism involving some kind of perceptual adaptation. We mention four lines of evidence.

First, recalibration appears with many psychophysical paradigms. Although initially observed in magnitude estimates (Marks 1988)—which suggested that it might reside in numerical, or other, labels—it is equally evident in paired comparison (Marks 1992a, 1994), in paired comparison of intervals (Schneider and Parker 1990), and as aftereffects of stimulus-specific exposure (Marks 1993).

Second, recalibration is evident in the judgment of loudness of tones differing in frequency (Marks 1988, 1992a, b, 1993, 1994; Marks and Warner 1991; Schneider and Parker 1990), but not, under comparable conditions, in the judgment of duration of such tones (Marks 1992b). Recalibration is evident in the judgment of visual extent of lines differing in orientation, but not in the judgment of visual extent of lines differing in color (Marks 1992b). Indeed, the bandwidth of loudness recalibration resembles the bandwidth of auditory peripheral nerve responses (see Marks 1994; Marks and Warner

1991). It is hard to reconcile these findings with a mechanism that relies solely on decisional processes. On the other hand, the findings are consistent with the hypothesis that recalibration reflects differential adaptation within channels. Thus we suggest that loudness is processed within channels that are selective for sound frequency (critical bands; see Zwicker and Scharf 1965), but duration is not (Allan 1979; but see Allan 1984; Walker and Irion 1979); and that visual length is processed within channels that are selective for orientation, but not within channels selective for color. When all stimuli are processed in the same channel, any change in responsiveness affects the stimuli equivalently, so that no recalibration is observed. Recalibration is always measured differentially. Being stimulus-specific, recalibration bears a generic resemblance to various contingent perceptual aftereffects (e.g., Dodwell and Humphrey 1990).

Third, in hearing, recalibration of loudness depends on absolute intensity levels and seems to occur only when recalibrating signals are sufficiently strong, exceeding at least 50 dB (Marks 1993). This finding too suggests a sensory basis.

Finally, Rankin (1993) made use of a well-known spatial "illusion" in the chemical senses—that when a person takes in the mouth a solution containing an odorant, which stimulates only olfactory but not gustatory receptors, the odorant is localized in the mouth rather than the nose—to demonstrate that recalibration in chemosensory perception depends on the modality of stimulation rather than qualitative similarity per se. Recalibration was absent when the stimuli comprised two tastants that were perceived as similar (much as it is absent from loudness when frequencies fall within the same critical band; see Marks 1994; Marks and Warner 1991). But recalibration was present when the stimuli comprised a tastant and an odorant, both sipped (and thus both localized in the mouth), even though they were perceived to be as similar as the two tastants that gave no recalibration. Gustatory and olfactory stimuli are processed within different neural channels, even when they are perceptually similar, whereas similar-tasting gustatory stimuli are processed within the same channel. Thus recalibration seems to rely on the activation of different neural channels.

What are the implications for the perception of visual and haptic spatial extents? A prime example of coding spatial information from different modalities within a common space is found in the localization of flavor in the mouth. Foods and beverages generally activate olfactory receptors in the nasal epithelium, by retronasal flow, as well as gustatory receptors in the tongue. Rankin's (1993) findings imply that recalibration is specific to the modalities of taste and olfaction even when the stimuli are localized in a common space, and they suggest that recalibration takes place prior to the projection of gustatory and olfactory information onto a common spatial representation. The first two experiments reported here ask whether recalibration is similarly specific to vision and haptic touch. Does orientation-specific recalibration induced in vision or in haptic touch transfer to the other modality, when the same stimuli are presented to both modalities?

11.3 EXPERIMENT 1

Experiment 1 sought to compare within-modality and between-modality aftereffects using stimulus paradigms that should produce recalibration in vision and haptic touch. To this end, we induced recalibration by presenting different sets of stimuli in horizontal and vertical orientation, either visually or haptically. With haptic presentation, horizontal and vertical stimuli required the subjects to make tangential and radial arm movements, respectively. We measured the magnitude of recalibration with a scaling procedure (magnitude estimation), like that used by Potts (1991) in her study of visual recalibration of length, and tested for aftereffects in both modalities.

Method

Stimuli   Stimuli consisted of rectangular blocks, formed of wood and uniformly painted red, each 1.2 cm wide and high, and glued onto a separate blackened strips 51 cm long × 4 cm wide. The blocks came in 12 possible lengths: 4, 5, 6, 7, 8, 10, 12, 14, 16, 18, 21, and 24 cm. Each strip could be positioned appropriately in a square black tray for presentation to the subject, with the stimulus either visible (visual presentation) or hidden behind a curtain (haptic presentation).

The stimuli grouped into three main categories, two for inducing recalibration and one for measuring baselines and aftereffects. Set A comprised 8 short horizontals or tangentials (4–14 cm) and 8 long verticals or radials (8–24 cm), whereas set B comprised the complementary stimuli, 8 long horizontals or tangentials (8–24 cm) and 8 short verticals or radials (4–14 cm). The "common set," used for measuring baselines and aftereffects, consisted of the four stimuli (8–14 cm) common to sets A and B in both spatial orientations.

Procedure   The tray containing the stimulus was placed in the horizontal plane directly in front of the seated subject. The stimulus itself could be positioned either parallel or orthogonal to the subject's torso. In the former case, the stimulus was oriented horizontally to the eye and required tangential motion by the arm; in the latter, the stimulus was oriented vertically to the eye and required radial motion by the arm. With visual presentation, stimuli were exposed for about 4 seconds. With haptic presentation, arm movements were executed by having the subject explore the stimulus with the index finger of the right hand.

The experimental paradigm involved shifting between blocks of recalibration-inducing trials (which measured the magnitude of the induced intramodal recalibration effects) and blocks of test trials (which measured baselines and aftereffects in both the same modality and the other modality). Blocks of test trials were kept relatively brief because evidence at hand suggests that during the test trials subjects quickly begin to "readapt" (see Marks 1992a). Thus, after 6 initial practice trials (3 visual and 3 haptic) that were not counted, a given session contained 5 blocks, each of 16 trials. First came a baseline test, in which the 8 stimuli in the common set were presented horizontally and vertically to vision, and radially and tangentially for haptics, making a total of 16 randomly ordered trials in all; second came either set A (condition A) or set B (condition B), in which the 16 randomly ordered stimuli were presented either visually or haptically; third was the first test of aftereffects, comprising again the 16 trials of the common set; fourth was the second presentation of set A or B, as in block 2; the fifth and final block of trials comprised the second test of aftereffects, again using the common set.

The choice of psychophysical method was dictated by efficiency. In recalibration paradigms of this type, magnitude estimation and paired-comparison methods give similar results (Marks 1994); because magnitude estimation is more efficient, that method was used here. Subjects rated numerically the extent of each stimulus, with no designated standard or modulus. To the first stimulus, each subject assigned whatever number she or he deemed appropriate to represent the linear extent; then, to each succeeding stimulus, the subject assigned a number in proportion, using whole numbers and decimals as needed. Twenty-one women and eleven men (18–41 years old) served as paid subjects; all were right-handed as indicated by self-report. Sixteen of the subjects received the recalibrating stimuli visually, and the other sixteen received them haptically. Each subject served in two sessions, held on different days, judging stimuli of condition A in one session and those of condition B in the other (order of conditions counterbalanced over subjects in each modality).

Results

Baseline Besides providing baseline measures for examining aftereffects of recalibrating stimuli, judgments given in the very first block of trials make it possible to compare directly the visual and haptic judgments of spatial extent. Pooled geometrically over all subjects and all baseline sessions, the visual judgments exceeded the haptic judgments by 4.7 percent (6.01 vs. 5.74), a difference that is small but statistical reliable, as determined by analysis of variance (ANOVA) conducted on logarithmically transformed judgments, $F(1, 28) = 4.87$, $p < .04$, and that suggests a lack of complete spatial congruity between these two senses. Jastrow (1886) reported analogous findings more than a century ago.[1]

Recalibration Judgments given to the recalibrating stimuli, in the second and fourth blocks of trials, were averaged geometrically over subjects and plotted in the logarithmic coordinates of figure 11.1 (visual verticals and horizontals in the left panel; haptic radials and tangentials in the right panel). Within each panel, the functions on the left side show results obtained with set A, and those on the right side show results obtained with set B.

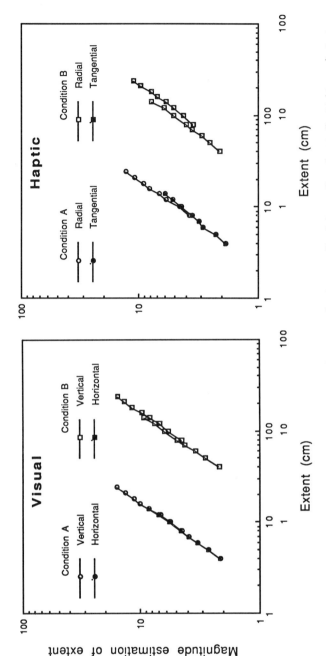

Figure 11.1 Magnitude estimates of spatial extent of stimuli presented either visually (left panel) or haptically (right panel), in two contextual conditions. In condition A (left side of each panel), stimuli presented horizontally to visual perception, or requiring tangential arm movements for haptic perception, were relatively great, whereas stimuli presented vertically or radially were relatively small. In condition B (right side of each panel), lengths presented in different orientations were switched.

It is clear that varying the distribution of stimulus lengths over orientations affected both visual and haptic judgments, and did so in a similar, albeit modest, fashion. Visual verticals were judged 9.4 percent longer than horizontals when subjects saw short verticals and long horizontals (condition B), but about equal to horizontals when subjects saw long verticals and short horizontals (condition A). Similarly, haptic radial extents were judged 23 percent greater than tangential extents when subjects made short radial movements and long tangential ones (condition B), but only 8.6 percent greater when subjects made long radial movements and short tangential ones (condition A). In each case, the displacement of the function with open symbols (visual verticals or haptic radials) from the function with filled symbols (horizontals or tangentials) reflects the degree of anisotropy—the magnitude of the VHI or RTI—characterizing that particular stimulus condition. Statistically, the changes in the ratio of perceived vertical to horizontal extent and in the ratio of perceived radial to tangential extent express themselves through the interaction of condition × orientation, $F(1, 30) = 38.7$, $p < .0001$, for all subjects together, and $F(1, 15) = 26.9$, $p < .0001$, and $F(1, 15) = 16.2$, $p < .0015$, for vision and haptics separately.[2]

Taken as a whole, that is, pooled over recalibrating conditions, the haptic RTI was substantially greater than the visual VHI, equal to 15.6 percent and 4.1 percent, respectively. Statistically, this difference is reflected in the interaction of modality × orientation, $F(1, 30) = 13.1$, $p < .0015$. Further, there was a reliable overall effect of orientation, $F(1, 30) = 39.5$, $p < .0001$, with a small and marginally reliable visual VHI, $F(1, 15) = 4.50$, $p = .05$, and a larger haptic RTI, $F(1, 15) = 40.5$, $p < .0001$.[3]

Aftereffects   Let us assume that the changes just described consist of adaptation-like decreases in perceived extent—that the greater the physical extent of the visual stimulus in a given orientation, or the greater the extent of the haptic arm movement in a given direction, the greater the adaptation. Such direction-specific adaptation is sufficient to account for the results just described. Given this, it seems natural to ask, What is it that adapts? Is adaptation specific to the modality in which the recalibrating stimuli are presented? Or does adaptation "generalize" to stimuli presented in the same location or orientation in space even when those stimuli are perceived through another modality? Is the "shrinking" of visual space in the vertical dimension associated with an analogous compression in space perceived through spatially corresponding radial movements of the arm? If "recalibration" is specific to the modality of exposure, aftereffects should be evident in the recalibrated modality but not in other modalities. Visual recalibration, for example, should produce visual aftereffects but not haptic ones. If "recalibration" affects some common mechanism, however, cross-modal effects should mimic intramodal ones, and recalibration should be evident haptically as well as visually.

Figure 11.2 shows the magnitude of the VHI (two upper panels) and the RTI (two lower panels) at baseline, after exposure to the two sets of visual

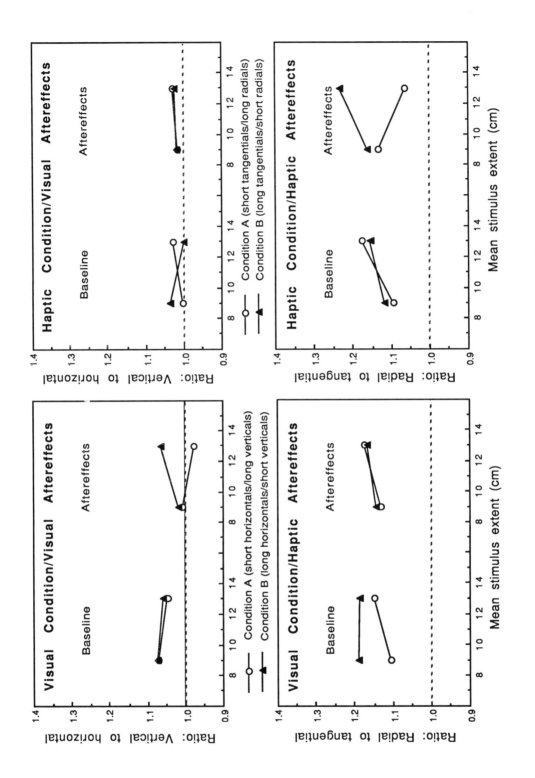

recalibrating stimuli (left panels), and after exposure to the two sets of haptic recalibrating stimuli (right panels). In each case, figure 11.2 plots the ratio of the mean judgments given to the stimuli presented vertically or radially to those presented horizontally or tangentially. To facilitate comparison, and to reduce noise, data have been pooled over the smallest two extents and over the largest two extents. In each panel, the dashed line at a ratio of 1.0 indicates the absence of any anisotropy (VHI or RTI).

Let us start with aftereffects of visual recalibration. At baseline, there was a modest visual VHI, amounting overall to a 6.2 percent greater judgment of verticals than horizontals (fig. 11.2, upper left-hand panel), which was modified only slightly by the introduction of the differential recalibrating trials. The ratio of judged vertical to horizontal extents dropped more in condition A (short horizontals and long verticals) than in condition B (long horizontals and short verticals), 8 percent versus 2.5 percent, respectively. Although these percentages changed in the direction expected if effects of recalibration linger, the interaction is not reliable, $F(1, 15) = 2.70$, $p < .15$. Given this lack of reliable intramodal aftereffects, it is not surprising that visual recalibration led to virtually no haptic aftereffects. Relative to baseline, where radials were judged 15.7 percent greater than tangentials (fig. 11.2, lower left-hand panel), subjects who had seen short horizontals and long verticals had their RTI increase by 2 percent, whereas those who had seen long horizontals and short verticals had their RTI decrease by 2 percent, a trivial change, $F(1, 15) = 1.175$, $p < .30$.[4]

Haptic recalibration led to more robust aftereffects, at least in haptic judgments. At baseline, there was a substantial haptic RTI, amounting to 13.5 percent (fig. 11.2, lower right-hand panel). Presenting the haptic recalibrating stimuli caused the RTI to decline by 8 percent in condition A (short tangential and long radial movements), but to increase by 5.5 percent in condition B (long tangentials and short radials). These direction-specific changes in the "calibration" of haptic space are reliable, $F(1, 15) = 6.24$, $p < .025$), and they concur with the changes measured in judgments of the contextually varying stimuli themselves (fig. 11.2, right), though they are slightly smaller in magnitude; this outcome is consistent with studies of loudness perception, which show that context-induced "recalibrations" tend to disappear during testing for aftereffects (Marks 1992a). On the other hand, visual judgments showed essentially no change after haptic recalibrating trials, with the VHI virtually invariant at 1–2 percent both at baseline and after haptic recalibration (fig. 11.2, upper right), $F(1, 15) < 1$. Presenting haptic recalibrating stimuli clearly had different effects on subsequent haptic and visual judgments, the difference

Figure 11.2 Ratios of judgments of stimuli presented vertically and horizontally (visual perception, upper panels) and of stimuli requiring radial and tangential arm movements (haptic perception, lower panels), at baseline and after exposure to stimuli in conditions A and B, as shown in figure 11.1.

between these intramodal and intermodal aftereffects itself being reliable, $F(1, 15) = 5.16$, $p < .04$.[5]

Discussion

The present results, taken together with earlier findings, support two broad generalizations. First, perceptual space has not one metric scale but many. Spatial scale depends on modality, the perception of spatial extent being slightly greater to the eye than to the moving arm; moreover, both visual and haptic space are directionally anisotropic, vertical extent often exceeding horizontal extent to the eye, and radial movement of the arm yielding greater perception of extent than does tangential movement. Second, the metric scales of visual and haptic space are dynamic and elastic—as if the percepts or judgments underwent some kind of length adaptation, or the two-dimensional representation of space underwent recalibration. Presenting greater magnitudes in one spatial direction or another reduces judgments of stimuli oriented in that direction. Although earlier studies revealed recalibration in vision (Armstrong and Marks 1995a; Potts 1991), experiment 1 provides the first empirical evidence, albeit not surprising, of analogous recalibration in haptic touch.

Unfortunately, with regard to the central issue of intermodal communality in recalibration, the results of experiment 1 make it is harder to draw strong conclusions. Although the recalibration in the metric spatial scale appears to be largely specific to the modality stimulated—at least, within the experimental and statistical power of the present paradigms—we make this conclusion cautiously, given that aftereffects of recalibration were modest at best. Presenting haptic recalibrating trials produced a relatively small haptic aftereffect, and presenting visual recalibrating trials, virtually no visual aftereffect. Lacking strong intramodal aftereffects, it is not surprising that cross-modal effects were absent.

11.4 EXPERIMENT 2

Although the first experiment demonstrated recalibration in both vision and touch, it was modest in size, and the lack of robust aftereffects speaks to the need for a more sensitive psychophysical method. Marks (1992a) noted that loudness aftereffects can diminish relatively quickly, perhaps because the recalibration itself simply dissipates over time, but more likely because the stimuli used to measure aftereffects themselves act to alter the state of perceptual adaptation (see Marks 1993). Consequently, experiment 2 made two significant changes in procedure. First, we now interspersed trials on the secondary, or transfer, modality amid the series of stimuli presented on the primary, recalibration-inducing modality. Intermixing the two kinds of stimuli should increase the likelihood of measuring changes in haptic perception during visual recalibration, and changes in visual perception during haptic recalibration. And second, we switched from a single-stimulus, magnitude-scaling procedure to a two-stimulus, paired-comparison procedure. This change, albeit at the cost of efficiency, should minimize the possibility that differential labeling contributes to the recalibration, without any sacrifice in its magnitude; in fact, the available evidence (Marks 1994) suggests that, if anything, under otherwise comparable stimulus conditions, the paired-comparison method gives slightly greater recalibration than does magnitude estimation.

Method

Stimuli (6, 7, 8, 9, 10, 12, and 14 cm in extent) were selected from those used in experiment 1 and presented in the same apparatus and setup. These stimuli were divided into three sets: two *recalibrating sets* and a single *transfer set*. Recalibrating set A comprised the five shortest stimuli (6–10 cm) oriented horizontally (vision) or tangentially (haptic touch), together with the five longest stimuli (8–14 cm) oriented vertically (vision) or radially (touch). Recalibrating set B reversed the assignment of lengths to orientations, comprising long stimuli (8–14 cm) in horizontal or tangential orientation and short stimuli (6–10 cm) in vertical or radial orientation. Note that three lengths—8, 9, and 10 cm—are common to both recalibrating sets, A and B, and to the transfer set. We define the modality of the condition as that of the recalibrating set. Thus, in the *visual conditions*, the recalibrating sets were presented visually and the transfer sets haptically, whereas in the *haptic conditions*, the recalibrating sets were presented haptically and the transfer sets visually. The present paradigm therefore makes possible direct comparison of the subjects' performance with the same stimuli presented to both modalities.

Trials containing stimuli from a given recalibrating set and the corresponding transfer set were intermixed within each test session. The method was paired comparison. On each trial, the subject received two stimuli in succession (interstimulus interval = about 0.5 sec), both in the same modality, and responded by indicating which stimulus was perceived to be greater in extent, the first or the second. There were 25 possible pairs of stimuli in each recalibrating set (5 possible lengths in first interval × 5 in the second interval) and 9 possible pairs in each transfer set (3 lengths × 3 lengths), making 34 pairs in all. These 34 pairs were ordered randomly within a single block of trials, with temporal order of orientations chosen randomly on each trial. Every session contained 4 such blocks of 34 pairs, for a total of 136 pairs of test stimuli per session. The 136 pairs immediately followed 4 practice trials, which were selected randomly from the set of stimulus pairs.

Each subject participated in two sessions, held on different days, condition A containing stimuli from recalibrating set A and condition B containing stimuli from recalibrating set B. Order of sessions was balanced across subjects. Eighteen women and six men, (18–33 years, all right-handed) participated. For twelve of the subjects, the recalibrating stimuli were visual and the transfer stimuli were haptic in both sessions, and for the other twelve, the recalibrating stimuli were haptic and the transfer stimuli were visual in both sessions.

Results

Results were summarized by computing, for each pair, the average probability that the stimulus oriented vertically was judged greater than the stimulus oriented horizontally, p(vertical > horizontal), in the case of visual trials, or, correspondingly, the probability that radial movements were judged greater than tangential movements, p(radial > tangential), in the case of haptic trials. All of the critical comparisons involve the nine stimulus pairs common to all of the stimulus sets, whether recalibrating stimuli or transfer stimuli, and whether presented visually or haptically.

The present results again revealed pervasive anisotropies in both vision and haptic touch. For instance, on those trials in which subjects compared equally long stimuli, both p(vertical > horizontal) and p(radial > tangential) generally exceeded 0.5. Looking at a larger subset of data, if we pool over the responses to the nine stimulus pairs common to all stimulus sets (averaging across both recalibrating sets, A and B), the mean proportions are 0.65 for visual recalibrating trials, 0.63 for visual transfer trials, 0.61 for haptic recalibrating trials, and 0.67 for haptic transfer trials. In each case, the mean proportion is reliably greater than 0.5, $X^2(1) = 81.9$, 56.1, 39.2, and 101.4, respectively, with all values of $p < .0001$. Thus the present results reveal once again the tendency for verticals to be perceived as greater than horizontals by vision, and for radial movements to be perceived as greater than tangential movements by haptic touch.

Figure 11.3 plots the results obtained in the visual conditions. The panel on the left gives data obtained in the visual recalibrating sets, and the panel on the right the corresponding data obtained in the haptic transfer sets. In each case, the probability is plotted against the extent of the vertically oriented stimulus, with each horizontally oriented stimulus represented by a separate function. Results obtained in condition A (short visual horizontals and long verticals) are given by open symbols, connected by solid lines, and those obtained in condition B (long horizontals and short verticals) by filled symbols, connected by dashed lines. To facilitate viewing the salient results, the symbols and connecting lines obtained with the nine common stimuli are darker in appearance than the other, contextual stimuli (left panel). The horizontal dotted line indicates equal response to the two alternatives ($p = 0.5$).

Results obtained with the visual recalibrating stimuli show the expected outcome. Given that the horizontal lengths are physically greater than the vertical lengths in condition B, but smaller in A, recalibration should consist of a reduction in perceived length of horizontals in B relative to that in A. And if horizontals are reduced in perceived length in B, then verticals should appear relatively greater in B than in A, hence the probabilities should be

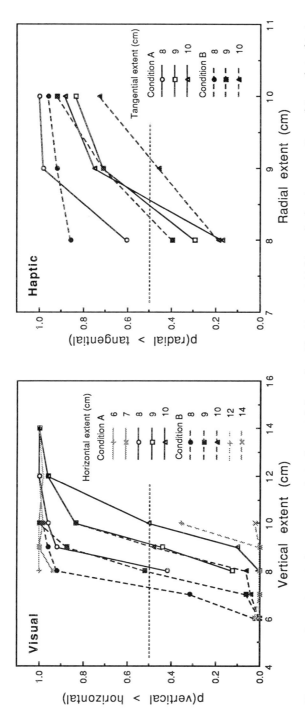

Figure 11.3 Successive paired comparisons of visual extent (left panel) and haptic extent (right panel), showing proportions of times that subjects judged vertically oriented stimulus to be longer than the horizontally oriented stimulus, or corresponding radial stimulus longer than tangential stimulus. In condition A, horizontals are relatively short and verticals long (open symbols, solid lines), and in condition B horizontals are long and verticals are short (filled symbols, dashed lines).

greater. They are. In each case, the filled symbols (condition B) tend to fall above the corresponding open symbols (condition A). For example, subjects judged the 8 cm vertical to be greater than the 8 cm horizontal 92 percent of the time in condition B (filled circle) but only 42 percent of the time in condition A. The present pattern of results resembles that found previously by Armstrong and Marks (1995a) with stimuli presented on a video monitor.

What about the responses to haptic transfer stimuli? By comparison, they show no recalibration. Overall, the small differences between judgments made in the two conditions reveal little or no systematic trend; if anything, there may be a very slight tendency for probabilities to be greater in condition A than in condition B, contrary to the direction expected if recalibration generalized to touch.

Figure 11.4 gives corresponding results obtained in the haptic conditions, where the recalibrating stimuli were haptic (left panel) and transfer stimuli visual (right panel). With the haptic recalibrating stimuli, as with the visual recalibrating stimuli in figure 11.3, the filled symbols tend to fall above the corresponding open symbols, indicating that the radials were judged especially great relative to tangentials when the subjects were presented long tangentials and short radials (condition B), rather than short tangentials and long radials (condition A). Again, the shifts in response are specific to the modality of the recalibrating stimuli. There is no evidence of cross-modal transfer to vision. The filled symbols and open symbols in the right-hand panel virtually overlap, with no systematic overall trend. Statistical evaluation by ANOVA supports these conclusions. In both the visual and haptic conditions, there is a highly reliable within-modality effect of recalibrating condition, $F(1, 11) = 77.3$ and 76.9, $p < .0001$, respectively, but no cross-modal transfer effect of condition, $F(1, 11) < 1$ in both cases.[6]

Discussion

The results of experiment 2 are both clear and straightforward. Augmenting the physical lengths of stimuli presented in one orientation relative to those presented in another orientation systematically affects perceptual judgments, consistent with the hypothesis that perceived extent diminishes in the orientation or direction in which the lengths are greater. Further, these recalibrations in spatial scale are specific to the modality of stimulation. Varying the physical extents of stimuli presented visually modifies visual judgments, but not haptic ones, and varying the extents of stimuli presented haptically modifies haptic judgments, but not visual ones.

11.5 EXPERIMENT 3

In several recent studies, Marks has argued that recalibration represents a kind of stimulus-specific perceptual adaptation, and not (or at least, not only) a general shift in response criteria or labels (Marks 1992a, 1993, 1994). The

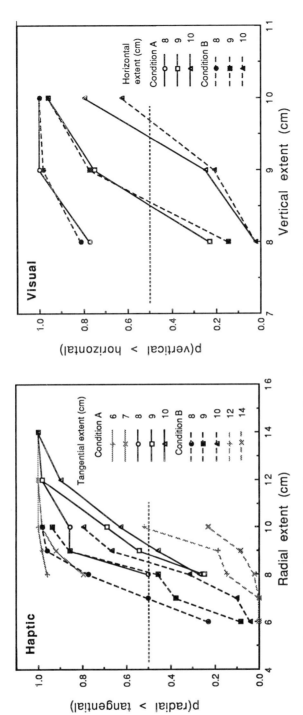

Figure 11.4 Successive paired comparisons of haptic extent (left panel) and visual extent (left panel), showing proportions of times that subjects judged radially oriented stimulus to be greater in length than tangentially oriented stimulus, or the corresponding horizontal stimulus greater in length than vertical stimulus. In condition A, tangentials are relatively short and radials long (open symbols, solid lines), and in condition B tangentials are long and radials are short (filled symbols, dashed lines).

argument rests in part on evidence that recalibration makes itself evident only in perceptual dimensions that are encoded by multiple, stimulus-specific sub-channels. Thus, loudness of tones differing in frequency showed recalibration only when the signal frequencies differ sufficiently (Marks 1992a, 1994; Marks and Warner 1991), reflecting frequency-specific coding of loudness within critical bands (e.g., Zwicker and Scharf 1965). By contrast, judgments of duration under comparable conditions showed no recalibration (Marks 1992b), consistent with the view that the auditory system uses a single channel to encode duration.

Recalibration appears to be modality-specific—at least under the limited set of conditions examined here in experiments 1 and 2. But to what degree is it also specific to the perception of space? In the visual system, for example, the present results are consistent with the hypothesis that the *lengths* of horizontally oriented and vertically oriented stimuli are encoded within different subchannels (although their orientational sensitivities may overlap). But it is likely that the *durations* of horizontally oriented and vertically oriented stimuli are encoded within a single channel, that is, information about duration is probably derived independently of a visual stimulus's spatial orientation. If so, then judgments of duration of stimuli presented in different orientations should reveal no recalibration when the average durations vary. Experiment 3 tests this prediction.

Method

Experiment 3 used the paired-comparison method. Stimuli were 2.70 cm vertical and 2.85 cm horizontal lines (which under present conditions, where the viewing frame was visible, made the lines appear approximately equal in length), presented on a Taxan monitor (white lines against a black background), and controlled in duration by a microprocessor (Apple IIe). Following the general paradigm of experiment 2, stimulus set A comprised horizontal lines of relatively short duration (0.4, 0.5, 0.6, 0.7, and 0.8 sec) and vertical lines of relatively long duration (0.7, 0.8, 1.0, 1.2, and 1.4 sec), whereas set B reversed the assignment of durations to orientations. Note that only two durations are common to the two sets, the small overlap between stimulus values reflecting our attempt to maximize the likelihood of finding any recalibration in perceived duration, should it exist.

Stimuli in each pair were presented sequentially (ordered randomly with respect to orientation), with 0.75 sec separating the offset of the first stimulus and the onset of the second. The subject's task was to indicate on each trial which stimulus appeared to last longer, the first or the second. Thus there were 25 possible pairs of stimuli; the entire set of 25 was presented in 10 randomly ordered replicates within a given test session, making 250 trials in all. Ten women and six men (18–34 years old) participated in condition A on one day and in condition B on another day. Order of conditions was balanced over subjects.

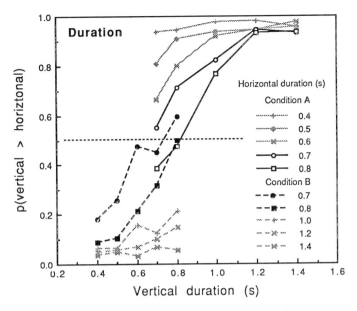

Figure 11.5 Successive paired comparisons of duration, showing proportions of times that subjects judged vertically oriented stimulus to last longer than horizontally oriented stimulus. In condition A, horizontal stimuli have relatively short durations and verticals long durations (open symbols, solid lines), and in condition B horizontals have long durations and verticals have short durations.

Results

Figure 11.5 gives the mean probabilities that the vertical line was judged greater in duration than the horizontal line, p(vertical > horizontal). Results obtained in condition A are given by open symbols, connected by solid lines, and results obtained in condition B given by filled symbols, connected by dashed lines. In general, the functions obtained in the two stimulus conditions appear to form a single, uniform series. Four stimulus pairs are critical, formed of the common durations, 0.7 and 0.8 sec. Values of p(vertical > horizontal) produced by each of these four pairs were similar though not identical in the two conditions. If anything, there is a slight tendency for the probability to be smaller in condition B than in condition A, opposite to the direction of recalibration. Statistically, only the effects of horizontal and vertical duration were reliable, $F(1, 15) = 33.1$, $p < .0001$, and $F(1, 15) = 15.0$, $p < .002$, respectively, though the effect of stimulus condition does approach reliability, $F(1, 15) = 4.425$, $p = .053$.

Discussion

As we anticipated, there is no evidence of differential adaptation (recalibration) in the perception of duration of lines presented in different spatial orientations. This outcome is compatible not only with the general hypothesis that recalibration resides in some kind of perceptual adaptation, rather than a general "bias" in responding, but also with the more specific hypothesis that recalibration fails to appear when all of the stimuli are processed within a single channel, as seems the case with duration (e.g., Allan 1979). The results of experiments 1–3 point to a fundamental difference between the mediation of spatial and temporal information, at least in vision. Whereas information about visual duration that arises from stimuli differing in spatial orientations appears to be processed through a single channel, analogous information about visual length appears to be processed through different channels that maintain some orientational selectivity. Although it would be difficult to perform a haptic analogue to experiment 3, we suspect that similar results would obtain and that the difference between temporal and spatial information processing would hold for haptic touch as well as vision.

11.6 MODALITIES AND SPATIAL REPRESENTATIONS

The integration of spatial information derived from different sensory modalities is central to perceptual processing. Nevertheless, every modality is to some extent like an island, entire unto itself. The psychological scale of length or distance, the unit magnitude of perceived extent, varies both within and between the visual and haptic modalities. Space is anisotropic, the perception of spatial extent of a physically constant stimulus object varying with its orientation or direction. Moreover, the findings reported here bear two implications. First, the spatial scales or metrics are not only directionally sensitive but elastic, that is, contingent on recent stimulation. And second, these adjustments or "recalibrations" in scale seem largely if not entirely specific to each modality. It is possible, of course, that modality-specific anisotropy and elasticity do not characterize all kinds of spatial perception; anisotropy and elasticity might only characterize, say, consciously given experiences of space. For example, the work of Bridgeman and colleagues (Bridgeman et al. 1979; Bridgeman, Kirch, and Sperling 1981) suggests a possible dissociation between spatial processing involved in motor activity and those in conscious perception, with spatial information being more "veridical" in motor activity. Thus it is conceivable that other measures of spatial information processing would not show elasticity in the VHI or RTI, or indeed any VHI or RTI at all.

Even so, it seems to us likely that anisotropy and elasticity are fundamental—and relatively "early"—properties of spatioperceptual processing. If not hard-wired, anisotropy seems virtually ineluctable. However often we have viewed objects in different orientations, vertical extents tend to appear greater than horizontal extents; however often we reach in different directions, radial movements appear greater than tangential movements; however often we have held an object in our hand while looking at it, the distance between thumb and forefinger appears larger than it feels (Jastrow 1886 reported data showing that proprioceptive extent and visual extent can be nonlinearly related, a finding later rediscovered by Stevens and Stone 1959; but see also van Doren 1995).

These intramodal and intermodal differences in scale presumably withstand long-term "correction" by experience. On the other hand, the differences in scale are readily modified in the short term, adapting to the characteristics of stimuli recent presented. Thus, in experiment 1, presenting longer vertical than horizontal objects served to equalize the visual scale in these two orientations (see fig. 11.1, left panel, condition A). Recalibration of this sort appears to be a widespread, adaptation-like perceptual phenomenon. As the results of experiment 3 showed, however, recalibration is neither universal nor inevitable, not being evident in judgments of duration of visual stimuli differing in orientation. Recalibration has similarly been absent from the perception of duration of low-frequency and high-frequency tones, the pitch of low-intensity and high-intensity tones, and the length of orange and green lines (Marks 1992b), but it has been readily observed in the perception of loudness of low-frequency and high-frequency tones (Marks 1988, 1992a, 1993, 1994; Schneider and Parker 1990), the perceived intensity of tastants differing in quality (Rankin 1993; Rankin and Marks 1991, 1992), and the perceived intensity of odorants differing in quality (Rankin 1993).

The contingent character of recalibration is reminiscent of various contingent perceptual aftereffects, the best known being the orientation-specific shifts in color known as "McCollough effects" (e.g., McCollough 1965; Dodwell and Humphrey 1990). It is not at all clear, however, whether related or identical mechanisms underlie both classes of phenomena. In any case, it is our view that recalibration reflects the outcome of differential adaptation in multiple subchannels. Frequency-dependent changes in loudness provide the best-studied, and probably the clearest, example. As is well known, the peripheral auditory system maps signal frequency spatially, onto location of maximal stimulation of the basilar membrane. One consequence is the relatively narrow tuning of peripheral auditory nerve fibers (e.g., Kiang et al. 1965). Recalibration of loudness may reflect selective adaptation (probably in the central nervous system, given unpublished evidence of Marks that it shows interaural transfer) within individual frequency channels. When the signal frequencies (used both to produce and test for recalibration) fall close together, they activate the same channel. Consequently, even though adaptation may take place under these circumstances, the adaptation is not differential but affects both signal frequencies equally, and thus no recalibration is evident in the comparisons of loudness. When the signal frequencies lie farther apart, however, each tends to activate a different channel. In this case, the adaptation is differential; the channel more sensitive to the stronger signal experiences greater adaptation, and the outcome is measured as a shift in relative responsiveness in the two channels (see Marks 1994).

An analogous model may apply to recalibration of perceived extent. We propose that length is processed both visually and haptically within orientation-selective channels that are susceptible to adaptation. Studies of loudness imply that recalibration may depend solely on the stimuli presented at high signal levels; presenting relatively loud signals at a single frequency, but not relatively soft ones, suffices to produce recalibration (Marks 1993). We speculate that this is likely true also for recalibration of length. Thus recalibration would depend critically on the longest stimuli presented. Whichever channel processes sufficiently larger objects would "adapt" more, thereby decreasing that channel's relative responsiveness.

Recalibration of perceived extent, we argue, arises relatively early in spatial processing, which is to say, before extent-related information from different modalities converges. That is, we propose that recalibration precedes convergent processing of visual and tactile spatial information such as that described by Graziano and Gross (chap. 8, this volume; see also Stein and Meredith 1993). This proposal must remain tentative, however, given the many possible ways to map spatial stimuli in visual and haptic space, and thus the many possible variants of the experiments described here. It would be valuable, for example, to repeat the present experiments, but with all of the stimuli oriented in the frontal plane (in which case the visual orientations would again be horizontal and vertical, but the corresponding arm movements would in both cases be tangential).

Less certain is the relation of recalibration to the locus of attentional selection. Recalibration itself has resisted manipulations of attention, at least in the perception of loudness (Marks 1992b). Perhaps recalibration of spatial extent is similarly independent of attention; if so, this would again be consistent with a relatively "early" locus—or at least, one that precedes the site or sites of attentional selection, particularly the sort that reflects multimodal processes (e.g., Driver and Grossenbacher, chap. 9, this volume; Hikosaka et al., chap. 10, this volume). Like some of the processes responsible for anisotropy itself, the processes underlying the modulations in spatial scale known as recalibration seem specific to sensory modalities. Perhaps this should come as no surprise, given that other mechanisms of spatial processing, such as memory (e.g., Abbott 1864; Connolly and Jones 1970; Posner 1967) are also specific to the visual and haptic senses.

NOTES

Preparation of this article was supported by National Institutes of Health grant DC 00818.

1. Also reliable in experiment 1 were (a) an overall effect of orientation, $F(1, 28) = 57.5$, $p < .0001$; (b) an interaction of orientation with modality, $F(1, 28) = 15.7$, $p < .001$ reflecting a larger RTI than VHI; (c) an overall effect of extent, $F(3, 84) = 728.0$, $p < .0001$; (d) an interaction of extent with modality, $F(3, 84) = 3.24$, $p < .03$; and (e) interactions of order of sessions with modality, $F(1, 28) = 4.50$, $p < .05$; condition with session, modality, and orientation, $F(1, 28) = 7.84$, $p < .01$; and condition with block of trials, modality, orientation, and extent, $F(3, 84) = 2.96$, $p < .04$. These interactions are not of special interest.

2. The VHI was evident in both contextual sets A and B of stimuli the first time they were presented (block 2); but in the second presentation (block 4), only set B gave a positive VHI, whereas set A gave a negative VHI, of roughly the same absolute magnitude, $F(1, 15) = 5.377$,

$p < .04$. By contrast, a positive RTI emerged in both sets A and B in both the first and second presentations. Also reliable were, for vision, (a) the effect of extent, $F(3, 45) = 241.5$, $p < .0001$, and (b) an interaction of condition with block of trials and orientation, $F(1, 15) = 5.912$, $p < .03$. And reliable for haptics were (a) an effect of extent, $F(3, 45) = 404.1$, $p < .0001$, and (b) an interaction of orientation with extent, $F(3, 45) = 4.68$; $p < .01$.

3. Also reliable were (a) an effect of block of trials, $F(1, 30) = 4.83$, $p < .04$; (b) an overall effect of extent, $F(3, 90) = 592.8$, $p < .0001$; and (c) an interaction of orientation with extent, $F(3, 90) = 4.302$, $p < .01$.

4. Five other terms were reliable: in vision, effects of (a) extent; $F(3, 45) = 387.7$, $p < .0001$; (b) orientation, $F(1, 15) = 6.05$, $p < .03$; and (c) an interaction of orientation with block, $F(1, 15) = 7.175$, $p < .02$; in haptic touch, effects of (a) extent, $F(3, 45) = 209.3$, $p < .0001$, and (b) orientation, $F(1, 15) = 50.2$, $p < .0001$.

5. Eight other terms were reliable: in haptic touch, effects of (a) extent, $F(3, 45) = 484.0$, $p < .0001$; (b) block, $F(1, 15) = 8.03$, $p < .02$; (c) an interaction of condition with block, $F(1, 15) = 6.875$, $p < .02$; (d) orientation, $F(1, 15) = 25.8$, $p = .0001$; and (e) interactions of condition with orientation, $F(1, 15) = 6.461$, $p < .025$, and condition with block and orientation, $F(1, 15) = 6.24$, $p < .025$. Reliable in vision were effects of (a) extent, $F(3, 45) = 570.5$, $p < .0001$, and (b) block, $F(1, 15) = 9.69$, $p < .01$.

6. The other reliable terms were (a) effects of extent, $F(3, 33) = 239.0$ and 126.7, $p < .0001$, for horizontal and vertical extent, respectively, in visual recalibrating trials; $F(3, 33) = 110.7$ and 117.7, $p < .0001$, for corresponding tangential and radial extent in haptic transfer trials; $F(3, 33) = 37.0$ and 58.1 for tangential and radial extent in haptic recalibrating trials; and $F(3, 33) = 273.9$ and 217.7, $p < .0001$, for horizontal and vertical extent in visual transfer trials; (b) extent × extent interactions in visual recalibrating trials, in corresponding haptic transfer trials, and in visual transfer trials, $F(4,66) = 6.80$, 7.82, and 16.7, all values of $p \leq .0002$; (c) condition × vertical extent and condition × radial extent interactions in the visual condition, $F(2, 22) = 3.94$ and 3.85, $p < .05$; (d) a condition × tangential extent interaction with haptic recalibrating stimuli, $F(2, 22) = 4.080$, $p < .05$; and (e) a condition × extent × extent interaction with visual recalibrating stimuli, $F(4, 44) = 9.60$, $p < .0001$. None of the higher-order interactions is of special interest; to a large degree, they reflect such factors as ceiling and floor effects. More importantly, there was no evidence for changes in the patterns of response over the course of the test session; in no case was there a reliable effect of block of test trials, nor any interaction involving block of trials. Thus, consistent with earlier findings (Marks 1993), recalibration develops quickly, within a small number of trials.

REFERENCES

Abbott, T. K. (1864). *Sight and touch: An attempt to disprove the received (or Berkeleian) theory of vision*. London: Longman, Green.

Allan, L. G. (1979). The perception of time. *Perception and Psychophysics, 26,* 340–354.

Allan, L. G. (1984). Contingent aftereffects in duration judgments. *Annals of the New York Academy of Sciences, 423,* 116–130.

Armstrong, L., and Marks, L. E. (1995a). Contextual effects in the visual perception of length. Forthcoming.

Armstrong, L., and Marks, L. E. (1995b). Haptic perception of linear extent. Working paper.

Auerbach, C., and Sperling, P. (1974). A common auditory-visual space. Evidence for its reality. *Perception and Psychophysics, 16,* 129–135.

Bridgeman, B., Kirch, M., and Sperling, A. (1981). Segregation of cognitive and motor aspects of visual function using induced motion. *Perception and Psychophysics, 29,* 336–342.

Bridgeman, B., Lewis, S., Heit, G., and Nagle, M. (1979). Relation between cognitive and motor-oriented systems of visual position perception. *Journal of Experimental Psychology: Human Perception and Performance, 5,* 692–700.

Cheng, M. F. H. (1968). Tactile-kinesthetic perception of length. *American Journal of Psychology, 81,* 74–82.

Connolly, K., and Jones, B. (1970). A developmental study of afferent-reafferent reintegration. *British Journal of Psychology, 61,* 259–266.

Davidon, R. S., and Cheng, M. F. H. (1964). Apparent distance in a horizontal plane with tactile-kinesthetic stimuli. *Quarterly Journal of Experimental Psychology, 16,* 277–281.

Deregowski, J., and Ellis, H. D. (1972). Effect of stimulus orientation upon haptic perception of the horizontal-vertical illusion. *Journal Experimental Psychology, 95,* 14–19.

Dodwell, P. C., and Humphrey, G. K. (1990). A functional theory of the McCollough effect. *Psychological Review, 97,* 78–89.

Finger, F. W., and Spelt, D. K. (1947). The illustration of the horizontal-vertical illusion. *Journal of Experimental Psychology, 39,* 548–551.

Green, B. G. (1982). The perception of distance and location for dual tactile pressures. *Perception and Psychophysics, 31,* 315–323.

Higashiyama, A. (1992). Anisotropic perception of visual angle: Implications for the horizontal-vertical illusion, overconstancy of size, and the moon illusion. *Perception and Psychophysics, 51,* 218–230.

James, W. (1890). *The principles of psychology.* New York: Henry Holt.

Jastrow, J. (1886). The perception of space by disparate senses. *Mind, 11,* 539–554.

Kiang, N.-Y.-S., Watanabe, T., Thomas, E. C., and Clark, L. F. (1965). *Discharge patterns of single fibers in the cat's auditory nerve.* Cambridge, MA: MIT Press.

Künnapas, T. M. (1955). An analysis of the "vertical-horizontal" illusion. *Journal of Experimental Psychology, 49,* 134–140.

Künnapas, T. M. (1957). The vertical-horizontal illusion and the visual field. *Journal of Experimental Psychology, 53,* 405–407.

Künnapas, T. M. (1959). The vertical-horizontal illusion in artificial visual fields. *Journal of Psychology, 47,* 44–48.

Lederman, S. J., Klatzky, R. L., Collins, A., and Wardell, J. (1987). Exploring environments by hand or foot: Time-based heuristics for encoding distance in movement space. *Journal of Experimental Psychology: General, 13,* 606–614.

Marchetti, F. M., and Lederman, S. J. (1983). The haptic radial-tangential effect: Two tests of Wong's "moments-of-inertia" hypothesis. *Bulletin of the Psychonomic Society, 21,* 43–46.

Marks, L. E. (1988). Magnitude estimation and sensory matching. *Perception and Psychophysics, 43,* 511–525.

Marks, L. E. (1992a). The contingency of perceptual processing: Context modifies equal-loudness relations. *Psychological Science, 3,* 285–291.

Marks, L. E. (1992b). The slippery context effect in psychophysics: Intensive, extensive, and qualitative continua. *Perception and Psychophysics, 51,* 187–198.

Marks, L. E. (1993). Contextual processing of multidimensional and unidimensional auditory stimuli. *Journal of Experimental Psychology: Human Perception and Performance, 19,* 227–249.

Marks, L. E. (1994). "Recalibrating" the auditory system: The perception of loudness. *Journal of Experimental Psychology: Human Perception and Performance, 20,* 382–396.

Marks, L. E., Girvin, J. P., Quest, D. O., Antunes, J. L., Ning, P., O'Keefe, M. D., and Dobelle, W. H. (1982). Electrocutaneous stimulation. II. The estimation of distance between two points. *Perception and Psychophysics, 32,* 529–536.

Marks, L. E., and Warner, E. (1991). Slippery context effects and critical bands. *Journal of Experimental Psychology: Human Perception and Performance, 17,* 986–996.

McCollough, C. (1965). Color adaptation of edge detectors in the human visual system. *Science, 149,* 1115–1116.

O'Connor, N., and Hermelin, B. (1981). Coding strategies of normal and handicapped children. In R. D. Walk and H. L. Pick, Jr. (Eds.), *Intersensory perception and sensory integration,* 315–343. New York: Plenum Press.

Posner, M. I. (1967). Characteristics of visual and kinesthetic memory codes. *Journal of Experimental Psychology, 75,* 103–107.

Potts, B. C. (1991). The horizontal-vertical illusion: A confluence of configural, framing, and contextual factors. Ph.D. diss., Yale University.

Prinzmetal, W., and Gettelman, L. (1993). Vertical-horizontal illusion: One eye is better than two. *Perception and Psychophysics, 53,* 81–88.

Rankin, K. M. (1993). Differential effects of context on intensity judgments of taste and smell: Perceptual change or judgmental bias? Ph.D. diss., Stockholm University.

Rankin, K. M., and Marks, L. E. (1991). Differential context effects in taste perception. *Chemical Senses, 16,* 619–629.

Rankin, K. M., Marks, L. E. (1992). Effects of context on sweet and bitter tastes: Unrelated to sensitivity to PROP (6-*n*-propylthiouracil). *Perception and Psychophysics, 52,* 479–486.

Rollman, G. B. (1974). Electrocutaneous stimulation. In F. A. Geldard (Ed.), *Cutaneous communication systems and devices,* 39–51. Austin, TX: Psychonomic Society.

Schneider, B., and Parker, S. (1990). Does stimulus context affect loudness or only loudness judgments? *Perception and Psychophysics, 48,* 409–418.

Stein, B. E., and Meredith, M. A. (1993). *The merging of the senses.* Cambridge, MA: MIT Press.

Stevens, S. S., and Stone, G. (1959). Finger span: Ratio scale, category scale, and jnd scale. *Journal of Experimental Psychology, 57,* 91–95.

Van Doren, C. L. (1995). Cross-modality matches of finger span and line length. *Perception and Psychophysics, 57,* 555–568.

Walker, J. T., and Irion, A. L. (1979). Two new contingent aftereffects: Perceived auditory duration contingent on pitch and on temporal order. *Perception and Psychophysics, 26,* 241–244.

Weber, E. H. (1834). *De pulsu, resorptione, auditu et tactu: Annotationes anatomicae et physiologicae.* Leipzig: Koehler.

Wong, T. S. (1977). Dynamic properties of radial and tangential movements as determinants of the haptic horizontal-vertical illusion with an *L* figure. *Journal of Experimental Psychology: Human Perception and Performance, 3,* 151–164.

Zwicker, E., and Scharf, B (1965). A theory of loudness summation. *Psychological Review, 72,* 3–26.

VI Integration for Motor Control

12 Are Proprioceptive Sensory Inputs Combined into a "Gestalt"?

Jean P. Roll, Jean C. Gilhodes, Regine Roll, and Françoise Harlay

ABSTRACT

In order to study the organization of the proprioceptive sensory codes subserving movement perception, complex hand-drawing illusions were elicited using various vibration patterns applied to the wrist muscles of human subjects. It was established that it is possible to elicit kinesthetic illusions involving spatially oriented lines and geometrical shapes such as rectilinear or curvilinear figures by activating four groups of muscle tendons at the wrist level. The vibration sequences specifically evoking each shape were determined by varying the vibration frequency, the duration of each stimulus, and the vibrator onsets, and by applying the vibrators either successively or simultaneously. The proprioceptive coding of a trajectory can be modeled in terms of a series of vectors, whose direction depends on the anatomical sites of the muscles stretched and shortened during the movement. The vector giving the spatial path of a movement is the sum of the vectors of the proprioceptive inputs originating from each muscle, and the modulus of the resulting vector is the instantaneous velocity of the movement. It therefore emerges from the results of this study that muscle proprioception is able to generate spatiotemporal afferent pattern that may mediate complex cognitive operations such as those involved in the memorizing and recognition of motor forms. Moreover, some experimental data indicate that proprioceptive inputs from all the muscles holding and moving the retina in space, from the foot up to the eyes, are used by the brain to process the visual information required to perform spatial localization and reaching tasks. It is suggested that proprioception may provide a link between personal and extrapersonal space.

12.1 INTRODUCTION

Simply looking at figure 12.1 reminds one of the extreme importance of the human muscular system, which forms a true chain running from one extremity of the body, the feet, which anchor the body to the floor, up to the eyes, which open onto extrapersonal space, where objects are located in relation to the body and possibly reached. This motor chain is also a proprioceptive sensory chain, however, running from eye to foot (Roll and Roll 1988).

In this chapter we discuss the use of a vibratory method to investigate how the brain processes muscular information for two main perceptual purposes: (1) the conscious representation of movement trajectories and (2) the use of proprioceptive cues to build up a functional link between the body and extrapersonal space. Accordingly, our chapter will be subdivided into two parts. In section 12.2, some recent results will be presented concerning the

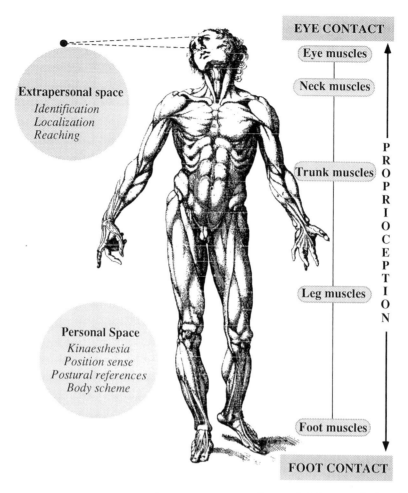

Figure 12.1 From "Eye to foot": proprioceptive chain as link between body space and extrapersonal space.

use of complex vibratory patterns to induce complex illusory drawing movements with predictable parameters in humans; on the basis of these results, a general theory of proprioceptive sensory coding will be proposed and discussed, according to which perception of a movement is mediated by a particular proprioceptive afferent pattern and can be formally described in terms of vectorial expressions. Scalar models of this kind can be used to set up an attractive relationship between the peripheral sensory code organization and the central mechanisms recently described at cortical levels, where populations of cells have been found to encode movement kinematics vectorially (Georgopoulos, Taira, and Lukashin 1993; Kalaska 1991; Schwartz 1994).

In section 12.3, some experimental data will be presented in support of the idea that proprioceptive inputs from all the muscles holding and moving the retina in space, from the feet up to the eyes, are coprocessed by the brain along with the retinal input during spatial localization and reaching activities. What is more, we would like to propose that the proprioceptive system may also constitute a link between personal and extrapersonal space (Roll, Velay, and Roll 1991).

12.2   HUMAN HAND VIBRATION-INDUCED VIRTUAL DRAWING

It has by now been clearly established that muscle information contributes to the conscious coding of positions and movements in humans (Goodwin, McCloskey, and Matthews 1972; Matthews, 1982; Roll and Vedel 1982; Gilhodes, Roll, and Tardy-Gervet 1986). This was first suggested by the finding that mechanical vibration applied to the arm muscles of human subjects, with no visual information available, induced the illusory sensation that the subjects' motionless forearm was actually moving. Numerous studies subsequently confirmed that kinesthetic illusions of this kind were generated in humans by the preferentially activated Ia afferents, and established the quantitative relationships existing between the parameters of the vibratory stimulus and those of the resulting sensation of movement. On the basis of microelectrode recordings performed directly on human Ia fibers, the spindle primary endings were found to be highly sensitive to vibration (Burke et al. 1976a, b; Roll and Vedel 1982). The existence of a one-to-one stimulus-response linkage within the 1 to 100 Hz frequency range means that by modulating the vibration frequency, it is possible to induce a proportional change in the primary ending discharge frequency. This makes tendon vibration a useful tool for experimentally eliciting proprioceptive signals with predetermined characteristics. Unlike the primary endings, the secondary endings and Golgi tendon organs are only slightly sensitive to vibration under our experimental conditions, where low-amplitude vibration (0.25 mm peak to peak) is applied to muscles at rest (Roll, Vedel, and Ribot 1989). It was also observed that the speed of illusory movements of this kind depends on the vibration frequency and reaches a maximum at frequencies of around 80 Hz (Roll and Vedel 1982; Jones 1988). In addition, the velocity of the illusory movements remains practically constant at slightly increasing vibration frequencies, and thus mimics the increasing discharge pattern of the muscle spindle primary endings observed when a movement is imposed on a joint at a constant speed (Roll, Vedel, and Ribot 1989; Vedel and Roll 1982), whereas vibration applied at decreasing frequencies gives rise to the illusion that a movement is being performed at a decreasing speed (Gilhodes et al. 1993).

These illusory movements are in the same direction as movement that would have resulted if the muscle had been stretched instead of being vibrated. This finding gave rise to the suggestion that the muscles stretched during the performance of real movements, namely, the antagonist muscles, may play an important role in movement parameter coding (Roll, Gilhodes, and Tardy-Gervet 1980; Roll 1981; Capaday and Cooke 1983; Roll and Vedel 1982). The respective contributions of the proprioceptive afferent messages arising from antagonist muscles to determining the direction and the velocity of the ensuing illusory sensations of movement were then analyzed. It has emerged from these studies that illusory sensations of movement are elicited only when there exists an imbalance between the proprioceptive afferent messages arising from two antagonistic muscles, and that the velocity of the illusory movements depends on the magnitude of this difference (Gilhodes, Roll, and Tardy-Gervet 1986; Gilhodes et al. 1993). These insights led to the development of tendon vibration as a means of selectively and quantitatively activating the human muscle proprioceptive channel and thus exploring, in the case of simple, single-joint movements, the exact relationships between the parameters of the vibratory stimulus, the patterns of the afferent proprioceptive inputs evoked, and the characteristics of the corresponding sensations of movement.

With a view to studying the kinesthetic sensations associated with the complex movements of one joint, the wrist, and with the set of muscles involved, we extended our previous use of tendon vibration by applying it to various groups of muscles to generate artificial muscle spindle afferent messages. The various muscles responsible for moving a joint were stimulated in the present case using predefined patterns of vibration to induce the perception of illusory movements with specific trajectories describing geometrical shapes. The idea underlying this procedure was that it might be possible to ascertain how the proprioceptive sensory codes mediating the perception of recognizable motor forms are organized.

It was established that it is possible to elicit kinesthetic sensations corresponding to definite geometrical shapes (such as lines, squares, circles, or triangles) by activating four groups of muscle tendons at the wrist level. The vibration sequences specifically evoking each shape were determined by varying the vibration frequency and the duration of each stimulus and by applying the vibrations either successively or simultaneously.

Material and Methods

Experiments were carried out on 9 subjects, who were blindfolded throughout the experiment; they were comfortably seated with their right forearm in a horizontal grooved support, grasping a pencil whose tip was in contact with a digitizing tablet (fig. 12.2A) when the vibration was applied to the wrist muscles. The tip of the pencil was fixed to the digitizing tablet in such a way that the hand was immobilized. After the vibration sequence, the tip of the pencil was released, and the subjects were asked to actively reproduce the kinesthetic sensations induced by the vibration as accurately as possible, paying attention to both the shape of the trajectory and the movement velocity. Before copying the illusory movements with their eyes closed, the subjects were asked to orally identify the figure they had just perceived.

The mechanical vibration was applied to the extensors, flexors, abductors, and adductors of the hand at wrist level by means of four computer-driven

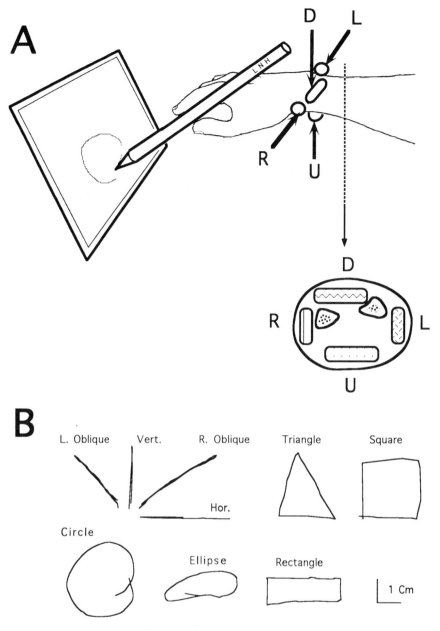

Figure 12.2 A. Experimental setup: Subject is grasping pencil whose tip is in contact with digitizing board. Four vibrators, denoted R, D, L and U, are applied to wrist tendons. Vibrator R induces illusory sensation that subject's hand is moving to right (D, downward; L, to left; and U, upward). Diagrams at bottom of A show 4 groups of muscles activated by each vibrator. B. Various illusory drawing movements perceived by subject in response to various patterns of vibration (see corresponding vibratory patterns on figs. 12.3 to 12.7).

Are Proprioceptive Sensory Inputs Combined into a "Gestalt"?

electromagnetic vibrators (vibralgic model, Ikar Cie Ltd.). Each vibrator was held by means of a flexible metal tube, with which it could be adjusted to a particular wrist tendon, and was connected to a high-power amplifier. Each rectangular pulse had a duration of 5 ms, the vibration amplitude was 0.25 mm peak to peak, and the duration of the vibration sequences varied between 3 and 18 seconds, depending on the sequence involved. The vibrators were activated either singly or in pairs, and the vibration frequency ranged between 40 and 80 Hz. The vibration patterns, defined as sequences of time intervals between the successive pulses, were stored in a computer (Bull SPS) and delivered to the various vibrators.

Thirteen patterns of vibration assumed to induce the illusory perception of simple geometrical shapes were used. These patterns were presented in a random order to the subjects, who they had no advance knowledge as to what the shapes might be or what sizes and orientations they might have. The subjects were asked to keep their eyes closed both while undergoing the vibration and while actively drawing the perceived movement trajectory with the pencil on the digitizing tablet. The vibration patterns used to induce illusory hand-drawing movements were determined on the basis of the stretching, costretching, and shortening of the muscles that occur when each of the geometrical figures in question is actually being drawn by hand. This information was then used to vibrate the various muscles involved so as to generate muscle spindle messages similar to those which would have arisen if real movements had been performed. The vibration frequency at which each vibrator was initially set and its subsequent time course were determined on the basis of the primary spindle activity analyses carried out in previous studies (Roll and Vedel 1982; Vedel and Roll 1983; Ribot-Ciscar et al. 1991; Roll et al. 1989). The data previously obtained on the kinaesthetic effects of vibrating more than one muscle were also taken into account (Gilhodes, Roll, and Tardy-Gervet 1986; Gilhodes et al. 1993). The drawings produced by the subjects on the digitizing tablet were sampled at a frequency of 250 Hz, and their characteristics were digitized and stored. Figure 12.1A shows the experimental setup and the vibrated muscle groups.

Results

In all the subjects the various patterns of vibration applied to the four groups of wrist muscles induced the illusory sensation that they were drawing geometrical figures with their hand. Depending on the pattern of vibration applied, these drawings were either straight lines with a specific spatial orientation (vertical, horizontal, or oblique lines), rectilinear figures (squares, rectangles, or triangles) or curvilinear figures (circles or ellipses). Figure 12.2B gives an example of the figures drawn by one subject to describe the illusory movements he had just perceived when subjected to the various patterns of vibration.

Beyond what was expected, the subjects correctly named the figures drawn in 90.6 percent of the trials. Among these, the orientation was correctly specified for 82 percent of the straight lines, for 96 percent of the rectilinear figures, and for 94 percent of the curvilinear figures. The results obtained will be presented and discussed according to the above three types or vibration-induced kinesthetic forms.

Virtual Oriented Line Drawing   The subjects reported that they felt as if they were drawing horizontal lines in the right or left direction depending on whether the hand abductors or adductors were vibrated at wrist level, and they felt as if they were drawing vertical lines in the upward or downward direction depending on whether the hand flexor or extensor muscle tendons were vibrated. The sensation that the subjects were drawing oblique lines moving upward to the left was elicited by vibrating the adductor and flexor muscles together; the sensation of drawing lines downward to the right was induced by vibrating the abductor and extensor muscles together. The oblique lines seemed to extend in the left direction downward when the adductor and extensor muscles were stimulated together, and to the right upward when the abductors and flexors were costimulated. The perceived hand movement velocity varied from one subject to another, averaging about 5 cm/sec at vibration frequencies ranging from 50 to 80 Hz. Whenever the subjects drew a line, the corresponding regression slope was calculated, the orientation of the line measured, and the mean velocity of the drawing movement was computed. Figure 12.3A gives the results obtained with horizontal, vertical, and oblique lines. Each vector corresponds to one trial performed by a given subject; the results of all the trials performed by all the subjects are included in this graph.

The direction of each vector was that of the line drawn by the subject during a trial, and the vector modulus was the mean velocity at which that line was drawn. In the case of the horizontal and vertical line-drawing sensations, the orientation of the vector populations could be clearly seen to be in two orthogonal directions. Figure 12.3B gives the mean vectors indicating the direction and the velocity of the line-drawing sensations induced by the six patterns of vibration indicated in the corresponding pictographs.

Although the dispersion of the vector orientations was greater with oblique than with horizontal and vertical lines, all the vectors expressing the sensations induced by a specific pattern of vibration nevertheless fell into the same quadrant of the graph. The mean vectors show that the mean directions of the lines drawn by the subjects copying the illusions they had perceived differed depending on the stimulus patterns (these are shown in the corresponding pictographs). The mean sensations elicited, in terms of the corresponding motor performance, are indicated by vectors that could be clearly seen to be oriented in two orthogonal directions, but at an angle of about 45° with respect to the coordinate axes.

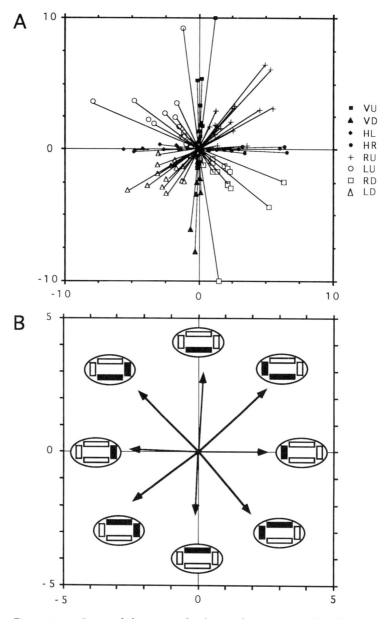

Figure 12.3 Perceived direction and velocity of movements induced by vibrating single muscle or two adjacent muscles. A. Results of individual trials, where each vector is obtained at one trial for each experimental condition. B. Velocity vectors obtained by averaging results of individual trials performed by all subjects with each pattern of vibration. Vibration site used to obtain each vector is indicated. Each vibratory stimulus, which had duration of 4 sec and frequency ranging between 50 and 80 Hz, was applied twice. (VU, vertical up; VD, vertical down; HL, horizontal left; HR, horizontal right; RU, right up; LU, left up; RD, right down; LD, left down). (units: cm/sec).

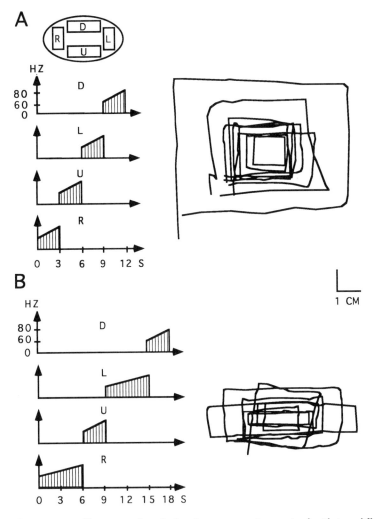

Figure 12.4 Illusory quadrangle-drawing movements perceived with two different patterns of vibration indicated on left: A (square pattern) and B (rectangular pattern).

These results show that it is possible by applying specific vibratory patterns to the wrist muscle tendons to induce in subjects the illusion that they are performing simple graphic gestures such as line-drawing in a clearly pre-defined spatial direction.

Virtual Rectilinear Figure Drawing   The subjects were made to feel as if they were drawing rectilinear geometrical shapes (triangles, squares, or rectangles) by successively applying three or four of the vibration patterns previously found to induce spatially oriented straight lines. When the four appropriate vibration patterns giving rise to illusory horizontal and vertical hand movements (upward vs. downward, or right vs. left) were applied successively, the subjects felt as if they were drawing a rough square (fig. 12.4A) if

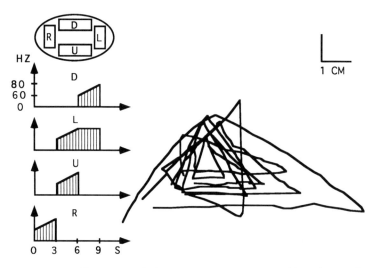

Figure 12.5 Illusory triangle-drawing movements perceived by subjects when subjected to pattern of vibration indicated on left. Graphs on left show vibration pattern applied with time to groups of muscles D, L, U and R (defined as in fig. 12.2).

the two vibration patterns were both applied for the same length of time (3 sec), or a rectangle (fig. 12.4B) if the duration of the sequence corresponding to a horizontal line was increased twofold (6 sec). Finally, the subjects felt as if they were drawing triangles when three specific vibration patterns were applied successively to particular groups of wrist muscles, that is, they felt as if they were drawing a horizontal right-to-left segment, followed by a segment drawn to the left in the upward direction, and completed by an oblique segment drawn to the left in the downward direction (figs. 12.4 and 12.5).

The subjects' statements showed that they always (100 percent of the time) clearly distinguished between sensations of quadrilateral and three-sided figure drawing, whereas square drawing was distinguished from rectangle drawing in only 82 percent of all the cases tested.

The ratio between the horizontal versus vertical size of the quadrilateral was calculated and mean values of 1.20 in the case of squares and 1.79 in the case of rectangles obtained. The ratio in the case of rectangles therefore amounted to approximately 2, as did the ratio between the durations of the corresponding vibration sequences. In the case of rectangles, the mean length of the long sides was 40.2 mm and that of the short sides, 22.4 mm, whereas in the case of squares, the mean length of the vertical sides was 27.4 mm and that of the horizontal sides, 33.3 mm. Finally, in the case of triangles, the mean value of the base was 43 mm and that of the height, 31.5 mm.

To summarize, by applying specific patterns of vibration to the four groups of wrist muscles, we established that it was possible to elicit in the subjects the illusion that they were drawing particular geometrical shapes.

Virtual Curvilinear Figure Drawing   In the previous experiments, the subjects were made to feel as if they were producing series of line segments, whereas in the subsequent experiments they were made to feel as if they were producing curvilinear figures. Specific patterns of vibration were applied successively to two of the four groups of wrist muscles in such a way that the frequency decreased gradually in the case of one muscle group, while either increasing or remaining constant in the case of the adjacent muscle group. Moreover, the radius of curvature was assumed to depend on the rate of increase or decrease in the frequency of the vibration applied to each of the covibrated muscles. In 95 percent of the subjects, these vibratory patterns induced the illusory sensation that they were drawing curvilinear geometrical figures with their hand. Two different patterns of vibration were used here, which were expected to induce sensations of circlelike or ellipselike drawing.

Figures 12.6A and B show all the superimposed individual shapes drawn by the subjects when asked to mimic the sensations elicited by the vibration and to give the characteristics of the corresponding vibration patterns. In 16 cases out of the 18 tested, these figures were identified by the subjects as being closed curvilinear figures (8 as circles and 8 as ellipses). Figures 12.7B and D give the mean shapes produced by the subjects with the two patterns of vibration used. The two patterns differed as follows: in the case of the "circle pattern" the vibration frequency applied to one muscle decreased as soon as that applied to the adjacent one increased, whereas in the case of the "ellipse pattern" the same frequency was applied to one muscle for four seconds. Each figure was obtained by analyzing the polar coordinates recorded after normalizing each individual drawing by scanning it in 9° steps. The maximum moduli of each figure were calculated using this angular step, and averaged. Each of the two patterns of vibration was found to give rise to an illusory sensation involving a different closed curvilinear figure. The mean of all the drawings of the first kind shown here (figure 12.7B) can be said to be circlelike in shape because the radius was fairly constant; whereas the mean drawing shown in figure 12.7D can be said to be ellipselike because its horizontal and vertical radii have markedly different lengths.

Discussion

What Do the Subjects Feel? Phenomenological Aspects   What exactly do subjects perceive, if one can tell at all, when they are receiving complex patterns of mechanical vibration applied around the wrist? This is an extremely interesting question, although the data available so far do not allow us to give any unequivocal answers. A precise phenomenological approach to kinesthetic illusions of this kind might certainly tell us something quite basic about voluntary actions in general and even about some of the controversial philosophical issues involved.

Analyses of this kind have been carried out for many years on information obtained by questioning large populations of subjects. In the present study,

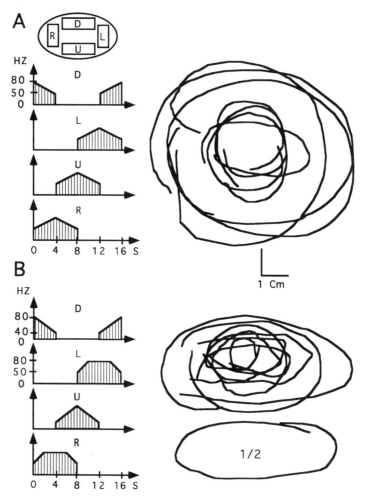

Figure 12.6 Illusory curvilinear drawing movements induced by applying patterns of vibration given in A ("circlelike" pattern) and B ("ellipselike" pattern; scale of drawing marked "1/2" is reduced by one-half).

the subjects were also presented with a questionnaire experiencing the vibration-induced illusory movements ($N = 25$).

The questionnaire brought to light the following facts: the vibration-induced illusory movements were clearly perceived by all the subjects as being limb segment movements. In most cases, the subjects were convinced that the illusory movement had actually occurred. The sensations of movement were always felt to be somewhat surprising because the movements were not intentional, that is, they were not initiated by the subjects themselves. This feeling of surprise was often expressed during the experiments by a smile, and the general impression was that the experience was a fairly pleasant one on the whole. Our analysis of the sensations of movement perceived by the subjects indicated that some of the characteristics were those of real move-

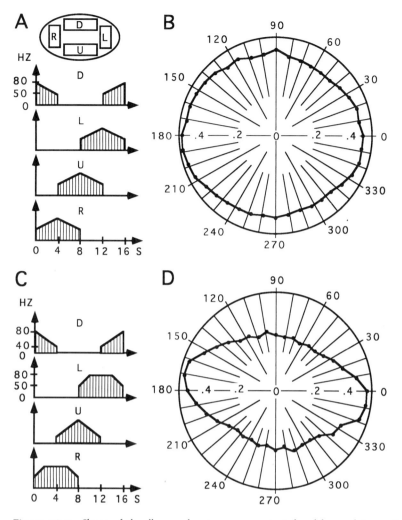

Figure 12.7 Shape of the illusory drawing movements induced by applying patterns of vibration A and C. Each of figures 12.7B and D was based on normalized data expressed in polar coordinates. Dots are mean coordinates obtained within 9° angular step.

ments: the subject's hand seemed to move in a given direction (i.e., the movement had a definite orientation). The movement seemed to begin and end at specific points in space. On the other hand, the sensation of movement was perceived as resulting from external forces by only 25 percent of the subjects, and as resulting from internal (although nonintentional) forces by the remaining 75 percent. Seventy-five percent of all the subjects experienced a feeling of strangeness, probably because they seemed to be performing an action without their own volition, but perhaps also because the proprioceptive sensory feedback triggered by the vibratory stimulus actually simulated only part of the sensorimotor context that normally surrounds a voluntary action.

Here no muscles were voluntarily activated (the movement was only illusory), and hence no feedback was generated, particularly not the feedback usually arising from the Golgi tendon receptors of active muscles. The tactile feedback normally elicited in response to deformation of the cutaneous and subcutaneous tissue was also lacking here because no movement actually occurred and the skin was therefore not deformed. Finally, because no motor command was involved, no "efferent copy" was obviously generated such as that which partly mediates the conscious awareness of real movements (Teuber 1972). These various lacking components might therefore explain why the kinesthetic illusions induced by vibration are both slightly unreal and slightly incomplete.

In the case of the illusory drawing movements induced in the present experiments, the subjects clearly perceived their hand drawing a geometrical figure on the digitizing tablet. The impression that they were drawing was probably facilitated by the postural context associated with holding a pencil.

The apparently somewhat contradictory conclusion to be drawn from the above findings is that from the perceptual point of view, the illusory sensations of movement were very close to those which normally accompany voluntary actions, although the subjects did not generate them intentionally.

Vector Modeling of Proprioceptive Sensory Codes   Although the basic principles underlying sensory coding have been established, no general theories have been advanced for coding in muscle proprioception. This should come as no surprise. Muscle receptors are widely distributed among the various muscles acting on a joint, and many if not all of them undergo different mechanical constraints, which tend furthermore to change during the performance of complex movements. The spindle afferent messages arising during the accomplishment of a movement, which constitute that movement's sensory signature, not only tend to be complex because they are generated by a whole set of muscles, but also vary during the time taken to perform the movement. How can we picture the proprioceptive "landscape" associated with a given movement, and what basic principles might be at work in the coding of a movement trajectory? The results of the present study provide a basis for formulating the general principles possibly underlying the organization of the proprioceptive messages involved in the perception of movements with complex trajectories.

Without excluding the possible contribution of efferent copy (Teuber 1972), that tendon vibration gives rise to the illusion the subject is performing complex drawing movements involving recognizable geometrical figures shows that proprioceptive feedback may constitute one of the bases for perceiving symbolic manual actions like writing and drawing, as well as the means of perceptually decoding the sensory products of these actions. Moreover, because it is possible to manipulate muscle sensitivity by applying peripheral vibration to induce sensations of movement with predictable kinematic and spatial characteristics in a limb segment, we felt it might be worth attempting to formulate the principles governing the proprioceptive sensory codes involved in the perception of ongoing movements.

Let us take, first of all, the simplest possible case, where a single vibration is applied to a single muscle tendon. The direction of the resulting illusory movement will depend on the anatomical site of the vibrated muscle and therefore on the role of this muscle in the joint space in which it operates. The vibrated muscle can therefore be said to be the muscle that is stretched by the movement it encodes. This suggests that movement direction coding depends on the stretching imposed on the antagonist muscles, which causes a considerable increase in the spindle afferent discharge (Capaday and Cooke 1983; Roll and Vedel 1982; Gilhodes, Roll, and Tardy-Gervet 1986). Concomitantly, the primary spindle discharge either decreases or stops altogether in the active agonist muscles (Vallbo 1973; Roll and Vedel 1982). The direction of a movement may therefore depend on the contrast between the two sets of spindle activity occurring in a pair of antagonistic muscles. This hypothesis is supported by the finding that vibration applied simultaneously at the same frequency to two antagonistic muscles never induces kinesthetic illusions, but simply the feeling that the position of the joint in question has been stabilized. Only when the frequencies differ does an illusory sensation of movement occur (Gilhodes, Roll, and Tardy-Gervet 1986). This difference in frequency actually reflects the spindle discharge level, which in turn is dictated by the speed at which a muscle is stretched during a movement (Matthews 1972; Roll and Vedel 1982) and the speed at which the agonists are shortened. The parameters of a vibration-induced sensation of movement can therefore be expressed by a vector, whose direction is given by the anatomical site of the vibrated (or stretched) muscle, and whose modulus is taken to be vibration-frequency-dependent, that is, velocity-dependent.

When a pair of antagonistic muscles is covibrated at the same frequency, we therefore have two vectors with the same modulus oriented in opposite directions whose sum vector is null. If the muscles are covibrated at different frequencies, the resulting illusory sensation can also be written as the sum vector resulting from the addition of the two initial vectors.

The subjects' feeling that they were drawing oblique lines was induced by covibrating adjacent groups of muscles that, when vibrated separately, gave rise to the illusion the subjects were drawing orthogonally oriented lines. The covibration therefore simulated the concomitant stretching of two adjacent groups of muscles. Our averaged data again suggest that the vector describing an illusory oblique hand trajectory corresponds in fact to the sum of the two separate vectors taken to formulate the sensations evoked upon vibrating each of the two adjacent muscles separately. It is worth mentioning here that applying two vibrations to two muscles at the same time does not give rise to two separate illusions, but to a single one. This means that the central nervous system permanently processes and integrates the spindle afferent messages arising from the various muscles which are coengaged in the movement. (Figure 12.8.)

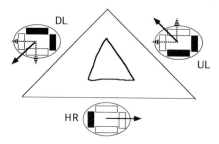

Figure 12.8 Vector coding of illusory triangle-drawing movement. (HR, horizontal right; UL, upward left; and DL, downward left.) Dashed vectors describe kinesthetic illusion obtained when vibrating each muscle in isolation. Solid vectors represent sum vectors describing kinesthetic illusion obtained when two adjacent muscles are covibrated (UL, DL).

Having previously determined the patterns of vibration required to induce spatially oriented line-drawing illusions, it was then only necessary to apply two or more of these patterns in succession in order to obtain triangular or quadrilateral figure–drawing illusions. The principles underlying the spatial orientation of each of the segments used to compose a linear figure were determined as described above. The length of each segment depended on the duration of the corresponding vibration sequence: in the case of a rectangle, it was twice as long when composing the longer sides as when composing the shorter sides. This hypothesis was confirmed by the experimented data: the mean length to width ratio in the case of rectangles turned out to be approximately 2.

As with oblique line drawing, illusions of curvilinear figure drawing can be elicited by covibrating two adjacent muscles; in this case, however, each of the muscles was subjected to a different pattern: an increasing vibration frequency was applied to the one muscle and a decreasing frequency to the other. By applying a single pattern of vibration to each pair among the four wrist muscle groups in succession, we succeeded in eliciting in the subjects the illusion that they were drawing a closed, circlelike figure.

From the theoretical point of view, the parameters of this illusory sensation can be expressed at any time by a vector whose origin coincides with the limb extremity and whose direction, in the case of a curvilinear figure, is the tangent to the drawing trajectory (rotating vector). The radius of curvature of the illusory drawing trajectory is determined by the rate at which the vibration frequency applied to the two covibrated muscles increases or decreases. If the rate of change is kept stable and the pattern of vibration is applied to all the successive pairs of adjacent wrist group muscles, the sensation elicited will be one of circlelike drawing. If the rate of change in the frequencies is varied from one pair to another, the sensation will be one of ellipselike drawing.

In addition, the use of a vector notation makes it possible to relate our results to the latest data obtained at the cortical level with a view to elucidating the brain mechanisms involved in cognitive activities, especially those which involve movement coding (Georgopoulos, Taira, and Lukashin 1993; Kalaska 1991). The authors of studies on the activity of shoulder-related cells in area 5 of the parietal cortex of behaving monkeys have reported that the proximal arm neurons were broadly tuned to the movement direction and that the tuning curves of various neurons overlapped considerably. The only possible source of information about the movement direction was the pattern of activity of the entire active population (Georgopoulos, Caminiti, and Kalaska 1984; Kalaska et al. 1990). This conclusion was confirmed using a formal vector model where the contribution made by each cell to the movement direction coding was simulated by a vector oriented toward the cell's preferred direction and depended on the level of discharge associated with a particular movement velocity. The resulting population vector, which was the sum vector of all the single vectors, accurately coded the direction and the velocity of the movement. These authors therefore suggested that a "joint space kinematic representation of natural movement trajectories" might be built up in parietal area 5 (Kalaska 1991, 320). Moreover, that the activity of the cells investigated often varied with the arm posture has suggested that area 5 may also be one of the possible sites for representing static body postures (Kalaska, Caminiti, and Georgopoulos 1983; Kalaska et al. 1990). Because many area-5 cells respond to passive proprioceptive inputs and are activated only after the onset of active movements, they can be presumed to deal only with sensory activities and to contribute to generating proprioceptive kinesthetic representations of body posture and movement (Sakata et al. 1973; Kalaska 1988). These propositions can now be reassessed in the light of recent findings by Schwartz (1994), who demonstrated that in monkeys, a direct cortical representation of drawing occurs. A population vector method providing a spatial map of neuronal activity was used to examine rhesus monkeys' motor cortical representation of the hand's trajectory as they drew spirals. These results again show that the movement trajectory was an important determinant of the cortical activity, although of course the data were obtained at the motor level. The similarities between the vector models that have been developed so far to describe the coding of movement trajectories at the proprioceptive periphery and at the cortical level strongly suggest that the pattern of the proprioceptive inputs at least partly determines the pattern of activity of the corresponding cortical neuronal sets.

It is also worth mentioning that, in addition to perceiving illusory movements in response to proprioceptive stimulation, the subjects were able to recognize and to accurately describe the motor forms elicited by the various vibratory patterns used. This means that the various instantaneous kinesthetic sequences must have been memorized and linked up into identifiable geometrical figures belonging to a repertoire of possible geometrical shapes (Jeannerod 1994). It therefore emerges that muscle proprioception is able to generate spatiotemporal inputs that may subserve complex cognitive operations such as those involved in the memorizing and recognition of motor forms, including symbolic actions performed with the human hand such as writing or drawing.

12.3 INTEGRATION OF PROPRIOCEPTIVE AND VISUAL CUES FOR LOCATING OBJECTS IN EXTRAPERSONAL SPACE

Although the first experiment provides some information about the brain's need to combine proprioceptive inputs from multiple muscles to sense the direction and velocity of complex body movements, the question remains, how does the brain process proprioceptive and visual cues together in order to relate our own movements to the location or movements of the objects in extrapersonal space?

Numerous recent results converge here to support the idea that muscular proprioception, along with vision, provides a link between personal and extrapersonal space (Roll and Roll 1987; Roll, Velay, and Roll 1991; Velay et al. 1994; Biguer et al. 1988). This statement implies that retinal information collected from the environment and proprioceptive information arising from the body itself may be processed together by the central nervous system in order to extract the spatial characteristics of objects in space and subsequently to organize visually guided activities. What remains to be established in particular is the kind of neurophysiological cues used by the central nervous system to process the absolute position of the retina in space so as to transform the retinotopic coordinates of an object into spatial coordinates.

Two types of extraretinal information are available for this purpose: the more classical type, "corollary discharge" or "efferent copy," originating from the central command (Howard 1982; Jeannerod 1982; Mittelstaedt 1989; Teuber 1972), and the proprioceptive type, based on the information arising from all the linked body segments that hold and move the retina in space, namely, the eyes, head, trunk, and legs. It is indeed possible the brain may at any moment process the absolute position of the retina in space on the basis of ongoing proprioceptive feedback from the whole "muscle chain" that links the eyes to the foot support. The following experiment provides evidence supporting these hypotheses.

Methods

The role of eye and neck proprioception in the egocentric localization of objects in extrapersonal space was studied in an open-loop visuomanual pointing task, during which vibration was applied to eye and/or neck muscles (Roll, Velay, and Roll 1991).

In ten seated subjects, vibration was applied to the neck, sternocleidomastoidus (SCM) or splenii, and/or extraocular muscles, inferior rectus (IR).

In the last case, the stimulus was applied to the periphery of the eyeball by means of minivibrators fixed to an external mechanical device with which the vibrators could be precisely adjusted. The duration of the vibration trains was 3 seconds, the frequency could vary from 20 to 100 Hz, and the peak-to-peak amplitude was 0.1 to 0.2 mm.

A pointing task was performed by the subjects under monocular viewing conditions. They were seated in complete darkness just in front of a vertical panel supplying a computer with the rectangular coordinates of the finger contact points. The subjects' heads were immobilized by means of combined head and chin rests. The subjects were required to gaze at a small luminous target that appeared for three seconds at the center of the panel and to point with their right hand at the place where the target had been before disappearing. In all the experimental series, each pointing sequence included ten trials. The rectangular coordinates of the pointing spots were then transformed into angular coordinates, taking into account that the subjects' eyes were 47 cm away from the pointing panel. Eye or neck muscles were vibrated only during the three-second period corresponding to the presentation of the luminous target.

Results

Vibrating the IR muscle of the right eye looking at a small visual target in darkness resulted, in all the tested subjects, in the illusion that the target was slowly moving upward. The direction and extent of this perceptual effect was measured in terms of the coordinates of the target position to which the subjects pointed immediately after the target had disappeared.

As shown in figure 12.9 (B and C), the mean upward pointing shift varied with the vibration frequency from 2.5 degrees at 20 Hz up to 4.5 degrees at 80 Hz and then remained unchanged at 100 Hz.

An illusory upward target movement was also induced by applying vibration to the tendons of the sternocleidomastoidus muscles for 3 seconds. This resulted in a mean pointing shift of 4.05 degrees which is very similar to that observed with IR vibration. When the inferior rectus and the SCM muscles were costimulated for 3 seconds, the subjects again reported perceiving an upward movement of the target, which resulted in a slightly greater mean pointing shift than those observed when the vibration was applied separately to each set of muscles (fig. 12.9D).

Finally, vibration applied concomitantly to both the splenius muscles resulted in all the subjects in an illusory downward movement of the target (mean pointing shift 5.4 degrees), and combined stimulation of the inferior rectus and neck (splenii) muscles resulted in a mean pointing shift which did not differ significantly from zero. The latter result is not surprising, since vibrating the IR and neck muscles separately resulted in illusory target movements in opposite directions.

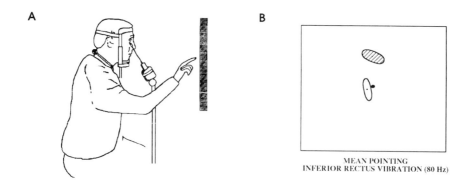

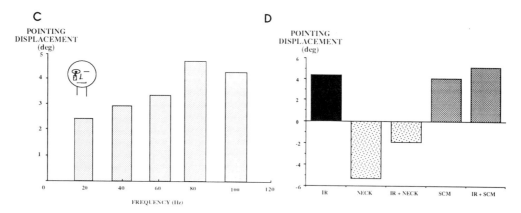

Figure 12.9 A. Experimental setup. B. Schematic representation of one subject's pointing areas under 80 Hz vibration of right inferior rectus (hatched confidence ellipse) and in control situation (empty ellipse). C. Mean upward pointing displacement as function of vibration frequency. D. Mean vertical pointing displacement under five vibration conditions (IR, inferior rectus; SCM, sternocleidomastoidus; Neck, splenii) (From Roll, Velay, and Roll 1991).

Discussion

The visual and visuomotor effects of eye and neck muscle vibrations observed here were fully consistent with the hypothesis that muscle proprioception from the muscles holding and moving the retina in space are coprocessed by the central nervous system along with retinal inputs. This proposition can indeed be extended to include the leg muscles because illusory visual target movements have also been elicited, in standing subjects by applying vibration to ankle muscles (Tibialis anterior or Soleus; Roll and Roll 1988). When no retinal information is available, muscle vibration elicits either whole-body movements or kinesthetic illusions, depending on the postural context (Roll et al. 1989), whereas when subjects are gazing at a given point in space, the vibration-induced illusions extend to the extrapersonal space, and the same proprioceptive message is taken to mean that the target is moving. In this situation, subjects no longer perceive illusions of movement involving parts of their own body. First, that the perceived velocity of the visual illusion was low and was found to increase within the 20 to 80 Hz frequency range constitutes major evidence that this visual illusion was of proprioceptive origin. Second, the direction of the illusory target movements described by the subjects undergoing muscle vibration and the direction of their mean pointing shifts were consistent with the idea that these muscle information may be involved in the spatial coding of retinal inputs, and therefore in the organization of visually oriented activities. In this respect, our results fit those obtained by Biguer et al. (1988), who reported that a rightward shift of the perceived position of a stationary target occurred when the posterior part of the neck was vibrated, and those by Cohen (1961), who established that after neck deafferentation, monkeys were unable to accurately perform visuomanual locating tasks. It is worth pointing out, moreover, that our assumptions and results are strongly supported by numerous recent findings, particularly clinical data by Campos, Chiesi, and Bolzani (1986), who reported that patients with pathological deafferentation of the ophthalmic branch of the trigeminal nerve performed target mislocations in an open loop pointing task. Pointing errors were also reported to occur (Gauthier, Nommay, and Vercher 1988) in normal subjects whose one covered eye was abducted by means of a suction lens, and in cats (Fiorentini, Berardi, ad Maffei 1982), where experimental deafferentation resulted in locating errors in a whole-body ballistic task.

Taken as a whole, our data seem to clearly demonstrate that eye and neck muscle proprioception contributes, as an extraretinal factor, to specifying the gaze direction in visually oriented activities. We would suggest that the proprioceptive feedback arising from eye and neck muscles might be part of a larger processing system involving all the body muscular feedbacks that serve to build up a directional reference frame accounting for the posture of the whole body. The presence of this body reference system might be the prerequisite for any action to be successfully performed in extrapersonal space (Roll, Velay, and Roll 1991).

To conclude, because complex hand-drawing illusions can be obtained by performing complex manipulations of the proprioceptive inputs, it can be said that these afferent messages are integrated into a single percept and that muscle proprioceptive cues may subserve complex cognitive movement coding and representation operations. Moreover, the occurrence of visual illusions and errors in visually guided behavior suggests that muscular proprioception may also act as unifying factor between personal and extra-personal space. These findings may throw some light on integration of multimodal information in the control of motor activities.

ACKNOWLEDGMENTS

The authors are grateful to H. Neiger, J. L. Demaria, J. P. Roman, N. Tir for their assistance, and to J. Blanc for revising the English. This work was supported by grants from C.N.R.S.-G.D.R Sport and INRS.

REFERENCES

Biguer, B., Donaldson, I. M., Hein, A., and Jeannerod, M. (1988). Neck muscle vibration modifies the representation of visual motion and direction in man. *Brain, 111*, 1405–1424.

Burke, D., Hagbarth, K. E., Lofstedt, L., and Wallin, B. G. (1976a). The responses of human muscle spindle endings to vibration of non-contracting muscles. *Journal of Physiology, 261,* 673–693.

Burke, D., Hagbarth, K. E., Lofstedt, L., and Wallin, B. G. (1976b). The responses of human muscle spindle endings to vibration of during isometric contraction. *Journal of Physiology, 261,* 695–711.

Campos, E. C., Chiesi, C., and Bolzani, R. (1986). Abnormal spatial localization in patients with herpes zoster ophtalmicus. *Archive Ophtalmic, 104,* 1176–1177.

Capaday, C., and Cooke, J. D. (1983). Vibration induced changes in movement-related EMG activity in human. *Experimental Brain Research, 52,* 139–146.

Cohen, L. A. (1961). Role of eye and neck proprioceptive mechanisms in body orientation and motor coordination. *Journal of Neurophysiology, 24,* 1–11.

Fiorentini, A., Berardi, N., and Maffei, L. (1982). Role of extraocular proprioception in the orienting behavior of cats. *Experimental Brain Research, 48,* 113–120.

Gauthier, G. M., Nommay, D., and Vercher, J. L. (1988). Ocular muscle proprioception and visual localization in man. *Journal of Physiology, London, 406.*

Georgopoulos, A. P., Caminiti, R., and Kalaska, J. F. (1984). Static spatial effects in motor cortex and area 5: Quantitative relations in a two-dimensional space. *Experimental Brain Research, 54,* 446–454.

Georgopoulos, A. P., Taira, M., and Lukashin, A. (1993). Cognitive neurophysiology of the motor cortex. *Science, 260,* 47–52.

Gilhodes, J. C., Coiton, Y., Roll, J. P., and Ans, B. (1993). Propriomuscular coding of kinesthetic sensation. Experimental approach and mathematical modeling. *Biological Cybernetics, 68,* 509–519.

Gilhodes, J. C., Roll, J. P., and Tardy-Gervet, M. F. (1986). Perceptual and motor effects of agonist-antagonist muscle vibration in Man. *Experimental Brain Research, 61,* 395–402.

Goodwin, G.-M., McCloskey, D.-I., and Matthews, P.-C.-B. (1972). The contribution of muscle afferents to kinesthesia shown by vibration induced illusions of movement and by the effect of paralyzing joint afferents. *Brain, 95,* 705–748.

Howard, I. (1982). *Human visual orientation.* New York: Wiley.

Jeannerod, M. (1982). How do we direct our actions in space? In A. Hein and M. Jeannerod (Eds.), *Spatially oriented behavior,* 1–13. New York: Springer.

Jeannerod, M. (1994). The representing brain: Neural correlates of motor intention and imagery. *Behavioral and Brain Sciences, 17*(2), 187–202.

Jones, A. L. (1988). Motor illusions: What do they reveal about proprioception? *Psychological Bulletin, 103,* 72–86.

Kalaska, J. F. (1988). The representation of arm movements in postcentral and parietal cortex. *Canadian Journal of Physiology and Pharmacology, 66,* 455–463.

Kalaska, J. F. (1991). What parameters of reaching are encoded by discharges of cortical cells? In D. R. Humphrey and H. J. Freund (Eds.), *Motor control: Concepts and issues,* 307–330.

Kalaska, J. F., Caminiti, R., and Georgopoulos, A. P. (1983). Cortical mechanisms related to the direction of two-dimensional arm movements: Relations in parietal area 5 and comparison with motor cortex. *Experimental Brain Research, 51,* 247–260.

Kalaska, J. F., Cohen, D. A. D., Prud'homme, M., and Hyde, M. L. (1990). Parietal area 5 neuronal activity encodes movement kinematics, not movement dynamics. *Experimental Brain Research, 80,* 351–364.

Matthews, P. B. C. (1972). *Mammalian muscle receptors and their central actions.* London: E. Arnold.

Matthews, P. B. C. (1982). Where does Sherrington's "muscular sense" originate? Muscles, joints, corollary discharges? *Annual Review of Neurosciences, 5,* 189–218.

Mittelstaedt, H. (1989). Basic solutions to the problem of head-centric visual localization. In R. Warren, A. H. Wertheim (Eds.), *The perception and control of self-motion,* 3–23. Hillsdale, NJ: Erlbaum.

Ribot-Ciscar, E., Tardy-Gervet, M. F., Vedel, J. P., and Roll, J. P. (1991). Post-contraction changes in human muscle spindle resting discharge and stretch sensitivity. *Experimental Brain Research, 86,* 673–678.

Roll, J. P. (1981). Contribution de la proprioception musculaire à la perception et au contrôle du mouvement chez l'Homme. *Ph.D. diss., Aix-Marseille I University.*

Roll, J. P., Gilhodes, J. C., Roll, R., and Velay, J. L. (1989). Contribution of skeletal and extraocular proprioception to kinesthetic representation. In M. Jeannerod (Ed.), *Attention and performance XIII,* 549–566. Hillsdale, NJ: Erlbaum.

Roll, J. P., Gilhodes, J. C., and Tardy-Gervet, M. F. (1980). Effets perceptifs et moteur des vibrations musculaires chez l'Homme normal: Mise en évidence d'une réponse des muscles antagonistes. *Archives Italiennes de Biologie, 118,* 51–71.

Roll, J. P., and Roll, R. (1987). Kinaesthetic and motor effects of extraocular muscle vibration in man. In K. O'Regan and A. Levy-Schoen (Eds.), *Eye movements,* 57–68. Amsterdam: North-Holland.

Roll, J. P., and Roll, R. (1988). From eye to foot: A proprioceptive chain involved in postural control. In B. Amblar, A. Berthoz, and F. Clarac (Eds.), *Posture and gait,* 155–164. Amsterdam: Elsevier.

Roll, J. P., and Vedel, J. P. (1982). Kinaesthetic role of muscle afferents in Man, studied by tendon vibration and microneurography. *Experimental Brain Research, 47,* 177–190.

Roll, J. P., Vedel, J. P., and Ribot, E. (1989). Alteration of proprioceptive messages induced by tendon vibration in man: A microneurographic study. *Experimental Brain Research, 76,* 213–222.

Roll, R., Velay, J. L., and Roll, J. P. (1991). Eye and neck proprioceptive messages contribute to the spatial coding of retinal input in visually oriented activities. *Experimental Brain Research, 85,* 423–431.

Sakata, H., Takaoka, A., Kawarasaki, A., and Shibutani, H. (1973). Somatosensory properties of neurons in superior parietal cortex (area 5) of the rhesus monkey. *Brain Research, 64,* 85–102.

Schwartz, A. B. (1994). Direct cortical representation of drawing. *Science, 265,* 540–542.

Teuber, H. L. (1972). Perception et mouvements, aspects neurophysiologiques et psycho-physiologiques. In *Neuropsychologie de la perception visuelle,* 187–221. Paris: Masson.

Vallbo, A. B. (1973). Muscle spindle afferent discharge from resting and contracting muscles in normal human subjects. In J. E. Desmedt (Ed.), *New developments in EMG and clinical neuro-physiology,* vol. 3, 251–262. Base 1: S. Karger.

Vedel, J. P., and Roll, J. P. (1982). Response to pressure and vibration of slowly adapting cutaneous mechanoreceptors in the human foot. *Neurosciences Letters, 34,* 289–294.

Vedel, J. P., and Roll, J. P. (1983). Muscle spindle contribution to the coding of motor activities in Man. *Experimental Brain Research, suppl. 7,* 253–265.

Velay, J. L., Roll, R., Lennerstrand, G., and Roll, J. P. (1994). Eye proprioception and visual localization in humans: Influence of ocular dominance and visual context. *Vision Research, 34*(16), 2169–2176.

13 Integration of Extrinsic and Motor Space

David A. Rosenbaum, Loukia D. Loukopoulos,
Sascha E. Engelbrecht, Ruud G. J. Meulenbroek, and
Jonathan Vaughan

ABSTRACT

When a reach is planned to a location in the external environment, a transformation must be made from extrinsic spatial coordinates to intrinsic motor coordinates. Understanding how the transformation is achieved is a central goal of research on perceptual-motor control. A core issue is how the transformation occurs, given that more degrees of freedom typically define a posture (e.g., 100 degrees of freedom for the joints) than typically define the position of an object in extrinsic space (e.g., the three spatial coordinates of the object's center of mass, and its pitch, roll, and yaw). This chapter reviews a theoretical model designed to solve the transformation problem. The model assumes that motor planning has two main stages: (1) selecting a target posture, and (2) performing a movement or series of movements that bridges the gap between the starting posture and target posture. The selection of a target posture is assumed to take into account how close the hand (or other contact point) will come to the target location and how costly the movement will be from the starting posture to the target posture. These costs provide constraints that help minimize the discrepancy between the degrees of freedom of the extrinsic and intrinsic reference frames. They also help rationalize observed efficiencies of movement. The achievements and limitations of the model are discussed.

13.1 INTRODUCTION

When a reach is planned to an external location, a transformation must be made from extrinsic spatial coordinates to intrinsic body coordinates. Given the desired external location of the hand, one must find joint angles, muscle lengths, and muscle forces that bring the hand to that location. Much is at stake in achieving this transformation. Prey will not be caught, mates will not be embraced, and offspring will not be plucked from harm's way if desired locations cannot be reached quickly and accurately.

In this chapter we consider how the transformation might be achieved. We couch the discussion in a theory of movement planning that has been the focus of our research for the past several years. We begin with a treatment of the difficulties inherent in the transformation problem. Then we present our model, reviewing its accomplishments and remaining challenges.

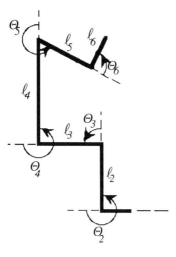

Figure 13.1 Limb segments and joint angles for a simple stick figure.

13.2   THE PERILS OF HAND LOCATION LOOK-UP

Let us begin with some mathematics. Consider a simple stick figure (fig. 13.1) that has a set of n linked limb segments, $s_1, s_2, \ldots, s_n$, where the subscript increases as one ascends the limb segment chain from the toe upward. If the ith segment has a fixed length l_i, and the joint angle linking the ith segment to its parent segment is θ_i, we can define the extrinsic spatial (Cartesian) coordinates, (x, y) of the jth joint as follows:

$$x_j = x_{j-1} + l_{j-1} \cos \sum_{i=1}^{j-1} \theta_i$$

$$y_j = y_{j-1} + l_{j-1} \sin \sum_{i=1}^{j-1} \theta_i.$$

(13.1)

This formulation provides a way of defining the location of the end of the nth limb segment. If a tool happens to be attached to the most distal joint, the location of its endpoint can be similarly derived, provided its length and angle of attachment to the last joint are known.

What we have outlined above is known, in robotics, as "forward kinematics" (Craig 1986). The term *kinematics* refers to the analysis of positions without regard to the forces that yield them (*Dynamics* is concerned with forces). The term *forward* refers, somewhat arbitrarily, to the derivation of locations from joint angles and limb lengths. *Inverse kinematics* involves finding a joint angle configuration (a posture) that permits a specified point along the limb segment chain to reach a desired location. In the discussion that follows, we use the term *contact point* to refer to this specified point. If the tip of the index finger needs to be brought to a location, then the tip of the index finger is the contact point.

The capacity to compute forward kinematics has great advantages. As indicated above, when one can compute forward kinematics, one can determine where the end of a tool will be in external space; because tool use is basic for survival, this ability is highly desirable. With the ability to compute forward kinematics, one can also determine where any point along the limb segment chain is located. Suppose, for example, that one has just been bitten by a mosquito on the left arm and wants to swat the mosquito as quickly as possible with the right hand. If one is going to hit the mosquito, it will not be enough to know which patch of skin was bitten; one must also know where in external space the patch of skin is located. Without this information, the swatting hand has no idea, so to speak, of where to go.

While it is desirable to be able to compute forward kinematics, if an actor can wield a tool or swat at mosquitoes, it does not follow that he or she can do the computations. Another possibility, which does not require the computation of forward kinematics, is that the actor has stored instances of previous reaches, along with information about the locations attained by one or more points along the limb segment chain at one or more times during those reaches. For example, if the actor stores the x-y location of the hand at the completion of one reach, and the x-y location of the hand at the completion of another reach, then later, when the hand must be brought to either of these two locations, the appropriate reach can be identified and then executed. We call this method "hand location look-up."

There are several problems with hand location look-up, however, and all of them bear on inverse kinematics. The first, most obvious, problem is that it is not clear what to do when the hand must be brought to a location that has not been learned. One way of avoiding this problem is to allow that the look-up table has many, many entries (Atkeson 1989), but this merely reduces the scope of the problem without eliminating it.

A second problem concerns aiming with parts of the body other than the hand. Suppose the elbow or shoulder must be brought to a target location. This might occur when one wants to switch on a light with one's shoulder when one's arms are loaded with packages. It would be convenient if the look-up table stored elbow and shoulder locations as well as hand locations, but then the problem would remain of how to cope with limited stored instances of elbow and shoulder locations, just as the problem arose before of how to cope with limited stored instances of hand locations. Moreover, one could ask why, if hand, elbow, and shoulder locations are stored, locations of other selected points along the body are not stored. Why not store locations of intermediate points along the forearm or upper arm, for example? If one assumed that only "landmark" anatomical locations are stored (e.g., just the wrist, elbow, and shoulder), then one could imagine that locations mapped to intermediate body points could be found by interpolation, based on their known distances from the landmark anatomical locations. However, if one were to postulate this computational ability, one might as well postulate the capacity for forward kinematics itself. Furthermore, interpolation would not allow for the localization of the end of an *extension* of the arm (i.e., a handheld tool).

A third problem with relying on hand location look-up is that there are generally an infinite number of reaches that can bring the hand (or other contact point) to a given location within the workspace. The reason is that there are more degrees of freedom (df) in the body than in the geometrical description of an external location. For a point in a plane, for example, there are just 2 df, its x and y coordinates, assuming a Cartesian reference frame. By contrast, the human joint system has about 100 mechanical df. Even if one considers a real object, such as a cylinder, in 3-D space, its position is specified completely by 6 df—the three spatial coordinates of the object's center of mass, and its pitch, roll, and yaw. But the arm alone (i.e., the shoulder, elbow, and wrist) has 7 df. Hence, even a handless arm has more degrees of freedom than a cylinder, and so an infinite number of arm positions permit the cylinder to be grasped, and an infinite number of arm positions permit an arbitrary contact point along the arm to reach a point in a plane. This complicates the hand-location look-up method because, in addition to all its other problems, it becomes unclear which of the reaches that maps to a location should be stored, and if more than one reach should be stored, which one should be selected.

All these considerations lead us to doubt that the nervous system relies on hand-location look-up. What is more likely, in our view, is that the nervous system can compute forward kinematics, and that through this ability, it can generate reaches to any location with any part of the body or with any extension of the body (i.e., with a tool). We do not know how forward kinematics is computed by the nervous system, nor how to test the hypothesis that forward kinematics is in fact computed, so we need to dispel the hope that we will resolve these questions here. What we will do instead is to describe, in the next section, the reasoning we have followed to develop a general model of movement planning, which assumes the capacity for forward kinematics. An earlier version of the model was described by Rosenbaum et al. (1993a, b), and a more detailed description of the current model is given in Rosenbaum et al. (1995).

13.3 STEPS TO A MODEL

Consider again the inverse kinematics problem, focusing on the fact that a location within the workspace can generally be reached with an infinite number of reaches. Given this one-to-many mapping, how can particular reaches be selected?

Trial-and-Error Planning

A first hypothesis is that the planning system simulates different random movements until a movement is found that brings the hand acceptably close to the target, at which time that movement is executed. In this scheme, forward kinematics is used to evaluate each simulated movement to determine whether the contact point will be acceptably close to the place it is supposed to go.

Such a model need not be dismissed out of hand; one has actually been developed and shown to work reasonably well for a 3 df robot manipulator (Mel 1990, 1991). On the other hand, the trial-and-error method may not be adequate for a system with more degrees of freedom. For a more complex system, the number of iterations needed to find an acceptable movement could become unacceptably large, making the solution time long. Another reason why it is doubtful that movements are planned through random simulation is that such a method fails to explain the reductions in planning speed that accompany practice.

Building on the Mass-Spring Model

A more realistic possibility is to build on the mass-spring model of motor control. The mass-spring model was independently proposed by Asatryan and Feldman (1965) in Russia and by Crossman and Goodeve (1963/1983) in the United States. The main idea of the model as it pertains to the inverse kinematics problem is that a desired joint angle can be specified in terms of an equilibrium position such that the muscle lengths allow the desired joint angle to be adopted, and the muscle forces sum to zero. An appealing feature of this model is that when all the joint angles of the body are specified, all the muscle lengths are implied (Shadmehr 1993), suggesting that if a *posture* (i.e., a vector of joint angles) is planned, muscle lengths follow from it. Furthermore, if the muscles can change from their initial lengths to their new target lengths simply by finding themselves in disequilibrium until the new equilibrium position is achieved, then, in principle, the details of the movement need not be spelled out explicitly. Only the target posture needs to be planned, and the movement from the starting posture to the target posture can come "for free."[1]

Finding a Target Posture

If the goal of planning is to find a target posture, how should that target posture be found? It is implausible to assume that postures are stored for all possible location because there are an infinite number of locations to which contact points can be brought. Moreover, for any location within the workspace, there are an infinite number of possible postures. These observations imply that if any postures are to be stored in memory, the number must be smaller than the number possible. How then can the panoply of postures that is performed be derived from the smaller number of postures that may be stored?

The answer lies in recognizing that postures may be regarded as vectors in a space whose dimensions are the mechanical degrees of freedom of the joints. An advantage of this approach is that the posture vectors can be linearly combined; for example, they can be summed to provide a resultant vector in the same space. When one sums vectors, the length of the resultant is greater than the length of any of the component vectors (provided that at least two of the component vectors have lengths greater than zero). Thus, if posture vectors are summed and if the components of those vectors extend from the minimum to the maximum of their respective ranges, the resultant will be a vector with physiologically unrealistic joint angles. This is not true, however, if the component vectors are first scaled down such that the scale factors applied to all the component vectors lie between 0 and 1 and also sum to 1. With this constraint, the length of the resultant vector will never be greater than the maximum of any of the component vector lengths.

What is gained by scaling the component vectors down and then summing them up? If each component vector represents a stored posture, the scale factor for each component vector can be viewed as a weight assigned to the stored posture for the task at hand. The weight of each stored posture can in turn can be viewed as an activation of the stored posture, based upon its suitability for the task to be performed. If the stored postures are assigned weights based on their suitability for completion of the task, and if the assigned weights lie between 0 and 1 and sum to 1, then the weighted-sum vector is a posture that occupies the same rage of values as the component vectors. Moreover, the weighted-sum vector can serve as a target posture.

How should weights be assigned to the stored posture? Suppose the pth stored posture, like any stored posture, has a nonnegative cost, c_p. The simplest way to assign a weight to the pth stored posture is to let the weight, w_p, of the pth stored posture be defined as $w_p = c_p / \sum c_p$. In our model, we use a slightly more complicated procedure. After the cost of each stored postures has been obtained (see below), the cost is passed through a Gaussian filter, yielding a value $g(c_p)$, which approaches 1 as c_p approaches 0. Once the Gaussian values have been found for all the stored postures, w_p is set to $g(c_p) / \sum g(c_p)$.

Our reason for using Gaussian filtering of the costs is that the standard deviation of the Gaussian can be set to the minimum cost of any stored posture. Thus, if there is a stored posture whose cost is 0 (the ideal cost), the standard deviation of the Gaussian is 0; this "perfect" stored posture then receives a weight of 1 and automatically becomes the target posture. However, if none of the stored postures is perfectly suited for the task, the standard deviation is greater than 0, and none of the stored postures is assigned all the weight. By allowing the target posture to be a weighted average when no stored posture is perfectly suited for the task, the planning system can generate novel target postures, as required in skilled performance. Moreover, the planning method allows the target posture to be selected either through a winner-take-all strategy when there is an ideal stored posture, or a weighted summing strategy when there is not. These two choice methods are different outcomes of the same underlying decision process, which is satisfying in view of the fact that both strategies are used by the brain (Erickson 1984; Saltzman and Newsome 1994); for evidence of weighted summing of kinesthetic input, see Roll et al., chap. 12, this volume).

How Many Stored Postures?

How many stored postures are there, and what are their identities? In linear algebra, the only vectors needed to span a space are the basis vectors for the space, that is, d orthogonal vectors corresponding to the d dimensions of the space, although one normally allows weights to take on all real values. In our system, where the weights lie between 0 and 1 and must sum to 1, the minimal number of vectors needed to span a space of d dimensions is 2^d. These 2^d vectors go to the minimum and to the maximum of each dimension. Thus, for a two-dimensional space whose dimensions are labeled a and b, 2^2 vectors are needed, going to $(\min a, \max b)$, $(\max a, \min b)$, $(\max a, \max b)$, and $(\min a, \min b)$, respectively.[2] For most of the simulations to be presented here, the minimal number of stored postures needed is $2^3 = 8$.

If 2^d vectors are needed to span a space of d dimensions, 2^{100} vectors are needed to span a space corresponding to the $d = 100$ df the human joint system. It has been estimated that there are no more than 2^{80} electrons in the universe, so it is hard to believe that there are more stored postures in one person's memory. The way to cope with this problem is to allow for posture *subspaces*; for example, there might be a subspace for the hand and a subspace for the foot. Postures occupying the same subspace would belong to the same synergy or coordinative structure (Kugler, Kelso, and Turvey 1980), whereas postures not occupying the same subspace would not belong to the same synergy or coordinative structure. From this point of view, the existence of synergies or coordinative structures is necessitated by storage limitations.

Granted that posture subspaces require fewer stored postures than strictly necessary, we also allow for the possibility that there can be more stored postures than are minimally required. The reason is that we model learning in terms of a survival-of-the-fittest mechanism. In our theory, at time $t = 0$, an individual has a random set of stored postures, each of which has an initial strength. As each stored posture is evaluated for the tasks that are encountered, stored postures that are consistently assigned high weights have high strengths, whereas stored postures that are consistently assigned low weights have low strengths. If the strength of a stored posture gets low enough, that stored posture "dies" and is replaced by another randomly chosen posture. Through this Darwinian process, the actor has more and more stored postures for tasks that have well-suited postures. On the other hand, because lost stored postures are replaced with other randomly chosen postures, the system as a whole can be preadapted for new tasks. (For more details and relevant simulations, see Rosenbaum et al., 1995.)

Evaluating Stored Postures

How are stored postures evaluated? What determines their suitability or cost? When we posit costs for stored postures, we assume that the degrees of freedom problem (the problem of finding unique solutions when many solutions are possible; see Bernstein 1967) cannot be solved by relying solely on mechanics or dependencies between effectors, even though both factors play significant roles in reducing the degrees of freedom problem (Bizzi et al. 1992; Kugler, Kelso, and Turvey 1980). Our emphasis on cost evaluation follows from the observation that when particular types of movements are performed though other types are possible, some selection criterion must be used (e.g., Cruse, Brüwer, and Dean 1993; Flash and Hogan 1985; Nelson 1983; Uno, Kawato, and Suzuki 1989). One need not assume that the cost is represented explicitly in the nervous system, any more than one must assume that the principle of least action is represented explicitly in the physical universe, thereby causing light to travel in straight lines. The costs can be implicit, although, in our theory, they may be used deliberately by the actor. In our view, a major aim of any planning theory should be to allow for a way of specifying what task needs to be performed. For a waiter carrying a tray, for example, it is important to keep the tray flat, but for that same person when he returns home, it is no longer important to hold his newspaper horizontally. In our view, a task is a set of weighted costs, and the capacity to set the weights for the costs is as important for effective planning as the capacity to satisfy the costs themselves. Satisfying costs need not require cost minimization. Often, minimization is computationally expensive, and all that is needed is to find a solution for which the cost is acceptably low (cf. Simon's 1979 notion of "satisficing").

Given our belief in the flexibility of cost specification, the costs used in our planning system are flexible. In general, we allow that any given task can be represented by a set of weights for all costs that are potentially relevant to performance. Thus, in speaking, costs pertaining to sound production have high weights, whereas costs pertaining to bringing the hand close to a spatial target have low weights; the opposite is true for most reaching tasks. By allowing for all types of costs and assuming that the weights assigned to them sum to 1, we have a common format for specifying all tasks, and the same planning system can be employed for dealing with all of them.

In our model of reaching control, we focus on just two of the costs that are possible in performance, implicitly setting the weights of all other possible costs to zero. Before saying here what these costs are, we wish to mention that in our system, each stored posture is evaluated for the costs it would incur, but we make no assumptions about whether the evaluations occur serially or in parallel. If the stored postures are represented by autonomous "demons" of the sort sometimes hypothesized for visual processing (Selfridge 1959; see Lindsay and Norman 1977), the entire system would work in parallel.

The two costs that we focus on for reaching are called the "spatial error cost" and the "travel cost". The *spatial error cost* is the distance that would lie between the contact point (e.g., the tip of the index finger) and the spatial target if the stored posture under consideration were adopted. For convenience, we express this distance as the Euclidean separation between the two points. We arbitrarily assume a Cartesian coordinate frame, noting that the geometry used by the perceptual-motor system for evaluating spatial error is as yet unknown.

The *travel cost* for each stored posture is the cost that would be incurred if the actor moved from the starting posture to the particular stored posture under evaluation. The travel cost is a function of the angular distances to be covered by the joints as well as the times in which those angular distances must be covered; the travel cost for a stored posture is determined in part by the *expense factors* for the individual joints. The expense factor for each joint reflects the difficulty of rotating it and can vary based on the health of the joint and the loads imposed on the limb segments it must rotate. We assume that a joint has a characteristic expense factor, which changes infrequently; the expense factor for the joint, the angular distances to be covered, and the times in which those angular distances must be bridged together imply the effort required to move from the starting posture to the stored posture. The greater the anticipated effort, the greater the travel cost. (For more details, see Rosenbaum et al., 1995.)

Once a stored posture's travel cost and spatial error cost are known, a total cost can be assigned to the stored posture. The total cost is simply the weighted sum of the stored posture's travel cost and spatial error cost, where the weights for the two costs lie between 0 and 1 and sum to 1 (the same constraint as for summing posture vectors). If a task requires high spatial accuracy, the weight assigned to the spatial error cost is high, and the weight assigned to the travel cost is low; if a task does not require great spatial accuracy, the weight assigned to the spatial error cost is low, and the weight assigned to the travel cost is high. We allow for the adjustment of the spatial error weight and travel cost weight because, as indicated above, we regard the assignment of weights to costs as essential for representing different tasks.

The final stage of planning is to specify a target posture by taking a weighted sum of the stored posture vectors. The weights assigned to each stored posture are equal to the Gaussian transformation of its total cost divided by the sum of the Gaussian transformations of the total costs of all the stored postures; the sum is obtained by linearly combining the weighted stored-posture vectors.[3]

Moving to the Target Posture

The final part of our theory concerns movement to the target posture. As we said earlier in discussing the mass-spring model, we were attracted to the possibility that when an equilibrium position is specified, movement to the equilibrium position falls out, because the limb is now in disequilibrium. The limb can in essence move passively to the new equilibrium position; a complete plan for the trajectory need not be laid out by a central programmer. Although questions have been raised about how plausible such trajectories are for multijoint movements (Hasan 1991), we find the general concept appealing and thus have adopted it in our model. Specifically, we assume that when a target posture is defined, each joint simply reduces the error between its starting angle and its target angle. We assume that each joint's angular displacement is achieved with a sinusoidal driving torque, as assumed in other models (Meyer, Smith, and Wright 1982). A sinusoidal torque profile yields a bell-shaped angular velocity profile for each joint. If the torques for all the joints start together and then stop together, the path from the starting posture to the final posture through joint space is a straight line. It is not crucial for our model that the movement occur this way—this is just a working hypothesis—although it is appealing to suppose that it does because then biological movement can be said to obey the principle of least action from physics, at least with respect to motion through joint space. More importantly, the assumption that the joints begin and end their motions together provides an empirically testable prediction about the timing of multijoint movement.

13.4 MODEL PERFORMANCE

How well does the model perform? Can it achieve basic aspects of everyday performance and account for more subtle findings in the literature? In addressing these questions, we should make clear that in developing our model, we have adopted something of an engineering strategy. We have tried to make explicit all the assumptions that permit us to solve the inverse kinematics problem posed by a creature with arbitrarily many degrees of freedom. We have sought to develop a model that, if not a perfect account of natural performance, is still complete enough to be useful for practical applications.

Based on computer simulations using a simple stick figure like the one shown in figure 13.1. We can say that our model does in fact satisfy the main objectives for which it was designed. Specifically, we have modeled the behavior of a 3 df stick figure that can bend at the hip, shoulder, and elbow to move in the sagittal plane. Below, we list the major capabilities of the stick figure, which we have named "INKI" (short for inverse kinematics).

1. INKI can simulate the reaching performance of human subjects (Vaughan et al. 1995); representative simulation results are shown in figure 13.2. In this experiment, human adults reached for targets in the sagittal plane. The target in each trial was a tennis ball, which simply had to be touched with the palm of the hand. The target occupied 12 possible locations, arranged in 3 rows and 4 columns. The subjects wore markers on the knee, hip, shoulder, elbow,

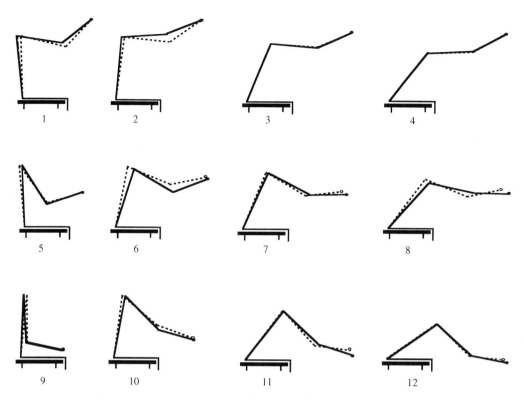

Figure 13.2 Actual postures (solid lines) and simulated postures (dashed lines) of typical subject reaching to each of 12 targets in sagittal plane. From Vaughan et al. (1995).

and wrist, and they reached to each of the 12 target locations while being videotaped from the side. Each reach was initiated from a resting position (the hand on the knee). For each trial, the videotaped positions of the markers were later digitized from the frozen video frame in which the subject first left the starting posture and from the frozen video frame in which the subject first arrived at the target posture. After we digitized the human performance, we had INKI reach to each of the same 12 target locations. INKI was given only the starting posture the subject adopted and the limb lengths of his or her body. The question was whether INKI would adopt the same target postures as the subject did. As shown in figure 13.2, the predicted target postures came very close to the actual target postures. The model accounted for more than 96 percent of the variance in the obtained data over the subjects. To fit the model to the data, we estimated four parameters—the expense factors of the hip, shoulder, and elbow and the spatial error weight. These four parameters were fitted to the full data set, consisting of 3 joint angles for each of 4 subjects reaching to each of 12 targets (i.e., 144 data points). The best-fitting expense factors for the hip, shoulder, and elbow were, respectively, 97.8 percent, 58.2 percent, and 82.3 percent of the maximum possible expense factor for all joints, and the best-fitting spatial error weight was .843.

(For more details about the experiment, fitting procedure, and robustness of the fit, see Rosenbaum et al. 1995 and Vaughan et al. 1995.) Because the model can account for the postures adopted by human subjects, we can take its other virtues more seriously; these are outlined below. All the following claims about the model have been checked using simulations in which INKI's expense factors and spatial error weight had the best-fitting values mentioned above.

2. INKI can bring any contact point along the limb segment chain to any point within the work space from any starting posture. Furthermore, INKI can do this even if the expense factor of one of its joints increases dramatically, simulating the effects of reluctance or inability to bend some joint following injury. Thus, if the hand can be brought to a target location when the expense factors of the 3 joints are normal, it can still reach that target location if, say, the hip is far more difficult to bend. This capacity for adapting to changes in joint mobility arises from the way planning is carried out. If the expense factor for a joint increases, stored postures requiring extensive rotations of that joint are assigned lower weights than usual, and thus the target posture requires only small rotation of the "damaged" joint. Being able to change the way one moves in order to achieve the same goals is, of course, essential for everyday performance.

3. Another demonstration of INKI's flexibility is that it can reach effectively with a tool. For example, if the tool is "held in the hand" (attached to the wrist), its end-point (or any specified point along its length) can be brought to a specified location within reach. This is possible because the planning system can compute forward kinematics; using stored postures, the planning system can determine where, for each stored posture, the contact point along the tool would end up if the stored posture were adopted.

4. Because of its capacity for forward kinematics, INKI can also respond adaptively to "amputation." If the forearm is shortened, provided the length of the forearm is known to the planner, forward kinematics can be used to determine where the end of the forearm would be if a particular stored posture were adopted. A spatial error cost can then be determined for that stored positive and a weight assigned to it based on its ability to achieve the spatial target. Finally, a target posture can be found to achieve the spatial target location if the length of the forearm, or for that matter, any limb segment, changes.

5. INKI can bring more than one contact point to more than one spatial target at a time, as long it is geometrically possible to do so. (In real life, a person might want to do this when laying a forearm on the armrest of a chair, bringing the elbow to the back of the armrest and the hand to the front.) This task is possible in the model because the planning system can have distinct spatial error costs for distinct contact points.

6. Another extension of the model permits INKI to reach for *series* of spatial targets by anticipating how it will reach for spatial target n when it reaches

for spatial target $n - 1$. The method that yields such *coarticulation* effects has INKI first plan its reach to spatial target n and then plan its reach to spatial target $n - 1$. Thus, in the first pass, INKI considers the spatial error cost of each of its stored postures relative to spatial target n, and the travel cost of each its stored postures relative to the starting posture. After the target posture for spatial target n is found, INKI selects a target posture for spatial target $n - 1$ evaluating three, rather than the usual two, costs for each stored posture. These three costs are (1) the spatial error cost relative to spatial $n - 1$ that would accrue if the stored posture were adopted; (2) the travel cost of moving from the starting posture to the stored posture under evaluation; and (3) the travel cost of moving from the stored posture under evaluation to the target posture for spatial target n. Because of this third cost, the target posture for spatial target $n - 1$ is chosen as an effective "detour" or "via posture" on the way to the final target posture.

7. Another extension of the model allows INKI to move any contact point along the limb segment chain *through* a location (a *via location*) on the way to some other location. This is achieved by aiming for a virtual spatial target location beyond the via location and superimposing a movement from the via location to the ultimate spatial target onto the movement from the starting location to the virtual target location. The assumption that movements can be superimposed has been supported in other studies (e.g., Flash and Henis 1991).

8. Additional extensions of the model make it possible for INKI to write and draw (Meulenbroek et al. 1994). The stick figure that implements writing and drawing is called "DINKI" (short for drawing inverse kinematics). DINKI has 6 df, in comparison to INKI's 3. DINKI can bend at the shoulder, elbow, wrist, and at three finger joints; these motions displace a pen held between the index finger and thumb. DINKI can bring the pen tip to any location within its workspace from any other location within its workspace, just as INKI can, and it has all the capabilities that INKI does. In addition, DINKI can generate strokes, as required in writing and drawing, by directing the pen tip to a series of target locations and via locations, defined, respectively, as points of maximal and minimal curvature in the strokes to be produced. Most important for present purposes, DINKI can produce essentially the same graphic output when the expense factors of its joints vary widely. Hence DINKI shows the capacity for motor equivalence in just the way that motor equivalence has been most classically characterized—producing the same written output through different means (Lashley 1942; Merton 1972).

9. The model can account for a number of learning effects. As mentioned earlier, because of the Darwinian character of the acquisition and retention of stored postures, those stored postures that allow a contact point to reach an often-tested region proliferate, whereas those that do not tend to dwindle. The demography of stored postures affects the time it takes to find acceptable target postures because of an aspect of planning not reviewed

earlier—*feedforward correction*—which occurs when there is an unacceptably high spatial error cost for a planned target posture. In such a case, the planning system aims for a second spatial target, chosen to counteract the biases in direction and amplitude that the initial target posture reflected. If, after planning, the second target posture is judged unacceptable as a means of aligning the contact point with the first spatial target, a third spatial target is chosen to counteract the bias in direction and amplitude of the second target posture relative to the first spatial target. This third target posture is then generated to bring the contact point to the third spatial target, and so forth until an acceptable target posture is found or until a deadline is reached. Our simulations have shown that through this process, the contact point gets closer and closer to the first spatial target. The number of feedforward correction cycles needed to bring the contact point to the first spatial target is smaller, the closer the location of the first spatial target is to the center of an often-tested spatial region. The presence of more stored postures for the often-tested region allows planned target posture to be acceptably close to spatial targets within that region in a small number of feedforward correction cycles (see Rosenbaum et al. 1995 for details).

10. The model accounts for a number of more subtle phenomena observed in the motor control literature. For example, it accounts for the fact that performance suffers when there is uncertainty about initial positions of the limbs, as observed in deafferentation studies (Polit and Bizzi 1979; Sanes 1990) and in studies that use tendon vibration to alter the perceived position of the limb (Sittig, Denier van der Gon, and Gielen 1987). According to the model, deficits in performance are predicted when there is greater uncertainty about initial positions because target postures are planned with respect to initial postures. Moreover, movement trajectories are generated by reducing the distance in joint space between the initial posture and the target posture, in which case movement execution is adversely affected by uncertainty about the starting position of the limb.

11. The model accounts for the change in the shape of the handpath that occurs when subjects make upward movements in the sagittal plane, as opposed to outward movements in the sagittal plane (Atkeson and Hollerbach 1985). The hand travels in a straighter path in outward movements than in upward movements. The model predicts this outcome because both outward and upward movements are most easily achieved with little hip rotation, assuming that the expense factor for the hip is larger than the expense factor for the shoulder and elbow; empirical support for this assumption has been obtained by Vaughan et al. 1995; see item 1 in this section. Owing to the geometry of the limbs, when there is little hip rotation, outward movements of the hand follow a straighter path than do upward movements.

12. Yet another phenomenon the model accounts for is the shape of the distribution of endpoints of blind reaching movements. Typically, when subjects make blind positioning movements with a handheld stylus, the distri-

bution of locations where the stylus ends up is skewed toward the starting position of the stylus (Ghez et al. 1990; Schmidt et al. 1979; Siddall, Holding, and Draper 1957). This outcome is explained in the model by referring to the combined effects of minimizing travel costs and spatial error costs. As stored postures are evaluated for the contributions they can make to an aiming task, the desire to minimize spatial error costs leads to the selection of target postures that are close to the target location but equally spaced around its center. The desire to minimize the travel cost favors stored postures close to the starting posture and leads to the skewed pattern that is observed.

13. Finally, the model allows for the planning of movements around obstacles (Loukopoulos et al. 1993). The method used involves the identification of via locations through which the contact point must be brought on its way to a final spatial target location if internal simulations of the initially planned movement suggest a collision. This method demands many planning iterations, however, and is not as simple as we would like. That obstacle avoidance fails as often as it does in everyday performance—witness the need for Band-Aids—does not assure us that the strategy used by natural actors is as complicated as the method we have developed so far. For example, the method we use can require the identification of whole series of via locations if there are multiple objects in the work space. The process of finding each via location and testing for possible collisions as movements are made through them may be too lengthy and computationally intensive to be taken seriously as a realistic model of natural obstacle avoidance.

13.5 CHALLENGES FOR THE FUTURE

Having just mentioned one challenge for our future work, it is appropriate to discuss others that remain. First, we need to seek a simpler means of avoiding obstacles, recognizing that the method may need to have some inherent complexity; obstacle avoidance, after all, takes years to be mastered (Bruner 1970) and even adults are prone to bump into tables, cut themselves, and so forth. A method that comes to mind is one used in robotics. The idea is to allow the motor system to find its own path to a specified target configuration through more passive means (Connolly and Grupen 1993; Khatib 1985). This can occur in much the same way that water finds its way to a basin of attraction; such a path can be found by solving the Laplacian (i.e., the second time derivatives must sum to zero). The process can be simulated on a digital computer as follows: (1) in a matrix of postures, assign a fixed low value to the target posture, assign a fixed high value to the starting posture, to postures at the edge of joint space, and to postures that would collide with obstacles, and assign an arbitrary intermediate but nonfixed value to all other postures; (2) allow each stored posture with a nonfixed value to take on the average of itself and its immediate neighbors, repeating this process until there are no numerical changes; and finally, (3) generate the trajectory by moving from the starting posture to postures with successively lower values until the target posture is reached. Because the solution to the Laplacian never runs into a local minimum, the planned path will avoid obstacles, provided forward kinematics can be used to determine which stored postures would collide with the obstacles in the work space (Lozano-Pérez 1981). The one difficulty with this approach is that the trajectories may not be physically realistic, in which case, it may be necessary to supplement the method with additional mechanical constraints.

Another challenge, closely related to the first, is to include costs related to dynamics. Here the work of Mitsuo Kawato (see chap. 14, this volume) is especially instructive because he and his colleagues have developed effective methods for modeling the generation of movements, both in humans and in robots. Most striking is Kawato's postulation of bidirectional influences between planning in extrinsic spatial coordinates and planning with respect to dynamics, which is, of course, very similar to our postulation of spatial error costs as well as travel costs. The emphasis on both types of costs holds considerable promise as a way of solving long-standing problems in perceptual-motor integration.

NOTES

This work was supported by grant SBR-94-96290 from the National Science Foundation, a University of Massachusetts Faculty Research Grant, a Research Scientist Development Award from the National Institute of Mental Health, the Dutch Organization for Scientific Research (NWO Stimulans Premie), the Royal Netherlands Academy of Science, and the Hamilton College Faculty Research Fund. Correspondence should be sent to David A. Rosenbaum at the Department of Psychology, 621 Moore Building, Pennsylvania State University, University Park, PA 16802, or via electronic mail to DAR12@CAC.PSU.EDU. Please do not quote without permission.

1. Hasan (1991) has pointed out that the trajectories that emerge when these movements are simulated are not physically realistic, which does not mean, however, that the planner could not plan movements by specifying new equilibrium positions. It may mean instead that a more realistic model of the physical plant is needed to explain how simple commands from the central nervous system have realistic effects at the periphery.

2. Because a zero-length vector scaled by any positive real still has zero length, it may not be obvious why the zero-length vector that goes to ($\min a$, $\min b$) should be included. The reason for including ($\min a$, $\min b$) can be appreciated by considering a space that has only one dimension, a. In that case, the only scalable vector would go to $\max a$, but the sum of the weights used to generate vectors spanning the space (i.e., the one weight) would only sum to 1 when the scaled vector went to $\max a$. Including the vector that goes to $\min a$ permits the sum of the weights always to sum to 1.

3. If it is costly to evaluate all stored postures, either because they must evaluated serially or because of resource limitations, then there are a number of ways to abbreviate the evaluation process. One way is to accept as the target posture the first stored posture whose total cost falls below some threshold. Another way is to stop evaluating stored postures as soon as enough stored postures have been evaluated that have total costs below a threshold; once these stored postures have been found, weights can be assigned to them, and a target posture

can be found through the method otherwise used for all the stored postures. We have not yet evaluated these alternative techniques, in part because we have been reluctant to add the additional parameter (the threshold term) needed to do so.

REFERENCES

Atkeson, C. G. (1989). Learning arm kinematic and dynamics. *Annual Review of Neuroscience, 12,* 157−183.

Atkeson, C. G., and Hollerbach, J. M. (1985). Kinematic features of unrestrained arm movements. *Journal of Neuroscience, 5,* 2318−2330.

Asatryan, D. G., and Feldman, A. G. (1965). Functional tuning of the nervous system with control of movement or maintenance of a steady posture: 1. Mechanographic analysis of the work of the joint on execution of a postural task. *Biophysics, 10,* 925−935.

Bernstein, N. (1967). *The coordination and regulation of movements.* London: Pergamon Press.

Bizzi, E., Hogan, N., Mussa-Ivaldi, F. A., and Giszter, S. (1992). Does the nervous system use equilibrium-point control to guide single and multiple joint movements? *Behavioral and Brain Sciences, 15,* 603−613.

Bruner, J. S. (1970). The growth and coordination of skill. In K. Connolly (Ed.), *Mechanisms of motor skill development,* 63−92. London: Academic Press.

Connolly, C. I., and Grupen, R. A. (1993). The applications of harmonic functions to robotics. *Journal of Robotic Systems, 10(7),* 931−946.

Craig, J. J. (1986). *Introduction to robotics.* Reading, MA: Addison-Wesley.

Crossman, E. R. F. W., and Goodeve, P. J. (1963/1983). Feedback control of hand-movement and Fitts' Law. *Quarterly Journal of Experimental Psychology, 35A,* 251−278.

Cruse, H., Brüwer, M., and Dean, J. (1993). Control of three- and four-joint arm movement: Strategies for a manipulator with redundant degrees of freedom. *Journal of Motor Behavior, 25,* 131−139. Special issue, ed. T. Flash and A. Wing: *Modeling the control of upper limb movement.*

Erickson, R. P. (1984). On the neural bases of behavior. *American Scientist, 72* (May−June), 233−241.

Flash, T., and Henis, E. (1991). Arm trajectory modification during reaching towards visual targets. *Journal of Cognitive Neuroscience, 3,* 220−230.

Flash, T., and Hogan, N. (1985). The coordination of arm movements: An experimentally confirmed mathematical model. *Journal of Neuroscience, 5,* 1688−1703.

Ghez, C., Gordon, J., Ghilardi, M. F., Christakos, C. N., and Cooper, S. E. (1990). Roles of proprioceptive input in the programming of arm trajectories. *Cold Spring Harbor Symposia on Quantitative Biology, 55,* 837−847.

Hasan, Z. (1991). Biomechanics and the study of multijoint movements. In D. R. Humphrey and H. J. Freund (Eds.), *Motor control: Concepts and issues,* 75−84. Chichester: Wiley.

Khatib, O. (1985). Real-time obstacle avoidance for manipulators and mobile robots. In *Proceedings of the 1985 IEEE International Conference on Robotics and Automation,* 500−505.

Kugler, P. N., Kelso, S., and Turvey, M. T. (1980). On the concept of coordinative structures as dissipative structures: I. Theoretical lines of convergence. In G. E. Stelmach and J. Requin (Eds.), *Tutorials in motor behavior,* 3−47. Amsterdam: North-Holland.

Lashley, K. S. (1942). The problem of cerebral organization in vision. *Biological Symposia, 7,* 301−322.

Lindsay, P. H., and Norman, D. A. (1977). *Human information processing: An introduction to psychology*. New York: Academic Press.

Loukopoulos, L. D., Rosenbaum, D. A., Meulenbroek, R. G. J., and Vaughan, J. (1993). Computations for obstacle avoidance. Paper presented at the Annual Meeting of the Psychonomics Society, Washington, DC.

Lozano-Pérez, T. (1981). Automatic planning of manipulator transfer movements. *IEEE Trans Syst, Man, Cybern SMC-11, 10*, 681–698.

Mel, B. W. (1990). *Connectionist robot motion planning*. Boston: Academic Press.

Mel, B. W. (1991). A connectionist model may shed light on neural mechanisms for visually guided reaching. *Journal of Cognitive Neuroscience, 3*, 273–292.

Merton, P. A. (1972). How we control the contraction of our muscles. *Scientific American, 226*(5), 30–37.

Meulenbroek, R. G. J., Rosenbaum, D. A., Thomassen, A. J. W. M., and Loukopoulos, L. (1994). A model of limb segment coordination in drawing behaviour. In C. Faure, P. Keuss, G. Lorette, and A. Vinter (Eds.), *Advances in handwriting and drawing: A multidisciplinary approach*, 349–362. Paris: Europia.

Meyer, D. E., Smith, J. E. K., and Wright, C. E. (1982). Models for the speed and accuracy of aimed movements. *Psychological Review, 89*, 449–482.

Nelson, W. L. (1983). Physical principles for economies of skilled movements. *Biological Cybernetics, 46*, 135–147.

Polit, A., and Bizzi, E. (1979). Characteristics of motor programs underlying arm movements in monkeys. *Journal of Neurophysiology, 42*, 183–194.

Rosenbaum, D. A., Engelbrecht, S. E., Bushe, M. M., and Loukopoulos, L. D. (1993a). A model for reaching control. *Acta Psychologica, 82*, 237–250.

Rosenbaum, D. A., Engelbrecht, S. E., Bushe, M. M., and Loukopoulos, L. D. (1993b). Knowledge model for selecting and producing reaching movements. *Journal of Motor Behavior, 25*, 217–227. Special issue edited by T. Flash and A. Wing: *Modeling the control of upper limb movement*.

Rosenbaum, D. A., Loukopoulos, L. D., Meulenbroek, R. G. J., Vaughan, J., and Engelbrecht, S. E. (1995). Planning reaches by evaluating stored postures. *Psychological Review, 102*, 28–67.

Saltzman, C. D., and Newsome, W. T. (1994). Neural mechanisms for forming a perceptual decision. *Science, 264*, 231–237.

Sanes, J. (1990). Motor representations in deafferented humans: A mechanism for disordered movement performance. In M. Jeannerod (Ed.), *Attention and performance XIII: Motor representation and control*, 714–735. Hillsdale, NJ: Erlbaum.

Schmidt, R. A., Zelaznik, H. N., Hawkins, B., Frank, J. S., and Quinn, J. T., Jr. (1979). Motor output variability: A theory for the accuracy of rapid motor acts. *Psychological Review, 86*, 415–451.

Selfridge, O. G. (1959). Pandemonium: A paradigm for learning. In *The mechanisation of thought processes*, London: H. M. Stationery Office.

Shadmehr, R. (1993). Control of equilibrium position and stiffness through postural modules. *Journal of Motor Behavior, 25*, 228–241.

Sidall, G. J., Holding, D. H., and Draper, J. (1957). Errors of aim and extent in manual point to point movement. *Occupational Psychology, 31*, 185–195.

Simon, H. (1979). *Models of thought*. New Haven: Yale University Press.

Sittig, A. C., Denier van der Gon, J. J., and Gielen, C. C. A. M. (1987). The contribution of afferent information on position and velocity to the control of slow and fast human forearm movements. *Experimental Brain Research, 67*, 33–40.

Uno, Y., Kawato, M., and Suzuki, R. (1989). Formation and control of optimal trajectory in human multijoint arm movement: Minimum torque-change model. *Biological Cybernetics, 61*, 89–101.

Vaughan, J., Rosenbaum, D. A., Loukopoulos, L. D., and Engelbrecht, S. E. (1995). Finding final postures. In preparation.

14 Bidirectional Theory Approach to Integration

Mitsuo Kawato

ABSTRACT

Fast and coordinated arm movements should be executed in the feedforward control model because the biological feedback loops are slow and have small gains. However, recent estimates of dynamic stiffness during movement have been low compared to those under posture maintenance, which suggests that biological feedforward control cannot rely solely on the muscle spring properties or spinal reflex characteristics. Thus neural internal models such as an inverse dynamics model are necessary for feedforward control. Multijoint point-to-point arm movement trajectories are characterized by roughly straight hand paths and bell-shaped speed profiles. Kinematic and dynamic optimization principles have been proposed to account for these invariant features so far. Experimental data have been found to support the dynamic optimization theory, which requires both forward and inverse models of the motor apparatus and the external world. In this chapter I propose a bidirectional theory for the integration in a hierarchical structure of representations in the brain, where both the upward and downward information flows are utilized for real-time computations in sensorimotor integration. The two direction flows are implemented by internal forward and inverse models, respectively.

14.1 INTRODUCTION

The problem of controlling goal-directed limb movements can be partitioned conceptually into a set of information-processing subproblems: trajectory planning, coordinate transformation from extracorporal space to intrinsic body coordinates, and motor command generation. Solutions to these subproblems are required to translate the spatial characteristics of the target or goal of the movements into an appropriate pattern of muscle activation. Over the past decade, computational studies of motor control concentrating on these three subproblems have become much more advanced.

One of the key findings in these computational studies is that all of the three problems are ill posed: the solution to each problem cannot uniquely be determined. This is because the more motoric representations must always specify the larger numbers of degrees of freedom than the more sensory representations. For trajectory planning, the visual system specifies the location of the target point or the location of obstacles, while the motor system needs to determine the whole time course of the trajectory that reaches the target and avoids the obstacles. For coordinate transformation, visual information about the target, the obstacles, or the movement trajectory should be translated into the corresponding coordinates attached to the body, such as joint angles and muscle lengths, whose degrees of freedom are always greater than those of the visual system. Determination of motor commands at level of the spinal cord or the cerebral cortex requires an even larger number of degrees of freedom (number of neurons) than the number of joints or muscles.

Several neural network models and conceptual models were proposed to resolve this computational difficulty at the level of hardware, as well as algorithms understanding. However, at the computational level, only the optimal theory explanations was successful. I believe that the ill-posed nature of the problems and the resulting optimal computational models are not restricted to visually guided reaching movements but play equally essential roles in the understanding of other broad brain functions, from the control of sequential movements, integration of different vision modules, and learning of new behaviors by imitation, to consciousness. In this chapter, visually guided reaching movements are treated as a good model system, much like the harmonic oscillator in physics; I derive a fundamental theoretical framework based on a study of visually guided reaching movements and then extend this to sensorimotor integration.

In section 14.2, I first introduce invariant features of multijoint arm movements. In section 14.3, I introduce several optimization models that can potentially reproduce these experimental data. In section 14.4, I compare the frameworks of the unidirectional theory and the bidirectional theory. In section 14.5, I develop the bidirectional theory for integration within motor control as well as integration in motion-perception linkage. In sections 14.6, 14.7, and 14.8, I summarize experimental data that, as a whole, support the bidirectional theory. Thus the general organizational plan of this chapter goes as follows: here are (1) a computationally difficult problem and experimental data that must be explained by theories (sections 14.1 and 14.2); (2) two alternative theories (sections 14.3 and 14.4); (3) my best solution to the problem (section 14.5); and (4) how I got there (sections 14.6, 14.7, and 14.8).

14.2 INVARIANT FEATURES OF A MULTIJOINT ARM TRAJECTORY

One interesting feature of human multijoint arm movements is that the hand paths between two points are roughly straight, and the hand speed profiles are bell-shaped (Kelso, Southard, and Goodman 1979; Morasso 1981; Abend, Bizzi, and Morasso 1982; Atkeson and Hollerbach 1985; Flash and Hogan 1985; Uno, Kawato and Suzuki 1989).

We reexamined human multijoint arm movements using the OPTOTRAK (Northern Digital Inc.) position measurement system. Subjects (3 males, aged 28–39) were asked to move their hands from one point to another using elbow and shoulder joint rotations while their wrists were braced. Arm movement was constrained in the horizontal plane at the shoulder level. We tested three methods for constraining the movement in the horizontal plane: (1) supporting subjects' elbows by a long strap from the ceiling; (2) attaching cuffs made of a low-friction material to subjects' wrists and covering the table with a low-friction Teflon sheet; and (3) asking subjects to hold their arms about 5 to 10 cm above the table before, during, and after the movement. The three different methods gave essentially the same results, but the third one gave the smoothest and most comfortable movement execution; thus we report here the results obtained under the third condition. The path data shown in figure 14.1 have already been published in Japanese (Koike and Kawato 1994), but the velocity and acceleration data shown in figure 14.2 have not. Similar but noisier data using the long strap (method 1) were previously published (Kawato et al. 1993).

Durations for movement were not given; instead, subjects could select their own comfortable duration, which ranged from 500 to 750 ms depending on the distances moved. Figure 14.1 shows hand paths for five different movements (T1 ⇒ T3, T2 ⇒ T6, T3 ⇒ T6, T4 ⇒ T1, T4 ⇒ T6) taken from one subject. The hand position was sampled at 400 Hz, and each point in figure 14.1 corresponds to one sampled position. Paths generated under 10 trials for each movement were overwritten. The positions of the initial and target points were the same as those used in Uno, Kawato, and Suzuki (1989). The origin of figure 14.1 is the shoulder position, the X-axis is toward the right, and the positive direction of the Y-axis is forward away from the body. One can see that the trajectories, while roughly straight for most movements, are significantly curved for some (e.g., T2 ⇒ T6). The observation that transverse paths are significantly curved but that radial paths (paths away from the frontal plane of the body) are considerably straighter will play an important

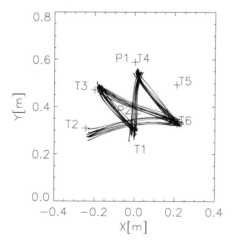

Figure 14.1 Hand paths for five different discrete point-to-point movements (T3 ⇒ T6, T2 ⇒ T6, T1 ⇒ T3, T4 ⇒ T1, T4 ⇒ T6) measured with OPTOTRAK position measurement system.

role in discriminating different computational theories in sections 14.3, 14.4, and 14.6.

We also calculated hand tangential velocities and accelerations. Figures 14.2A and B show them for the movement from T2 to T6 shown in figure 14.1. Note that velocity and acceleration profiles of other movements are very similar (see fig. 3 of Uno, Kawato, and Suzuki 1989 for velocity profiles for different paths). A second-order Butterworth filter with a cutoff frequency of 10 Hz was used to make numerical calculations of the velocity from the position data. The same filter was again used to obtain the acceleration from the velocity.

The shape of the velocity profile agrees with previous studies, and is characterized by a single peak and bell-shaped profile. The acceleration profile is noisier because of numerical differentiation, but reveals very important characteristics which can be used to reject some computational models for trajectory planning and control. When the hand is in a static state either before or after the movement, the acceleration is zero. During the movement, it is of course not zero except at the time of peak velocity, as can be seen from figure 14.2B. It should be emphasized that the acceleration gradually increases from zero at the beginning of the movement, and also that it gradually increases (decreases in magnitude) to zero at the end of the movement (conceptually depicted in the right column of figure 14.2C). It is not discontinuous at the beginning or end of the movement. Consequently, optimization models such as minimum acceleration or minimum torque that predict the discontinuity of acceleration at the beginning and end of movement as explained below are rejected.

From the Euler-Poisson equation derived from the minimum acceleration model, the fourth time derivative of the position must be zero. This implies that the trajectory is represented as the third polynomial in time. If the initial and final positions are specified and zero velocities are required at the beginning and at the end of movement, all four free parameters of the third polynomial are uniquely determined, and there is no room to control the acceleration at the beginning and end of the movement, which is not zero in general. In other words, the acceleration profile for the minimum acceleration model is a linear function of time as shown on the left in figure 14.2C, and it has large discontinuities at the beginning and at the end of movement. A very similar logic can be developed to reject the minimum torque model.

The endpoint control hypothesis (Bizzi, Polit, and Morasso 1976) is also rejected because it predicts the discontinuity of acceleration at the beginning of movement. In this hypothesis the equilibrium position jumps from the start posture to the target posture at the initiation of movement. The force or torque generated in this hypothesis is the difference between the actual position and the equilibrium position, multiplied by the mechanical stiffness of the motor apparatus. Because the force jumps from zero just before movement initiation to a large value just after the movement, the acceleration, which covaries with the force, has a large discontinuity at the beginning of the movement.

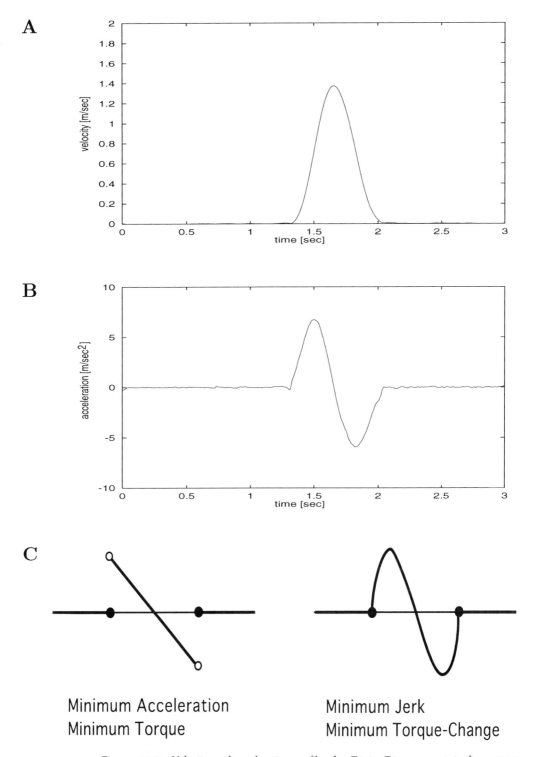

Figure 14.2 Velocity and acceleration profiles for T2 to T6 movement in figure 14.1. A. Velocity profile. B. Acceleration time course. C. Theoretical predictions of acceleration profile made by the minimum acceleration model and minimum torque model (left) and by minimum jerk model and minimum torque change model (right).

14.3 KINEMATIC VERSUS DYNAMIC OPTIMIZATION MODELS FOR TRAJECTORY PLANNING

This section briefly reviews several optimization models which have been experimentally examined, and describes their relative ability to resolve ill-posed issue in sensorimotor computational problems.

Minimum Jerk Model

Flash and Hogan (1985) proposed a mathematical model, the minimum jerk model, which assumes that the trajectory followed by a subject's arm tends to minimize the square of the movement jerk (rate of change in acceleration), integrated over the entire movement:

$$C_J = 1/2 \int_0^{t_f} \left\{ \left(\frac{d^3 X}{dt^3} \right)^2 + \left(\frac{d^3 Y}{dt^3} \right)^2 \right\} dt. \tag{14.1}$$

Here, (X, Y) are the Cartesian coordinates of the hand, and t_f is the movement duration. The predicted trajectory for a discrete point-to-point movement is a straight line. The trajectory is also characterized by a perfectly symmetrical bell-shaped speed profile. Thus the prediction is in qualitative agreement with the data shown in figures 14.1 and 14.2.

The reason for the straightness can be illustrated in at least two ways. The first, more analytical explanation is as follows. In equation 14.1, X and Y do not interact with each other; thus optimization can be done separately for X and Y. We then obtain the same functional form for X and Y, that is, the same fifth-order polynomial in time. This indicates that the path in the (X, Y)-plane is straight. The other, more geometrical explanation for a wider class of kinematic optimization models will be given in section 14.6.

The minimum jerk model was the first optimization model to be experimentally confirmed; this was epoch-making for biological optimization theories. The minimum jerk model is based solely on the kinematics of movement, independent of the dynamics of the musculoskeletal system. It is successful only when formulated in terms of the motion of the hand in extracorporeal space and fails when defined in terms of, for example, the joint angles. This is because the minimum jerk model predicts straight trajectories in the space where the objective function is defined. The minimum jerk model defined in joint angle space predicts straight paths in the joint angle space, but these are overly curved in Cartesian space when compared with the experimentally observed data. Thus the minimum jerk model implies that the trajectory is first planned in extrinsic space.

The minimum jerk model is simple and beautiful, but the uniqueness of the solution seems too strong in the sense that the model predicts a unique trajectory regardless of various conditions which may be present in the environment or in the motor task itself.

If a major objective of motor control is merely to decrease the degrees of freedom in the system, this can be easily achieved by introducing very strong couplings between all independent variables so that the system behaves in a stereotyped, single, fixed-action pattern. However, this is not at all desirable. The solutions adopted by the motor control network should be flexible and should adapt to various environmental conditions; otherwise, humans would not have the capacity for *motor equivalence* or *equifinality*—the ability to achieve the same physical objective in more than one way. However, because the minimum jerk model is a kinematic model, it cannot adapt planned trajectories in extrinsic space to different dynamic aspects involved in the motor task, environment, and the motor apparatus, such as the inertial characteristics of manipulated objects, force field, or physical parameters of the arm.

Minimum Torque Change Model

Based on the idea that movement optimization must be related to movement dynamics, Uno, Kawato, and Suzuki (1989) proposed the following alternative quadratic measure of performance:

$$C_\tau = 1/2 \int_0^{t_f} \sum_{i=1}^{m} \left(\frac{d\tau_i}{dt} \right)^2 dt, \tag{14.2}$$

where τ_i is the torque fed to the ith of m actuators. Here, the performance measure (objective function) is the sum of the square of the rate of change of the torque, integrated over the entire movement. One can see that C_τ (14.2) is related to C_J (14.1) because the rate of change of torque is locally proportional to the jerk. In particular, if the controlled object is a point mass, then the force is equal to the product of the mass and the acceleration. Thus the minimum jerk (rate of change of acceleration) is identical to the minimum force change (minimum torque change). However, for a multijoint, non-linear-controlled object, the two criteria are different. In particular, C_τ depends critically on the dynamics of the musculoskeletal system, not just on the kinematics.

For unconstrained movements between pairs of targets in front of the body, predictions made by both these models have agreed closely with experimental data. However, movement trajectories predicted by the minimum torque change model (14.2) are quite different from those predicted by the minimum jerk model (14.1) in the following four behavioral situations: (1) movements in a vertical plane, (2) mirror-reflected via-point movements, (3) movements from the side of the body to in front, (4) movements between two points while resisting a spring. For vertical movements, past data have already been found to support the minimum torque change model (Atkeson and Hollerbach 1985). When Uno, Kawato, and Suzuki (1989) dealt with the other three, they found that predictions of the minimum torque change model matched the data better than did those of the minimum jerk model.

Minimum Motor Command Change Model

Musculoskeletal systems possess muscle tension sensors (Golgi tendon organs) as well as muscle length and velocity sensors (muscle spindles) but no direct joint torque sensors; joint capsule mechanoreceptor afferents are not sensitive to intermediate joint angles, but are sensitive to extremes of joint angles (Kandel, Schwartz, and Jessell 1991). Considering these physiological constraints, Uno, Suzuki, and Kawato (1989) proposed a minimum muscle tension change model.

This evolution of the minimum torque change model to the minimum muscle tension change model can be interpreted as a proximal shift of the space where the smoothness constraint is given (see fig. 14.3): from more extrinsic space (joint torques) to more intrinsic space (muscle tensions). Because of several theoretical and computational reasons given below, this proximal shift seems to be further extended so that the smoothness constraint is defined in the intrinsic space even for the brain.

I proposed the minimum motor command change model (Kawato 1992) that minimizes the following criterion:

$$C_M = 1/2 \int_0^{t_f} \sum_{i=1}^{n} \left(\frac{dM_i}{dt}\right)^2 dt, \tag{14.3}$$

where M_i, is the ith motor command out of n commands. Several definitions of motor commands are possible. At the lowest level, we could define the ith muscle motor command by the instantaneous frequency of nerve pulses arriving at the ith muscle. At the spinal cord level, the firing frequency of each alpha motoneuron could be denoted by M_i. In this case, summation in the above equation is taken over all motoneurons related to the investigated movements. Thus both the rapid change in individual firing rate and rapid recruitment are penalized. At an even higher level, firing frequencies of corticomotoneurons in the cerebral motor cortex could be represented by M_i.

In order to understand the theoretical reasons for the preference of the minimum motor command change model, it is necessary to recall that all three subproblems involved in visually guided reaching movements (trajectory planning, coordinate transformation, motor command generation) encounter computational difficulty: the redundancy problem. The above optimization principles were proposed to resolve the ill-posed nature of one or more of these problems. It is very important to realize that if the smoothness criterion of some optimization model is defined at a specific space, then the model can only solve ill-posed computational problems that are defined at or above that level (fig. 14.3). The minimum jerk model defined at the task space can thus resolve only the ill-posed trajectory formation problem. Because the minimum torque change model specifies the smoothness criterion at the joint torque coordinates, it can determine unique torque waveforms when the target position is specified. Because joint angles and the corresponding Cartesian coordinates are uniquely determined from the torque waveforms,

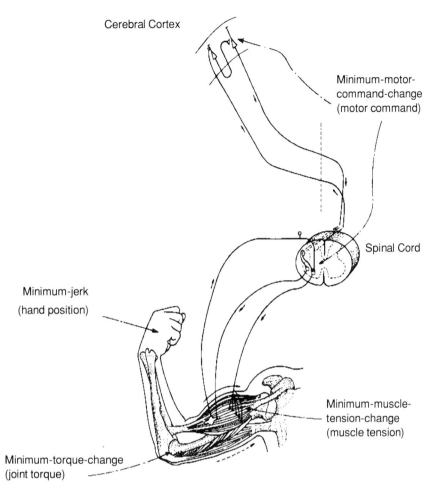

Cerebral Cortex

Minimum-motor-
command-change
(motor command)

Spinal Cord

Minimum-jerk
(hand position)

Minimum-muscle-
tension-change
(muscle tension)

Minimum-torque-change
(joint torque)

Figure 14.3   Schematic diagram illustrating components involved in visually guided reaching movements and different spaces where different variables are represented. Four different spaces are used to represent movement conditions, movement trajectories, and motor commands. Positions of target or obstacles are represented in three-dimensional Cartesian space (extrinsic space). Hand position in this coordinate system can be measured by visual system. During movements, joint torques are generated from muscle tensions. Muscle activation levels are controlled by nervous system. Minimum jerk model is defined at Cartesian coordinates of hand position and can solve trajectory formation problem. Minimum torque change model is defined at joint torque coordinates and can solve trajectory formation problem, inverse kinematics problem, and inverse dynamics problem up to joint torque. Minimum muscle tension change model is defined at muscle tension coordinates and solves above three problems up to muscle tension. Minimum motor command change model is defined in motor command coordinates of central nervous system and can solve above three problems up to motor commands in brain. It is possible to impose smoothness constraint on motor commands at different levels such as motoneuron firing in spinal cord, or pyramidal tract neuron firing in cerebral motor cortex.

both the ill-posed inverse kinematics problem (coordinate transformation from visual to joint space), which is formulated between the joint space and the visual space, and the trajectory formation problem are said to be simultaneously solved by the minimum torque change model. Similarly, the minimum muscle tension change model, which specifies the smoothness criterion at the muscle level, can resolve the ill-posed inverse dynamics problem (the problem of determining muscle tensions from desirable joint motions) as well as the inverse kinematics problem and trajectory formation problem. And finally, the minimum motor command change model, which specifies the smoothness criterion in the central nervous system, can resolve excess degrees of freedom at that motor command level as well as all of the above three problems (trajectory formation, inverse kinematics, and inverse dynamics).

The following gives three reasons for extending the minimum muscle tension change model to the minimum motor command change model. First, in order to solve the ill-posed problem posed by the enormous excess degrees of freedom in the central nervous system (larger numbers of motoneurons or corticomotoneurons than the number of muscles), it is necessary to use the smoothness principle in the state space of the central nervous system (i.e., firing frequency of neurons).

Second, in view of the nature of the neural network hardware that executes trajectory planning and control, it can be said that the origin of the smoothness resides in the central nervous system rather than in the periphery. Thus it would seem more plausible to impose the smoothness constraint at the central nervous system level rather than at the peripheral level.

Finally, Uno and Kawato (1994), in response to Flash's (1990) criticism of the link inertia parameter values used in Uno, Kawato, and Suzuki (1989), found that the minimum torque change model can reproduce human data well if measured dynamic viscosity values (Bennett et al. 1992) are combined with correct inertia parameter values in the simulation. But if zero-viscosity values are assumed as in Flash (1990), the predicted hand paths are too concavely curved from the body compared with the human data. Because the musculoskeletal system's viscosity properties arise mainly from muscle velocity-tension relationships and spinal reflex characteristics, the measured viscosity coefficients used can not be interpreted as a viscoelastic component of the dynamical properties of the arm. Thus, if we are really talking about the torque actually generated at the joint, there is only a little viscosity in the controlled object. Consequently, the "torque" in this simulation should be interpreted as the motor command arriving at the muscles determining muscle-generated torques. In this sense, the original minimum torque change model should be renamed the minimum *commanded* torque change model.

14.4   UNIDIRECTIONAL VERSUS BIDIRECTIONAL THEORY

Many of the computational models for trajectory planning and control can be broadly classified into one of two contrasting theories: unidirectional and

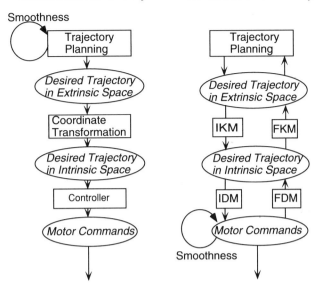

Unidirectional theory   **Bi-directional theory**

Figure 14.4 Hierarchical arrangement of computational problems and internal representations of visually guided arm movements. Left side shows block diagram of unidirectional theory; right side, block diagram of the bidirectional theory.

bidirectional. In both theories, a hierarchical structure of information representations and the three problems involved in visually guided movements (trajectory planning, coordinate transformation, motor command generation) are assumed as shown in figure 14.4. The fundamental difference between the two theories is the direction of information flows allowed for solving the three computational problems.

In the unidirectional theory, information flows only downward from the higher level to the lower level. As a result, a higher-level computational problem is solved without any reference to lower-level computational problems. For example, trajectory planning is solved without using any knowledge about coordinate transformations or motor command generation. Thus the three problems are solved sequentially, step by step (table 14.1). That is, first the trajectory planning problem is solved to compute the desired trajectory in extrinsic space (in many cases, task-oriented visual coordinates). Next the coordinate transformation problem is solved to obtain the desired trajectory in intrinsic space (joint angles, muscle lengths, etc.) from the trajectory in the extrinsic space. Finally, the necessary motor commands for the desired trajectory in the intrinsic space are calculated by a controller.

On the other hand, in the bidirectional theory, upward information flows as well as downward flows are allowed and are actually essential for solving the three computational problems (table 14.1). As a result, a higher-level computational problem can be solved while taking account of events at lower levels. For example, trajectory planning is executed by requiring the

Table 14.1 Comparison of Unidirectional and Bidirectional Theories for Goal-Directed Arm Movements

Theory	Unidirectional	Bidirectional
How to solve three computational problems	Sequential	Simultaneous
Spaces where trajectory is planned	Extrinsic space (task-oriented visual coordinates)	Intrinsic space (body coordinates) and extrinsic space
Optimization principle (example)	Kinematic (minimum jerk)	Dynamic (minimum torque change)
Control	Virtual trajectory control	Inverse dynamics model
Internal models of motor apparatus and environment	Not necessary	Forward dynamics model and inverse dynamics model
Motor learning	No specific prediction	Acquisition of internal models
Curved path	• Incomplete control • Visual misperception • Virtual trajectory	Optimal (planned) trajectory itself is curved
Stiffness during movement	High stiffness	Low stiffness
Altered visual environments	• Invariant in extrinsic space • Variant in intrinsic space	• Invariant in intrinsic space • Variant in extrinsic space
Force field adaptation (new dynamic environment)	No adaptation	Adaptation
Trajectory under translation, rotation, relfection	Invariant	Variant

smoothness of motor commands. Thus the three problems are solved simultaneously rather than sequentially (table 14.1).

This section briefly summarizes comparisons between the unidirectional theory and the bidirectional theory according to table 14.1. Some of the different predictions made by the two theories have recently been tested in experiments by our laboratory and others. In sections 14.6, 14.7, and 14.8 we will discuss these experimental examinations of the two theories and in general provide experimental data supporting the bidirectional theory.

One of the most fundamental differences between the two theories concerns the spaces in which the trajectory is first planned; consequently, there is a controversy about the coordinate system in which trajectories are planned: whether it is extrinsic (kinematic) or intrinsic (dynamic). In the unidirectional theory the trajectory is assumed to be planned solely in the extrinsic space (usually task-oriented visual coordinates), while all the kinematic and dynamic factors at the lower levels are neglected. On the other hand, in the bidirectional theory the trajectory is planned in both intrinsic space (body coordinates) and extrinsic space. Goals of movements such as the endpoints of reaching are given in the extrinsic space, while necessary constraints to select a unique trajectory (i.e., to resolve the ill-posed issue) are given in the intrinsic space. Thus the two spaces are used simultaneously for trajectory planning.

The above explanation to the controversy might be too simple and slightly misguided. The difference between the unidirectional theory and bidirectional theory surely is not simply whether or not there is only planning in extrinsic space; somehow those high-level plans must be passed down to a system that deals with forces and motor commands, in which case there must be a lower-level planner (or controller). Actually, as an illustrative example, we can imagine a unidirectional strategy in which first the minimum jerk model in Cartesian coordinates specifies the path in extrinsic space, next the minimum torque change model transforms this desired trajectory into joint angle motions, and finally the minimum motor command change model determines the necessary motoneuron firings from the desired joint angle motions. In this extreme case, motor planning (or in a wider sense, trajectory planning) is done at all of the three different levels, but the information flow is unidirectional. The lower-level planner obeys the commands (path constraints or desired joint angle motions) from the higher level strictly, and the higher-level planner ignores the lower-level planner. Thus the distinction between the unidirectional and bidirectional theories is neither directly coupled to kinematic versus dynamic optimization models nor to extrinsic versus intrinsic trajectory planning. The essential difference between the two theories is whether different-level motor planners and controllers are arranged in a purely hierarchical manner (unidirectional) or whether they talk to each other (bidirectional) to determine motor behaviors.

However, in most of the biologically plausible models studied, the optimization principles for trajectory planning developed by the two theories, which are inseparably coupled to the spaces for the first trajectory planning, are markedly different. In the unidirectional theory, because the planning process does not take the lower levels into account, the optimization principle has to be kinematic at the highest level, and all of the dynamic factors are therefore neglected at this first planning stage. One representative example is the minimum jerk model defined in Cartesian coordinates. On the other hand, in the bidirectional theory it is possible to use principles on the optimization of dynamics that take lower levels into account. One representative example is the minimum torque change model.

In the bidirectional theory both the forward dynamics model and the inverse dynamics model are necessary for fast computation in trajectory planning; these two kinds of models correspond to downward and upward information flows, respectively (fig. 14.4). These internal models should be learned and stored somewhere in the brain. Acquisition of internal models could form a major part of motor learning. A biologically plausible learning scheme to acquire the inverse dynamics model was earlier proposed (Kawato, Furukawa, and Suzuki 1987; Kawato and Gomi 1992), and we have already obtained some experimental evidence that internal models reside in the cerebellum (Shidara et al. 1993).

As already explained in section 14.2, some point-to-point arm trajectories such as lateral (transverse) motions are markedly curved. In the unidirectional theory the curvature of these paths is ascribed to one or several of the listed reasons. In section 14.6, I describe recent experimental examinations of these reasons, which have led me to conclude that a major portion of the observed curvature cannot be explained by these factors.

The bottom three items in table 14.1 indicate experimental tests of predictions made by the two theories. Experiments examining predictions about altered visual environments are described in section 14.7. In section 14.8 we discuss experimental data obtained in the force field adaptation paradigm, which overall support the bidirectional theory predictions.

In closing this section, I explain why intuitively the unidirectional strategy cannot solve a large class of optimization problems, which appear in vision and motor computations, and in which constraints are given in multiple, different spaces.

The general formulation of the problem can be given as follows. Let us assume that there are several spaces $\mathscr{S}_1$, $\mathscr{S}_2$, ..., $\mathscr{S}_n$, hierarchically arranged and represented by different areas of the brain. Suppose $\mathscr{S}_1$ is attached to the input interface of the brain (such as vision, audition, somatosensory system) and $\mathscr{S}_n$ is attached to the output interface of the brain (descending motor commands to motoneurons, muscle tensions, joint torques). Let $x_1, x_2, \ldots, x_n$ be states of representations at these different spaces. There exist functional relationships between these representations. If the mapping is one-to-one, then $x_{i+1} = f(x_i)$ and $x_i = f^{-1}(x_{i+1})$ hold. But, in the general case, the correspondence is many-to-many, and thus only the following inclusion relationships hold: $x_{i+1} \in \mathscr{G}(x_i)$ and $x_i \in \mathscr{H}(x_{i+1})$. Let us suppose that different constraints $C_1, C_2, \ldots, C_n$ are given at different spaces $\mathscr{S}_1, \mathscr{S}_2, \ldots, \mathscr{S}_n$, respectively. We assume that there exists a unique optimal solution $x_1^*, x_2^*, \ldots, x_n^*$, that satisfies several hard constraints and minimizes (or maximizes) several soft constraints. This optimal solution also satisfies inclusion relationships given above between different hierarchies.

In the unidirectional theory framework, at each space a unique solution must be calculated. But apparently this cannot be done. For example, the constraint C_1 at $\mathscr{S}_1$ cannot determine a unique solution if it is a hard constraint (for example, a target point in reaching movements, or retinal images in vision computation). On the other hand, if C_1 is a soft constraint, it determines the unique solution, which does not satisfy other constraints in other spaces (for example, the smoothest possible trajectory in the space is not to move, or the smoothest 2-D surface is a frontoparallel plane). Consequently, different spaces and different constraints given there must talk each other to find the optimal solution while taking account of the inclusion relationships between different spaces.

The simplest example is the minimum torque change trajectory. Here, the trajectory X is represented in the Cartesian space $\mathscr{S}_1$; the torque τ is represented in the torque space $\mathscr{S}_2$. The relationship between X and τ is given by the Lagrangean equation of motion. If there is no kinematic or dynamic redundancy, the mapping is one-to-one, but if redundancy exists, the mapping is one-to-many. The hard constraint in the Cartesian space is that the trajectory must reach the target at a fixed time, $X(t_f) = X_{target}$, while the soft constraint in the torque space is that the rate of change of the torque integrated over the entire movement (14.2) must be minimized. The hard constraint in $\mathscr{S}_1$ cannot uniquely determine the solution because there is an infinite number of possible trajectories that end at the specified target at the specified time. On the other hand, if we seek the smoothest solution in the torque space $\mathscr{S}_2$, the solution is without any movement, which apparently does not reach the target. Thus we should deal with the two spaces simultaneously in order to find the torque and the trajectory that reach the specified target with the smoothest torque time course. Furthermore, any algorithm to calculate this optimal solution either implicitly or explicitly must use both the two direction inclusion relationships $x_{i+1} \in \mathscr{G}(x_i)$ and $x_i \in \mathscr{H}(x_{i+1})$ (inverse dynamics and forward dynamics in this example).

14.5 INTEGRATION BY NEURAL NETWORK IN A HIERARCHICAL AND PARALLEL SYSTEM

In this chapter I first introduced invariant features of multijoint arm movements, then several optimization models that can potentially reproduce these experimental data. In the previous section, I proposed the framework of the bidirectional theory and noted predictions of the theory that could be experimentally tested. In sections 14.6, 14.7, and 14.8, I summarize experimental data obtained in tests by our and other labs. The experimental data, as a whole, support the bidirectional theory, although I admit they are still not conclusive in some respects and there remain several controversial points. But, in this section, I further describe the theoretical advantage of the bidirectional theory for integration within motor control as well as integration in motion-perception linkage.

Bidirectional Neural Network Architecture

We have been developing several neural network models that can generate the optimal trajectory and its corresponding motor command in the framework of the dynamic optimization model. Early models either used only the forward or inverse model of the controlled object and thus had several difficulties, such as a large number of relaxation steps required for calculation, the necessity of spatial representation of time (e.g., torques at different times are represented by different neurons), or the necessity of backpropagation calculation (Kawato et al. 1990). These difficulties can theoretically all be resolved by utilizing both the forward and inverse models of dynamics and kinematics (Kawato 1992). Based on this idea, Wada and Kawato (1993) developed the FIRM (forward-inverse relaxation model) neural network model for optimal trajectory generation and control. By computer simulation, we confirmed that FIRM can generate an arm trajectory within a few iterations; some mathematical proofs of its optimality and convergence were also given. FIRM contains both the forward dynamics model and the inverse dynamics model of the controlled object. Figure 14.5 shows the hierarchical and bidirectional structure of our hardware implementation. FIRM is just one achievement of this general structure. In general, inverse models are necessary for fast computation, while forward models are necessary to resolve redundancy problems, or in more intuitive terms, to improve the adaptability of behaviors.

The reason why the bidirectional and hierarchical structure shown in figure 14.5 is advantageous in resolving several difficulties in the dynamic optimization theory is as follows. Mathematically speaking, the essential difficulty of computation required in the dynamic optimization theory is that two different constraints for optimization are represented in different spaces. In reaching movements, the location of the starting points and endpoints provides the two-point boundary conditions for the optimization problem, while the performance index is the time integral of the sum of the squares of the rate of motor commands. The nonlinear dynamics of the arm govern the relationship between the motor command and the trajectory. The hard constraints (target points) are represented in the task space, although the soft constraint (smoothness) is represented in the motor command space. Because these two conditions should be satisfied simultaneously, if only one type of internal model is used and if simultaneous optimization is actually done on the two constraints, several difficulties, such as a long convergence time, arise.

The essential mathematical idea behind the bidirectional theory is to divide the optimization calculation into two parts, corresponding to the task targets and the smoothness, by using the forward and inverse models. The approximated inverse model can transform all visual information about the task into a tentative motor command (downward information flow); the motor command can then be smoothed in the motor command space, and the extent of deviation of the hard constraint predicted by the forward model (upward information flow). Based on this error, a compensatory and additive motor command is calculated by the inverse model (downward again). This cycle of computation rapidly converges to a suboptimal solution.

Because the output of the network model is a time-varying sequence of motor signals, I assume that the bidirectional computation actually involves internal generation of the time-varying sequence and feeding this back for error correction through a few iterations before allowing the time-varying sequence to generate overt movements. Here, I defend this as a plausible method for generating movements in real time; I believe that we run through planned movements internally and correct them before acting.

Relaxation Neural Network Model
for Trajectory Formation

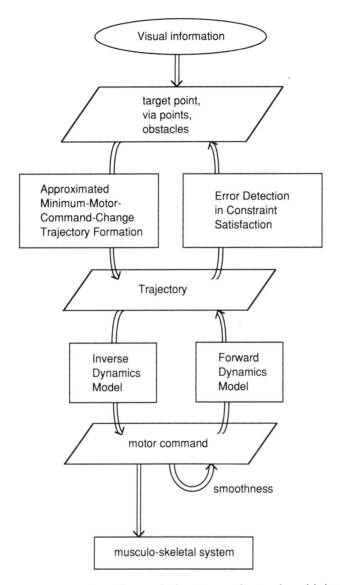

Figure 14.5 General type of relaxation neural network model that can generate optimal trajectory and its corresponding motor command. FIRM is one specific example of this type of network.

I know that this sounds biologically implausible; I suppose the main reasons are twofold. The first reason is the timing problem. Does the brain have enough computation time before generating movement to circulate information through different levels? Our answer is yes, because the relaxation computation quickly reaches the equilibrium within two or three iterations. And, even if there is no time for signal circulation, our model calculates a quasi-optimal solution in one-shot manner (unidirectional calculation).

The second reason for the strangeness of the bidirectional model has to do with simulation of forthcoming movement in the brain. But we do know of the existence of corollary discharge or the efference copy of the motor commands in the brain. Because a forward model of the motor apparatus (internal simulator of the movement) would greatly enhance the computational capability of the brain, from mental movement imagery, mental training of motor skills, and prediction of behavior, to real-time control, I believe that this computational model is utilized in the brain.

Bidirectional Theory for Sequential Movements

We have hypothesized that our computational theory for reaching movements can be extended to other classes of voluntary movements such as handwriting or speech. For this extension of the theory, the computational theory (dynamic optimization) and the hardware (bidirectional and hierarchical structure) are easily transferred, but the representation level needs careful consideration. Here, extension of the via-point idea is crucial. For speech, we believe that each phoneme determines the via-point target location. For handwriting, we developed an algorithm to extract the minimum number of via points from a given trajectory X_{data} with some level of error threshold θ. If a fixed number of via points $\mathscr{S} = \{P_1, P_2, .., P_N\}$, is given and the arm dynamics are known, we can calculate the optimal trajectory $X_{opt}(\mathscr{S})$ passing through these via points. The via-point extraction problem is formulated to find the value of $\mathscr{S}$ that gives the minimum value of N while satisfying $\|X_{data} - X_{opt}(\mathscr{S})\| < \theta$. If the error threshold θ is satisfied for the minimum N, then the problem is to find the value of $\mathscr{S}$ that gives the minimum error level $\|X_{data} - X_{opt}(\mathscr{S})\|$. Note that this via-point extraction problem is again a nonlinear optimization problem. Our via-point extraction algorithm uses FIRM again, and this suggests a duality between movement pattern formation and movement pattern perception (Wada and Kawato 1995).

We succeeded in reconstructing a cursive handwriting trajectory quite accurately from about 10 via points for each character. The extracted via points included not only kinematically definable feature points with maximum curvature and lowest velocity but also other points not easily extracted by any purely kinematic method not taking account of the dynamics of the arm or the dynamic optimization principle. A simple word recognition system from cursive connected handwritings was constructed based on this via-point representation, and it worked without a word dictionary (Wada et al. 1995).

When the same algorithm was applied to speech articulator motion during natural speech, the extracted via points corresponded fairly well to phonemes that were determined from a simultaneously recorded acoustic signal. Natural speech movement was reconstructed well from those phoneme-like via points.

Bidirectional Theory for Sensory-Motor Integration

Thus we have accumulated evidence that the bidirectional theory approach is a promising computation model for several types of movements. We have proposed the same bidirectional architecture for fast computation in early vision and for fast and reliable integration of different vision modules in middle-vision problems, including the integration of surface normal estimation, boundary detection, and light source estimation in shape from shading (Kawato, Hayakawa, and Inui 1993; Hayakawa et al. 1994). It is also encouraging to note that in the field of word perception the classical unidirectional view has also been challenged by the more powerful bidirectional theory (McClelland and Rumelhart 1981).

The mathematical structure of the vision and motor-control models is almost identical; furthermore, we have neuroanatomical support for our bidirectional model. Patterns of anatomical connections within cerebral cortical areas must form the structural basis for solving sensorimotor integration problems. A hierarchical flow of connections within the sensory, motor, and association areas is characterized by a specific organization of a laminar origin and termination of reciprocal cortico-cortical connections (Pandya and Yeterian 1988). Rostrally directed feedforward connections originate mainly from neurons in layer III and terminate in and around layer IV of the higher areas. In contrast, caudally directed (backprojection) connections originate in layers V and VI and, to a lesser extent, in layer IIIa and terminate mainly in layer I. Thus, although we do not have any strong physiological data, it is very tempting to propose that the same bidirectional architecture might be applicable to the integration of different modules ranging from sensory information processing to motor control.

First, encouraged by the finding that our computational framework can be extended to different types of movements and, second, tempted to unify our previous models of motor control (Kawato 1992, Wada and Kawato 1993) and of vision, I propose a general bidirectional and hierarchical scheme for module integration as shown in figure 14.6. The essential proposal is that the feedforward connection from the more sensory cortical area to the more motor cortical area provides an approximated inverse model of a physical process in the external world such as arm movement or the imaging process, while the backprojection connection from the more motor area to the more sensory area provides a forward model of the same physical process. By mathematical analysis and computer simulation, we can show that a small number of relaxation computations circulating this forward-inverse hierarchy achieves fast and reliable integration of different sensory and motor modules,

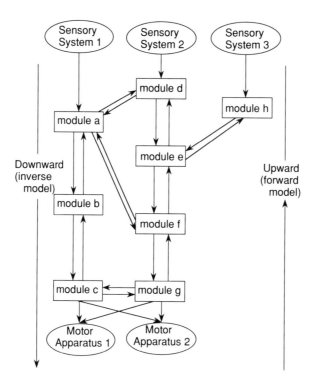

Figure 14.6 General bidirectional and hierarchical scheme for module integration both in sensory and motor information processing.

and therefore might resolve the following two problems. (1) How are parallel computational modules (multiple visual and motor cortical areas) integrated to allow a coherent scene perception and coordinated behavior? (2) How can ill-posed sensorimotor problems be solved by the brain within several hundreds of milliseconds?

The basic assumption in this proposal is that the brain consists of a number of modules that correspond roughly to different cortical areas and are organized in a hierarchical yet parallel manner. We do not assume a single gigantic map playing the central role in integration; rather, we are proposing a parallel distributed way of integrating different modules. It is well known in neuroanatomy that if one area is connected to another by a feedforward connection, backward or feedback connections always exist. My main proposal is that the downward information flow implemented by the feedforward connection constitutes an approximate inverse model of some physical process outside the brain such as kinematic transformations, dynamic transformations, or optics, that is, the image generation process. On the other hand, the upward information flow implemented by the feedback connections provides a forward model of the corresponding physical process.

What are the advantages of this bidirectional architecture? The first advantage is its fast computation. The cascade of inverse models results in a feedforward and one-shot calculation, which can execute reflexes and fixed-action patterns triggered by specific stimuli. But if we do not have forward models, and if we must rely solely on computational machinery provided by the unidirectional theory, our behavior repertoire is very limited. Equifinality, optimality, or adaptability to different environmental situations can be done only if the brain uses some kind of internal forward models, in other words, emulators or predictors of external events. The network relaxation in the circle of the inverse and forward models converges very rapidly, within a few iterations, to a suboptimal solution. This is the second computational advantage; a third is that integration of parallel modules can be done rapidly. Thus the bidirectional theory may provide an understanding about how the large number of different visual cortical areas can nevertheless produce a coherent percept of the visual world. Finally, the bidirectional theory may provide a concrete computational algorithm for the motor theory of movement pattern perception as outlined below.

In the motor theory of speech perception (Liberman et al. 1967), a neural network for motor control is supposed to play an essential role in the perception of speech. Our algorithm gives one specific computational achievement of this psychological theory. Human movement data, either visual (e.g., handwriting, biological motion) or auditory (e.g., speech) is very severely constrained by the dynamics of the controlled objects and interactions with the external world as well as the motor control strategy adopted by the central nervous system. Thus any efficient motor pattern perception scheme must either implicitly or explicitly take account of these physical and physiological constraints. Here, we advocate a rather radical approach by stating that the movement pattern generation network actively participates in movement pattern perception in a dualistic way. The proposed theory of movement pattern perception based on dynamic optimization extracts via points from a given movement pattern trajectory. In this process of via-point extraction, motor control constraints such as the optimization principle and motor apparatus dynamics play the essential role. Furthermore, the same neural networks used in motor control can be used because they contain bidirectional information flows. The computational framework of this bidirectional theory of movement pattern perception is schematically depicted in figure 14.7. This is still a preliminary computational model and should not be taken as a formal psychological or physiological model. Nevertheless, it is quite attractive because we can demonstrate the potential computational power of the bidirectional theory for motion-perception linkage in several experiments, which include, as already explained, reconstruction of cursive handwritten characters and natural speech movement.

Our most recent engineering demonstration was in the domain of robot task learning by imitation (Kawato 1995). Learning Japanese Kendama by imitation was implemented in a robot eye-hand system to exemplify the integration of perception of biological motion and motor learning. In this example, we examined the potential power of the following learning strategy:

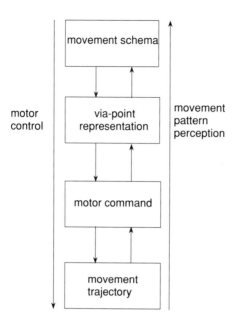

movement schema

motor
control

via-point
representation

movement
pattern
perception

motor command

movement
trajectory

Figure 14.7 Computational schema to achieve motor theory of movement pattern perception based on bidirectional approach.

(1) begin with a human demonstrating the task, (2) perceive the demonstrated movement trajectory based on the dynamics of the controlled object and the dynamic optimization theory, (3) extract via points from which FIRM can reconstruct trajectories, (4) learn the functional relationship between via points and task performance using multiple examples, (5) treat via points as abstract control variables while using a fixed trajectory generation and control scheme, and (6) adaptively modify locations and timing of via points so that the task can be executed while continuing to use the above learning rules.

14.6 POSSIBLE EXPLANATIONS FOR CURVED PATHS

The curvature of movement paths depends on the location in the work space where the trajectory is generated. For example, the movement paths, whose starting point is an outstretched arm to the side of the body and whose endjoint is in front of the body, have high curvatures (Uno, Kawato, and Suzuki 1989). These high curvatures, at first sight, seem to support the bidirectional theory rather than the unidirectional theory because kinematic optimization models such as the minimum jerk model predict perfectly straight paths for point-to-point movements.

The reason why kinematic optimization models defined in extrinsic space predict straight optimal paths is as follows. Invariance of objective functions under translation, rotation, or reflection is the consequence of any kinematic model with symmetry, and thus curved paths cannot be unique optimal solutions. If a curved path were the unique optimal solution, the symmetrically reflected curved path with respect to the line connecting the starting points and endpoints should have exactly the same objective function value, and thus should become another unique optimal solution. This is a contradiction. Thus the optimal trajectory in a kinematic optimization model with symmetry must be strictly straight. This strong property would appear to contradict the actual data mentioned above unless some explanation can be given to salvage the unidirectional theory.

Wolpert, Ghahramani, and Jordan (1994) listed the following three possible explanations for the observed curvature in the unidirectional theory framework (see also table 14.1).

1. The first possibility is that the reference trajectory is straight but that imperfections in the control system lead to a curvature that is dependent on the dynamics of the arm.

2. The second possibility is that the curvature seen is due to visual misperception.

3. The third possibility is that the central nervous system, rather than the directly computing torque, specifies the trajectory in terms of an intermediate representation, such as a series of equilibrium positions (Flash 1987) or desired muscle lengths. The actual trajectory produced then depends on the dynamics of the arm. This possibility differs from imperfect control in that it is this intermediate representation, rather than the outcome, that is matched to the reference trajectory.

The following subsections discuss these three possible explanations while referring to recent experimental data and theoretical studies.

Incomplete Control and Visual Misperception

Wolpert, Ghahramani, and Jordan found a significant correlation between curvature perceived as straight and the curvature of actual arm movements. They suggested that subjects try to make straight-line movements, but that actual movements are curved because visual misperception makes the movements appear to be straighter than they really are. This explanation is quite interesting and also seems to be closely related to the well-known visual distortion effect *horopter*; that is, rods on the horizontal plane appearing to lie parallel to the frontoparallel plane are convex to the body at a far distance and concave to the body at a near distance (Foley 1980). However, the correlation between visual misperception and movement curvature in itself cannot tell us whether there exists a causal relationship.

In order to examine visual misperception as well as incomplete control as explanations of curvature, Osu et al. (1994) conducted two experiments. In the first, subjects were asked to move their right hand from the starting point where their arm was at the side of their body to the endpoint in front of their body. The following four types of instructions were given to the subjects.

1. Move your hand from the starting point to the endpoint.

2. Move your hand from the starting point to the endpoint along the curved path drawn on the table, which is actually the average path in the above first paradigm (we did not say this to the subjects).

3. Move your hand straight from the starting point to the endpoint.

4. Move your hand along the straight path drawn on the table from the starting point to the endpoint.

The above four instructions were used to define a set of four corresponding experimental conditions that were given in the following order: $1 \rightarrow 2 \rightarrow 3 \rightarrow 4 \rightarrow 3 \rightarrow 2 \rightarrow 1$. Figure 14.8 shows the averaged hand paths and their standard deviation for each test block and one subject. The upper plot shows movements without a visual reference (instructions 1 and 3). In the upper plot, from the top, are movement spontaneously generated (instruction 1), instructed straight trajectory before learning (instruction 3 before instruction 4), and instructed straight trajectory after learning (instruction 3 after instruction 4). The lower plot shows movements (top is instruction 2 and bottom is

SM

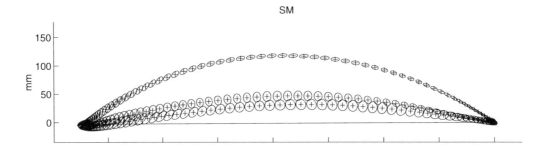

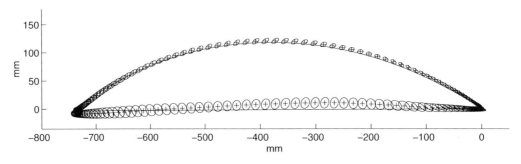

Figure 14.8 Averaged hand paths and standard deviation under different instructions for one subject. Point (0,0) denotes initial position of movements. Cross denotes average $X - Y$ positions normalized and resampled at 80 Hz. Orientation of long axis of ellipses surrounding crosses denotes direction of principal component of position variation at that time. Radius of ellipses denotes standard deviation of position at that time. Solid line in upper plot denotes start-to-goal straight line.

instruction 4) with visual references denoted by solid curves. The experimental procedures, relevant statistics about the data and detailed results are presented elsewhere (Osu et al. 1995).

In instruction 1, normal trajectories generated under the most natural condition were measured; instruction 2 was used to examine the effect of imposing path constraints. No significant difference between instructions 1 and 2 was observed. Instruction 3 was used to test the first and second explanations for curvature. The difference between instructions 3 and 4 was whether to give visual guidance about the straight path, thus the visual misperception effect could be examined by comparing trajectories made under instructions 3 and 4. It was found that subjects generated much straighter trajectories under condition 3 than they did under condition 1. The difference was not only statistically significant but also very marked. This simply disproved the incomplete control hypothesis.

Trajectories made under condition 4 were only a little bit straighter than those made under condition 3. This slight difference could be ascribed to the visual misperception effect or, in our preferred interpretation, imperfect ability to internally generate a straight path. That subjects were able to generate almost straight paths under condition 3 indicates that visual misperception, even if it has some causal relationship to movement curvature, does not have a large effect.

Osu et al. (1994) then examined point-to-point movements constrained in the frontoparallel plane within 3-D space. The instructions given to subjects were like those in conditions 1 and 3 in experiment 1. It was further required that the movement paths be contained in the frontoparallel plane about the eye level. The reason for this requirement was that no strong visual distortion effect such as horopter is known to exist within this plane (Indow and Watanabe 1988). Under instruction 1, subjects generated a significantly upward convex path in the frontoparallel plane and showed a slight curvature (outward convexity) in the horizontal plane when the 3-D path was projected onto these two planes. On the other hand, under instruction 3, trajectories projected onto the frontoparallel plane were significantly and markedly straighter than those projected under instruction 1. The same conclusions can be drawn from this experiment as were drawn from the above experiment. Furthermore, because visual distortion was not expected in the frontoparallel plane the observed movement curvatures under instruction 1 could not be ascribed to visual misperception.

Another source of evidence supporting the major role of link dynamics in observed curvature comes from comparing curvatures within the horizontal plane (e.g., fig. 14.1) and within the vertical plane (Atkeson and Hollerbach 1985). For movements shown in figure 14.1, only shoulder and elbow extension and flexion were involved. Transverse movements were curved, but radial movements were relatively straighter. Atkeson and Hollerbach (1985) also examined movements in which only elbow and shoulder flexion and extension were involved. They found that up-and-down movement paths are outwardly convex while fore-and-aft movement paths are relatively straight. If we rotate the vertical plane 90 degrees around the anterior-posterior axis passing through the shoulder joint, it exactly matches the horizontal plane at the shoulder level. This rotation can actually be achieved by 90° shoulder abduction. Then, fore-and-aft movements in the vertical plane correspond to radial movements in the horizontal plane, and up-and-down movements in the vertical plane correspond to transverse movements in the horizontal plane. This conceptual yet interesting coincidence of observed curvatures by 90° shoulder abduction makes perfect sense if the curvature difference associated with different paths comes from dynamic interactions between the forearm and upper arm. For this discussion, we neglected the effect of gravity on path shapes based on a previous computer simulation (Uno, Kawato, and Suzuki 1989), and additionally adopted the theoretical argument given by equation 14.5 in section 14.8. Note that the same visual misperception effect was not expected for the up-and-down movements in the vertical plane and the corresponding 90°-rotated transverse movements in the horizontal plane.

Virtual Trajectory Control Hypothesis

Flash (1987) explained slight curvatures observed in point-to-point paths in front of the body by combining the minimum jerk model with the virtual trajectory control hypothesis (Bizzi et al. 1984; Hogan 1984). That is, the virtual trajectory, and not the real trajectory, was assumed to be planned as the minimum jerk trajectory. Although the virtual trajectory is straight, the real trajectory is slightly curved because of imperfect control by the virtual trajectory control. However, the stiffness values assumed in Flash's (1987) simulation could be controversial. Bennett et al. (1992), Bennett (1993), Gomi, Koike, and Kawato (1992), and Gomi and Kawato (1995) found that dynamic stiffness during movement was much less than assumed by Flash (1987) and occasionally less than during posture control. Based on these measured values of stiffness during movement, Katayama and Kawato (1993) showed that, to reproduce roughly straight hand paths, the virtual trajectory must be wildly curved.

The differences between Flash's (1987) and Katayama and Kawato's (1993) simulations can be readily understood if one recalls that the required joint torques are generated as the product of mechanical stiffness and the difference between the virtual and real trajectories under the virtual trajectory control hypothesis. If physical parameters such as the moment of inertia, mass, and link length are given, and if the desired hand trajectory is fixed, the required joint torques can be uniquely determined from the inverse dynamics equation. When the stiffness is large, the difference between the virtual and real trajectories is small, but if the stiffness is small, this difference becomes large. Human multijoint hand paths are roughly straight for point-to-point movements. Consequently, in Flash's simulation, where relatively high stiffness was assumed, the virtual trajectory could be close to the real trajectory; that is, it could be a simple straight trajectory. In Katayama and Kawato's simulation, however, where relatively low stiffness was assumed, the virtual trajectory was very different from the real trajectory and was wildly curved. Conversely, if the virtual trajectory is planned as the minimum jerk trajectory, real trajectories are overly curved and do not get close enough to the target point (Katayama and Kawato 1993). Thus, if we consider the low mechanical stiffness values recently measured during movement, it would seem difficult to reproduce slightly curved hand paths by combining the virtual trajectory control hypothesis with the minimum jerk model.

Furthermore, Koike and Kawato (1993, 1995) provided experimental data that supports the low stiffness values and complicated virtual trajectory shapes using a completely different and independent methodology. They constructed a forward dynamic neural network model that can estimate dynamic joint torques from 10 surface EMG (electromyogram) signals by using intensive training based on a vast amount of physiological data collected during multijoint arm movements as well as posture control. The trained network is very accurate in reproducing the isometric as well as the dynamic torques and also the trajectories. It contains muscle nonlinear properties such as the length-tension curve and the velocity-tension curve. The network can be readily used to calculate virtual trajectories without any further assumption about the musculoskeletal system and its controller. The predicted virtual trajectories for slow movements are close to the actual trajectories but those for medium speed movements are considerably different from the actual trajectories, and the predicted complicated virtual trajectories are very different from the minimum jerk trajectory.

14.7 ALTERED VISUAL ENVIRONMENTS

Logic Underlying Kinematic Transformation Test

Trajectories generated in altered visual environments can be used to discriminate between the unidirectional and bidirectional theories. Let $X = (x, y)$ and $P = (p, q)$ denote the hand position on the CRT (computer remote terminal) and the hand position on a board or a table. Generally, functional relationships exist between the two coordinates as follows:

$$X = f(P). \tag{14.4}$$

We are interested in the case where f is a nonlinear function that causes a straight path on a CRT to become curved on the hand plane and vice versa. Let us assume that the subjects learned this nonlinear mapping from repeated trials. On a CRT screen, the starting point X_S, the target point X_T, and the hand cursor $X = f(P)$ are presented.

Let us assume first, as per the unidirectional theory, that subjects plan their trajectories in task-oriented visual coordinates, in this case, on the CRT screen. Given this assumption, a straight trajectory should be observed connecting the starting and target points on the CRT screen. The corresponding trajectory on the hand plane can be obtained using the inverse of f, and is curved since the inverse of nonlinear function f distorts the straight line into a curve.

Next, as per the bidirectional theory, let us assume that the smoothness constraint is given in the intrinsic body space. Then, calculation and control of the optimal trajectory can be done in exactly the same manner as under the normal condition. If the two points are in front of the body, roughly straight paths in the hand plane are generated. The corresponding trajectory on the CRT screen can be obtained using f, and it is markedly curved.

Adaptation in Altered Visual Environments

Wolpert, Ghahramani, and Jordan (1995) examined shapes of paths in an experimental paradigm that, while roughly similar, differed from the paradigm described in the previous section in two important aspects. First, an LCD (liquid crystal display) projector was used to present the finger positions as virtual images on the plane of the digitizing tablet. Second, the magnitude of visual distortion was started at zero (no perturbation) and was increased linearly.

When they increased the perceived curvature of normally straight sagittal movements, subjects showed significant corrective adaptation (25 percent) in the curvature of their actual hand movement. Increasing the curvature of the normally curved transverse movements also produced a significant corrective adaptation (17 percent): the hand movement became straighter, thereby reducing the visually perceived curvature. By contrast, when the curvature of naturally curved transverse movements was reduced, there was no significant adaptation (-2 percent).

As described in the previous subsection, the unidirectional theory predicts 100 percent adaptation in the hand space for all of these experiments, so that no (0 percent) change is observed on the LCD screen. On the other hand, the bidirectional theory predicts 0 percent adaptation, resulting in no change in the hand space and 100 percent change on the LCD screen. Experimental data show 25 percent, 17 percent and -2 percent adaptation in the hand space and hence 75 percent, 83 percent, and 102 percent change, respectively, on the LCD screen. Nevertheless, Wolpert, Ghahramani, and Jordan concluded from their experiment results that trajectories are planned in extrinsic visual space and are incompatible with models such as minimum torque change.

Uno, Imamizu, and Kawato (1994) also examined trajectories under a visually altered environment. Subjects moved their right hand (shoulder and elbow) at the level of the shoulder. The hand, elbow, and shoulder positions were measured with the OPTOTRAK position measurement system, and the shoulder joint angle and the elbow joint angle were calculated. Direct vision of the hand was not allowed; the hand cursor, the starting point, and the target point were presented on a 33-inch CRT located vertically in front of the subject; and a simple linear transformation in joint angles was introduced that actually corresponded to a strongly nonlinear transformation between the hand plane and the CRT screen.

Experiments were conducted with more than 10 subjects altogether, and with only a few exceptions, the bidirectional theory prediction (hand trajectory is preserved, not CRT trajectory) was observed. Significantly, there was no single case where the unidirectional theory prediction (CRT trajectory is preserved, not hand trajectory) was supported. Furthermore, the exceptions were observed only when the subjects could not attain endpoint accuracy, even after 320 training trials. The experimental procedures and relevant statistics about the data will be presented fully elsewhere.

Although the conclusions drawn by the above two groups of authors contrasted, the experimental data themselves were not that different. However, it should be emphasized that in Uno, Imamizu, and Kawato (1994), (1) the training session was longer, (2) subjects were informed of the existence and characteristics of the transformation, (3) subjects could not attain the goal unless they acquired the internal model of the transformation, (4) the location of the CRT screen was different from that of the hand position, (5) the transformation was turned on at full strength from the beginning of the training session, and (6) the transformation was very simple at body coordinates and was relatively easily learned. All these differences helped and encouraged the subjects to acquire internal models of the imposed transformations. The bidirectional theory requires that the central nervous system possess both forward and inverse internal models of kinematics and dynamics of the normal environment. Consequently, in order to fairly compare predictions of the two theories, it is critical to provide sufficient information so that subjects can acquire internal models of the imposed environments.

14.8 FORCE FIELD ADAPTATION

Trajectories under externally applied force fields can be used to discriminate between the unidirectional and bidirectional theory. The underlying logic is very simple. Because the kinematic optimization principle defined in extrinsic space does not take account of any dynamic effect of the external force field, the desired trajectory in that situation is exactly the same as it is under the normal condition. Thus, once the controller regains its capability to achieve the optimal trajectory after a short period of adaptation, the central nervous system achieves exactly the same shapes of trajectories as it did under the control condition without the force field. On the other hand, the dynamic optimization principle defined in intrinsic space takes account of the new dynamic environment imposed by the external force field. Thus it recalculates a different optimal trajectory from that calculated without the force field, once the central nervous system acquires the internal model of both the forward and inverse dynamics of the arm in combination with the environment. Thus, too, after a relatively longer duration of adaptation, different trajectories than the control trajectories are predicted. Although this logic underlying the force field adaptation experiment is simple, it turns out that the practical design of proper experimental conditions actually needs careful consideration.

Uno, Kawato, and Suzuki (1989) first used this paradigm to support the dynamic optimization principle. They used a strong rubber band attached to the subject's hand to induce an elastic force field. After about 50 trials, subjects produced significantly curved paths with asymmetrical speed profiles that were in good agreement with the prediction made by the minimum torque change model. Although we did not fully realize it at that time, this experimental paradigm satisfied two important prerequisites of the force field adaptation experiment needed to test the two theories on fair ground. Namely, (1) the force field must be strong enough and sharply variable along a generated trajectory to induce large effects on optimal trajectory shapes that can be detected even in the presence of experimental variations; and (2) the experimental setting must allow subjects to learn both the forward and inverse dynamics model of the arm under the external force field. In order to satisfy the second prerequisite, the number of training trials must be sufficiently large. In addition, it is probably better for subjects to directly see the mechanical apparatus that induces external force fields and to understand its actions and nature; it is also helpful to inform subjects about the characteristics of the force field as well as its existence; and finally, if subjects have had previous experience with similar force fields, their experience should greatly facilitate the acquisition of internal models.

Unfortunately, the two prerequisites were not satisfied in the experimental examinations of force fields by Flash and Gurevich (1991) and Shadmehr and Mussa-Ivaldi (1994). Both teams reported failure to observe significant changes in trajectory shapes in the force field. Uno and Kawato (1994) simulated the minimum torque change trajectory based on Shadmehr and Mussa-Ivaldi's (1994) numerical values of force field and found that optimal trajectories under their own force field differed only slightly from those without the force field. Thus, according to these experiments, there should be no significant difference in trajectories. By contrast, in simulation, we succeeded in reproducing large distortions of the trajectories after the first exposure to the force field; our simulation result, that the optimal trajectory is not so much affected but the first exposed trajectory is very much affected, is quite counterintuitive. This is because of the combined effects of relatively small forces (0 to 6 N), the small movement distance (10 cm), and most importantly the quasi-uniform force field along a single trajectory, peculiar to the viscous force field used. Details of this simulation study will be presented elsewhere.

It must be noted that any uniform force field, even if it is very strong, has no influence on the optimal trajectory of the minimum motor command change model because the time derivative of such a uniform field vanishes in the criterion as shown below.

$$C_M = 1/2 \int_0^{t_f} \sum_{i=1}^n \left(\frac{dM_i^{\text{comp}}}{dt} \right)^2 dt$$

$$= 1/2 \int_0^{t_f} \sum_{i=1}^n \left(\frac{dM_i^{\text{WO}}}{dt} + \frac{dM_i^{\text{unif}}}{dt} \right)^2 dt \qquad (14.5)$$

$$= 1/2 \int_0^{t_f} \sum_{i=1}^n \left(\frac{dM_i^{\text{WO}}}{dt} \right)^2 dt,$$

where M_i^{comp} is the total motor command necessary for compensating the arm inherent dynamics and canceling the imposed force field. M_i^{WO} the motor command in the normal condition without the force field. M_i^{unif} is the motor command that compensates the applied uniform force field. It might be quite large but its time derivative vanishes.

Regarding the discrepancy between Flash and Gurevich (1991) and Uno, Kawato, and Suzuki (1989), possible reasons for the failure to detect significant changes in the former study might be (1) the fixed point of the spring was a little far from the trajectory and thus the force direction did not sufficiently change (again, quasi-uniform force field), (2) the force magnitude was not large enough, and/or (3) the training number of less than 15 was not large enough for acquisition of internal forward models. We plan to examine these factors in our future experiments.

ACKNOWLEDGMENTS

I would like to thank Dr. Yoh'ichi Tohkura of ATR Human Information Processing Research Laboratories for his continuing encouragement. Preparation of this manuscript was supported by a Human Frontier Science Project grant to Mitsuo Kawato.

REFERENCES

Abend, W., Bizzi, E., and Morasso, P. (1982). Human arm trajectory formation. *Brain, 105,* 331–348.

Atkeson, C. G., and Hollerbach, J. M. (1985). Kinematic features of unrestrained vertical arm movements. *Journal of Neuroscience, 15,* 2318–2330.

Bennett, D. J. (1993). Torques generated at the human elbow joint in response to constant position errors imposed during voluntary movements. *Experimental Brain Research, 95,* 488–498.

Bennett, D. J., Hollerbach, J. M., Xu, Y, and Hunter, I. W. (1992). Time-varying stiffness of human elbow joint during cyclic voluntary movement. *Experimental Brain Research, 88,* 433–442.

Bizzi, E., Accornero, N., Chapple, W., and Hogan, N. (1984). Posture control and trajectory formation during arm movement. *Journal of Neuroscience, 4,* 2738–2744.

Bizzi, E., Polit, A., and Morasso, P. (1976). Mechanism underlying achievement of final head position. *Journal of Neurophysiology, 39,* 435–444.

Flash, T. (1987). The control of hand equilibrium trajectories in multijoint arm movements. *Biological Cybernetics, 57*, 257–274.

Flash, T. (1990). The organization of human arm trajectory control. In J. M. Winters and S. L. Y. Woo (Eds.), *Multiple muscle systems: Biomechanics and movement organization*, 282–301. New York: Springer.

Flash, T., and Gurevich, I. (1991). Arm stiffness and movement adaptation to external loads. *Proceedings of IEEE Engineering in Medicine and Biology Society, 13*, 885–886.

Flash, T., and Hogan, N. (1985). The coordination of arm movements: An experimentally confirmed mathematical model. *Journal of Neuroscience, 5*, 1688–1703.

Foley, J. M. (1980). Binocular distance perception. *Psychological Review, 87*, 411–434.

Gomi, H., and Kawato, M. (1995). The change of human arm mechanical impedance during movements under different environmental conditions. *Society for Neuroscience Abstracts, 21*, 686.

Gomi, H., Koike, Y., and Kawato, M. (1992). Human hand stiffness during discrete point-to-point multijoint movement. *Proceedings of IEEE Engineering in Medicine and Biology Society, 14*, 1628–1629.

Hayakawa, H., Nishida, S., Wada, Y., and Kawato, M. (1994). A computational model for shape estimation by integration of shading and edge information. *Neural Networks, 7*, 1193–1209.

Hogan, N. (1984). An organizing principle for a class of voluntary movements. *Journal of Neuroscience, 4*, 2745–2754.

Indow, T., and Watanabe, T. (1988). Alleys on an extensive apparent frontoparallel plane: A second experiment. *Perception, 17*, 647–666.

Kandel, E. R., Schwartz, J. H, and Jessell, T. M. (Eds.). (1991). *Principles of neural science*. 3d ed. New York: Elsevier.

Katayama, M., and Kawato, M. (1993). Virtual trajectory and stiffness ellipse during multijoint arm movement predicted by neural inverse models. *Biological Cybernetics, 69*, 353–362.

Kawato, M. (1992). Optimization and learning in neural networks for formation and control of coordinated movement. In D. Meyer and S. Kornblum (Eds.), *Attention and performance, XIV: Synergies in experimental psychology, artificial intelligence, and cognitive neuroscience—A silver jubilee*, 821–849. Cambridge, MA: MIT Press.

Kawato, M. (1995). A bidirectional theory approach to prerational intelligence. In *Proceedings of ZiF Conference on Prerational Intelligence*, Bielefeld, Germany, 16–20 May 1994.

Kawato, M., Furukawa, K., and Suzuki, R. (1987). A hierarchical neural-network model for control and learning of voluntary movement. *Biological Cybernetics, 57*, 169–185.

Kawato, M., and Gomi, H. (1992). The cerebellum and VOR/OKR learning models. *Trends in Neurosciences, 15*, 445–453.

Kawato, M., Gomi, H., Katayama, M., and Koike, Y. (1993). Supervised learning for co-ordinative motor control. In E. B. Baum (Ed.), *Computational learning and cognition*, 126–161. SIAM Frontier Series. Philadelphia: Society for Industrial and Applied Mathematics.

Kawato, M., Hayakawa, H., and Inui, T. (1993). A forward-inverse optics model of reciprocal connections between visual areas. *Network: Computation in Neural Systems, 4*, 415–422.

Kawato, M., Maeda, Y, Uno, Y., and Suzuki, R. (1990). Trajectory formation of arm movement by cascade neural network model based on minimum torque change criterion. *Biological Cybernetics, 62*, 275–288.

Kelso, J. A. S., Southard, D. L., and Goodman, D. (1979). On the nature of human interlimb coordination. *Science, 203,* 1029–1031.

Koike, Y., and Kawato, M. (1993). Virtual trajectories predicted from surface EMG signals. *Society for Neuroscience Abstracts, 19,* 543.

Koike, Y., and Kawato, M. (1994). Trajectory formation from surface EMG signals using a neural network model. *Transactions of Institute of Electronics, Information, and Communication Engineers, DII77,* 193–203. In Japanese.

Koike, Y., and Kawato, M. (1995). Estimation of dynamic joint torques and trajectory formation from surface EMG signals using a neural network model. *Biological Cybernetics, 73,* 291–300.

Liberman, A. M., Cooper, F. S., Shankweiler, D. P., and Studdert-Kennedy, M. (1967). Perception of the speech code. *Psychological Review, 74,* 431–461.

McClelland, J. L., and Rumelhart, D. E. (1981). An interactive activation model of context effects in letter perception. I. An account of basic findings. *Psychological Review, 88,* 375–407.

Morasso, P. (1981). Spatial control of arm movements. *Experimental Brain Research, 42,* 223–227.

Osu, R., Uno, Y., Koike, Y., and Kawato, M. (1994). *Examinations of possible explanations for trajectory curvature in multijoint arm movements.* ATR technical report TR-H-069. Also submitted to *Journal of Experimental Psychology.*

Pandya, D. N., and Yeterian, E. H. (1988). Architecture and connections of cortical association areas. In A. Peters and E. G. Jones (Eds.), *Cerebral cortex.* Vol. 4, *Association and auditory cortices,* 3–61. New York: Plenum Press.

Shadmehr, R., and Mussa-Ivaldi, F. A. (1994). Geometric structure of the adaptive controller of the human arm. *Journal of Neuroscience, 14,* 3208–3224.

Shidara, M., Kawano, K., Gomi, H., and Kawato, M. (1993). Inverse-dynamics model eye movement control by Purkinje cells in the cerebellum. *Nature, 365,* 50–52.

Uno, Y., Imamizu, H., and Kawato, M. (1994). *Exploration of space where arm trajectory is planned by experiments in altered kinematics.* ATR technical report TR-H-070. Also submitted to *Experimental Brain Research.*

Uno, Y., and Kawato, M. (1994). *Dynamic performance indices for trajectory formation in human arm movements.* ATR technical report TR-H-071.

Uno, Y., Kawato, M., and Suzuki, R. (1989). Formation and control of optimal trajectory in human multijoint arm movement—minimum torque change model. *Biological Cybernetics, 61,* 89–101.

Uno, Y., Suzuki, R., and Kawato, M. (1989). Minimum muscle tension change model that reprouces human arm moement. In *Proceedings of the 4th Symposium on Biological and Physiological Engineering,* 299–302. In Japanese.

Wada, Y., and Kawato, M. (1993). A neural network model for arm trajectory formation using forward and inverse dynamics models. *Neural Networks, 6,* 919–932.

Wada, Y., and Kawato, M. (1995). A theory for cursive handwriting based on the minimization principle. *Biological Cybernetics, 73,* 3–13.

Wada, Y., Koike, Y., Vatikiotis Bateson, E., and Kawato, M. (1995). A computational theory for movement pattern recognition based on optimal movement pattern generation. *Biological Cybernetics, 73,* 15–25.

Wolpert, D. M., Ghahramani, Z., and Jordan, M. I. (1994). Perceptual distortion contributes to the curvature of human reaching movements. *Experimental Brain Research, 98,* 153–156.

Wolpert, D. M., Ghahramani, Z., and Jordan, M. I. (1995). Are arm trajectories planned in kinematic or dynamic coordinates? An adaptation study. *Experimental Brain Research, 103,* 460–470.

15 One Visual Experience, Many Visual Systems

Melvyn A. Goodale

ABSTRACT

Evidence from both neurological patients and intact subjects suggests that our perception-based knowledge of the world depends on visual processes quite independent from those mediating the visual control of skilled motor acts, such as manual prehension. This division of labor can be mapped onto the two main streams of visual projections in primate cerebral cortex: the ventral stream from striate cortex to inferotemporal cortex and the dorsal stream from striate cortex to the posterior parietal region. Although both streams process information about the orientation, size, and shape of objects, and about their spatial relations, each stream uses visual information in different ways. Transformations carried out in the ventral stream permit the formation of perceptual and cognitive representations that embody the enduring characteristics of objects and their spatial relations with each other; those carried out in the dorsal stream, which utilize moment-to-moment information about the disposition of objects within egocentric frames of reference, mediate the control of a number of different goal-directed actions. Thus the production of normal goal-directed behavior in the visual world depends on the integration of at least two relatively independent input-output visual systems.

15.1 INTRODUCTION

Vision is often identified with visual experience. Conscious sight, however, is only one of the functions of vision, and much of the work done by the visual system is quite inaccessible to experiential perception. The size of our pupils, for example, can change dramatically as our eyes move from one part of the visual array to another; yet, try as we might, we cannot "experience" either the reflexive contraction of the iris muscles or the change in the visual array that produces that contraction. Similarly, even though much of our behavior and physiology is strongly linked to circadian and circannual light cycles, we have no direct experience of that visual modulation. Moreover, the neural circuits controlling these reflexive or "vegetative" visual functions are not only independent of one another but are also quite separate from the neural circuitry mediating visual perception. But, as we shall see in this chapter, even complex visually guided behavior, such as reaching out and grasping an object, appears to depend on visual mechanisms that are functionally and neurally separate from those mediating our perception of that object.

The idea of modularity in the visual system is not new. It has been known for many years that the retinal projections to the brain show considerable variation in their physiological characteristics, and it has been convincingly demonstrated that this physiological variation reflects functional differences in the nature of the visual information conveyed to the brain by these different projections. Within the brain itself, the multiplicity of visual pathways and areas, particularly within the cerebral cortex, has been seen as a reflection of the different kinds of information processing that the visual system carries out on the basic retinal array. Different modules are responsible for different kinds of visual processing, and these modules are, for the most part, quite independent of one another. For example, some modules appear to be dedicated to the processing of color, others to the processing of form and contour, and still others to the processing of motion or depth (for review, see Zeki 1993). Nevertheless, despite the emphasis on modularity, most contemporary accounts of vision make the implicit assumption that the function of all these modules is to deliver some sort of integrated representation of the external world, which can then serve as the perceptual foundation for all visually based thought and action. In this chapter, I will challenge this idea of a monolithic visual system (albeit one with modular inputs); I will argue instead that modularity in the visual system is largely a reflection of the different requirements of the output systems that vision serves and that vision is anything but monolithic in function. I will argue, in other words, that despite the apparent unity of our visual experience, the visual system is really a collection of relatively independent modules linked to different output systems. These different input-output modules can be grouped, on functional grounds, into two broad divisions. One set of modules delivers our visual perception of objects and events in the world; another set mediates the visual control of actions directed at those objects and events. It is this latter set that includes the visuomotor modules that mediate the control of goal-directed reaching and grasping movements.

15.2   NEUROPSYCHOLOGICAL DISSOCIATIONS BETWEEN PERCEPTION AND ACTION

In the intact brain, of course, the visual system appears to work as an integrated whole. Objects are identified and actions are executed within a visual world that is unified and seamless. Evidence from neurological patients, however, tells a very different story. Consider the case of the patient D.F., a young woman who developed a profound visual form agnosia following carbon monoxide–induced anoxia (Goodale et al. 1991; Milner et al. 1991). While the damage in D.F.'s brain is quite diffuse, the ventrolateral regions of her occipital lobe are particularly compromised, although primary visual cortex appears to be largely spared (for details, see Milner et al. 1991). Even though D.F.'s "low-level" visual abilities are reasonably intact, she can no longer recognize everyday objects or the faces of her friends and relatives;

nor can she identify even the simplest of geometric shapes. (If an object is placed in her hand, of course, she has no trouble identifying it by touch.) Remarkably, however, D.F. shows strikingly accurate guidance of her hand and finger movements when she attempts to pick up the very objects she cannot identify. Thus, when she reaches out to grasp objects of different sizes, her hand opens wider midflight for larger objects than it does for smaller ones, just as it does in people with normal vision (Goodale et al. 1991). Similarly, she rotates her hand and wrist quite normally when she reaches out to grasp objects in different orientations. At the same time, she is quite unable to describe or distinguish between the size or orientation of different objects when they are presented to her in simple discrimination tests. In fact, as figure 15.1 illustrates, this is true even when D.F. is asked to indicate the size or orientation of an object manually. Thus she cannot indicate the size of an object by opening her index finger and thumb a matching amount; nor can she rotate a handheld card to match the orientation of an visual stimulus placed in front of her. In other words, D.F.'s visual system is no longer able to

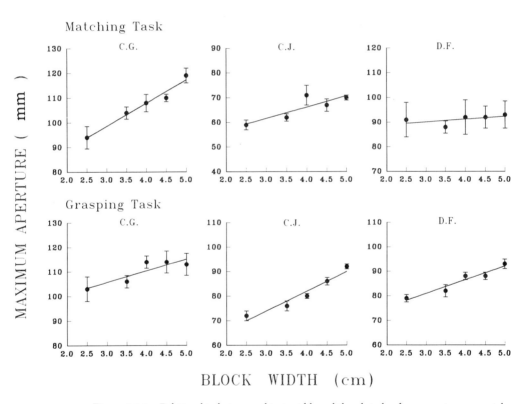

Figure 15.1 Relationship between object width and thumb-index finger aperture on matching task and grasping task for patient D.F. and two age-matched control subjects (C.G. and C.J.). When D.F. was required to indicate how wide block was by opening her finger and thumb, her matches were unrelated to object width and showed considerable trial-to-trial variability. When she picked up block, however, size of her grasp was well correlated with width of block.

One Visual Experience, Many Visual Systems

deliver any perceptual information about the size and orientation of objects in the world. Yet at the same time, the visuomotor systems in D.F.'s brain that control the programming and execution of visually guided actions remain quite sensitive to these same object features.

There is evidence that patients with damage to other visual areas in the cerebral cortex, such as the superior regions of the posterior parietal cortex, show a pattern of visual behavior that is essentially the mirror image of that of D.F. Such patients are often unable to use visual information to rotate their hand or to scale the opening of their fingers when reaching out to pick up an object, even though they have no difficulty describing the size or orientation of objects in that part of the visual field (Jakobson et al. 1991; Perenin and Vighetto 1988).

These neurological observations, together with evidence from electrophysiological and behavioral studies in the monkey, have led David Milner and me to propose a new interpretation of the division of labor between the two streams of visual pathways that leave the primary visual cortex and project to distinct regions of the primate cerebral cortex. These two streams, which were identified in the macaque monkey over ten years ago by Ungerleider and Mishkin (1982), consist of a ventral stream arising in primary visual cortex and projecting to inferotemporal cortex, and a dorsal stream also arising from primary visual cortex but projecting instead to the posterior parietal cortex (see fig. 15.2). Although one must always be cautious when drawing homologies between monkey and human neuroanatomy (Crick and

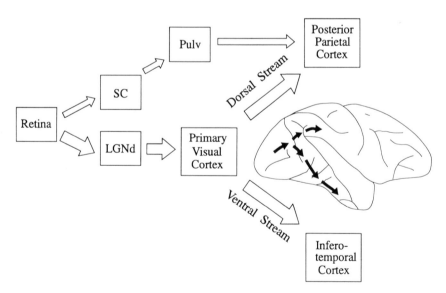

Figure 15.2 Schematic diagram showing major routes whereby retinal input reaches dorsal and ventral streams. Diagram of macaque brain (right hemisphere) on right of figure shows approximate routes of cortico-cortical projections from primary visual cortex to posterior parietal and inferotemporal cortex, respectively. (LGNd: lateral geniculate nucleus, pars dorsalis; Pulv: pulvinar: SC: superior colliculus.)

Jones 1993), it seems likely that the visual projections from the primary visual cortex to the temporal and parietal lobes in the human brain may involve a separation into ventral and dorsal streams similar to that seen in the macaque brain. Ungerleider and Mishkin (1982) originally proposed that the ventral stream plays a special role in the identification of objects, whereas the dorsal stream is responsible for localizing objects in visual space.

Our reinterpretation of this story places less emphasis on the differences in the visual information received by the two streams (object features versus spatial location) than it does on the differences in the transformations the streams perform upon that information. In our view, both streams process information about object features and about their spatial relations, but each stream uses this visual information in different ways. In the ventral stream, the transformations focus on the enduring characteristics of objects and their relations, permitting the formation of long-term perceptual representations that can be used to identify and recognize objects. In the dorsal stream, the transformations deliver the instantaneous and egocentric coordinates of objects and thereby mediate the visual control of skilled actions, such as manual prehension, directed at those objects. Such a division of labor in the cortical visual pathways accounts rather well for the neurological dissociations we and others have observed in the perception of object size and orientation, and for the use of these object features in the control of manual prehension.

Analysis of Object Shape for Perception and Action

The size and orientation of objects are not the only features that control the parameters of a grasping movement. To pick up an object successfully, it is not enough to orient the hand and scale the grip appropriately; the fingers and thumb must also be placed at appropriate opposition points on the object's surface. Computation of these "grasp points" must take into account the surface boundaries or shape of the object. In fact, even casual observations of grasping movements suggest that the posture of the fingers and hand are remarkable sensitive to object shape. But does the visual analysis of object shape for grasping, like the related analyses of object size and orientation, depend on neural mechanisms that are relatively independent of those underlying the perceptual identification of objects? To answer this question, my colleagues and I compared the ability of the patient D.F. to discriminate objects of different shape with her ability to position her fingers correctly on the boundaries of those same objects when she was required to pick them up (Goodale, et al. 1994). In addition, we contrasted D.F.'s performance on these tasks with that of another patient, R.V., a fifty-five-year-old woman who developed optic ataxia after strokes that left her with large bilateral lesions of the occipitoparietal cortex, with no involvement of the temporal cortex (for details of the lesion, see Goodale et al. 1994). The optic ataxia, which was evident clinically as difficulty in directing her grasping or pointing movements toward objects presented in different parts of the visual field, had resolved to some extent before we saw R.V., although it was still clear that she had visuomotor problems. She showed poor scaling of her grasp for object size, for example, even though she was able to indicate the size of the object quite well manually by adjusting the opening of her index finger and thumb to match the width of the object (Goodale et al. 1993). Nevertheless, despite her visuomotor deficits, R.V.'s resolution acuity was in the normal range (although she did have a small quadrantanopsia in her lower right visual field due to invasion of the calcarine fissure in the left hemisphere). R.V. was not apraxic; she had no difficulty following simple commands such as "show me how you would eat soup with a spoon," and her hand movements during the execution of this actions seemed quite normal. Moreover, her hand strength and finger-tapping abilities also appeared normal, suggesting that she had no motor deficits per se. R.V. also achieved a perfect score on a twenty-item test of object recognition in which she was asked to identify line drawings of common objects; D.F. was able to identify only two items correctly on this same test.

Twelve different shapes (two of each, for a total of twenty-four) were used to compare D.F.'s and R.V.'s ability to discriminate between shapes and to use shape information to control grasping (see fig. 15.3). The shapes were con-

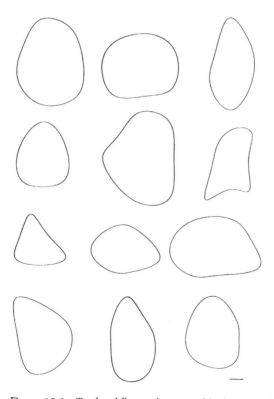

Figure 15.3 Twelve different shapes used both in same/different visual discrimination tasks and in grasping task. Line on bottom right indicates one centimeter.

structed out of wood 0.6 cm in thickness, painted enamel white; they were presented on a table covered with a black cloth. The shapes were based on the templates used by Blake (1992) to develop algorithms for the control of grasping in two-fingered robots working in novel environments. These shapes were chosen because they have smoothly bounded contours and an absence of clear symmetry. Thus the determination of stable grasp points requires an analysis of the entire contour envelope of the shape. Moreover, in a normative study, where the grasping of these shapes was examined in ten neurologically intact subjects, we observed a remarkable consistency in the grasp points selected by different subjects when they were asked to pick up the shapes using their index finger and thumb in a "precision grip" (see fig. 15.4).

In the discrimination tests, D.F. and R.V. were presented with a series of pairs of these shapes and were simply asked to indicate whether the shapes in each pair were the "same" or "different." For one discrimination test, the relative orientation of the two shapes on "same" trials was identical; for the other discrimination test, the relative orientation of the two shapes on "same" trials varied from one trial to the next. It did not matter which test was used; D.F. and R.V. showed remarkably different discrimination abilities on both of them. As can be seen in figure 15.5, D.F.'s performance hovered just above chance and she seemed quite unable to distinguish one shape from another. In contrast, R.V. achieved a score of 90 percent correct when the relative orientation of the two shapes on "same" trials was identical, falling to 80 percent correct when the relative orientation of the two shapes was varied from trial to trial. In other words, whereas D.F. apparently failed to perceive whether two objects had the same or different outline shapes, R.V. had little difficulty in making such a discrimination.

We observed quite the opposite pattern of results when D.F. and R.V. were asked to pick up these objects. Even though D.F. had failed to discriminate between these different objects, she had no difficulty in placing her finger and thumb on stable grasp points on the circumference of any of these objects when any one of them was placed in different orientations in front of her. In fact, the grasp points she selected were remarkably similar to those chosen by a neurologically intact control subject (see fig. 15.6). In addition, D.F. showed the same systematic shift in the selection of grasp points as the control subject when the egocentric orientation of the object was changed. Moreover, there were other similarities between D.F.'s grasps and those of the control subject: the line joining the two grasp points tended to pass through the center of mass of the object; these "grasp lines" often corresponded to the axes of minimum or maximum diameter of the object; and finally, the grasp points were often located on regions of the object boundary that would be expected to yield the most stable grip—regions of maximum convexity or concavity (Iberall, Bingham, and Arbib 1986; Blake 1992). This dissociation between profoundly disturbed perception and intact visuomotor control

Figure 15.4 "Grasp lines" (joining points where index finger and thumb first made contact with shape) for ten normal subjects for four of twelve shapes. Each of four orientations in which shapes were presented is plotted separately. Small line at end of grasp line indicates point where the thumb made contact with shape. Subjects tended to pick up shape so that grasp line intersected center of mass of shape. In addition, they selected grasp lines that fell across maximum or minimum diameter of object. They also chose points of maximum convexity.

parallels earlier observations that looked at D.F.'s ability to deal with object size and orientation (Goodale et al. 1991).

R.V.'s grasping was very different from D.F.'s (see fig. 15.6); R.V. often chose very unstable grasp points, and she stabilized her grasp only after her finger and thumb made contact with the object. Thus, despite her apparent ability to perceive the shape of an object, R.V. was unable to use visual information about object shape to control the placement of her finger and thumb as she attempted to pick up that object. Once she had made contact

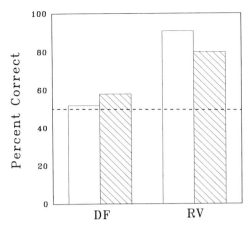

Figure 15.5 Performance of D.F. and R.V. on same/different discrimination tests. Open bars show performance on task in which relative orientation of two shapes on the "same" trial was identical; hatched bars show performance on task in which relative orientation of twin shapes varied between "same" trials. Control subject scored perfectly on both tests although she took longer when two shapes on same trials were presented at different orientations. Dotted line indicates chance performance.

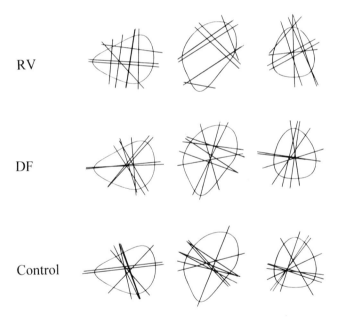

Figure 15.6 "Grasp lines" (joining points where index finger and the thumb first made contact with the shape) selected by optic ataxic patient (R.V.), visual-form agnosic patient (D.F.), and control subject when picking up three of twelve shapes. Four different orientations in which each shape was presented have been rotated so that they are aligned. No distinction is made between points of contact for thumb and finger in these plots.

One Visual Experience, Many Visual Systems

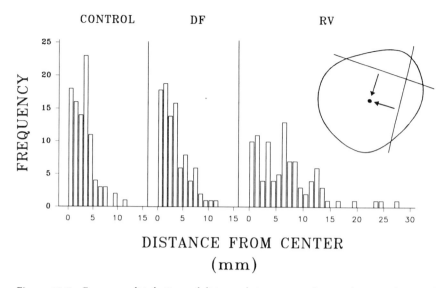

Figure 15.7 Frequency distributions of distances between grasp lines and center of mass of shape for D.F., R.V., and control subject for all twelve shapes. Inset shows how those distances were calculated for two different grasp lines.

with the object, however, her manipulation of it appeared essentially normal. This suggests that, despite her problems in visuomotor control, she was able to use tactile and haptic information to control the placement of her fingers; it was just her visuomotor performance that was disturbed. In order to quantify differences between the performance of R.V. and D.F. (and the control subject), we measured the shortest distance between the grasp line (connecting opposing grasp points) on each trial and the object's center of mass. As figure 15.7 illustrates, whereas D.F. and the control subject did not differ on this measure, both differed significantly from R.V.

The striking double dissociation observed in D.F. and R.V. parallels the results of earlier studies (Goodale et al. 1991; Goodale et al. 1993; Perenin and Vighetto 1988), which focused on object size and orientation rather than object shape. The question remains, however, as to whether or not this pattern of deficits and spared visual abilities in the two patients can be tied to the functional distinction between the dorsal and ventral streams that David Milner and I have proposed.

In D.F.'s case, the brain damage that she suffered as a consequence of anoxia appears to have interrupted the normal flow of shape and contour information into her perceptual systems without affecting the processing of shape and contour information by her visuomotor control systems. But where is the damage in D.F.'s brain? If, as was suggested earlier, the perception of objects and events is mediated by the ventral stream of visual projections to inferotemporal cortex, then D.F. should show evidence for damage relatively early in this pathway. Certainly, the pattern of damage revealed by MRI (magnetic resonance imaging) is consistent with this interpretation; the major focus of cortical damage is in the ventrolateral region of the occipital cortex, an area that is thought to be part of the human homologue of the ventral stream. At the same time, her primary visual cortex, which provides input for both the dorsal and ventral streams, appears to be largely intact; although input from primary visual cortex to the ventral stream has been compromised in D.F., input from this structure to the dorsal stream appears to be essentially intact. In addition, the dorsal stream, unlike the ventral stream, also receives input from the superior colliculus via the pulvinar, a nucleus in the thalamus (see fig. 15.2). Thus input to the dorsal stream from both the superior colliculus (via the pulvinar) and the lateral geniculate nucleus (via primary visual cortex) could continue to mediate well-formed visuomotor responses in D.F.

One must be cautious, however, about drawing strong conclusions about anatomy and pathways from patients like D.F. Her deficits arose, not from a discrete lesion, but from anoxia. As a consequence, the brain damage in D.F., while localized to some extent, is much more diffuse than it would be in a patient with a stroke or tumor. Thus, while the striking dissociation between perceptual and visuomotor abilities in D.F. can be mapped onto the distinction between the ventral and dorsal streams of visual processing proposed by Goodale and Milner, that mapping can be only tentative. The proposal is strengthened, however, by observations in patients like R.V. whose pattern of deficits is complementary to D.F.'s and whose brain damage can be confidently localized to the dorsal stream.

R.V., who had no difficulty discriminating between the different shapes used in this experiment, could not use information about object shape to guide the placement of her fingers. The damage in R.V.'s brain is largely confined to the occipitoparietal region, an area thought to be homologous to the dorsal stream in monkeys. R.V.'s inability to use shape information to guide her precision grip is probably due to damage to these dorsal stream pathways; her ability to discriminate between different shapes (and to recognize line drawings) can be attributed to the fact that the ventral stream of projections to her temporal cortex was spared.

But what other evidence is there to suggest that the ventral stream, which is apparently damaged in D.F. but spared in R.V., has a special role to play in the perception of objects and object features? As it turns out, there is a long history of electrophysiological and behavioral work in the monkey linking this pathway with object recognition. For example, visually responsive neurons in the ventral stream, particularly in inferotemporal cortex and neighboring regions of the superior temporal sulcus, are often sharply tuned for object features such as shape, color, and visual texture (for review, see Goodale 1993; Goodale and Milner 1992; Milner and Goodale 1993, 1995). In fact, ensembles of cells sensitive to particular object features appear to be organized into columns, where each column consists of cells that are responsive to the visual appearance of similar objects (Fujita et al. 1992). Some cells in these regions are quite category-specific and will respond to a particular object, such as a monkey face, over a broad range of lighting conditions, viewpoints, and retinal image sizes (e.g., Hasselmo et al. 1989; Perrett et al. 1991; Hietanen et al. 1992). Moreover, these and other cells in inferotemporal cortex typically have exceptionally large receptive fields, usually including the fovea and often extending across the vertical meridian. Not surprisingly, bilateral lesions of inferotemporal cortex typically produce severe deficits in visual recognition and discrimination learning (for review, see Ungerleider and Mishkin 1982), a finding which is again consistent with the idea that the ventral stream is concerned with providing the raw material for recognition memory and other long-term representations of the visual world. Although the concurrent motor behavior of the monkey has little or no effect on the activity of the cells in the ventral stream, there is good evidence to suggest that the responsivity of cells can be modulated by attention (e.g., Chelazzi et al. 1993) and by the reinforcement history of the stimuli employed to study them (e.g., Richmond and Sato 1987; Sakai and Miyashita 1992). Indeed, it has recently been suggested that cells in this region might play a role in comparing current visual inputs with internal representations of recalled images (Eskandar, Richmond, and Optican 1992; Eskandar, Optican, and Richmond 1992), which are themselves presumably stored in other regions, such as neighboring regions of the medial temporal lobe and related limbic areas (Fahy, Riches, and Brown 1993; Nishijo et al. 1993).

But what about the dorsal stream, which is damaged in R.V. and presumably spared in D.F.? Is there evidence in the monkey to suggest that this pathway has a special role to play in the visual processing of object shape for the control of manual prehension? Of course, ever since the pioneering work of Hyvärinen, Mountcastle, and their colleagues, we have known that, in sharp contrast to cells in the ventral stream, visually sensitive cells in posterior parietal cortex are modulated by the concurrent motor behavior of the animal (Hyvärinen and Poranen 1974; Mountcastle et al. 1975). Thus the activity of some visually driven cells in this region has been shown to be linked to saccadic eye movements; the activity of others, to whether the animal is fixating a stimulus; and the activity of still other cells, to whether the animal is engaged in visual pursuit or is making goal-directed reaching movements (for a review of saccade-modulated activity in posterior parietal cortex, see Colby, chap. 7, this volume).

It is likely that such cells are important components in networks that provide the necessary egocentric spatial frames of reference (retina-centered, head-centered, trunk-centered, shouldered centered, and so on) for the visual control of specific visuomotor outputs (see also Graziano and Gross, chap. 8, this volume). But what is of most interest in the present context is that some cells in the posterior parietal area that fire when monkeys reach out to pick up objects are selective not for the spatially directed movement of the arm but for the movements of the wrist, hand, and fingers made prior to and during the act of grasping the target (Hyvärinen and Poranen 1974; Mountcastle et al. 1975). Furthermore, it has been shown recently that many of these cells are visually selective and are tuned for objects of a particular shape and/or orientation (Sakata et al. 1992; Taira et al. 1990). These manipulation neurons thus appear to be tied to the properties of the goal object as well as to the distal movements that are required for grasping that object. The manipulation neurons are strongly linked with areas in premotor cortex that contain cells whose activity is associated with grasping behavior (Gentilucci and Rizzolatti 1990). Indeed, it has been suggested that the reciprocal connections between these two regions may permit a "matching" between sensory input and the required motor output for grasping (Sakata et al. 1992).

The route by which the visual information required for the coding of the object shape reaches the posterior parietal cortex is at present unknown. It is unlikely, however, that the shape coding in manipulation cells is dependent on input from the higher-level modules within the ventral stream that support the *perception* of object qualities. Evidence against this possibility is that monkeys with profound deficits in object recognition following inferotemporal lesions are nevertheless as capable as normal animals at picking up small food objects (Klüver and Bucy 1939), at catching flying insects (Pribram 1967), and at orienting their fingers in a precision grip to grasp morsels of food embedded in small oriented slots (Buchbinder et al. 1980). In short, these animals behave much the same way as D.F.: they are unable to discriminate between objects on the basis of visual features they can clearly use to control their grasping movements.

There is good convergence then between the neuropsychological evidence in humans and the electrophysiological work in monkeys. Both support the division of labor that David Milner and I have proposed for the two streams of visual processing in the primate brain. The ventral stream appears to mediate the visual perception of objects, while the dorsal stream plays the major role in the visual control of motor acts, such as manual prehension, directed at those objects. Moreover, this functional distinction extends to the analysis of object shape; both streams, it appears, have access to visual information about the shape of objects, but each stream uses this information for different purposes.

15.3 DISSOCIATIONS BETWEEN PERCEPTION AND ACTION IN NORMAL VISUAL SYSTEMS

Although the evidence with neurological patients discussed above points to a clear dissociation between the visual pathways supporting perception and action in the cerebral cortex, one might also expect to see, under certain circumstances, evidence for such a dissociation in neurologically intact individuals. In other words, the visual information used to calibrate and control a skilled motor act directed at an object might not always match the perceptual judgments made about that object. After all, the control of skilled actions imposes requirements on visual processing that are different from those demanded of the mechanisms supporting visual recognition. Efficient grasping, for example, demands rapid and accurate computation of the size, shape, orientation, and location of the object, and the required computations for action must be organized within egocentric frames of reference. For example, while we might *perceive* that one object is larger or closer than another, such relative judgments of size and distance are not enough to calibrate the grasping movement directed at that object; to grasp the object accurately, it is necessary to know its *exact* size and distance.

Object Location

There are several studies showing clear dissociations in normal subjects between perceptual judgments of the location (or apparent change in location) of visual stimuli and the motor acts directed at those stimuli. Bridgeman, Kirch, and Sperling (1981), for example, have shown that even though a fixed visual target surrounded by a moving frame appears to drift in a direction opposite to that of the frame (which appears stationary), subjects persist in pointing to the actual location of the target. Wong and Mack (1981) have obtained similar dissociations but with saccadic eye movements rather than pointing. In their experiments, a small target was presented within a surrounding frame; after a 500 ms blank period, the frame and target reappeared, but now the frame was displaced a few degrees to the left or right. The target itself was presented at exactly the same location as before, yet instead of perceiving the frame as having changed position, subjects had the strong illusion that it was the target that had changed position, in a direction opposite to that of the actual displacement of the frame. This illusion was maintained even when the target was displaced in the same direction as the frame, but by only one third the distance. In this latter condition, the perceived change in target position after the blank period was still in the direction opposite to the change in the position of the frame and, even more remarkably, in the direction opposite to the actual change in position of the target. Yet despite the presence of this strong illusory displacement of the target, subjects consistently directed their saccades to the true location of the target (in other words, to its location in egocentric or retinocentric coordinates rather than to its location in perceptual or frame-based coordinates).

Complementary dissociations have also been observed in experiments in which the perception of a visual stimulus remains quite stable despite large displacements of its actual position—displacements that have a clear effect on the final position of both eye and hand movements directed at that target. In one such experiment, in which a target was moved unpredictably during a saccadic eye movement, subjects were unable to report, even in forced-choice testing, whether or not a target had changed position, even though correction saccades and manual aiming movements directed at the target showed near-perfect adjustments for the unpredictable target shift (Goodale, Pelisson, and Prablanc 1986). In other words, an illusory perceptual constancy of target position was maintained in the face of large amendments in visuomotor control.

These experiments suggest that the mechanisms mediating the perception of object location operate largely in *allocentric* coordinates, whereas those mediating the control of object-directed actions operate in egocentric coordinates. In other words, perception uses a world-based coordinate system in which objects are seen as changing location relative to a stable or constant world; the systems controlling action systems, however, cannot afford these kinds of constancies and must compute the location of the object with respect to the effector directed at that target. Thus, in the experiments by Bridgeman et al. (1981) and Wong and Mack (1981), the target within the moving or displaced frame was perceived as moving *relative* to the frame, while the frame itself, which was the only large visible feature in the field of view, was perceived as a stable background. The visuomotor systems computing the saccadic eye movements (or the aiming movements) directed at the target simply ignored the movement of the frame and computed the actual position of the target in retinocentric (and perhaps also in head- and/or shoulder-centered) coordinates. In the experiments by Goodale, Pelisson, and Prablanc (1986), where the position of the target was sometimes changed during a saccade, the subjects' failure to perceive the displacement of the target was probably a reflection of the broad tuning of perceptual constancy mechanism that preserve the identity of a target as its position is shifted on the retina during an eye movement. When no other reference points are available in the field of view, the perceptual system assumes that the position of the target (which was stable at the beginning of the saccade) has not changed. Such an assumption has little consequence for perception and is computationally efficient. But the visuomotor systems controlling saccadic eye movements and manual aiming movements cannot afford that luxury. At the end of the first saccade, they must recompute the position of the target (within egocentric frames of reference) so that the appropriate correction saccade and amendment to the trajectory of the moving hand can be made. In short, visuomotor control demands different kinds of visual computations than visual perception.

Object Size

Just as the perception of object location appears to operate within relative or allocentric frames of reference, so does the perception of object size. Although we often make subtle relative judgments of object size, we rarely make absolute judgments. Indeed, our judgments of size appear to be so inherently relative that we can sometimes be fooled by visual displays in which visual stimuli of the same size are positioned next to comparator stimuli that are either much smaller or much larger than the target stimuli. Such size-contrast illusions are a popular demonstration in many introductory textbooks in psychology and perception. One such illusion is the so-called Titchener circles (or Ebbinghaus illusion), in which two target circles of equal size, each surrounded by a circular array of either smaller or larger circles, are presented side by side (see fig. 15.8). Subjects typically report that the target

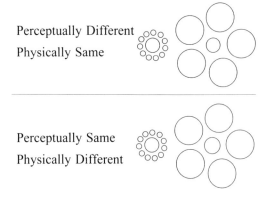

Perceptually Different
Physically Same

Perceptually Same
Physically Different

Figure 15.8 Diagram showing Titchener circles illusion. In top figure, two central disks are same actual size; in bottom figure, disk in annulus of large circles has been made somewhat larger in size.

circle surrounded by the array of smaller circles appears larger than the one surrounded by the array of larger circles, presumably because of the difference in the contrast in size between the target circles and the surrounding circles. Although the illusion is usually depicted as I have just described, it is also possible to make the two target circles appear identical in size by increasing the actual size of the target circle surrounded by the array of larger circles (see fig. 15.8).

While perception is clearly affected by these manipulations of the stimulus array, there is good reason to believe that the calibration of size-dependent motor outputs, such as grip aperture during grasping, would not be. After all, when we reach out to pick up an object, particularly one we have not seen before, our visuomotor system must compute its size accurately if we are to pick it up efficiently, that is, without fumbling or readjusting our grip. It is not enough to know that the target object is larger or smaller than surrounding objects; the visuomotor systems controlling hand aperture must compute its real size. For this reason, one might expect grip scaling to be refractory to size contrast illusions.

To test this idea, my colleagues and I (Aglioti, DeSouza, and Goodale 1995) developed a variation of the Titchener circles illusion in which two thin "poker chip" disks were used as the target circles. The disks were white, 3 mm thick, and varied in size from 27 to 33 mm in diameter; a thin black line was drawn around the circumference of each disk on the extreme edge of its top surface. The disks were arranged as pairs on a standard Titchener annular circle display (see fig. 15.8) drawn on a white background and positioned directly in front of the subject.

In a preliminary session, each subject was tested with the entire series of disks to establish which pair of disks would be consistently reported as identical in size for that subject (by increasing the actual size of the disk in the array of large circles as illustrated in fig. 15.8); in subsequent test sessions, each subject was tested with those particular disks. For the fourteen subjects tested, an average increase of 2.5 mm in the diameter of the disk surrounded by large circles was required for the subjects to perceive the two disks as identical in size. In subsequent test session, then, trials in which the two disks appeared perceptually identical but were physically different in size could be randomly alternated with trials in which the disks appeared perceptually different but were physically identical (for half of these latter trials, a pair of the small disks was used and for the other half, a pair of the larger disks was used). The left-right position of the arrays of large and small circles was of course randomly varied throughout. On each trial, the two target disks were presented for 3 seconds (by illuminating the table with an overhead lamp). Subjects were given the following instructions: if you think the two disks are the same size, pick up the one on the left; if you think they are different in size, pick up the one on the right. (In a subsequent test session, these instructions were reversed.) All subjects were asked to pick up the disk with the index finger and thumb of their right hand. Three infrared light–emitting diodes (IREDs) were attached to the hand; one on the tip of the index finger, one on the tip of the thumb, and one on the wrist. By tracking the position of these IREDs (at 100 Hz) with two infrared sensitive cameras, the size of the opening between the index finger and thumb as the subject reached toward the disk could later be reconstructed off-line.

Although there was considerable individual variation, all the subjects remained sensitive to the size-contrast illusion throughout testing. In other words, their choice of disk was affected by the contrast in size between the disks and the surrounding circles. As a consequence, they treated disks that were actually physically different in size as perceptually equivalent and they treated disks that were physically identical as perceptually different. Remarkably, however, the scaling of their grasp was affected very little by these beliefs; instead, the maximum grip aperture, which was achieved approximately 70 percent of the way through the reach towards the disk, was almost entirely determined by the true size of that disk. As figure 15.9 illustrates, the difference in grip aperture for large and small disks was the same for trials in which the subject believed the two disks were equivalent in size (even though they were different) as it was for trials in which the subject believed the two disks were different in size (even though they were identical). In short, the calibration of grip size seemed to be largely impervious to the effects of the size-contrast illusion.

Of course, the control of skilled movements is clearly not isolated from perceptual information. The perceived functions of objects such as hammers, telephones, and wine glasses have clear effects on the nature of the grasps we adopt when we pick them up. And even in the task above, one can see some influence of perception on grip scaling—at least for those trials where subjects perceived the two disks as different in size when in fact they were identical. On some of these trials, some subjects did open their fingers slightly more for the disk surrounded by the small circles than they did for

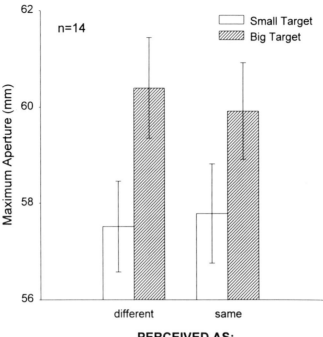

Figure 15.9 Maximum aperture between index finger and thumb on trials where subjects reached to one of target disks when these appeared to be different in size but were actually identical (on half of trials, both were identical small disks; on other half, both were identical large disks) and when they appeared to be same but were actually different in size.

the disk surrounded by the large circles. Nevertheless, this perceptual effect on grip aperture circles was quite variable—and significantly smaller than the size difference required to achieve perceptual equivalence between the two disks in judgment tasks. In other words, the effect of the illusion on grip size was much smaller and more variable than the effect of the illusion on perceptual judgments of size. In contrast, as we have already seen, all subjects showed a strong effect of real object size on the calibration of their grip—independent of whether it was on perceptually different or perceptually identical trials.

But why should perception be so susceptible to the illusion, while the calibration of grasp is not. The mechanisms underlying the size illusion are not well understood. It is possible that the illusion arises from a straightforward relative-size-scaling mechanism, whereby an object that is smaller than its immediate neighbors is assumed to be smaller than a similar object that is larger than its immediate neighbors. It is also possible that some sort of image-distance equation is contributing to the illusion in which the array of smaller circles is assumed to be more distant than the array of larger circles. As a consequence, the target circle within the array of smaller circles would also be perceived as more distant (and therefore larger) than the target circle of equivalent retinal image size within the array of larger circles. In other words, the illusion may be simply a consequence of the perceptual system's attempt to make size constancy judgments on the basis of an analysis of the entire visual array (Gregory 1963).

The idea that some sort of relative size judgment is crucial to the illusion is supported by experiments showing that the strength of the illusion increases as the size difference between the target circles and the elements of the surrounding arrays is increased (Massaro and Anderson 1971; Girgus, Coren, and Agdern 1972). Decreasing the number of elements in the array (Massaro and Anderson 1971) or increasing the distance between the target circles and the elements in the array (Girgus, Coren, and Agdern 1972) reduces the strength of the illusion. Other experiments have shown that changing the form of the elements in the surrounding array so that they no longer resemble the target circles also reduces the strength of the illusion (Coren and Miller 1974). This latter finding in particular has been interpreted as evidence that the illusion arises rather late in perceptual processing—certainly at a stage after some parsing of the visual scene into elements with distinct forms (Coren and Girgus 1978).

Mechanisms such as these, in which the relations between object in the visual array play a crucial role in scene interpretation, are clearly central to perception. In contrast, the execution of a goal-directed act like prehension depends on metrical computations that are centered on the target itself. Moreover, the visual mechanisms underlying the control of the grasping movements must compute the real distance of the object (presumably on the basis of reliable cues such as stereopsis and retinal motion). As a consequence, computation of the retinal image size of the object coupled with an accurate estimate of distance will deliver the true size of the object for calibrating the grip. Thus the very act by means of which subjects indicate their susceptibility to the illusion (i.e., picking up one of the two target circles) is itself unaffected by the visual information driving that illusion.

Such paradoxes show that what we think we "see" is not always what guides our actions; they provide powerful evidence for the parallel operation, within our everyday life, of two types of visual processing, each apparently designed to serve quite different purposes, and each characterized by quite different properties. The evidence from neurological patients described earlier suggests that these two types of processing may depend on quite separate (but interactive) visual pathways in the cerebral cortex.

15.4   PANTOMIME: A ROLE FOR PERCEPTION IN "REPRESENTATIONAL" ACTIONS

Although the experiments described above provide clear evidence that the control of actions can operate quite independently of perception, not all actions are immune to such influences. For example, on occasions when a subject pantomimes an action in the absence of a goal object, the output parameters may be specified more by a stored perceptual representation than by the normal visuomotor route to action. In this last section of the chapter, differences in the visual control of natural and pantomimed actions are examined.

Because observers (and sometimes objects) are often moving, the egocentric coordinates of a goal object can change considerably from moment to moment. As a consequence, it would be efficient to compute the required coordinates for action immediately before the movements are initiated, and it would be quite inefficient to store such coordinates (or the resulting motor programs) for more than a few milliseconds before executing the action; after all, the actual coordinates of the goal object could change dramatically in that time. For this reason, the visuomotor systems in the dorsal stream might be expected to work almost entirely on-line. Thus movements directed to remembered objects (objects that were present, but are no longer) might be expected to look rather different from movements directed to objects in real time. In fact, as I have already indicated, the control of movements to remembered objects might depend much more on stored perceptual representations of the goal object than on the transformations delivered by the normal visuomotor route.

In a recent experiment (Goodale, Jakobson, and Keillor 1994), we examined the kinematics of grasping movements made by normal subjects to a "remembered" object. The experiment was run as follows. The subjects were first shown a rectangular block, whose size and distance varied from trial to trial. Automated shutters located in front of their eyes were closed for 2 seconds, and the block was removed; when the shutters opened, the subjects were required to reach out and pretend to pick up the block as if it were still there. In other words, subjects were being asked to pantomime a grasping movement 2 seconds after last seeing the intended goal object. Subjects performed these pantomimed actions in a manner quite different from the way they executed natural, goal-directed grasping movements. Their mimed actions consistently reached lower peak velocities, tended to last longer, followed more curvilinear trajectories, and undershot target location, compared to normal reaches. Moreover, subjects consistently opened their hand less when miming than when reaching for objects that were physically present. Nevertheless, their grip aperture was still highly correlated with the size of the object they had viewed just 2 seconds before.

The programming of pantomimed movements such as these must rely, not on current visual information, but rather on a stored representation of the previously seen object and its spatial location. But what is the nature of this representation? If, as was argued above, visuomotor systems operate only in real time, the stored information driving pantomimed actions must depend on another system, one designed specifically for representing objects in their spatial locations over longer periods of time—in short, the "perceptual" system presumed to mediate object recognition. If this is the case, then D.F., who appears to have no perception of object size, shape, and orientation,

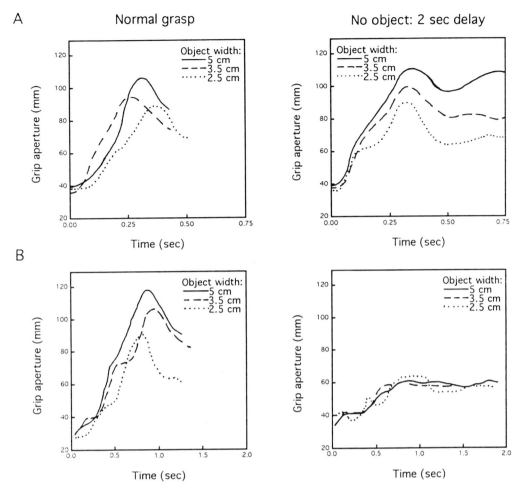

Figure 15.10 Graphs illustrating changes in grasping movements shown by normal subject and D.F. when asked to reach toward an object that they had been shown 2 seconds earlier but that was is no longer present. Although normal subjects continue to show grip scaling in absence of object, no such scaling is evident in grasps shown by D.F.

should have real trouble pantomiming grasping movements to objects seen only 2 seconds earlier. This indeed is the case. As figure 15.10 illustrates, after a delay of 2 seconds, D.F. appeared to have "lost" all information about object size needed to preshape her hand in flight. Of course, this was to be expected because D.F. had no "percept" of the object in the first place. Thus, when no object was present to drive her real-time visuomotor control systems, she could not fall back on the stored information about object size available to normal subjects.

For the perceptual systems (i.e., those involved in visual learning and recognition), a retention interval of 2 seconds is trivial. Clearly we are capable of remembering the characteristics of objects we have seen only once for extremely long periods of time. The visuomotor coordinates needed to program a given movement, however, may have to be updated even over intervals as short as 2 seconds when the relative positions of the observer and the object change. Thus it would be counterproductive to store these coordinates for any significant period of time; far better that they be calculated immediately before each action occurs. It is perhaps not surprising, then, that increasing the delay from 2 to 30 seconds had no appreciable effect on the performance of either the normal subjects or D.F.

The control of manual prehension depends on visuomotor systems that not only operate in real time but work with coordinate systems that locate the object in egocentric frames of reference. Thus we would expect them to be ill equipped to deal not only with a *temporal* delay between "seeing" the object and directing an action toward it but also with a significant *spatial* displacement of the required output coordinates. Not surprisingly then, requiring normal subjects to pantomime a grasping movement *beside* an object, as opposed to grasping it directly, resulted in the same kind of change in the kinematics of the movements seen in the movements directed to remembered objects. Moreover, because these pantomimed movements were presumably also driven by perceptual representations of the target object rather than online visuomotor control systems, D.F. was unable to perform them convincingly (Goodale, Jakobson, and Keillor 1994). Results such as these provide convincing evidence that the visuomotor systems underlying goal-directed actions are different from those underlying pantomimed actions, which appear to depend more on the perceptual systems mediating object recognition.

15.5 CONCLUSIONS

The evidence outlined in this chapter suggests that the apparent cohesion of our visual world depends on input-output systems working in parallel. The visual processing that delivers our world of meaningful objects and their interrelations are quite distinct from those mediating the visual control of actions directed at those objects. In addition, this division of labor in visual processing can be mapped onto the anatomical distinction between the ventral and dorsal streams of processing in the primate cerebral cortex. Nevertheless, the two systems must work together in the control of everyday behavior. Thus, even though the execution of a goal-directed action may depend on dedicated, on-line, control systems in the dorsal stream, the selection of appropriate goal objects and the action to be performed must depend in part on the perceptual machinery of the ventral stream. In short, the two systems must integrate their outputs in the production of normal goal-directed behavior.

REFERENCES

Aglioti, S., DeSouza, J. F. X., and Goodale, M. A. 1995. Size-contrast illusions deceive the eye but not the hand. *Current Biology, 5,* 679–685.

Blake, A. 1992. Computational modelling of hand-eye coordination. *Philosophical Transactions of the Royal Society, London, 337,* 351–360.

Bridgeman, B., Kirch, M., and Sperling, A. 1981. Segregation of cognitive and motor aspects of visual function using induced motion. *Perception and Psychophysics, 29,* 336–342.

Buchbinder, S., Dixon, B., Hyang, Y.-W., May, J. G., and Glickstein, M. 1980. The effects of cortical lesions on visual guidance of the hand. *Society for Neuroscience Abstracts, 6,* 675.

Chelazzi, L., Miller, E. K., Duncan, J., and Desimone, R. 1993. A neural basis for visual search in inferior temporal cortex. *Nature, 363,* 345–347.

Coren, S., and Girgus, J. S. 1978. *Seeing in deceiving: The psychology of visual illusions.* Hillsdale, NJ: Erlbaum.

Coren, S., and Miller, J. 1974. Size contrast as a function of figural similarity. *Perception and Psychophysics, 16,* 355–357.

Crick, F., and Jones, E. 1993. Backwardness of human neuroanatomy. *Nature, 361,* 109–110.

Eskandar, E. M., Richmond, B. J., and Optican, L. M. 1992. Role of inferior temporal neurons in visual memory. I. Temporal encoding of information about visual images, recalled images, and behavioral context. *Journal of Neurophysiology, 68,* 1277–1295.

Eskandar, E. M., Optican, L. M., and Richmond, B. J. 1992. Role of inferior temporal neurons in visual memory. II. Multiplying temporal waveforms related to vision and memory. *Journal of Neurophysiology, 68,* 1296–1306.

Fahy, F. L., Riches, I. P., and Brown, M. W. 1993. Neuronal signals of importance to the performance of visual recognition memory tasks: Evidence from recordings of single neurons in the medial thalamus of primates. In T. P. Hicks, S. Molotchnikoff, and T. Ono (Eds.), *The visually responsive neuron: From basic neurophysiology of behavior, Progress in Brain Research,* Vol. 95. 401–416. Amsterdam: Elsevier.

Fujita, I., Tanaka, K., Ito, M., and Cheng, K. 1992. Columns for visual features of objects in monkey inferotemporal cortex. *Nature, 343,* 343–346.

Gentilucci, M., and Rizzolatti, G. 1990. Cortical motor control of arm and hand movements. In M. A. Goodale (Ed.), *Vision and action: The control of grasping,* 147–162. Norwood, NJ: Ablex.

Girgus, J. S., Coren, S., and Agdern, M. 1972. The interrelationship between the Ebbinghaus and the Delboeuf illusions. *Journal of Experimental Psychology, 95,* 453–455.

Goodale, M. A. (1993). Visual pathways supporting perception and action in the primate cerebral cortex. *Current Opinion in Neurobiology, 3,* 578–585.

Goodale, M. A., Jakobson, K. S., and Keillor, J. M. 1994. Differences in the visual control of pantomimed and natural grasping movements. *Neuropsychologia, 32,* 1159–1178.

Goodale, M. A., Meenan, J. P., Bülthoff, H. H., Nicolle, D. A., Murphy, K. S., and Racicot, C. I. 1994. Separate neural pathways for the visual analysis of object shape in perception and prehension. *Current Biology, 4,* 604–610.

Goodale, M. A., and Milner, A. D. 1992. Separate visual pathways for perception and action. *Trends in Neurosciences, 15,* 20–25.

Goodale, M. A., Milner, A. D., Jakobson, L. S., and Carey, D. P. 1991. A neurological dissociation between perceiving objects and grasping them. *Nature, 349,* 154–156.

Goodale, M. A., Murphy, K. S., Meenan, J. P., Racicot, C. I., and Nicolle, D. A. 1993. Spared object perception but poor object-calibrated grasping in a patient with optic ataxia. *Society for Neuroscience Abstracts, 19,* 775.

Goodale, M. A., Pelisson, D., and Prablanc, C. 1986. Large adjustments in visually guided reaching do not depend on vision of the hand or perception of target displacement. *Nature, 320,* 748–750.

Gregory, R. L. 1963. Distortions of visual space as inappropriate constancy scaling. *Nature, 199,* 678–680.

Hasselmo, M. E., Rolls, E. T., Baylis, G. C., and Nalwa, V. 1989. Object-centered encoding by face-selective neurons in the cortex in the superior temporal sulcus of the monkey. *Experimental Brain Research, 75,* 417–429.

Hietanen, J. K., Perrett, D. I., Oram, M. W., Benson, P. J., and Dittrich, W. H. 1992. The effects of lighting conditions on responses of cells selective for face views in the macaque temporal cortex. *Experimental Brain Research, 89,* 157–171.

Hyvärinen, J., and Poranen, A. 1974. Function of the parietal associative area 7 as revealed from cellular discharges in alert monkeys. *Brain, 97,* 673–692.

Iberall, T., Bingham, G., and Arbib, M. A. 1986. Opposition space as a structuring concept for the analysis of skilled hand movements. In H. Heuer and C. Fromm (Eds.), *Generation and modulation of action pattern,* Experimental Brain Research Series, vol. 15, 158–173. Berlin: Springer.

Jakobson, L. S., Archibald, Y. M., Carey, D. P., and Goodale, M. A. 1991. A kinematic analysis of reaching and grasping movements in a patient recovering from optic ataxia. *Neuropsychologia, 29,* 803–809.

Klüver, H., and Bucy, P. C. 1939. Preliminary analysis of functions of the temporal lobes of monkeys. *Archives of Neurological Psychiatry, 42,* 975–1000.

Massaro, D. W., and Anderson, N. H. 1971. Judgmental model of the Ebbinghaus illusion. *Journal of Experimental Psychology, 81,* 147–151.

Milner, A. D., and Goodale, M. A. 1993. Visual pathways to perception and action. In T. P. Hicks, S. Molotchnikoff, and T. Ono (Eds.), *The visually responsive neuron: From basic neurophysiology to behavior, Progress in Brain Research,* vol. 95, 317–338. Amsterdam: Elsevier.

Milner, A. D., and Goodale, M. A. 1995. *The visual brain in action.* Oxford: Oxford University Press.

Milner, A. D., Perrett, D. I., Johnston, R. S., Benson, P. J., Jordan, T. R., Heeley, D. W., Bettucci, D., Mortara, F., Mutani, R., Terazzi, E., and Davidson, D. L. W. 1991. Perception and action in visual form agnosia. *Brain, 114,* 405–428.

Mountcastle, V. B., Lynch, J. C., Georgopoulos, A., Sakata, H., and Acuna, C. 1975. Posterior parietal association cortex of the monkey: Command functions for operations within extrapersonal space. *Journal of Neurophysiology, 38,* 871–908.

Nishijo, H., Ono, T., Tamura, R., and Nakamura, K. 1993. Amygdalar and hippocampal neuron responses related to recognition and memory in monkey. In T. P. Hicks, S. Molotchnikoff, and T. Ono (Eds.), *The visually responsive neuron: From basic neurophysiology to behavior, Progress in Brain Research,* vol. 95, 339–358. Amsterdam: Elsevier.

Perenin, M.-T., and Vighetto, A. 1988. Optic ataxia: A specific disruption in visuomotor mechanisms. I. Different aspects of the deficit in reaching for objects. *Brain, 111,* 643–674.

Perrett, D. I., Oram, M. W., Harries, M. H., Bevan, R., Hietanen, J. K., Benson, P. J., and Thomas, S. 1991. Viewer-centred and object-centred coding of heads in the macaque temporal cortex. *Experimental Brain Research, 86,* 159–173.

Pribram, K. H. (1967). Memory and the organization of attention. In D. B. Lindsley and A. A. Lumsdaine (Eds.), *Brain function and learning*, vol. 4 of *UCLA forum in medical sciences 6*, 79–112. Berkeley: University of California Press.

Richmond, B. J., and Sato, T. 1987. Enhancement of inferior temporal neurons during visual discrimination. *Journal of Neurophysiology, 58*, 1292–1306.

Sakai, K., and Miyashita, Y. 1992. Neural organization for the long-term memory of paired associates. *Nature, 354*, 152–155.

Sakata, H., Taira, M., Mine, S., and Murata, A. 1992. Hand-movement-related neurons of the posterior parietal cortex of the monkey: Their role in visual guidance of hand movements. In R. Caminiti, P. B. Johnson, and Y. Burnod (Eds.), *Control of arm movement in space: Neurophysiological and computational approaches*, 185–198. Berlin: Springer.

Taira, M., Mine, S., Georgopoulos, A., Murata, A., and Sakata, H. 1990. Parietal cortex neurons of the monkey related to the visual guidance of hand movement. *Experimental Brain Research, 83*, 29–36.

Ungerleider, L. G., and Mishkin, M. 1982. Two cortical visual systems. In D. J. Ingle, M. A. Goodale, and R. J. W. Mansfield (Eds.), *Analysis of visual behavior*, 549–585. Cambridge, MA: MIT Press.

Wong, E., and Mack, A. 1981. Saccadic programming and perceived location. *Acta Psychologica, 48*, 123–131,

Zeki, S. 1993. *A vision of the brain*. Oxford: Blackwell Scientific.

VII Integration in Language

16 Integration of Multiple Sources of Information in Language Processing

Dominic W. Massaro

ABSTRACT

It is now indisputable that language processing is influenced by multiple sources of information. Understanding spoken language is constrained by a variety of sensory cues, as well as lexical, semantic, syntactic, and pragmatic constraints. Research questions include the nature of the sources of information, how each source is evaluated and represented, how the multiple sources are treated, whether or not the sources are integrated, the nature of the integration process, how decisions are made, and the time course of processing. The fuzzy logical model of perception (FLMP) is shown to give a better description of performance than a formalized horse race (RACE) model and a postperceptual guessing (PPG) model; research findings also falsify the predictions of the interactive activation model. Research in a variety of domains and tasks supports the conclusions that (1) perceivers have continuous rather than categorical information from each source; (2) each source is evaluated with respect to the degree of support for each alternative; (3) each source is treated independently of other sources; (4) the sources are integrated to give an overall degree of support for each alternative; (5) decisions are made with respect to the relative goodness of match; (6) evaluation, integration, and decision are necessarily successive but overlapping stages of processing; and (7) cross talk among the sources of information is minimal. The FLMP, which embodies these properties, gives the best extant account of language processing.

It is worth reflecting on the theme of Attention and Performance XVI, integration, which is more or less the antithesis of attention. Attention has traditionally been viewed as a screening device to protect information-challenged actors from environmental overload: we attend to some information at the expense of processing other information or we even actively filter out some input so that other input can be more accurately processed. Integration provides an alternative perspective because it stresses the combination of the many inputs or sources of information available to the perceiver. Although the attention metaphor has dominated much of the research since the birth of this organization, today it is more commonplace to give less emphasis to attentive processes and to accept an organism's ability to combine several seemingly disparate pieces of information. The study of how multiple sources of information are put together to guide performance has been the theme of our work for almost two decades (Massaro and Cohen 1976; Oden and Massaro 1978; see also Oden and Anderson 1974; Anderson 1981). The present chapter continues this theme in the domain of perceiving and understanding language; it begins with a brief description of our general perspective and paradigm of inquiry.

16.1 INFORMATION PROCESSING ANALYSIS OF LANGUAGE

Stages of information processing and hierarchical processing have been central to our approach to the study of psychological phenomena (Massaro 1975a,b, 1987). It is assumed, for example, that there are at least four stages of processing a language pattern: sensory transduction, sensory cues, perceived attributes, and conceptual understanding. Human sensory systems transduce linguistic input and make available a configuration of sensory cues. Perceived attributes correspond to the outcome of processing these cues. As in other domains of pattern recognition, there is a many-to-one relationship between sensory cues and perceived attributes (Bennett, Hoffman, and Prakash 1989; Massaro and Cowan 1993). For example, information about the syntactic structure of a spoken utterance is conveyed not only by pitch but also by duration and the actual words being used. In turn, there is a one-to-many relationship between a sensory cue and the resulting perceived attributes. The pitch of the speaker's voice provides segmental information and information about the syntactic structure of the utterance, as well as the age, gender, and affective state of the speaker (Murray and Arnott 1993). In an analogous fashion, perceived attributes and conceptual understanding are not necessarily uniquely associated. Identical percepts can take on different meanings, and the same meaning can be created by entirely different percepts. The plethora of homophones in English, such as *see* and *sea*, produce different meanings with the same phonological form, while the different phonological forms *sea* and *ocean* can produce more or less the same meaning.

Language processing can be viewed as highly analogous to visual perception and recognition. Our current understanding of perception might be summarized as (1) perception is a process of inference; (2) perceptual inference is not deductively valid; and (3) perceptual inferences are biased (Bennett, Hoffman, and Prakash 1989) Assumptions 1 and 2 go back to at least Helmholtz and are easily illustrated. Given the statement,

Biting alligators can be dangerous,

the perceiver might infer that alligators that bite are a threat when the speaker might actually be referring to the new sport of people biting alligators. Assumption 3 simply means that the perceptual system is biased toward some interpretations in preference to others. A homograph ("kind") appears to be initially interpreted in terms of its most frequent meaning (see MacDonald, chap. 17, this volume). These three assumptions confront the inverse mapping problem. In language processing, we seek the intended meaning, given the multiple linguistic and situational cues.

We operate on the assumption that general principles of pattern recognition provide a productive approach to the study of language processing.

What message is intended, given the multidimensional language input? Thus language processing is also envisioned as a biased inferential process. Given some linguistic event, the best interpretation is usually supported by several cues in addition to being biased. For example, if the many different cues are made ambiguous to create a phonological form between a word and a nonword, we will tend to perceive it as the word (Ganong 1980). Given the assumption that language processing is best conceptualized as pattern recognition, it is worthwhile to consider the most appropriate definition of language recognition.

16.2 LANGUAGE RECOGNITION

What does it mean to recognize a linguistic pattern such as a word? I assume that word recognition is a part of the broader concept of language comprehension. Consider the popular riddle "How many animals did Moses bring on the ark?" Most people find this a perfectly acceptable question and give some quantitative reply. They do not notice or understand at the time of the question that the lead character in the riddle's version of this biblical event is not Noah but Moses (Erickson and Mattson 1981; Reder and Kusbit, 1991). Aspects of the appropriate biblical event are quickly called to mind even if the main player or other details are incorrect. Comprehension appears to be a matter of degree (graded); there are different degrees of understanding of our example riddle. For example, one person answered 40 animals, 20 of each sex, confusing the 40 days of rain with the number of animals. In addition, understanding is dynamic in that it fluctuates across time—for example, the change in understanding when we become aware of the misplaced biblical character. (MacDonald, chap. 17, this volume, presents analogous arguments for graded and dynamic activation of meaning. Similarly, sentence interpretation is more ambiguous than the discrete interpretations usually given by psycholinguists; see Altmann, chap. 19, this volume.)

At issue is whether word recognition is any different from comprehension in terms of its graded quality. Of course, my view is that the outcome of word recognition is graded in the same way that comprehension is graded. Most investigators, on the other hand, have assumed that the outcome of word recognition either occurs or does not. This all-or-none property is also reflected in our models of word recognition, beginning with Morton's (1969) seminal logogen model with a threshold for each word and Forster's (1985) search model of lexical access to the more recent cohort (Marslen-Wilson 1984) and activation-verification models (Paap et al. 1982). Much of contemporary research also reflects the implicit assumption of discrete word recognition. There is a good deal of debate about the number of activated meanings given presentation of a polysemous word, but the all-or-none property of a given meaning is not usually questioned.

However, there are hints of evidence for graded word recognition. Abrams and Balota (1991), for example, found that the strength of a key press was related to the frequency of the test word. Connine, Blasko, and Wong (1994) demonstrated that word recognition might be graded. An ambiguous prime was made by modifying the initial phoneme before /ent/ to be ambiguous between /d/ and /t/; in this case, the prime was an ambiguous word between *dent* and *tent*. Ambiguous primes of this type facilitated lexical decisions for both meanings of the prime, indicating perhaps multiple and graded activation. Thus we should keep in mind the caveat that word recognition is unlikely to be all-or-none. The next section reviews two opposing views of language processing.

16.3   AUTONOMOUS VERSUS INTEGRATION MODELS

Like many other investigators, my research has addressed a distinction between autonomous and integration models of language processing (Massaro 1987, 1989a). Although this distinction can be formulated around a variety of characteristics, a major difference has to do with how several linguistic variables influence performance. Early, strictly modular views proposed that a linguistic process such as phoneme recognition is triggered by a primary source of information (e.g., auditory speech in terms of phonetic features) and is not perturbed by other sources such as lexical, syntactic, and semantic context (Fodor 1983). Integration models, on the other hand, proposed that these multiple sources of information are combined during linguistic processing (Massaro 1975b; Oden 1977). Thus much of the debate has centered on how bottom-up and top-down sources are processed. Bottom-up sources correspond to those sources that have a direct mapping between the sensory input and the representational unit in question; top-down sources come from contextual constraints that are *not* directly mapped onto the unit in question. As an example, a bottom-up source would be the stimulus presentation of a test word after the presentation of a top-down source, a sentence context. A critical question for both integration and autonomous (modularity) models is how bottom-up and top-down sources of information work together to achieve word recognition. For example, an important question is how early can contextual information be integrated with acoustic-phonetic information. A large body of research shows that several bottom-up sources are evaluated in parallel and integrated to achieve recognition (Massaro 1987, 1994). An important question is whether top-down and bottom-up sources are processed in the same manner.

Previous theories have not always been clear about how bottom-up and top-down sources are processed. Marslen-Wilson (1987) distinguishes among access, selection, and integration. *Access*, or activation, corresponds to the mapping of the speech input onto lexical representations; *selection* involves selecting the word form that best matches the input and context; and *integration* means associating the syntactic and semantic information at the word level onto higher levels of processing. For Marslen-Wilson, a bottom-up source would necessarily influence access, and the top-down source would influence only selection. Early selection "means that the acoustic-phonetic and the contextual constraint on the identity of a word can be integrated together at a point in time when each source of constraint is inadequate, by itself, to uniquely specify the correct candidate" (Marslen-Wilson 1987, 77). Needless to say, the selection process has to be specified exactly to describe how the bottom-up and top-down sources work together to achieve performance of this kind.

Tyler (1990) observes that top-down context cannot affect activation or selection if autonomous models are correct but must somehow play a role later in processing. It has been shown that subjects are more likely to identify an ambiguous phoneme as one that makes a word (Ganong 1980). Given Tyler's reasoning, lexical context must somehow influence performance after activation and selection of the phoneme have occurred in an autonomous fashion. This reasoning is not necessarily true, however; in the RACE model (Cutler et al. 1987), for example, subjects can respond at the word level even if activation and selection at the phoneme level are not yet finished. That is, the response can be based on only the word information without any additional influence from the test segment in the test word.

Thompson and Altmann (1990) make a distinction between selection and instruction in the framework of a speech recognition system. A word lattice is created based on bottom-up processing, and selection only allows filtering of candidates after they have entered the word lattice. Syntactic processing does not influence which words are placed in the word lattice. Instruction, on the other hand, allows syntactic processing to influence which words are entered into the word lattice. It is assumed, for example, that analysis by synthesis of candidates occurs on the basis of grammatical information. In the instruction case, processing at the grammatical level penetrates the processing at the word level; within this framework, the issue of autonomous versus integrative processes might boil down to whether instruction occurs.

I take the critical characteristic of autonomous models to be the language user's *inability* to integrate bottom-up and top-down information. Integration will be defined within a formal model of language processing. To attempt to add some order to the plethora of possibilities, we consider integration of top-down and bottom-up information as the touchstone distinguishing between autonomous and nonautonomous models. In my view, the autonomous model must necessarily predict no perceptual integration of top-down with bottom-up information.

As perhaps apparent in the debate between autonomous and integration viewpoints, specific predictions and tests are not easy. It is proposed that our science will make progress only with the formalization and test of specific models of language processing. In this chapter I formalize and test two prototypical autonomous models as well as an integration model. The integration model is the fuzzy logical model of perception (FLMP), which has been tested extensively in a broad number of domains. The autonomous models are a horse race model (RACE), and a postperceptual guessing (PPG) model, which are new formalizations of existing autonomous views. Thus I use a falsification and strong-inference strategy of inquiry (Massaro 1987, 1989a; Platt 1964; Popper 1959). Results are informative only to the degree that they distinguish among alternative theories. The experimental task, data analysis, and model testing are devised specifically to attempt to reject some theoretical alternatives. Our first goal, of course, is to distinguish between autonomous and integration models. The FLMP has been very successful, and I begin with the description of this model.

16.4   FUZZY LOGICAL MODEL OF PERCEPTION (FLMP)

The results from a wide variety of experiments have been described within the framework of the FLMP. Within the framework shown in figure 16.1, language processing is robust because there are usually multiple sources of information that the perceiver evaluates and integrates to achieve perceptual recognition. According to the FLMP, patterns are recognized in accordance with a general algorithm, regardless of the modality or particular nature of the patterns. The assumptions central to the model are (1) each source of information is evaluated to give the degree to which that source supports the relevant alternatives; (2) the sources of information are evaluated independently of one another; (3) the sources are integrated to provide an overall degree of support for each alternative; and (4) perceptual identification follows the relative degree of support among the alternatives.

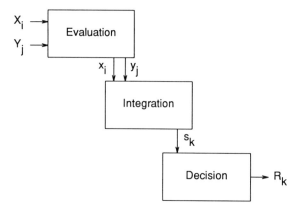

Figure 16.1   Schematic representation of three stages involved in perceptual recognition. Three stages are shown to proceed left to right in time to illustrate their necessarily successive but overlapping processing. Sources of information are represented by uppercase letters (indicated by uppercase letters X_i and Y_j). Evaluation process transforms these sources of information into psychological values (indicated by lowercase letters x_i and y_j) These sources are then integrated to give overall degree of support for given alternative s_k. Decision operation maps this value into some response, R_k, such as discrete decision or rating.

16.5 FLMP ACCOUNT OF LEXICAL CONTEXT

The experimental task we use was first tested by Ganong (1980), who established that lexical identity could influence phonetic judgments. A continuum of test items was made by varying the voice onset time (VOT) of the initial stop consonant of CVC syllables; the VC was also varied. For example, subjects identified the initial consonant as /d/ or /t/ in the context /æʃ/ (where /d/ makes a word *dash* and /t/ does not), or in the context /æsk/ (where /t/ makes a word *task* and /d/ does not). Both the segmental information of the initial phoneme and the lexical context influenced performance. The top panel of figure 16.2 shows that the percentage of voiced judgments decreased as the initial segment was changed from /t/ to /d/. A lexical context effect was also observed because there were more voiced judgments /d/ in the context /æʃ/ than in the context /æsk/. The bottom panel of figure 16.2 shows similar results for the contexts supporting the words *dirt* and *turf*. Significantly, this lexical effect was largest at the most ambiguous intermediate levels of VOT, which is consistent with the general principle that the least

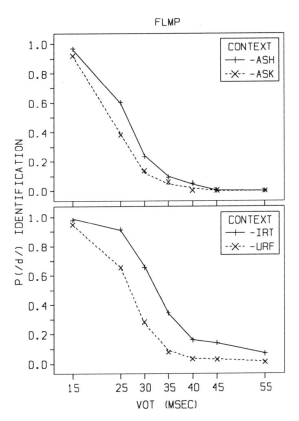

Figure 16.2 Observed (points) and predicted (lines) proportion of /d/ identification for *-ash* and *-ask* contexts (top panel) and *-irt* and *-urf* contexts (bottom panel) as function of VOT. (Observed data from Ganong 1980). Predictions of FLMP.

ambiguous source has the most influence on perception. Ganong's original results have been replicated and extended by several investigators (Connine and Clifton 1987; McQueen 1991; Pitt and Samuel 1993).

According to the FLMP, there are two sources of information in the Ganong (1980) task: the bottom-up information from the initial speech segment and the following top-down context. It is assumed that both of the sources are evaluated and integrated to achieve perceptual identification. The evaluation process provides continuous information indicating the degree to which each source of information supports each alternative. This continuous information is represented in terms of fuzzy truth values that lie between 0 (no support) and 1 (complete support); with two response alternatives, as in the Ganong (1980) task, .5 is completely ambiguous support. Furthermore, with just two response alternatives, the support of a source of information for one alternative is 1 minus its support for the other alternative. At the integration operation, the total support for a given alternative is given by the multiplicative combination of the two separate sources of support. Finally, the decision operation follows a relative goodness rule (RGR): a response is based on the total support for that alternative relative to the total support for both alternatives.

Assume that s_i is the information supporting the voiced alternative given by the initial segment and that c_j is the support for the voiced alternative given by the following context. The subscripts i and j index the different levels of the segment and the context. In this case, the total support S for the voiced alternative, given segmental information S_i and lexical context C_j, would be

$$S(voiced|S_i \text{ and } C_j) = s_i \times c_j. \tag{16.1}$$

The total support for the voiceless alternative would be

$$S(voiceless|S_i \text{ and } C_j) = (1 - s_i) \times (1 - c_j). \tag{16.2}$$

Given the RGR at the decision stage, the predicted probability of a voiced response, $P(voiced|S_i \text{ and } C_j)$, is equal to

$$P(voiced|S_i \text{ and } C_j) = \frac{s_i \times c_j}{[s_i \times c_j] + [(1 - s_i) \times (1 - c_j)]}. \tag{16.3}$$

This model was applied to two sets of results from Ganong's original study (Massaro and Oden 1980). With 7 levels of bottom-up information and 2 different contexts, 7 values of s_i and 2 values of c_j must be estimated to predict the results. Thus 9 free parameters are used to predict the 14 independent data points in each of two different experiments; these parameters are estimated by a search routine that minimized the squared differences between the observed and predicted values (Chandler 1969). As can be seen from the close match between the observed points and predicted lines in figure 16.2, the FLMP gives a good description of the results. Thus the model captures the observed interaction between segmental information and lexical context: the effect of context is greater to the extent that the segmental information is ambiguous. This yields two curves in the shape of an American football, which is a trademark of the FLMP.

16.6 INDIVIDUAL VERSUS GROUP RESULTS

Until recently, the Ganong (1980) task has not been carried out to allow individual subject analyses; indeed, most, if not all, psycholinguistic studies of top-down and bottom-up sources of information only present results pooled across subjects. In general, we have found that average results are fairly representative of the subjects that make up the average, although there is reason to be cautious with average results (Massaro and Cohen 1993). For example, average results tend to favor linear over nonlinear models. In any event, a high priority in psycholinguistic research should be to test extant models against results of individual subjects. The primary modifications of the typical research strategy would require a much larger number of observations for each subject and the testing of formal models against the individual results. Although the interaction of bottom-up and top-down sources of information has been of central interest in the last decades of research on language processing, the number of studies with individual results can be counted on a single hand. We hope that future research will test individuals more thoroughly so that competing models can be developed and tested against individual performance.

Pitt (1995) carried out an extensive study of lexical context effects in the Ganong task. Contrary to tradition, a large number of observations were recorded for each subject providing an opportunity to test formal models against individual performance. In Pitt's task, the initial consonant was varied along six steps between /g/ and /k/ and the following context was either /Ift/ or /Is/. In this case, the context /Ift/ would bias subjects to perceive /g/ as in *gift* and the context /Is/ would bias subjects to perceive /k/ as in *kiss*. Massaro and Oden (1995) tested the FLMP against the identification results of the 12 individual subjects in Pitt's experiment 3a for which a very large number of observations (104) were obtained for each data point for each subject. The points in figure 16.3 give the observed results for each of the 12 subjects in the task; for most of the subjects, the individual results tend to resemble the average results reported by Pitt and earlier investigators. Ten of the 12 subjects were influenced by lexical context in the appropriate direction. Subject 1 gave an inverse context effect, and subject 7 was not influenced by context.

In producing predictions for the FLMP, it is necessary to estimate parameter values for the 6 levels of bottom-up information and the 2 lexical contexts. Thus 8 free parameters are used to predict the 12 independent probabilities of a voicing judgment: 6 values of s_i and 2 values of c_j. The lines in figure 16.3 give the predictions of the FLMP; the good description of the results is apparent in the figure and in the small root mean squared deviation

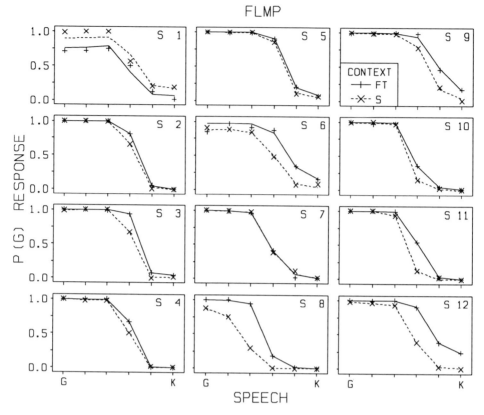

Figure 16.3 Observed (points) and predicted (lines) proportion of /g/ identifications for /lft/ and /ls/ contexts as function of speech information of initial consonant. Results from Pitt's (1995) experiment 3a. Predictions are for FLMP.

(RMSD) between predicted and observed values. The RMSD is .017 on the average across all 12 independent fits.

Subject 1 showed a context effect in the opposite direction to the other subjects (and to reasonable expectation). The FLMP gave a very poor description of this subject's results, yielding an RMSD of .066. This poor fit is impressive because it demonstrates that the FLMP is not so powerful that it can fit any possible result. The repeated success of the model appears to have led some researchers to suspect that it uses excessive free parameters or has some other "unfair" advantage that somehow makes it effectively unfalsifiable. Such suspicions were argued to be wholly unfounded (see Massaro and Cohen 1993), and this result supports this argument.

Although the FLMP provides a good description of the results, it is worthwhile to have a benchmark indicating how good is good. Even if a model is perfectly correct, we cannot expect it to fit observed results exactly. Reasonably accurate models must be stochastic or have built-in variability, as do observed results. The current FLMP is deterministic (has no variability) at the feature evaluation and integration processes, and becomes stochastic only at the decision process. The variability at the decision process is due to the RGR, in which the probability of a response alternative is equal to the merit of a particular alternative, relative to the sum of the merits of all relevant alternatives. If we know the observed probabilities and the number of observations, a benchmark RMSD can be determined and compared to the observed RMSD (see Massaro and Cohen 1993). The average of these 12 benchmarks for the results in figure 16.3 was .024, not significantly different from the observed RMSDs that averaged .017. Thus we can conclude that the FLMP described the results as accurately as could be expected from any correct model; for Pitt's results, we cannot expect an autonomous model to do any better than the FLMP. The question must be reformulated to ask whether there is an autonomous processing model that can do as well. We now examine two such autonomous viewpoints.

16.7 POSTPERCEPTUAL GUESSING (PPG) MODEL

One autonomous explanation of context effects in speech perception is that they occur only when the bottom-up information is ambiguous. An important property of this model is discreteness: recognition either occurs via the bottom-up information or it does not. When it does not, top-down information is used to make a judgment. This model appears to represent the more general view that context effects are postperceptual. Some investigators have argued that certain context effects are indeed postperceptual. For example, Samuel (1981) claims that bias effects, but not sensitivity effects, in the phonemic restoration task are postperceptual. Connine (1990) claimed that RTs of perceptual judgments can distinguish between perceptual and postperceptual effects; her task evaluated sentence context and segment processing in an extension of the Ganong (1980) task. The speech continuum consisted of syllables varying between *dent* and *tent*. The sentence context could be biased toward either of these two alternatives. The identification judgments were analogous to those found in the lexical studies; there was a strong bottom-up influence and a small effect of context for the ambiguous tokens between the two alternatives. Based on an analysis of the RTs, Connine argued that the influence of sentence context was necessarily postperceptual. If this is the case, then her results do not challenge autonomous models. More generally, advocates of modularity are quick to interpret positive findings of top-down context on putative bottom-up processing as postperceptual. Without formal models, deciding between perceptual and post-perceptual effects is not at all easy.

Instantiation of the PPG model for Ganong (1980) task assumes that context has a possible influence *only* when the sensory input from the initial phoneme is not identified. There are two types of trials: those when the voicing of the initial phoneme is identified and those when it is not. When voicing identification of the segmental source is successful, the perceiver responds with the appropriate alternative. When no identification is made, the perceiver uses the context to identify the initial segment. It is assumed that the probability of a voiced judgment, given a lexical context C_j, is g_j, labeled as such to emphasize its postperceptual guessing origin. The predicted probability of a voiced response is thus equal to

$$P(voiced|S_i \text{ and } C_j) = v_i + (1 - v_i - vs_i)c_j. \tag{16.4}$$

where v_i is the probability of identifying the segmental source as a voiced response, and vs_i is the probability of identifying the segmental source as voiceless. The term $(1 - v_i - vs_i)$ is the probability of not identifying the voicing of the segmental source, and g_j is the bias to respond with the voiced alternative when the voicing of the segmental source is not identified. Equation 16.4 represents the postperceptual theory that the voicing of the initial segmental source is either identified or else lexical context is used. The lexical context has an influence only when the initial segment is not identified. The model requires v_i, vs_i, and c_j parameters.

In Pitt's (1995) study with 6 levels of bottom-up segmental information, 6 free parameters are necessary for identifying the initial segment as the voiced alternative and 6 as the voiceless one; the bias g_j must be estimated for each of the two lexical contexts. Unfortunately, a total of $6 + 6 + 2 = 14$ free parameters are necessary to predict just 12 independent data points. Thus it appears that the PPG model cannot be fairly tested against the results because the number of free parameters exceeds the number of independent data points.

Another strategy is to impose some constraints on the model to reduce the number of free parameters. One possibility is to assume that the two endpoint stimuli on each of the two ends of the segmental continuum are never identified as the inappropriate alternative. That is, the two stimuli at the voiced end are never identified as voiceless, and the two stimuli at the voiceless end are never identified as voiced. This constraint reduces the number of free parameters to 10, which is still 2 more than the FLMP; it seems reasonable because it still allows for the possibility that the voicing of the 2 middle levels of the segment is not identified. The constrained model does a poor job of describing the results, with an RMSD of .068, significantly worse than the FLMP. Another constraint is to assume that the perceiver *always* responds in accordance with the lexical context when the segmental information is not identified. This model, with 12 parameters, does equally poorly with an RMSD of .067. Given that potential advocates of the PPG model might reject these constrained models as being unrealistic, we are fortunate to have a set of results in which the number of free parameters for the PPG model does not exceed the number of data points.

16.8 PHONOLOGICAL CONTEXT

The role of phonological context has been studied in the same manner as lexical context. Massaro and Cohen (1983) studied the contribution of phonological constraints in a speech identification task. Subjects were presented with CCV syllables, with the first consonant being /p/, /v/, /t/, or /s/, the second consonant being one of seven glides equally spaced on a continuum between /l/ and /r/, and with the vowel being /i/. The glide was changed from /l/ to /r/ by changing its initial third formant frequency from high to low. The rationale was that perceivers have two sources of information: the segmental information about the glide and the phonological context. In English the segment /r/ is admissible when it follows initial /p/ and /t/, but not initial /s/ and /v/. Similarly, the segment /l/ is admissible when it follows initial /p/ and /s/, but not initial /t/ and /v/. Seven subjects were tested on the 7 times 4 = 28 experimental conditions, with 40 observations per condition. The percentages of /r/ identifications for three of the subjects are shown in figure 16.4, along with the predictions of the FLMP. Both the bottom-up glide information and the top-down phonological context influenced performance; in addition, the contribution of one source was larger to the extent the other source was ambiguous. The FLMP provided a good description of these results of the individual subjects, with an average RMSD of .055 (see Massaro and Cohen 1991).

Instantiation of the PPG model for this task assumes that context has a possible influence *only* when the bottom-up input from the glide is not

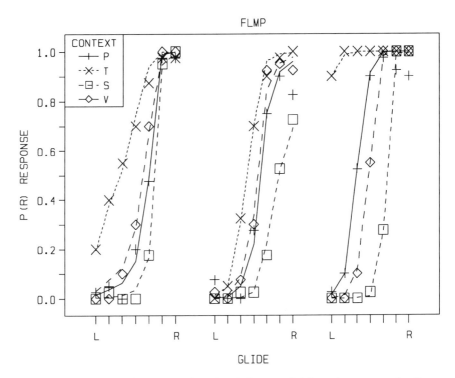

Figure 16.4 Observed (points) and predicted (lines) probability of *r* response for three typical subjects as function of glide F_3 onset level and context (after Massaro and Cohen 1983, experiment 2). Predictions are for FLMP.

identified. When identification of the bottom-up input is successful, the perceiver responds with the appropriate alternative. Where no identification is made, the perceiver uses the top-down phonological context to identify the initial segment. It is assumed that the probability of a /r/ judgment, given a phonological context C_j, is g_j. The predicted probability of a /r/ response is thus equal to

$$P(/r/|S_i \text{ and } C_j) = r_i + (1 - r_i - l_i)g_j, \qquad (16.5)$$

where r_i is the probability of identifying the bottom-up source as /r/; l_i is the probability of identifying the bottom-up source as /l/; and g_j is the bias to respond with /r/ when the the bottom-up source is not identified. The phonological context has an influence only when the bottom-up source is not identified. The model requires 7 r_i, 7 l_j, and 4 g_j parameters. These 18 free parameters are fewer than the 28 independent data points, but still 7 more than the 11 free parameters required by the FLMP. The fit of the PPG model is shown in figure 16.5. The fit to the individual subjects gave an average RMSD of .085, significantly larger than the average RMSD for the fit of the FLMP.

One might wonder why a PPG model is necessary because bottom-up dominance could be built into the FLMP. However, the central assumption of

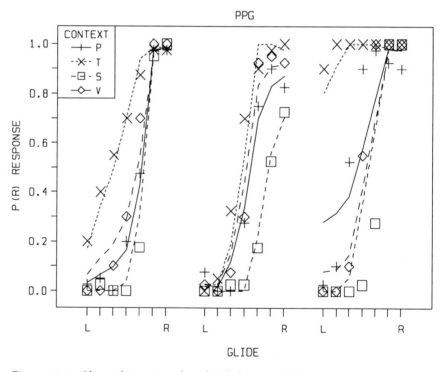

Figure 16.5 Observed (points) and predicted (lines) probability of r response for three typical subjects as function of glide F_3 onset level and context (after Massaro and Cohen 1983, experiment 2). Predictions are for PPG model.

the PPG model is qualitatively different from the FLMP. In the FLMP, both modalities are always integrated in speech perception, while only a single source is used on a given trial in the PPG model. That is, the response is either determined by the bottom-up information or by context when the bottom-up information is not identified. Thus the FLMP and PPG model provide distinctly different accounts of language perception. We will see that the PPG model also differs from another model grounded in modularity, namely, the RACE model.

16.9   RACE MODEL

Variations of a horse RACE model have been around for decades in a variety of guises such as the dual route model of reading. The version we consider is related to the one articulated by Cutler et al. (1987) and reinforced by McQueen (1991). In most speech-processing tasks, there are several possible routes to an interpretation of the input. In reading, for example, we can recognize a word directly from its orthographic form or by translating its letters into a speech code that is then used for lexical access. In another task involving spoken language, phoneme monitoring, subjects might report the occurrence of a phoneme either directly from the phonological level or indirectly from the spoken word containing the phoneme (Cutler and Norris 1979; Foss and Gernsbacher 1983). Similarly, in the Ganong lexical context task, the subject might report the first segment directly from the phonological representation or indirectly from the lexical activation or access of a particular word. The initial phoneme could be reported as voiced solely from the activation at the phonological level, or it could be reported from the activation of a lexical item. The route that is responsible for the judgment occurs probabilistically and is a function of task variables.

As emphasized by Frauenfelder, Segui, and Dijkstra (1990), the activation of the word via the lexical route occurs at a discrete moment in time, which also accepts the assumption that word recognition is all-or-none. In the spirit of a horse race, the RACE model also must assume that discrete information about the test segment (via the phonological route) is made available at a discrete point in time. This assumption stands in sharp contrast to the continuous sources of information available to the perceiver in the FLMP (Massaro and Cohen 1994). The RACE model appears to be related to a simple (perhaps too simple) quantitative account of the joint effects of stimulus and context. This model is the antithesis of integration, and has been called a "single-channel model" (Massaro 1985). It is necessarily assumed that only one of the two sources of information determines the response on any given trial. The emitted response is based on one source or the other. We define the probability of making a response on the basis of the initial segmental information as p. Given only two sources of information, and given that a response must come from one source or the other, the probability of making a response on the basis of lexical information is $1 - p$. Thus predicted performance is given by

$$P(voiced|S_i \text{ and } C_j) = (p)(s_i) + (1 - p)g_j. \tag{16.6}$$

The value s_i is equal to the probability of a voiced decision made at the segmental level, and g_j is equal to the probability of a voiced decision made at the word level. The value i indexes the ith level along the stimulus continuum of the segmental information and j indexes the context. This formalization of the RACE model assumes a fixed p across all conditions, a s_i value that varies with the segmental information in the initial consonant, and g_j value that varies with the lexical context.

Advocates of the RACE model will quickly notice that equation 16.6 does not have the necessary complexity of verbal descriptions of the model. For example, p is expected to decrease to the extent the segmental information is ambiguous. In the Cutler and Norris (1979) model, the probability of making a decision on the basis of the segmental information depends critically on the relative speeds of the two routes. It seems reasonable to assume that the relative speed of the segmental route is an inverted U-shaped function of the levels of the segment between the voiced and voiceless alternatives. That is, the segmental route would be slow to the extent the segmental information is ambiguous. In this case, p should also depend on the level of segmental information. The subscript i is used to index the probability of responding on the basis of the segmental information (the prelexical route). Generalizing equation 16.6 gives

$$P(voiced|S_i \text{ and } C_j) = (p_i)(s_i) + (1 - p_i)g_j. \tag{16.7}$$

In this case, the value of p_i depends on S_i. To describe Pitt's results, this model requires 6 values of p_i, 6 values of s_i, and 2 values of g_j, for a total of 14 free parameters to predict just 14 independent data points. This makes the model untestable; there are no results using the Ganong task in which the full RACE model can be tested.

Because constraining the parameters of the RACE model did not seem justified, we are left with testing the model against the phonological constraints study. In this case, we simply envision that phonological constraints operate in the same manner in the RACE model as do lexical constraints. There are independent segmental glide and phonological admissibility routes and the winner is responsible for the response. Equation 16.7 was used to fit the results so that 7 values of p_i, 7 values of s_i, and 4 values of g_j, for a total of 18 free parameters to predict the 28 data points. As can be seen in figure 16.6, the RACE model gave a poor description of the results; the average RMSD was .085. Considering that the fit of the FLMP gave an average RMSD of .055, with just 11 rather than 18 free parameters, we have strong evidence for integration of bottom-up and top-down sources of information. Modular, strictly autonomous models are greatly damaged by the same results.

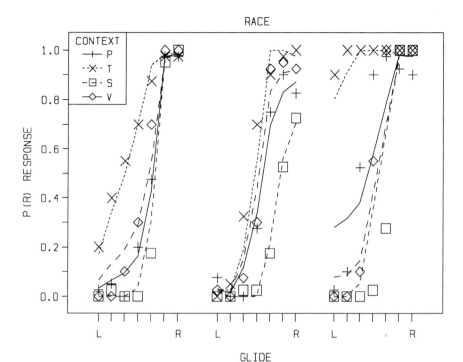

Figure 16.6 Observed (points) and predicted (lines) probability of *r* response for three typical subjects as function of glide F_3 onset level and context (after Massaro and Cohen 1983, experiment 2). Predictions are for RACE model.

16.10 INTEGRATING SENTENCE CONTEXT IN THE GATING TASK

The gating task (Grosjean 1980, 1985) has been a method developed to assess speech perception and word recognition. As indicated by the name of the task, portions of the spoken message are eliminated or gated out. Successive presentations involve longer and longer portions of the word; subjects attempt to name the word after each presentation. Warren and Marslen-Wilson (1987), for example, presented words such as *school* or *scoop*. The probability of correct recognition of a test word increases as additional word information is presented in the gating task.

The gating task appears to have promise for the investigation of speech perception and spoken language understanding. Investigators have shown that two features of the gating task do not limit its external validity. Multiple presentations of the test word on a given trial (Cotton and Grosjean 1984; Salasoo and Pisoni 1985) and unlimited time to respond in the task (Tyler and Wessels 1985) are not essential for the results. Thus the results appear to be generalizable to the on-line recognition of continuous speech.

Tyler and Wessels (1983) used the gating paradigm to assess the contribution of various forms of sentence context to word recognition. Subjects heard a sentence with its final word gated out. This test word was increased in

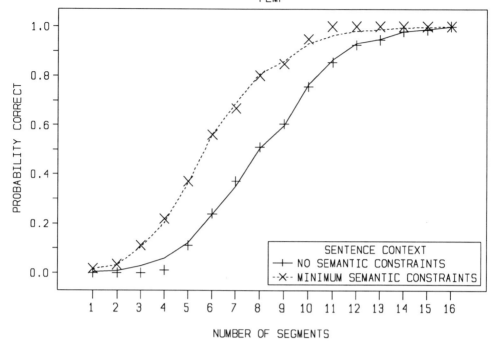

Figure 16.7 Observed (points) and predicted (lines) probability of identifying test word correctly as function of sentential context and number of segments of test word. Minimum semantic constraints refers to minimum semantic and weak syntactic constraints. No semantic constraints refers to no-semantic and weak syntactic constraints (results of Tyler and Wessels 1983; predictions of FLMP).

duration by adding small segments of the word until correct recognition was achieved. The sentence contexts varied in syntactic and semantic constraints. Some sentence contexts had minimal semantic and weak syntactic constraints in that the target word was not predictable in a test, given the sentence context and the first 100 ms of the target word. Performance in this condition can be compared to a control condition in which no semantic and weak syntactic constraints were present. If sentential context contributes to recognition of the test word, then accuracy should be better for the sentence context with minimum semantic constraints.

Figure 16.7 gives the probability of correct word recognition as a function the number of segments in the test word and the context condition. Both variables had a significant influence on performance. In addition, the interaction between the two variables reveals how word information and context jointly influence word recognition. Semantic constraints influence performance most at intermediate levels of word information. Their contribution is most apparent when there is some but not complete information about the test word. The lines in figure 16.7 give the predictions of the FLMP (see Massaro 1994). As can be seen in the figure, the FLMP captures the exact form of the improvement in performance as a function of segmental information and sentential context.

As in the Ganong (1980) task, the PPG and RACE models would require more free parameters than data points in this study. Future studies should increase the number of context conditions in order to make the factorial design more symmetrical, and thus provide a test of these models with respect to the contribution of sentential context.

A positive effect of sentence context in this situation is very impressive because it illustrates a true integration of word and context information. The probability of correct recognition is zero when the minimum semantic context is given with very little word information (one segment). Similarly, the probability of correct recognition is zero with three segments of the test word presented after a sentence context with no semantic constraints. That is, neither minimum semantic constraints nor three segments are capable of producing a correct answer. Together, however, they allow a correct answer 1 out of 10 times; three segments of the test word preceded by a sentential context with semantic constraints produce about 10 percent accuracy. Although neither the semantic context alone nor the limited segmental information permits word recognition, when presented jointly, word recognition is above chance. This superadditive combination of bottom-up and top-down information is even more apparent when overall performance is intermediate. With seven segments, for example, semantic context improves accuracy from 40 to 70 percent. The superadditive combination of bottom-up and top-down information cannot be predicted by either the PPG or the RACE models because performance on any given trial must come from one source of information or the other. Thus the strong effect of minimum semantic context illustrated in figure 16.7 can be considered to reflect true integration of bottom-up and top-down sources of information.

The form of the interaction of stimulus information and context is also relevant to the prediction of the cohort model. Marslen-Wilson (1987) assumes that some minimum cohort set must be established on the basis of stimulus information *before* context can have an influence. In terms of FLMP description, this assumption implies that the output of the evaluation of context should change across different levels of gating. To test this hypothesis, another model was fit to the results; in this model, semantic context was assumed to have an influence only after some minimum gating interval. Because it is not known what this minimum interval should be, an additional free parameter was estimated to converge on the interval that gave the best description of the observed results. The model did not improve the description of the results, weakening the claim that semantic context has its influence only after some minimum stimulus information has been processed. This result is another instance of the general finding that there are no discrete points in psychological processing (see Tanenhaus et al., chap. 18, this volume, for analogous arguments). The system does not seem to work one way at one point in time (i.e., no effect of context), and another way in another point in time (i.e., an effect of context).

16.11 NATURE OF INTEGRATION

The model tests have established that perceivers integrate top-down and bottom-up information in language processing, as described by the FLMP, which means that sensory information and context are integrated in the same manner as several sources of bottom-up information. The goal now is to address the nature of this integration process. Many investigators appear to believe that interactive activation is the only viable alternative to autonomous models. However, the FLMP allows integration while maintaining independence among the sources (at the evaluation stage). Because our concern has been with spoken language, I will discuss previous tests comparing the FLMP and a specific instantiation of interactive activation—the TRACE model.

16.12 INTERACTIVE-ACTIVATION—THE TRACE MODEL

The most popular form of integration is interactive activation. The TRACE model of speech perception (McClelland and Elman 1986) is one of a class of connectionist models in which information processing occurs through excitatory and inhibitory interactions among a large number of simple processing units. The units, arranged hierarchically, and putatively representing the functional properties of neurons, correspond to features, phonemes, and words. Features activate phonemes, and phonemes activate words, whereas activation of one type of units inhibits other units of the same type. In addition, activation of higher-order units activates their lower-order units; for example, activation of the word *gift* would activate the phonemes making it up.

A bottom-up source of information is processed sequentially through the feature, phoneme, and word units. Because of interactive activation, however, a top-down word context can modify the activation of the same lower-order units. Bottom-up activation from the phoneme units activates word units, which in turn, activate the phoneme units that make them up. Integration of bottom-up and top-down sources of information is achieved through interactive activation. Interactive activation appropriately describes this model because it is clearly an interaction between the two levels that is postulated. The amount of bottom-up activation modifies the amount of top-down activation, which then modifies the bottom-up activation, and so on.

In support of the TRACE model, Elman and McClelland (1988) carried out an ingenious demonstration of context effects in speech perception. Because of coarticulation—the influence of producing one speech segment on the production of another—a given speech segment has different acoustic forms in different contexts. The phonemes /s/ and /ʃ/ are necessarily produced differently, and will differentially influence the production of the following speech segment. Perceivers not only recognize the different speech segments /s/ and /ʃ/; they apparently are able to compensate for the influence of these segments in recognizing the following speech segment. During production of speech, coarticulation involves the assimilation of the acoustic characteristics of one sound in the direction of the characteristics of the neighboring sound. The production of /s/ contains higher-frequency energy than /ʃ/ and coarticulation will give the sound following /s/ higher-frequency energy than the same sound following /ʃ/.

Perceivers apparently take this assimilative coarticulatory influence into account in their perceptual recognition of /t/ and /k/ (and /d/ and /g/). Mann and Repp (1981) showed that recognition of the same segment as /t/ or /k/ is dependent on whether the preceding segment is /s/ or /ʃ/. The energy in /k/ is somewhat lower in frequency than that in initial /t/—the /t/ has a high burst. Using synthetic speech, a continuum of speech sounds ranging from *tapes* to *capes* was made by varying the onset properties of the sounds; these sounds were placed after the words *Christmas* and *foolish*. Subjects were more likely to identify the stop as /k/ than /t/ if the preceding fricative was /s/ than if it was /ʃ/ (for this contrast effect, see Mann and Repp 1981), a result that contributes to the validity of top-down effects on perceptual processing by making the hypothesis of a postperceptual decision less likely. There is no obvious guessing state based on the context that would produce the observed contrast effect.

Elman and McClelland's (1988) study induced the same contrast effect, mediated by the lexical identity of the first word rather than the acoustic structure of its final syllable. As expected from the Mann and Repp (1981) study, there were more judgments of *capes* following *Christmas* than following *foolish*, although this dependency could have been triggered directly by the acoustic differences between /s/ and /ʃ/. To eliminate this possibility, Elman and McClelland (1988) created an ambiguous sound halfway between /s/ and /ʃ/ to replace the original fricatives in *Christmas* and *foolish*. Given a lexical context effect, we would expect that the ambiguous segment would tend to be categorized as /s/ when it occurred in *Christmas* and as /ʃ/ when it occurred in *foolish*. Would the same contrast effect occur given the same ambiguous segment in *Christmas* and *foolish*? Figure 16.8 shows that it did: subjects were more likely to report the test word *capes* following the context word *Christmas* than following the context word *foolish*, and this effect was larger when the segmental information about the /k/-/t/ distinction in the test word was ambiguous.

Given interactive activation, the contrast effect can be described by assuming connections from the phoneme level in one time slice to the feature level in adjacent time slices (as in TRACE I, Elman and McClelland 1986, 1988). The units corresponding to /s/ and /ʃ/ phonemes would be connected laterally and downward to feature units, which in turn would be connected upward to the phoneme units /t/ and /k/. The downward activation from the fricative phoneme to the feature level would modulate the upcoming upward

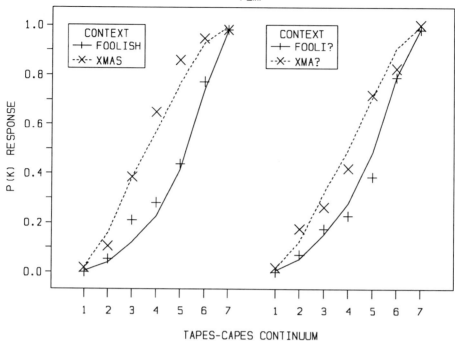

Figure 16.8 Observed (points) and predicted (lines) probability of /k/ identification as function of stimulus and preceding context for original and ambiguous preceding consonant. Results from Elman and McClelland (1988). Predictions are for FLMP.

activation from the feature level to the stop phonemes. To describe the lexical effect for the case in which the two words *Christmas* and *foolish* have the same ambiguous final fricative segment, top-down connections from the word level to the phoneme level would activate the appropriate phoneme unit—/s/ and /ʃ/ in *Christmas* and *foolish*, respectively. These units would then activate downward to the feature level, leading to a contrast effect. Because of the assumed top-down activation modulating the bottom-up activation, interactive activation is central to their explanation.

Description of the result does not require interactive activation, however. The result simply shows that information from the lexical level of the preceding word can influence the identification of the following word. Lexical context disambiguates the final segment of the context word, which in turn biases identification of the first segment of the following word. In this case, the top-down context influences the interpretation of the bottom-up information of the following segment. This perceptual bias has the same outcome as if the word context and the test segment function were two independent sources of information. Figure 16.8 gives the fit of the FLMP to the results (Elman and McClelland 1988, experiment 1; Massaro 1992). Nine free parameters were estimated to predict the 28 data points: 7 for the 7 levels along the *tapes-capes* continuum, 1 for /s/ or /ʃ/ in the intact context word condition, and 1 for lexical context with the ambiguous final segment. The pure lexical context effect is seen in the left panel and the combined effect of lexical context and context segment (/s/ or /ʃ/) is shown in the right panel. The FLMP gave an acceptable description of the results, with an RMSD of .048. The good fit of the FLMP emphasizes the point that lexical context and segmental information can both contribute to word recognition *without* the context modifying the representation of the segmental information.

Because the context effects appear to be equally well accounted for by FLMP and by TRACE, it is important to test between them. The primary difference between TRACE and FLMP involves the joint effects of bottom-up and top-down information. The predictions of the models have been contrasted in the phonological constraints study described previously (Massaro 1989b; Massaro and Cohen 1991). Recall that subjects were asked to identify a glide consonant in syllables beginning with one of the four consonants /p/, /v/, /t/, or /s/ followed by a liquid consonant ranging from /l/ to /r/, followed by the vowel /i/.

A simulation of the phonological context experiment using TRACE was compared with the observed results (Massaro 1989b). A simulation of TRACE involves presentation of a pattern of activation to the units at the feature level. The input is presented sequentially in successive time slices, as would be the case in real speech. The processing of the input goes through a number of cycles in which all of the units update their respective activations at the same time, based on the activations computed in the previous update cycle. These activations are mapped into predicted responses, following McClelland and Elman (1986). Although the results of the simulation showed effects of both the bottom-up and top-down sources of information, the quantitative predictions of TRACE did not follow the form of the observed results (Massaro 1989b). These results might imply that interactive activation, the central premise of TRACE, is not a psychologically plausible mechanism for combining several sources of information.

More recently, several investigators have attempted to place the FLMP and the TRACE on more equal footing to allow more direct comparisons. One method has been to reduce the complexity of the TRACE by using miniature neural networks. A network designed to predict context effects is shown in figure 16.9 (McClelland 1991; Massaro and Cohen 1991). Three levels of units are assumed: "target," "context," and "word." The target and context levels can be considered to contain units activated by the target letter and the contextual letters, respectively; these are analogous to the bottom-up and top-down sources of information in the FLMP. Activation of context units and target units activates word units. Consistent with the TRACE assumption of interactive activation, all units within the context and target levels are bidirectionally connected to all word units. Only the excitatory connections are shown in the figure. Within each of the three levels, each unit also has inhibitory connections to all other units within that level.

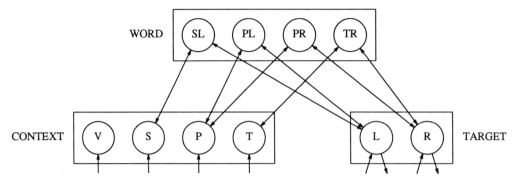

Figure 16.9 Network used in simulation of TRACE model applied to phonological constraints experiment of Massaro and Cohen (1983). Inhibitory connections between units within Word, Context, and Target levels are not shown in network.

The target units R and L are activated to varying degrees by the critical speech segment. As in the FLMP, we can assume that changes in the glide will change the activation of the L unit relative to the R unit. The context units are activated by the different contexts. The word unit labeled "SL" corresponds to all words that begin with /sl/ and so on for the other word units. Because of the interactive-activation assumption, the word units in turn send their activation downward to the context and target units.

In the network, the effects of stimulus and context are combined via the units in the word layer. The activations of word units are fed back to the target and context units, changing their activations in a manner that reflects the activations of both target and context units. In this manner, the joint effects of target and context units are reflected in the activations of units in both the target and context layers. This passing of activation occurs for a number of cycles until a sufficient amount of activation occurs at the target units. The activations are mapped into strength values, which are then mapped into a response using the RGR.

The simplest model to fit to the study requires 11 parameters: 7 R target value inputs (with the L target receiving the additive complement), 4 context inputs (with the nonselected contexts set to 0). The simulation of the TRACE is completely deterministic; the outcome of a simulation under a given set of conditions will produce the same results each time the simulation is run. The TRACE outcome was fit to the observed data by minimizing the differences between the predicted and observed values. For each of the 28 experimental conditions, a simulation trial was run with a hypothetical set of parameter values, and a goodness of fit was computed. As in the fit of the FLMP, the parameter values were changed systematically to maximize the goodness of fit of the TRACE. As can be seen in figure 16.10, the TRACE is not capable of describing the influence of the different types of context, and does a poor job describing the results, with an average RMSD value of .083, significantly larger than the fit of the FLMP.

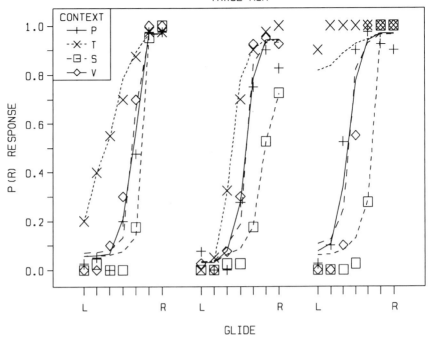

Figure 16.10 Observed (points) and predicted (lines) probability of *r* response for three typical subjects as function of glide F_3 onset level and context (after Massaro and Cohen 1983, experiment 2). Predictions are for TRACE model with RGR decision process.

McClelland (1991) placed the blame for the TRACE's failure to predict Massaro's (1989b) results on the decision stage of the model rather than on some other process such as interactive activation. The TRACE was modified by (1) adding noise to the inputs, thus making the initial processing in the model probabilistic rather than deterministic; and (2) changing the RGR decision rule to a best-one-wins (BOW) rule in which the response alternative corresponding to the most active unit would always be chosen (McClelland 1991). With these two modifications, McClelland (1991) argued that the predictions of the TRACE are consistent with the empirical observations (and with the predictions of the FLMP). However, this new model was not actually tested against any empirical results.

To provide an empirical test of the new TRACE, Massaro and Cohen (1991) ran simulation trials by adding normal noise samples to both the target and context input values. For each of the simulated trials, a BOW decision was made on the final target activations. The simulated trials gave the predicted proportion of responses at each of the experimental conditions. The fit of this model did not improve on the fit of the deterministic TRACE with the RGR decision rule. The RMSD obtained for this model was .111, about twice that found for the FLMP. Figure 16.11 shows the fit of this 11-parameter TRACE. A second, 12-parameter TRACE was run (starting with the parameters

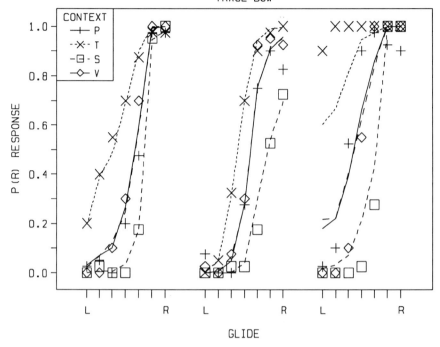

Figure 16.11 Observed (points) and predicted (lines) probability of *r* response for three typical subjects as function of glide F_3 onset level and context (after Massaro and Cohen 1983, experiment 2). Predictions are for TRACE model with BOW decision process.

of the 11-parameter model), which added the standard deviation of the noise as a free parameter. Only a small improvement was seen with an RMSD of .099, still significantly poorer than the fit of the FLMP. The TRACE model with intrinsic noise added at each processing cycle also gave a poor description of the results, relative to the FLMP. This model-fitting exercise shows that the FLMP gives a better description of the results than the TRACE; thus we can conclude these results support the FLMP over the TRACE.

Advocates of interactive activation, and researchers more generally, might not be easily persuaded by the differences in goodness of fit to empirical results. It is thus important to emphasize that interactive activation appears to have the incorrect dynamics to accurately describe the time course of perceptual processing. The influence of context necessarily lags behind the influence of bottom-up information in interactive activation models. However, there is strong evidence that context can have an influence at any time relative to the bottom-up information (Massaro and Cohen 1991). Moreover, interactive activation models must predict that context can eventually dominate bottom-up information with increases in processing, although this prediction fails empirical tests (Massaro and Cohen 1991) and goes against everyday behavior. If processing followed interactive activation, slow reading would permit top-down context to override bottom-up information. Readers slow down to proofread, however, which makes the detection of misspellings easier to spot.

Other empirical results support the conclusion that interactive activation is not an appropriate process to account for the influence of context on perception (Massaro and Cohen 1991). One set of results comes from a phoneme monitoring task by Frauenfelder et al. (1990). They first found that reaction time (RT) to a target phoneme in a word decreased when the phoneme occurred near or after the uniqueness point—the point when only one word was consistent with the input up to that point. This result is consistent with the TRACE model because top-down activation from the lexical level would activate the word's phonemes. In a second study, they replaced one of the phonemes in the word with the target phoneme. Given that the word context should have activated the lexical representation in TRACE, top-down activation from the lexical level to the phoneme level should have occurred. Because of the lateral inhibition between phonemes, the target phoneme should have been inhibited and thus more difficult to detect. However, there was no increase in RT, even when the substituted phoneme differed by just the voicing feature. This result weakens TRACE's central assumptions about how activation and inhibition operate to combine top-down and bottom-up information. The results are consistent with the FLMP because there are no inhibitory processes in the model. A word context can facilitate processing of the segments making it up, but not inhibit the processing of other segments.

Another source of evidence against TRACE comes from McQueen (1991), who studied the influence of lexical context on the identification of a final segment, such as in *kiss-kish* and *fiss-fish*. Because top-down activation takes time to build up, TRACE predicts a larger context effect for slow responses than for fast responses for these syllable final distinctions. As also noted by Massaro and Cohen (1991), the presence of top-down activation requires several cycles of processing after activation from bottom-up sources; thus there would be less time for top-down activation with fast responses than with slow response, and a larger context effect should be found with slow responses. The actual results were just the opposite of this prediction: larger context effects with fast responses. These same results can be described by a dynamic version of the FLMP (Massaro and Cohen 1991; Massaro and Oden 1995). Lexical information and segmental information function as two sources of information processed continuously over time. When lexical context comes before the segmental information, there is more processing time available for the context, relative to the segmental information; in this case, fast responses are predicted to show a larger effect of lexical context than slow responses. On the other hand, when lexical context comes after the segmental information, there is *less* processing time available for the context relative to the segmental information; in this case, the FLMP predicts a larger effect of lexical context with slow, relative to fast, responses. These predictions hold up, as illustrated in McQueen's (1991) study with early lexical context and by Pitt's (1995) results with late lexical context.

Pitt (1995) used test items, such as /gIft/ or /kIs/, in which the lexical information occurs later in the test word than the phonological information in the initial consonant. The FLMP predicts that support for /g/ from the bottom-up and top-down sources grows with processing time, although there is necessarily a delay in the arrival of the lexical information, relative to the stimulus information from the initial consonant. To provide a quantitative test of this interpretation, the FLMP was fit to the 14 individual subjects and to the average results in Pitt's experiment 1. The model was fit to the three identification conditions in the slow, middle, and fast RT conditions. It was assumed that the available processing time differed in the three conditions. The available processing time was taken to be the mean RT for each subject under each of the three conditions; the mean RTs across the 14 subjects were 345, 445, and 663 ms, respectively. The mean RTs for individual subjects were taken to be the available processing time for the phonological information. These same values, minus a constant delay c_l, for the arrival of the lexical information, were taken to be the available processing time for the lexical information.

We assume that evaluation of the speech information follows the function in equation 16.8, which gives the amount of support s for /g/, defined as $S(s)$:

$$S(s) = \alpha(1 - e^{-\theta t}) + .5(e^{-\theta t}). \tag{16.8}$$

Equation 16.8 describes the evaluation process as a negatively accelerated growth function of processing time t; it is assumed that the information provided by this source of information can be represented by α, and that the rate of processing this information, θ, is independent of the information value. The values of α, which represents the asymptotic support for the alternative /g/, are equal to the parameter values indicating the degree of support in the typical fit of the model when processing time is not a factor. If α corresponds to the amount of support for the voiced alternative /g/, then the speech syllable changed from a somewhat ambiguous /g/ to a less ambiguous /g/ would have a larger α value but would be processed with a fixed θ. The three RT conditions would necessarily have different processing times. The same type of equation would describe the growth of the lexical context information c, except that the constant delay c_l for its arrival would be subtracted from the available processing time.

Integration of the outputs of evaluation occurs continuously, producing a overall goodness of match for each of the test alternatives. Given two sources of information, the output of integration, $S(s, c)$, is given by equation 16.9:

$$S(s, c) = [\alpha_s(1 - e^{-\theta t}) + .5(e^{-\theta t})] \times [\alpha_c(1 - e^{-\theta(t-c_l)}) + .5(e^{-\theta(t-c_l)})], \tag{16.9}$$

where α_s is the asymptotic support from the initial consonant stimulus and α_c is the asymptotic support from the lexical context. The value of θ is assumed to be the same for both the stimulus information and the lexical context and c_l is the delay between the onset of the processing and the onset of the lexical information. The RGR at decision is simply instantiated when the feature evaluation and integration are completed, as constrained by the RT condition. The same operations occur at all 3 RT conditions; only the available processing time differs across the conditions.

To provide a baseline for the fit of this dynamic FLMP, the FLMP was first fit to each of the three RT conditions separately, with a unique set of 10 parameters for each RT condition. The average RMSD for the fit of the 14 individual subjects was .017, whereas the RMSD for the fit of the average subject was .010. Thus the static FLMP provides an excellent description of the results. The fit of the dynamic FLMP reduces the number of free parameters from 30 to 12; in this case, the FLMP is being tested against three times as many data points (16 versus 48 observations) with only 2 additional parameter values (θ corresponding to the rate of processing and c_t). Figure 16.12 gives the predictions of this dynamic FLMP to the average results; as can be seen, the dynamic FLMP nicely describes the increase in the influence of lexical context with increases in processing time. The average RMSD for the fit of the 14 individual subjects was .046, whereas the RMSD for the fit of the average subject was .020. Considering the savings in the number of free

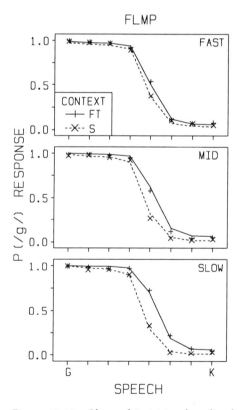

Figure 16.12 Observed (points) and predicted (lines) proportion of /g/ identifications for /lft/ and /ls/ contexts as function of speech information of initial consonant. Three panels give results for fast, middle, and slow identifications. Predictions of FLMP.

Table 16.1 Domains of Language Processing That Provide Evidence for FLMP

Domain	Sources of Information
Speech perception	Acoustic features
	Visible speech
	Gesture
	Tactile speech
	Electrical speech
	Phonological constraints
	Lexical constraints
	Syntactic constraints
	Semantic constraints
Reading	Letter features
	Orthographic constraints
	Lexical constraints
	Spelling-to-sound constraints
	Sentential constraints
Sentence Interpretation	Semantic information
	Syntactic information
	Prosodic information

parameters, the dynamic FLMP does a respectable job of describing the results. The average value of θ was 8.59 and the average value constant delay c_l was 297 ms. It is encouraging that the value of c_l is a reasonable estimate of the time between the onset of the syllable and the onset of the lexical context. The good description given by the dynamic FLMP reveals that the influence of lexical context as a function of RT is most parsimoniously described as due to processing time. Postulating different strategies or some other qualitative influence is not necessary.

Although we have been concerned with empirical results from only a few domains, it is important to remind the reader that there is evidence for the FLMP framework from a much broader set of domains. Table 16.1 lists the domains of language processing that provide evidence for the FLMP. Supporting results come from reading as well as from spoken language, and also from the more cognitive task of sentence interpretation (Bates and Mac-Whinney 1987). As can be seen in the table, the FLMP has been able to account for the influence of a broad range of information sources in language processing.

16.13 PARALLELS IN VISUAL PERCEPTION

In vision, the perceiver's goal is to solve the problem of what environmental situation exists, given the current conflux of sensory cues. This conceptualization of visual perception is exemplified by several authors in this volume (see Bülthoff and Yuille, chap. 3; Frisby, Buckley, and Freeman, chap. 4). Their work is based on the assumption that the combination or integration of several depth cues or visual modules is fundamental for successful visual processing. The Bayesian framework of Clark and Yuille (1990) used by Bülthoff and Yuille is in many ways analogous to the framework used in our research. It is striking that two very similar frameworks would be developed in very different domains—claimed to fundamentally different modules (Fodor 1983). As we have seen, the language-processing literature is consistent with the idea that the cues are first treated independently before being integrated to achieve perceptual recognition. Bülthoff and Yuille, (chap. 3), on the other hand, argues for some type of stronger coupling between the cues supporting vision. In Clark and Yuille's (1990) terms, strong coupling implies that "the operation of one sensory module is affected by the output of another sensory module so that the outputs of the two sensory modules are no longer independent" (p. 72). We have yet to see convincing evidence of strong coupling in vision, whereas some research clearly supports the assumption of cue independence (Cutting and Bruno 1988; Massaro 1988; Massaro and Cohen 1993).

Bülthoff and Yuille (chap. 3, this volume) use results such as those shown in figure 3.5 of their chapter as evidence for strong coupling. The results are interpreted to mean that the combination of two cues produces more accurate perception than could be predicted from the two cues. Stated another way, perception of shape, given each cue presented alone, is too poor to account for the accurate shape perception, given both cues. The implicit assumption in this interpretation is that one of these cues can be presented without the other, for example, shading can be presented without texture; however, a shape will always have some information about texture and shading (see Massaro 1988 for a more thorough description of this point). It is simply the case that the presentation of a single cue actually involved presentation of the other cue, but at a value that supported the "incorrect" frontoparallel projection. From this perspective, the poor shape judgments in the "single-cue" conditions reflect the integration of two opposing cues; it follows that the good shape judgments, given two consistent cues, do not demand a "strong coupling" interpretation.

16.14 PHENOMENAL EXPERIENCE IN LANGUAGE PROCESSING

Psycholinguistics is perhaps too wedded to our phenomenal experience in seeking explanations. One phenomenal experience in speech perception is that of categorical perception. Listening to a synthetic speech continuum of syllables varying between /ba/ and /pa/ provides an impressive demonstration: students and colleagues usually agree that their percept changes qualitatively from one category to the other in a single step or two, with very little fuzziness in between. Another misleading impression is that we hear substantial silent periods between the words of an utterance, when in fact very little silence exists. We also wonder, regardless of our native language, why foreign languages do not have these silences, whereas our language does; we impose our speech categories on other languages. This author has had several experiences of hearing certain German, Spanish, and Japanese phonological categories in terms of similar English ones. Our phenomenal experience, however, may reveal very little of the hidden processes supporting perception and understanding. As noted by Marcel (1983), phenomenal experience might be dependent on linking current hypotheses with sensory information. If the sensory information is lost very quickly, continuous information could participate in the perceptual process but might not be readily accessible to introspection. As in most matters of psychological inquiry, we must find methods to tap the processes involved in cognition without relying on only introspective reports.

Dennett (1991) has clarified an important distinction between "filling in" and "finding out," which is highly relevant to our phenomenal experience of categorical perception. In the categorical perception viewpoint, there seems to be significant filling in: we perceive two different speech events as the same category because a speech-is-special module makes them equivalent at the sensory/perceptual level. On the other hand, it is possible that categorization is simply finding out. That is, the goal of speech perception is categorization; we are able to find out which category best represents the speech event without necessarily modifying the sensory/perceptual representation of that event. In terms of the FLMP, we evaluate, integrate, and make a decision, if necessary, without necessarily modifying the sensory/perceptual representations of the speech event.

Perceptual effects can arise from sources of information other than the modality in question. For researchers like myself who spend a good deal of time looking at a talking face as well as listening to it, the most convincing result is that the speaker's face influences our "auditory" perceptual experience (McGurk and MacDonald 1976). I interpret this type of influence as analogous to the influence of top-down sources of information in speech perception (Massaro 1994). Although a strong interpretation of autonomous processing might argue that auditory perception should not be penetrated by visual information, visual information and auditory information are integrated to achieve perceptual recognition. Analogously, the experimental results described in this chapter show that bottom-up and top-down sources of information are integrated in word and sentence processing.

Filling in might appear to be an attractive explanation of our phenomenal experience of contradictory auditory and visual speech. We are told to report what we hear, and the visible speech biases our experience relative to the unimodal auditory case. Because it is our auditory experience we are reporting, it seems only natural to believe that the representation of the auditory speech has been changed—filled in—by the visual. Another interpretation, however, is that we do not have veridical access to the auditory representation. As Marcel (1983) has pointed out, we report interpretations—finding out—and not representations. Thus we must be careful about equating phenomenal reports with representations.

Not only can we be misled by our perceptual experience, we also are fallible with respect to our understanding of language. The illusion of knowing has been well documented (Glenberg et al. 1987). Students are asked to read a passage and indicate if they understand it. They read it and then claim it is perfectly clear—even though the passage contains a blatant contradiction. They presume knowledge and coherence when in fact there is very little. The same might be said of our reaction to political speeches. We too often nod our heads in agreement in circumstances where we do not know what we are agreeing with. This takes our interpretation of the Japanese "yes" or nod of agreement one step farther. Westerners have learned that "yes" from a Japanese does not mean their listener agrees—only that he or she understands. We must also realize that "yes," or even an apparently informed answer from any listener, might not signify understanding, as in our illusory understanding of the Moses question.

ACKNOWLEDGMENTS

The research reported in, and the writing of, this chapter were supported in part by Public Health Service grant PHS R01 NS 20314 and National Science Foundation grant BNS 8812728. The author would like to acknowledge Norman H. Anderson and Gregg Oden for their important influence on this work. The comments of Michael Cohen, Maryellen MacDonald, James McClelland, and an autonomous reviewer are greatly appreciated. Michael Cohen also provided expert help on the model testing.

REFERENCES

Abrams R. A., and Balota, D. A. (1991). Mental chronometry: Beyond reaction time. *Psychological Science, 2*, 153–157.

Anderson, N. H. (1981). *Foundations of information integration theory.* New York: Academic Press.

Bates, E., and MacWhinney, B. (1987). Competition, variation, and language learning. In B. MacWhinney (Ed.), *Mechanisms of language acquisition, 157–193.* Hillsdale, NJ: Erlbaum.

Bennett, B. M., Hoffman, D. D., and Prakash, C. (1989) *Observer mechanics: A formal theory of perception.* San Diego: Academic Press.

Chandler, J. P. (1969). Subroutine STEPIT—Finds local minima of a smooth function of several parameters. *Behavioral Science, 14*, 81–82.

Clark, J. J., and Yuille, A. L. (1990). *Data fusion for sensory information processing systems.* Dordrecht: Kluwer.

Connine, C. M. (1990). Effects of sentence context and lexical knowledge in speech processing. In G. T. M. Altmann (Eds.) *Cognitive models of speech processing: Psycholinguistic and computational perspectives, 281–294.* Cambridge, MA: MIT Press.

Connine, C. M., Blasko, D. G., and Wong, J. (1994). Vertical similarity in spoken word recognition: Multiple lexical activation, individual differences, and the role of sentence context. *Perception and Psychophysics, 56*, 624–636.

Connine, C. M., and Clifton, C. (1987). Interactive use of lexical information in speech perception. *Journal of Experimental Psychology: Human Perception and Performance, 13,* 291–299.

Cotton, S., and Grosjean, F. (1984). The gating paradigm: A comparison of successive and individual presentation formats. *Perception and Psychophysics, 35,* 41–48.

Cutler, A., Mehler, J., Norris, D., and Segui, J. (1987). Phoneme identification and the lexicon. *Cognitive Psychology, 19,* 141–177.

Cutler, A., and Norris, D. (1979). Monitoring sentence comprehension. In W. E. Cooper and E. C. T. Walker (Eds.), *Sentence processing: Psycholinguistic studies presented to Merrill Garrett,* 113–134. Hillsdale, NJ: Erlbaum.

Cutting, J. E., and Bruno, N. (1988). Minimodularity and the perception of layout. *Journal of Experimental Psychology: General, 117,* 161–170.

Dennett, D. C. (1991). *Consciousness explained.* Boston: Little, Brown.

Elman, J., and McClelland, J. (1986). Exploiting lawful variability in the speech wave. In J. S. Perkell and D. H. Klatt (Eds.), *Invariance and variable in speech processes,* 360–385. Hillsdale, NJ: Erlbaum.

Elman, J., and McClelland, J. (1988). Cognitive penetration of the mechanisms of perception: Compensation for coarticulation of lexically restored phonemes. *Journal of Memory and Language, 27,* 143–165.

Erickson, T. D., and Mattson, M. E. (1981). From words to meaning: A semantic illusion. *Journal of Memory and Language, 20,* 540–551.

Fodor, J. A. (1983). *Modularity of mind.* Cambridge, MA: Bradford Books.

Forster, K. I. (1985). Lexical acquisition and the modular lexicon. *Language and Cognitive Processes, 1,* 87–108.

Foss, D. J., and Gernsbacher, M. A. (1983). Cracking the dual code: Toward a unitary model of phoneme identification. *Journal of Verbal Learning and Verbal Behavior, 22,* 609–632.

Frauenfelder, U. H., Segui, J., and Dijkstra, T. (1990). Lexical effects in phonemic processing: Facilitatory or inhibitory? *Journal of Experimental Psychology: Human Perception and Performance, 16,* 77–91.

Ganong, W. F., III. (1980) Phonetic categorization in auditory word recognition. *Journal of Experimental Psychology: Human Perception and Performance, 6,* 110–125.

Glenberg, A. M., Sanocki, T., Epstein, W., and Morris, C. (1987). Enhancing calibration of comprehension. *Journal of Experimental Psychology: General, 116,* 119–136.

Grosjean, F. (1980). Spoken word recognition processes and the gating paradigm. *Perception and Psychophysics, 28,* 267–283.

Grosjean, F. (1985). The recognition of words after their acoustic offset: Evidence and implications. *Perception and Psychophysics, 38,* 299–310.

Mann, V. A., and Repp, B. H. (1981). Influence of preceding fricative on stop consonant perception. *Journal of the Acoustical Society of America, 69,* 548–558.

Marcel, A. J. (1983). Conscious and unconscious perception: An approach to the relations between phenomenal experience and perceptual processes. *Cognitive Psychology, 15,* 238–300.

Marslen-Wilson, W. D. (1984). Function and process in spoken word recognition: A tutorial review. In H. Bouma and D. G. Bouwhuis (Eds.), *Attention and performance X: Control of language processes,* 125–150. Hillsdale, NJ: Erlbaum.

Marslen-Wilson, W. D. (1987). Functional parallelism in spoken word recognition. In U. H. Frauenfelder and L. K. Tyler (Eds.), *Spoken word recognition*, 71–102. Cambridge, MA: MIT Press.

Massaro, D. W. (1975a). *Experimental psychology and information processing*. Chicago: Rand McNally.

Massaro, D. W. (Ed.). (1975b). *Understanding language: An information processing analysis of speech perception, reading, and psycholinguistics*. New York: Academic Press.

Massaro, D. W. (1985). Attention and perception: An information-integration perspective. *Acta Psychologica, 60*, 211–241.

Massaro, D. W. (1987). *Speech perception by ear and eye: A paradigm for psychological inquiry*. Hillsdale, NJ: Erlbaum.

Massaro, D. W. (1988). Ambiguity in perception and experimentation. *Journal of Experimental Psychology: General, 117*, 417–421.

Massaro, D. W. (1989a). Multiple book review of *Speech perception by ear and eye: A paradigm for psychological inquiry. Behavioral and Brain Sciences, 12*, 741–794.

Massaro, D. W. (1989b). Testing between the TRACE model and the fuzzy logical model of perception. *Cognitive Psychology, 21*, 398–421.

Massaro, D. W. (1992). Connectionist models of speech perception. In R. Reilly and N. Sharkey (Eds.) *Connectionist approaches to language processing*, 321–350. Hillsdale, NJ: Erlbaum.

Massaro, D. W. (1994). Psychological aspects of speech perception: Implications for research and theory. In M. Gernsbacher (Ed.), *Handbook of psycholinguistics*, 219–263. New York: Academic Press.

Massaro, D. W., and Cohen, M. M. (1976). The contribution of fundamental frequency and voice onset time to the /zi/-/si/ distinction. *Journal of the Acoustical Society of America, 60*, 704–717.

Massaro, D. W., and Cohen, M. M. (1983). Phonological context in speech perception. *Perception and Psychophysics, 34*, 338–348.

Massaro, D. W., and Cohen, M. M. (1991). Integration versus interactive activation: The joint influence of stimulus and context in perception. *Cognitive Psychology, 23*, 558–614.

Massaro, D. W., and Cohen, M. M. (1993). The paradigm and the fuzzy logical model of perception are alive and well. *Journal of Experimental Psychology: General, 122*, 1–10.

Massaro, D. W., and Cohen, M. M. (1994). Visual, orthographic, phonological, and lexical influences in reading. *Journal of Experimental Psychology: Human Perception and Performance, 20*, 1107–1128.

Massaro, D. W., and Cowan, N. (1993). Information processing models: Microscopes of the mind. *Annual Review of Psychology, 44*, 383–425.

Massaro, D. W., and Oden, G. C. (1980). Speech perception: A framework for research and theory. In N. J. Lass (Ed.), *Speech and language: Advances in basic research and practice*, vol. 3, 129–165. New York: Academic Press.

Massaro, D. W., and Oden, G. C. (1995). Independence of lexical context and phonological information in speech perception. *Journal of Experimental Psychology: Learning, Memory, and Cognition, 21*, 1053–1064.

McClelland, J. L. (1991). Stochastic interactive processes and the effect of context on perception. *Cognitive Psychology, 23*, 1–44.

McClelland, J. L., and Elman, J. L. (1986). The TRACE model of speech perception. *Cognitive Psychology, 18*, 1–86.

McGurk, H., and MacDonald, J. (1976). Hearing lips and seeing voices. *Nature, 264,* 746−748.

McQueen, J. M. (1991). The influence of the lexicon on phonetic categorization: Stimulus quality in word-final ambiguity. *Journal of Experimental Psychology: Human Perception and Performance, 17,* 433−443.

Morton, J. (1969). Interaction of information in word recognition. *Psychological Review, 76,* 165−178.

Murray, I. R., and Arnott, J. L. (1993). Toward the simulation of emotion in synthetic speech: A review of the literature on human vocal emotion. *Journal of the Acoustical Society of America, 93,* 1097−1108.

Oden, G. C. (1977). Integration of fuzzy logical information. *Journal of Experimental Psychology: Human Perception and Performance, 3,* 565−575.

Oden, G. C., and Anderson, N. H. (1974). Integration of semantic constraints. *Journal of Verbal Learning and Verbal Behavior, 13,* 138−148.

Oden, G. C., and Massaro, D. W. (1978). Integration of featural information in speech perception. *Psychological Review, 85,* 172−191.

Paap, K. R., Newsome, S. L., McDonald, J. E., and Schvaneveldt, R. W. (1982). The activation-verification model for letter and word recognition: The word-superiority effect. *Psychological Review, 89,* 573−594.

Pitt, M. A. (1995). The locus of the lexical shift in phoneme identification. *Journal of Experimental Psychology: Learning, Memory, and Cognition, 21,* 1037−1052.

Pitt, M. A., and Samuel, A. G. (1993). An empirical and meta-analytic evaluation of the phoneme identification task. *Journal of Experimental Psychology: Human Perception and Performance, 19,* 699−725.

Platt, J. R. (1964). Strong inference. *Science, 146,* 347−353.

Popper, K. (1959). *The logic of scientific discovery.* New York: Basic Books.

Reder, L. M., and Kusbit, G. W. (1991). Locus of the Moses illusion: Imperfect encoding, retrieval, or match? *Journal of Memory and Language, 30,* 385−406.

Salasoo, A., and Pisoni. D. (1985). Interaction of knowledge sources in spoken word identification. *Journal of Memory and Cognition, 2,* 210−231.

Samuel, A. G. (1981). Phonemic restoration: Insights from a new methodology. *Journal of Experimental Psychology: General, 110,* 474−494.

Thompson, H., and Altmann, G. T. M. (1990). Modularity compromised: Selecting partial hypotheses. In G. T. M. Altmann (Eds.), *Cognitive models of speech processing: Psycholinguistic and computational perspectives,* 324−344. Cambridge, MA: MIT press.

Tyler, L. K. (1990). The relationship between sentential context and sensory input: Comments on Connine's and Samuel's chapters. In G. T. M. Altmann (Eds.), *Cognitive models of speech processing: Psycholinguistic and computational perspectives,* 315−323. Cambridge, MA: MIT press.

Tyler, L. K., and Wessels, J. (1983). Quantifying contextual contributions to word-recognition processes. *Perception and Psychophysics, 34,* 409−420.

Tyler, L. K., and Wessels, J. (1985). Is gating an on-line task? Evidence from naming latency data. *Perception and Psychophysics, 38,* 217−222.

Warren, P., and Marslen-Wilson, W. D. (1987). Continuous uptake of acoustic cues in spoken word recognition. *Perception and Psychophysics, 41,* 262−275.

17 Representation and Activation in Syntactic Processing

Maryellen C. MacDonald

ABSTRACT

Syntactic processing, traditionally thought to be the province of an autonomous module, is argued to be one of several constraint satisfaction processes that constitute language comprehension. The importance of nonlinear activation to this approach is reviewed, and recent data concerning syntactic ambiguity resolution are shown to be comparable to findings from other domains, particularly speech perception, in suggesting that ambiguity resolution can be viewed as a constraint satisfaction process over partially activated alternative interpretations of the ambiguity. This approach is pursued in more detail in two investigations. First, studies of individual differences in syntactic ambiguity resolution suggest that representations and/or activation functions may vary across comprehenders in important ways. Second, effects of postambiguity context on ambiguity resolution show that context that arrives during the period of partial activation affects the nature of the ambiguity resolution process, as expected from an activation-based account.

17.1 CONSTRAINTS ON REPRESENTATION AND ACTIVATION

One of the primary theoretical domains in psycholinguistics affected by research in linguistics has been the architecture of language comprehension. Much of this research has argued for representational autonomy, claiming that linguistic representations are isolated from nonlinguistic representations and that certain linguistic representations, particularly syntactic representations, are autonomous from other linguistic representations (e.g., Chomsky 1982). A logical (though not necessary) consequence of this approach is that the processes operating on these representations are also autonomous—that they are modular processes in the sense embraced by Fodor (1983). This modular approach has been widely adopted in psycholinguistics and appears in models of word recognition (e.g., Forster 1979), lexical ambiguity resolution (Swinney 1979), and syntactic processing or *parsing* (Frazier 1987). This chapter will critically evaluate this approach, focusing on syntactic processes, which have provided some of the best evidence for the modular framework. The alternative view proposed here retains the levels of representation common to many linguistic and psycholinguistic theories but departs from these accounts in its claim that the general properties of partial activation and constraint satisfaction guide comprehension at all the different levels of representation.

Modular versus Constraint-based Syntactic Processing

Beyond the claim for the autonomy of syntactic representations, there are several other reasons why syntactic processing has been so closely identified with modular architectures. The first of these is the powerful intuitive evidence for modularity that arises from comprehenders' surprising failures to comprehend so-called garden path sentences, which contain temporary syntactic ambiguities that are resolved with an interpretation that the comprehender does not expect. When this unexpected interpretation is revealed at the disambiguation of the ambiguity, comprehenders have a conscious feeling of surprise, even in the presence of contextual information that should have aided their comprehension. The best-known example of a garden path sentence is from Bever (1970) and is shown in (1) with its alternative interpretations.

(1) a. The horse raced past the barn fell.
    b. The horse raced past the barn. (main verb interpretation)
    c. The horse (that was) raced past the barn fell. (reduced relative interpretation)

Sentence 1a is a garden path sentence because most comprehenders who read it are surprised to encounter the verb "fell," and they have difficulty interpreting the sentence. The two alternative interpretations that are temporarily available for this sentence are often called the "main verb" and "reduced relative" interpretations and are shown in (1b) and (1c) respectively. Most comprehenders initially interpret the input as a simple sentence in which "raced" is the past tense main verb of the sentence, as in (1b). The correct interpretation, illustrated in (1c), is that "raced" is a past participle introducing a relative clause meaning "the horse that was raced past the barn," and "fell" is the main verb of the sentence. Relative clauses of this sort can appear in English without being introduced by "that was," hence the term *reduced relative* for this construction.

Comprehenders' inability to interpret sentences such as (1a), even in the presence of a discourse context in which it would be very sensible to utter a sentence of this sort, has promoted the claim that the syntactic processor is an autonomous module, immune to potentially helpful context and other outside influences. In this sense, garden path sentences are the psycholinguistic analogue of visual illusions, in which the perceiver knows that the percept is illusory, yet the seemingly autonomous visual system continues to report the illusion.

Another reason for the favored modular status of the syntactic parser is that one particular model with a modular architecture has been well specified in a number of details, making it an attractive framework for exploring language comprehension. This account is the "garden path model" of parsing developed by Lyn Frazier and her colleagues (Ferreira and Clifton 1986; Frazier 1987; Rayner, Carlson, and Frazier 1983). There are three key features of Frazier's account that distinguish it from alternative proposals. First, it specifies exactly what information is and is not handled by the parser. In this model, the parser receives information only about the lexical categories of the input, such as *noun* and *verb*. The parser builds one syntactic structure for the string of categories. All information about word meanings, plausibility, and context is not available to the parser. Second, it specifies the parser's routines for handling ambiguity. When the parser encounters input that could be parsed in more than one way, it immediately chooses exactly one interpretation for the input, guided by two built-in heuristics that force the simplest and most local interpretation to be built. Third, Frazier's model provides for a second-stage "thematic processor" that has access to all the information hidden from the parser. This processor has the capability to detect the parser's misanalyses of ambiguities and guide reanalysis. The model yields predictions about which interpretations of ambiguities will be preferred (the ones selected by the parsing heuristics) and about the effects of context on syntactic processing, namely, that such effects will always be limited to the second-stage thematic processor and will thus be evident only after the initial operation of the autonomous parser. Frazier's (1987) review of her approach in *Attention and Performance XII* offers a sizable list of syntactic ambiguities and experimental results of parsing in context that seem to fit well within her modular approach.

A rapidly developing alternative view questions whether the syntactic processor is an autonomous module. This alternative view holds that syntactic ambiguities are resolved via the application of graded constraints at many different levels of representation, including constraints such as the relative frequency and plausibility of alternative interpretations (Burgess 1991; MacDonald, Pearlmutter, and Seidenberg 1994a; 1994b; Spivey-Knowlton, Trueswell, and Tanenhaus 1993; Taraban and McClelland 1988; Trueswell and Tanenhaus, 1994; Trueswell, Tanenhaus, and Garnsey 1994; Trueswell, Tanenhaus, and Kello 1993). According to this view, there is no special parsing stage or structural preference algorithms as in the garden path model.

The precise claims of the various constraint-based models differ in detail, but many have suggested that much or all of syntactic ambiguity resolution can be seen as a special case of ambiguity resolution over individual lexical items (e.g., MacDonald, Pearlmutter, and Seidenberg 1994a; Trueswell and Tanenhaus 1994; Trueswell, Tanenhaus, and Garnsey 1994). The relevant lexical ambiguities in this case are not semantic (as in the various meanings of *calf*) but are instead ambiguities concerning a word's syntactic functions. For example, some verbs in English have different morphological forms in the simple past tense (e.g., *rode, went*) and the past participle tense (e.g., *ridden, gone*), but most English verbs have the same form in both tenses, typically though not always an *-ed* ending (e.g., *raced, pushed*, but *bought*). Whenever one of these tense-ambiguous verbs is encountered, the comprehender must use some frequency and contextual information to determine the tense of the sentence, in the same way that comprehenders use frequency and contextual information to resolve semantic ambiguities such as *calf* (Burgess 1991; Simpson 1984). The important claim in constraint-based theories of syntactic ambiguity resolution is that all syntactic ambiguities, including garden path sentences such as (1a), are triggered by one or more lexical ambiguities of this sort. Moreover, each alternative syntactic interpretation is linked to exactly one interpretation of the lexical ambiguities triggering the syntactic ambiguity. Thus the syntactic ambiguities can be resolved to the extent that frequency and contextual information can resolve the lexical ambiguities that trigger them.

This approach is an important departure from the purely rule-based parser, in that it suggests that both lexical and syntactic ambiguities are constrained in the same way by lexical frequency and discourse context. A more general claim, extending beyond these two types of ambiguity, is that ambiguity resolution at all levels of representation proceeds in the same basic way, guided by probabilistic information about alternative frequencies and the surrounding context. The constraint-based approach therefore makes important claims for theories of linguistic representation, in that each type of representation must be subject to the graded effects of frequency and context.

If syntactic processing and other psycholinguistic processes do have the same character, then we should be able to see clear parallels between syntactic processes, such as syntactic ambiguity resolution, and other seemingly distinct processes, such as phoneme ambiguity resolution within speech perception. The next section reviews several examples. Comparisons between speech and syntactic processing phenomena will be carried over into the second part of the chapter, in which several new directions will be explored in domains that modulate the nature of constraint use during syntactic processing. These include individual differences in comprehension and the temporal distribution of contextual information and ambiguities, particularly the interesting case in which contextual information follows the ambiguity.

Activation and Representations

Most of the recent work supporting a constraint-based approach to syntactic ambiguity resolution has been presented in empirical papers demonstrating the effects of constraint use during ambiguity resolution (e.g., MacDonald 1994; Pearlmutter and MacDonald 1992, 1995; Spivey-Knowlton, Trueswell, and Tanenhaus 1993; Trueswell, Tanenhaus, and Garnsey 1994). Although the notion that alternative interpretations of ambiguities may be activated to varying degrees is shared by all these papers, the confines of an experimental article do not permit extended discussion of the nature of activation and representation, particularly when the basic claim about use of probabilistic constraints has been so controversial in this field. MacDonald, Pearlmutter, and Seidenberg 1994a did present a more extended discussion of some lexical-level representations and lexical frequency information that the authors suggested were crucial to lexical and syntactic ambiguity resolution, but even this long review article does not contain much discussion of how these lexical representations accrue activation. It is important to recognize that all of this work makes particular assumptions about the nature of activation, even if these assumptions are not discussed in great detail.

The assumption inherent in the constraint-based models is that lexical representations may be activated to varying degrees, and the extent to which a representation is activated constrains how rapidly it can accrue additional activation. This is the assumption of *nonlinear activation*, which is an important component of interactive activation models of processing (McClelland and Rumelhart 1981; see McClelland 1987 for additional discussion of nonlinear activation and language processing), and it is also a component of other noninteractive architectures, such as Massaro's fuzzy logical model of perception (FLMP; Massaro 1989; see also chap. 16, this volume).[1] In this view, when a representation (of a phoneme, word, etc.) receives excitatory input from some source, such as from contextual constraints, the extent to which activation accrues in the representation is a function of the extent to which the representation was already activated when the excitatory input was received. At a low asymptote of activation, new input will cause the activation to accrue slowly, such that a large amount of excitatory input is required to yield much increase in activation. The same result obtains at the high asymptote of activation—additional excitatory input yields little additional activation. At a moderate level of activation, however, excitatory input results in rapid activation accrual.

The importance of the nonlinear activation claim for language processing emerges in the effects of contextual information on processing linguistic input. The extent to which context can influence processing at some level is argued to be a function of the activation of the representation of the input. Contextual information should have a very strong effect during the period in which activation can accrue rapidly, namely, the period in which a representation is partially activated, but it should have little effect on a representation that is either strongly activated or has very little activation. Specifically within ambiguity resolution, contextual information should have its strongest effects when alternative interpretations of an ambiguity are each partially activated, such that contextual support to one interpretation results in a rapid accrual of activation for that interpretation. If one interpretation strongly dominates the other(s), however, such that the dominant interpretation has a large amount of activation and the others a very small amount, then contextual support for one of these interpretations will not result in much change of activation. This account, if it is a general property of language processing systems, should be evident in ambiguity resolution at a number of different levels. We will briefly consider three.

Phonemic Ambiguity   A clear demonstration of the relationship between the degree of ambiguity and the effectiveness of context can be seen in much speech perception research, where it is possible to manipulate precisely both the context and the ambiguity in the acoustic signal. For example, Connine (1987) examined perception of pairs of words that differed by only the voicing feature in one phoneme, for example, *dent* versus *tent*. Auditory stimuli were synthesized on a continuum of voice onset time (VOT), so that when presented in isolation, the stimuli with the shortest VOTs were clearly perceived as *dent*, the tokens with the long VOTs were clearly perceived as *tent*, and the ones in the middle were ambiguous. In the view proposed here, these ambiguous stimuli should result in partial activation of both the *dent* and *tent* representations, whereas the stimuli at each end of the VOT continuum should result in strong activation of one representation and weak activation of the other. When the stimuli were presented within a sentence context that biased one of the two words (e.g., "The fender had a..."), the effect of the context depended on the ambiguity inherent in the stimulus: the clear stimuli at the ends of the VOT continuum were unaffected by the context, but identification of the ambiguous items in the middle of the continuum was reliably influenced by context (see Massaro, chap. 16, this volume, for similar examples). This is the result we would expect given nonlinear activation: The partially activated stimuli were more influenced by context than the less ambiguous stimuli.

Lexical Ambiguity   Other clear examples of the context-ambiguity relationship can be found within lexical ambiguity resolution, which arises when a word has several alternative meanings, such as *calf*, *pitcher* or *port*. Here the degree of ambiguity cannot be manipulated with the acoustic signal; rather, the extent to which alternative interpretations are partially activated appears to be a function of the relative frequency of the alternative meanings in past usage, a factor that varies widely across ambiguous words. For example, the two meanings of *pitcher* (a container for liquids; a ballplayer) are roughly equal in frequency, whereas for *port*, the "harbor" meaning is more frequent than the meaning "fortified wine." There is now substantial evidence that the frequency of the alternative interpretations guides the resolution of such ambiguities in neutral contexts (Simpson 1984) and also modulates the extent to which contextual information can influence the interpretation of the ambiguity. For example, Duffy, Morris, and Rayner (1988) measured reading times for ambiguous words in sentences and found that the effect of prior context in the sentence on reading times for the ambiguous words was modulated by the frequency of the alternative meanings of the ambiguity. They examined reading times for both "equibiased" words such as *pitcher* and biased words such as *port* in neutral contexts and contexts supporting the lower-frequency meaning (or in the case of the equibiased words, one randomly chosen meaning). Prior contexts were found to promote the randomly chosen meaning they supported in equibiased words, but not to promote the lower-frequency meaning they supported in biased words (e.g., the "wine" meaning of *port*). Again, contexts are effective when the alternatives are at roughly equal activation, and not effective when one alternative strongly dominates (see Kawamoto 1993 for additional discussion).

Syntactic ambiguity   In contrast to the resolution of phonemic and lexical ambiguity, where the relationship between ambiguity, activation levels, and context seems relatively straightforward, it has not always been clear how to apply these insights to the resolution of syntactic ambiguity. The difficulty arises in syntactic processing because claims about activation levels naturally presuppose activated representations, and syntactic representations have not generally been considered candidates for activation. Unlike the "stored" representations of the phonemes and lexical items in a language, syntactic representations have traditionally been viewed as being built anew, via the operation of generative rules, for each new sentence that the comprehender encounters (Frazier 1987). When confronted with an ambiguity, a structure-building syntactic parser has the option of either building one structure for the input, as in the garden path model (Frazier 1987), or building all alternative structures in parallel (Altmann and Steedman 1988); the partial activation notion is not really compatible with these two traditional alternatives.

On the other hand, lexical constraint−based accounts of syntactic ambiguity resolution offer a way to apply the principle of nonlinear activation to syntactic processing. The claim that syntactic ambiguities are triggered by lexical ambiguities can be realized in several different types of representations. For example, activation levels of alternative interpretations of lexical items could control which syntactic structure gets built, such that only the structure appropriate for the most active interpretation of a lexical item can be built. Ford, Bresnan, and Kaplan's (1982) approach offers this possibility, although they do not discuss activation levels directly. Given nonlinear activation, however, relatively unambiguous lexical interpretations, in which one interpretation had far more activation than the other(s), would be relatively insensitive to context, whereas more ambiguous, partially activated lexical alternatives would be very sensitive to context. In this way, contextual information would have a measurable, though indirect, effect on syntactic ambiguity resolution, because the "winning" lexical interpretation would determine the syntactic structure. Alternatively, in the approach adopted by MacDonald, Pearlmutter, and Seidenberg (1994a), the knowledge about permissible syntactic structures is contained within the lexical representation itself and is not constructed separately. In this approach, each lexical item is connected to "X-bar structures," which are representations of grammatical linkages between words and phrases in a given language. Just as semantically ambiguous words like *calf* are hypothesized to activate several alternative semantic interpretations, and just as morphologically ambiguous verbs such as *raced* are hypothesized to activate both past and past participle tense representations, words that can participate in alternative syntactic interpretations activate alternative X-bar structures. Thus syntactic structures themselves can be partially activated in the MacDonald, Pearlmutter, and Seidenberg (1994a) approach, unlike the Ford, Bresnan, and Kaplan (1982) position, where one syntactic structure is built. The MacDonald and colleagues position therefore suggests that the frequency with which a word participates in various syntactic structures should constrain ambiguity resolution. Given the inherent confounding of alternative syntactic structures and alternative lexical representations, such as past versus past participle tenses for morphologically ambiguous verbs, it is difficult to design a clear test of this hypothesis.[2] Because the outcome of this debate is not crucial to the issues of interest here, claims for activation of syntactic structures themselves will not be addressed further.

As an illustration of the workings of a lexical activation account of syntactic ambiguity resolution, consider again the main verb/reduced relative (MV/RR) ambiguity, as in the garden path sentence "The horse raced past the barn fell" for the RR interpretation, and the simple MV interpretation in "The horse raced past the barn yesterday." MacDonald, Pearlmutter, and Seidenberg (1994a) have suggested that there are (at least) three lexical ambiguities in the representations of verbs (such as "raced") that trigger this syntactic ambiguity. First, as discussed above, the -ed ending on these verbs is ambiguous between past and past participle tenses. The main verb interpretation requires the past tense, as in "The horse went past the barn yesterday." The reduced relative interpretation, however, requires the past participle tense, as in "The horse ridden past the barn fell." Second, the verb is ambiguous in voice. The main verb interpretation requires the active voice, whereas the reduced relative is a kind of passive, which can be seen more clearly in its "unreduced" form, with "be" as the passive marker: "The horse that was raced past the barn fell." Third, "raced" is ambiguous in its argument structure, which refers to the kinds of noun arguments the verb takes and the kinds of thematic roles it can assign to these arguments. The verb "raced" participates in a several of different argument structures, including transitive, in which there is both an Agent of the action and a Theme (or Patient) that is acted upon, as in the active sentence "The horse [Agent] raced the donkey [Theme]" or in the passive sentence "The horse [Theme] was raced...," and intransitive, in which there is only one noun argument, as in "The horse [Agent] raced well." The main verb interpretation permits a variety of argument structures, including transitive and intransitive, but the reduced relative interpretation, a type of passive, requires a transitive argument structure: "The horse [Theme] raced past the barn fell."

The fact that the MV/RR ambiguity is triggered by a set of lexical ambiguities in the verb yields the prediction that, like ambiguities at other levels of representation, these lexical-syntactic ambiguities should be resolved via a process of partial activation and constraint satisfaction. More specifically, two important results observed with other ambiguities should also be observed with syntactic ambiguity. The first of these is the effect of frequency of the alternative interpretations on ambiguity resolution. The three lexical ambiguities that trigger the MV/RR syntactic ambiguity (verb tense morphology, voice, and argument structure) each have alternative interpretations that occur with varying frequency. As with lexical semantic ambiguities, the frequency of the alternative interpretations of the ambiguous verb in the MV/RR ambiguity should affect the activation level of the alternative interpretations.

The clearest test of this frequency hypothesis would be to compare ambiguity resolution in the situation most favorable for the MV interpretation (the conjunction of high-frequency past tense, intransitive argument structure, and active voice) to that in the situation most favorable for the RR interpretation (high-frequency past participle, transitive argument structure, and passive voice). Because this sort of comparison requires more detailed information about the frequency of alternative verb representations than is currently available, most investigations of lexical frequency effects have been limited to the frequencies of only one feature. For example, MacDonald (1994) examined the effect of argument structure frequencies on resolution of the MV/RR ambiguity. The verbs that trigger the MV/RR ambiguity differ widely in the relative frequency of their alternative argument structures. The verb *raced* occurs much more frequently in an intransitive argument structure than in a transitive argument structure, whereas the verb *carried* is more frequent in transitive uses than intransitive (Connine et al. 1984). Because the reduced relative interpretation of the MV/RR ambiguity requires the transitive argument structure, low transitive frequency verbs such as *raced* should be very difficult to interpret within a reduced relative construction, whereas high transitive frequency verbs such as *carried* should be relatively easy to resolve with this structure. MacDonald (1994) contrasted ambiguity resolution in a *biased transitive* condition, which contained ambiguous verbs (e.g., *carried*, *pushed*) that were selected to have a higher-frequency transitive than intransitive argument structure, compared to a *biased intransitive* condition, in which ambiguous verbs (e.g., *raced*, *moved*) were more frequent in intransitive than transitive structures. The critical data were self-paced reading times in the disambiguation region of the sentence, which revealed the RR interpretation, compared to reading times in an unambiguous control condition. The effect of ambiguity on reading times varied with argument structure frequency. The biased intransitive (*moved*) sentences had reading times that were significantly longer in the disambiguation region than in the unambiguous condition, whereas sentences with the biased transitive verbs (*pushed*) had reading times at the disambiguation that did not differ from unambiguous times. These and other findings for lexical frequency effects in syntactic ambiguity resolution (e.g., Trueswell, Tanenhaus, and Kello 1993) support the important role of lexical representations in syntactic ambiguity resolution.

The second prediction to emerge from claims for nonlinear activation and a lexically based account of syntactic ambiguity resolution concerns context effects during ambiguity resolution. As with ambiguity resolution at other levels, contexts should be most helpful in syntactic ambiguity resolution when alternative lexical interpretations are partially activated, and less helpful when one alternative has a substantial amount of activation and others do not. Specifically for the MV/RR syntactic ambiguity, contextual information should be most successful in promoting the reduced relative interpretation when the alternative interpretations for the three lexical ambiguities (verb tense, voice, argument structure) are equibiased.

MacDonald, Pearlmutter, and Seidenberg (1994b) examined this prediction with a meta-analysis of twelve published studies that had previously investigated the effect of context on MV/RR ambiguity resolution. These studies all measured reading times for ambiguous sentences that were resolved with the reduced relative interpretation, compared to unambiguous controls. All of the studies also manipulated contextual information prior to the ambiguity, such that a helpful context condition promoted the ultimately correct reduced relative interpretation of the ambiguity, whereas an unhelpful context condition promoted the ultimately incorrect main verb interpretation of the ambiguity. Four of the studies provided evidence for the garden path model's prediction that the syntactic parser operates autonomously from contextual information; they found that ambiguous sentences resolved with the reduced relative interpretation had longer reading times than unambiguous controls, regardless of context (Britt et al. 1992; Ferreira and Clifton 1986; Rayner, Carlson, and Frazier 1983; Rayner, Garrod, and Perfetti 1992). The other eight studies found that ambiguities resolved in the presence of helpful context were no more difficult than unambiguous controls, a pattern interpreted to show that contextual information constrains parsing operations (Burgess 1991; MacDonald 1994; Ni and Crain 1990; Pearlmutter and MacDonald 1992; Spivey-Knowlton, Trueswell, and Tanenhaus 1993; Tabossi et al. 1994; Trueswell and Tanenhaus 1991, 1992; Trueswell, Tanenhaus, and Garnsey 1994). The twelve studies vary widely in the type of contextual information provided to promote the reduced relative interpretation of the ambiguity, the type of reading time measure used, and the strength of context manipulations (though context strength is not quantified with normative or other data for most of these studies).

MacDonald et al. investigated whether the pattern of results reflected variations in the frequency of alternative interpretations of one of the lexical ambiguities triggering the MV/RR ambiguity—past versus past participle tense frequency. Using the Francis and Kucera (1982) norms, they calculated the relative frequency of the past versus past participle uses for the ambiguous verbs in each study, on the assumption that contextual information should be more influential when the alternative tenses were partially activated and roughly as frequent, and less influential in the situation in which one alternative strongly dominated. The results can be seen in figure 17.1, where studies supporting the modular position are represented with open circles, and those supporting the constraint-based position, with filled circles. There are two important findings. First, the percentage of past participle tense use was reliably higher in those studies supporting context effects than in

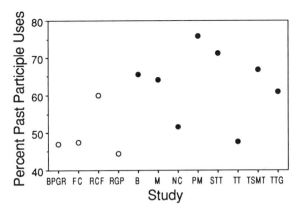

Figure 17.1 Mean percentage of past participle uses for ambiguous verbs used in twelve studies of context effects in MV/RR ambiguities. In order, the studies on *x*-axis are as follows: BPGR: Britt, Perfetti, Garrod, and Rayner (1992); FC: Ferreira and Clifton (1986); RCF: Rayner, Carlson, and Frazier (1983); RGP: Rayner, Garrod, and Perfetti (1992); B: Burgess (1991); M: MacDonald (1994); NC: Ni and Crain (1990); PM: Pearlmutter and MacDonald (1992); STT: Spivey-Knowlton, Trueswell, and Tanenhaus (1993); TT: Trueswell and Tanenhaus (1991; 1992); TSMT: Tabossi, Spivey-Knowlton, McRae, and Tanenhaus (1994); TTG: Trueswell, Tanenhaus, and Garnsey (1994). See MacDonald, Pearlmutter, and Seidenberg (1994b) for additional details.

those finding no context effects. This result supports the claim that context effects in ambiguity resolution are modulated by the nature of the activation of alternative interpretations, with greater context effects more evident in the case of roughly equal partial activation of alternatives. The fact that the results shown in figure 17.1 emerged despite substantial variation across studies in important factors such as dependent measure and context strength underscores the importance of these frequency analyses.

A second finding shows the picture to be somewhat more complicated, however, in that the actual percentages are such that the four no-context studies at the left of the figure are the ones that have roughly equal percentages of alternative tenses. This point emphasizes the need to study frequency effects for the *conjunction* of lexical features thought to be important here. Tense is only one of three or more lexical features that differ in the main verb and reduced relative interpretations, and we would expect that partial activation of the alternative syntactic interpretations would be a function of the frequency of all lexical features.

Summary

The general notion of activation levels can go a long way toward accounting for the character of ambiguity resolution processes. The principle of nonlinear activation was seen to be particularly important in accounting for the role of contextual information in ambiguity resolution, such that the same pattern of context and frequency effects was found in phonemic ambiguity resolution

(Connine 1987), lexical ambiguity resolution (Duffy, Morris, and Rayner 1988), and syntactic ambiguity resolution (MacDonald, Pearlmutter, and Seidenberg 1994b). In addition to the claim for nonlinear activation, a second crucial component for the linkage in ambiguity resolution between these different levels of representation was an account of how to represent syntactic ambiguities at least in part as lexical ambiguities (MacDonald, Pearlmutter, and Seidenberg 1994a; Trueswell, Tanenhaus, and Kello 1993; Trueswell, Tanenhaus, and Garnsey 1994; Trueswell and Tanenhaus 1994), without which it is not clear how to apply the insights about activation levels to syntactic representations. The combined account suggests that syntactic processing, far from being the prototypical discrete, symbolic system, is just as compatible with an activation account as are other language comprehension processes.

17.2 MORE CONSTRAINTS ON REPRESENTATION AND ACTIVATION

The constraint-based account described above is of course preliminary in many respects, in that it is limited by a lack of knowledge about crucial aspects of the representations. For example, it is not clear what sorts of frequency information are available to comprehenders. It is clear that comprehenders know a great deal of simple frequency information (e.g., the frequency of a word, phoneme, etc., in the language), but it is less clear how far frequency information extends into the range of combinatorial frequencies (e.g., those of words, phonemes, etc.) in a given phrase, sentence, or discourse). Answers to questions such as these are essential for understanding the nature of the representations that comprehenders activate during language comprehension; the questions themselves serve to focus research within a constraint-based framework of language processing.

One way to investigate the limits on constraint use is to provide far richer contexts than are typically available in the standard psycholinguistics experiment; Altmann (chap. 19, this volume) discusses the role of larger discourse contexts, and Tanenhaus et al. (chap. 18, this volume) investigate language comprehension in conjunction with information from the visual world. In the sections below, two other domains are considered in which questions arise concerning the nature of frequency, context, and activation during language comprehension, particularly during syntactic processing. The first is the nature of individual differences in comprehenders and how these differences appear to affect ambiguity resolution. The second is the nature of the linguistic signal, specifically the time course of the arrival of contextual information and the ambiguity during comprehension. As we will see, both domains add significant complications to the simple story of partial activation and context introduced above. Far from weakening the constraint-based approach, the complications posed by these two domains move the approach forward, revealing new facets of the linguistic representations and activation functions that are pail of syntactic processing.

Individual Differences in Ambiguity Resolution

If ambiguities are resolved through weighing a number of probabilistic constraints, then it is possible that constraint use may vary substantially across individuals, as a function of some differential capacity to use constraints and/or through exposure to different kinds of linguistic input. This would allow us to better specify two central parts of any constraint-based theory: (1) an account of the kinds of constraints comprehenders can or cannot use during language comprehension; and (2) the source of any limitations on constraint use. In investigating what kinds of frequency data comprehenders do or do not encode and use, research into individual differences may reveal that there is not one fixed answer to this question but rather that different comprehenders may use some constraints to different degrees. The source of any such deferences—in different computation abilities across individuals versus different exposure to relevant input—could tell us much about how —and to what extent—probabilistic constraints are used to guide language comprehension. Thus individual differences research may help us explore the nature and limits of constraint use.

The clearest articulation of the role of individual differences in syntactic ambiguity resolution is offered by Just and Carpenter (1992). They suggest that individual differences in Daneman and Carpenter's (1980) reading span task (a test of linguistic working memory capacity) have measurable effects on syntactic ambiguity resolution, in that comprehenders with high reading span scores are better able to use contextual information to resolve syntactic ambiguities than subjects with low reading span scores. They suggested that whereas all subjects would be able to use simple contextual information, only high-span subjects would be able to use subtle contextual constraints during ambiguity resolution. Just and Carpenter tested this claim in a study that investigated comprehenders' use of context in resolving MV/RR ambiguities in favor of the RR interpretation. They found that high-span subjects were sensitive to constraints provided by the animacy of the subject noun in the sentence, whereas low-span subjects were not (cf. Trueswell, Tanenhaus, and Garnsey 1994). It was less clear whether this different sensitivity resulted in different patterns of ambiguity resolution in the two span groups, but several other results confirm Just and Carpenter's claim. First, Connine, Blasko, and Wang (1994) found that high-span subjects were better able than low-span subjects to use prior semantic context to resolve phonemic *dent/tent* ambiguities. Second, Pearlmutter and MacDonald (1995) obtained evidence that high-span subjects were better able to use contextual information when resolving MV/RR ambiguities in favor of the simple MV interpretation. They found that high-span subjects' reading times at the disambiguation were reliably correlated with the plausibility of the MV intransitive interpretation revealed at the disambiguation, relative to alternative interpretations. By contrast, the low-span subjects' reading times showed no correlation with the plausibility of the alternative interpretations of the ambiguity. Low-span subjects were not impervious to all probabilistic information in the signal, however; reading times for both groups of subjects correlated with simple word frequency information that typically influences reading times.

These results reintroduce the question of the source of these individual differences—in different knowledge of the constraints, in different activation functions, or in different computational capacities (see also Kutas and King, chap. 20, this volume). Although the data are not definitive, additional results suggest that some of these alternative explanations are less likely than others. First, Pearlmutter and MacDonald (1995) found that high- and low-span subjects were equally sensitive to the plausibility constraints when the constraints were measured with an off-line rating task. This shows that the low-span subjects were not completely ignorant of the constraints affecting ambiguity resolution for these sentences, but it does not rule out the possibility that high-span subjects are more familiar with subtle constraints than are low-span subjects, so that the constraining information becomes available earlier for high-span subjects.

A second piece of evidence for the source of individual differences comes from a comparison of older and younger adults' abilities to use contextual information to resolve lexical category ambiguities such as *fires*, which may be interpreted as either a noun or a verb. Stevens et al. (1995) examined subjects' abilities to use context to resolve ambiguities in which the crucial context appeared immediately before the ambiguous word. In a cross-modal naming task measuring the early stages of ambiguity resolution, they found that only younger subjects showed good use of context, that the older subjects showed no evidence of being sensitive to contextual information. In an off-line sentence completion task and in cross-modal naming experiments where the contextual information appeared well in advance of the ambiguity, however, both groups showed sensitivity to the contextual information in the stimuli. This pattern of results is interesting in light of other evidence concerning the effects of aging on cognitive processes. Many studies of semantic knowledge (e.g., assessments of vocabulary size) show that older adults equal or outperform college-aged subjects (e.g., Burke and Yee 1984), but older adults have repeatedly been found to perform cognitive operations more slowly than younger subjects (Salthouse 1982). These results suggest that processing speed, including the speed with which activation is passed from one representation to another, may be an important component in the individual differences in context use during ambiguity resolution, at least those differences that appear through the lifespan.

In sum, the individual differences research, while still in its infancy, offers some important information for the investigation of representation and activation during language processing. First, this research again points to the parallels in ambiguity resolution across many different levels of representation; there are now studies pointing to individual differences in use of context in lexical category ambiguities (Stevens, et al. 1995) and syntactic ambiguities (Pearlmutter and MacDonald 1995). Second, this research has implications for questions concerning representation, such as what kinds of information comprehenders can use to guide ambiguity resolution. The individual differences research not only suggests that there may not be one simple answer to such questions but also that the nature of the answer may depend on properties such as speed of activation.

Partial Activation and the Locus of Context

When psychologists think about context effects in cognitive processing, they generally envision a situation in which contextual information is available prior to the target information, where "target information" refers to the information whose processing is of interest in an experiment, such as an ambiguity. The situation in which contextual information precedes the target has dominated research within psycholinguistics, including studies of priming in word recognition and investigations of prior context on lexical and syntactic ambiguity resolution. This situation need not hold within speech perception, where the coarticulatory information in the speech signal is such that identification of a phoneme may be influenced by both preceding and subsequent segments. Here the phoneme to be identified and the subsequent context (the next phoneme) are very close together in time and are even overlapping, given the way that speech is produced. It is therefore not surprising that comprehenders make use of subsequent context in this case, although it is not difficult to imagine situations where subsequent context would have a more limited effect. We have hypothesized that contextual information has its strongest effect when alternative interpretations of an ambiguity are partially activated. This claim yields the prediction that subsequent context should have similar effects to prior context if the subsequent context arrives during the time in which alternative interpretations are partially activated, but it should have little effect if it arrives too late, after frequency information, other contextual information, or competition between alternatives has caused one interpretation to become far more activated than the others. This possibility suggests that studies of subsequent context could be used as a tool for investigating the nature of the activation process, by providing evidence concerning the time course during which subsequent context can constrain the interpretation of an ambiguity. Two investigations are reported below.

Speech Perception   The relationship between degree of ambiguity and effect of context can be seen clearly from a study of subsequent context effects in speech perception. Connine, Blasko, and Hall (1991) examined comprehenders' perception of *dent/tent* phonemic ambiguities that varied on a VOT continuum, such that the stimuli at the ends of the continuum were less ambiguous than stimuli in the middle. When these stimuli were followed by a context that favored one interpretation over the other (e.g., "the ?ent in the fender") they found a pattern of results that clearly replicated the effects

Connine (1987) found with prior context, namely, that subsequent contexts had a reliable effect on identification of the *dent/tent* stimulus when the acoustic signal was ambiguous between *dent* and *rent*, but no effect on identification of the unambiguous stimuli at the ends of the VOT continuum. This result suggests that for ambiguous stimuli, there is a period of competition during which subsequent contextual information can affect the activation of the alternative interpretations.

Connine, Blasko, and Hall also manipulated the time course of the contextual information. They found that context affected the interpretation of their ambiguous stimuli if it arrived within three syllables of the ambiguous word, but that it had no effect if it appeared six syllables after the ambiguous word (e.g., "the ?ent was noticed in the woods"). This result provides information about the period of time over which alternative interpretations may be partially activated, though of course this exact time course would not apply to all ambiguities or modalities; see Potter et al. (1993) and Potter, Stiefbold, and Moryadas (1995) for a similar investigation using visual presentations.

Syntactic Ambiguity Resolution   Given the contention that syntactic ambiguities are triggered by lexical ambiguities, it should be possible to find subsequent-context effects for these ambiguities as well. That is, there should be some period during which alternative interpretations of an ambiguity are partially activated, and competing and subsequent contextual information is able to promote one interpretation over others. In the case of the MV/RR ambiguity in sentences such as "The horse raced past the barn fell," the ambiguity is introduced at "raced," disambiguated at "fell," and the intervening words, "past the barn," could be a site in which postambiguity constraints could appear.

There is evidence for a subtle subsequent-context effect for the MV/RR ambiguity that emerges from English speakers' knowledge about "heavy–NP shift," namely, that long direct object NPs (but not short ones) may appear at the end of a sentence rather than in their traditional location next to the main verb (see note 2). Given that the NP shifting is optional for long direct object NPs and forbidden for shorter ones, the direct object of a verb almost always immediately follows its verb in English, as illustrated in sentences (2–4). In the *a* versions, the verb and direct object are adjacent, but in the *b* versions, a phrase intervenes between the verb and its object. The presence of an intervening phrase in the *b* versions yields sentences that native speakers of English typically judge to be awkward or ungrammatical, indicated here by asterisks. The exception is example (4b), which has a very long direct object NP. The intervening phrases in the *b* versions, such as " yesterday," "into the room," and "to Mary," vary in structure and meaning, but they are all clearly not the direct objects of their verbs and so will be termed *not–direct object* (not–DO) phrases (this terminology was introduced in MacDonald 1994).

(2) a. The dictator captured his enemy yesterday.
    b. *The dictator captured yesterday his enemy.

(3) a. The child carried a toy into the room.
    b. *The child carried into the room a toy.

(4) a. The teacher explained the very complicated geometry problem about the four triangles to Mary.
    b. The teacher explained to Mary the very complicated geometry problem about the four triangles.

The knowledge that a verb and its direct object are typically adjacent in English provides the following constraint to a comprehender who has encountered a verb followed by a not–DO phrase: The verb + not–DO sequence indicates that a direct object is not likely to appear later in the sentence, because NP–shifted very long direct objects, such as in (4b), are very rare in English. In this way, the presence of the not–DO phrase promotes other syntactic structures that do not have a direct object later in the sentence. One of these alternative structures is the reduced relative, as in "The child carried into the room was crying." Here the verb "carried" is followed by the not–DO phrase "into the room". There is no direct object later in the sentence because being a form of passive, the reduced relative has the direct "the child" preceding the verb.

Because the MV/RR ambiguity is triggered at the verb, the not–DO phrase is a form of postambiguity context that might constrain the interpretation of the ambiguity. MacDonald (1994) investigated comprehenders' use of the not–DO context in several self-paced reading experiments. She presented MV/RR ambiguous sentences that were disambiguated with the RR interpretation. Some examples can be seen in (5). All ambiguous sentences contained a not–DO phrase after the ambiguous verb (e.g., "in the coup", "just after dawn"), followed by the disambiguating verb of "was". The nature of the postambiguity context was manipulated at two levels. Example 5a shows the early context condition that provided a very constraining context, in that the very first word after the ambiguous verb (in this case, *in*) clearly signaled a not–DO phrase and thus clearly promoted a reduced relative interpretation. Because the word immediately after the ambiguity is informative, this constraint is likely to arrive while the alternative interpretations of the ambiguity are still in a state of partial activation and competition. Example 5b shows a late context in "just after dawn." In this case, the first few words do not signal clearly that the phrase is not a direct object (e.g., "just" could begin a direct object phrase, as in "captured just one town"). By the time constraining information arrives toward the end of the not–DO phrase, much of the processing of the ambiguity may already be complete, presumably with a more frequent MV interpretation accruing more activation than the RR interpretation. Late constraints should therefore have little effect on ambiguity resolution. This hypothesis was tested by comparing reading times in sentences such as (5a–b) to unambiguous control sentences such as (5c). This

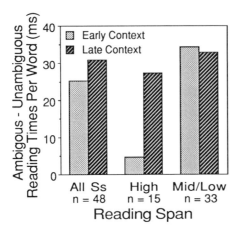

Figure 17.2 Size of ambiguity effect at disambiguation in MacDonald (1994), experiment 1. Right portion of figure shows subjects' performance within span group, which is not reported in MacDonald (1994).

sentence is unambiguous because the verb "overthrown" is unambiguously a past participle tense and forces the reduced relative interpretation.

(5) a. *Early context*: The ruthless dictator captured *in the coup* was hated throughout the country.

b. *Late context*: The ruthless dictator captured *just after dawn* was hated throughout the country.

c. Unambiguous controls: The ruthless dictator overthrown {in the coup / just after dawn} was hated throughout the country.

The critical region for reading times is at the definitive disambiguation "was heated"; an increase in reading times here, in comparison to times for the unambiguous controls, should reflect any difficulty that readers are having with the reduced relative interpretation. The ambiguous-unambiguous differences for the good and poor Context conditions are presented in figure 17.2. The bars at the left of the figure show the data as reported in MacDonald (1994); they reveal only a small, nonsignificant effect of the early/late context manipulation. Both conditions yield reliably longer reading times than the unambiguous control condition; the postambiguity context does not seem to be effective in this case.

The pattern changes, however, when individual differences are considered. Fifteen of the subjects tested in the experiment scored in the high-span range in the Daneman and Carpenter (1980) reading span task, and the rest were in the middle and low ranges. The data on the right of figure 17.2 show the effects of the postambiguity constraint for the two different span groups. The high-span subjects were substantially helped by the early context condition compared to the late context condition, whereas the other subjects showed no differences between the two conditions; both good and poor context conditions yielded longer reading times than unambiguous controls for these subjects. This result indicates that postambiguity context can be used during syntactic ambiguity resolution, but that some subjects may be better able than others to utilize this information, at least for this particular ambiguity and context. The differences between early and late context for the high-span readers also suggests that the time course of activation is such that if the postambiguity context is not available within the first one or two words following the ambiguity, the context will have little effect (see Burgess 1991 for a similar point concerning context that is or is not in the foveal region while fixating on the ambiguous verb during reading). This result is not greatly surprising, given the speed of language processing, but it does suggest the potential for using more precise manipulations of the ambiguity-context interval to chart the time course of activation during ambiguity resolution.

The differences between the low- and high-span subjects underscores the importance of considering individual differences when investigating the nature of the constraints that affect ambiguity resolution. It also makes the point that a simple, processing speed account of these individual differences is not likely to be correct. That is, a simplistic view of differences in processing speed would predict that high-span subjects would more rapidly activate one interpretation of an ambiguity and inhibit others, compared to low-span subjects. If so, high-span subjects would have a smaller window of time during which subsequent context effects could be observed than would low-span subjects, who would have a longer period of partial activation. The opposite result was obtained, however.

This demonstration that subsequent context is useful in syntactic ambiguity resolution, as in speech perception (Connine, Blasko, and Hall 1991), suggests that subsequent context information may be an important constraint on interpretation at many levels of linguistic representation. These postambiguity constraints, which are largely unexplored to date, may prove to be particularly useful in syntactic ambiguity resolution of so-called head-final languages, such as Japanese, in which verbs follow their arguments (subjects, objects, prepositional phrases, etc.) In most accounts of sentence processing, much of which has been developed in the study of English, information from the verb (its meaning, tense, position in the sentence, etc.) is considered crucial for full interpretation of the surrounding phrases, including assigning thematic roles such as Agent and Theme and assigning grammatical roles such as subject and object. From this perspective, a Japanese comprehender encountering a string of nouns and other phrases with no verb until the end of the sentence would seem to be faced with insurmountable syntactic ambiguities while awaiting the verb (Inoue and Fodor, 1995). The fact that Japanese comprehenders are not overwhelmed by ambiguity suggests that this perspective is incorrect. Although work on Japanese sentence processing is limited, it seems likely that a large number of probabilistic constraints are guiding comprehension and that many of these constraints are from subsequent context, for example, constraints that arrive between the introduction of an ambiguous phrase at the start of the sentence and the disambiguation at the sentence-final verb.

17.3 CONCLUSIONS

This chapter has explored the claim that a crucial part of language comprehension, ambiguity resolution, can be viewed as the outcome of constraint satisfaction processes modulating the activation of alternative interpretations of ambiguities. This account was argued to apply as much to syntactic ambiguities as to other types of ambiguity such as phonemic and lexical ambiguities, in contrast to previous accounts that have treated syntactic processing as an autonomous module sharing no architectural characteristics with other levels. The key feature in the extension of the activation account to syntactic processes was a representational claim, that much syntactic information can be represented in the lexicon, so that it may be partially activated like other lexical information.

This activation-based account was shown to be compatible with new research on the roles of individual differences and subsequent context on ambiguity resolution. Indeed, the research was prompted by the constraint-based approach and is not a natural avenue of investigation within a modular framework. Frazier's (1987) universal parsing heuristics do not readily suggest individual differences as a line of inquiry, nor does Frazier's parser, which immediately adopts one interpretation at the introduction of a syntactic ambiguity, readily provide a role for probabilistic postambiguity contexts in ambiguity resolution. The existence of this new research is noteworthy in light of claims that constraint-based accounts are too unconstrained to provide a good basis for further research in syntactic processing (e.g., Clifton and Ferreira 1989). The research presented here, however, clearly shows that the constraint-based framework can provide a basis for detailed exploration into syntactic processing operations, and it also demonstrates that there are observable limits on the use of probabilistic constraints, such that constraint use may vary across individuals and across the time course of processing. Further exploration of these limits should continue to illuminate the nature of the representations and processes that constitute syntactic comprehension.

NOTES

This research was supported by National Science Foundation grant DBS-9120415. Correspondence should be directed to M. C. MacDonald, Hedco Neuroscience Building, University of Southern California, Los Angeles, CA 90089-2520. E-mail: mcm@gizmo.usc.edu.

1. The competing claims of interactive activation models and the FLMP model have been tested in several domains, including speech perception (Massaro 1989 and chap. 16, this volume; McClelland 1991). Because syntactic processing research has focused on the use of

graded constraints, a claim that is compatible with both the interactive and FLMP architectures, syntactic ambiguity resolution has not yet provided any evidence that clearly favors one or the other type of model.

2. Stallings, MacDonald, and O'Seaghdha (1995) have provided some suggestive data supporting the hypothesis that syntactic structures may be activated. They investigated the phenomenon of "heavy–NP shift," namely, that it is grammatical in English to place a long (or "heavy") direct object noun phrase (NP) either directly after the verb (which is the obligatory location for short direct object NPs) or later in the sentence, after some other constituent, such as a prepositional phrase (PP). Such "shifted" structures (e.g. "Mary revealed [to Sue]$_{PP}$ [her secret ambitions to be president of the company]$_{NP}$) have the same meaning and the same lexical representations (such as the same verb tense) as the "unshifted" structure in which the direct object is adjacent to the verb ("Mary revealed [her secret ambitions to be president of the company]$_{NP}$ [to Sue]$_{PP}$"). The essential difference between the two sentence types is in the *phrase structure*, specifically the ordering of the two phrases. If words activate alternative X-bar structures as a function of the frequency with which they have previously participated in the structures, then English speakers' usage and comprehension of shifted versus unshifted structures should be a function of the frequency with which the words to be uttered or comprehended have previously participated in the alternative structures. Stallings, MacDonald, and O'Seaghda's results support this position. They found that in on-line production studies where subject uttered sentences composed of phrases that appeared on a computer screen, in off-line rating tasks where subjects rated the acceptability of shifted versus unshifted structures, and in analyses of text corpora, there were substantial effects of the frequency with which a sentence's main verb had previously participated in shifted versus unshifted structures. Verbs with higher shifting frequencies were more likely to elicit shifted structures in spoken and written production, compared to verbs that rarely participate in shifted structures; in the rating task, shifted structures were rated as better sentences when they contained a verb with a higher shifting frequency than when they contained a verb with low shifting frequency. These results suggest that the frequency of a word's participation in various syntactic structures (shifting frequency) is being encoded in the representation of the verbs, supporting the claim that syntactic representations can themselves be activated (MacDonald, Pearlmutter, and Seidenberg 1994a).

REFERENCES

Altmann, G. T. M., and Steedman, M. (1988). Interaction with context during human sentence processing. *Cognition, 30,* 191–238.

Bever, T. G. (1970). The cognitive basis for linguistic structure. In J. R. Hayes (Ed.), *Cognition and the development of language.* New York: Wiley.

Britt, M. A., Perfetti, C. A., Garrod, S., and Rayner, K. (1992). Parsing in discourse: Context effects and their limits. *Journal of Memory and Language, 31,* 293–314.

Burgess, C. (1991). *Interaction of semantic, syntactic and visual factors in syntactic ambiguity resolution.* Ph.D. diss., University of Rochester.

Burke, D. and Yee, P. L. (1984). Semantic priming during sentence processing by young and older adults. *Developmental Psychology, 20,* 903–910.

Chomsky, N. (1982) *Lectures on government and binding,* Dordrecht: Foris.

Clifton, C. and Ferreira, F. (1989). Ambiguity in context. *Language and Cognitive Processes, 4,* SI 77–104.

Connine, C. M. (1987). Constraints on interactive processes in auditory word recognition: The role of sentence context. *Journal of Memory and Language, 26,* 527–538.

Connine, C., Blasko, D. G., and Hall, M. (1991). Effects of subsequent sentence context in auditory word recognition: Temporal and linguistic constraints. *Journal of Memory and Language, 30,* 234–250.

Connine, C. M., Blasko, D. G., and Wang, J. (1994). Vertical similarity in spoken word recognition: Multiple lexical activation, individual differences, and the role of sentence context. *Perception and Psychophysics, 56,* 624–636.

Connine, C., Ferreira, F., Jones, C., Clifton, C., and Frazier, L. (1984). Verb frame preferences: Descriptive norms. *Journal of Psycholinguistic Research, 13,* 307–319.

Daneman, M., and Carpenter, P. A. (1980). Individual differences in working memory and reading. *Journal of Verbal Learning and Verbal Behavior, 19,* 450–466.

Duffy, S. A., Morris, R. K., and Rayner, K. (1988). Lexical ambiguity and fixation times in reading. *Journal of Memory and Language, 27,* 429–226.

Ferreira, F., and Clifton, C. (1986). The independence of syntactic processing. *Journal of Memory and Language, 25,* 348–368.

Fodor, J. A. (1983). *Modularity of mind.* Cambridge, MA: MIT Press.

Ford, M., Bresnan, J., and Kaplan, R. M. (1982). A competence-based theory of syntactic closure. In J. Bresnan (Ed.), *The mental representation of grammatical relations,* 727–796. Cambridge, MA: MIT Press.

Forster, K. I. (1979). Levels of processing and the structure of the language processor. In W. Cooper and E. Walker (Eds.), *Sentence processing: Psycholinguistic studies presented to Merrill Garrett.* Hillsdale, NJ: Erlbaum.

Francis, W. N., and Kucera, H. (1982). *Frequency analysis of English usage: Lexicon and grammar.* Boston: Houghton-Mifflin.

Frazier, L. (1987). Sentence processing: A tutorial review. In M. Coltheart (Ed.), *Attention and performance XII: The psychology of reading.* Hillsdale, NJ: Erlbaum.

Frazier, L. (1994). Sentence (re-)analysis. Unpublished manuscript, University of Massachusetts.

Inoue, A. and Fodor, J. D. (1995). Information-paced parsing of Japanese. In R. Mazuka, and N. Nagai (Eds.), *Japanese Sentence Processing.* Hillsdale, NJ: Erlbaum.

Just, M. A., and Carpenter, P. A. (1992). A capacity theory of comprehension: Individual differences in working memory. *Psychological Review, 98,* 122–149.

Kawamoto, A. (1993). Nonlinear dynamics in the resolution of lexical ambiguity: A parallel distributed processing account. *Journal of Memory and Language, 32,* 474–516.

MacDonald, M. C. (1994). Probabilistic constraints and syntactic ambiguity resolution. *Language and Cognitive Processes, 9,* 157–201.

MacDonald, M. C., Pearlmutter, N. J., and Seidenberg, M. S. (1994a). The lexical nature of syntactic ambiguity resolution. *Psychological Review, 101,* 676–703.

MacDonald, M. C., Pearlmutter, N. J., and Seidenberg, M. S. (1994b). Syntactic ambiguity resolution as lexical ambiguity resolution. In C. Clifton, L. Frazier, and K. Rayner (Eds.), *Perspectives on sentence processing.* Hillsdale, NJ: Erlbaum.

Massaro, D. W. (1989) Testing between the TRACE model and the fuzzy logical model of perception. *Cognitive Psychology, 21,* 398–421.

McClelland, J. L. (1987). The case for interactionism in language processing. In M. Coltheart (Ed.), *Attention and performance XII: The psychology of reading,* 3–36. London: Erlbaum.

McClelland, J. L. (1991). Stochastic interactive processes and the effect of context on perception. *Cognitive Psychology, 23,* 1–44.

McClelland, J. L., and Rumelhart, D. E. (1981). An interactive activation model of context effects in letter perception: 1. An account of basic findings. *Psychological Review, 88,* 375–407.

Ni, W., and Crain, S. (1990). How to resolve structural ambiguities. In *Proceeding of the 20th annual meeting of the North Eastern Linguistic Society,* 414–427. Amherst, MA: Graduate Linguistics Students Association.

Pearlmutter, N. J., and MacDonald, M. C. (1992). Plausibility and syntactic ambiguity resolution. In *Proceedings of the 14th Annual Conference of the Cognitive Society,* 498–503. Hillsdale, NJ: Erlbaum.

Pearlmutter, N. J., and MacDonald, M. C. (1995). Individual differences and probabilistic constraints in syntactic ambiguity resolution. *Journal of Memory and Language, 34,* 521–542.

Potter, M. C., Moryadas, A., Abrams, I., and Noel, A. (1993). Word perception and misperception in context. *Journal of Experimental Psychology: Learning, Memory and Cognition, 19,* 3–22.

Potter, M. C., Stiefbold, and Moryadas, A. (1995). Word selection in reading sentences: Preceding versus following contexts. Unpublished manuscript, MIT.

Rayner, K., Carlson, M., and Frazier, L. (1983). The interaction of syntax and semantics during sentence processing. *Journal of Verbal Learning and Verbal Behavior, 22,* 358–374.

Rayner, K., Garrod, S., and Perfetti, C. A. (1992). Discourse influences during parsing are delayed. *Cognition, 45,* 109–139.

Salthouse, T. A. (1982). *Adult cognition: An experimental psychology of human aging.* New York: Springer.

Simpson, G. B. (1984). Lexical ambiguity and its role in models of word recognition. *Psychological Bulletin, 96,* 316–340.

Spivey-Knowlton, M. J., Trueswell, J. C., and Tanenhaus, M. K. (1993). Context and syntactic ambiguity resolution. *Canadian Journal of Experimental Psychology, 47,* 276–309.

Stallings, L., MacDonald, M. C., and O'Seaghdha, P. G. (1995). Constraints on phrase order: Effects of length and verb disposition. Submitted.

Stevens, K., MacDonald, M. C., Schuster, S. P., and Harm, M. (1995). Aging and the use of context in ambiguity resolution. Poster presented at the Seventh Annual CUNY Conference on Human Sentence Processing, Tucson, Arizona.

Swinney, D. A. (1979). Lexical access during sentence comprehension: (Re)consideration of context effects. *Journal of Verbal Learning and Verbal Behavior, 18,* 645–659.

Tabossi, P., Spivey-Knowlton, M. J., McRae, K., and Tanenhaus, M. K. (1994). Semantic effects on syntactic ambiguity resolution: Evidence for a constraint-based resolution process. In C. Umiltà and M. Moscovitch (Eds.), *Attention and performance XV,* 589–616. Cambridge, MA: MIT Press.

Taraban, R., and McClelland, J. L. (1988). Constituent attachment and thematic role assignment in sentence processing: Influences of content-based expectations. *Journal of Memory and Language, 27,* 597–632.

Trueswell, J. C., and Tanenhaus, M. K. (1991). Tense, temporal context, and syntactic ambiguity resolution. *Language and Cognitive Processes, 6,* 339–350.

Trueswell, J. C., and Tanenhaus, M. K. (1992). Consulting temporal context during sentence comprehension: Evidence from the monitoring of eye movements in reading. In *14th Annual Conference of the Cognitive Science Society,* 492–497.

Trueswell, J. C., and Tanenhaus, M. K. (1994). Toward a lexicalist framework of constraint-based syntactic ambiguity resolution. In C. Clifton, L. Frazier and K. Rayner (Eds.), *Perspectives on sentence processing*, 155–179. Hillsdale, NJ: Erlbaum.

Trueswell, J. C., Tanenhaus, and Garnsey, S. M. (1994). Semantic influences on parsing: Use of thematic role information in syntactic disambiguation. *Journal of Memory and Language, 33,* 285–318.

Trueswell, J. C., Tanenhaus, M. K., and Kello, C. (1993). Verb-specific constraints in sentence processing: Separating effects of lexical preference from garden paths. *Journal of Experimental Psychology: Learning, Memory, and Cognition, 19,* 528–553.

18 Using Eye Movements to Study Spoken Language Comprehension: Evidence for Visually Mediated Incremental Interpretation

Michael K. Tanenhaus, Michael J. Spivey-Knowlton, Kathleen M. Eberhard, and Julie C. Sedivy

ABSTRACT

When subjects followed spoken instructions to touch or manipulate real objects (e.g., "Pick up the candle"), their eye movements to objects in the visual display were closely time-locked to referential expressions in the instructions. Subjects established reference incrementally, making an eye movement to the target object as soon as sufficient linguistic information was available to identify the referent from among the visual alternatives. Thus, with well-defined tasks, eye movements can be used to monitor the rapid mental processes that accompany spoken language comprehension in natural contexts. Under these conditions, visual context clearly affected the processing of the linguistic message itself, including the resolution of temporary ambiguities within individual words. The speed with which linguistic and nonlinguistic information are integrated is interpreted as strong support for models where multiple constraints are simultaneously coordinated during ongoing comprehension.

18.1 INTRODUCTION

This chapter reports initial results from a project in which we are using eye movements to monitor the rapid mental processes that accompany spoken language comprehension in simple well-defined behavioral tasks, such as following instructions to manipulate real objects. Before turning to the details of this work, let us briefly place the program of research in the context of current work on the integration of information in language processing.

Since George Miller's classic studies in the early 1960s (e.g., Miller 1962), most work on sentence processing has been rooted in what Clark (1992) has called the "language-as-product" tradition (for a recent review, see Tanenhaus and Trueswell, 1995). Research in this tradition has focused primarily on how readers and listeners recover the linguistic structure of a written sentence or a spoken utterance.

An important consequence of linguistic input unfolding over time is that words and sentences typically contain brief ambiguities. As a result, ongoing comprehension necessarily involves ambiguity resolution. For example, the beginning of the spoken word "candy" is consistent with several lexical alternatives, including the word "candle." Similarly, in the unambiguous sentence "Put the apple on the towel," in which the prepositional phrase "on the towel" specifies the destination or goal where the apple is to be put, the phrase is also temporarily consistent with an interpretation in which it modifies "the apple," as it does in the sentence "Put the apple on the towel into the box."

The central issue that arises in ambiguity resolution is how readers and listeners integrate different types of constraints to resolve the numerous local ambiguities that arise during language processing. One influential hypothesis, which has largely dominated research during the last decade or so, is that linguistic information is initially structured by a modular grammatical processing system that is "encapsulated" from information provided by other cognitive and perceptual systems (Fodor 1983; Frazier 1987), much as early visual processing is often claimed to be structured by autonomous processing modules (Cavanagh 1989; Livingstone and Hubel 1983; Marr 1982). In contrast, more "interactive" or constraint-based models have emphasized that multiple constraints are simultaneously integrated to arrive at partial interpretations as the input unfolds (e.g., Rumelhart 1977; McClelland 1987). For more detailed discussion, see the chapters in this volume by Altmann (chap. 19), MacDonald (chap. 17), and Massaro (chap. 16).

Modular and constraint-based models are most sharply distinguished by when context is used during the comprehension process. In modular models, initial processing within a module is assumed to take place independently of context. In contrast, interactive models assume that context affects even the earliest moments of language processing. These different views have led to numerous empirical studies examining the time course with which different types of context influence linguistic processing (for recent reviews, see MacDonald, Pearlmutter, and Seidenberg 1994; Spivey-Knowlton, Trueswell, and Tanenhaus 1993). This work relies heavily on on-line experimental methods that can provide fine-grained temporal information about the comprehension process.

The notion of context dominating this literature is primarily that of a "correlated" constraint. Correlated constraints for an ambiguity of a certain type occur when context provides information from another domain that is strongly correlated with one of the alternatives, for example, semantic information that is potentially relevant for resolving a syntactic ambiguity. Although a number of studies in the 1980s seemed to show that correlated constraints affected ambiguity resolution only after an initial encapsulated stage of processing, recent results suggest a different picture, as discussed by MacDonald (chap. 17, this volume). For example, local semantic constraints as well as constraints provided by the discourse context of an utterance, have clear effects on even the earliest moments of syntactic processing. However, these contextual effects are mediated by local factors, such as lexical frequency, so that contextual effects are strongest when local biases are weakest. Previous failures to find effects of context thus appear to be due to a combination of weak constraints and strong local biases.

Given the central role context has played in recent work, it is important to note that the view of context dominating the language-as-product tradition differs from the view of context within a second tradition in language processing research, which focuses on the pragmatics of language use. According to this "language-as-action" tradition, the interpretation of an utterance, including the interpretation of individual words, is inextricably contextualized to a particular time, place, and circumstance (Clark 1992). Crucially, from the language-as-action perspective, the linguistic processing that accompanies comprehension cannot be divorced from the relevant behavioral context in which comprehension takes place.

Work in the language-as-product and language-as-action traditions has not proceeded completely independently. For example, the referential theory of garden paths developed by Altmann and his colleagues (Altmann and Steedman 1988), which emphasizes the importance of pragmatic discourse context for ambiguity resolution, is largely compatible with the language-as-action view (see Altmann, chap. 19, this volume). Nonetheless, work in sentence processing has largely ignored the richer notion of behavioral context that is central to the language-as-action tradition.

The mode of language processing studied by researchers in the language-as-product and language-as-action traditions is also quite different. In the language-as-action tradition, researchers often study interactive conversation in clearly circumscribed behavioral contexts, in which the linguistic expressions have referents in the real world, and in which the participants have clearly defined behavioral goals. By contrast, the typical language-as-product study uses written language with single sentences or short texts in which the linguistic expressions do not have real-world referents and the subjects are told to "comprehend" the linguistic input, but not actually to use it for a goal-directed behavior.

The differences in what mode of language processing a researcher chooses to study stem partly from theoretical biases. For example, if one assumes that recovering the linguistic structure of a sentence proceeds for the most part independently of behavioral context, then it makes little sense to study stimuli more complex than individual sentences. However, another, more practical reason for why scientists interested in information integration in language processing have focused on "decontextualized" language is that the experimental methods most informative about the time course of spoken language comprehension cannot be easily used in more natural contexts. One of the primary goals of the current work was to use eye movements to develop such a methodology.

Putting methodological considerations aside, there are also important theoretical reasons for studying language processing with well-defined comprehension tasks in situations where the language has clear real-world referents, as a complement to more traditional psycholinguistic studies. We will focus on two of these reasons.

The first reason is that the relative weighting of local factors, such as lexical frequency, compared to more global contextual constraints, may differ, depending on the mode of language processing. We can illustrate this point using the example, "Bill put the apple on the towel into the box." When readers and listeners encounter the second preposition "into" in this sentence they are momentarily confused because they initially assume that "on the towel" specifies the destination where the apple is to be put. In the type of constraint-based lexicalist model that we and MacDonald have been developing, this bias can be understood as arising from the fact that "put" always occurs with a goal argument specifying a location. Moreover, the goal argument is typically introduced by a preposition. Thus, for the fragment "put the apple on," the system will be strongly biased to treat "on" as introducing the goal.

Experiments using reading time measures have found that confusion at the second preposition persists even when the preceding discourse context introduces two potential referents for "the apple" (Britt 1994), thus giving the reader a reason to expect that "the apple" will be modified in order for its referent to be made clear, as in the following example:

There are two apples and a box. One apple is on a towel and the other is on a napkin. Bill put the apple on the towel into the box.

This result might mean that strong lexical constraints necessarily have more immediate effects on language processing than referential context established by prior discourse context. On the other hand, it could mean that the context needs to be maintained in memory and thus may not be immediately accessible. In addition, for the context to be maximally effective, the reader would have to assume that it will be relevant to the ambiguous linguistic expression the moment that expression is first encountered.

Now consider a situation in which a person is being told to rearrange the same few objects on a coffee table and to "put the apple on the towel into the box." "Put" now refers to an action that must involve one of the objects, "the apple" has real-world referents that can be interrogated as the expression is heard, and the need to determine which apple is to be moved develops prior to hearing the word "on." Under these conditions, referential context might well have stronger and more immediate effects.

Note, we are not suggesting that results from one type of situation are giving us the "right" answer about how context is used in language processing and that results from another situation are misleading. Rather, models of language processing must be able to naturally accommodate both types of results. This is particularly important, given that the prevailing bias in the field has been to appeal to information encapsulation to explain why the effects of certain types of contextual information are delayed.

The second reason for examining language processing in natural contexts is that focusing only on decontextualized language encourages us to couch our explanations primarily in terms of linguistic forms. For example, it becomes easy to think of ambiguity as a problem the language system needs to solve on the way to having a unified representation, and of context as useful primarily for resolving local indeterminacy. This leads us to tacitly accept a form of "perceptual encapsulation" in which the product of language perception is a unified representation that subserves cognition and action. While this view of language processing could be correct, it is important to note that the traditional view of perception is being strongly challenged in recent work in vision and in the neurosciences (cf. Ballard, Hayhoe, and Pook 1995, and references therein; and Goodale, chap. 15, this volume). The alternative view is that the visual system constructs representations closely tied to the particular behavioral tasks the brain is trying to accomplish. Thus one cannot understand the visual system without taking into account the relevant behavioral context. This contextualized view of visual processing seems broadly compatible with some of the fundamental tenets of the language-as-action tradition.

If this line of argument is correct, it will be important to study language processing with well-defined behavioral tasks in circumscribed situations, because these are the conditions in which we have the best chance of understanding what the relevant context is. Although these ideas are broadly compatible with the class of constraint-based models we think is most promising, they also suggest that the strength of a correlated constraint cannot be determined in isolation from the relevant behavioral context for comprehension (Clark and Carlson 1982).

This argument, we should note, runs counter to the prevailing bias in the language-as-product tradition, namely, that the most general explanations will come from understanding comprehension independently of the constraining behavioral context. It also directly challenges Fodor's (1983) claim that progress in language processing will come from understanding it as an encapsulated "input system."

The research program we have been developing uses eye movements to study spoken language comprehension in simple tasks where subjects follow instructions to manipulate real objects. Before reaching for an object, people typically move their eyes to fixate on it (e.g., Abrams et al. 1991). We reasoned that if subjects were instructed to manipulate objects in a work space, then their eye movements to relevant objects might be closely time-locked to referential expressions in the spoken instructions. If so, then eye movements could be used to monitor the rapid mental processes that accompany spoken language comprehension, making it possible to investigate spoken language processing in natural behavioral contexts where the language has clear real-world referents. Having subjects perform an action also creates a well-defined behavioral context in which the information provided by the visual context is clearly relevant.

We hypothesized that, under these conditions, subjects would seek to establish reference with respect to their behavioral goals incrementally as the spoken language unfolded, rapidly integrating the spoken language with the information provided by the visual context. We were also interested in determining whether referentially relevant visual context would influence the earliest moments of linguistic processing. If so, this would provide strong evidence against the hypothesis that fully encapsulated processing modules play a central role in language processing.

18.2   EXPERIMENT 1: VISUALLY MEDIATED COMPETITOR EFFECTS

In a classic set of experiments, Marslen-Wilson (1987) demonstrated that, to a first approximation, recognition of a word occurs shortly after the auditory input uniquely specifies a lexical candidate. For polysyllabic words, this is often prior to the end of the word. For example, the word "elephant" would be recognized shortly after the phoneme /f/. Prior to that, the auditory input would be consistent with the beginnings of several words, including "elephant," "elegant," "eloquent," and "elevator." Thus recognition of a spoken word is strongly influenced by the words it is phonetically similar to, especially those which share initial phonemes. Marslen-Wilson referred to the set of lexical candidates activated in the same phonetic environment as a "cohort" (for review, see Marslen-Wilson 1987).

Evidence from several experimental paradigms indicates that these candidates are partially activated as a word is being processed. For example, cross-modal lexical priming experiments demonstrate that semantic information associated with cohort members is temporarily activated as a word unfolds. The prior context of the utterance and subsequent input provide evidence that is used to evaluate the competing alternatives (cf., Marslen-Wilson 1987; Zwisterlood 1988). Although current models differ in how they account for these data, nearly all models incorporate the idea that the time it takes to recognize a word depends on a set of potential lexical candidates (See Cutler 1995 for a recent review).

This experiment had two goals. The first goal was to determine how closely time-locked eye movements to a target object would be to the name of the object in a spoken instruction. The second goal was to determine whether the presence of a "competitor" object with a similar name would influence eye movement latencies to the target object. A visually mediated "competitor" or "cohort" effect would provide strong evidence that lexically based information associated with lexical candidates is partially activated. In addition, it would demonstrate that relevant visual context affects even the early moments of spoken language processing.

Method

Subjects   Eight subjects participated in the experiment.

Apparatus   Eye movements were monitored using an Applied Scientific Laboratories (ASL) eye tracker. The ASL is a head-mounted, video-based system. Monocular eye position is determined by monitoring the locations of the center of the pupil and the first Purkinje image. The pupil is illuminated with an infrared light-emitting diode (IR LED) coaxial with a video "eye camera" placed above an IR reflecting beam splitter. The beam splitter allows the subject an unobstructed view of the visual field, and eye movements can be tracked over the entire range. The locations of the center of the pupil and the first Purkinje image are calculated at video rates (60 Hz). The accuracy of the ASL's eye-in-head record is about a degree over a range of ± 20 degrees. The ASL provides two data streams: a digital record containing monocular eye-in-head values and a video record on which crosshairs indicating gaze position are superimposed on the subject's field of view provided by a color (charge-coupled device) scene camera mounted on the headband. The video record was coordinated with the audio record for all data analysis.

Procedure   Subjects were seated in front of a 1-meter-square horizontal work space that was divided into 25 squares, as shown in figure 18.1. Subjects were seated at arm's length from the work space. The entire work space subtended about 60 degrees of visual angle horizontally, and about 40 degrees vertically (due to foreshortening). A black cross in the center square served as a fixation point.

Each trial block consisted of ten instruction sets. An instruction set directed the subject to pick up an object and then put it in the square above or below another object. A sample instruction set is given in example 1:

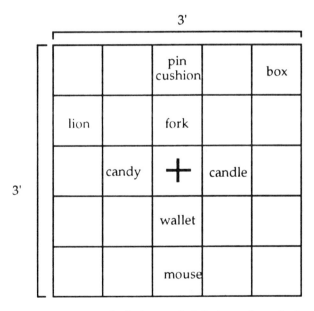

Figure 18.1   Example display in which both members of cohort pair are present in work space. Sample instruction is "Look at the cross. Pick up the candle. Now hold it over the cross. Now put it above the candy."

(1) a. Look at the cross.
     b. Pick up the candle.
     c. Now hold it over the cross.
     d. Now put it above the candy.

Four pairs of critical objects with names that were phonetically similar until late in the word (*candy/candle*, *car/carton*, *penny/pencil*, and *doll/dolphin*) were the critical stimuli. Six trial blocks were generated for each critical cohort pair. Each object appeared without its cohort member on two trial blocks and both objects were present on the other four trial blocks. A trial block consisted of two or three instructions that referred to critical objects plus instructions that referred to the filler objects.

Each subject was assigned to twelve trial blocks generated from two of the four cohort pairs. For the "pick up" instruction, each subject was presented with a total of eight trials on which a cohort member occurred without its competitor, and sixteen trials on which the competitor was present. For trials involving cohort members, the objects were always in one of the six squares that shared a boundary to the left or the right of the center square.

Figure 18.1 shows the work space at the beginning of the instruction set given in example (1). The instructions and the positions of the objects were varied to prevent strategies; in particular, we avoided creating any contingencies that would have resulted in predictable instructions.

A session began with a calibration routine to map eye-in-head coordinates to scene camera coordinates. Calibration was checked after each instruction set, and, if necessary, minor adjustments were made. At the start of a trial block, ten objects were placed in squares on the board, and the experimenter named each object once during a calibration check. The objects not used on that trial block were then removed. This was done to ensure that the subjects began the trial blocks for a cohort pair with equivalent exposure to the names of all of the objects in the set. The experimenter then read the instruction sets from a prepared script.

Results

The data were analyzed using video recordings, with crosshairs indicating the position of the eye superimposed on each frame. The experimenter's voice was recorded on the audio channel of the tape. We matched each video frame, sampled at 30 Hz, to the corresponding 33 ms chunk of the speech stream using a VCR with frame-by-frame playback and synchronized audio. For each of the critical trials, we determined the frame on which the critical word in the instruction began and the frame on which it ended. The mean duration for the cohort members was 300 ms. The frame on which a saccade to the target was *launched* was determined by when the crosshairs left the square with the fixation cross en route to the target object. *Launch time* was defined as the latency from when the target word began until when the saccade to the target was launched. When the first fixation was to an object other than the target, the trial was scored as a *false launch*.

On all of the critical trials, the movement of the hand to pick up the target object was preceded by a saccade to that object. False launches occurred on 33 percent of the trials. For correct trials, the mean launch time for the "pick-up" instruction was 487 ms from the onset of the target word. Saccade latencies were longer when the display contained a competitor (530 ms) than when it did not (445 ms). This difference was reliable, $F(1, 7) = 9.27; p < .02$. If we assume that the interval between a saccade launch and when programming of a saccade began is about 200 ms, then we can estimate that the programming of a saccade to the target object began an average of 55 ms before the end of the word in the noncompetitor condition.

More false launches were made when a competitor was present than when it was absent, but this difference was not reliable (37 percent compared to 29 percent). Of the false launches in the competitor-present condition, 61 percent were to the competitor object. In contrast, in the competitor-absent condition, only 25 percent of the false launches were to the object that occupied the same square as the competitor object in the corresponding competitor-present condition. This difference was reliable in an analysis for six subjects $F(1, 5) = 14.90; p < .02$. Two subjects did not make any false launches in the noncompetitor condition and thus were excluded from the analysis.

The timing of the false launches to the competitor object was also informative. The mean latency when the first eye movement was a false launch to the competitor object was 415 ms, compared to 530 ms when the first launch was to the correct object in the competitor condition and 445 ms to the correct object in the noncompetitor condition. That the mean latency for false launches to competitor objects was as fast as the correct launches in the unambiguous conditions suggests that these eye movements were being programmed while the spoken input was still ambiguous between the target and the competitor.

Additional data were provided by trials on which subjects were instructed to put the object they were holding above a cohort member. A noncohort object could be put above a cohort member ("Now put it [wallet in hand] above the candle") when both the candy and candle were on the board (competitor present) or when just one of the cohort members was on the board (competitor absent). The data for these trials are less reliable than the "pick up" data because there were fewer observations per subject. Nonetheless, it is worth noting that they showed the same pattern. In the competitor-absent condition, latencies with "put above" instructions were 370 ms with 22 percent false launches, compared to 450 ms with 37 percent false launches when the competitor was present.

The "put above" instruction allows for a third condition in which subjects holding the cohort member are instructed to put it above its competitor (e.g., "Now put it [candle in hand] above the candy"). The results for this "in hand" condition patterned with the competitor-present condition. Launch times and the percentage of false launches were 470 ms and 38 percent, respectively. This result suggests that subjects were not adopting a simple strategy to anticipate the next command. The reason is that the competitor effect appeared even when one of the cohort members was in the subject's hand and thus was not a possible target location for a "put above" instruction.

Discussion

Three primary results emerged from this experiment. First, eye movements to the target object were closely time-locked to the linguistic expression referring to that object. Thus the eye movements provide an informative measure of ongoing comprehension. Second, the latency with which the saccades to the target object were launched provides clear evidence that retrieval of lexical information begins before the end of a word. The launch latencies are especially striking because programming of the saccade cannot begin until the referent and its location have been identified with some degree of confidence.

Third, the names of the possible referents in the visual context clearly influenced the speed with which a referent was identified. This demonstrates that the instruction was interpreted incrementally, taking into account the set of relevant referents present in the visual work space. The high rate of false launches to competitors also lends further support to the idea that multiple lexical candidates are activated early on in recognition. That information from another modality influences the early moments of language processing is consistent with constraint-based models of language processing, but problematic for models holding that initial linguistic processing is encapsulated. While proponents of an encapsulated linguistic system might argue that visual influences are not problematic as long as they are restricted to effects on lexical processing, a sharp boundary between lexical and syntactic processing is becoming increasingly difficult to defend, given the type of theoretical framework described by MacDonald (chap. 17, this volume; see also Trueswell and Tanenhaus 1994).

Finally, the relatively high rate of false launches highlights how natural and inexpensive saccadic eye movements are for information gathering. Subjects did not seem to require strong evidence about the correct target before moving their eyes. In contrast, subjects never made "false reaches" with their hand. In fact, the cost of a false launch in terms of delay in eventually selecting the correct target was surprisingly small. When subjects made false launches to a competitor, the mean latency for the final saccade to the correct target was 750 ms, which was only 220 ms longer than when there was not a false launch. This delay corresponds approximately to the time it takes to program an additional eye movement. The frequency of false launches suggests that, in this paradigm, eye movements are launched even when the subject has only partial information. This bodes well for the sensitivity of eye movements as a response measure for examining ongoing processing.

18.3   EXPERIMENT 2: REFERENTIAL NOUN PHRASES

The goal of this experiment was to determine whether subjects would incrementally identify the object referred to in a syntactically complex phrase, simultaneously taking into account both the information provided by the unfolding linguistic input and the set of alternatives present in the visual context. Subjects were instructed to touch one of four blocks mounted on an upright board. The blocks differed along three dimensions: marking, color, and shape. The instructions referred to the block using a noun phrase with adjectives (e.g., "Touch the starred yellow square"). The display determined what word in the noun phrase disambiguated the target block with respect to the visual alternatives.

From a syntactic perspective, adjectives modify the head noun in a noun phrase. Thus one might expect that interpretation of an adjective does not occur until the head noun. However, what is being modified in the interpretation of the utterance is *not* the head noun itself, but rather the entity in the discourse model to which the noun refers. Thus, under conditions where the context circumscribes the domain of referents, interpretation of an adjective could take place as soon as it was encountered. That is, if "yellow" provides disambiguating information, then subjects should make eye movements to the starred yellow square shortly after hearing "yellow."

Method

Subjects   The subjects were five University of Rochester students, who were paid for participating in the experiment.

Materials   The experimental materials consisted of four critical target commands given in example (2):

(2)   a.   Touch the plain red square.
     b.   Touch the plain blue rectangle.
     c.   Touch the starred yellow square.
     d.   Touch the starred pink rectangle.

Each command was given in six types of visual displays. Each display contained four Duplo blocks mounted vertically on a plastic Duplo board. The blocks differed along three dimensions: *marking* (plain or starred), *color*, (red, blue, yellow, and pink) and *shape* (square or rectangle). The six displays for the instruction "Touch the plain red square" are presented in figure 18.2.

The display determined the "point of disambiguation" in the instruction, i.e., which word in the instruction uniquely identified the target block. There

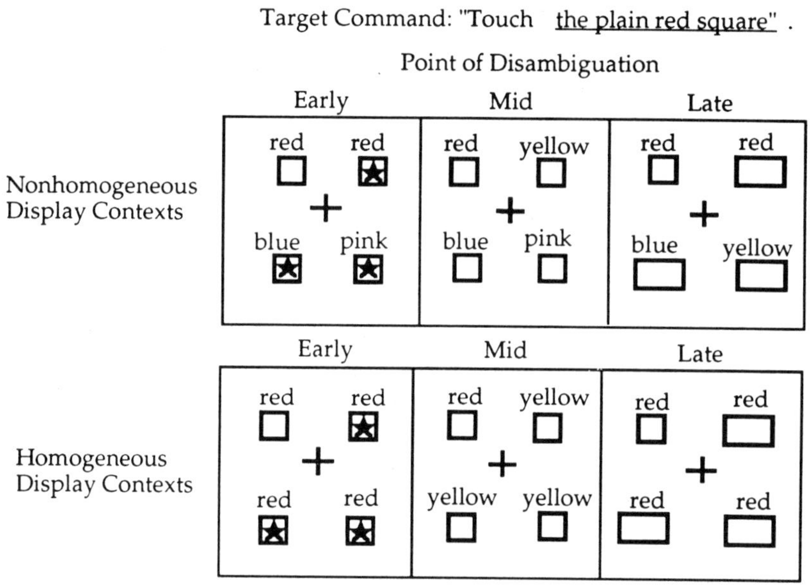

Target Command: "Touch the plain red square" .

Point of Disambiguation

Figure 18.2 Example of displays representing three "point of disambiguation" conditions in homogeneous and nonhomogeneous display contexts for instruction "Touch the plain red square." In early condition, target object is disambiguated by word "plain" in spoken command. In mid condition, target is disambiguated by "red"; in late condition, it is disambiguated by "square." In homogeneous displays, the target is the only unique block in display.

were three points of disambiguation: *early* (after the marking), *mid* (after the color) and *late* (after the noun). The homogeneity of the display was also varied. In nonhomogeneous displays, all of the distractor objects were different, whereas in the homogeneous displays, all of the distractor objects were identical. This manipulation was included in order to see whether definiteness information conveyed by the determiner "the" is helpful in establishing reference. In natural discourse, English speakers use the definite determiner when the referent of the noun phrase can be uniquely identified by the listener. In the homogeneous displays, there is only one unique referent, whereas all of the possible referents are unique in the heterogeneous display. Thus immediate use of definiteness would facilitate identification of the referent in the homogeneous display. We should note, however, that definiteness may be confounded with the complexity of the display. The homogenous displays might be easier to encode because three of the objects were identical.

The 24 test trials were generated by combining each of the four instructions in example 2 with the six display types depicted in figure 18.2. The instructions were embedded in instruction sets that began with "Look at the cross," followed by three further instructions. The critical instruction could appear as the first, second, or third instruction in the set. The test trials were interspersed with 28 filler displays, 12 of which were homogeneous and 16 of which were nonhomogeneous. The filler trials were constructed to avoid strategies by varying the position of the blocks as well as the locations that the subject was instructed to touch.

Subjects were seated at arm's length from the board, approximately 50 cm from the display. The fixation cross covered an area of approximately 1 cm. Squares were approximately 3.5 cm, horizontally and vertically, whereas the rectangles were 3.5 cm by 7 cm. The blocks were on a diagonal, 10 cm from the fixation cross in the orientation shown in figure 18.2.

The subjects were told that each display would be accompanied by three commands that would instruct them to touch one or more of the blocks in the display. Subjects were instructed to follow each command as quickly as possible without making errors. They were instructed to rest their hands in their lap between instructions and look at the fixation cross. The experimenter placed the blocks on the board before each trial and then read the instruction set from a script. The instructions were spoken into a microphone and recorded on Hi8 videotape on a VCR along with the video input from the scene camera.

A session began with a calibration routine to map eye-in-head coordinates to scene camera coordinates. Calibration was checked periodically, and, if necessary, minor adjustments were made. Before each trial block, the experimenter placed the blocks on the board and then read the instruction sets from a prepared script.

Results

The data were analyzed using the same procedure as in experiment 1. Only data from trials in which the subject made an eye movement to the correct target block were included in the analyses. Forty-eight of the 120 observations were eliminated because the subject did not make an eye movement to the target (26 observations), made false launch to a block other than the target (17 observations), or because of experimenter or equipment error (5 observations). The results for each of the six conditions are summarized in figure 18.3.

The launch times for the 72 trials on which the first fixation was to the target were analyzed using a 2 × 3 analysis of variance (ANOVA). Launch times were measured from the beginning of the word "the." There was a main effect of homogeneity of display, $F(1, 4) = 13.03$; $p < .03$ with faster launch times in homogeneous displays than nonhomogeneous displays (730 ms vs. 869 ms). There was also a main effect of Point of Disambiguation, $F(2, 8) = 5.94$, $p < .03$. Planned comparisons showed that launch times were faster in the early disambiguation condition (600 ms) than either the mid condition (830 ms) or the late condition (969 ms), which did not differ from each other (the 95 percent confidence interval was 228 ms). The point of disambiguation effect reflects the fact that subjects initiated eye movements to the target shortly after hearing the word in the instruction that disambiguated it from the other blocks in the display. This is clearly illustrated in figure 18.4, which

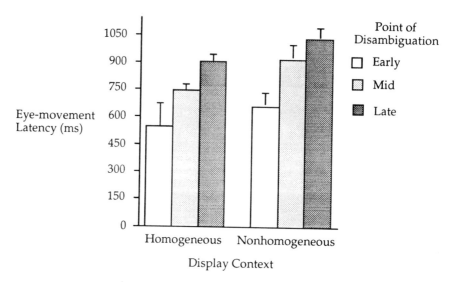

Figure 18.3 Mean latencies for correct eye movement and standard errors, measured from onset of spoken determiner "the."

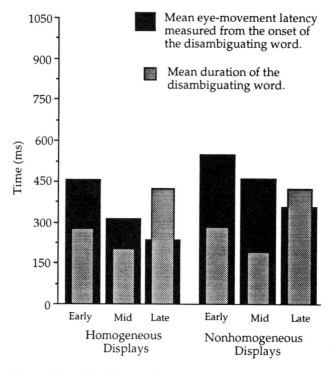

Figure 18.4 Mean latencies for correct eye movements, measured from onset of disambiguating word, and mean duration of disambiguating words in each of six conditions. Mean durations of disambiguating words are superimposed over mean eye movement latencies. In early and mid disambiguation conditions, eye movements occurred shortly after offset of disambiguating word. In late disambiguation conditions, eye movements occurred before offset of disambiguating word.

gives the latency of the launch with respect to the beginning and end of the disambiguating word, for the early, mid, and late conditions. It takes approximately 200 ms from the point that programming of an eye movement is initiated to when the eye begins to move. Thus figure 18.4 shows that subjects often began programming eye movements prior to the end of the word. The latency from the onset of the disambiguating word to when the eye movement was launched decreased throughout the instruction, presumably because constraints became stronger as the instruction unfolded and fewer blocks remained as possible referents prior to the point of disambiguation.

Discussion

The point of disambiguation as determined by the instruction in conjunction with the display clearly influenced when eye movements occurred; moreover, eye movements to the target object began shortly after the disambiguating word. Both of these results strongly support the conclusion that the noun phrase was interpreted incrementally with respect to the referents in the visual model. The strong effects of homogeneity would seem to suggest that subjects also made use of definiteness information. However, we have two serious reservations about the data that make this conclusion premature. First, as we mentioned, homogeneity is likely to be confounded with complexity. Second, an examination of the data from the first and second half of the experimental sessions suggested that at least some of the homogeneity effect was strategic, that is, it developed during the course of the experiment, presumably because subjects learned that "the" in a homogeneous display always referred to the unique referent. In contrast, the point of disambiguation results showed no evidence of being affected by strategies that developed during the experiment.

One surprising result was that subjects often initiated hand movements without first making a saccade to the target. It is likely that a combination of several factors was responsible for why trials without fixations were so frequent. First, the displays contained only four blocks and subjects had plenty of time to scan the display before the instructions. Second, subjects could clearly identify the characteristics of the blocks while maintaining fixation on the cross. Finally, subjects were only required to touch the objects and not to grasp them. Informal experimentation showed that even subjects who frequently touched a block without first fixating on it, would invariably fixate on the block if they were instructed to pick it up.

18.4 EXPERIMENT 3: CONTRASTIVE FOCUS

One of the potential advantages of exploring spoken language in visual contexts is that the paradigm allows one to study model-language interactions that depend upon the prosodic characteristics of the utterance. This experiment investigated the interaction between visual information and linguistic information conveyed by contrastive focus. We presented instructions such as "Touch the LARGE blue triangle," with contrastive stress on the word "large," in the context of visual displays with four shapes that could differ in size, color, and shape. Intuitively, the assertion in the sentence is understood as standing in contrast to an instruction to touch a shape that shares all of the properties of the large blue triangle except for the property marked by contrastive focus, that is, a small blue triangle. The notion of a contrast set is made explicit in recent work in formal semantics (Krifka 1991; Rooth 1985). The basic idea is that a proposition with contrastive focus is understood as standing in contrast with an inferred contrast set.

The hypothesis that a contrast set is established when stress is encountered predicts that eye movements to the referent of a spoken expression should be faster when the expression contains contrastive stress than when it does not. This is because, under the assumption that processing is incremental, contrastive stress should provide disambiguating information. For example, when a subject hears the stressed adjective "LARGE" in the instruction "Touch the LARGE blue triangle," given in the context of the display depicted in figure 18.5, the presence of stress delimits the set of potential target shapes to a large shape with a contrast member that differs from it only in size. Because our displays typically contained only one large shape with a contrast member, there is sufficient information for the subject to resolve the reference shortly after hearing the word "LARGE." However, when large is uttered with neutral stress, additional information is required to resolve reference because there are two large shapes in the display.

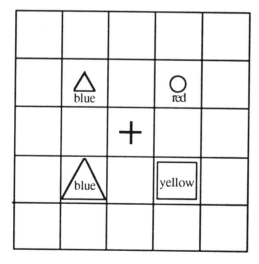

Figure 18.5 Sample display of shapes for contrastive stress experiment. Example instructions accompanying dislay are "Look at the cross. Touch the large/LARGE blue triangle. Now, touch the small one/red circle."

Method

Subjects   The subjects were sixteen University of Rochester students, who were paid for participating in the experiment.

Procedure   Subjects were seated in front of the horizontal work space described in experiment 1; the cross in the center square again served as a fixation point. As in all of the experiments, each instruction set began with the command "Look at the cross."

Figure 18.5 shows the positioning of the shapes with respect to the fixation cross.

The shapes varied in *size* (large or small), *color* (red, blue, and yellow), and *shape* (triangle, square, and circle). There were a total of 32 instruction sets: 16 were experimental trials and 16 were fillers that were designed to minimize the likelihood that subjects would develop strategies; each instruction set contained four instructions. A sample instruction set is given in example (3).

(3)   a.   Look at the cross.
      b.   Touch the LARGE blue triangle.
      c.   Now, touch the small one.
      d.   Now, touch it again.

On the 16 test trials, the display contained two shapes that differed only in size (e.g., a large blue triangle and a small blue triangle), one large shape of a different color and shape (e.g., a large yellow rectangle) and one small shape of a different color and shape (e.g., a small red circle). The first instruction either contained contrastive stress on the size adjective or normal stress (e.g., "LARGE"/"large blue triangle"). Filler trials were constructed to minimize strategies by avoiding any predictable sequences across the experiment.

For six of the subjects we also systematically manipulated whether the display contained a single contrast, as illustrated in figure 18.5, or two potential contrasts. A sample two-contrast display would be one with a large and a small blue triangle as well as a large and small red squares. With two potential contrasts, contrastive stress no longer provides additional information, compared to neutral stress. This condition was included to rule out the possibility that contrastive stress merely served to more strongly direct the subject's attention to the size dimension. If this were the case, then contrastive stress should have similar effects with both the single-contrast and double-contrast displays.

The experimenter placed the shapes on the board and then read the instructions from a script. The experimental session was preceded by three practice trials.

Results

Latency data for trials in which the initial fixation was to the correct shape were analyzed from the videotapes, using the same procedure described for experiment 1. Latencies were measured from the onset of the color adjective. When the size adjective on the first instruction had contrastive stress, latencies to launch a saccade to the referent shape took an average of 431 ms, compared to 545 ms when the first instruction had normal stress. This difference was reliable, $F(1, 15) = 6.17; p < .05$. An ANOVA on the subset of six subjects for whom we included the two-contrast set condition showed a reliable interaction between the type of display and the effect of contrastive stress, $F(1, 5) = 18.04; p < .01$. When the display contained only one potential contrast set, launch latencies were 472 ms with constrastive stress, compared to 635 ms with neutral stress, whereas when the display contained two contrast sets, the launch latencies were 588 ms with contrastive stress and 555 ms with neutral stress.

Discussion

The effects of contrastive stress provide a further example of how reference is established incrementally when the visual context makes the potential referents accessible as the speech is being processed. The results replicate the "point of disambiguation" effect we found in experiment 2. They also support the analysis of contrast sets central to current semantic theories of contrastive focus and show that listeners compute contrast sets immediately when they encounter an expression with contrastive stress.

18.5 GENERAL DISCUSSION

Each of the experiments that we have reported is clearly preliminary in several respects. The experiments require replication with more subjects and with better-controlled conditions. For example, it will be important to use digitized speech in future studies in order to have better control over the acoustic characteristics of the speech and to avoid contamination from possible experimenter biases. It will also be important to use finer-grained analyses of both the eye movement record and the speech stream. We are presently planning extensions and replications with digitized speech and finer temporal resolution using a 200 Hz eye movement camera. Each experiment also raises specific theoretical issues that need to be explored in detail.

Nonetheless, the results clearly demonstrate that when subjects are instructed to manipulate objects, eye movements to the objects are closely time-locked to referential expressions in the spoken instructions. Thus the eye movements can be used to monitor the rapid mental processes that accompany spoken language comprehension, making it possible to investigate spoken language processing in natural behavioral contexts where the language has clear real-world referents. Under these conditions, we found that listeners established reference incrementally as the spoken instruction unfolded, rapidly integrating the information in the visual model with the speech. We also found that the visual context immediately affected how the linguistic input itself was initially processed. Objects in the visual context affected the time course with which temporary ambiguities within unambiguous words were resolved. These results complement the McGurk effect discussed by Massaro (chap. 16, this volume), where visual information is integrated with acoustic information in phoneme identification.

Taken together, these results highlight the incremental and referential nature of spoken language in real-world contexts. In addition, the nearly seamless integration of visual and linguistic information revealed by these experiments provides strong support for models of language processing in which multiple constraints are rapidly integrated.

Our experiments relied heavily on the fact that subjects typically make a saccadic eye movement to an object prior to reaching for it. This raises the possibility that the paradigm might be limited to simple commands with highly restricted displays, thus placing severe limits on the usefulness of the methodology and perhaps the extent to which the results can be generalized.

However, in recent experiments we have explored more complex instructions. Under these conditions, the time to reach for an object is still closely time-locked to its point of disambiguation. More important, subjects make sequences of eye movements that are highly informative about the ongoing comprehension process. For example, in one experiment, a subject was given a complex instruction such as "Put the five of hearts that is below the eight of clubs above the three of diamonds," with a display of seven miniature playing cards, including *two* five of hearts mounted in slots of an upright board.

As the subject heard "the five of hearts," she successively looked at each of the two cards that were potential referents. After hearing "below the," the subject immediately looked at a ten of clubs, which was above the five that she had been fixating on. Before the word "clubs" had ended, her eye moved to interrogate the card above the other five of hearts, which was the eight of clubs, thus identifying that five as the target. The eye then immediately shifted to the target card and remained there until the hand grasped it. Results like these encourage us to believe that the paradigm we have been exploring will be useful for topics ranging from early processes in spoken word recognition to conversational interactions during cooperative problem solving.

We began this chapter by suggesting that in reading studies where context is established by a short linguistic context, contextual effects might be weaker, compared to conditions where the contextual constraint is both clearly relevant and "copresent" with the utterance. We conclude by briefly describing recent evidence we have obtained that provides striking support for this claim.

Spoken instructions containing the ambiguity with perhaps the strongest preference in English were presented to subjects in visual contexts that provided referential support of the type discussed by Altmann (chap. 19, this volume) for either the preferred or the unpreferred interpretation.

As we discussed earlier, the prepositional phrase "on the apple" in a sentence such as "Put the apple on the towel into the box" is briefly ambiguous between an argument of the verb "put" that specifies the destination (goal) where the apple is to be put and a modifier that specifies the location of the apple to be moved. In the absence of context, readers have a strong preference to initially interpret the phrase "on the towel" as the goal, resulting in temporary confusion when a second preposition is encountered, as in example (4):

(4) Put the apple on the towel in the box.

Recall that from a constraint-based lexicalist perspective, this bias arises because the verb "put" almost always occurs with both a noun phrase that specifies its theme (the object to be moved) and a prepositional phrase that specifies the goal location (MacDonald et al. 1994; Spivey-Knowlton and Sedivy 1995). Thus lexical frequency strongly biases the goal reading. It comes as no surprise then that even when a linguistic referential context similar to those described by Altmann (chap. 19, this volume) clearly specifies a need for noun phrase modification (e.g., "There are two apples on the table... Put the apple on the towel..."), readers continue to initially process "on the towel" as the goal (e.g., Britt 1994; Spivey-Knowlton and Sedivy 1995).

However, we found clear effects of referential contexts when similar contexts were presented visually (Tanenhaus et al. 1995). Subjects were presented with instructions similar to the one presented in example 4 in contexts containing four sets of objects. In the one-referent context, the objects were an apple on a towel, a pencil, another towel, and a box. In the two-referent context, the pencil was replaced by a second apple which was on a napkin. Thus "the apple" could refer to either of the two apples, and the phrase "on the towel" provides modifying information that specifies which apple is the correct referent. As a control condition, we used the instruction "Put the apple that's on the towel in the box," in which the word "that" unambiguously indicates that "on the towel" is a modifier.

The eye movement patterns and latencies clearly showed that the first phrase was initially misinterpreted as the destination in the one-referent context, but not in the two-referent context. In the one-referent context, subjects typically looked at the incorrect destination (the towel) shortly after hearing the ambiguous prepositional phrase, whereas they rarely looked at the incorrect destination in the two-referent context. The fixation pattern and timing of eye movements to the target object (the apple on the towel) and the correct destination (the box) clearly differed in the one-referent context for the ambiguous and unambiguous instructions, whereas there were no differences between the ambiguous and unambiguous instructions in the two-referent context. Thus, in a well-circumscribed task, referential context controls the initial interpretation of even the most strongly biased lexical/syntactic ambiguities.

In sum, we have introduced a new paradigm in which spoken language processing can be studied using natural tasks where the language has clear real-world referents, and we have argued that there are important theoretical reasons for examining language processing under these conditions. In our preliminary studies, we find that the linguistic input is rapidly integrated with relevant information provided by the visual context. In addition, we find that the visual context strongly influences even the earliest moments of language processing, providing strong evidence against the idea that linguistic input is initially structured by a fully encapsulated linguistic processing system.

NOTE

This research was partially supported by NICHD grant HD-27206 and NIH resource grant RR06853. Spivey-Knowlton was supported by an NSF predoctoral fellowship and Sedivy by a Canadian SSHRC predoctoral fellowship. We would like to thank Dana Ballard and Mary Hayhoe for encouraging us to use their laboratory and Jeff Pelz for assistance in learning how to use the equipment. Alex Reed, Greg Stevens, and Kenzo Kobashi assisted in data collection. We would like to thank Gerry Altmann and James McClelland for helpful feedback on a preliminary version of this chapter.

REFERENCES

Abrams, R. A., Meyer, D. E., and Kornblum, S. (1990). Eye-hand coordination: Oculomotor control in rapid aimed limb movements. *Journal of Experimental Psychology: Human Perception and Performance, 16,* 248–276.

Altmann, G. T. M., and Steedman, M. (1988). Interaction with context during human sentence processing. *Cognition, 30,* 191–238.

Ballard, D. H., Hayhoe, M. M., and Pook, P. K. (1995). Deictic codes for the embodiment of cognition. Forthcoming.

Britt, M. A. (1994). The interaction of referential ambiguity and argument structure in the parsing of prepositional phrases. *Journal of Memory and Language, 33,* 251–283.

Cavanagh, P. (1989). Multiple analyses of orientation in the visual system. In D. Lam and C. Gilbert (Eds.), *Neural Mechanisms of Visual Perception.* Houston: Gulf Publishing.

Clark, H. H. (1992). *Arenas of language use.* Chicago: University of Chicago Press.

Clark, H. H., and Carlson, T. B. (1981). Context for comprehension. In J. Long and A. Baddeley (Eds.), *Attention and Performance IX.* Hillsdale, NJ: Erlbaum.

Cutler, A. (1995). Spoken language comprehension and production. In J. Miller and P. Eimas (Eds.). *Handbook of Cognition and Perception: Volume 11: Speech, Language, and Communication,* 97–136. New York: Academic Press.

Fodor, J. A. (1983). *Modularity of mind.* Cambridge, MA: MIT Press.

Frazier, L. (1987). Sentence processing: A tutorial review. In M. Coltheart (Ed.), *Attention and performance XII.* Hove, England: LEA.

Krifka, M. (1991). A compositional semantics for multiple focus constructions. *Proceedings of Semantics and Linguistic Theory* (SALT) 1, Cornell University Working Papers 11.

Livingstone, M., and Hubel, D. (1983). Specificity of cortico-cortical connections in monkey striate cortex. *Nature 304,* 531 (1983).

MacDonald, M. C., Pearlmutter, N., and Seidenberg, M. S. (1994). The lexical nature of syntactic ambiguity. *Psychological Review, 101,* 676–703.

Marr, D. (1982). *Vision.* New York: Freeman.

Marslen-Wilson, W. D. (1987). Functional parallelism in spoken word recognition. *Cognition, 25,* 71–102.

Matin, E., Shao, K. C., and Boff, K. R. (1993). Saccadic overhead: Information processing time with and without saccades. *Perception and Psychophysics, 53,* 372–380.

McClelland, J. (1987). The case for interactionism in language processing. In M. Coltheart (Ed.), *Attention and Performance XII.* Hove, England: LEA.

Miller, G. (1962). Some psychological studies of grammar. *American Psychologist, 17,* 748–762.

Rooth, M. (1985). *Association with focus.* Ph.D. diss. University of Massachusetts at Amherst.

Rumelhart, D. (1977). Toward an interactive model of reading. In S. Dornic (Ed.), *Attention and Performance VI.* Hillsdale, NJ: Erlbaum.

Spivey-Knowlton, M. J., and Sedivy, J. (1995). Parsing attachment ambiguities with multiple constraints. *Cognition, 55,* 227–267.

Spivey-Knowlton, M. J., Trueswell, J. C., and Tanenhaus, M. K. (1993). Contexts effects in syntactic ambiguity resolution: Discourse and semantic influences in parsing reduced relative clauses. *Canadian Journal of Experimental Psychology, 47,* 276–309.

Tanenhaus, M. K., Spivey-Knowlton, M. J., Eberhard, K. M., and Sedivy, J. C. (1995). Integration of visual and linguistic information in spoken language comprehension. *Science, 268,* 1632–1634.

Tanenhaus, M. K., and Trueswell, J. C. (1995). Sentence comprehension. In J. Miller and P. Eimas (Eds.). *Handbook of Cognition and Perception: Volume 11: Speech, Language, and Communication,* 217–262. New York: Academic Press.

Trueswell, J., and Tanenhaus, M. (1994). Toward a lexicalist constraint-based framework of syntactic ambiguity resolution. In C. Clifton, L. Frazier, and K. Rayner (Eds.), *Perspectives on Sentence Processing.* Hillsdale, NJ: Erlbaum.

Zwitserlood, P. (1988). The locus of the effects of sentential semantic context in spoken word processing. *Cognition, 32,* 25–64.

19 Accounting for Parsing Principles: From Parsing Preferences to Language Acquisition

Gerry T. M. Altmann

ABSTRACT

The predominant trend in sentence-processing research, and syntactic ambiguity resolution, has been to consider sentence processing as an isolated process, divorced from the (conversational and real-world) contexts within which sentences are produced and comprehended. In this chapter I adopt an alternative approach and assume that sentence processing cannot be considered apart from the processes responsible for interpreting the real-world context. Specifically, I suggest that the adult behaviors we see concerning the resolution of syntactic ambiguity reflect an attentional mechanism driven, in part, by processes responsible for establishing the mapping between language and world. The origins of these behaviors are thus rooted in early language acquisition. Connectionist simulations are described that illustrate the manner in which such mappings may be acquired, and that further illustrate the notion of "attention" as applied to sentence interpretation. An implicit artificial grammar–learning experiment with human subjects, motivated by the simulations, demonstrates the manner in which the mapping of regularities across different domains (e.g., linguistic/visual) can, under certain circumstances, take place. Taken together, the various findings suggest that the interdependence between events in the real world and the language used to describe those events necessarily guides the processes that underlie their interpretation.

19.1 PARSING PREFERENCES

A property of all languages is that they tolerate ambiguity. Almost as remarkable as the fact that languages tolerate *so much* ambiguity, is the fact that people tend to interpret certain kinds of ambiguity in systematic ways, systematic both across different instances of the same class of ambiguity *and* across different people. It is this systematicity that gives rise to the so-called garden path phenomenon exemplified by the sentences 1 and 2 below:

(1) a. The horse raced past the barn fell.
    b. He told the patient that he was worried about to visit again in two weeks.

(2) He said he ate it yesterday.

In (1a) the verb "raced" is ambiguous between a main verb and a past participle, and yet there is a consistent preference to interpret it as a main verb; hence the difficulty on encountering "fell" which would require a past participle interpretation of "raced." In (1b) the word "that" can either introduce a complement clause (what was told the patient) or it can introduce a relative clause (something more about the patient). The preference here is to interpret "that" as introducing a complement clause, and hence the difficulty with "to visit...," which is compatible only with a relative clause interpretation. In (2a) there is a *recency effect*; a preference to interpret "yesterday" as being when the eating happened, as opposed to when the saying happened. In each one of these cases, the preferred interpretation leads the reader "up the garden path."

The existence of these preferences is well established (e.g., J. D. Fodor and Frazier 1980; Frazier 1979; Frazier 1987; Frazier and J. D. Fodor 1978; Frazier and Rayner 1982; Kimball 1973). What is less well established is their cause. There are currently two broad approaches to understanding these preferences. One approach has been to assume that because the ambiguities themselves can be classified in terms of syntactic structures, the preferences for one interpretation or another must be due to processes involved in computing those syntactic structures. For instance, Frazier (1979) explained the preferences in terms of two syntactic parsing principles: *minimal attachment* and *late closure*. The principle of minimal attachment states that the processor attempts to build the least complex syntactic structure possible; when faced with a choice between a simple noun phrase interpretation of "the patient": [$_{NP}$ the patient]; or a complex noun phrase interpretation: [$_{NP}$[$_{NP}$ the patient]...], the processor will opt for the simple analysis.[1] Hence the preferences in (1). The late closure principle states that the processor attempts to incorporate new material in the phrase currently being processed. In (2a), when "yesterday" is encountered, the current phrase is [$_{VP}$ ate it...], and hence the preference to modify "ate" instead of "said." A crucial component of such claims (henceforth referred to as the "garden path theory") is that although semantic and contextual factors may in principle determine the *final* interpretation arrived at, the *initial* interpretation is governed by purely structural considerations.

The alternative approach to understanding these preferences, however, is to assume that the content of the items concerned *does* influence the choice of initial analysis. After all, the purpose of sentence comprehension is to establish, in effect, who did what to whom, and not to build syntactic structures per se. Consequently, the kinds of ambiguity that give rise to garden path effects need not be characterized solely at the level of syntactic description—they can also be characterized in terms of alternative (local) interpretations regarding the nature of the relationships between the whos, the whats, and the whoms. And this in turn means that their resolution may depend on what relationships have been discovered, or anticipated, up until the point at which the ambiguity must be resolved. For example, Crain and Steedman (1985) proposed that during normal sentence processing individual sentences are interpreted with respect to the preceding context, and that in a sentence fragment such as (3) below, the decision about how to interpret the ambiguous sequence "that he was worried about" (as a relative clause or as part of a complement) is made on *referential* grounds.

(3)   The doctor told the patient that he was worried about...

They claimed that whichever analysis resulted in the identification of a unique referent for "the patient" would be the one chosen by the sentence processor. Thus, if this fragment were embedded in a context in which there were more than one patient, but in which the doctor was worried about just one of them, the relative clause interpretation should be chosen. If, on the other hand, this fragment were embedded in a context in which there were just one patient (or just one patient were "foregrounded"; Chafe 1972), the complement clause interpretation would be chosen. That is, the relative clause interpretation would be rejected because it would *presuppose* that more than one patient had been identified on the basis of the referring expression "the patient" (Crain and Steedman 1985 assumes that the processor abides by a principle whereby it avoids violating unsatisfied presuppositions).

Considerable evidence has been amassed in recent years to suggest that referential factors *do* influence the initial decisions of the processor in the manner just outlined (Altmann, Garnham, and Dennis 1992; Altmann and Steedman 1988; Britt 1994; Britt et al. 1992; Spivey-Knowlton, Trueswell, and Tanenhaus 1993; but see also Altmann, Garnham, and Henstra 1994; Mitchell and Corley 1994; Mitchell, Corley, and Garnham 1992). The data are complicated by the finding that local factors, such as the frequency of occurrence of alternative attachments, or alternative argument structures, can also influence the decision process (see MacDonald, chap. 17, this volume; for review MacDonald, Pearlmutter, and Seidenberg 1994). MacDonald accounts for parsing preferences in terms of lexical biases concerning the statistical predominance of the alternative meanings (and associated syntactic forms) of the ambiguous items—she assumes that sentence processing is essentially a constraint satisfaction problem (lexical biases being one of the constraints to be satisfied), with contextual manipulations being more readily apparent when the lexical biases are weakest (see also Trueswell and Tanenhaus 1994). When ambiguities are encountered, they are resolved according to constraints imposed by, among other things (including local lexically based factors), the interpretive and integrative processes that map the surface form of the sentence onto its (context-dependent) meaning.

It is unclear, given the evidence regarding referential and lexical factors, whether a purely structural principle like minimal attachment *ever* determines initial attachments. The late closure principle, on the other hand, is less easily dismissed. Unlike the presuppositional account developed by Crain and Steedman (1985) for the resolution of the simple/complex NP ambiguities, there are few accounts of late closure that translate easily into empirically testable predictions concerning the influence of contextual factors (but see Altmann 1986; Niv 1993a, b). MacDonald et al. (1994) account for recency effects in terms of the differential activation of alternative attachment sites for the incoming item. They interpret alternative attachment sites as alternative (lexically derived) argument structures, each available for the incorporation of the incoming constituent; they propose that the argument structure associated with the most recent attachment site will be more highly activated than an argument structure associated with a less recent attachment site (and whose activation will have decayed with time). And because the most highly activated site is also the most accessible, it follows that there will exist a preference to associate with the most recent (and most active) structure.[2]

Although part and parcel of the constraint-satisfaction approach to sentence processing, this activation-based account of the closure preferences explains the closure preference not in terms of constraints as such but rather as a by-product of the architecture of an interactive activation device (and specifically, as a by-product of decaying activation). However, there does exist an alternative approach, based on a fundamental constraint on language processing; namely, that the linguistic input be mapped onto some representation of the world. The mapping between language and world requires that there exist an interdependence between what is attended to in the language, and what is attended to in the world (some minimal dependence is required; otherwise, the language could not be learned—see below). The referential effects described earlier are one by-product of this interdependence; the closure preferences may in fact be another.

A number of alternative versions of syntactic parsing preferences have been formulated that can account for the closure preferences (with varying degrees of success), but that do not suppose the preferences to be a by-product of the processor's architecture (e.g., Abney 1989; Carreiras and Clifton 1993; Frazier and Clifton, 1995; Gilboy et al. 1995; Pritchett 1992). What they each have in common is that verbs, and verblike constituents, are taken to play a major role in determining attachment preferences. Specifically, the processor attempts to attach incoming material within the current *theta domain*, or that part of the syntactic structure in which verb arguments are assigned whatever roles are appropriate given the meaning of the verb. In (4) below, the verb "found" is the current "role giver," and hence the preference to associate "yesterday" with "found" and not "left."

(4) Tom left with the dog he found yesterday

The notion of a theta domain is important because it acknowledges that verbs are not the only kinds of things that assign roles to the participants/objects referred to in a sentence. For instance, the final prepositional phrase in (5) below tells us a property of the restaurant, namely, that it is located near the High Street.

(5) He ate in the restaurant near the High Street

The same property/role information can be provided by using the stative verb "is," as in "the restaurant is near the High Street"; the preposition "near" is a theta-assigner. However, the preference to associate incoming items within the current theta-domain can be (re)interpreted as a preference to associate them within the current *predicate*.

The notion of predicates, and different predicate *types*, is fundamental to contemporary theories of semantics, for example, Davidsonian event semantics (Davidson 1980) and extensions of discourse representation theory (Kamp 1981), based on Davidson 1980 and Mourelatos 1978. An analysis of the sentences in which late closure–like preferences appear to hold suggests that attachments are preferred to *event* and *state* predicates (e.g., "ate" and "in the restaurant," respectively). But what are the advantages of replacing one theoretical device (a preference to associate within the current theta-domain) with another (a preference to associate to predicates)? First, the property that makes something a predicate is not structural; it is semantic—the burden of explanation shifts from being purely structural in origin to being semantic in origin (the principle of late closure and the alternative theta domain–based accounts are *syntactic*, not semantic). We thus return to the claim that syntactic ambiguities are resolved on the basis of some integration between the syntactic and the semantic. Second, it permits consideration of the developmental origins of the device. We can ask (and indeed, we must ask) *why* there should exist a preference to associate incoming items with the current predicate. And it is in response to this question that we can relate issues in sentence processing to issues of attention (and performance).

One approach to human sentence processing is to suppose that it consists in the processor "attending" to the different entities being described, and to the events in which those entities participate (or to the states in which those entities exist). During acquisition, for instance, the child must attend not simply to the linguistic input but also to the real world (and specifically, to those aspects of the real world being described by the linguistic input). This notion of attention and the interdependence between what is attended to in the linguistic input and what is attended to in the world being described (during acquisition, at least) are central to theories concerned with the acquisition of word meaning (e.g., Fisher et al. 1994; Landau and Gleitman 1985). It follows then that language processing will be constrained not simply by the contextual factors outlined earlier (including properties of both the linguistic and referential context) but also by the attentional processes implicated in such theories (unless these processes somehow "switch off" once the adult state is reached). To explain the closure preferences, we need simply suppose that the focus of attention is limited to the current event or state (or predicate) and that the processor avoids shifting the focus of attention away from the current focus of attention. To attach an incoming item to anything other than the current predicate would constitute a shift in the focus of attention. Such an account predicts that only certain kinds of contextual information could overcome the closure preference. But what kind of information could possibly signal to the processor that a shift in attention is appropriate? First, a local cue, such as prosody in the spoken form, or punctuation in the written form (for discussion of the relationship between prosody and issues of focus, see Bock and Mazzella 1983; Halliday 1967; Needham 1990), and second, a contextual cue that explicitly focuses attention on one particular predicate rather than another. We are currently exploring this possibility using materials such as (6) below, where the function of the context is to set up a question that *focuses attention* on a particular predicate within the sentence.

(6) a. When will Tom shampoo the dog he found?
     b. He'll shampoo the dog he found tomorrow.

We shall return to consider this case further below.

The work of Gleitman and colleagues (e.g., Fisher et al. 1994) suggests that, during acquisition, what is attended to in the world constrains the child's interpretation of the linguistic input, but that the linguistic input also constrains the child's interpretation of the world—the two kinds of interpretation are interdependent (as has to be the case if a mapping is to be established between the two). An example (albeit simulated) of such constraints can be seen in recent work in the connectionist modeling of sentence processing. Indeed, the notion of what constitutes "attention" in the context of sentence processing, and the role of predicates as "attentional units," can perhaps be better explicated in terms of a concrete example, a simulation reported by Sopena (1991).

19.2 CONNECTIONIST MODELS OF ATTENTION AND LANGUAGE ACQUISITION

Despite a number of well-publicized criticisms of the connectionist approach to cognitive modeling (e.g., J. A. Fodor and Pylyshyn 1987), several important insights have been gleaned from such modeling. For instance, the work of Jeffrey Elman (Elman 1990a, b, 1993) has demonstrated how a simple recurrent network (SRN) (see fig. 19.1), whose task is simply to predict what the next input will be, develops "hidden" representations of the input items that reflect their syntactic form class (and even certain "semantic" features) based on the co-occurrences of the individual words in the input sequences. In effect, the system performs a distributional analysis of the input, with syntac-

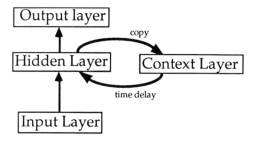

Figure 19.1 Simple recurrent network (SRN). The activation pattern at the hidden layer is copied to the context layer, and at the next time step, this pattern is input to the hidden layer.

tic types emerging as a function of their distributional characteristics (this is in contrast to claims concerning the unfeasibility of such an approach; e.g., Pinker 1987). Moreover, the distinction between different syntactic structures is captured in the system as a distinction between different trajectories through the state space as each word is encountered; identical structures lead to similar trajectories, whereas nonidentical structures lead to dissimilar trajectories.

Sopena (1991) used a slight variation of this network to model, initially, the manner in which a subject's eyes travel around a visual scene while listening to a description of that scene. In effect, the position of the eyes reflects what is currently being attended to.[3] One can think of his model as being trained on the sentential input, with the associated output at any one moment being the object on which the eye fixates. Sopena's insight was to realize the analogy between this task and the task involved in reading/hearing a sentence. Consider, for example, the sentence in (7) below (taken from Sopena 1991).

(7)   The man that is looking at the woman with a handbag is leaning against the streetlight.

When subjects looked at the corresponding visual scene while listening to this sentence, their eyes would travel from the man to the woman with the handbag and then *back* to the man during the main clause continuation "is leaning against the streetlight" (for further data on eye movements in response to verbal input, see Tanenhaus et al., chap. 18, this volume). Sopena argued that the process of sentence comprehension proceeds according to shifts in the focus of attention in much the same way a visual scene is scanned when it is described verbally. In (7) the focus of attention shifts back to the man when "is" is encountered (cf. "antecedent reactivation"). In order to reflect this equivalence, Sopena trained his network on a variety of sentence structures, and at each moment in time, the network's task was to represent at its output layer the proposition that constituted the focus of attention. Each proposition was represented as a set of entities, actions, and thematic roles (associated with each entity), and was therefore constructed "on the fly." In (7) there are three propositions (corresponding to three predicates):

(8)   a.   The man is leaning against the streetlight
      b.   The man is looking at the woman
      c.   The woman has a handbag

Over the time course of the sentence, the propositions in (8) become activated in the order *a-b-c-a* (bearing in mind that each proposition is initially incomplete). A consequence of this activation sequence is that the output representation of "man," for instance, disappears from the output representation during proposition 8c, but reactivates when the auxiliary "was" is encountered (signaling proposition 8a). Similarly, the output representation of "woman" remains active from when "woman" is first encountered in the input (part of proposition 8*b*), through to when "was" is encountered (that is, through proposition 8*c*, until proposition 8*a* is signaled). The order of activation/deactivation changes slightly in the case of (9):

(9) The man that the woman with a handbag is looking at is leaning against the streetlight.

In this case, the output representation of "man" is deactivated when "the woman" is encountered, and reactivates (with the agent role) when "is leaning" is encountered.

After an initial period of training, during which the network was explicitly trained to activate the appropriate sequences, Sopena's (1991) network activated the appropriate sequences in response to a wide variety of syntactic structures. The network was even able to generalize to novel structures (and hence, novel propositional sequences) that it had not encountered during training. For instance, from sequences such as shown in (10), the network would generalize to (11):

(10) a. The nurse loves the colonel that was smoking.
     b. The nurse loves the carpenter that bought the car.
     c. The son of the colonel loves the nurse.
     d. The carpenter loves the nurse that the colonel offended.

(11) a. The son of the colonel loves the nurse that was smoking.
     b. The nurse loves the carpenter that offended the son of the colonel.

And from sequences such as in (12), and other simpler structures, it could generalize to (13):

(12) John loves the woman that Peter thought was a multimillionaire.

(13) John loves the woman that Peter thought Mary said was a multimillionaire.

There are two fundamental assumptions that underlie Sopena's work. The first is that the linguistic input constrains the interpretation of that input in much the same way as linguistic input can constrain the interpretation of a visual scene. In effect, the interpretation of the real world is constrained by the form of the linguistic input (which is explicitly demonstrated in Sopena's 1991 study of visual scanning in response to verbal input). This is the converse of the (referential) constraints described earlier, in which context (i.e., knowledge of the world) constrains the interpretation of the linguistic input. That the interpretation of the world and the interpretation of the linguistic input describing that world are mutually constraining is a simple consequence of the necessary dependence between the two. The second assumption is that the mapping of sentences onto mental representations is an attentional process, with the focus of attention being limited to "a simple argumental grid, or predicate, or to each 'node' in a semantic structural tree" (Sopena 1991, 11). Such an assumption, the same as that introduced in the preceding section, helps explain what would be required to correctly parse the answer to the question in (6a), reproduced below:

(6) b. He'll shampoo the dog he found tomorrow.

To associate "tomorrow" with "will shampoo" would require that the focus of attention shift away from the current focus (the thematic argument structure associated with "found") and relocate to "will shampoo." And just as Sopena's network learns to shift its focus of attention as a result of systematic shifts in attention during training/acquisition, so we can suppose that the tendency to avoid certain shifts in focus results from attentional processes during early (infant) language acquisition.

In Sopena's simulations, only those actions, entities, and associated roles that correspond to a single argument grid or predicate are simultaneously activated. Thus the predicate comes to function as an attentional unit simply because the network is *trained* to treat predicates as such. But is this simply an arbitrary constraint on the network's training? Or might it reflect a more fundamental property of the manner in which language acquisition must proceed? If infants' role as language acquirers is to establish the entities being referred to and their roles in the events being described, then the only contention is whether they simultaneously attend to (cf. "activate") more than one event/predicate at a time, or whether, a little like Sopena's subjects scanning a visual scene, they attend to just the one, before shifting their attention to another.

Language acquisition requires that infants associate meanings to the words they hear. To do this, an infant must in some sense attend to the objects being referred to. If, during early language acquisition, the infant's attention is directed to the objects being talked about, and to whatever is happening to those objects (cf. how the attention of Sopena's (1991) network is directed during training), the result may be an automatic tendency to establish what is being talked about and attend to what is happening to it until something comes along to shift the focus of attention onto something new. Indeed, it is hard to understand how anything else could be the case; if infants do not attend to the objects being talked about, how could they learn the mapping between the tokens of the language and their meaning? And if infants do not attend to what happens to the objects being described (or to what state the objects are in) but shift their attention before being cued to do so, what guarantee is there that they will establish the mapping between the *appropriate* real-world event (or state) and the linguistic device used to describe the intended event? Similarly, if infants simultaneously attended to the entities/actions/roles constituting more than one event or state, what guarantee would there be that they establish the appropriate mappings between the events and their corresponding linguistic descriptions?

Fisher et al. (1994) propose that sentence/world pairings are acquired on the basis of previously experienced linguistic-structural observations as well as real-world observation (and that unconstrained real-world observation alone would not enable the appropriate sentence/world pairings to be learned). In their view, the sentence structure itself focuses attention on relevant aspects of the world context. An implicit component of their hypothesis, concerning the acquisition of verb meaning and argument structure, is that argument structures are attended to.

Although clearly speculative, an approach to sentence processing based on shifting attention leads naturally to the suggestion that adult parsing strategies have their origins in early acquisition. The referential considerations discussed earlier arise because of an attendance to the referents of the language (without which acquisition could not occur). The tendency to avoid shifting the focus of attention away from the current predicate also arises as a generalization of attentional phenomena in acquisition, and the manner in which the infant's attention is drawn (both intrinsically and as a consequence of implicit/explicit cuing) to relevant real-world events. The burden of explanation is thus shifted away from the traditional forum within which parsing preferences have been discussed, and toward theories or models of acquisition. Hence an answer to the earlier question, What are the advantages of replacing one theoretical device with another? The closure preferences do not reflect an arbitrary design feature, but reflect fundamental properties of language use and language acquisition. In short, they reflect the acquisition of the language/world mapping and the manner in which that acquisition proceeds.

The emphasis has therefore shifted considerably; language processing cannot be divorced from the real-world context onto which the language must be mapped. Nor can it be divorced from the manner in which the mapping is first acquired. Language learning requires more than simply learning about the structure of the language itself (cf. Elman's simulations 1990a, b); it is a process that goes hand in hand with learning about the structure of the world and about the relations between the world and language. Without a common structure between language and events in the world, and without the ability to establish a mapping between the two, the concept of language would be meaningless. In the next section, I describe some recent work on the acquisition of (artificial) grammars that explores further the acquisition of, and mapping between, common structures.

19.3 MODELING THE ACQUISITION AND MAPPING OF STRUCTURES ACROSS DOMAINS

In Elman's simulations (1990a, b), the task of the network was simply to predict the next input. From an "ecological" perspective, this task is attractive, not least because of the obvious evolutionary advantages that it offers. But this task is also attractive because of the insights it offers regarding the notion of relevance in the input. Specifically, sensitivity to structure in the input is a function of the degree to which that structure is predictive of the next input (see Cleeremans 1993 for further discussion). Moreover, this

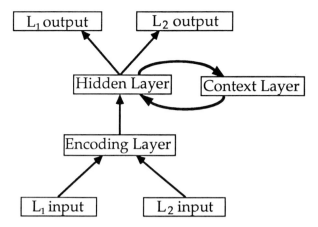

Figure 19.2 Modified SRN with two sets of inputs and two sets of outputs (from Altmann, Dienes, and Goode 1995; Dienes, Altmann, and Gao 1994). Weights on all connections are initially set to random values; thus weights between L_1 and the encoding layer, and between L_2 and the encoding layer, initially differ.

sensitivity may underlie more than just the acquisition of sequential (linguistic) structure; it may also underlie the establishment of the mapping between structures in one domain (e.g., variation in the linguistic input) and structures in another (e.g., variation in the world).

Figure 19.2 shows a modified SRN in which two tasks have to be performed simultaneously—learning the sequential structure of the language labeled "L_1" and learning to *map* this language onto some other input/output pairing, labeled, "L_2." Thus L_1 could be input to the SRN as a sequence of words (cf. Elman's 1990a, b simulations), and L_2 could represent the *semantics* of L_1 (in some as yet unspecified way, but possibly including some real-world correlate of L_1).

In a variety of simulations, we (Dienes, Altmann, and Gao 1994) have explored the efficacy of such an architecture with respect to the acquisition of mappings from tokens in one domain to structures extracted on the basis of exposure to another domain. In effect, we aimed to establish whether a single network can simultaneously learn about the structure of a language and the mapping between variation in that language and variation in some other domain. In each case, the sequences that made up L_1 and L_2 were *correlated* but not identical. In effect, we assumed that the semantics of L_1 would be a structure that reflected underlying aspects of the structure of L_1. What we actually had was a single grammar generate sequences of nonsense syllables, some of which were assigned to L_1 and some of which were assigned to L_2. Thus the sequences of L_1 and L_2 differed both in surface form (no two sequences of syllables were the same) and in terms of structure (no two sequences of form classes generated by the grammar, and to which the individual syllables were assigned, were the same). However, the grammar underlying the two sets of sequences was the same. We assumed, therefore, that whatever would be abstracted on the basis of exposure to the L_1 sequences would map onto, in a fairly direct way, whatever was abstracted on the basis of exposure to the L_2 sequences. In real-language terms, we assumed that the semantic structure evoked by hearing/reading "The man that is looking at the woman with a handbag is leaning against the streetlight" would be similar to the (semantic) structure evoked by seeing the event the sentence describes (cf. Sopena's 1991 view of narrative/scene processing). Clearly, variation in the language must map onto (i.e., must be correlated with) variation in the world. Otherwise, one could not predict how the world would be, for example, if described by the alternative sentence "The woman with the handbag that is looking at the man is leaning against the streetlight."

The mapping between L_1 and L_2 is a function of the connectivity between the input and hidden layers. If the weights on these connections are completely arbitrary, then the mapping is random. At issue is whether an architecture such as this can learn the appropriate configuration of weights that will allow the appropriate mapping of different structures in L_1 onto different structures in L_2. We found, first, that training the network on sequences from L_1 and L_2 simultaneously improved learning of L_1 compared to just training on L_1 alone, Learning proceeded by backpropagating the errors at both the L_1 *and* L_2 outputs, and learning was assessed on the basis of the match between the L_1 prediction at each time step and the actual L_1 input at the next time step. We calculated the mean square error between the L_1 prediction at each time step during learning and the actual L_1 input at the next time step and found that the error was consistently smaller at each time step when L_2 was present than when it was absent. This result may at first appear unsurprising because the information that needs to be abstracted on the basis of L_1 to perform the prediction task overlaps with the information that would be abstracted on the basis of L_2. Thus providing L_2 at the same time simply provides more information on which basis to abstract the necessary structure. On the other hand, the structures induced on the basis of L_2 can only be useful during the learning of L_1 if the tokens of L_2 can be mapped onto the appropriate tokens of L_1. One can imagine the problem as follows. The network has to predict the L_1 output partly on the basis of the L_2 input (otherwise, no advantage could accrue); if the network could not acquire the appropriate mapping between the tokens of L_1 and L_2, there could be no predictive advantage of utilizing the L_2 input. Consequently, the network has done more than simply acquire the structure underlying L_1 and L_2; it has also acquired (an approximation to) the appropriate mapping between the two.

We also found that training on L_2 *before* training on L_1 improved learning of L_1 (that is, speeded it up) compared to just training on L_1 alone.[4] Again, this may seem unsurprising, as the structure abstracted on the basis of exposure to L_2 is common to the structure abstracted on the basis of L_1. So having induced the appropriate structure on the basis of L_2, the network is already "set up" with (a subset of) the appropriate structures required for L_1. But again, for this prior "knowledge" to be useful, the network must be able to map between tokens of L_1 and L_2.

In the simulations reported above, the sequences from L_1 would be presented to the L_1 input units, and the sequences from L_2 would be presented to the L_2 input units. Similarly, L_1 and L_2 would be separated at the output layer. The weights on the connections between these various layers would all be initialized to different random values; thus in its "initial" state the network has no knowledge about the relationship between the elements of L_1 and the elements of L_2—it has no prior knowledge of the mapping that exists between L_1 and L_2. But the network is agnostic as to the actual *physical* form the sequences of L_1 and L_2 take. In other words, the input to L_1 at any one time step is simply a vector that could represent anything at all; likewise, for the input to L_2. Indeed, this is in part the motivation for the network; the input vectors can represent variation in quite distinct *domains*. So the following prediction is straightforwardly made. If the L_1 vectors represent sequences of, for instance, nonsense *syllables*, and the L_2 vectors represent, for instance, sequences of nonsense *symbols* (see table 19.1), the network will learn about the *syllable* sequences faster following exposure to the *symbol* sequences, so long as the underlying grammar generating the sets of sequences is the same.

In further simulations, we modified the testing regime so that the network performed a classification task, distinguishing between grammatical and ungrammatical sequences (this simply involves applying a simple function to the mean square errors generated by each sequence). Our prediction was that the network would be able to distinguish between grammatical and ungrammatical sequences of *syllables* if previously trained on the sequences of *symbols*, even though it would have no a priori knowledge of how the syllable world mapped onto the symbol world. The network was first trained on symbol sequences (recoded onto the L_2 input units, with the weights adjusted by backpropagation from the L_2 output units). When testing the network in the new domain (e.g., with syllable sequences recoded onto the L_1 input units), the recurrent weights and the weights between the encoding and

Table 19.1 Example Sequences Used in Altmann, Dienes, and Goode 1995

Syllables	Symbols
vot kav pel	
hes vot kav jix pel kav jix	
jix hes pel rud	
jix pel dup kav	

Note: There is no correspondence, in these examples, between the two sets of sequences, although all were generated by the same grammar.

hidden layers were frozen, or their learning rates reduced (we assumed an optimization rule that would reduce the learning rate as a function of the sign and magnitude of the backpropagated error), and only the "mapping" weights between the L_1 input and the encoding layer, and between the hidden layer and the L_1 output layer, were changed. As each syllable was applied to the L_1 input units, the network attempted to predict the next one, and the error was backpropagated through the network, changing the mapping weights. We found in this case that the network more successfully predicted successive syllables of grammatical than ungrammatical sequences—it successfully distinguished between the L_1 syllable sequences and ungrammatical control sequences (matched for length and frequency of individual elements) having previously been trained on only the L_2 symbol sequences. It had successfully learned the mapping between the syllables and the symbols such that it could perform the classification task. What remained to be seen was whether *human* subjects could do the same.

In the following section, I describe some results taken from Altmann, Dienes, and Goode 1995 that explore our prediction.

19.4   IMPLICIT LEARNING OF ARTIFICIAL GRAMMARS: MAPPING ACROSS DOMAINS

In a variety of studies we have explored the extent to which exposure to regular variation in one domain (e.g., sequences of nonsense syllables) can influence the acquisition of grammatical knowledge concerning regular variation in another domain (e.g., sequences of arbitrary graphic symbols). We used the implicit learning paradigm (e.g., Reber 1967, 1989) in which subjects are first exposed to sequences generated by an artificial grammar prior to being given a classification task in which they have to distinguish between (novel) sequences generated by that same grammar and other sequences that do not obey the rules of the grammar. During the first stage of the experiment, subjects are not informed about the existence of a set of rules but are informed they are taking part in a memory task (or alternatively, they may be told simply to attend to the sequences prior to being asked some unspecified questions about the sequences). In the second stage, subjects are informed that the sequences they have just seen/heard were generated by a set of rules and that some of the new sequences they are about to see/hear were also generated by this same set. The subjects' task is to mark which test sequences were rule-generated, and which were not. Typically, subjects cannot report the rules they have used during the classification stage of the task (and even when they can, their rules tend not to be good predictors of their actual performance), and the confidence with which they make each response does not correlate with whether that response was correct (see Berry and Dienes 1993 for review). Nonetheless, subjects can classify the test sequences with up to 70 percent accuracy.

In one experiment (experiment 4 from Altmann, Dienes, and Goode 1995), we generated 120 sequences of symbols for the learning phase (see table 19.1 for example sequences). The 120 sequences were made up of four repetitions of just 30 different sequences generated by a relatively small phrase structure grammar (taken from Morgan, Meier, and Newport 1987). A further 40 sequences (each different again) generated by this grammar were used in the test phase. For each grammatical test sequence, an ungrammatical sequence was generated by reordering the elements in the sequence. This guaranteed preserving the exact frequency distribution of the individual elements, the length of the individual sequences, and the frequency-by-length properties of the grammatical and ungrammatical test items. The resulting 80 sequences were translated into sequences of *symbols* (the same mapping between symbol and underlying form class was used as in the learning phase) or sequences of *nonsense syllables* (with an arbitrary, but constant mapping between syllable and form class). See Table 19.1 for examples. There were two groups of subjects. One group of 12 subjects was given 120 sequences of symbols to study (for around 10 minutes) and then given the 80 test sequences to classify. Half the subjects classified the symbol sequences first, and half classified the syllable sequences first. They were told to classify the sequences according to which ones they believed had been generated by the same set of rules used to generate the first sequences they had seen. A second group of 12 subjects acted as controls, and they were simply given the 80 test sequences to classify (symbol or syllable in fully counterbalanced order; there was, subsequently, no effect of order of classification); they were told that some sequences had been created using a complex set of rules, while others had been created using no rules at all.[5]

The control subjects performed at around 50 percent. In other words, they failed (unsurprisingly) to distinguish between the grammatical and ungrammatical sequences (whether syllables or symbols). The subjects who were first shown the 120 symbol sequences distinguished between grammatical and ungrammatical *symbol* sequences with 71 percent accuracy, in keeping with other implicit learning studies of this kind. Of crucial interest, however, was how they performed on *syllable* sequences. Recall that they had never seen these nonsense syllables before—the learning sequences had consisted of *symbols*, not syllables. They in fact performed at 65 percent (a statistically significant improvement relative to the controls, but significantly below the 71 percent level of the subjects who saw symbols in both the learning and test phases). Similar results were found in another study in which the learning sequences were auditory sequences of nonsense syllables and the test sequences were sequences of symbols (Altmann, Dienes, and Goode 1995, experiment 3).

These results suggest that a grammar acquired through experience of regular variation in one domain can be used to categorize structures experienced in another domain (where the term *grammar* refers simply to whatever knowledge is induced over the course of the learning period). In principle, then, sensitivity to grammatical structure can be demonstrated within a domain of variation even in the absence of any prior exposure to that domain; all that is required is prior exposure to equivalent variation (or some subset of it) in some other domain. In the extreme, what could be taken for innate knowledge of variation in one domain might simply reflect the mapping onto this domain of knowledge previously acquired in another.

This has interesting implications for early language acquisition. For instance, there is considerable evidence that newborn infants are sensitive to the prosodic structures of their language (e.g., Cooper and Aslin 1989; DeCasper and Spence 1986; Mehler et al. 1988). This ability is no doubt due to in utero experience (the fetal auditory system starts functioning by around thirty weeks' gestation, although the tissue and fluid surrounding the fetus act as a low-pass filter, allowing only the lower frequencies, below around 800 Hz, to reach the fetus). It is conceivable that whatever structure is induced over the course of this early exposure to prosodic variation will influence or shape whatever structures must subsequently be induced during exposure to unfiltered speech stimuli.

Of course, if the system were totally unconstrained, there would be enormous potential for interference; it might not be advantageous for the regularities extracted during early *visual* experience to interact with the regularities extracted during early speech processing.[6] On the other hand, it *would* be advantageous to be able to derive a mapping between the speech signal and the real world events that the speech refers to, just as it might in fact be advantageous in certain circumstances to map the auditory and visual signals onto a common underlying representation—the "McGurk effect" (McGurk and MacDonald 1976; Massaro, chap. 16, this volume) perhaps being a by-product of one such advantageous mapping.

The very fact that there exists an interdependence (i.e., a mapping) between events in the real world and the language used to describe them means that our interpretation of language, and our interpretation of the world, must be mutually constraining. Our data, if they generalize beyond the artificial situation from which they were derived, support this view; they suggest that the interpretation of one domain (e.g., the world) will be influenced by the extent to which a mapping can be established between structures acquired in that domain and structures acquired in another domain (e.g., language). Sopena's 1991 finding regarding eye movements in response to verbal descriptions is one (laboratory) example of this. An important feature of the earlier simulations is that a mapping is derived only insofar as it permits appropriate *predictions* to be made. In terms of the Fisher et al. 1994 account of how sentence structure focuses attention on the relevant aspects of the world context, the kinds of sentence/world pairings with which they are concerned constitute a kind of mapping. These pairings, they suggest, are acquired on the basis of linguistic-structural observations, as well as real-world observations. A problem for any such account concerns which actual aspects of the real-world observation should feed into the acquisition of a specific meaning/argument structure. And presumably, one constraint (there are others; see Fisher et al. 1994) is that the acquisition device must converge on a sentence/world mapping that has predictive value. Consequently, only those features of the real-world context will be entertained which can both map onto linguistic structure and in so doing enable predictions regarding subsequent structure. Linguistic structure focuses attention on relevant aspects of the world context because those aspects, mapped onto the linguistic structure, have predictive value regarding not simply the linguistic structure but also the world itself.

19.5 CONCLUSIONS

An important aspect of language processing that has largely (and surprisingly) been ignored is that the sentences of a language are not simply abstract patterns waiting to be discerned. Instead, they are abstract patterns that map onto some intended meaning. The task for the developing infant (indeed, for the neonate) is both to discern those patterns (whether acoustic or morphosyntactic) and to map them onto whatever is perceived (by the infant) to be the appropriate meanings. In early infancy the attentional devices provided by "motherese" and a host of other nonverbal gestures presumably function to direct the infant to at least a subset of the intended meanings. As the infant develops a rudimentary understanding of language, the language itself further constrains the intended meanings. If there is one lesson we have learned from contemporary research into connectionist models, it is that the input to the learning device and the manner in which the learning device is made to react to that input have profound implications for the "adult state." Sopena's 1991 research suggests how, so long as the attentional spotlight is somehow driven during acquisition, the resulting generalization may be to a self-driven spotlight that shifts its focus of attention automatically in response to particular "cues" in the input. I have suggested here that an inevitable consequence of such a generalization process may be that certain syntactic ambiguities are resolved in ways determined by the attentional process.

If parsing is an attentional process, how does the processing system know when to shift its focus of attention? The empirical work on language acquisition, and Sopena's 1991 modeling work, suggests that linguistic form comes to guide which aspects of the world (or its representation) the infant/adult should attend to. Attentional shifts become correlated with certain linguistic forms. This sounds, on the face of it, to have much in common with the constraint-based approaches to sentence processing described earlier. However, the attentional approach attempts to address the origins of certain of the constraints. While certain parsing phenomena almost certainly reflect the greater statistical preponderance of certain structures over certain others, some phenomena (e.g., closure) may reflect something more fundamental than simple statistics divorced from the real-world contexts in which those statistics first arise.

One consequence of the attentional hypothesis is that contextual influences on parsing take on a slightly different flavor. According to the accounts developed in Altmann and Steedman 1988 and Crain and Steedman 1985, the influence of context (specifically, referential context) comes about because certain parsing decisions are based on whether the context supports the presuppositions conveyed by the structure being processed. According to the attentional account developed here, the influence of context (including referential context) comes about because the context, coupled with structural form, guides the attentional mechanism. In the "when will Tom shampoo the dog he found?" case, the *wh-* questions set up a strong expectation regarding where the relevant information will occur in the answer "he'll shampoo the dog he found tomorrow." In processing terms, this expectation is simply the manifestation of attentional cuing by the context and, subsequently, by the form of the linguistic structure that precedes the answer "tomorrow."[7] In the case of the referential contexts studied by Crain, Steedman, and colleagues, the "expectation" simply concerns the identification of (or attention to) a protagonist (or other entity) currently within the focus of attention— together, context and linguistic form constrain the direction of attention. In many respects, this approach to contextual influences is little different from the constraint-based approaches argued for by MacDonald and by Tanenhaus. In both approaches, different sources of information, whether contextual or statistical, constrain the actions of the processor. By grounding the attentional mechanism in early acquisition, we can start to build up a picture of why those actions come to be constrained in this manner.

The emphasis in this chapter has been to (re)consider that language takes place, and is acquired, in the context of the world to which it refers. At some level within the system, the representations elicited in response to the verbal input must meet up with those elicited in response to the visuomotor input. Hand-eye movements in response to verbal input (cf. Tanenhaus et al., chap. 18, this volume) are an example of such a requirement. Similarly, early language learning must proceed at least in part by the formation of an association—a mapping—between the verbal and visual inputs. The simulations described above were a first attempt to explore some of the consequences of such a requirement. The result was a model in which the language input interacts, at a common level of representation, with inputs from other domains (although what may at first appear to be nonlinguistic inputs may well be put to linguistic use; cf. the McGurk effect). Much further work remains to be done, specifically, to explore further the attentional account of parsing preferences discussed in the first part of this chapter and the consequences of cross-domain mapping as described in the second part. Both avenues of research converge on the view that acquiring and understanding knowledge of language is an integral and inseparable part of acquiring and understanding knowledge of the world.

ACKNOWLEDGMENTS

I am particularly grateful to Toshio Inui and James McClelland for suggesting I contribute to *Attention and Performance XVI*. Aspects of this chapter would not have been conceived had I not been thinking about the themes of the meeting. I am also grateful to my colleagues Alan Garnham and Zoltán Dienes for the fruitful collaborations that have led to the work described here, and to James McClelland, Mark Seidenberg, and Michael Tanenhaus for their comments on an earlier version of this chapter. This work was supported by JCI grants SPG8920151 and G9110951, and by the U.K. component of the Human Frontiers in Science Program project on Processing Consequences of Language Phonologies.

NOTES

1. In this discussion I consider only simple/complex NP examples of minimal attachment preferences, although the reader should refer to Clifton and Ferreira 1989 for other examples.

2. An equivalent account holds if adverbs such as "yesterday" are treated as functions whose arguments are the structures they modify (cf. Pareschi and Steedman 1987; Steedman 1987). In this case the account need simply be reframed in terms of the relative activations of the alternative verb structures; the most active being the most readily available argument for the adverb-as-function.

3. The reader will find elsewhere in this volume a number of succinct reports showing that attention can be directed to a point that is *not* currently being fixated. Whether or not the term *attention* is being used here to refer to the same underlying processes as described in the other chapters in this volume is a moot point, and one on which I am agnostic. It is likely that attentional processes (or effects that can be described in such terms) operate at many different levels of cognitive processing.

4. Noel Sharkey, in a personal communication, has found similar effects in simulations inspired by our studies with human subjects described below.

5. In other studies, the control group has been exposed to stimuli generated by a *different* grammar, but the pattern of results remains unchanged.

6. Dienes, Altmann, and Kwan 1995 demonstrate that the knowledge acquired during implicit artificial grammar learning can be strategically applied, even though the actual rules remain opaque to conscious introspection. There may therefore be a strategic element to the mapping mechanism implicated in our studies of the transfer of knowledge across domains. During early acquisition, the strategic application of knowledge across domains may conceivably be signaled by the attention-directing mechanisms of "motherese."

7. Unfortunately, at the time of writing, the relevant experimental data were unavailable.

REFERENCES

Abney, S. P. (1989). A computational model of human parsing. *Journal of Psycholinguistic Research, 18*(1), 129–144.

Altmann, G. T. M. (1986). *Reference and the resolution of local syntactic ambiguity: The effect of context in human sentence processing.* Ph.D. diss., Edinburgh University.

Accounting for Parsing Principles

Altmann, G. T. M., Dienes, Z., and Goode, A. (1995). On the modality independence of implicitly learned grammatical knowledge. *Journal of Experimental Psychology: Learning, Memory, and Cognition, 21*(4).

Altmann, G. T. M., Garnham, A., and Dennis, Y. (1992). Avoiding the garden path: Eye movements in context. *Journal of Memory and Language, 31,* 685–712.

Altmann, G. T. M., Garnham, A., and Henstra, J. A. (1994). Effects of syntax in human sentence parsing: Evidence against a structure-based proposal mechanism. *Journal of Experimental Psychology: Learning, Memory, and Cognition, 20*(1), 209–216.

Altmann, G. T. M., and Steedman. M. J. (1988). Interaction with context during human sentence processing. *Cognition, 30*(3), 191–238.

Berry, D., and Dienes, Z. (1993). *Implicit learning.* Hove, England: Erlbaum.

Bock, J. K., and Mazzella, J. R. (1983). Intonational marking of given and new information: Some consequences for comprehension. *Memory and Cognition, 11,* 64–76.

Britt, M. A. (1994). The interaction of referential ambiguity and argument structure. *Journal of Memory and Language, 33,* 251–283.

Britt, M. A., Perfetti, C. A., Garrod, S., and Rayner, K. (1992). Parsing in discourse: Context effects and their limits. *Journal of Memory and Language, 31,* 293–314.

Carreiras, M., and Clifton, C. (1993). Relative clause interpretation preferences in Spanish and English. *Language and Speech, 36*(4), 353–372.

Chafe, W. L. (1972). Discourse structure and human knowledge. In J. B. Carroll and R. O. Freedle (Eds.), *Language comprehension and the acquisition of knowledge,* 41–69. New York: Winston.

Cleeremans, A. (1993). *Mechanisms of implicit learning.* Cambridge, MA: MIT Press.

Clifton, C., and Ferreira, F. (1989). Ambiguity in context. *Language and Cognitive Processes, 4*(3/4), SI 77–104.

Cooper, R. P., and Aslin, R. N. (1989). The language environment of the young infant: Implications for early perceptual development. *Canadian Journal of Psychology, 43*(2), 247–265.

Crain, S., and Steedman, M. J. (1985). On not being led up the garden path: The use of context by the psychological parser. In D. Dowty, L. Karttunen, and A. Zwicky (Eds.), *Natural language parsing: Psychological, computation, and theoretical perspectives,* 320–358. Cambridge: Cambridge University Press.

Davidson, D. (1980). *Essays on actions and events.* Oxford: Oxford University Press.

DeCasper, A. J., and Spence, M. J. (1986). Prenatal maternal speech influences newborns' perception of speech sounds. *Infant Behaviour and Development, 9,* 133–150.

Dienes, Z., Altmann, G. T. M., and Gao, S.-J. (1994). Mapping across domains without feedback: A neural network model of transfer of implicit knowledge. *Cognitive Science.* Forthcoming.

Dienes, Z., Altmann, G. T. M., Kwan, L., and Goode, A. (1995). Unconscious knowledge of artificial grammars is applied strategically. *Journal of Experimental Psychology: Learning, Memory, and Cognition, 21*(5).

Elman, J. L. (1990a). Finding structure in time. *Cognitive Science, 14,* 179–211.

Elman, J. L. (1990b). Representation and structure in connectionist models. In G. T. M. Altmann (Ed.), *Cognitive models of speech processing: Psycholinguistic and computational perspectives,* 345–382. Cambridge, MA: MIT Press / Bradford Books.

Elman, J. L. (1993). Learning and development in neural networks: The importance of starting small. *Cognition, 48*(1), 71–99.

Fisher, C., Hall, G., Rakowitz, S., and Gleitman, L. (1994). When it is better to receive than to give: Syntactic and conceptual constraints on vocabulary growth. *Lingua, 92*, 333–375.

Fodor, J. A., and Pylyshyn, Z. W. (1987). Connectionism and cognitive architecture: A critical analysis. *Cognition, 28*, 3–71.

Fodor, J. D., and Frazier, L. (1980). Is the human sentence parsing mechanism an ATN? *Cognition, 8*, 417–459.

Frazier, L. (1979). *On comprehending sentences: Syntactic parising strategies.* Bloomington, Ind.: Indiana University Linguistics Club.

Frazier, L. (1987). Theories of sentence processing. In J. Garfield (Ed.), *Modularity in knowledge representation and natural language processing*, 493–522. Cambridge, MA: MIT Press / Bradford Books.

Frazier, L., Clifton, C. (1995). *Construal.* Cambridge, MA: The MIT Press.

Frazier, L., and Fodor, J. D. (1978). The sausage machine: A new two-stage parsing model. *Cognition, 6*, 291–325.

Frazier, L., and Rayner, K. (1982). Making and correcting errors during sentence comprehension: Eye movements in the analysis of structurally ambiguous sentences. *Cognitive Psychology, 14*, 178–210.

Gilboy, E., Sopena, J. M., Clifton, C., and Frazier, L. (1995). Argument structure and association preferences in Spanish and English complex NPs. *Cognition, 54*(2), 131–167.

Halliday, M. A. K. (1967). Notes on transitivity and theme in English: II. *Journal of Linguistics, 3*, 199–244.

Kamp, H. (1981). A theory of truth and semantic representation. In J. Groenendijk, T. Janssen, and M. Stokhof (Eds.), *Formal methods in the study of language*, 277–322. Amsterdam: Mathematics Center Tracts.

Kimball, J. (1973). Seven principles of surface structure parsing in natural language. *Cognition, 2*, 15–47.

Landau, B., and Gleitman, L. R. (1985). *Language and experience: Evidence from the blind child.* Cambridge, MA: Harvard University Press.

MacDonald, M. C., Pearlmutter, N. J., and Seidenberg, M. S. (1994). The lexical nature of syntactic ambiguity resolution. *Psychological Review, 101*(4), 676–703.

McGurk, H., and MacDonald, J. (1976). Hearing lips and seeing voices. *Nature, 264*, 746–748.

Mehler, J., Jusczyk, P. W., Lambertz, G., Halsted, N., Bertoncini, J., and Amiel-Tison, C. (1988). A precursor of language acquisition in young infants. *Cognition, 29*, 143–178.

Mitchell, D. C., and Corley, M. M. B. (1994). Immediate biases in parsing: Discourse effects or experimental artefacts? *Journal of Experimental Psychology: Learning, Memory, and Cognition, 20*(1), 217–222.

Mitchell, D. C., Corley, M. M. B., and Garnham, A. (1992). Effects of context in human sentence parsing: Evidence against a discourse-based proposal mechanism. *Journal of Experimental Psychology: Learning, Memory and Cognition, 18*(1), 69–88.

Morgan, J. L., Meier, R. P., and Newport, E. L. (1987). Structural packaging in the input to language learning: Contributions of prosodic and morphological marking of phrases to the acquisition of language. *Cognitive Psychology, 19*, 498–550.

Mourelatos, A. (1978). Events, processes and states. In P. Tedeschi and A. Zaenen (Eds.), *Syntax and semantics. Vol. 14, Tense and aspect*, 191–212. New York: Academic Press.

Needham, W. P. (1990). Semantic structure, information structure, and intonation in discourse production. *Journal of Memory and Language, 29*, 455–468.

Niv, M. (1993a). A computational model of syntactic processing: Ambiguity resolution from interpretation. Ph.D. diss., University of Pennsylvania, Philadelphia.

Niv, M. (1993b). Resolution of syntactic ambiguity: The case of new subjects. In *Proceedings of the Fifteenth Annual Meeting of the Cognitive Science Society*, Hillsdale, NJ: Erlbaum.

Pareschi, R., and Steedman, M. (1987). A lazy way to chart-parse with categorial grammars. In *Proceedings of the 25th Annual Meeting of the Association of Computational Linguistics*, Stanford, CA: ACL.

Pinker, S. (1987). The bootstrapping problem in language acquisition. In B. Macwhinney (Ed.), *Mechanisms of language acquisition*, 399–441. Hillsdale, NJ: Erlbaum.

Pritchett, B. L. (1992). *Grammatical competence and parsing performance*. Chicago: University of Chicago Press.

Reber, A. S. (1967). Implicit learning of artificial grammars. *Journal of Verbal Learning and Verbal Behaviour, 77*, 317–327.

Reber, A. S. (1989). Implicit learning and tacit knowledge. *Journal of Experimental Psychology: General, 118*(3), 219–235.

Sopena, J. M. (1991). *ERSP: A distributed connectionist parser that uses embedded sequences to represent structure*. Technical report no. UB-PB-1-91. Department de Psicologia Basica, Universitat de Barcelona.

Spivey-Knowlton, M., Trueswell, J., and Tanenhaus, M. (1993). Context and syntactic ambiguity resolution. *Canadian Journal of Experimental Psychology, 47*, 276–309.

Steedman, M. J. (1987). Combinatory grammars and parasitic gaps. *Natural Language and Linguistic Theory, 5*, 403–439.

Trueswell, J. C., and Tanenhaus, M. K. (1994). Towards a lexicalist framework of constraint-based syntactic ambiguity resolution. In C. Clifton, L. Frazier, and K. Rayner (Eds.), *Perspectives on sentence processing*, 155–179. Hillsdale, NJ: Erlbaum.

20 The Potentials for Basic Sentence Processing: Differentiating Integrative Processes

Marta Kutas and Jonathan W. King

ABSTRACT

We show that analyzing voltage fluctuations known as "event-related brain potentials," or ERPs, recorded from the human scalp can be an effective way of tracking integrative processes in language on-line. This is essential if we are to choose among alternative psychological accounts of language comprehension. We briefly review the data implicating the N400 as an index of semantic integration and describe its use in psycholinguistic research. We then introduce a cognitive neuroscience approach to normal sentence processing, which capitalizes on the ERP's fine temporal resolution as well as its potential linkage to both psychological constructs and activated brain areas. We conclude by describing several reliable ERP effects with different temporal courses, spatial extents, and hypothesized relations to comprehension skill during the reading of simple transitive sentences; these include (1) occipital potentials related to fairly low-level, early visual processing, (2) very slow frontal positive shifts related to high-level integration during construction of a mental model, and (3) various frontotemporal potentials associated with thematic role assignment, clause endings, and manipulating items that are in working memories.

In it comes
out it goes
and in between nobody knows
how flashes of vision
and snippets of sound
get bound to meaning.
From percepts to concepts
seemingly effortless integration
of highly segregated
streams of sensory information
—with experiences past
out of the neural closet
and in use at last.
—M. K.

20.1 INTRODUCTION

Pulling the external world apart and putting the pieces back together internally, differentiating and integrating, assimilating and accommodating to a torrent of information arriving from multiple senses, acting and reacting to a world we both experience and change—these are the sensory, perceptual, and cognitive processes that make our brains among the most metabolically active tissue in the body (Plum 1975). Thus, when we speak of integrative processes, we are clearly talking about processes of perception and of action, multiply instantiated in different brain regions according to the modality of input and level of processing, whose neural connections have been sculpted by the history of the organism and the history of the species (the prewired and the postwired together).

Language comprehension in general, and reading in particular, are good examples of activities involving a wide range of analytic and synthetic operations. In this chapter we will argue that event-related brain potentials (ERPs) can give us insight into the time course and intensity of the integrative processes involved in reading, not merely at the level of the single word, but at the level of whole phrases and clauses as well. Moreover, we will show how judiciously combining electrophysiological data with other functional imaging data can help ground these integrative processes to their neural generators, an essential step in our goal of unifying cognitive theory with biology.

As we are clearly in the first throes of an admittedly ambitious project, this chapter serves primarily to spell out which integrative aspects of language processing might be most amenable to electrophysiological study and to pose hypotheses about the connection between specific ERP features and (chiefly) syntactic features of sentences. We begin with a brief discussion of working memory (WM), which we view as the arena for integrative processing. In particular, we discuss how properties of the WM system might determine the way in which thematic roles (e.g., agent, patient, theme, instrument) are mapped onto the linguistic representation of discourse participants to yield the intended meaning of a clause. Next, we consider what the neuroanatomy of the cortex tells us about the structure of language processing. We suggest that evidence from a functional analysis of language processing and from brain imaging of language processes together have revealed that computations like thematic role assignment are both functionally and anatomically distributed. We briefly introduce the basics of cognitive electrophysiology, including those components of the ERP to words which most directly relate to potential integrative processes. We also discuss the most heavily investigated component of the ERP sensitive to semantic features of words—the N400. We conclude with a description of an experiment involving basic transitive clauses, which we performed in order to see how easily electrophysiological correlates of language processing could be mapped onto linguistic concepts. In summary, we think our results provide preliminary evidence that the ERP approach to sentence processing can help in the examination and analysis of linguistic concepts such as thematic role assignment, thereby deepening our understanding of how discourse representations of clauses are constructed on-line.

20.2 INTEGRATION, ARGUMENT STRUCTURE, AND WORKING MEMORY

Integration in language processing goes beyond simply assigning hierarchical structure to what are essentially one-dimensional strings of linguistic tokens (themselves built up from patterns of light and sound). Full comprehension of a message requires that the comprehender arrive at an interpretation that yields information not already known, causing a change in the comprehender's state of knowledge and possibly also behavior. Precisely how this integration occurs is both unknown and highly controversial. For the purposes of our argument, however, we will assume that the cognitive outcome of integration is a (re)depiction of the activity of various discourse entities as expressed by the speaker in the listener's mind. Creating this mental redepiction presumably entails selecting discourse entities and encoding their interactions within a dynamic mental model that supports the kinds of inferences required to yield new information to the comprehender; this is the discourse level of representation.

In this chapter we will focus on processes that obtain syntactic and thematic role information from word representations and apply it to the construction of temporary syntactic and more long-lived, discourse-level representations. We assume that lexical access, thematic role assignment, and construction of a discourse representation are heavily interleaved, rather than strictly sequential, and that partial information is routinely used as it becomes available. On this assumption, for instance, a reader would form a discourse representation of a noun phrase (NP) such as "the secretary," even though it may subsequently be refined by a prepositional phrase or relative clause (e.g., "the secretary at the reception desk," "the secretary who typed the memo").[1] We also discuss the interface between working memory and thematic role assignment. Specifically, we outline the proposal that unintegrated syntactic constituents impose a load on working memory until they are integrated by extending Gibson's (1990, 1991) model of syntactic ambiguity resolution to unambiguous sentences.

20.3 WORKING MEMORY

While the concept of working memory (WM) as a constraint to processing has long been a key to psycholinguistic theories, going back at least to the collaboration of Miller and Chomsky (1963), its use has been largely intuitive. There is still no generally agreed-upon mechanistic account of exactly how WM constrains language processing, although no one doubts that it does (but see Just and Carpenter 1992 for a promising approach). For instance, despite the universal acceptance of the idea that WM is *capacity-limited*, rarely is this property defined precisely, presumably due to the difficulties in identifying the relevant "units" of storage in language. At present, it simply is unclear whether working memory is best quantified in terms of discrete, chunklike entities (e.g., Simon 1974), levels of activation within a production system (e.g., Anderson 1983) or across units of a neural network (e.g., St. John and McClelland 1990), or as the products of more specific processes coded as a function of articulatory parameters or visuospatial structure (Baddeley 1986). Although we also provide no definitive answer on this, we suggest that itemlike and patternlike views are in many cases complementary.

Another, perhaps too obvious, characteristic of working memory is that its contents are *temporary*. Items can only be active, that is, remain a part of working memory, only so long; once activated, they can and often should be suppressed as soon as the computations for which they were needed have run their course. Indeed, it is from the temporal sequencing of computations that a type of self-organization of processing emerges—an organization that enforces some degree of separation between processes that would otherwise lead to confusion and ambiguity. The active suppression of "irrelevance" in large part serves to guarantee that working memory contains only necessary information, with the practical consequences that processing is simpler, faster, and less error-prone than it might otherwise be.[2] More important for present purposes, we should expect both the capacity limitation and the temporal characteristics of WM to impact language processing inasmuch as we believe WM is needed for successful comprehension.

Comprehension of even the simplest sentences requires successful mapping between representations at different levels. This is not an easy problem. For one thing, linguistic inputs, while perhaps not strictly one-dimensional strings, are undeniably more "linear" than the higher-order representations they must be mapped onto.[3] Moreover, many kinds of natural language structures can be conceived of as requiring multiple arguments to complete their meaning—in other words, of having several "slots" that need to be "filled." Or, from the inverse perspective, some structures can be construed as isolated "chunks" or "fillers" that need to be "connected" or "slotted" to form higher-level units. But given that linguistic input is serial in nature, "fillers" will not necessarily precede their "slots." Accordingly, during the processing of structures requiring multiple arguments, some "slots" may remain unfilled until their expected "fillers" are encountered, leading to the generation of expectancies.[4] Likewise, some "fillers" may remain unattached until their expected "slots" are encountered, requiring active maintenance of the filler. Thus successful comprehension entails storage or *maintenance* of activation,[5] generation of *expectations* for future items, and assignment of fillers to slots or *integration*. These are in fact generally considered to be basic operations of working memory and, as such, would be subject to its capacity limitations and temporal characteristics.

This understanding of the operations on WM is not unique to language processing; such operations would appear instead to be "central" to many different cognitive problems in Fodor's (1983) sense of that term. This perceived centrality notwithstanding, their existence in a cognitive system may be quite specialized in function and distributed in character. In fact, Baddeley's (1986) influential model of WM points toward a degree of specificity in storage components (e.g., phonological store, articulatory loop, visuospatial scratch pad), although it has been criticized primarily for its underspecification of central executive processes. Both psychological and neurophysiological evidence as well as computational arguments now converge to suggest that Baddeley's underspecification of the central executive may reflect a real weakness in the theory, and that the executive may not be as central as originally proposed.[6] For example, recent studies in cognitive neuroscience by Goldman-Rakic (1987) and her colleagues (e.g., Wilson, Scalaidhe, and Goldman-Rakic 1993) suggest that working memory storage systems are so highly fractionated as to render it next to impossible to lesion central "executive" processes while sparing storage, and vice versa. Thus, while the frontal cortex has been implicated in the so-called executive functions, in practice, these have proven intractable to separation from storage components behaviorally (reviewed by Fuster, 1989, 1993); they appear not to be centralized in the sense of being localized to a single, distinct, amodal cortical area (Sereno 1991).

In line with the neuroscience view of working memory, Kimberg and Farah (1993) demonstrated via computer simulations of frontal lobe functioning how the notion of a central executive may be superfluous. Using a model of WM that does not include any central executive module, they were able to simulate both normal and abnormal performance on at least four tasks sometimes impaired by frontal lobe damage. The beauty of their working computer model is that it accounts for abnormal performance in a variety of so-called frontal tasks by changing only a single parameter without recourse to a central executive; the frontal cortex modulates (maintains and controls) the strength of associations among various (broadly defined) elements of different information types. Thus merely weakening associations among elements mimics frontal patients' performance in seemingly disparate areas such as motor sequencing tasks, the Stroop test, the Wisconsin card sorting task, and tests of source memory. In the next section, we argue that at least one prominent aspect of integration in language processing, namely thematic role assignment, can be similarly analyzed.

20.4 THEMATIC ROLES IN PRINCIPLE

The field of syntax has long felt a tension between theoreticians who sought to enforce a strict division of syntactic and semantic processing (e.g., Chomsky 1965) and those who sought to unify the two (e.g., Fillmore 1968). A limited rapprochement between these two positions has occurred over the last decade with the development of Chomsky's "Government and Binding" (GB) framework (1981), which places more emphasis on general principles of language processing (than on highly specific, tightly ordered rules) and on the centrality of semantic argument structure (in the guise of thematic role assignment) in syntactic analysis. Although we do not have space to do this issue justice, we raise it to justify our particular position here: because something akin to thematic role assignment occurs during parsing, it is reasonable to track the progress of processing simple, single clauses by examining thematic roles.

In essence, thematic role assignment expresses the creation of a bridge between the linguistic representation of a participant in a discourse and the specific role the participant is expected to take. Given that much of the information needed to make these participant-action correspondences is carried by verbs, once the possible roles associated with a verb are revealed, we can conceive of a process that maps these thematic roles onto the discourse participants. In other words, information in the verb can be used to map explicit associations between particular, previously unassociated items in working memory. (This characterization might remind some readers of Kimberg and Farah's 1993 theory of the frontal cortex.)

Our position on the relationship between thematic role assignment and working memory owes much to Gibson (1990), who has used (limited) working memory capacity both to sanction and to constrain the pursuit of parallel analyses in cases of syntactic ambiguity. Specifically, Gibson proposed that readers were free to pursue multiple parallel analyses of a temporarily ambiguous syntactic structure with two provisos: first, that the capacity required to maintain multiple parsings did not exceed readers' total WM capacity and, second, that readers be allowed to discard analyses whenever these were significantly more costly to maintain than the "easiest" reading. Gibson proposed that cost (thematic or working memory load) was incurred by NPs temporarily lacking a thematic role and by thematic roles that were momentarily unassignable. Because both these types of load on working memory were presumed to be similar in nature and equal in magnitude, thematic load was calculated as a simple sum of NPs not yet assigned roles and thematic roles not yet assigned to NPs.

Although Gibson's (1990) theory was intended to account for garden path effects, we think it can be extended to language processing in general. For example, Gibson's purposes required only that readings exceeding total WM capacity or consuming much more memory than a rival reading lead to observable behavioral effects. However, with more sensitive dependent measures even "subcritical" thematic loads might have observable effects. Furthermore, the proposed equality of the two types of thematic loads (NPs without roles, unassigned thematic roles) posited by Gibson was more a matter of convenience than a theoretical necessity. Thus the WM loads induced by NPs without roles and by unassigned thematic roles might be psychologically and physiologically distinguishable, in a way parallel to our previous suggestion for the WM processes required to maintain "passive" memory loads and to project or expect future events. Accordingly, we anticipate that this psychological decomposition of WM operations will have reliable electrophysiological signatures, as will be detailed in our discussion of the brain and its electrophysiological message.

20.5 LIMITATIONS OF THE CORTEX: SIZE MATTERS

Our brief discussion of thematic role assignment suggests how one might begin to map highly complex linguistic concepts onto simpler psychological primitives. We will motivate our mapping of the interactions among these same psychological primitives onto electrophysiological effects at the scalp by pointing out some neuroanatomical constraints on processing. That is, we will detail the manner in which neural circuitry in general might delimit the ways that language and working memory processes (and the associated ERPs) could and could not work. Our conclusions support the idea that there are multiple "language areas," that these areas subserve both language-specific and non-language-specific subprocesses, and that they are widely but not randomly distributed in the brain.

Textbook models of language imply the existence of specifically linguistic processes instantiated in a neural system that includes a single pair of inter-connected cortical areas, namely Broca's area in frontal cortex, and Wernicke's area in the temporal lobe near its junction with the parietal lobe. This anatomically bipartite language-processing model has suggested a number of ways to construe language as a dichotomous entity. As mood or fashion suits us, we see various dichotomous pairings of production versus comprehension, of syntax versus semantics, of grammar versus lexicon, and of regularity versus exception, with one term of each pair assigned to Broca's area and the other to Wernicke's area, respectively. Indeed, this is more than just idle theorizing; neuropsychologists working with both normal and aphasic populations do find evidence in favor of such dichotomies (see, for example, Caplan 1994). However, it has proven exceedingly difficult to move beyond descriptions of aphasic symptomatology and to reify these dichotomies in a satisfying model of what is processed in, say, Broca's area.

Moreover, the anatomical definition of cortical language areas has tended to be surprisingly loose; rarely are their size, shape, or evolutionary history relative to adjoining areas of cortex discussed in any detail (but see Deacon 1992). Some of this looseness might be ascribed to a sort of (wishful?) thinking that because these areas are supposed to be highly flexible, higher-order association cortex, they should be more variable (than, say, primary sensory areas). Recent work, however, has cast doubt in particular on the very existence of purely "associative" brain areas of any sizable extent (e.g., Sereno 1991). This leads us to reconsider some basic questions: how many language areas are there, where are they located, what are their particular functions, how are they connected to each other in time and space, and is there any principled order to their activity? Before we address these questions directly, we outline the logic behind a reliably informative, if uncommon, approach to cortical organization that uses information about the size, number, and connectivity of individual areas to appreciate the integrative problems they help to solve.

In an average person, the cortical surface area of a single hemisphere measures approximately 80,000 mm^2 (e.g., Cherniak 1994)[7] which Brodmann's (1909) influential work divided into 47 architectonically distinct brain areas. It is now clear this was a conservative parcellation, although it was in fact less conservative than other contemporary schemes. To cite a clear example of a likely undercount, Brodmann defined only 6 areas in what is now considered the human visual cortex; this is 4 times less than the current estimate of the number of cortical visual areas (about 25) found in a visually sophisticated primate like the macaque (Felleman and Van Essen 1991). Furthermore, many of the visual areas that Brodmann missed were far from exotic, including such well-established areas as MT (responsible for processing motion) and V4 (responsible for processing color and other higher-order features). While we would hesitate to suggest that this factor-of-4 difference would apply to Brodmann's total, we can with high confidence add to his 47 areas the number of "extra" areas so far demonstrated in visual, auditory, and somatosensory cortex (as briefly reviewed by Felleman and Van Essen 1991) and suggest there are at least 80 human cortical brain areas, defined cytoarchitectonically and by patterns of interareal connections. Thus the "average" brain area even in the human brain would at best cover about 1,000 mm^2 of the cortex, which is only slightly larger than two ordinary postage stamps. Even primary visual cortex (V1) measures only approximately 2,500 mm^2 (Horton and Hoyt 1991), and can be further divided into upper and lower visual field "subareas" on the basis of separate connections to higher visual areas (Felleman and Van Essen 1991).

The point of this exercise was to give us a ballpark estimate of the size of an average cortical area and see how the so-called language areas measure up. The size and location of Broca's area, as usually depicted, varies substantially from source to source, but certain "minimal" areas are universally included; namely, a substantial amount of the cortex along the inferior frontal gyrus, almost all of the pars opercularis and pars triangularis, and also parts of the more anterior pars orbitalis (e.g., Penfield and Jasper 1954; Ojemann 1991). The pars triangularis alone, at approximately 3,500 mm^2 is 40 percent larger than V1, and over three times the size of the average brain area.[8] Similar rough estimates of several different "textbook" depictions of Broca's area yield similar results.[9]

All in all, these depictions of Broca's area (even in the more advanced texts cited here, which show relatively "punctate" areas) would appear to make it by far the largest known cortical brain area in the human. In our opinion, this is highly unlikely. Even Brodmann divided this region into two areas, and we might expect four or more to be found, based on the size of the "average" brain area (also see Deacon 1992). A similar argument can be made concerning Wernicke's area, which is more variable in its size and placement than Broca's (see, for example, Sereno 1991).[10]

We have argued that the number of distinct brain areas within the classical language regions is larger than previously supposed. Accordingly, it is not surprising that the correlation between damage to Broca's and Wernicke's areas and aphasic symptomatology is so low (Willmes and Poeck 1993). As suggested by Alexander, Naeser, and Palumbo (1990), a larger number of brain areas would suggest more principled reasons for the variability of damage to language processing following lesions to Broca's area. Some of the more selective cases reported in the literature may in fact reflect selective damage to particular cortical fields within the anterior language-processing region, or the disconnection of these areas from each other or from posterior areas. This would also be consistent with the remarkable variability across positron-emission tomography (PET) studies of exactly which areas appear to change their activity during supposedly "language"-processing tasks (e.g., Roland 1993).

If there actually are many cortical language areas, as we have argued, we would also expect a *decrease* in the relative degree of interconnectivity among them, especially between those not adjacent on the cortical sheet (Cherniak 1990, 1994).[11] The important point is that, even if there were only two language *regions* comprising a larger number of language subareas, limitations on their interconnectivity should not be underestimated. Yet a further wrinkle in the cortical language area story has been added by the discovery of a *third* language area on the bottom of the temporal lobe, called the "basal temporal language area" (Luders et al. 1986). In summary, if language regions are mosaics of subareas, the functional and electrical responses from, say, left anterior brain areas would be expected to generate multiple observable activity patterns that we could associate with distinct processing factors. In general, the pattern of electrical activity over the scalp during the processing of a sentence should be quite complex. We now turn to a discussion of the electrophysiological pattern actually observed.

20.6   BRIEF INTRODUCTION TO ERPS

Ever since Berger's (1929) discovery that brain electrical activity can be measured at the human scalp, the electroencephalogram (EEG) has been used as a research tool to investigate the functioning of the central nervous system in both mental and physical terms. The EEG can be used in a variety of ways as a dependent measure of changes either in its frequency content or in the brain activity triggered (evoked) by some transient event. We will briefly sketch these two approaches, and then introduce the ERP components most commonly associated with reading.

The spectral analysis of resting EEG is widely known because of its clinical applications (see, for example, Spehlmann 1981). Of greater relevance to our research are recent efforts that correlate regionalized alterations in the spectral (frequency) composition of the EEG with differences in cognitive tasks (e.g., Klimesch, Schimke, and Pfurtscheller 1993). The typical measure is an attenuation in the amount of power within specific frequency bands, mostly alpha (10 Hz) but also beta (20–50 Hz) and others in association with the processing of some event, hence, the term *event-related desynchronization*.[12] These techniques are less commonly known to most cognitive psychologists, but we mention them here because recently they have been applied to investigations of "intensive" dimensions of processing and working memory use (Pfurtscheller and Klimesch 1990; see also Gevins and Cutillo 1993 for a related approach).

The other common use of EEG information as a dependent measure is based on the concept of evoked potentials, whereby it is assumed that some triggering event causes a change in the brain's response in a way that can be related to its content and/or context. The most common way to analyze such data is to form averages from the EEG of many individual trials, time-locked to the trigger (generally an external stimulus or a subject-generated movement). The assumption behind this approach is that transient activity not specific and therefore not synchronized to the triggering event is random and will average out over the course of many repetitions, leaving an event-related potential (ERP) signal that presumably reflects activity causally time-locked to the event.[13] Brain activity measured in this way is an extremely sensitive index of changes in brain state or operations, as a function of the environment or otherwise (reviewed extensively by Regan 1989).

Given what is known about the organization and activation of the neural circuitry necessary to generate a sizable ERP at the scalp, the best candidate generator for most of what is seen are the pyramidal cells in the cortical layers. Calculating from this potential distribution at the scalp exactly which generators are active is known as the "inverse problem." The general inverse problem is, in principle, insoluble (no matter how dense the recording electrode array) because there are infinitely many combinations of neural generators that could yield the same distribution of electrical activity at the scalp (Nunez 1981). This is why merely locating the largest peak amplitude at some point over the scalp *cannot* be given as sole evidence that the generator is located in the cortical patch right beneath that electrode, or that what looks like a local tangential dipole is such. Sometimes that it true, but sometimes it is not. Fortunately, as Dale and Sereno (1993) have suggested, adding a few constraints (i.e., external structure or more information) to the problem renders it soluble in practice.[14]

While the mapping of generators onto mental functions is not straightforward (as the mapping may be other than one to one), knowing the minimum number of possible generators can give us a starting point for hypothesizing about the minimum number of mental processes necessary to explain performance in some task. The ERP provides a good link between the physical and mental world because it is brain activity whose parameters are sensitive to manipulations of psychological variables.

An important division in the study of ERPs is usually made between "fast" activity, which generates most of the response we see to single words,

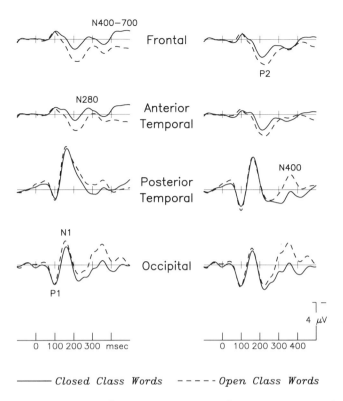

N400–700

Frontal

P2

N280

Anterior
Temporal

Posterior
Temporal

N400

N1

Occipital

P1

4 μV

0 100 200 300 msec

0 100 200 300 400

————— *Closed Class Words*   – – – – – *Open Class Words*

Figure 20.1 Grand average ERPs ($N = 24$) from 8 representative electrode sites for open-class (solid line) and closed-class (dashed line) words from recent ERP language study (King and Kutas 1995). Left hemisphere is plotted on left, and in this and all subsequent figures, negative voltages are plotted up. ERP features labeled on this figure are mentioned in text.

and "slow" activity in very low frequency bands of the ERP (less than 1 Hz). Both fast and slow potentials can be characterized in terms of their morphology (waveshape), latency and/or time course, amplitude, and distribution across the scalp. We recommend that duration be added, at least until it is shown to be uninformative. To date, virtually all of the research on the ERPs related to language processing has focused on the faster, transient responses triggered by individual words; these include the P1, N1, P2, N2, N280 or lexical processing negativity (LPN),[15] P300, N400, and N400–700 (see fig. 20.1 for illustration; Hillyard and Picton 1987 and Kutas and Van Petten 1994 for reviews).[16] A thumbnail sketch of the relation between psychological processes and these ERP components, in our opinion, would link the earliest components (P1, N1) to early visual processing (e.g., feature extraction) and attentional modulations thereof; the LPN to lexical access; the P2 and the family of P3-like components[17] to encoding and memory storage–related operations; the N400 to aspects of semantic analyses; and the N400–700 to anticipatory processes. In addition, these faster responses are superimposed on much slower (lower-frequency) voltage modulations.

Until relatively recently, cognition-related modulations of very slow cortical potentials (SCPs) have been explored primarily in the realm of memory (especially working memory) and vigilance research (for review, see McCallum and Curry 1993; Ruchkin et al. 1988; Rosler and Heil 1991). We will not summarize this work here, but merely emphasize for present purposes that the slow cortical potentials are not simply a sum of overlapping transient ERP components but a reflection of brain activity in their own right.

Previously, we reviewed evidence demonstrating that language processing is widely distributed in the brain. We now turn to the question of what implications this distribution might have for our ability to record electrical activity specific to language processing. Insofar as the various cortical language areas are in close proximity to each other and do cooperate to process the same kinds of information, we might expect them to be extensive enough to have distinct electrophysiological signatures even with a modest number of sensors. Moreover, if there are three (or more) language regions as well as other brain regions playing a supporting role in language processing, we should be able to see multiple and differentiable ERP effects caused by differences in linguistic input or differences in the performance of the subjects. We start our discussion of language-related ERPs by reviewing the work on the N400 and its use in psycholinguistic research.

20.7 ELECTROPHYSIOLOGY OF SEMANTIC PROCESSING: THE N400

The event-related potential technique has been used for over thirty years in investigations of cognition. And, over this period, we have discovered facts about phonological, lexical, semantic and syntactic analyses (see the special issue of *Language and Cognitive Processes* edited by Garnsey, vol. 8, no. 4, 1993). We begin with a very brief review of the work related to semantic processing and then describe a new way of using ERPs to study reading (and ultimately speech comprehension).

Much of the early work in the electrophysiology of language capitalized on the sensitivity of the ERP to violations of semantic expectancies—failures of integration at the level of meaning. A larger percentage of the more recent work has focused on violations of various syntactic rules or constraints, with the aim of determining the extent to which there exist separate semantic and syntactic levels of representation (e.g., Neville et al. 1991; Osterhout and Holcomb 1992; Munte, Heinze, and Mangun 1993; Rosler et al. 1993; Hagoort, Brown, and Groothusen 1993). Such studies rest on the assumption that if semantic and syntactic processing and violations thereof yield qualitatively different patterns of brain activity, then they must be subserved by different brain systems whose very existence is proof of their separate identities. And, indeed, the results to date show that semantic violations on the whole differ from syntactic ones in some way, although the story is clearly more complicated because the brain's responses to various syntactic violations also differ from one another in ways that are still poorly understood (e.g., Neville et al. 1991). For the moment, we cannot be certain that it is always syntax which has been violated. But, rather than dwelling on this issue, let us briefly review what has been learned from the ERP investigations of a class of semantic violations.

The ERP to a word that is semantically anomalous within a sentence is characterized by a negative-going wave between 200 and 600 ms, peaking around 400 ms, with a somewhat posterior, slightly right-hemisphere amplitude maximum; this is the so-called N400. The N400 elicited by a semantic violation is large and remarkably similar (albeit not identical) in its distribution whether the violation occurs in sentences being read (e.g., Kutas and Hillyard 1980), listened to (e.g., McCallum, Farmer, and Pocock 1984), or interpreted from hand shapes and movements of American Sign Language (e.g., Kutas, Neville, and Holcomb 1987). Moreover, the amplitude of the N400 effect (the difference between responses to anomalous and congruent words) appears to be similarly sensitive to a number of factors including semantic relationship whether the sentences are presented visually one word at a time at relatively slow rates (e.g., one word every 700 to 1,100 ms), as was frequently done in early work, or at somewhat faster rates (e.g., between 250 and 500 ms), as is more typical today (e.g., Gunter, Jackson, and Mulder 1992; Kutas 1993).

The ERP to a clear-cut semantic violation has the largest N400. However, fifteen years of research has revealed that the ERPs to all words contain some N400 activity whose amplitude is determined by a variety of factors (for review, see Kutas and Van Petten 1994). Chief among these is how expected or predictable a word is, given its *current context*. We take current context to include not only sentential contexts but also paragraphs and texts, on the one hand, and word pairs and lists on the other, as we shall describe. Further, the N400 effect is not strictly limited to real words because large N400s also characterize the ERPs to pseudowords—letter strings that both look and sound as though they could be words, and give a reader the sense that they ought to have meaning. Pseudoword N400 effects occur both in the context of word-nonword pairs and in lists of words (e.g., Bentin, McCarthy, and Wood 1985; Holcomb 1993; Holcomb and Anderson 1993; Holcomb and Neville 1990; Rugg, Doyle, and Melan 1993). By contrast, the ERPs to nonwords (orthographically illegal combinations of unpronounceable letter strings) do not seem to show any N400 activity (Holcomb and Neville 1990; Nobre and McCarthy 1994) Thus the extremes in the distribution of N400 amplitudes elicited by single-word stimuli are marked by pseudowords at one end and nonwords at the other. The amplitudes of the N400s to all other words fall somewhere in between, with the exact distribution being determined by a combination of different factors as detailed below.

The reality that multiple factors affect N400 amplitude is made especially salient when we seek to explain the modulation of an N400 due to the lexical class of the eliciting word. Thus, while we see larger N400s to open-class or content words (e.g., nouns, verbs, adjectives and -*ly* adverbs) than to closed-class or function words (Kutas and Van Petten 1994; Neville, Mills, and Lawson 1992), some or all of this difference may be caused by factors such as word frequency, abstractness, and repetition that are correlated with, but distinct from, lexical class. In experiments using lists of unrelated words, one sees larger N400s elicited by lower frequency words than by high-frequency words (e.g., Rugg 1990), larger N400s to concrete words than to abstract words (e.g., Kounios and Holcomb 1992) and larger N400s to the first occurrences of words in a session than to subsequent occurrences of the same word in both word lists and in text (Rugg 1985; Karayanidis et al. 1991; Van Petten et al. 1991). Notice that each of the simple effects of frequency, abstractness, and repetition alone could account for the larger N400s in open-class than in closed-class words, without the need to resort to the possible interactions among them.[18]

The factors described above have effects on the N400 *independent* of context, but many other factors are richly *dependent* on context, especially the semantic and pragmatic context. Thus in list contexts we find N400s to words preceded by an associatively or semantically related word are smaller than those to words preceded by an unrelated word (e.g., Bentin, McCarthy, and Wood 1985; Kutas and Hillyard 1989; Holcomb 1988; Holcomb and Neville 1990). Although this effect could be explained in terms of item-to-item priming alone, such an explanation seems less plausible when we consider the effects of sentence contexts, where we find smaller N400s to words that are more semantically constrained by their context (Van Petten and Kutas 1991) even when there is little direct semantic association between the eliciting word and other words in the sentence. Also note that the type of constraint effective in dampening the N400 effect is far from general; accumulating syntactic constraints by themselves do *not* reduce N400 amplitude (Van Petten and Kutas 1991).

Overall, the N400 is very sensitive to many of the factors shown to have behavioral effects in studies of word recognition. Moreover, it appears that these factors can interact to influence the amplitude of the N400. For instance, the N400 frequency effect is reduced as a function of accumulating semantic constraints; clear frequency effects are seen on the N400 to the first few open-class words in a sentence, but none are seen on the N400 to congruent open-class words late in a sentence (Van Petten and Kutas 1991). Another robust finding is that the N400 congruity effect is reduced by repetition (Kutas, Van Petten, and Besson 1988; Besson and Kutas 1993; Mitchell, Andrews, and Ward 1993), although the precise pattern of effects is complex.[19]

In our opinion, one of the most important consequences of this research has been the suggestion that the way the brain deals with semantic violations is not *qualitatively* different from the semantic analyses it routinely carries out during reading or speech comprehension in the absence of obvious violations. Thus we view the apparent failures of semantic integration that people experience when a "real" violation occurs as merely an end point on a continuum of processing for meaning. This realization was brought home by the data showing different amplitude N400s to the final words of the following two sentences:

(1) The bill was due at the end of the hour.

(2) She locked the valuables in the safe.

These are both perfectly normal, comprehensible sentences, and yet the N400 to "hour" was significantly larger than that to "safe." In fact, Kutas and Hillyard (1984) found that the amplitude of the N400 was inversely correlated (r = −.9) with the cloze probability of the eliciting word.[20] This correlation has led to the hypothesis that N400 amplitude may merely index a word's predictability (subjective conditional probability). If these were the only data available, this would be a viable hypothesis. However, in the same paper as well as others since (e.g., Kutas 1993), it was demonstrated that words with equivalent predictability (i.e., identical cloze probabilities) were nonetheless associated with N400s of different amplitudes. In other words, when cloze probability was held constant, N400 amplitude was a function of the semantic or associative relation between the expected word and the word actually presented.[21] For instance, if the sentence fragment "The better students thought the test was too" were completed not by the expected word "easy" but by one of two words with equally low subjective conditional probability (p < .03) such as "simple" or "short," the ERP to both of these would contain a sizable N400; however, the N400 to the word "simple" would be smaller, presumably because of its closer semantic tie to "easy." A similar effect has been observed for outright semantic incongruities (Kutas, Lindamood, and Hillyard 1984). Thus N400 amplitude goes beyond sheer indexing of subjective conditional probability.[22]

Our knowledge of what factors do and do not modulate the amplitude of the N400 has allowed us to address some specific questions within psycholinguistics. For example, Garnsey, Tanenhaus, and Chapman (1989) used the fact that N400s are reliably elicited by semantic anomalies to evaluate two alternative hypotheses about the strategies that guide parsing sentences when there is a momentary ambiguity about their syntactic structure. The strategy used in the study was to construct sentences that were semantically anomalous, but where the anomaly would become obvious at different points in the sentence depending upon which parsing strategy was followed. Consider the following *wh-* question:

(3) What bread did he read at the library?

This sentence is clearly anomalous, and our knowledge of the N400 congruity effect predicts a clear N400 difference between some word in (3) and an appropriate control sentence. The relevant and controversial issue, however, is where in the course of this question the N400 would be elicited. From a "first resort strategy" (Frazier and Fodor 1978), it follows that the N400 would be elicited at the first location where one could assign a thematic role to the filler NP (e.g., "what bread," which fills the gap following "read"). In (3) this would be at the word "read" because books, newspapers, and maybe even palms can be read but "bread" cannot; the N400 would thus reflect the unsuitability of "bread" as an object of "read." An alternative strategy, which can be called the "last resort strategy," predicts that the language system waits until the last possible gap could have occurred, and only then attempts to perform the thematic role assignment. On this view, one can argue that an N400 would not be elicited at "read" but rather at "library," when the end of the sentence precludes the possibility of finding a second possible gap, and the sentence is without doubt anomalous. Some version of the last resort strategy would clearly be more effective in the case where the question presented turned out to be not (3) but (4):

(4)   What bread did he read about at the library?

Here, attempting to fill the first possible gap at "read" would lead to an immediate semantic anomaly, while the very next word would have allowed the parser to posit a second, more semantically plausible gap, thereby disambiguating the structure. Garnsey, Tanenhaus, and Chapman (1989) found an N400 at the earliest possible point in the sentence time-locked to the word "read," and took this as evidence for the "first resort strategy." Because this is a psycholinguistics experiment touching on fairly subtle issues, there are other viable interpretations for this outcome.[23] These issues, however, are not unique to this study, nor are they raised by the use of the N400 as an electrophysiological index of anomaly processing. Accordingly, we offer it as an illustration of how the N400 in particular and ERPs in general can be used in psycholinguistic research to limit the number of possible explanations for certain phenomena.

Another application of the N400 is as an index of the integrity of certain normal functions in special populations. For example, Kutas, Hillyard, and Gazzaniga (1988) used the fact that semantic anomalies elicit N400s to assess the sentence-processing capabilities of the right hemisphere of split-brain patients. ERPs were recorded to very brief flashes of bilateral presentations of two words each of which was either congruent or incongruent with a preceding spoken sentence frame.[24] Briefly, Kutas, Hillyard, and Gazzaniga (1988) found that all patients produced N400s when the semantic violation was presented to the left hemisphere, but only the two patients whose right hemispheres showed a capacity for controlling speech output also generated N400s when the anomalous word was flashed to the right hemisphere. Thus Kutas and colleagues speculated that the proposed semantic organization of the lexicon may be more a consequence of the need for speeded output from a concept to actual words (i.e., for speech production) than the more standard view, which emphasizes this organization for comprehension.

Another result of this experiment was that the distribution of the N400 in these split-brain patients was most consistent with a deep neural generator.

Recently, evidence for just such a generator was reported by McCarthy and his collaborators (McCarthy et al. 1995; Nobre, Allison, and McCarthy 1994) based on depth recordings from patients with intractable epilepsy undergoing evaluation for possible surgical treatment. Specifically, they found a component in their depth recordings that behaved like a surface N400 in many of the ways listed above, that was quite focal, and that was electrophysiologically most consistent with a source in the anterior fusiform gyrus on the underside of the temporal lobe.[25] This is apparently the same region of the fusiform gyrus that Luders has shown includes a previously unknown "language area"—a patch of cortex that, when stimulated electrically, hinders a patient's ability to name objects or, in some cases, to speak at all (Luders et al. 1986). Surgical resection of this area is associated with aphasia, which does, however, usually fully resolve (Luders et al. 1991).

20.8   THE ELECTROPHYSIOLOGY OF BASIC SENTENCE PROCESSING

Unspoken in this story of the N400 is an implicit assumption about what kinds of processes are likely to trigger language ERP components, namely the sensory registration, encoding, and interpretation of individual words. We would expect to see these reflected in transient ERP components such as the P1, N1, P2, LPN, P3, and N400 to varying degrees. But as we noted in the introduction, this is not the complete story of language processing, which also entails the computation of the syntactic, semantic, and thematic relationships among single words. Thus, in addition to attentional focusing, visual feature extraction, lexical access, and activation of semantic memory, which are triggered by each lexical item with a certain urgency, the activated words and concepts must somehow be functionally linked so as to support a discourse representation and the inferences it affords. Aspects of these latter processes are by their nature cumulative, integrative, and more variable in their time course relative to individual words; thus we might expect to see them reflected in brain potential activity that is less reliably time-locked (than transient ERPs) to any given word with a time course that is slower and in some cases also either continuous or cumulative.

We take the continued activation, suppression, reactivation, and interaction of elements of these representations during sentence comprehension to be the province of working memory. Moreover, we presume that such links and integrative processes constitute the various temporary representations in phrases and clauses as well as in discourse. The basic building blocks for representations at the level of clauses (e.g., NPs and VPs) and at the level of discourse (e.g., actions and entities) are provided by linguistic theories; previously, we proposed an account of how these might rely on WM operation. Because various WM functions have different expected time courses and different relations to lexical items and sentence-level processes, we might expect them to be reflected in ERP effects with different time courses and distributions at the scalp. Specifically, (1) articles at the beginning of a noun phrase can reliably be used to anticipate the impending arrival and storage of a noun phrase (as reflected in the N400–700, which would resolve); (2) noun phrases can be assigned to a thematic role if one is unfilled and the link is obvious, or must be maintained for future use if it is not; (3) verbs can be used to delimit the possible thematic roles and make assignments to actors that are available in WM; and (4) clause endings can provide a good opportunity to perform WM operations before the next lexical onslaught. Thus we might expect different ERP patterns loosely time-locked to articles, nouns, verbs, and clause endings.

Theoretically, components that index integration should be present during the processing of virtually any kind of sentence, possibly modulated by a host of structural factors. There is, however, a great attraction to simplicity. Thus, for the following ERP analysis during reading, we concentrate on processing very simple transitive clauses (subject, verb, object) throughout their extent. This analysis reveals four potentially critical ERP effects, reflecting aspects of lexical access, the addition of noun phrases into working memory, thematic role assignment, and high (discourse) level integration; these effects have different time courses, distinct spatial distributions across the scalp, and are differentially affected by a number of within and between subject variables. A glimpse of ERP records to more complex sentence structures is also presented as an additional test of the hypothesized link between the various ERP effects and the underlying cognitive operations.

Our approach was to record the ERPs from a number of sites spread evenly across the scalp as subjects read 256 sentences, which included our critical materials, namely, multiclausal sentences that began with simple transitive clauses and continued with a causative conjunction, such as:

(5)   The   secretary answered the   phone because . . .
      [article] [noun]   [verb]   [article] [noun] [conjunction]

There are several advantages to using such simple materials. First, it is easy to construct vast numbers of these syntactically simple sentences so as to obtain good signal-to-noise ratios even for single subjects. Second, unlike some special syntactic constructions, such sentences do not draw attention to themselves and yet still require orthographic, lexical, semantic, syntactic, and pragmatic analyses. Likewise, they must also tap limited working memory resources and long-term memory for ultimate comprehension even if they are not taxing. That is, these materials are essentially nonreactive when compared with sentences including more complex clauses (e.g., "The boat sailed down the river sank"; "The German people hated was Hitler"; "The cat the dog the boy kicked chased died") or outright anomalies ("I like coffee with cream and dog"; "The broker persuaded to sell the stock"; "She was happy to get himself a drink"; "They was not pleased by the outcome"; "The scientist criticized the of proof the theorem."). Clearly, such sentences do draw attention to themselves by virtue of their incomprehensibility, strangeness or ungrammaticality and thus elicit ERPs that may reflect this aspect of the stimuli. By contrast, we think the ERP waveforms elicited by simple transitive clauses are unlikely to reflect the output of any specialized or abnormal processing strategies.

We expect that, just as the value of the N400 as an index of semantic analysis rose when it was shown to be characteristic of the ERP to every word,[26] so the utility of other language-related potentials will increase insofar as they are shown not to be processing violations per se. Finally, simple transitives might be less controversially used as a benchmark for sentence-processing investigations with special populations (e.g., nonfluent aphasics, patients suffering from various types of dementia, etc.) than other sentence types.

Method

Eighteen right-handed, monolingual English speakers (nine women, all between 18 and 29 years of age) were paid for their participation. Six of these participants reported having at least one left-handed family member, a factor known to influence ERPs to language stimuli, and particularly the laterality of the N400 (Kutas, Van Petten, and Besson 1988). None of the subjects reported any history of reading problems or any neurological disorder, and all had normal or corrected-to-normal vision.

Participants were asked to read sentences presented one word at a time (200 ms duration, with a 500 ms word onset asynchrony) for comprehension. There were a total of 256 sentences ranging between 12 and 18 words in length. Of these, 72 were the critical materials, namely multiclausal sentences beginning with a pure transitive clause followed by a causative conjunction. The remaining 184 sentences were fillers including 20 sentences whose first clauses contained a complex complement object (detailed below). It should be noted that just over half of the total sentences in this experiment began with the category sequence [det]-[N]-[V], which made our critical materials all the more unexceptional by comparison. Comprehension was tested on a random 50 percent of the sentences by having subjects respond to true/false probes querying the sentence material; 24 critical and 104 filler sentences were so probed. The true/false comprehension probe appeared 1,500 ms after the sentence-final word and remained on the screen for 2,500 ms, during which eye movements were explicitly allowed. A half-second fixation interval then preceded the next trial.

Recordings were made with 26 geodesically arranged electrode sites on a standard electrocap (see fig. 20.2) and from electrodes over both mastoid processes. In addition, electrodes placed at the outer canthi and under both eyes were used to record eye movements and blinks. All recordings were taken relative to a noncephalic reference, that is, a cardiac artifact—adjusted average of electrodes placed at the sternoclavicular junction and on top of the seventh cervical vertebra.

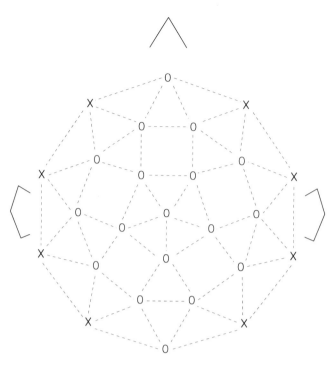

Figure 20.2 Schematic representation of location of each of 26 recording sites on scalp. In this and in all subsequent 26-electrode figures, nose is pointing toward top of page and topmost electrode is in center of forehead. Four lateral pairs of electrodes used in analyses that follow (frontal, anterior temporal, posterior temporal, and occipital) are shown as Xs.

The electroencephalographic and electro-oculographic recordings were analog-filtered between .01 and 100 Hz (TC ≈ 8 sec), digitized at a sampling rate of 250 Hz, and decimated[27] to 83.3 Hz prior to averaging over the longer epochs reported in this chapter. Epochs with blinks, eye movements and other artifacts such as amplifier blocking were rejected off-line before averaging (approximately 39 percent of all trials); epochs with correctable blinks (i.e., without amplifier blocking) were corrected using an adaptive filtering algorithm developed by Dale (1994) and included in the relevant ERP averages.

Results and Discussion

Comprehension Performance As expected, subjects had little difficulty comprehending the sentences that these transitive clauses initiated. Average comprehension rates were over 95 percent; however, six subjects did show comprehension rates markedly lower than 90 percent, which is rather striking for sentences of this nature. Hereafter we refer to these six subjects as "poor comprehenders" (relative to the twelve so-called good comprehenders.)[28]

^{1} The ^{2}secretary ^{3}answered ^{4}the ^{5}phone ^{6}because...

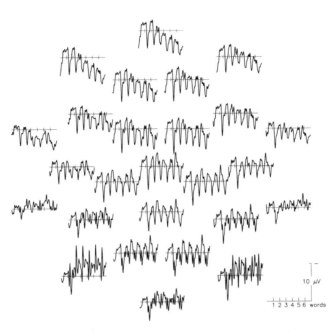

Figure 20.3 Grand average ($N = 18$) ERPs across simple transitive clause (i.e., first five words) and following word at all 26 scalp recording sites. Superscripts in example sentence refer to serial position indicated in calibration legend.

Event-related Brain Potentials (ERPs)   ERP waveforms to simple transitive clauses were derived from an average of 44 blink-corrected trials per subject (range: 28 to 58) with an epoch length of 3,500 ms, including a 500 ms presentence baseline. This epoch included all five words in the initial transitive clause and the following causative conjunction (e.g., "because"). Thus the contribution of any given lexical item to the average at each position was reduced while at the same time the lexical class and functional similarities among words at each position were highlighted.

Typically, such data are examined by averaging the ERP to each word in a sentence, forming subaverages as a function of experimental conditions, and measuring the amplitudes of peaks (or over some longer range) and latencies of the positive and negative peaks and troughs in the various waveforms. However, because our focus here is on processes that go beyond the single-word level, we will concentrate on measures of clause-length ERPs. The resultant grand average ERPs ($N = 18$) across the entire clause at all 26 electrode locations are shown in figure 20.3. Although this display highlights the regularity of the ERP response to each word and shows how it varies with scalp location to some degree, it does not easily yield to a visual

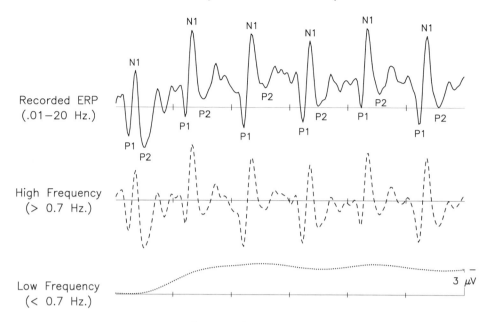

Figure 20.4 Cross-clause grand average ERP from left occipitotemporal site showing originally recorded and averaged data in first row (solid line), digitally high-pass filtered data in second row (>0,7 Hz, dashed line), and digitally low-pass filtered data in third row (<0.7 Hz, dotted line).

analysis of topographical distinctions. In order to tease apart the relatively punctate processes from those with a more prolonged and/or cumulative time course, we digitally filtered the recorded waveforms with a low-pass filter (<.7 Hz). Figure 20.4 shows the consequences of such digital filtering in separating the high- and low-frequency components of the recorded ERP for a single site (left occipitotemporal). Clearly, there is substantial slow activity across the course of the sentence that is independent of the transient P1-N1-P2 components triggered by each incoming word (see fig. 20.4, third row).

As can be seen in figure 20.5, even a cursory examination of the electrical signatures of these slow components of whole-clause averages reveals a rich landscape of differentiable potentials. The most remarkable aspect of these potentials is their systematic inhomogeneity over the scalp, with both anterior-posterior and left-right differences in polarity, time course, and amplitude. Presumably these electrical patterns were sculpted by the various nontransient demands of visual sentence processing, with their richness paralleling the complexity and multitude of the underlying neural processes.

The diversity of the whole-clause ERPs is especially striking when one compares analogous locations over the left and right hemispheres at the most lateral recording sites, that is, the outermost ring going from the front (top) to the back (bottom) of the head.[29] Ideally, we would employ statistical

The secretary answered the phone because...

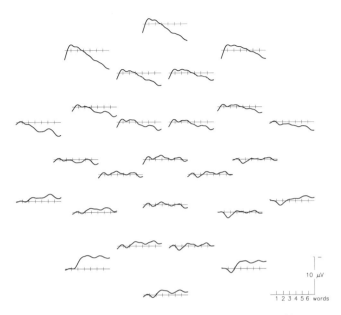

Figure 20.5 Same data as in figure 20.3 subjected to low-pass filtering at 0.7 Hz, resulting in emphasis of slow potential activity across transitive clause.

procedures tailored for making inferences about maps with rich spatiotemporal structure, but the commonly accepted and available methods are far from ideal, especially from the point of view of statistical power. For this chapter, we restrict our analysis to well-known factorial analyses of variance (ANOVAs) with repeated measures performed on the four pairs of most lateral electrodes, with the factors being hemisphere (left, right) and electrodes (four levels as described above). Individual analyses of pairs of sites were then performed after the omnibus ANOVA as indicated. All analyses, unless otherwise noted, were performed on the mean amplitude of the region between 2000 and 2500 ms post sentence onset, that is, on the clause-ending word.

Overall, the strong visual impression of voltage differences along an anterior-posterior axis that are shaped by laterally asymmetric factors is confirmed by the omnibus ANOVA (main effect of electrodes: $F(3, 51) = 5.19$, $p < .001$; interaction of electrodes and hemisphere: $F(3, 51) = 8.28$, $p < .001$). Over the front of the head, the slow potential is negative for the first two words but thereafter slowly becomes more and more positive over the course of the clause; this positive drift is significantly larger over left- than right-hemisphere sites by the end of the clause at prefrontal sites ($F(1, 17) = 7.92$; $p < .05$). At anterior temporal sites, superimposed on a subtle version of this slow positivity there is a more phasic positive change coincident with the appearance of the verb, and maximal in the range of 1300 to 1800 ms. This positivity is in turn followed by a negative-going wave that peaks at the clause-final word. Both the positivity and the subsequent negativity are better articulated over the left- than the right-hemisphere sites. Thus, for the verb-related positivity, we have a main effect of hemisphere at anterior temporal sites in the region between 1300 and 1800 ms, with the left hemisphere being more positive ($F(1, 17) = 6.45; p < .02$). For the clause-ending negativity at anterior temporal sites, we take the clause ending effect as the difference between the mean voltage at the end of the clause and the mean voltage on the following word, where we find a similar effect of hemisphere, with the left-hemisphere effect being larger ($F(1, 17) = 11.02; p < .01$).

Turning our attention to sites over the back of the head, the most obvious change is in the overall polarity of the ERP from positive-going over the front of the head to negative-going over the back; this effect is more pronounced over the left hemisphere. Thus, if we add an additional factor, grouping electrodes into anterior and posterior sets, we find a significant main effect of this anterior-posterior factor ($F(1, 17) = 9.00; p < .01$), and an interaction of this factor with hemisphere ($F(1, 17) = 14.64; p < .01$). At the posterior temporal sites (third pair of most lateral sites from front to back), this negativity builds slowly from the second word of the sentence to a peak around the clause ending, similar to that at anterior temporal sites. More prominent is the slow negative potential over the occipitotemporal sites that begins with the first word and is sustained at a steady level across the entire clause; this negative shift is also reliably larger over the left than the right hemisphere by the end of the clause ($F(1, 17) = 7.50; p < .02$). In summary, the slow components visible at frontal, anterior temporal, posterior temporal, and occipitotemporal sites show a left-right asymmetry consistent with the specialized role in language processing ascribed to the left hemisphere in the standard teachings of neuropsychology. It is important to note, however, that these data do not rule out involvement of the right hemisphere.[30]

20.9 PARSING THE ERP BY LOCATION AND FUNCTION

But what is the brain doing? What is the mind doing? We start our explanation with a discussion of the sensory, perceptual, and cognitive processes we know from behavioral, psychological, and psycholinguistic studies of word recognition and reading. We combine this with the spatial and temporal information provided by the patterns of the electrical activity at the scalp, and integrate this knowledge with data from other neuroscience studies to put forward some testable working hypotheses. Clearly, the first thing that subjects must do in this reading task is to process the words as visual input, analyzing the relevant visual features and forming representations at the word-form level sufficient to support the phenomena described by lexical access. By lexical access, we mean activation that leads to the availability of

Kutas and King

the syntactic specifications (e.g., word class, arguments, etc.) and core semantic attributes associated with each letter string.

Visual Processing and Occipitotemporal Cortex

A good place to start, therefore, is over the visual areas, the occipital cortex, because anatomical and neurophysiological research on visual processing has demonstrated that it is these areas which perform the initial visual analyses to provide the language system with input for further processing. It is here that the ERPs show the earliest time-locked activity following each word, namely, the P1 component of the visual evoked potential (EP). As seen in figure 20.6, the ERP to each word is characterized by the P1, N1, and P2 components (also see fig. 20.4). The earliest component, P1, occurs between 70 to 100 ms post word onset. The P1 and N1 have together been implicated in early sensory visual and vision-related attentional processing (reviewed by Hillyard and Picton 1987). Both have been found to vary in amplitude with manipulations in the physical parameters of visual stimuli as well as with attention, especially when attentional allocation is based on spatial location.

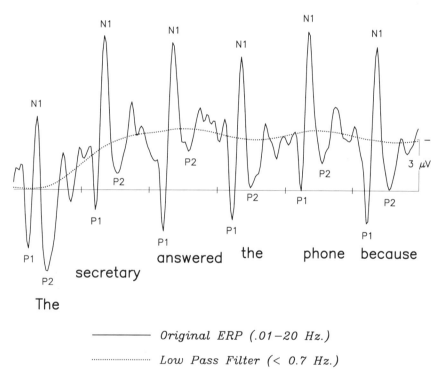

Original ERP (.01–20 Hz.)

Low Pass Filter (< 0.7 Hz.)

Figure 20.6 Cross-clause grand average ERP from left occipitotemporal site as originally recorded and averaged (solid line), and after application of a low-pass (<0.7 Hz) digital filter that emphasizes slow activity (dotted line). Early, visually specific P1, N1, and P2 components elicited by each word are labeled throughout clause.

For example, the amplitude of the P1 over the right occipital area is enhanced when attention (but not the eyes) is directed to a specific location to the left of fixation, and the opposite pattern holds when attention is focused to the left of fixation. Indeed, the behavior of the P1 component in a variety of visuospatial selective attention tasks has led Hillyard and his collaborators to propose that the P1 reflects the activity of a sensory gate mechanism that modulates the beam width of the attentional "spotlight" (Mangun, Hillyard, and Luck 1993). Recently, Mangun et al. (1993) combined individual subject magnetic resonance images (MRIs), brain electrical source localization (BESA), and current source density analysis (CSD) to localize the P1 generator to the extrastriate cortex contralateral to the visual field stimulated. While there is likely to be a family of P1s with slightly different functions and localizations, the class of P1 potentials is a good candidate for an early sensory potential that reflects decoding of visual input such as the letter strings subjects were asked to read in this experiment.

A good functional account of the next positive component, the P2, is lacking, but it is known that its amplitude is sensitive to pattern in the visual input. Thus, for example, the P2 is larger for patterned visual stimuli than for unstructured light flashes and larger when the visual features are coherent, as in a real face, than when all the facial features are present but scrambled (Jeffreys and Tukmachi 1992). All in all, it is reasonable to assume that the P1, N1, and P2 components of the visual EP reflect neural activity involved in early sensory analyses including visual feature extraction and its modulation by attention.

Consistent with previous reports, both the P1 and the P2 components to each word were asymmetric in amplitude, being larger over the right hemisphere (e.g., Kutas, Van Petten, and Besson 1988; Compton et al. 1991). If we are justified in assuming that these P1s are generated in the extrastriate cortex as per Mangun, Hillyard, and Luck's (1993) analysis, then this component falls close to the region identified by Petersen et al. (1990) via positron-emission tomography (PET) as specialized for processing the attributes of visually presented wordlike stimuli. Specifically, across a number of studies, Petersen and his colleagues found increased blood flow in this region of the extra-striate cortex when subjects viewed real words, nonsense strings, and so-called false fonts (i.e., stimuli that looked like words comprising fragments that looked somewhat like letters) but not when they listened to spoken words. Moreover, this is essentially the same area where Squire et al. (1992) observed significant decreases in blood flow when words were repeated within an experimental session (in an implicit priming task), presumably because aspects of visual feature extraction were facilitated (primed) by exposure during a prior study episode.

Figure 20.6 also shows that at the occipitotemporal sites, these transient sensory responses are superimposed on a sustained negativity. This standing negativity took approximately one second to reach its eventual plateau of approximately -3 μV. Thus, at this site, the nature of the visual processing was insensitive to lexical class (e.g., open or closed class) and was laterally asymmetric, being larger over the left than the right hemisphere. As a working hypothesis, we suggest that this negative shift reflects processing and integration of the visual features necessary to activate a word-form representation. If so it may be related to the activation in the ventral occipital areas proposed by Petersen et al. (1990) to be involved in processing word forms. Fiez and Petersen (1993) described a region in the lower side of the occipital lobe that showed increased blood flow both following visually presented words and orthographically regular pseudowords but *not* following either so-called false fonts or unpronounceable consonant strings. Because Fiez and Petersen did not use very familiar visual patterns such as pictures of objects or faces as a control, their identification of this area as specific to word form may be premature.[31] Nonetheless, the general region undoubtedly has a role in early visual processing.

The time course of the slow negativity fits with the proposal that it mirrors the use of resources dedicated to the continued processing of visual features, or the continuous activation of word-form representations supporting higher-level computations. A further testable hypothesis is that the asymmetry in this component may reflect lexical processes; it would thus be informative to determine whether a similar negativity would distinguish the processing of lists of pseudowords (where it would be expected) from lists of nonwords (where it would not). Moreover, examining the elicitation of this negativity during extended presentations of complex visual scenes, faces, or real pictures would further test its specificity to lexical level analysis. Finally, if the negativity is uniquely tied to lexical-level processes, then we might expect a similarly prolonged potential during speech reflecting acoustic-phonetic analyses and segmentation. Based on the available neuropsychological, neurophysiological, and neuroimaging data, these operations would most likely be carried out in the superior temporal gyrus and nearby brain regions, thereby resulting in a more central scalp distribution typical of that obtained for early sensory auditory components (Naatanen 1992).

A somewhat surprising aspect of these occipital potentials is highlighted in the comparison between good and poor comprehenders in figure 20.7. Because the absolute level of performance was relatively high (over 80 percent for all subjects), and the differences between good and poor comprehenders were therefore relatively small, we were surprised to find that the ERPs from the two groups differed in several respects. First, the sensory components were on the whole larger peak-to-peak (e.g., P1-N1, N1-P2) for the poor than good comprehenders. Second, both the amplitudes of the sensory components and the slow negativity exhibited greater hemispheric asymmetry in the poor comprehenders (for the slow negativity at occipitotemporal sites, $F(1, 16) = 5.31; p < .05$). In a previous report, we have suggested that the larger visual EPs in the poorer comprehenders might indicate that they allocated more attentional resources to fairly low-level visual processing of the words (feature extraction) than the better comprehenders (King and Kutas

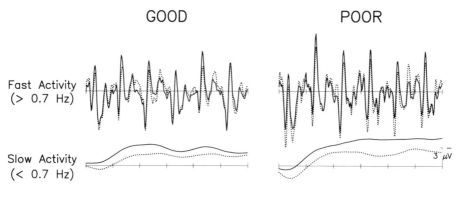

GOOD   POOR

Fast Activity
(> 0.7 Hz)

Slow Activity
(< 0.7 Hz)

—————— *Left Hemisphere*   ············· *Right Hemisphere*

Figure 20.7 Comparison of lateral distribution of cross-clause ERPs from over occipito-temporal sites for good ($N = 12$, left column) and poor comprehenders ($N = 6$, right column). Left (solid line) and right (dotted line) hemispheres are shown superimposed in top row after high-pass digital filtering and in bottom row after low-pass digital filtering.

1995a). The present data are in line with this suggestion, perhaps indicating that the poorer comprehenders also devoted more processing resources to the integration of the visual features into a representation (word form) that could be used to access a word's syntactic specifications and semantic attributes.

As mentioned previously, these occipital potentials were not especially sensitive to lexical class or word meaning. Typically, ERPs over more anterior regions are more sensitive indices of lexical class and semantic relationships both at the word and sentence levels. The factors that influence this N400 potential were noted in the introduction. As we did not explicitly manipulate the amplitude of the N400 in this study, we merely point out its presence as an index of semantic analysis at the interface between lexical and sentential levels.

Semantic and Syntactic Processing: Frontal and Temporal Electrode Sites

By contrast to the early feature extraction that takes place transiently between 80 and 100 ms post stimulus onset, the effects of semantic and structural variables tend to be reflected transiently in the ERP almost 100 ms later between 200 and 600 ms post word onset. We think that it is at this time that the specific word meanings derived from an interplay between the "core" characteristics of a word and the context in which it is currently embedded emerge. Thus at the same time as the visual areas are engaged with early visual processing functions, accessing visual word forms, and keeping these word forms active for further processing, frontal and temporal regions are

GOOD   POOR

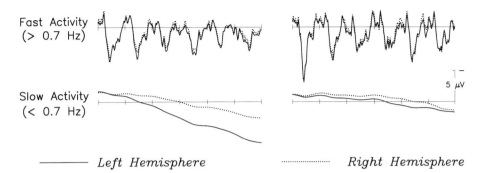

Fast Activity
(> 0.7 Hz)

Slow Activity
(< 0.7 Hz)

5 μV

——————— *Left Hemisphere*   ················· *Right Hemisphere*

Figure 20.8 Comparison of lateral distribution of the cross-clause ERPs from over the prefrontal sites for good ($N = 12$, left column) and poor comprehenders ($N = 6$, right column). Left (solid line) and right (dotted line) hemispheres are shown superimposed in top row after high-pass digital filtering and in bottom row after low-pass digital filtering. Note that ultraslow positive drift is almost twice as large over left hemisphere, while faster potentials are almost identical over two hemispheres.

involved in analyzing word meanings and the sentence constituents, setting up a mental model of the situation or delimiting a mental space (Johnson-Laird 1983; Fauconnier 1985), and keeping all of these information sources active as working memory. Noun phrases and verbs are presumed to be especially important here in that they provide the players, the roles, and the actions—who did what to whom (when and where).

We now turn to the slow activity at the most frontal recording sites,[32] where we found that reading the transitive clauses was associated with a slow-growing, cumulative positivity; this positive drift was almost twice as large over the left than the right frontal sites (see also fig. 20.9). By contrast, the transient EPs at these same frontal sites were bilaterally symmetric. The frontal maximum of these potentials taken together with the known role of the frontal lobes in the "executive" functions of working memory suggest that they reflect integration between items in WM with information from long-term memory to form a coherent mental model essential both to understanding and to the laying down of a retrievable memory trace.

Just as with the posterior slow potential effects, the good and poor comprehenders could be differentiated on the basis of the amplitude and asymmetry of this frontal positivity (see fig. 20.8). It was much larger for the good than the poor comprehenders; the difference being mostly due to its absence in the left-hemisphere ERPs of the poor comprehenders, causing a reliable interaction of comprehension skill and hemisphere at the frontal lateral sites ($F(1, 16) = 5.06$; $p < .05$). Note that this is exactly the opposite of the pattern we observed for the occipital negativity, where poorer comprehenders

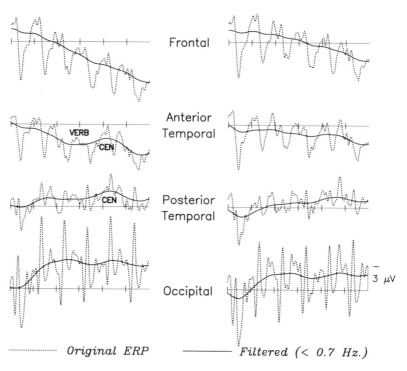

Frontal

Anterior
Temporal

VERB

CEN

Posterior
Temporal

CEN

Occipital

‾
3 μV

·········· *Original ERP*   ——— *Filtered (< 0.7 Hz.)*

Figure 20.9 Superimposed are originally recorded cross-clause grand average ($N = 18$) ERPs and the slow activity only (low-pass-filtered at 0.7 Hz) for 4 pairs of sites going from front to back of head over left and right hemispheres, separately. Note phasic positivity at left anterior temporal sites that peaks just following the verb and is itself immediately followed by negativity at clause ending (i.e., clause-ending negativity or CEN).

showed larger effects. We take this pattern as indicative of a possible trade-off in the poor comprehenders between resources devoted to early visual processing and those devoted to higher-level integrative processing (e.g., Perfetti and Lesgold 1977); one might expect such a trade-off to be imposed by the time constraints of working memory operations. Although we did not test their memory for the experimental materials, we would expect poor comprehenders to perform worse on recognition memory or recall tests for these sentences if less time was devoted to "deeper" processing. Of some interest to this reciprocity hypothesis is what would happen in the poor comprehenders if the sentences were spoken instead of read. Insofar as their comprehension problem is solely a consequence of impaired early visual processing, poor comprehenders should show normal ERPs during speech processing, assuming that their early auditory processing is within normal limits. Of course, it is also possible that the early processing difficulties are due to a fault in a domain-general operation such as temporal synchrony or sequencing, and would therefore be manifest in both reading and speech processing (see, for example, Tallal, Miller, and Fitch 1993).

The extreme slowness of the frontal activity is very striking. Indeed, its time course is more in line with that of neuromodulatory, metabolic, or blood flow processes than postsynaptic activity. One obvious temptation is to seek some connection of these slower frontal potentials and the activity of a neuromodulatory neurotransmitter known to impact working memory performance, namely, dopamine. There is substantial evidence that both the frontal lobes and its dopamine innervations are critical for proper execution of WM functions (e.g., Sawaguchi and Goldman-Rakic 1991). In short, both the frontal region and dopamine appear to be necessary to allow humans to stop and think without always reacting in a reflexive fashion—to determine what is relevant and requires attentional resources, and what is immaterial, given the current situation. Certainly part of the frontal lobe must be involved in maintaining the frontal attentional system (Posner and Petersen 1990) and in holding onto the sense of continuity that characterizes most immediate thought.[33] We should also note the possibility that this slow scalp-positive shift could be due to a cortical surface negative shift within a deep convolution of the frontal cortex or along a medial surface such as the anterior cingulate, which would reverse in polarity over the ipsilateral scalp.[34]

In either case, our working hypothesis is that this growing anterior positivity is a cumulative index of the construction of a coherent sentence-level schema or the delimitation of a mental space (e.g., Fauconnier 1985). Clearly, this integrative process would be most easily achieved and most readily completed for simple transitive constructions and would be more difficult for sentences with embedded clauses (which we will discuss later). Insofar as such integration is difficult, the slow frontal positivity should grow less rapidly. In general, we have found that loading unassigned noun phrases into working memory and possibly holding onto thematic role placeholders in working memory were associated with negative-going potentials superimposed on this slow frontal shift (King and Kutas 1995a). On the other hand, operations within working memory, such as uncovering argument structure information from a verb and making preliminary role assignments to the subject NP, seem to be associated with a positive-going potential. This phasic positivity is superimposed on the slower, more anterior positivity; thus, coincident with the verb there was a phasic positivity more prominent over left temporal sites (see fig. 20.9). Also at the left anterior temporal recording site, this phasic positivity was almost immediately followed by a negativity that appeared time-locked to the end of the clause (we will dub this the "CEN" for clause-ending negativity). The CEN also was most prominent at temporal sites over the left hemisphere.

Clause boundaries are known to be loci where changes related to language processing have large effects on working memory. For example, clause boundaries and sentence-final words are typically associated with increases in reading times measured via button presses and eye movements (Just and Carpenter 1980; Aaronson and Ferres 1986). Further, Levin and Kaplan (1970) reported that the eye-voice span became shorter at clause boundaries, in agreement with other results indicating that secondary task performance suffers insofar as it competes with clause closure processes. Without additional manipulations, we cannot be certain whether the CEN reflects successful wrap-up of the clause or processes that detect would-be clause endings based on structural considerations. In other words, we cannot distinguish theories that posit specialized wrap-up or integrative processes at clause boundaries from those that argue against any special or additional processing at a clause boundary. In this latter view, clause boundary effects would simply reflect the frequent coincidental co-occurrence of clause endings and finalizing multiple thematic role assignments.

Comparing Simple with Embedded Clauses

In other recent work (King and Kutas 1995a), we proposed that updating one's mental model by adding elements and/or forming functional links between them in WM were manifest in ERP modulations over frontal and temporal regions, especially in the left hemisphere. In that study we examined WM operations during reading by comparing sentences that contained embedded relative clauses. The critical materials were closely matched pairs of sentences both of which contained a relative clause modifying the main clause subject but differing in the role that the subject of the main clause played in the relative clause:

(6) a. The reporter who harshly attacked the senator admitted the error.
     b. The reporter who the senator harshly attacked admitted the error.

In (6a) "the reporter" is also the agent-subject of the relative clause, and the sentence is referred to as a "subject subject (SS) relative." By contrast, in (6b) "the reporter" is the object of the relative clause verb and the sentence is referred to as a "subject object (SO) relative." Neither of these sentence types is ambiguous, but they do differ in processing difficulty, with the object relative (SO) causing greater difficulty. Participants tend to be slower when reading object relatives and also make more comprehension errors when questioned on who did what to whom. The difficulty is seemingly concentrated on the verbs of the relative clause and main clause ("attacked" and "admitted") (e.g., King and Just 1991). These processing differences have been attributed to the greater working memory load imposed by object relative sentences, wherein not all information can be used as immediately upon occurrence, as it can in the subject relative sentences.

Our ERP data corroborated these behavioral findings in revealing large ERP differences (i.e., a left anterior negativity, or LAN effect; see also Kluender and Kutas, 1993a, 1993b) where the greatest processing times are typically reported for both word-by-word reading time (Ford 1983; King and Just 1991) and eye fixation studies (Holmes and O'Regan 1981), namely, at the main verb just following the relative clause. Our linking of modulations in this negativity with WM load is supported by the data in figure 20.10,

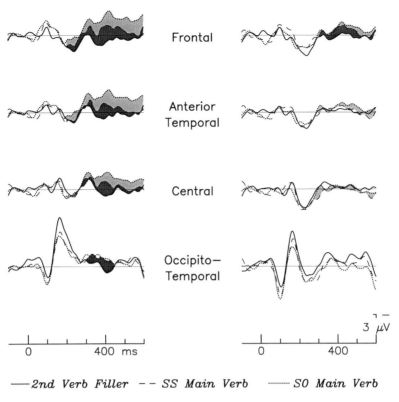

——— *2nd Verb Filler* — — *SS Main Verb* ·········· *SO Main Verb*

Figure 20.10 Grand average ($N = 24$) ERPs to main clause verb from subject relative (SS) and object relative (SO) sentences contrasted with the ERPs to second verbs in multiclausal sentence without any embeddings (e.g., "The secretary answered the phone and scribbled a message on the legal paper"). This difference in relative negativity over left frontal sites is known as "left anterior negativity" (LAN) effect. Data from King and Kutas (1995a).

showing the greatest LAN for the verbs in the more difficult SO sentences, the least negativity for the second verb in sentences without any embedded clauses, and a negativity of intermediate amplitude for the main verb of SS sentences. Further evidence for this position is given in Kluender and Kutas (1993a). More important, however, across-sentence ERP averages unambiguously demonstrated that the brain deals with subject and object relative sentences differently, well before the verbs (see figure 20.11). That is, we observed significant differences between the two sentence types much earlier than typical reading time effects.

One striking ERP feature distinguishing SS from SO sentences was the relatively larger slow frontal positive shift in SS sentences; in this case, the ERPs to the two sentence types diverged as soon as the reader was obliged to add a second noun phrase (NP) to working memory in object relative sentences. This frontal shift grew over the course of these sentences most quickly for the structurally simpler sentence type (e.g., the first clause of coordinate transitive clauses similar to the ones we discussed previously) and

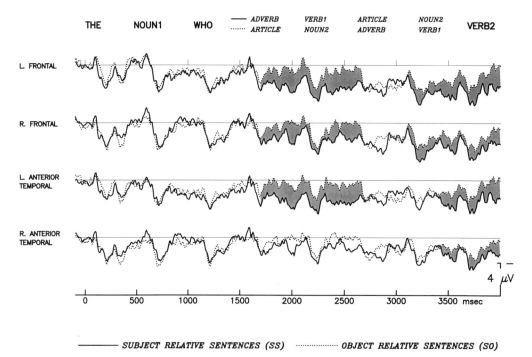

| THE | NOUN1 | WHO | —— ADVERB
······· ARTICLE | VERB1
NOUN2 | ARTICLE
ADVERB | NOUN2
VERB1 | VERB2 |

L. FRONTAL

R. FRONTAL

L. ANTERIOR TEMPORAL

R. ANTERIOR TEMPORAL

4 μV

0   500   1000   1500   2000   2500   3000   3500 msec

—— SUBJECT RELATIVE SENTENCES (SS)   ········· OBJECT RELATIVE SENTENCES (SO)

Figure 20.11 Comparison of grand average ($N = 24$) ERPs elicited by subject (SS) and object (SO) relative sentences at four anterior recording sites. Recordings span first two words of the main clause, the embedded clause, and next few words of main clause. Difference between two ERPs is shaded for emphasis. Data taken from King and Kutas (1995).

least quickly for the structurally more complex sentence type, reaching the smallest amplitude offset for the most difficult (SO) sentence type. As mentioned earlier, we linked this slow frontal positive drift with sentence level integration and hypothesized that negative-going deflections from it occurred with each additional demand on working memory: the heavier the load, the more negative (i.e., less positive) the slow potential shift. Note that at the end of the SS relative clause we see a phasic negativity, which we take to be the CEN for the relative clause. The CEN for the SO clause is not apparent, but, then again, neither is the actual end of the relative clause, which ends with a gap. One interesting possibility is that the left frontal negativity we observe following the relative clause is primarily an enlarged CEN, possibly prolonged through time, as also suggested by Kluender and Kutas (1993b). This pattern of effects is reasonable not only because the detection of the gap in the relative clause may not be closely time-locked to any word onset, but also because clause-ending processes in SO sentences may take longer, as has been suggested by reaction time and eye movement data (e.g., King and Just 1991; Ford 1983; Holmes and O'Regan 1981).

We observed a similar effect in the present data when comparing the simple transitive clauses with more complex sentence types; loading items into WM was associated with enhanced frontotemporal negativities. Note

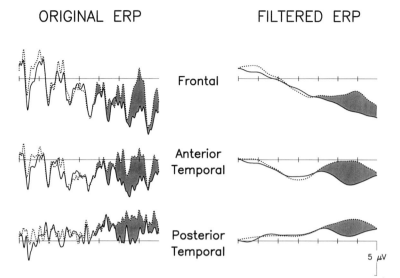

ORIGINAL ERP   FILTERED ERP

Frontal

Anterior
Temporal

Posterior
Temporal

5 μV

——————— *The secretary answered the phone because...*

·················· *The secretary answered that the phone...*

Figure 20.12   Grand average ERPs to simple transitive clauses plotted against clauses where object is complex complement structure (i.e., embedded sentence). Note that shaded difference between two sentence types becomes substantial after point at which it is clear that object of verb in nonsimple case is complex complement.

that this WM-related negativity is different from the CEN. This contrast is depicted in figure 20.12, where the ERPs to simple transitives are overlaid with those to clauses whose object is a complex complement. The ERP difference between these two sentence types becomes substantial after the point at which it is obvious that the object of the verb in the nonsimple case is an embedded sentence. Thus, in the case of the simple transitives, the clause ending is demarcated by a negativity with a left temporal focus. By contrast, in the case of the more complex sentence type, the waveform also goes more negative as information is loaded into WM, although this negativity seems to include both a prolongation of the CEN and a more frontal component reflecting the additional WM load.

As would be predicted from a variety of working memory-based theories of comprehension, the ERP slow potential differences between subject and object relative sentences were correlated with comprehension. Unlike good comprehenders (87 percent accuracy), the poorer comprehenders (68 percent accuracy) showed the positive shift *only* for simple transitive clauses and not for the subject relative sentences. Moreover, poor comprehenders showed relatively little difference in their ERPs to subject and object relative sentences (see fig. 20.13). They appeared to be loaded down simply in comprehending sentences with embedded clauses per se, without much regard for the additional demand the SO sentences made on WM resources. Note that

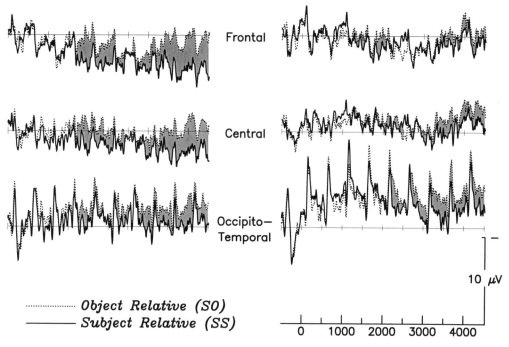

GOOD COMPREHENDERS   POOR COMPREHENDERS

Frontal

Central

Occipito—
Temporal

10 µV

·············· *Object Relative (SO)*
———— *Subject Relative (SS)*

0   1000   2000   3000   4000

Figure 20.13 Comparison of the cross-clause ERPs from the SS versus SO sentences in good ($N = 12$, left column) and poor ($N = 12$, right column) comprehenders at three left-hemisphere sites. Data taken King and Kutas (1995).

the ERPs from the occipital leads also show the previously discussed differences in the visual EPs of good versus poor comprehenders; both the sensory EPs and the slow negativity were larger and more asymmetric in the poor than in the good comprehenders.

20.10 SUMMARY

In this this chapter we have described the patterns of electrical activity recorded from the subjects' scalp as they read through the initial transitive clause in a series of thematically unrelated, multiclausal sentences. We linked the electrical activity to phenomena within the psycholinguistic literature on sentence processing as well as to brain areas defined by research on nonhuman animals, brain-damaged individuals, and various human brain–imaging techniques. We proposed electrophysiological markers for relatively early, low-level processes such as visual feature extraction and integration into a word form, as well as for later processes such as thematic role assignment, clause closure, and the construction and integration of a more complete discourse model. We also presented evidence for an ERP index of maintaining items in working memory. Throughout, we highlighted the differences in these processes as they related to comprehension skill, suggesting a possible trade-off between resources for low-level visual analysis versus higher-level integration. Although our results must be regarded as preliminary, they have suggested to us several working hypotheses that seek to unify concepts in the cognitive and biological studies of language processing, and offer the prospect of achieving a true cognitive neuroscience integration.

ACKNOWLEDGMENTS

This research was supported by NICHD grant HD22614 and NIA grant AG08313. Jonathan W. King was supported by a fellowship from the San Diego McDonnell-Pew Cognitive Neuroscience Institute and training grant NIH/NIDCD T32 DC00041-01 to the Center for Research in Language at UCSD. We also thank the members and organizers of the NICI Cognitive Neuroscience Summer School held at Berg en dal, Netherlands in July 1994 for their inspiration, Jill Weckerly for endless hours as an interactive sounding board, and Elizabeth Bates for her comments.

NOTES

1. Because they do not arise in the simple materials used in the present experiment, we will not discuss the complexities of establishing that a particular noun phrase or pronoun actually refers to an antecedent. Nevertheless, these issues are clearly very important in language processing and elegantly underscore the need for a flexible model of working memory.

2. This account has the added benefits of explicit computational modularity (Fodor 1983) without actually encapsulating functional subsystems.

3. This is true whether we prefer to think of linguistic inputs in terms of highly distributed neural networks, explicit tree structures or something in between.

4. Within English, which has too few case markings to indicate case roles for nouns, multiple-slot structures like verbs tend to have greater control over the eventual meaning of their fillers than the reverse, thereby establishing specific "expectations" concerning their fillers even in the absence of much pragmatic information.

5. That is, with respect to fillers or open slots, whether achieved via an articulatory loop or by passive spreading of activation.

6. Note that this characterization of WM is simultaneously at variance with functionally modular models of processing like Fodor's (1983) as well as those that attempt to make all processing dependent on a unified working memory like Newell's SOAR (1990). Fodor's hypothesis depends critically on central processes (e.g., general WM) to digest the output of its perceptual and linguistic modules, while Newell's depends on a universally convertible working memory to feed its more specialized problem spaces that control processing.

7. While 80,000 mm^2 is by no means small, it is actually smaller than even many neuroscientists have guessed in the past (Cherniak 1990).

8. We estimated the area of the pars triangularis by measuring its lateral extent from an actual size figure of the brain printed in DeArmond, Fusco, and Dewey's (1989) atlas and correcting for the amount of folding in this region of the cortex (estimated as a factor of almost 3 from an

inspection of the horizontal sections through this region, and by data presented in Dale and Sereno 1993).

9. The version of Broca's area appearing in Kandel, Schwartz, and Jessel 1991 on page 10 would appear to be over 4,000 mm², while the one on page 844 would be perhaps slightly larger. The version of Broca's area shown in Kolb and Whishaw 1990 on page 570 is slightly smaller, although it hardly overlaps those depicted in Kandel, Schwartz, and Jessel 1991.

10. In fact, Wernicke's account of his eponymous brain area shows it as occupying the cortex on the superior temporal gyrus anterior rather than posterior to the primary auditory cortex; see, for example, de Bleser, Cubelli, and Luzzatti 1993 for a facsimile of Wernicke's original figure and a discussion of his work.

11. Cherniak's (1990) work on quantitative neuroanatomy shows, for example, that long fiber connections between ipsilateral brain areas must be relatively scarce, or at best less dense than generally assumed, because there is simply not enough physical (actual) space within the white matter to allow them to be more common or to support them. A somewhat less stringent constraint also applies to the connectional budget between adjacent areas.

12. The use of the term *desynchronization* in these techniques may be misleading because it is not clear how or to what extent alpha activity (for example) is synchronized in the cortex, or what its desynchronization means.

13. We must assume when we use the average ERP approach that the response function to the trigger is stationary and that the "random" activity is completely uncorrelated with the true response. These strong assumptions are at best only partially fulfilled but do not vitiate the entire approach, judging by the number and variety of highly replicable effects in the field.

14. While an infinite number of configurations of a variable number of neural generators may account for any given pattern of electrical activity at the scalp, only some combinations are actually likely if we assume that the potential at the scalp is a sum of the excitatory post-synaptic potentials (EPSPs) and inhibitory postsynaptic potentials (IPSPs) from cortical pyramidal cells firing in synchrony. Moreover, because for the purposes of this analysis brain waves are just (no more than) electrical signals within a physical system, they can be deciphered in terms of the laws of physics. There are proven mathematical techniques available for determining the minimum number of separate generators needed to explain the pattern of electrical activity at the scalp at any given moment, and certainly at moments correlated in time. Thus, while certain assumptions must be made, they seem eminently reasonable. Still further constraints to delimit the solution space (i.e., the number of possible solutions) are available if findings from depth recordings are added. In all cases, the more electrodes, the better (although point sources would be preferable to large cup electrodes) because until at least the number of underlying generators is known (unless the minimum number of generators is considerable), high spatial sampling is needed to get localization precision. The number of recording electrodes should exceed at minimum (preferably, by a factor of 4) the number of generators assumed to be active. For one thing, you do not want to distort the signal; for another, it would be nice if you could still tell what color hair someone had (if any).

15. The LPN refers to the lexical processing negativity which King and Kutas (1995b) have proposed as an alternative to the N280 (Neville et al. 1992) because its latency varies systematically as a function of the length and frequency of the eliciting word. The LPN thus is an ERP component elicited by a word that marks the upper limit by which lexical access must have occurred.

16. Note that not all and perhaps none of these potentials are language-specific.

17. The P2 and P3-like components are often considered as part of the late positive complex (LPC), which includes both a preceding negativity (N2) and a subsequent slow wave (SW) that is negative frontally and positive posteriorly.

18. Although in fact it may be necessary to resort to such interactions to account for all of the ERP differences between open- and closed-class words. Thus, while not all the relevant analyses have been done, Neville, Mills, and Lawson (1992) used median splits of the open-class ERPs on length and frequency of usage to argue that neither one nor both of these factors were sufficient to account for the observed N400 differences between the two lexical classes.

19. Complicating factors include the nature of the stimuli, repetition lag, subject's task, and number of repetitions.

20. *Cloze probability* refers to the probability that a given word will be used by a subject to "fill in the blank," given a context with a missing word. We find it more than a little reassuring that probabilistic approaches to on-line parsing have recently enjoyed greater popularity both practically and theoretically (see, for example, MacDonald 1994 and chap. 17, this volume).

21. Of course it is possible that our estimates of cloze probability based on the cloze procedure are less sensitive than the brain's on-line estimates of a word's predictability.

22. The sensitivity of N400 amplitude to repetition also suggests that it is more than a measure of subjective conditional probability.

23. See, for example, Fodor (1989) for a thorough review of the issues involved in processing empty categories. More recent work has favored models where the parser maintains parallel syntactic analyses in certain situations (e.g., Gibson 1990). Moreover, MacDonald, Just, and Carpenter (1992) provide evidence that there are WM–related individual differences in the computation of such multiple analyses, thereby muddying the interpretation of Garnsey, Tanenhaus, and Chapman's (1989) data. If subjects were maintaining multiple syntactic analyses, the N400 observed may simply have meant that the "first resort" was *one* analysis being pursued. In this case, it would be informative to see if manipulating the content of the filler NP to change the plausibility of its filling the first gap affected N400 amplitude (e.g., "What bread" versus "What variety of bread" versus "What breads").

24. Thus there were four conditions: two where the words in the two visual fields were identical (one congruous and one incongruous) and two where the words in the two visual fields were different (one congruous and the other incongruous).

25. The component was a positivity on the cortex surface, but reversed in polarity and presumably would generate a negativity at the scalp surface.

26. With an amplitude determined by the extent to which the word was expected given the context.

27. In this context, *decimation* refers to a reduction in the EEG sampling rate between the time of acquisition and the time of analysis; for the integral decimation factor in this case, this corresponds to taking every third point of the data collected at 250 Hz.

28. It may be worth noting that four of these six poor comprehenders had at least one left-hander in their immediate family. We have observed group differences related to family history of left-handedness in previous language studies (e.g., Kutas, Van Petten, and Besson 1988; Kluender and Kutas 1993), and work by Bever and his colleagues (Bever, Carrithers, Cowart, and Townsend 1989) suggests that family sinistrality may be a biological factor reflecting a real aspect of the subject's language processing capabilities.

29. Note that these homologous sites are the farthest away from each other in the two hemispheres and therefore least susceptible to contamination by volume conduction from activity in the other hemisphere.

30. By way of contrast, the more medial recording sites (i.e., those nearer the vertex or center electrode) show much less left-right differentiation from each other. This overall pattern suggests that the generators underlying these slow potentials may be arranged asymmetrically.

Without additional evidence, however, we cannot be sure whether the asymmetry is due to a difference in dipole strength between the right and left hemisphere or to differences in dipole orientation between the two sides.

31. In particular, extremely recent functional magnetic resonance imagery (fMRI) work by Sereno and collaborators (personal communication) and other groups should greatly enrich our knowledge of these early visual areas.

32. Note that these most frontal recording sites have typically not been included in most ERP studies of language processing.

33. We reiterate our caution in inferring the underlying generators from maxima in the potentials at the scalp; we offer these primarily as working hypotheses for the moment.

34. Interestingly, Grossman et al. (1992) have provided PET evidence in favor of a role for the anterior cingulate in sentence processing; they suggest that processing deficits in this brain region play an important role in the (subtle) sentence-processing deficits seen in patients suffering from Parkinson's Disease.

REFERENCES

Aaronson, D., and Ferres, S. (1986). Reading strategies for children and adults: A quantitative model. *Psychological Review, 93*, 89−112.

Alexander, M. P., Naeser, M. A., and Palumbo, C. (1990). Broca's area aphasias: Aphasia after lesions including the frontal operculum. *Neurology, 40*(2), 353−362.

Anderson, J. R. (1983). *The architecture of cognition.* Cambridge, MA: Harvard University Press.

Baddeley, A. D. (1986). *Working memory.* Oxford: Clarendon Press.

Bentin, S., McCarthy, G., and Wood, C. C. (1985). Event-related potentials, lexical decision, and semantic printing. *Electroencephalography and Clinical Neurophysiology, 60*, 343−355.

Berger, H. (1929). Über das Elektroenzephalogramm des Menschen. *Archiv für Psychiatrie und Nervenkrankheiten, 87*, 527−570.

Besson, M., and Kutas, M. (1993). The many facets of repetition: A cued-recall and event-related potential analysis of repeating words in same versus different sentence contexts. *Journal of Experimental Psychology: Learning, Memory, and Cognition, 19*, 1115−1133.

Bever, T. G., Carrithers, C., Cowart, W., and Townsend, D. J. (1989). Language processing and familial handedness. In A. M. Galaburda (Ed.), *From reading to neurons: Issues in the biology of language and cognition,* 331−357. Cambridge, MA: MIT Press.

Brodmann, K. (1909). *Vergleichende Lokalisationslehre der Grosshirnrinde.* Leipzig: Barth.

Caplan, D. (1994). Language and the brain. In M. A. Gernsbacher (Ed.), *Handbook of psycholinguistics,* 1023−1053. San Diego: Academic Press.

Cherniak, C. (1990). The bounded brain: Toward quantitative neuroanatomy. *Journal of Cognitive Neuroscience, 2*, 58−68.

Cherniak, C. (1994). Component placement optimization in the brain. *Journal of Neuroscience, 14*(4), 2418−2427.

Chomsky, N. (1981). *Lectures on government and binding.* Dordrecht: Foris.

Chomsky, N. (1965). *Aspects of the theory of syntax* (Special technical report, Massachusetts Institute of Technology Research Laboratory of Electronics no. 11). Cambridge, MA: MIT Press.

Compton, P. E., Grossenbacher, P., Posner, M. I., and Tucker, D. M. (1991). A cognitive-anatomical approach to attention in lexical access. *Journal of Cognitive Neuroscience, 3*(4), 304–312.

Dale, A. (1994). Source localization and spatial discriminant analysis: Linear approaches. Ph.D. diss., University of California, San Diego, La Jolla, CA.

Dale, A. M., and Sereno, M. I. (1993). Improved localization of cortical activity by combining EEG and MEG with MRI cortical surface reconstruction: A linear approach. *Journal of Cognitive Neuroscience, 5*(2), 162–176.

Deacon, T. W. (1992). Cortical connections of the inferior arcuate sulcus cortex in the macaque brain. *Brain Research, 573*, 8–26.

De Armond, S. J., Fusco, M. M., and Dewey, M. M. (1989). *Structure of the human brain: A photographic atlas.* 3d ed. New York: Oxford University Press.

de Bleser, R., Cubelli, R., and Luzzatti, C. (1993). Conduction aphasia, misrepresentations, and word representations. *Brain and Language, 45*(4), 475–494.

Fauconnier, G. (1985). *Mental spaces: Aspects of meaning construction in natural language.* Cambridge, MA: MIT Press.

Felleman, D. J., and Van Essen, D. C. (1991). Distributed hierarchical processing in the primate cerebral cortex. *Cerebral Cortex, 1*, 1–47.

Fiez, J. A., and Petersen, S. E. (1993). PET as a part of an interdisciplinary approach to understanding processes involved in reading. *Psychological Science, 4*, 287–292.

Fillmore, C. (1968). The case for case. In E. Bach and R. T. Harms (Eds.), *Universals in linguistic theory*, 1–88. New York: Holt, Rinehart, and Winson.

Fodor, J. A. (1983). *Modularity of mind: An essay on faculty psychology.* Cambridge, MA: MIT Press.

Fodor, J. D. (1989). Empty categories in sentence processing. *Language and Cognitive Processes, 4*, 155–209.

Ford, M. (1983). A method of obtaining measures of local parsing complexity throughout sentences. *Journal of Verbal Learning and Verbal Behavior, 22*, 203–218.

Frazier, L., and Fodor, J. D. (1978). The sausage machine: A new two-stage parsing model. *Cognition, 6*, 291–325.

Fuster, J. M. (1989). *The prefrontal cortex: Anatomy, physiology, and neuropsychology of the frontal lobe.* New York: Raven Press.

Fuster, J. M. (1993). Frontal lobes. *Current Opinion in Neurobiology, 3*, 160–165.

Garnsey, S. M. (1993). Event-related brain potentials in the study of language: An introduction. *Language and Cognitive Processes, 8*(4), 337–356.

Garnsey, S. M., Tanenhaus, M. K., and Chapman, R. M. (1989). Evoked potentials and the study of sentence comprehension. *Journal of Psycholinguistic Research, 18*, 51–60.

Gevins, A., and Cutillo, B. (1993). Spatiotemporal dynamics of component processes in human working memory. *Electroencephalography and Clinical Neurophysiology, 87*, 128–143.

Gibson, E. (1990). Recency preference and garden path effects. In *Program of the Twelfth Annual Conference of the Cognitive Science Society*, 372–379. Hillsdale, NJ: Erlbaum.

Gibson, E. F. (1991). A computational theory of human linguistic processing: Memory limitations and processing breakdown. Ph.D. diss., Carnegie Mellon University, Pittsburgh.

Goldman-Rakic, P. S. (1987). Circuitry of primate prefrontal cortex and regulation of behavior by representational memory. In F. Plum and V. Mountcastle (Eds.), *Handbook of physiology: The nervous system*. Bethesda, MD: American Physiological Society.

Grossman, M., Crino, P., Reivich, M., Stern, M. B., and Hurtig, H. I. (1992). Attention and sentence processing deficits in Parkinson's disease: the role of anterior cingulate cortex. *Cerebral Cortex, 2*, 515–525.

Gunter, T. C., Jackson, J. L., and Mulder, G. (1992). An electrophysiological study of semantic processing in young and middle-aged academics. *Psychophysiology, 29*, 38–54.

Hagoort, P., Brown, C., and Groothusen, J. (1993). The syntactic positive shift (SPS) as an ERP measure of syntactic processing. *Language and Cognitive Processes, 8*, 439–483.

Hillyard, S. A., and Picton, T. W. (1987). Electrophysiology of cognitive processing. *Annual Review of Psychology, 34*, 33–61.

Holcomb, P. J. (1988). Automatic and attentional processing: An event-related brain potential analysis of semantic priming. *Brain and Language, 35*, 66–85.

Holcomb, P. J. (1993). Semantic priming and stimulus degradation: Implications for the role of the N400 in language processing. *Psychophysiology, 30*(1), 47–61.

Holcomb, P. J., and Anderson, J. E. (1993). Cross-modal semantic priming: A time course analysis using event-related brain potentials. *Language and Cognitive Processes, 8*(4), 379–411.

Holcomb, P. J., and Neville, H. J. (1990). Auditory and visual semantic priming in lexical decision: A comparison using event-related brain potentials. *Language and Cognitive Processes, 5*, 281–312.

Holmes, V. M., and O'Regan, J. K. (1981). Eye fixation patterns during the reading of relative-clause sentences. *Journal of Verbal Learning and Verbal Behavior, 20*, 417–430.

Horton, J. C., and Hoyt, W. F. (1991). The representation of the visual field in human striate cortex: A revision of the classic Holmes map. *Archives of Ophthalmology, 109*(6), 816–824.

Jeffreys, D. A., and Tukmachi, E. S. (1992). The vertex-positive scalp potential evoked by faces and by objects. *Experimental Brain Research, 91*(2), 340–350.

Johnson-Laird, P. N. (1983). *Mental models*. Cambridge, MA: Harvard University Press.

Just, M. A., and Carpenter, P. A. (1980). A theory of reading: From eye fixations to comprehension. *Psychological Review, 87*, 329–354.

Just, M. A., and Carpenter, P. A. (1992). A capacity theory of comprehension: Individual differences in working memory. *Psychological Review, 99*, 122–149.

Kandel, E. R., Schwartz, J. H., and Jessel, T. M. (Eds.). (1991). *Principles of neural science*. 3d ed. New York: Elsevier.

Karayanidis, F., Andrews, S., Ward, P. B., and McConaghy, N. (1991). Effects of inter-item lag on word repetition: An event-related potential study. *Psychophysiology, 28*, 307–318.

Kimberg, D. Y., and Farah, M. J. (1993). A unified account of cognitive impairments following frontal lobe damage: The role of working memory in complex, organized behavior. *Journal of Experimental Psychology: General, 122*(4), 411–428.

King, J., and Just, M. A. (1991). Individual differences in syntactic processing: The role of working memory. *Journal of Memory and Language, 30*, 580–602.

King, J. W., and Kutas, M. (1995a). Who did what and when? Using word- and clause-related ERPs to monitor working memory usage in reading. *Journal of Cognitive Neuroscience, 7*, 378–397.

King, J. W., and Kutas, M. (1995b). A brain potential whose latency indexes the length and frequency of words. *Program of the Cognitive Neuroscience Society Second Annual Meeting, 68.*

Klimesch, W., Schimke, H., and Pfurtscheller, G. (1993). Alpha frequency, cognitive load, and memory performance. *Brain Topography, 5,* 241–251.

Kluender, R., and Kutas, M. (1993a). Subjacency as a processing phenomenon. *Language and Cognitive Processes, 8*(4), 573–633.

Kluender, R., and Kutas, M. (1993b). Bridging the gap: Evidence from ERPs on the processing of unbounded dependencies. *Journal of Cognitive Neuroscience, 5,* 196–214.

Kolb, B., and Whishaw, I. Q. (1990). *Fundamentals of human neuropsychology,* 3d ed. New York: W. H. Freeman.

Kounios, J., and Holcomb, P. J. (1992). Structure and process in semantic memory: Evidence from event-related brain potentials and reaction times. *Journal of Experimental Psychology: General, 121,* 459–479.

Kutas, M. (1993). In the company of other words: Electrophysiological evidence for single-word and sentence context effects. *Language and Cognitive Processes, 8*(4), 533–572.

Kutas, M., and Hillyard, S. A. (1980). Reading senseless sentences: Brain potentials reflect semantic incongruity. *Science, 207,* 203–205.

Kutas, M., and Hillyard, S. A. (1984). Brain potentials during reading reflect word expectancy and semantic association. *Nature, 307,* 161–163.

Kutas, M., and Hillyard, S. A. (1989). An electrophysiological probe of incidental semantic association. *Journal of Cognitive Neuroscience, 1,* 38–49.

Kutas, M., Hillyard, S. A., and Gazzaniga, M. S. (1988). Processing of semantic anomaly by right and left hemispheres of commissurotomy patients: Evidence from event-related brain potentials. *Brain, 111,* 553–576.

Kutas, M., Lindamood, T., and Hillyard, S. A. (1984). Word expectancy and event-related brain potentials during sentence processing. In S. Kornblum and J. Requin (Eds.), *Preparatory states and processes,* 271–238. Hillsdale, NJ: Erlbaum.

Kutas, M., Neville, H. J., and Holcomb, P. J. (1987). A preliminary comparison of the N400 response to semantic anomalies during reading, listening and signing. *Electroencephalography and Clinical Neurophysiology, supplement, 39,* 325–330.

Kutas, M., and Van Petten, C. (1994). Psycholinguistics electrified. In M. A. Gernsbacher (Ed.), *Handbook of psycholinguistics,* 83–143. San Diego: Academic Press.

Kutas, M., Van Petten, C., and Besson, M. (1988). Event-related potential asymmetries during the reading of sentences. *Electroencephalography and Clinical Neurophysiology, 69,* 218–233.

Levin, H., and Kaplan, E. L. (1970). Grammatical structure in reading. In H. Levin and J. P. Williams (Eds.), *Basic studies on reading.* New York: Basic Books.

Luders, H., Lesser, R. P., Hahn, J., Dinner, D. S., Morris, H., Resor, S., and Harrison, M. (1986). Basal temporal language area demonstrated by electrical stimulation. *Neurology, 36,* 505–510.

Luders, H., Lesser, R. P., Hahn, J., Dinner, D. S., Morris, H. H., Wylie, E., and Godoy, J. (1991). Basal temporal language area. *Brain, 114,* 743–754.

MacDonald, M. C. (1994). Probabilistic constraints and syntactic ambiguity resolution. *Language and Cognitive Processes, 9,* 157–201.

MacDonald, M. C., Just, M. A., and Carpenter, P. A. (1992). Working memory constraints on the processing of syntactic ambiguity. *Cognitive Psychology, 24,* 56–98.

Mangun, G. R., Heinze, H. J., Burchert, W., Hinrichs, H., Munte, T. F., Scholz, M., Gos, A., Hundeshagen, H., Gazzaniga, M. S., and Hillyard, S. A. (1993). Combined PET and ERP studies of visual spatial selective attention in humans. *Society for Neuroscience Abstracts, 19*(2), 1288.

Mangun, G. R., Hillyard, S. A., and Luck, S. J. (1993). Electrocortical substrates of visual selective attention. In D. E. Meyer and S. Kornblum (Eds.), *Attention and performance XIV: Synergies in experimental psychology, artificial intelligence, and cognitive neuroscience,* 219–243. Cambridge, MA: MIT Press.

McCallum, W. C., and Curry, S. H. (Eds.) (1993). *Slow potential changes in the human brain.* NATO ASI series A: Life Sciences, vol. 254. New York: Plenum Press.

McCallum, W. C., Farmer, S. F., and Pocock, P. V. (1984). The effects of physical and semantic incongruities of auditory event-related potentials. *Electroencephalography and Clinical Neurophysiology: Evoked Potentials, 59,* 477–488.

McCarthy, G,, Nobre, A, C., Bentin, S., and Spencer, D. D. (1995). Language-related field potentials in the anterior-medial temporal lobe: I. Intracranial distribution and neural generators. *Journal of Neuroscience, 15,* 1080–1089.

Miller, G. A., and Chomsky, N. (1963). Finitary models of language users. In D. Luce, R. Bush, and E. Galanter (Eds.), *Handbook of mathematical psychology.* New York: Wiley.

Mitchell, P. F., Andrews, S., and Ward, P. B. (1993). An event-related potential study of semantic congruity and repetition in a sentence-reading task: Effect of context change. *Psychophysiology, 30,* 496–509.

Munte, T. F., Heinze, H.-J., and Mangun, G. R. (1993). Dissociation of brain activity related to syntactic and semantic aspects of language. *Journal of Cognitive Neuroscience, 5,* 335–344.

Naatanen, R. (1992). *Attention and brain function.* Hillsdale, NJ: Erlbaum.

Neville, H., Nicol, J. L., Barss, A., Forster, K. I., and Garrett, M. F. (1991). Syntactically based . sentence-processing classes: evidence from event-related brain potentials. *Journal of Cognitive Neuroscience, 3,* 151–165.

Neville, H. J., Mills, D. L., and Lawson, D. S. (1992). Fractionating language: Different neural subsystems with different sensitive periods. *Cerebral Cortex, 2*(3), 244–258.

Newell, A. (1990). *Unified theories of cognition.* Cambridge, MA: Harvard University Press.

Nobre, A. C., Allison, T., and McCarthy, G. (1994). Word recognition in the human inferior temporal lobe. *Nature, 372,* 260–263.

Nobre, A. C., and McCarthy, G. (1994). Language-related ERPs: Scalp distributions and modulation by word type and semantic priming. *Journal of Cognitive Neuroscience, 6*(3), 233–255.

Nunez, P. L. (1981). *Electric fields of the brain.* New York: Oxford University Press.

Ojemann, G. A. (1991). Cortical organization of language. *Journal of Neuroscience, 11,* 2281–2287.

Osterhout, L., and Holcomb, P. (1992). Event-related brain potentials elicited by syntactic anomaly. *Journal of Memory and Language, 31,* 785–806.

Penfield, W., and Jasper, H. (1954). *Epilepsy and the functional anatomy of the human brain.* Boston: Little, Brown.

Perfetti, C. A., and Lesgold, A. M. (1977). Discourse comprehension and sources of individual differences. In M. A. Just and P. A. Carpenter (Eds.), *Cognitive processes in comprehension,* 141–184. Hillsdale, NJ: Erlbaum.

Petersen, S. E., Fox, P. T., Snyder, A. Z., and Raichle, M. E. (1990). Activation of extra-striate and frontal cortical areas by visual words and wordlike stimuli. *Science, 249,* 1041–1043.

Pfurtscheller, G., and Klimesch, W. (1990). Topographical display and interpretation of event-related desynchronization during a visual-verbal task. *Brain Topography, 3,* 85–93.

Plum, F. (1975). Metabolic encephalophathy. In D. B. Tower (Ed.), *The nervous system,* vol. 2, 193–203. New York: Raven Press.

Posner, M. I., and Petersen, S. E. (1990). The attention system of the human brain. *Annual Review of Neuroscience, 13,* 25–42.

Regan, D. (1989). *Human brain electrophysiology: Evoked potentials and evoked magnetic fields in science and medicine.* New York: Elsevier.

Roland, P. E. (1993). *Brain activation.* New York: Wiley-Liss.

Rosler, F., and Heil, M. (1991). A negative slow wave related to conceptual load which vanishes if the amount of load is increased? A reply to Ruchkin and Johnson. *Psychophysiology, 28,* 363–364.

Rosler, F., Putz, P., Friederici, A. D., and Hahne, A. (1993). Event-related brain potentials while encountering semantic and syntactic constraint violations. *Journal of Cognitive Neuroscience, 5*(3), 345–362.

Ruchkin, D. S., Johnson, R., Mahaffey, D., and Sutton, S. (1988). Toward a functional categorization of slow waves. *Psychophysiology, 25,* 339–353.

Rugg, M. D. (1985). The effects of semantic priming and word repetition on event-related potentials. *Psychophysiology, 22,* 642–647.

Rugg, M. D. (1990). Event-related brain potentials dissociate repetition effects of high- and low-frequency words. *Memory and Cognition, 18,* 367–379.

Rugg, M. D., Doyle, M. C., and Melan, C. (1993). An event-related potential study of the effects of within- and across-modality word repetition. *Language and Cognitive Processes, 8*(4), 357–377.

Sawaguchi, T., and Goldman-Rakic, P. S. (1991). D1 dopamine receptors in prefrontal cortex: Involvement in working memory. *Science, 251,* 947–950.

Sereno, M. I. (1991). Language and the primate brain. In *Proceedings, Thirteenth Annual Conference of the Cognitive Science Society,* 79–84. Hillsdale, NJ: Erlabum.

Simon, H. A. (1974). How big is a chunk? *Science, 183,* 482–488.

Spehlmann, R. (1981). *EEG primer.* Amsterdam: Elsevier/North-Holland.

Squire, L. R., Ojemann, J. G., Miezin, F. M., Petersen, S. E., Videen, T. O., and Raichle, M. E. (1992). Activation of the hippocampus in normal humans: A functional anatomical study of memory. *Proceedings of the National Academy of Sciences, 89,* 1837–1841.

St. John, M. F., and McClelland, J. L. (1990). Learning and applying contextual constraints in sentence comprehension. *Artificial Intelligence, 97,* 332–361.

Tallal, P., Miller, S., and Fitch, R. H. (1993). Neurobiological basis of speech: A case for the preeminence of temporal processing. In P. Tallal, A. M. Galaburda, R. R. Llinas, and C. von Euler (Eds.), *Temporal information processing in the nervous system: Special reference to dyslexia and dysphasia,* 27–47. Annals of the New York Academy of Sciences, vol. 682. New York: New York Academy of Sciences.

Van Petten, C., and Kutas, M. (1991). Influences of semantic and syntactic context on open- and closed-class words. *Memory and Cognition, 19*, 95–112.

Van Petten, C., Kutas, M., Kluender, R., Mitchiner, M., and McIsaac, H. (1991). Fractionating the word repetition effect with event-related potentials. *Journal of Cognitive Neuroscience, 3*, 131–150.

Willmes, K., and Poeck, K. (1993). To what extent can aphasic syndromes be localized? *Brain, 116*, 1527–1540.

Wilson, F. A., O'Scalaidhe, S. P., and Goldman-Rakic, P. S. (1993). Dissociation of object and spatial processing domains in primate prefrontal cortex. *Science, 260*, 1955–1958.

VIII Attention

21 Cooperating Brain Systems in Selective Perception and Action

John Duncan

ABSTRACT

A neuropsychological hypothesis—the integrated competition hypothesis—is introduced to account for visual attention in the context of distributed brain activity engendered by visual input. Relevant data concern attentional modulation of single-neuron activity in the macaque, extinction phenomena following human and animal brain lesions, and the time course of the attentional state in normal human vision. According to the hypothesis, objects compete for representation in multiple brain systems, sensory and motor, cortical and subcortical. Competition is integrated, however, such that multiple systems converge to work concurrently on the same object. Local priming of target-selective units is used to give a competitive advantage to currently relevant objects. In single cells of monkey cortex, we see direct evidence for both priming and competition. In the human and monkey, multiple brain lesions produce a tendency to extinction, or bias against objects most affected by the lesion. Both spatial and nonspatial forms of extinction are described. In normal behavior, interference between two attended objects lasts for hundreds of milliseconds. These findings suggest that "attention" is a slowly evolving state in which multiple brain systems settle together on the selected object, making its different properties available together for control of behavior.

Multiple brain systems are concurrently activated by visual input. In the primate brain, these include the multiple cortical "visual areas" specialized for different purposes and, at least in part, for the analysis of different visual attributes such as motion, spatial arrangement, and shape (Desimone and Ungerleider 1989; Zeki 1978). Among visually responsive subcortical structures are the superior colliculus, involved in multimodal orienting (Stein, Wallace, and Meredith 1995), and several subdivisions of the pulvinar (Petersen, Robinson, and Keys 1985). Among motor systems activated by visual input are premotor cortex, important in reaching and grasping (Rizzolatti and Camarda 1987), and the frontal eye fields and associated structures (Goldberg and Colby 1989), involved in oculomotor control. The situation is shown schematically in figure 21.1. Visual input (left) activates multiple brain systems (center) and on this basis affords a variety of motor output (right). On the center left are shown representative sensory systems coding different visual properties, including spatial location (top) and object attributes such as color (here black or white) and shape (bottom); many other examples could be shown. On the center right are shown two representative motor systems,

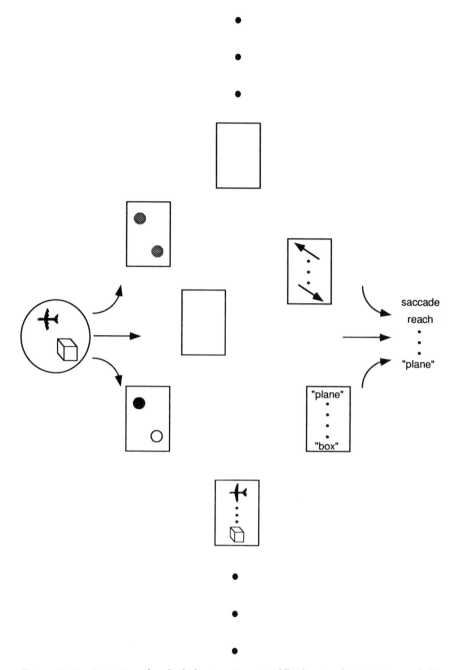

Figure 21.1 Activation of multiple brain systems (middle) by visual input (extreme left), affording variety of motor output (extreme right).

controlling, respectively, directional saccades (top) and naming (bottom); again many others could be shown.

In this chapter, I consider the problem of visual attention from the perspective of distributed brain activity. Vision is selective: at any given moment, only a small fraction of the total available visual input can be consciously identified or used in the control of behavior. Subjectively, attention is paid to some things but withheld from others. How is selectivity implemented in the multiple brain systems activated by visual input?

According to one common approach, a unified "attentional system" modulates activity in many parts of the brain, gating visual input so that only a selected part gains control of response systems (e.g., Posner and Petersen 1990). Often, this system has been supposed to select input by facilitation of a certain region of visual space. The parietal lobe and associated spatial processing structures have been seen as central (De Renzi 1982; Mesulam 1981). Parietal lesions commonly produce a tendency to disregard or neglect inputs from the contralateral side of space, and this has often been ascribed to difficulty in directing attention to that side.

A different approach has emphasized diversity of selective visual operations. In fact, a wide variety of cortical and subcortical lesions can lead to forms of unilateral neglect (Rizzolatti and Camarda 1987); similarly, activity in a wide variety of brain systems is modulated by attention or behavioral relevance (e.g., Bushnell, Goldberg, and Robinson 1981; Moran and Desimone 1985). According to the multiple-system approach, there are many different forms of visual selectivity. Different anatomical systems, for example, may be involved in selection of visual input for control of different effectors (Rizzolatti and Camarda 1987; Wurtz and Mohler 1976).

The view offered here has elements in common with both of these approaches. There is no unified attentional "system"; instead, attention reflects distributed activity in the multiple brain systems responding to visual input. At the same time, there is an element of unity in this attentional *function*. Though some have suggested that multiple forms of visual selectivity might be independent or autonomous (Allport 1993; Rizzolatti and Camarda 1987), the need for coordination has also often been mentioned (e.g., Kinsbourne 1987; Mesulam 1981; Rizzolatti and Berti 1990). According to the present view, indeed, attention emerges as an integrated state in which multiple brain systems converge to work on the different properties of a selected object and its implications for action. The ideas build on the account of Desimone and Duncan (1995), and owe much to the work of Farah (1990) and Phaf, van der Heijden, and Hudson (1990).

21.1 INTEGRATED COMPETITION HYPOTHESIS

The integrated competition hypothesis rests on three general proposals:

1. Of the many brain systems responding to visual input, perceptual and motor, cortical and subcortical, many and perhaps most are *competitive*

(Rizzolatti and Camarda 1987). Within each system, a gain in activation or representation for one object is bought at a loss to others; for example, representations of different objects may be mutually inhibitory.

2. Between systems, however, competition is *integrated*. As an object gains ascendancy in one system, this ascendancy tends also to be transmitted to others. "Attention" is the state that emerges as different brain systems converge to work on the same dominant object (e.g., Duncan 1993; Farah 1990; Kinsbourne 1987).

Integration of this sort is a general property of many "pattern completion" schemes (e.g., McClelland and Rumelhart 1981). The general idea is that nodes, units, or neurons responding to the same object support one another's activity. There are many possible ways to achieve such support (see below); one simple example is to positively connect units responding to the same spatial location because activations from the same location will usually concern the same object. If units within a pattern (i.e., responding to the same object) are mutually supportive, while units from different patterns (objects) are inhibitory, the system tends to settle into a state in which all units of one pattern are active, while others are suppressed.

More generally, of course, there is good reason to suppose that more than one pattern or object representation can be kept active at a time, though perhaps with mutual interference. The capacity of visual short-term memory, for example, is often estimated at three to four items (e.g., Sperling 1967). Among different ways to allow this within a pattern completion scheme, one is to assign different patterns to different phase slots in an oscillating system (see Hummel and Stankiewicz, chap. 5, this volume); for present purposes, such extensions need not be considered.

3. Competition is *controlled*, finally, by advance priming of units responding to one kind of object rather than another (see Harter and Aine 1984; Walley and Weiden 1973). Suppose, for example, that the animal searches for fruit of a particular color. Units selectively responsive to that color are preactivated in one or more brain systems in which color is coded. Inputs with the desired color gain a competitive advantage in the primed system; as such an input gains ascendancy in that system, it tends also to take control of others.

All of these principles are illustrated by the SLAM model of Phaf, van der Heijden, and Hudson (1990). In this model, the problem is to name, say, the object having a certain color. Separate subsystems contain units for shapes, colors, and color-shape conjunctions. (Only pairwise conjunctions are needed for the scheme to work.) Within each subsystem, units responding to different shapes, colors, or conjunctions are mutually inhibitory. Between subsystems, consistent colors and color-shape conjunctions (e.g., green, green square) are mutually supportive, while inconsistent colors and color-shape conjunctions (e.g., green, red square) are mutually inhibitory; the same goes for consistent and inconsistent shapes and conjunctions. Consider a display consisting of a green square and a red circle. If the instruction is to name the green object, green units in the color system are preactivated. Green thus gains an advantage over red in the color system; this translates to an advantage for the green square units in the conjunction system, and hence for square in the shape system. The model illustrates the principles of competition in multiple systems, of integration through support between units responding to the same object, and of control by preactivation.

Irrespective of the merits of this particular implementation, the general integrated competition scheme has two properties that are required by behavioral data. First, "attention" is a state in which the different attributes of a selected whole object gain ascendancy together for control of behavior. Many findings support such an object-based approach (see Kahneman and Henik 1977; Neisser 1967). Duncan (1984), for example, found that two attributes of a single object could be identified simultaneously without mutual interference, while attributes of two different objects could not. Second, however, many different single attributes can be used to control (whole) object selection. Given a brief display of alphanumeric characters, subjects can report just the letters in a certain row (selection by location), just the letters in a certain color, just letters ignoring digits, and so on; in all of these cases, selective processing is indicated by the finding that targets compete strongly with one another, while nontargets have little effect (Bundesen, Shibuya, and Larsen 1985; Duncan 1980). Depending on current concerns, visual inputs of any kind can be relevant to behavior; selection must accordingly be controlled by a flexible advance description of the kind of input currently required (Bundesen 1990; Duncan and Humphreys 1989). According to the integrated competition hypothesis, different selection rules can be implemented by different patterns of advance priming, probably within different brain systems.

In this chapter I consider the broad implications of the general integrated competition scheme. Section 21.2 considers behavioral modulation of single-unit responses in the monkey. These data concern competition and priming in spatial and nonspatial selection. Section 21.3 considers unilateral extinction and neglect, along with a range of related phenomena. The final sections deal with normal vision, including the time course of the attentional state, and implications of the integrated competition hypothesis for some standard issues in the cognitive literature.

21.2 COMPETITION AND PRIMING IN THE EXTRASTRIATE CORTEX OF THE MACAQUE

The first data to consider concern behavioral modulation of visual responses in the high-level visual cortex of the macaque. These data come from a collaborative project with Leo Chelazzi, Earl Miller, and Bob Desimone at NIMH in Bethesda (Chelazzi, Miller, Duncan, and Desimone 1993). Several previous studies had shown the influence of spatial selection cues on the responses of single neurons in various regions of extrastriate cortex. Responses

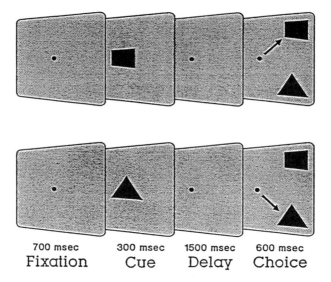

| 700 msec | 300 msec | 1500 msec | 600 msec |
| Fixation | Cue | Delay | Choice |

Figure 21.2 Visual search task used for recordings from inferotemporal neurons in macaque. Of two stimuli chosen for work with each cell (here, square and triangle), one produced strong positive response, while other did not. Arrow on choice display indicates saccade; no arrow was actually presented. Reprinted by permission from Chelazzi, Miller, Duncan, and Desimone 1993.

to a given input were enhanced when that input occurred at a relevant location, or suppressed when it occurred at an irrelevant location (Bushnell, Goldberg, and Robinson 1981; Moran and Desimone 1985). To examine nonspatial selection cues, we trained monkeys in a form of visual search using complex objects. Single-cell activity was recorded in anterior inferotemporal (IT) cortex; units in this region have large receptive fields and are selective for complex object properties (Schwartz et al. 1983), in accord with IT's role in complex object recognition (Ungerleider and Mishkin 1982).

The task we used is illustrated in figure 21.2. On the basis of a pretest, two objects were chosen for work with each cell: one (*effective stimulus*) gave a strong positive response, while the other (*ineffective stimulus*) did not. Each trial began with central fixation, followed by a brief foveal cue. On some trials, this cue was the effective stimulus; on others, it was the ineffective stimulus. Following a short delay, the search display was presented. The animal's task was to make an immediate saccade from the fixation point to whichever object matched the preceding cue. The display always contained both effective and ineffective stimuli; on some trials, however, the effective stimulus was the target to be fixated, while on others, it was the nontarget to be ignored.

The first prediction from the integrated competition hypothesis concerns activity in the delay between cue and search display. According to the hypothesis, search or selection should be controlled by preactivation of units responsive to a current target. In figure 21.3a, this priming is shown by enhanced activity in the object recognition system for cells responsive to one object (plane) rather than the other (box). Indeed this was the result for the majority of more than 100 IT cells recorded. Though only the fixation point was present in the delay, a cell's activity was slightly enhanced when its effective stimulus was the current target. These results match other reports of selective delay activity in IT units recorded in similar tasks (Fuster and Jervey 1981; Miyashita and Chang 1988).

The second prediction concerns competition in responses to the search display. According to the integrated competition hypothesis, units responsive to target and nontarget objects should compete. Preactivation of target units should give them a competitive advantage. Correspondingly, we found that responses to the effective stimulus in the test display were sustained when that stimulus was the target to be fixated. In contrast, responses to the same stimulus were suppressed (following an initial positive discharge) when it was the nontarget. Suppression began 100–200 ms following display onset, that is, around 100 ms before the animal's saccade.

In this experiment, we could only observe activity within IT itself. According to the hypothesis, however, the competitive advantage for the target, beginning initially in the object recognition system, is distributed eventually to systems dealing with many other properties (fig. 21.3b). Among other systems, the target object acquires control over those dealing with spatial location (fig. 21.3b, upper left) and saccades (fig. 21.3b, upper right), allowing a saccade to the target position.

In support of this more general proposal may be cited two further observations. The first concerns activity in cells of extrastriate region V4 in the object search task (Chelazzi and Desimone 1994). V4 is a major input area to IT; its cells have smaller receptive fields and simpler stimulus preferences (e.g., for bars of a certain size, color, and orientation; Desimone and Schein 1987; Zeki 1978). In V4 there was little selective delay activity, and the initial response to the effective stimulus in the search display was much the same whether this stimulus was target or nontarget. In the late phase of the response, however, immediately before the saccade, V4 cells began to show the same suppression of nontarget responses that we had seen in IT. Such findings provide tentative support for the idea that an initially local competitive bias—perhaps initiating in IT—ultimately has generalized consequences across extrastriate cortex.

The second set of findings concerns spatial cues. As mentioned above, in many studies an animal is told not which object to select but which location. According to the integrated competition hypothesis, the initial bias will now be set up in systems coding spatial information. The final result, however, will be the same generalized competitive advantage for the whole selected object: the scheme we need if many different attributes of an object can be used to select that whole object for control of behavior. Spatially specific priming is unlikely in IT, where receptive fields are large and spatial information accordingly poor. Instead, spatially specific delay activity, analogous to the

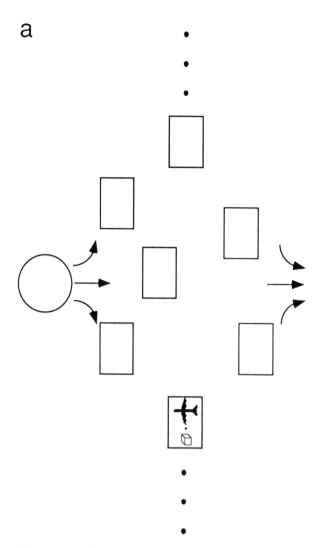

Figure 21.3 Selection by priming according to integrated competition hypothesis. Precue to search for plane (panel *a*) produces enhanced activity in corresponding neurons (plane larger than box) in object recognition system. Competition within this system means that neurons responding to other possible objects (box) are somewhat suppressed. When visual input arrives (panel *b*), competitive advantage for plane is eventually distributed to multiple brain systems.

object-specific activity we saw in IT, has been reported in areas specialized for spatial processing, including area 7 of the parietal lobe (Gnadt and Andersen 1988), and the closely related area 46 of the frontal lobe (Funahashi, Bruce, and Goldman-Rakic 1989). Indeed, in a spatial selection task, priming of cells with an appropriate spatial receptive field has also been seen in V4 (Luck et al. 1993). Taken together, such findings support the view that, depending on the selection task, priming in different regions of cortex can be used to give an initial competitive advantage to the desired or relevant object.

b

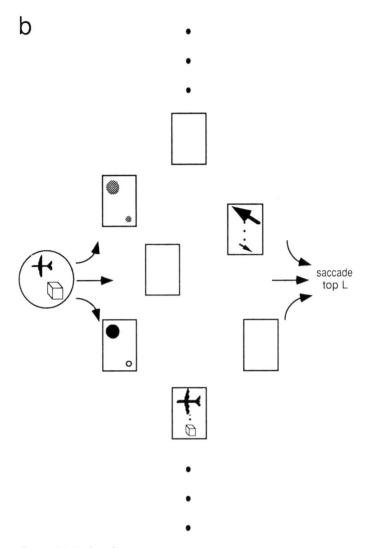

Figure 21.3 (cont.)

Despite its attractions, of course, the integrated competition hypothesis leaves many questions unresolved, three of which will be mentioned here. Returning first to the object search task, it seems unlikely that a competitive advantage for targets derives solely from the modest target-selective delay activity that we observed in IT. More recent data (Chelazzi, Miller, Lueschow, and Desimone 1993) show that selective delay activity is even stronger in the inferior convexity of the frontal lobe. In a similar task of matching objects across a delay, Fuster, Bauer, and Jervey (1985) found that cooling frontal cortex diminishes selective responses in IT, while cooling IT diminishes selectivity in the frontal lobe. Just as parietal area 7 and frontal area 46 may work together in spatial priming, so may IT and inferior frontal cortex work together in object search. More generally, different brain systems may support one another in selective priming, just as they do in competition between one object and another in the visual input.

A second point concerns limitations in the attentional modulation of visual responses in regions concerned specifically with the control of saccades, including superior colliculus and the frontal eye fields. Lesions to either colliculus or frontal eye field can produce a behavioral bias against the contralesional side (e.g., Latto and Cowey 1971), suggesting that these regions contribute to visual competition. In both these regions, however, single-cell data suggest much the same visual response to attended and unattended stimuli when no saccades are allowed; marked enhancement of the response occurs only with preparation of an eye movement (Goldberg and Bushnell 1981; Wurtz and Mohler 1976). Such data suggest that, when a particular form of motor output (e.g., foveation) is disallowed, enhanced response to an attended stimulus is somehow kept out of corresponding motor systems.

The third point concerns the domain of competition in extrastriate neurons. According to the data of Moran and Desimone (1985), competition in V4 may be spatially local: for any given cell, the response to an unattended effective stimulus is only suppressed if the attended, ineffective stimulus also falls within the receptive field. The interpretation might be that, at least in V4, competition occurs predominantly within each cell's receptive field. For each cell or cell cluster, it would be this predominantly local competition that was biased by the attentional state manifested in the visuomotor network as a whole.

21.3 SPATIAL AND NONSPATIAL EXTINCTION: COMPETITIVE IMBALANCE AFTER SELECTIVE BRAIN LESIONS

In unilateral neglect, there is a tendency to ignore input from the side of space contralateral to a brain lesion (Bisiach and Vallar 1988). The disorder has different manifestations and components, not all of which may be well correlated or require the same explanation (Halligan and Marshall 1992). For present purposes, the key aspect is competitive imbalance against the contralesional side (Kinsbourne 1987). In many cases, neglect of that side is enhanced by concurrent input on the unimpaired or ipsilesional side, a phenomenon termed *unilateral extinction* (e.g., Karnath 1988). Similarly, neglect may be diminished by strong cues to consider the contralesional side (e.g., Posner et al. 1984). In present terms, contralesional inputs gain control of behavior only when they have no strong competitors, or are strongly favored by the selection context. It is this specific element of competitive imbalance, rather than neglect construed more broadly, that is relevant to the present discussion.

As we have said, a common role of parietal lesions in extinction has led to a conventional view that visual attention is largely controlled by the parietal lobe, or at least by a broader circuit linking parietal cortex—with its central role in spatial processing—to closely associated cortical (dorsolateral prefrontal, anterior cingulate) and subcortical (pulvinar, colliculus) structures, similarly involved in spatial perception and action (e.g., Mesulam 1981; Posner and Petersen 1990). According to the present hypothesis, in contrast, "attention" to an object emerges as a result of integrated competition in multiple brain systems (see especially Kinsbourne 1987). One prediction is that a tendency to unilateral extinction should be the common consequence of many different brain lesions (Bender 1952). As shown in figure 21.4, if a lesion gives any one brain system a bias to one side, the dominant (unaffected) object in that system will tend also to take control of others. *Spatial* extinction should be common simply because brain lesions are commonly unilateral, and many brain systems have a predominantly contralateral representation of visual input. More generally, any lesion affecting the representation of one object more than another should produce a generalized competitive bias against that object.

One set of relevant data comes from a study I have recently been conducting with Glyn Humphreys and his group in Birmingham, Claus Bundesen in Copenhagen, and Robert Ward in Cambridge. Conventionally, the occipitoparietal component of the visual system, involved in spatial vision and visuomotor behavior, is distinguished from the occipitotemporal component, involved in object recognition (Ungerleider and Mishkin 1982). According to our hypothesis, extinction should result from lesions to either system. In our study, patients are shown brief displays of red and green letters. The task is to report red letters (targets), while ignoring green letters (nontargets). Displays have either a single target, a target accompanied by a nontarget, or two targets. By using brief exposures and vocal responses, we aim to study visual competitive biases, rather than a preference to move eyes or hand toward the ipsilesional side. In the full study, various patient groups are compared on a number of distinct measures of visual processing capacity and selectivity. Here I shall present illustrative data from only two patients and only a subset of the displays, those with a target in the left or right lower visual field, accompanied by nothing, a simultaneous nontarget, or a second target in the opposite lower field.

The first set of data (fig. 21.5a) comes from a typical patient with a stroke affecting the right parietal cortex; the data, as expected, show contralesional extinction. A target occurring alone was reported well whether presented to the ipsilesional or contralesional field. For an ipsilesional target, furthermore, there was little effect of an accompanying letter in the contralesional field, whether this letter was a nontarget or a second target. For a contralesional target, in contrast, an accompanying ipsilesional letter had a clear harmful effect. This extinction was strongest when the ipsilesional item was a target itself, but was marked even for a nontarget.

These are exactly the results we should expect if a parietal lesion produces a competitive bias against contralesional letters. Net competitive weights will be determined by two factors: a bias to targets caused by task-specific priming, and a bias to the ipsilesional field. Strong competition from an ipsilesional

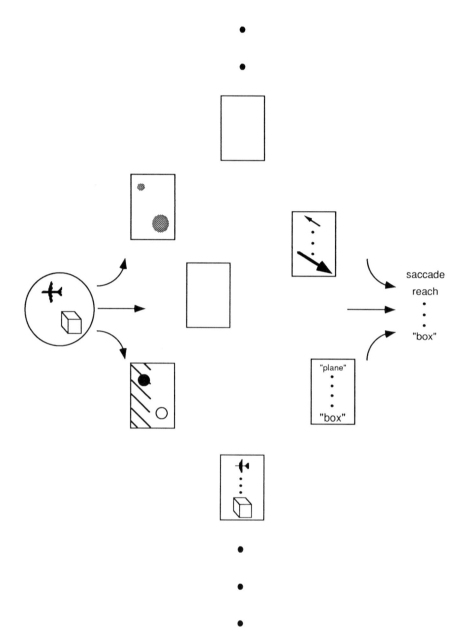

Figure 21.4 Extinction according to integrated competition hypothesis. If it affects one object selectively, lesion in many parts of the network (here, crosshatching in color system) will produce generalized competitive bias.

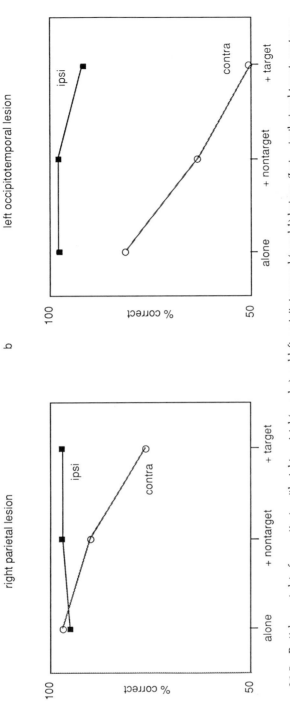

Figure 21.5 Partial report data from patients with right parietal (panel *a*) and left occipitotemporal (panel *b*) lesions. (Ipsi = ipsilesional target; contra = contralesional target.) As shown on abscissa, targets could be presented alone, or accompanied by nontarget or second target in opposite hemifield.

letter will always be harmful to a contralesional target, especially when the ipsilesional letter is a target itself.

Equivalent data from a patient with an occipitotemporal lesion are shown in figure 21.5b. This patient's stroke had affected the whole distribution of the left posterior cerebral artery, producing a pattern of upper right quadrantanopsia, reading difficulties, and simultanagnosia that is characteristic of such a lesion (Levine and Calvanio 1978). For this patient, the extinction data were almost equally clear: impairment in the contralesional field was striking with an accompanying ipsilesional letter. As predicted by the integrated competition hypothesis, extinction may be a very common consequence of unilateral lesions, whether these affect primarily occipitoparietal (spatial vision) or occipitotemporal (object vision) systems (see also Shelton, Bowers, and Heilman 1990).

In fact, this conclusion is consistent with a number of other findings. In an early monograph, Bender (1952) concluded that no one anatomical system was fundamental to extinction; even lesions to the spinal cord or trigeminal nerve could produce extinction when a stimulus on the affected part of the body was accompanied by a second stimulus elsewhere. A recent study similarly documented extinction following a wide variety of cortical and subcortical lesions (Vallar et al. 1994). Data from monkeys suggest a similar picture. In one study, V4 lesions produced a strong deficit only when the stimulus in the lesioned field quadrant was accompanied by an irrelevant distractor in an unlesioned quadrant (Desimone, Li et al. 1990). Much the same followed from lesions in the lateral pulvinar, a thalamic nucleus linked to V4 and IT, and the superior colliculus (Desimone, Wessinger, et al. 1990). Extinction-like results from spatial cuing studies (Posner et al. 1984) suggest a similar conclusion. In these studies, the subject makes a speeded response to onset of a light anywhere in the visual field. An initial cue indicates that the target is especially likely to occur in either the left or the right field. In human subjects, parietal lesions impair detection of contralesional targets, especially when they are unexpected, that is, when the cue indicates the *ipsilesional* side. The results are somewhat analogous to extinction (Posner et al. 1984); they show that contralesional targets are detected especially poorly in the presence of a strong bias to the ipsilesional side, or in our terms, in the presence of strong priming of ipsilesional units (Farah 1994). In the monkey, again, similar results are produced by a variety of cortical and subcortical lesions (Colby 1991). In all these cases, a competitive bias against the lesioned region of the field emerges as a common consequence of damage to many spatially mapped structures (Desimone and Duncan 1995).

More broadly, unilateral extinction following occipitotemporal lesions is only one of several related phenomena predicted by the integrated competition hypothesis. In the remainder of this section I shall illustrate with three further sets of data concerning integration of visual and motor biases in neglect, integration in normal behavior, and nonspatial rather than spatial extinction.

According to the integrated competition hypothesis, many different biases, cortical and subcortical, visual and nonvisual, should influence extinction and neglect. If any one of many brain systems can be made to favor the neglected side, this should have a generalized ameliorating effect on bias against that side. As envisaged by Kinsbourne (1987), one interesting possibility is feedback from motor to visual bias. Relevant data from Robertson and North (1994) are shown in figure 21.6. In this experiment, a neglect patient with a large right-hemisphere lesion attempted to read letters and numbers from a visual array, with free viewing and unlimited display time. Omissions from the left (contralesional) side were substantially reduced by irrelevant, concurrent movements of the left hand, but reinstated by concurrent movements of

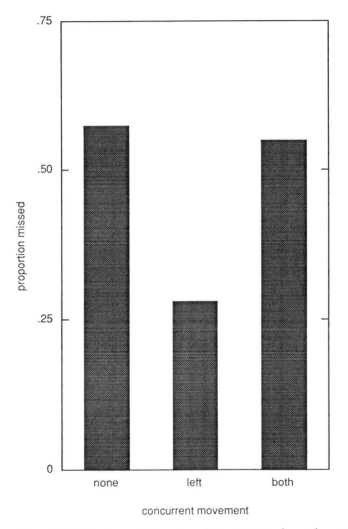

Figure 21.6 Reading omissions in neglect patient. Reading task was performed alone, or with concurrent, irrelevant movements of left or both hands. Replotted by permission from Robertson and North 1994.

Cooperating Brain Systems

both left and right hands. Biases initiating in other systems may have similar effects. In the superior colliculus, inputs from each side of space come predominantly from the eye on that side. Patching the eye ipsilateral to a lesion should thus produce a collicular bias to the contralateral (impaired) side, and has been shown to relieve neglect (Butter and Kirsch 1992); the same has been found for unilateral vestibular stimulation, producing a turning bias toward the neglected side (Rubens 1985).

"Premotor" theories of neglect assert primacy of motor over visual biases (Rizzolatti and Camarda 1987). Selective attention to inputs from one side of space directly reflects preparation to look, turn, or reach in that direction. According to the integrated competition hypothesis, the initial bias toward one object or another can arise in either motor or visual systems, as directly suggested by extinction following an occipitotemporal lesion. When competition is integrated, no part of the system is necessarily primary; an initial bias in any part has generalized consequences.

Turning next to studies of normal behavior, we find that here, too, there is evidence for integration between multiple forms of lateral bias. Morais (1978), for example, asked subjects to listen to one of two syllables played simultaneously from separate loudspeakers. Selection of the relevant syllable was facilitated by turning eyes, head, or even trunk in its direction. Driver and Spence (1994) found that simultaneous monitoring of visual and auditory events was easiest when they arose at the same spatial location. In this volume, related examples are presented by Driver and Grossenbacher (chap. 9), and by Shimojo et al. (chap. 23). At the same time, exceptions should be noted. Klein (1980), for example, found that preparing an eye movement to left or right had no measurable effect on lateralized visual detection. Spence and Driver (1995) found that an irrelevant auditory cue on one side biases visual detection; the reverse effect, however, was not seen.

A final prediction concerns nonspatial extinction. According to the integrated competition hypothesis, extinction should arise whenever a brain lesion affects the representation of one object more than another. A common case is unilateral extinction following lateralized brain damage, but equally, a lesion selectively affecting one type of object rather than one location should have a similar result. Good data on this question are yet to be obtained. As one example, a lesion selectively affecting tactile input may produce extinction when a touch on the body is accompanied by stimuli in another modality (Bender 1952). Here I shall provide two sets of data: a case of nonspatial extinction in Balint's syndrome, and extinction-like data produced in normal subjects by manipulation of stimulus contrast.

The Balint's patient was tested again in collaboration with Glyn Humphreys and his group in Birmingham (Humphreys et al. 1995). Balint's syndrome is a result of bilateral parietal lesions (e.g., Luria 1959). One aspect of the syndrome is severe restriction of awareness to one object at a time; Luria's (1959) patient, for example, had difficulty marking the center of a cross because his pencil seemed to disappear when attention was paid to the cross. In our case, there was severe extinction when two objects were presented, but extinction was determined by nonspatial rather than spatial factors. A word or a picture, for example, could be identified well when presented alone. When both were presented together, the patient tended to report the picture and deny the presence of the word, even when the word always appeared at fixation and the picture was irrelevant. Another task dealt with extinction between open and closed forms (fig. 21.7). The forms were squares and diamonds: "open" versions, which are relatively hard to identify (Biederman 1987), were made by removing corners, while "closed" versions, relatively easier, were made by removing side segments. The task was simply to decide whether any square

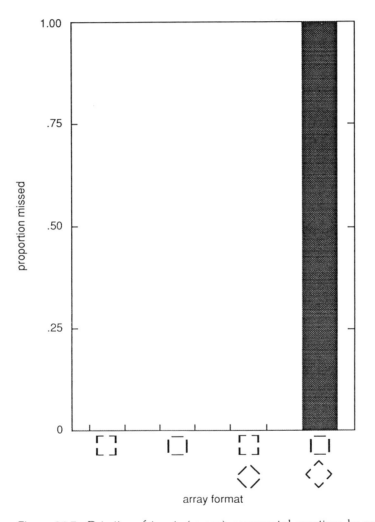

Figure 21.7 Detection of targets (squares), accompanied sometimes by nontargets (diamonds), in patient with bilateral parietal lesions. Target present trials only. Either closed or open targets were detected perfectly when presented alone (left); with two forms in array, subject behaved as though only closed form were present (right). Replotted by permission from Humphreys et al. 1995.

was present; the data in figure 21.7 come only from target-present trials. Performance was perfect with single open or closed forms, or when a closed square accompanied an open diamond. In the presence of a closed diamond, in contrast, an open square was never detected.

Although these data certainly show that an exaggerated competitive bias after brain lesion can be determined by nonspatial rather than spatial factors, they are an imperfect illustration of our main point because, in this case, it is unclear that the lesion itself produced the preference for pictures and for closed forms. In the latter case, closed forms may gain an advantage simply because their shape is more quickly derived. This leads on to our final demonstration of extinction-like behavior in normal vision.

In this experiment, carried out in collaboration with Hal Pashler and Manuel Sanches at the University of California in San Diego, normal subjects were asked to decide whether the target letter *A* was present in a 2- to 8-letter array. In different conditions, all letters were bright, all dim, or half bright and half dim. Mean reaction times and error rates for target present trials are shown in figure 21.8. The effects of brightness were modest, provided that the brightness of all letters was the same. In particular, all-bright and all-dim arrays produced similar search slopes, or decrements in speed and accuracy as additional nontargets were added. A dim target in the presence of mixed bright and dim nontargets, however, was very poorly detected. As the number of nontargets increased, the miss rate rose above 20 percent. Though other interpretations of the data are possible, it is tempting to see this result as a normal counterpart to (nonspatially determined) extinction. When a difference in brightness gives a competitive advantage to some display elements over others, a target in the disadvantaged set is very hard to detect. According to Bender (1952), the result was anticipated by Hippocrates: "Of simultaneous pains in two places, the lesser is obliterated by the greater."

All of these data suggest a tendency for competition to be integrated in multiple brain systems. Despite their separate functions and separate competitive interactions between one object and another, multiple systems tend to converge on dominance by the same object. At the same time, the tendency to integrate cannot be absolute; sometimes, for example, we may need to pay attention to auditory inputs from the left but visual inputs from the right, and of course this is perfectly possible (Driver and Spence 1994). With suitable differential priming, it must be possible for one brain system to settle on one winning object, while another system settles on another.

In recent years, correspondingly, many forms of neglect have been dissociated, including neglect of different sensory modalities (Bender 1952; Guariglia and Antonucci 1992), neglect of near versus far space (Rizzolatti, Gentilucci, and Matelli 1985), sensory versus motor neglect (Tegnér and Levander 1991), and so on. Generalized neglect may be strongest immediately after a lesion, when widespread functional imbalance between one side of the brain and the other follows even restricted cortical damage (Deuel 1987); rapid recovery of neglect, which is typical in the human, is accom-

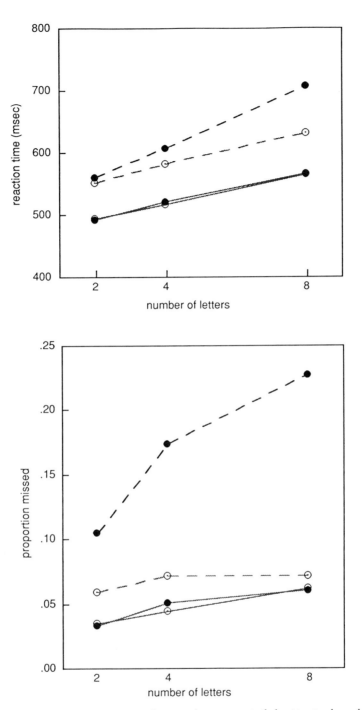

Figure 21.8 Reaction time (above) and omission rate (below) in visual search for target letter *A*. Target present trials only. (○——— all bright; ○ - - - all dim; ●——— mixed, target bright; ● - - - mixed, target dim.)

panied by resolution of these widespread functional imbalances in the monkey (Deuel 1987). According to the integrated competition hypothesis, a unilateral lesion in one brain system will perhaps produce the strongest and most permanent competitive imbalance in functions specifically dependent on that system. Though this imbalance will tend to generalize, such generalization may not be clinically obvious; for example, a lesion in the auditory representation of left space may produce strong auditory extinction, yet the tendency for this imbalance to generalize to competition in visual modules may easily be overcome by the normal process of priming and bias to relevant inputs. Bender (1952), for example, described a patient who was amused by the extinction of a tactile stimulus he could see being applied when a second touch was made on an unaffected part of his body. In this case, much of cognition was applied selectively to the affected stimulus; only the tactile imbalance could not be overcome. To put this another way, the imbalance produced by direct lesion in a system may be much greater than the imbalance produced by generalization from a lesion elsewhere.

Again, there are many further issues to be addressed. For example, I have said nothing about the predominance of left- over right-sided neglect in humans (Bisiach and Vallar 1988), about stimulus interactions not captured by a simple competitive model (e.g., Grabowecky, Robertson, and Treisman 1993; Halligan and Marshall 1994), or about differential competition within and between complex objects (Humphreys and Riddoch 1994). Moreover, though a competitive imbalance may be the common result of unilateral brain lesions, its limits remain to be explored. Dorff, Mirsky, and Mishkin (1965), for example, obtained only ambiguous results following anterior temporal lobe removals; such results may reflect increasingly bilateral representation at higher levels of the visual system (Desimone and Ungerleider 1989).

Finally it should be reemphasized that the broad spatial deficit following parietal lobe lesions may indeed be very different from the deficit produced by other lesions also associated with a generalized tendency to extinction. As I have said, the common result of a unilateral lesion may be a generalized competitive imbalance, accompanied by specific effects characteristic of the particular systems that are damaged. In typical "unilateral neglect," the contralesional space is disregarded even with unlimited exposure and free viewing, suggesting a particularly severe imbalance in spatial exploratory behavior (De Renzi 1982). Also included may be a variety of spatial distortions and misinterpretations. While some tendency to extinction may follow many unilateral lesions, this is not to question a specific parietal involvement in numerous spatial functions (Vallar et al. 1994).

21.4 TIME COURSE OF THE SELECTIVE STATE

Visual attention has often been conceived as a high-speed serial process, dealing with one object after another at rates of a few dozen milliseconds per item (e.g., Bergen and Julesz 1983; Schneider and Shiffrin 1977; Treisman and

Gelade 1980). In light of the integrated competition hypothesis, this is rather an uncomfortable view. If "attention" to an object develops as the interactive settling of cortical and subcortical, perceptual and motor, systems onto that object, it is perhaps rather hard to believe that the process could complete and reset every 50 ms or so,

In our IT data (Chelazzi, Miller, Duncan, and Desimone 1993), we took competition between objects to be reflected in suppression of responses to nontargets. This suppression did not begin until 100–200 ms from display onset; it developed slowly and was sustained up to the time of the response. While serial models with variable onset latencies might be fit to such data, the most natural conclusion is that the state of "attention" evolves over hundreds rather than tens of milliseconds.

Conventional serial models are based largely on visual search data. The increase in search time for each nontarget added to a display is taken to reflect the time for that nontarget to be scanned. The ambiguity of such data is well known, however (Townsend 1971); the data can also be fit by limited-capacity parallel models (see, for example, Ward and McClelland 1989). According to such models, added nontargets increase search time not because of serial scanning, but because limited processing capacity is more thinly divided (e.g., Atkinson, Holmgren, and Juola 1969; Bundesen 1990; Duncan and Humphreys 1989). In present terms, each nontarget competes for activation with the other elements of the display. To resolve the ambiguity of these data, the time course of interference between two attended objects must be measured more directly.

A recent set of studies, carried out in collaboration with Rob Ward in Cambridge and Kimron Shapiro in Calgary, shows how this might be done. Our method was simply to present two alphanumeric characters in rapid succession. Each was briefly (< 100 ms) displayed and masked. The interval between characters (stimulus onset asynchrony, or SOA) varied from 0 to 900 ms. In control conditions, only one character was to be identified; the other character appeared in an irrelevant location and, in most cases, differed also in other attributes (e.g., color) from the target. In the experimental condition, both characters were to be identified, allowing us to plot the time course of interference between them. In all cases, responses were unspeeded; we measured only the accuracy of stimulus identification.

Typical data (Duncan, Ward, and Shapiro 1994) are shown in figure 21.9. In the control condition (open circles), target identification was independent of SOA. In the experimental condition, the first character presented (negative SOAs) was identified well, but the second suffered sustained interference, lasting at least 300–400 ms. Measured directly by this method, competition between one object and another lasts around ten times longer than serial models would predict. In other studies, comparable data have been obtained when two targets are embedded in a stream of nontargets, presented rapidly one after the other at a single location (Broadbent and Broadbent 1987; Raymond, Shapiro, and Arnell 1992).

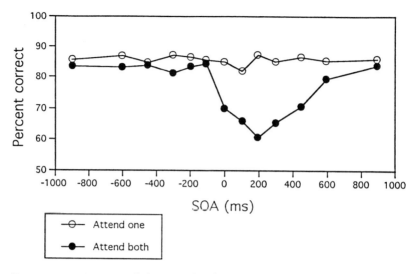

Figure 21.9 Accuracy of character identification at variable SOA. Two characters were presented on each trial; negative SOAs refer to first character, positive SOAs to second character. Open circles are trials where subjects identified single character while ignoring other. Filled circles are trials where subjects had to identify both characters. Reprinted by permission from Duncan Ward, and Shapiro 1994.

One question concerns the importance of response processes in this extended time course. When two speeded responses must be chosen in rapid succession, it is well known that the second suffers sustained interference (Welford 1968). In large part, this "psychological refractory period" (PRP) reflects queueing in a serial response selection device (Pashler 1989). Though we had used unspeeded responses to avoid such effects (Pashler 1989), a further experiment was run to check on our success. In unspeeded-response accuracy studies, two attributes of a single object can be identified without mutual interference (Duncan 1984). In speeded-response studies, however, choosing independent responses to different attributes of the same object produces a full-scale PRP (Fagot and Pashler 1992). To investigate this contrast, we had subjects identify either one or two attributes of the first object in our displays. As before, the measure of interest was interference with the *second* object. Again, responses were unspeeded. The data replicated closely the results in figure 21.9; in particular, the time course of interference was completely independent of the number of attributes identified on the first object (Ward, Duncan, and Shapiro in press). Thus interference does not reflect the duration of response selection; it is sensitive simply to the number of relevant visual objects.

These data show that competition between attended visual objects is not well explained by high-speed serial models. Instead it has a time course of hundreds of milliseconds, consistent with our physiological data, and fitting comfortably with the integrated competition hypothesis.

21.5 RELATIONSHIP TO COGNITIVE MODELS

It is worth considering the relationship between the integrated competition hypothesis and some standard cognitive models. Indeed, this hypothesis suggests useful perspectives on a variety of standard questions from the literature.

In general, the hypothesis is a development of several previous biased competition models (e.g., Bundesen 1990; Duncan and Humphreys 1989; Rumelhart 1970). According to these models, visual inputs compete for limited processing capacity. In the integrated competition hypothesis, "capacity" translates to activation in the sensorimotor network. In the functional models, relevant inputs are selected by comparing each input against some advance description of the kind of information currently needed in behavior (the "attentional template"; Duncan and Humphreys 1989); processing capacity is allocated preferentially to inputs matching this description. In the integrated competition hypothesis, the attentional template is implemented by advance priming. Functional models have also emphasized the grouping and segmentation processes that create perceptual objects; according to Duncan and Humphreys (1989), grouped parts of the input tend to gain or lose processing capacity together. In the integrated competition hypothesis, units responding to the same object support one another's activation. As we have said, many of these properties of integrated competition are illustrated by the SLAM model of Phaf, van der Heijden, and Hudson (1990).

In the cognitive literature, a number of issues have been debated under the general distinction between "early" and "late" selection models. Evidence for "early" selection comes, for example, from evoked potential studies, showing that focused attention to one side of space modulates visual responses from < 100 ms post–stimulus onset (Hillyard, Munte, and Neville 1985). Such results suggest that behavioral context intervenes early in visual activity. Evidence for late selection comes from findings that even irrelevant inputs receive some semantic analysis (e.g., Eriksen and Eriksen 1974), or that even complex stimulus characteristics such as the distinction between letters and digits can be used to determine where attention is directed (e.g., Duncan 1980; Schneider and Shiffrin 1977). Such results suggest that visual selectivity follows substantial prior analysis. Both kinds of result are easily accommodated by the integrated competition hypothesis. Spatial priming may be implemented early in the system; *some* difference between primed and unprimed responses may be expected early on. This is not to say, however, that unprimed inputs will produce *no* activity in semantic systems or that, when the task requires it, competition cannot be resolved by priming letter-digit rather than spatial representations.

A second major contrast has been drawn between "object"- and "space"-based models of visual attention. According to the object-based view, parts and properties of the same object tend to be selected together (Duncan 1984; Neisser 1967). This is a central aspect of the integrated competition hypothesis: "attention" is a state in which multiple brain systems work concurrently on the same object. According to the space-based view, attention is seen as a mental spotlight favoring inputs from one spatial region (e.g., Eriksen and Hoffman 1973; Posner, Snyder, and Davidson 1980). Space-based experiments ask how large the spotlight is, whether it can be divided, how quickly it can be moved, and so on. In most cases, they test the effects of advance cues showing where forthcoming targets will appear. According to the integrated competition hypothesis, these are experiments on the properties of spatial priming; they fit sensibly into the hypothesis without questioning its object-based aspects. Again, the integrated competition hypothesis interrelates apparently discrepant findings and models within a single, coherent framework.

A third major distinction concerns "general capacity" versus "multiple-resource" accounts of dual task interference. According to the general capacity view (Moray 1967), most instances of dual task interference reflect competition for a single, central pool of processing capacity. According to the multiple-resource view (Allport 1980), there are many separate sources of dual task conflict, depending on the particular processing systems that tasks require in common. As it stands, the integrated competition hypothesis deals only with the restricted domain of competition between perceived visual objects. Similar principles, however, might easily be applied to representations in other domains: to competition between retrieved facts, action plans, goals, and so on. According to the hypothesis, competition takes place separately in many separate brain systems; in this respect, the hypothesis adheres clearly to the multiple-resource approach. Indeed, there is no need for a restriction in parallel processing as long as two tasks activate no brain systems in common. At the same time, any strong tendency to integration will severely limit the ability of multiple systems to work concurrently on different problems. Attention to a single visual object, for example, may have some tendency to activate representations in a diverse network of brain systems, including those representing alternative actions, implications (Shastri and Ajjanagadde 1993) and so on. An investigation of interactions between visual and action-related activity might be particularly rewarding; among other things, it might allow us to address the question of how a particular behavioral setting allows establishment of appropriate priming activity for control of visual selection. Overall, the greater is the generalized consequence of selection in any one brain system, the more closely the processing network as a whole will approximate generalized, limited-capacity function.

21.6 CONCLUSIONS

The integrated competition hypothesis combines elements of several previous views. Though there is no unified attentional "system," neither is there the anarchy of multiple, independent selective visuomotor systems. The main principles of the hypothesis and the data they help to explain may be summarized as follows:

1. According to the hypothesis, objects compete in multiple brain systems, sensory and motor, cortical and subcortical, yet competition is integrated such that multiple systems tend to converge on processing the same object. This scheme is motivated by general requirements of visual selection. It must be possible to guide the selection of visual inputs using many different attributes; depending on the current task, different kinds of input (red objects, moving objects, objects in a certain location, etc.) may be relevant. This requires that selection be *initiated* from within many different brain systems. At the same time, behavior may depend on multiple properties of the selected object. This requires coordination across brain systems. In the integrated competition hypothesis, local priming gives the target object an initial advantage in the primed system; integration produces a generalized result.

2. In line with the view of Rizzolatti and Camarda (1987), dissociations between multiple forms of extinction and neglect imply multiple competitive systems. At the same time, many of the findings we have reviewed indicate a tendency to integration. In the monkey, nontarget suppression in IT may generalize to V4. In human patients and monkeys, visual extinction follows multiple lesions, occipitotemporal as well as occipitoparietal, and takes both spatial and nonspatial forms. Treatments based on lateral activation of several different systems, motor as well as visual, relieve unilateral neglect. In normal behavior, too, there is evidence for integration between lateral biases in sensory and motor systems, and in different input modalities.

3. In the monkey, there is direct evidence for priming of neurons responsive to a current target. This priming has a very different distribution in spatial and object selection tasks.

4. Direct measurement suggests that "attention" to an object is a sustained state, evolving over hundreds of milliseconds. In this state, the different properties of the selected object become available together for control of behavior.

ACKNOWLEDGMENTS

This research was supported by a grant from the Human Frontier Science Program. I am grateful to numerous collaborators and colleagues for their contribution to the ideas and for permission to use published and unpublished data and figures, including Claus Bundesen, Leo Chelazzi, Bob Desimone, Glyn Humphreys, Earl Miller, Andrew Olson, Hal Pashler, Jane Riddoch, Ian Robertson, Cristina Romani, Manuel Sanches, Kimron Shapiro, and Rob Ward.

REFERENCES

Allport, D. A. (1980). Attention and performance. In G. Claxton (Ed.), *Cognitive psychology: New directions*, 112–153. London: Routledge and Kegan Paul.

Allport, D. A. (1993). Attention and control: Have we been asking the wrong questions? A critical review of twenty-five years. In D. E. Meyer and S. Kornblum (Eds.), *Attention and performance XIV*, 183–218. Cambridge, MA: MIT Press.

Atkinson, R. C., Holmgren, J. E., and Juola, J. F. (1969). Processing time as influenced by the number of elements in a visual display. *Perception and Psychophysics, 6*, 321–326.

Bender, M. B. (1952). *Disorders in perception*. Springfield, IL: Charles C. Thomas.

Bergen, J. R., and Julesz, B. (1983). Parallel versus serial processing in rapid pattern discrimination. *Nature, 303*, 696–698.

Biederman, I. (1987). Recognition-by-components: A theory of human image understanding. *Psychological Review, 94*, 115–147.

Bisiach, E., and Vallar, G. (1988). Hemineglect in humans. In F. Boller and J. Grafman (Eds.), *Handbook of Neuropsychology*, vol. 1, 195–222. Amsterdam: Elsevier.

Broadbent, D. E., and Broadbent, M. H. P. (1987). From detection to identification: Response to multiple targets in rapid serial visual presentation. *Perception and Psychophysics, 42*, 105–113.

Bundesen, C. (1990). A theory of visual attention. *Psychological Review, 97*, 523–547.

Bundesen, C., Shibuya, H., and Larsen, A. (1985). Visual selection from multielement displays: A model for partial report. In M. I. Posner and O. Marin (Eds.), *Attention and performance XI*, 631–649. Hillsdale, NJ: Erlbaum.

Bushnell, M. C., Goldberg, M. E., and Robinson, D. L. (1981). Behavioral enhancement of visual responses in monkey cerebral cortex. I. Modulation in posterior parietal cortex related to selective visual attention. *Journal of Neurophysiology, 46*, 755–772.

Butter, C. M., and Kirsch, N. L. (1992). Combined and separate affects of eye patching and visual stimulation on unilateral neglect following stroke. *Archives of Physical Medicine and Rehabilitation, 73*, 1133–1139.

Chelazzi, L., and Desimone, R. (1994). Responses of V4 neurons during visual search. *Society for Neuroscience Abstracts, 20*, 1054.

Chelazzi, L., Miller, E. K., Duncan, J., and Desimone, R. (1993). A neural basis for visual search in inferior temporal cortex. *Nature, 363*, 345–347.

Chelazzi, L., Miller, E. K., Lueschow, A., and Desimone, R. (1993). Dual mechanisms of short-term memory: Ventral prefrontal cortex. *Society for Neuroscience Abstracts, 19*, 975.

Colby, C. L. (1991). The neuroanatomy and neurophysiology of attention. *Journal of Child Neurology, 6*, S90–S118.

De Renzi, E. (1982). *Disorders of space exploration and cognition*. Chichester: Wiley.

Desimone, R., and Duncan, J. (1995). Neural mechanisms of selective visual attention. *Annual Review of Neuroscience, 18*, 193–222.

Desimone, R., Li, L., Lehky, S., Ungerleider, L., and Mishkin, M. (1990). Effects of V4 lesions on visual discrimination performance and on responses of neurons in inferior temporal cortex. *Society for Neuroscience Abstracts, 16*, 621.

Desimone, R., and Schein, S. J. (1987). Visual properties of neurons in area V4 of the macaque: Sensitivity to stimulus form. *Journal of Neurophysiology, 57*, 835–868.

Desimone, R., and Ungerleider, L. G. (1989). Neural mechanisms of visual processing in monkeys. In F. Boller and J. Grafman (Eds.), *Handbook of Neuropsychology*, vol. 2, 267–299. Amsterdam: Elsevier.

Desimone, R., Wessinger, M., Thomas, L., and Schneider, W. (1990). Attentional control of visual perception: Cortical and subcortical mechanisms. *Cold Spring Harbor Symposia on Quantitative Biology, 55,* 963–971.

Deuel, R. K. (1987). Neural dysfunction during hemineglect after cortical damage in two monkey models. In M. Jeannerod (Ed.), *Neurophysiological and Neuropsychological Aspects of Neglect,* 315–334. Amsterdam: North-Holland.

Dorff, J. E., Mirsky, A. F., and Mishkin, M. (1965). Effects of unilateral temporal lobe removals in man on tachistoscopic recognition in the left and right visual fields. *Neuropsychologia, 3,* 39–51.

Driver, J., and Spence, C. J. (1994). Spatial synergies between auditory and visual attention. In C. Umiltà and M. Moscovitch (Eds.), *Attention and performance XV,* 311–331. Cambridge, MA: MIT Press.

Duncan, J. (1980). The locus of interference in the perception of simultaneous stimuli. *Psychological Review, 87,* 272–300.

Duncan, J. (1984). Selective attention and the organization of visual information. *Journal of Experimental Psychology: General, 113,* 501–517.

Duncan, J. (1993). Coordination of what and where in visual attention. *Perception, 22,* 1261–1270.

Duncan, J., and Humphreys, G. W. (1989). Visual search and stimulus similarity. *Psychological Review, 96,* 433–458.

Duncan, J., Ward, R., and Shapiro, K. (1994). Direct measurement of attentional dwell time in human vision. *Nature, 369,* 313–315.

Eriksen, B. A., and Eriksen, C. W. (1974). Effects of noise letters upon the identification of a target letter in a nonsearch task. *Perception and Psychophysics, 16,* 143–149.

Eriksen, C. W., and Hoffman, J. E. (1973). The extent of processing of noise elements during selective encoding from visual displays. *Perception and Psychophysics, 14,* 155–160.

Fagot, C., and Pashler, H. (1992). Making two responses to a single object: Implications for the central attentional bottleneck. *Journal of Experimental Psychology: Human Perception and Performance, 18,* 1058–1079.

Farah, M. J. (1990). *Visual agnosia: Disorders of object recognition and what they tell us about normal vision.* Cambridge, MA: MIT Press.

Farah, M. J. (1994). Neuropsychological inference with an interactive brain: A critique of the "locality" assumption. *Behavioral and Brain Sciences, 17,* 43–61.

Funahashi, S., Bruce, C. J., and Goldman-Rakic, P. S. (1989). Mnemonic coding of visual space in the monkey's dorsolateral prefrontal cortex. *Journal of Neurophysiology, 61,* 331–349.

Fuster, J. M., Bauer, R. H., and Jervey, J. P. (1985). Functional interactions between inferotemporal and prefrontal cortex in a cognitive task. *Brain Research, 330,* 299–307.

Fuster, J. M., and Jervey, J. P. (1981). Inferotemporal neurons distinguish and retain behaviorally relevant features of visual stimuli. *Science, 212,* 952–955.

Gnadt, J. W., and Andersen, R. A. (1988). Memory related motor planning activity in posterior parietal cortex of macaque. *Experimental Brain Research, 70,* 216–220.

Goldberg, M. E., and Bushnell, M. C. (1981). Behavioral enhancement of visual responses in monkey cerebral cortex. II. Modulation in frontal eye fields specifically related to saccades. *Journal of Neurophysiology, 46,* 773–787.

Goldberg, M. E., and Colby, C. L. (1989). The neurophysiology of spatial vision. In F. Boller and J. Grafman (Eds.), *Handbook of neuropsychology*, vol. 2, 301–315. Amsterdam: Elsevier.

Grabowecky, M., Robertson, L. C., and Treisman, A. (1993). Preattentive processes guide visual search: Evidence from patients with unilateral visual neglect. *Journal of Cognitive Neuroscience, 5,* 288–302.

Guariglia, C., and Antonucci, G. (1992). Personal and extrapersonal space: A case of neglect dissociation. *Neuropsychologia, 30,* 1001–1009.

Halligan, P. W., and Marshall, J. C. (1992). Left visuospatial neglect: A meaningless entity? *Cortex, 28,* 525–535.

Halligan, P. W., and Marshall, J. C. (1994). Focal and global attention modulate the expression of visuospatial neglect: A case study. *Neuropsychologia, 32,* 13–21.

Harter, M. R., and Aine, C. J. (1984). Brain mechanisms of visual selective attention. In R. Parasuraman and D. R. Davies (Eds.), *Varieties of attention.* Orlando, FL: Academic Press.

Hillyard, S. A., Munte, T. F., and Neville, H. J. (1985). Visual-spatial attention, orienting, and brain physiology. In M. I. Posner and O. S. M. Marin (Eds.), *Attention and performance XI,* 63–84. Hillsdale, NJ: Erlbaum.

Humphreys, G. W., and Riddoch, M. J. (1994). Attention to within-object and between-object spatial representations: Multiple sites for visual selection. *Cognitive Neuropsychology, 11,* 207–241.

Humphreys, G. W., Romani, C., Olson, A., Riddoch, M. J., and Duncan, J. (1995). Nonspatial extinction following lesions of the parietal lobe in man. *Nature, 372,* 357–359.

Kahneman, D., and Henik, A. (1977). Effects of visual grouping on immediate recall and selective attention. In S. Dornic (Ed.), *Attention and performance VI,* 307–332. Hillsdale, NJ: Erlbaum.

Karnath, H.-O. (1988). Deficits of attention in acute and recovered visual hemineglect. *Neuropsychologia, 26,* 27–43.

Kinsbourne, M. (1987). Mechanisms of unilateral neglect. In M. Jeannerod (Ed.), *Neurophysiological and neuropsychological aspects of neglect,* 69–86. Amsterdam: North-Holland.

Klein, R. (1980). Does oculomotor readiness mediate cognitive control of visual attention? In R. S. Nickerson (Ed.), *Attention and performance VIII,* 259–276. Hillsdale, NJ: Erlbaum.

Latto, R., and Cowey, A. (1971). Visual field defects after frontal eye-field lesions in monkeys. *Brain Research, 30,* 1–24.

Levine, D. N., and Calvanio, R. (1978). A study of the visual deficit in verbal alexia-simultanagnosia. *Brain, 101,* 65–81.

Luck, S., Chelazzi, L., Hillyard, S., and Desimone, R. (1993). Effects of spatial attention on responses of V4 neurons in the macaque. *Society for Neuroscience Abstracts, 19,* 27.

Luria, A. R. (1959). Disorders of "simultaneous perception" in a case of bilateral occipitoparietal brain injury. *Brain, 82,* 437–449.

McClelland, J. L., and Rumelhart, D. E. (1981). An interactive activation model of context effects in letter perception. I. An account of basic findings. *Psychological Review, 88,* 375–407.

Mesulam, M. M. (1981). A cortical network for directed attention and unilateral neglect. *Annals of Neurology, 10,* 309–325.

Miyashita, Y., and Chang, H. S. (1988). Neuronal correlate of pictorial short-term memory in the primate temporal cortex. *Nature, 331,* 68–70.

Morais, J. (1978). Spatial constraints on attention to speech. In J. Requin (Ed.), *Attention and performance VII*, 245–260. Hillsdale, NJ: Erlbaum.

Moran, J., and Desimone, R. (1985). Selective attention gates visual processing in the extratriate cortex. *Science, 229*, 782–784.

Moray, N. (1967). Where is capacity limited? A survey and a model. In A. F. Sanders (Ed.), *Attention and performance I*, 84–92. Amsterdam: North-Holland.

Neisser, U. (1967). *Cognitive psychology*. New York: Appleton-Century-Crofts.

Pashler, H. (1989). Dissociations and dependencies between speed and accuracy: Evidence for a two-component theory of divided attention in simple tasks. *Cognitive Psychology, 21*, 529–574.

Petersen, S. E., Robinson, D. L., and Keys, W. (1985). Pulvinar nuclei of the behaving rhesus monkey: Visual responses and their modulation. *Journal of Neurophysiology, 54*, 867–886.

Phaf, R. H., van der Heijden, A. H. C., and Hudson, P. T. W. (1990). SLAM: A connectionist model for attention in visual selection tasks. *Cognitive Psychology, 22*, 273–341.

Posner, M. I., and Petersen, S. E. (1990). The attention system of the human brain. *Annual Review of Neuroscience, 13*, 25–42.

Posner, M. I., Snyder, C. R. R., and Davidson, B. J. (1980). Attention and the detection of signals. *Journal of Experimental Psychology: General, 109*, 160–174.

Posner, M. I., Walker, J. A., Friedrich, F., and Rafal, R. D. (1984). Effects of parietal injury on covert orienting of attention. *Journal of Neuroscience, 4*, 1863–1874.

Raymond, J. E., Shapiro, K. L., and Arnell, K. M. (1992). Temporary suppression of visual processing in an RSVP task: An attentional blink? *Journal of Experimental Psychology: Human Perception and Performance, 18*, 849–860.

Rizzolatti, G., and Berti, A. (1990). Neglect as a neural representation deficit. *Revue Neurologique, 146*, 626–634.

Rizzolatti, G., and Camarda, R. (1987). Neural circuits for spatial attention and unilateral neglect. In M. Jeannerod (Ed.), *Neurophysiological and neuropsychological aspects of neglect*, 289–313. Amsterdam: North-Holland.

Rizzolatti, G., Gentilucci, M., and Matelli, M. (1985). Selective spatial attention: One center, one circuit, or many circuits? In M. I. Posner and O. S. M. Marin (Eds.), *Attention and performance XI*, 251–265. Hillsdale, NJ: Erlbaum.

Robertson, I. H., and North, N. T. (1994). One hand is better than two: Motor extinction of left hand advantage in unilateral neglect. *Neuropsychologia, 32*, 1–11.

Rubens, A. B. (1985). Caloric stimulation and unilateral visual neglect. *Neurology, 35*, 1019–1024.

Rumelhart, D. E. (1970). A multicomponent theory of the perception of briefly exposed visual displays. *Journal of Mathematical Psychology, 7*, 191–218.

Schneider, W., and Shiffrin, R. M. (1977). Controlled and automatic human information processing. I. Detection, search, and attention. *Psychological Review, 84*, 1–66.

Schwartz, E. L., Desimone, R., Albright, T. D., and Gross, C. G. (1983). Shape recognition and inferior temporal neurons. *Proceedings of the National Academy of Sciences, 80*, 5776–5778.

Shastri, L., and Ajjanagadde, V. (1993). From simple associations to systematic reasoning: A connectionist representation of rules, variables and dynamic bindings using temporal synchrony. *Behavioral and Brain Sciences, 16*, 417–494.

Shelton, P. A., Bowers, D., and Heilman, K. M. (1990). Peripersonal and vertical neglect. *Brain, 113*, 191–205.

Spence, C. J., and Driver, J. (1995). Audiovisual links in exogenous covert spatial orienting. Submitted to *Perception and Psychophysics*.

Sperling, G. (1967). Successive approximations to a model for short-term memory. In A. F. Sanders (Ed.), *Attention and performance I*, 285–292. Amsterdam: North-Holland.

Stein, B. E., Wallace, M. T., and Meredith, M. A. (1995). Neural mechanisms mediating attention and orientation to multisensory cues. In M. S. Gazzaniga (Ed.), *The cognitive neurosciences*, 683–702. Cambridge, MA: MIT Press.

Tegnér, R., and Levander, M. (1991). Through a looking glass: A new technique to demonstrate directional hypokinesia in unilateral neglect. *Brain, 114*, 1943–1951.

Townsend, J. T. (1971). A note on the identifiability of parallel and serial processes. *Perception and Psychophysics, 10*, 161–163.

Treisman, A. M., and Gelade, G. (1980). A feature integration theory of attention. *Cognitive Psychology, 12*, 97–136.

Ungerleider, L. G., and Mishkin, M. (1982). Two cortical visual systems. In D. J. Ingle, M. A. Goodale, and R. J. W. Mansfield (Eds.), *Analysis of visual behavior*, 549–586. Cambridge, MA: MIT Press.

Vallar, G., Rusconi, M. L., Bignamini, L., Geminiani, G., and Perani, D. (1994). Anatomical correlates of visual and tactile extinction in humans: A clinical CT scan study. *Journal of Neurology, Neurosurgery, and Psychiatry, 57*, 464–470.

Walley, R. E., and Weiden, T. D. (1973). Lateral inhibition and cognitive masking: A neuropsychological theory of attention. *Psychological Review, 80*, 284–302.

Ward, R., Duncan, J., and Shapiro, K. (in press). The slow time course of visual attention. *Cognitive Psychology*.

Ward, R., and McClelland, J. T. (1989). Conjunctive search for one and two identical targets. *Journal of Experimental Psychology: Human Perception and Performance, 15*, 664–672.

Welford, A. T. (1968). *Fundamentals of skill*. London: Methuen.

Wurtz, R. H., and Mohler, C. W. (1976). Organization of monkey superior colliculus: Enhanced visual response of superficial layer cells. *Journal of Neurophysiology, 39*, 745–765.

Zeki, S. M. (1978). Uniformity and diversity of structure and function in rhesus monkey prestriate visual cortex. *Journal of Physiology, 277*, 273–290.

22 Different Patterns of Popout for Direction of Motion and for Orientation

Asher Cohen and Richard Ivry

ABSTRACT

We used the visual search paradigm to demonstrate that popout of features in the dimensions of orientation and motion may be different. A series of experiments compared a directional motion task to an orientation task. When the target in the motion task was defined by particular direction of movement and all the distractors were defined by a second, homogeneous direction of movement, search time was minimally affected by the number of distractors. However, when the direction of motion for the distractors was heterogeneous, reaction time was dramatically affected by the number of distractors. By contrast, varying distractor heterogeneity in the orientation task had little effect on performance. Search for a target defined by one orientation was minimally affected by the number of distractors when the orientation of the distractors was heterogeneous.

The results suggest that the mechanism that leads to a popout of direction of movement may be different from the one that leads to a popout of orientation. We suggest that the popout for the direction of motion is due to a global analysis of a homogeneity of the display, whereas the popout for orientation is mediated by local analyses of differences between stimuli.

22.1 INTRODUCTION

Subjects in the visual search paradigm have to detect whether a target is present among a varying number of distractors. This paradigm has often been used to demonstrate a qualitative difference between search for a target defined by the presence of a single feature and search for a target defined by the presence of a conjunction of features. Typically, the reaction time (RT) for detecting a single-feature target is minimally affected by the number of distractors in the visual field (e.g., Egeth, Jonides, and Wall 1972; Ivry and Cohen 1990; Treisman and Gelade 1980). Single-feature targets are said to "pop out" from the field of distractors. The RT for detecting a conjunctive target, however, is typically a linearly increasing function of the number of distractors (Egeth, Virzi, and Garbart 1984; Treisman and Gelade 1980). In other words, the slope of the function between RT and set size is flat in the single-feature target search and steep in the conjunctive target search.

These studies have provided one of the primary lines of evidence for the feature integration theory proposed by Treisman and Gelade (1980). One of the main claims of this theory is that the processing of individual features and the conjoining of these features into objects involve separate processing stages. Although a number of recent visual search studies (e.g., Cohen and Ivry 1991; Houck and Hoffman 1986; McLeod, Driver, and Crisp 1988; Nakayama and Silverman 1986; Pashler 1987; Wolfe, Cave, and Franzel 1989) have blurred the distinction between feature and conjunction search, most current models of visual search (e.g., Cohen 1993; Treisman and Sato 1990; Wolfe, Cave, and Franzel 1989; but see Duncan and Humphreys 1989) still make a qualitative distinction between processing single features and processing conjunctions of features.

In our study we use the visual search paradigm for a different purpose. Our goal is to use this paradigm to demonstrate a further distinction at the level of single-feature processing between different dimensions. Specifically we show that the popout of a target defined by a particular direction of movement among distractors moving in other directions is different from the popout of a target defined by a particular orientation among distractors having other orientations. By doing so we emphasize that although the distinction between processing features and processing conjunction of features may be fundamental in visual perception, differences between features from different dimensions are also important.

The visual search paradigm has been used previously to demonstrate differences between features from different dimensions. Treisman and Gormican (1988) reported asymmetries within certain dimensions. For example, consider the dimension of size. Subjects find it easier to detect a long object among short distractors in comparison to searching for a short target among long distractors. This asymmetry is much less apparent within the color dimension. Reversing the mapping of target and distractor for a pair of colors such as yellow and lime green produces only a small change in the slope of the search function. Thus the comparison of feature variation within the size and color dimensions demonstrates that the processes involved in simple feature detection can be quite different for different dimensions (see Treisman and Gormican 1988 for a fuller discussion).

Driver and McLeod (1992) used the visual search paradigm to show differences in processing of stationary and moving stimuli. They compared search of conjunctive targets defined by movement and orientation. In one condition, the target was a tilted line that moved in the vertical direction. The distractors were either stationary tilted lines or vertical lines that also moved in the vertical direction. In the second condition, the target was a stationary tilted line and the distractors were stationary vertical lines or moving tilted lines. There were two levels of discriminability along the orientation dimension: an easy discrimination in which the tilted lines were at 45 degrees and a hard discrimination in which the tilted lines were just 9 degrees off of the upright orientation. When the discrimination was easy ($45°$ tilt), search for the moving target was much easier than the search for the stationary large, but when the discrimination was hard ($9°$ tilt), the pattern of results was reversed. The slope of the search function was much flatter for the stationary conjunction target in comparison to the moving conjunction target. Driver and McLeod concluded that there are substantial differences in the processing of moving and stationary stimuli.

The difference in processing between features from different dimensions has implications not just for detection of features but also for detection of more complex objects defined by conjunctions of features. Cohen (1993) found that differences in feature perception may lead to asymmetries in detection of conjunctive targets without any detectable asymmetries in the detection of single-feature targets. Asymmetries between large and small stimuli are obtained only when the difference in size is relatively small. Cohen (1993) employed horizontal and vertical stimuli that could be either large or small. The difference in size was chosen so that there would be no asymmetry in the search functions when the target was either small or large. Consider two tasks. In one task, the target was a large horizontal line and the distractors consisted of small horizontal lines and large vertical lines; in the second task, the target was a small horizontal line and the distractors were either large horizontal or small vertical lines. The target in both tasks was defined by a conjunction, with the only difference being that in the first task the target was large and in the second task the target was small. While there was no asymmetry between the features that formed the conjunctive targets, there was a marked asymmetry between the two conjunctive targets. Search for the large conjunctive target was much less affected by the number of distractors than search for the small conjunctive target (Cohen 1993). Despite observing this asymmetry only for conjunctive targets, however, the asymmetry was caused by the type of processing performed within the size dimension. Thus differences in processing features in different dimensions may have consequences for searches of more complex objects as well.

Popout can occur for targets defined on the basis of a difference in orientation (e.g., Treisman and Gormican 1988). Similarly, other studies have reported popout for targets defined by a particular direction of motion such as with a horizontally moving target among vertically moving distractors (Dick, Ullman, and Sagi 1987; Ivry and Cohen 1990). The dimensions of orientation and direction of movement appear to have at least a superficial similarity. Stimuli in both dimensions extend spatially in a similar manner, the difference being that orientation is static, whereas direction of movement is dynamic. We now report three experiments that demonstrate an important difference between these two cases of popout.

General Method

Subjects and Apparatus   All of the experiments were conducted in a dimly lit room. The subjects were undergraduate psychology students from Indiana University, who either received course credit or were paid for their participation. The stimuli were presented on a NEC MultiSynch SD color monitor that was controlled by a CompuAdd microcomputer. A chin rest was used to stabilize the viewing position and the subjects viewed the display from a distance of 100 cm.

Design All the experiments used a visual search task. The display for all tasks contained 3, 7, 9, or 13 items. A single target was included in the display on half of the trials for each array size; on the other half, all of the items were distractors. The positions of the stimuli were randomly selected with the constraint that the minimum distance between any two stimuli was at least 1.43 degrees of visual angle in any direction. On target-present trials, one of the distractors, chosen at random, was replaced by the target. Subjects received a short practice block of 48 trials, followed by 4 experimental blocks of 96 trials each.

Procedure Each trial began with the presentation of an asterisk in the center of the screen, serving as a fixation point. 1,000 ms later, the stimulus display replaced the asterisk and remained present until the subject responded. Subjects were instructed to respond as fast as they could while minimizing their mistakes. Responses were made by pressing one of two keys mounted on a response board interfaced with the computer. Subjects were instructed to respond with the left key if the target was present and to respond with the right key if the target was absent. The intertrial interval was 2 seconds, during which the screen was blank.

22.2 EXPERIMENT 1

The purpose of this experiment was to replicate the finding that a target defined by a particular direction of motion pops out from distractors that move in different directions (Dick, Ullman, and Sagi 1987; Ivry and Cohen 1990). Ivry and Cohen (1990) used a target that oscillated along the horizontal direction and distractors that oscillated in a vertical direction. Under these conditions, reaction time to detect the target was minimally affected by the number of distractors. In experiment 1, various directions of motion were used for the target and distractors to demonstrate the generality of this phenomenon.

In experiment 1a, the distractors oscillated in a horizontal direction and the target oscillated diagonally. For half of the subjects the target oscillated along a 45° diagonal, going from the lower right side of the screen to the upper left side and back. For the other half of the subjects, the target moved along the opposite diagonal (which will be referred to as the "135° condition"). In experiment 1b, the distractors oscillated vertically. Again, the target oscillated along one of two diagonals for separate groups of subjects. Finally, in experiment 1c, both the target and distractors oscillated along the diagonals. For half of the subjects, the target oscillated along the 45° diagonal; for the other half of the subjects, the target oscillated along the 135° diagonal. Note that in experiments 1a and 1b, the difference in orientation between the target and distractors is 45 degrees, whereas in experiment 1c, the difference is 90 degrees. 10 subjects participated in each experiment.

Stimuli   The stimuli consisted of small achromatic rectangles subtending 0.09 degree horizontally and 0.1 degree vertically of visual angle. Apparent motion was created by presenting a different screen every 50 ms in which each object was displaced 0.32 degree (center to center) in a direction determined by the conditions of the experiment. The amplitude of each half cycle of oscillation spanned 1.31 degrees. Oscillatory movement was created by reversing the direction of movement when an object reached the end of this distance. Each object would move three times in one direction before reversing and moving three times in the opposite direction. The starting phase within the oscillatory cycle was randomly determined for each object.

Results and Discussion

The pattern of the RT and error data was similar for all the experiments of this study; therefore, we focus on the RT data. The mean RT data of the target-present trials for the three experiments are shown in the top panel of figure 22.1. The mean RT data of the target-absent trials are shown in the bottom panel of figure 22.1; only correct responses are included. Table 22.1 shows the results of the intercept and slope of the set size functions as revealed by a regression analysis for all tasks.

The results are in accord with previous visual search studies of motion (Dick, Ullman, and Sagi 1987; Ivry and Cohen 1990) and demonstrate the generality of the popout of a target defined by a particular direction of movement. Although there are considerable differences among the absolute RTs of the three target-present conditions, in all three conditions RT was minimally affected by the number of distractors. The slopes were all under 5 ms/item, and none of the three values were significantly different from 0. The results of the target-absent trials are less consistent, as is often the case for these conditions (e.g., Ivry and Cohen 1990; Treisman and Gelade 1980). Shallow slopes were also found on the target absent trials in experiments 1a and 1b, the experiments in which the distractors moved along either the horizontal or vertical axes. However, in experiment 1c, reaction time rose quite steeply as more distractors moving along the off-diagonal were added to the display. Generally these results are similar to other findings of visual search for a target defined by a single feature.

22.3   EXPERIMENT 2

In most previous studies with targets defined by a direction of movement, the distractors were homogeneous with respect to the axis of direction of movements, that is, all the distractors oscillated along the same direction. In this

Ex. 1 - Target Present Trials

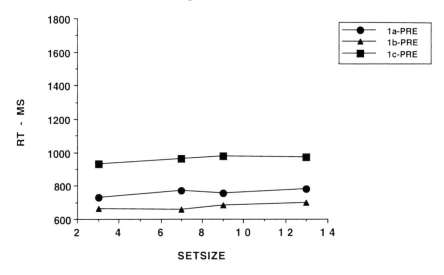

Ex. 1 - Target Absent Trials

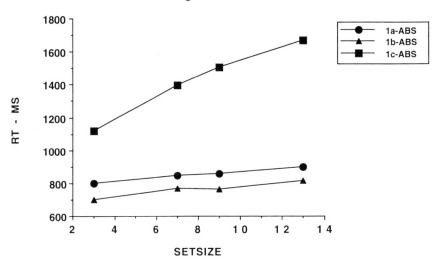

Figure 22.1 RTs for directional motion target in three tasks of experiment 1, with homogeneous distractors. Top panel depicts results of target-present trials; bottom panel depicts results of target-absent trials.

Table 22.1 Intercepts, Slopes, and R^2 of Array Size Functions in Various Tasks of Experiment 1

Experiment	1a	1b	1c
Target present			
Intercept	723	643	928
Slope	4.7	3.9	4.3
R^2	.78	.81	.74
Target absent			
Intercept	772	676	983
Slope	9.7	10.6	55.0
R^2	.99	.92	.98

experiment, we examine visual search for an oscillating target when the distractors move in two other directions. The three directions of movement (one for the target and two for the distractors) were selected from four alternatives: horizontal, vertical, and the two diagonals. As shown by previous studies and experiment 1, a target defined by any of these directions of motion will pop out when the distractors move along one of the other axes. Thus these directions of motion are clearly distinct.

What can we predict for this experiment with regard to the slope of the relation between RT and the number of distractors? Previous research leads to ambiguous answers. On the one hand, a large number of studies have shown that the degree of heterogeneity of distractors is an important factor in visual search (see Duncan and Humphreys 1989). Indeed, Duncan and Humphreys (1989) have proposed that the heterogeneity among the distractors is one of the primary determinants of the slope of the search function. On the other hand, there are certain situations in which a feature target pops out from among distractors that are heterogeneous among the critical dimension (e.g., Treisman and Gelade 1980). Furthermore, a study by Driver, McLeod, and Dienes (1992) that directly examined search for a target defined by a particular direction of movement among distractors moving in three other directions obtained a modest slope (around 15 ms/item). However, the method used by Driver, McLeod, and Dienes is different from ours in several important ways, as noted in the general discussion (section 22.5).

In experiment 2a, the target oscillated in a vertical direction. Half of the distractors oscillated along the 45° diagonal and the other half along the 135° diagonal; 20 subjects participated. In Experiment 2b, the target oscillated horizontally and the distractors were the same as in experiment 2a; 10 subjects participated. In experiment 2c, the target oscillated in a 45° direction. Half of the distractors oscillated vertically and the other half oscillated horizontally; 20 subjects participated. In experiment 2d, the target oscillated along the 45° axis. Half of the distractors oscillated along the horizontal axis and the other half oscillated along the 135° off-diagonal; 10 subjects participated. The stimuli were the same as those of experiment 1.

Results and Discussion

The mean correct RTs of the target-present trials in the 4 experiments are shown in the top panel of figure 22.2. The bottom panel shows the results for the target-absent trials. Table 22.2 shows the results of the intercept and slope of the set size functions as revealed by a regression analysis for all tasks.

The results are very different from those of experiment 1. In all four tasks, reaction time was markedly affected by the number of distractors, with slopes ranging from 63 ms/item to 81 ms/item. The set size slopes obtained in this task are unusually high even when compared to slow searches with conjunctive targets; these values are also considerably higher than that reported by Driver, McLeod, and Dienes (1992). The difficulty of these search tasks is most surprising when it is noted that search for any of these targets is quite easy when the distractors oscillate along a single axis.

The results of experiment 2 demonstrate that inclusion of a second axis of oscillation for the distractors dramatically changes the search requirements. This result was found with a variety of target-distractor pairings and does not seem to be unique to any particular pairing.

22.4   EXPERIMENT 3

The preceding experiment convincingly demonstrated that when the distractors oscillate along more than one axis, search for a target defined by the direction of motion is disrupted. Does this result reflect a general consequence of increasing the heterogeneity of the display? As mentioned before, manipulating the heterogeneity of the distractors can affect the slope of the array size function (see Duncan and Humphreys 1989). However, increasing heterogeneity does not always lead to increased difficulty on visual search tasks. For example, Treisman and Gelade (1980) obtained popout for targets defined by either color or shape (e.g., letters) among displays containing two types of color distractors and shape distractors. Comparisons between studies, however, may be problematic. There could be several idiosyncratic aspects to our method that may lead to different results. Experiment 3 was designed to demonstrate that heterogeneous distractors do not necessarily prevent a popout of a single-feature target with a method identical to that of experiment 2.

The targets and distractors in this experiment were all static objects that varied in terms of their orientation. A number of experiments have shown that orientation is a salient feature. Popout occurs for displays in which the target is of a different orientation than the distractors (e.g., Cohen 1993; Treisman 1988). In addition, as mentioned previously, direction of movement and orientation extend spatially in a similar manner.

In experiment 3a, the target was a vertical line. Half of the distractors were oriented along the 45° diagonal (from lower right to upper left), and the other

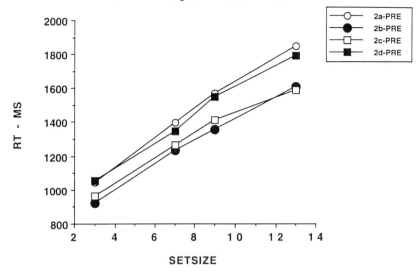

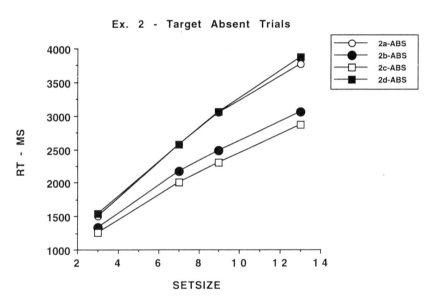

Figure 22.2 RTs for directional motion target in four tasks of experiment 2, with heterogeneous distractors. Top panel depicts results of target-present trials; bottom panel depicts the results of target-absent trials.

Patterns of Popout for Direction of Motion and Orientation

Table 22.2 Intercepts, Slopes, and R^2 of Array Size Functions in Various Tasks of Experiment 2

Experiment	2a	2b	2c	2d
Target present				
Intercept	819	729	804	836
Slope	81	68.9	62.8	75.2
R^2	.99	.99	.98	.99
Target absent				
Intercept	902	885	820	886
Slope	227.6	171.6	160.3	234.3
R^2	.99	.99	.99	.99

distractors were oriented along the 135° diagonal. The target in experiment 3b was a horizontal line and the distractors were the same as in experiment 3a. In experiment 3c, the target was oriented along the 45° diagonal and the distractors were oriented along either the vertical or horizontal axis. 10 subjects participated in each of the experiments.

Stimuli and Design The stimuli were stationary lines subtending 0.09 degree in width and 1.31 degrees in length. The length of the stimuli matched exactly the amplitude of the oscillating stimuli used in experiments 1 and 2; all other aspects of the design were similar to those of experiments 1 and 2.

Results and Discussion

The top panel of figure 22.3 depicts the correct mean RT of the target-present trials in the three tasks of this experiment. The bottom panel shows the results for the target-absent trials. Table 22.3 provides the details of the regression analyses of the set size functions.

Unlike the findings of experiment 2, the number of distractors had little effect on the search time. Although there is a small difference in slope between the three tasks, search in all three tasks falls within the common definition of a popout.

22.5   GENERAL DISCUSSION

The findings of this study demonstrate a different pattern of popout between the direction of motion task and the orientation task. When the distractors were homogeneous on the relevant dimension, a popout was obtained in the motion task, but when two types of distractors were used, a clear difference between the motion and orientation dimensions emerged. A static target defined on the basis of its orientation was rapidly detected even among arrays containing heterogeneous distractors with two different orientations. By contrast, the addition of a second axis of oscillation to the distractor set

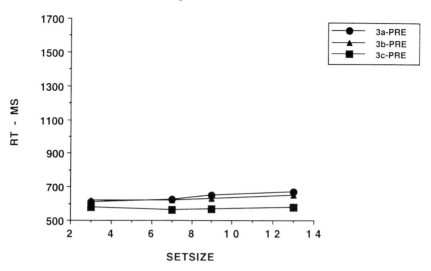

Ex. 3 - Target Present Trials

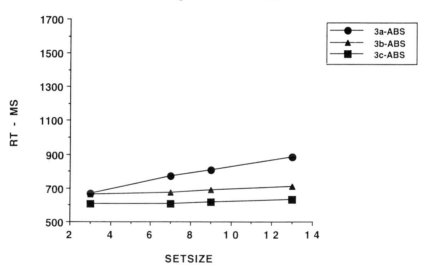

Ex. 3 - Target Absent Trials

Figure 22.3 RTs for orientation target in three tasks of experiment 3, with heterogeneous distractors. Top panel depicts results of target-present trials; bottom panel depicts results of target-absent trials.

Patterns of Popout for Direction of Motion and Orientation

Table 22.3 Intercepts, Slopes, and R^2 of Array Size Functions in Various Tasks of Experiment 3

Experiment	3a	3b	3c
Target present			
Intercept	586	602	569
Slope	6.5	3.4	0
R^2	.95	.90	.0
Target present			
Intercept	608	643	594
Slope	21.7	5.1	2.6
R^2	.99	.98	.87

led to a large increase in the slope of the search function for a target defined by direction of motion.

What is the reason for the different pattern of results in the motion and orientation tasks? One possible explanation is that the distinction between features is coarser in the motion dimension than in the orientation dimension. Put differently, the tuning profile for motion detectors may be broader for motion detectors than for orientation detectors. Broad tuning may be sufficient to allow popout when all of the distractors move along a single axis of oscillation because there may still remain some detectors that are uniquely activated by the target. For example, if the bandwidth extended to 90 degrees and the distractors oscillated along the 45° diagonal, the presence of a vertically oscillating target might be detected by examining the output of detectors maximally tuned to motion at 145 degrees. However, with such coarse coding, any pairing of two directions of oscillation for the heterogeneous distractors would produce activation across the full range of motion detectors. Therefore, the appearance of the target would not activate unique detectors and no popout would be obtained. If the bandwidth for orientation detectors was narrower, popout might still hold with heterogeneous distractors.

This explanation seems tenuous because it has to assume a very coarse tuning profile to account for the steep search functions in all the tasks of experiment 2. In particular, to account for the results of experiment 2d, in which the target oscillated in a 45° direction and the distractors oscillated horizontally and in a 135° direction, one has to assume a tuning profile of at least 67.5 degrees. With a less coarse tuning profile there would be detectors that would be uniquely activated by the target. Although there is no direct behavioral evidence that contradicts such an assumption, this magnitude of coarse coding seems rather extreme because it encompasses more than a third of all possible directions of motion. In addition, the tuning profile of single cells that are sensitive to motion is typically much less coarse (Maunsell and Van Essen 1983). Note, however, that properties of single cells do not necessarily generalize to behavioral properties.

There is a related explanation, proposed by Treisman (e.g., 1991; see also Wolfe et al. 1992) that seems to fit the findings better.[1] According to this account, early processes can lead to activation of only a few (e.g., four) detectors or categories per dimension. The choice of which four values are adopted for any search task may be flexible, but the total number of values detected at any one point is limited. Assume also that opposite directions of movement are detected separately; hence an oscillating stimulus has two directions of motion. Two oscillating distractors require four sets of detectors and the target requires two other sets of detectors. Therefore, detecting the target in experiment 2 requires the detection of at least five different directions of motion. This may be too difficult a load for the early processing, and consequently the target can only be detected by a conjunction of the two directions of movement from which it is composed. This explanation accounts also for the relatively easy search in the orientation task because this task requires the detection of only three values.

Although this explanation qualitatively fits the findings, we still find it tenuous. The slopes of the set size functions in experiment 2 are much steeper than slopes found in typical conjunctive searches (e.g., Egeth, Virzi, and Garbart 1984; Treisman and Gelade 1980). It is not clear why the addition of one more distractor (i.e., two values) leads to a shift from a flat slope to a very steep slope of set size functions; therefore, we suggest a different explanation.

To account for our findings we follow the terminology proposed by Duncan and Humphreys (1989, 1992). Duncan and Humphreys suggested that responses in visual search are made only to elements selected by the attentional system, and that this selection is determined by a weight assigned to each element in the display during search (see Cohen 1993 and Wolfe, Cave, and Franzel 1989 for similar proposals). Two different factors are important in determining the ease of visual search. The first factor is the similarity of the target and the distractors to a search template consisting of the internal description of the target by the subjects. During the search, each element in the display is compared to the search template and accumulates a weight as a function of its similarity to the search template. The rate of search is dependent on both the similarity between the target and the search template and the dissimilarity between the distractors and the search template. A second factor is perceptual grouping of elements present in the display. There is a spreading of weights among elements that can be joined to form a perceptual group (e.g., on the basis of common orientation or direction of motion). Linking the distractors into a group would be beneficial because all the members of the group could be suppressed as a single entity. In contrast, grouping the target with the distractors would be harmful and would increase response time.

Popout of a target among homogeneous distractors can be caused by either one of the two factors suggested by Duncan and Humphreys (1989, 1992). A target can be efficiently detected by a match to a search template if it is similar to the search template and the distractors are sufficiently dissimilar. Alternatively, the homogeneous distractors can be grouped and eliminated as a group. It is, of course, possible that both factors contribute to the popout; thus the source of the popout in search among homogeneous distractors is ambiguous.

When the distractors are heterogeneous, on the other hand, the situation may be different. If the heterogeneity of the distractors prevents their grouping, popout can be obtained only via the first factor of matching each element (or a group with just a few items) to the search template. Thus one way to examine the source of a popout for a particular target is to make the distractors heterogeneous and to find out whether the target still pops out. Importantly, when making the distractors heterogeneous, two added assumptions have to hold. First, the heterogeneous distractors cannot be grouped as efficiently as the homogeneous distractors. Second, the target can pop out among any one of the distractors. If popout still occurs with heterogeneous distractors, it suggests that matching the elements in the display to a search template is sufficient to create such a popout. If a popout does not occur with heterogeneous distractors, it suggests that matching the individual elements in the display to the search template is not sufficient for a popout. Furthermore, this latter situation suggests that the popout obtained when the distractors are homogeneous is due to perceptual grouping.

These arguments lend insight into the current findings. Consider first the results in the direction of motion task. The search functions were nearly flat with homogeneous distractors, but increased quite steeply with heterogeneous distractors. These results indicate that popout with homogeneous distractors must have been caused by grouping of the distractors. Presumably, neighboring items that have a similar axis of oscillation can be grouped together. In experiment 1, the only item that cannot be grouped with its neighbors is the target, and thus its detection is efficient. Making the distractors heterogeneous in experiment 2 appears to have interfered with grouping and led to a steep set size function.

Contrast these findings with those obtained in the orientation task of experiment 3. Here shallow search functions were found across all of the conditions. This would suggest that in searching for a target defined by a unique orientation, subjects compare the display to a search template.[2]

One of the main themes of this Attention and Performance meeting is integration within and between modalities. Our findings have implications not just for processing individual features but also for processing conjunctions of features within the modality of motion, as well as between motion and other modalities. Based on the present study, we have proposed that it is difficult to detect the presence or absence of a particular direction of movement. Making such a detection requires an examination of the elements by a limited-capacity system and may even have to be serial. This would suggest that finding a target composed of a conjunction of direction of movement with another feature may be difficult, as well, because the display in such situations is not homogeneous. An experiment in which the target is defined by a conjunction of direction of movement and velocity would illustrate this point.

We (Ivry and Cohen 1992) have previously found that a target defined by its velocity pops out among distractors moving with lower velocity. In an unpublished follow-up experiment Ivry and Cohen (1992), subjects had to detect a fast item oscillating in the horizontal direction among slow distractors oscillating horizontally and fast distractors oscillating vertically. The velocity of the fast items was 2.75 deg/sec and the velocity of the slow items was 1.38 deg/sec. The amplitude of oscillation was 41.2 minutes of arc horizontally and 45.9 minutes of arc vertically. The four display sizes used in this experiment were 3, 7, 11, and 15 items. The apparatus was the same as that used by Ivry and Cohen (1992); 12 subjects participated.

If grouping cannot be done efficiently when the distractors oscillate along more than one axis, this conjunction search should be slow. This is indeed the result we obtained. The estimated slope of the set size function for the target-present trials was 45.8 ms/item. The estimated slope for the target-absent trials was 155.4 ms/item.

The results reported in this chapter appear to be at odds with those obtained by Driver, McLeod, and Dienes (1992). Subjects in one of their experiments had to detect a target defined by one direction of motion among distractors moving in three other directions of motion. Although not flat, the slope of the search function in this experiment was quite shallow (around 15 ms/item for the target-present trials). This value is considerably below those found in the current experiment 2, even though the distractors in our display only contained motion along two axes. Moreover, Driver, McLeod, and Dienes (1992) reported a shallow slope for a target defined by the conjunction of direction of motion and velocity, whereas subjects in our unpublished study produced a steep set size slope in search for such a target.

A closer comparison of the two studies reveals a critical difference. The stimuli in our experiment oscillated, that is, each element moved in two opposing directions on each cycle. Furthermore, the distractors were out of phase with one another. By contrast, the stimuli in the Driver, McLeod, and Dienes (1992) study moved continuously in a specific direction. It may be that grouping is possible when objects move in phase and in a common direction. Thus, in the Driver, McLeod, and Dienes (1992) experiment where the target was moving in one direction and the distractors were moving in three other directions, the search might have approximated search among three distractors because distractors that had the same direction of movement were grouped. In the experiment where the target was defined by a conjunction of direction of movement and velocity, there were only two types of direction of movement, and search for the fast target could be done efficiently within each group.

Finally, our results emphasize that although the distinction between processing features and processing conjunctions of features is essential, it may also be important to distinguish between processing particular features from different dimensions. Our results suggest that the visual system can detect the appearance of specific features in the orientation dimension. By contrast, the visual system may not be able to detect the appearance of particular directions of motion; instead, items that move in the same direction may be grouped together, and this grouping may also lead to a popout. The different style of processing in the orientation and direction of motion dimensions may not only be essential for the detection of individual features but it may also have clear implications for integration of features.

NOTES

This study was supported by NSF grant BNS 90-12471 and by a grant from the Israel Foundations Trustees to Asher Cohen. We thank Anne Treisman for her useful comments on this manuscript.

1. We thank Anne Treisman for pointing out this alternative explanation.

2. Note that we take no stand on the type of processing needed to distinguish the target from the distractors. Some researchers (e.g., Nothdurft 1992) have claimed that finding the target requires finding a local contrast between different features. Others (e.g., Treisman and Gormican 1988) have claimed that the activation created by the target itself is sufficient for its detection.

REFERENCES

Cohen, A. (1993). Asymmetries in visual search for conjunctive targets. *Journal of Experimental Psychology: Human Perception and Performance, 19,* 775−797.

Cohen, A., and Ivry, R. (1991). Density effects in conjunction search: Evidence for a coarse location mechanism of feature integration. *Journal of Experimental Psychology: Human Perception and Performance, 17,* 891−901.

Dick, M., Ullman, S., and Sagi, D. (1987). Parallel and serial processes in motion detection. *Science, 237,* 400−402.

Driver, J., and McLeod, P. (1992). Reversing visual search asymmetries with conjunctions of movement and orientation. *Journal of Experimental Psychology: Human Perception and Performance, 18,* 22−33.

Driver, J., McLeod, P., and Dienes, Z. (1992). Are direction and speed coded independently by the visual system? Evidence from visual search. *Spatial Vision, 6,* 133−147.

Duncan, J., and Humphreys, G. W. (1989). Visual search and stimulus similarity. *Psychological Review, 96,* 433−458.

Duncan, J., and Humphreys, G. W. (1992). Beyond the search surface: Visual search and attentional engagement. *Journal of Experimental Psychology: Human Perception and Performance, 18,* 578−588.

Egeth, H. E., Jonides, J., and Wall, S. (1972). Parallel processing of multielement displays. *Cognitive Psychology, 3,* 674−698.

Egeth, H. E., Virzi, R. A., and Garbart, H. (1984). Searching for conjunctively defined targets. *Journal of Experimental Psychology: Human Perception and Performance, 10,* 32−39.

Houck, M. R., and Hoffman, J. E. (1986). Conjunction of color and form without attention: Evidence from an orientation-contingent color aftereffects. *Journal of Experimental Psychology: Human Perception and Performance, 12*, 186–199.

Ivry, R. B., and Cohen, A. (1990). Dissociation of short and long range apparent motion in visual search. *Journal of Experimental Psychology: Human Perception and Performance, 16*, 317–331.

Ivry, R. B., and Cohen, A. (1992). Asymmetry in visual search for targets defined by differences in movement speed. *Journal of Experimental Psychology: Human Perception and Performance, 18*, 1045–1057.

Ivry, R. B., and Cohen, A. (1992). Search for conjunctive targets defined by speed and direction of movement is limited. Unpublished manuscript. University of California, Berkeley.

Maunsell, J. H. R., and Van Essen, D. C. (1983). Functional properties of neurons in middle temporal visual area of the Macaque monkey. I. Selectivity for stimulus direction, speed, and orientation. *Journal of Neurophysiology, 49*, 1127–1147.

McLeod, P., Driver, J., and Crisp, J. (1988). Visual search for a conjunction of movement and form is parallel. *Nature, 332*, 154–155.

Nakayama, K., and Silverman, G. H. (1986). Serial and parallel processing of visual feature conjunctions. *Nature, 320*, 264–265.

Nothdurft, H. C. (1992). Feature analysis and the role of similarity in preattentive vision. *Perception and Psychophysics, 52*, 355–375.

Pashler, H. (1987). Detecting conjunctions of color and form: Reassessing the serial search hypothesis. *Perception and Psychophysics, 41*, 191–201.

Treisman, A. M. (1988). Features and objects: The fourteenth Bartlett memorial lecture. *Quarterly Journal of Experimental Psychology, 40A*, 201–237.

Treisman, A. M. (1991). Search, similarity, and the integration of features between and within dimensions. *Journal of Experimental Psychology: Human Perception and Performance, 17*, 652–676.

Treisman, A. M., and Gelade, G. (1980). A feature integration theory of attention. *Cognitive Psychology, 12*, 97–136.

Treisman, A. M., and Gormican, S. (1988). Feature analysis in early vision: Evidence from search asymmetries. *Psychological Review, 95*, 15–48.

Treisman, A. M., and Sato, S. (1990). Conjunction search revisited. *Journal of Experimental Psychology: Human Perception and Performance, 16*, 459–478.

Wolfe, J. M., Cave, K. R., and Franzel, S. L. (1989). Guided search: An alternative to the feature integration model for visual search. *Journal of Experimental Psychology: Human Perception and Performance, 15*, 419–433.

Wolfe, J. M., Friedman-Hill, S. R., Stewart, M. L., and O'Connel, K. M. (1992). The role of categorization in visual search for orientation. *Journal of Experimental Psychology: Human Perception and Performance, 18*, 34–49.

23 Vision, Attention, and Action: Inhibition and Facilitation in Sensory-Motor Links Revealed by the Reaction Time and the Line Motion

Shinsuke Shimojo, Yasuto Tanaka, Okihide Hikosaka, and Satoru Miyauchi

ABSTRACT

To investigate critical factors for local inhibition and facilitation in visual-motor tasks, we randomized stimulus dimensions (location, color, and orientation) and response-stimulus interval across trials. The subject performed four different tasks. Reaction times at the same location were longer, that is, "inhibition of return" (IOR) occurred, in the detection and location discrimination tasks. Reaction times at the same location were shorter in the color and orientation discrimination tasks. IOR was observed also in arm-reaching and saccadic eye movement tasks. Moreover, the task-dependent difference of RTs was observed also with popout displays. The results indicate a dissociation of two visual functions: detection/orienting and fine feature analysis.

To investigate whether motor readiness could draw attention to the target location and have an influence on visual information processing, we employed the "line motion" illusion; we showed that mere preparation for a motor response, such as arm reaching or saccade, would be sufficient to yield local facilitation at the prepared target location.

In this chapter, we discuss issues related to functional links between the visual and the motor systems. For this purpose, we will present two sets of findings: one employing the reaction time paradigm and indicating functional segregation of two visual functions, and the other employing the "line motion" paradigm and indicating effects of motor readiness on the visual information processing.

23.1 REACTION TIME AND ATTENTION

Spatial attention is an indispensable aspect of visual information processing: indispensable because the brain has a limited capacity, whereas the constant flows of sensory inputs could be infinite in theory. Without selection and filtering by attention, it would be impossible to perceive what is important and to respond to it appropriately (James 1890; Helmholtz 1910; Broadbent 1958). On the other hand, some authors have recently argued that there is no limit to the brain's capacity for visual information processing (Van der Heijden 1991). Limited capacity may, instead, concern "selection for action." This view of spatial attention may be a part of the reason why reaction time (RT) has been often employed as a sensitive measure to access the selection and filtering processes, and it has revealed various effects in a spatiotemporal context.

For instance, consider a situation where a cue and a target are presented sequentially, either at the same or different locations. When the target is presented at the same location as the cue, RT is larger than that at the different location. This is so particularly when the interval between the onset of the cue and the target (stimulus onset asynchrony, or SOA) is relatively large (300–1500 ms; Posner and Cohen 1984). This has been called "inhibition of return" (IOR) and repeatedly duplicated (Maylor 1985; Nissen 1985; Kwak and Egeth 1992; Tassinari et al. 1994; Gibson and Egeth 1994; Tipper et al. 1994).[1]

23.2 INHIBITION OF RETURN AND ITS UNDERLYING MECHANISM

The underlying mechanism of IOR is unknown, however. Because the reaction task involves various levels of processing, it is unclear at which level the effect occurs.[2] Some researchers suggest that inhibition occurs when location of the target alone is changed (Kwak and Egeth 1992), that IOR is therefore closely related to spatial location, rather than to any other visual attributes, of the target (Nissen 1985; Kwak and Egeth 1992). They argue that this effect occurs in the visual orienting process, for which a "spotlight" would be a good metaphor (Posner 1980). Meanwhile, others suggest that facilitation, instead of inhibition, may occur in the different conditions or tasks (Terry, Valdes, and Neill 1994).

To understand the mechanisms more inclusively, we first tried to duplicate the inhibitory effect in a simple detection task, which was similar to that employed by Kwak and Egeth (1992).

A Pilot Study

A single target was presented in either the top left or top right position of the display, while the subject fixated at a point (FP) in the bottom center. The location of the target was randomized between these two locations across trials. The interval between the button-pushing response and the next target appearance (reaction stimulus interval, or RSI) was also randomized across the trials (200/400/1,000/2,000 ms). The distance between the target and FP was 12 degrees. Note that there was no cue in this experiment, and we were mostly interested in the positional effect of the previous target on RT to the present target. Four subjects (two naive and two nonnaive (authors)) were asked to detect a target, and to press a mouse button as quickly as possible.

In results, strong inhibition of return was obtained for all subjects at all RSIs, except the longest (2,000 ms). Thus the cue/target distinction is not a necessary condition for IOR, as originally suggested by Tassinari and his colleagues (Tassinari et al. 1987).

23.3 TASK DEPENDENCY OF INHIBITION AND FACILITATION

What are the critical conditions for the IOR effect, then? Could the distinction between detection and discrimination be critical? Or rather, could the type of visual information, say, spatial versus nonspatial attributes be critical (Kwak and Egeth 1992; Tassinari et al. 1994; Terry, Valdes, and Neill 1994)? To address these issues, we conducted experiment 1.1.

Experiment 1.1: Task Dependency of Inhibition and Facilitation of Return in Button Pressing

Subjects Six subjects participated in the experiment: four naive and two nonnaive (authors).

Stimuli and Apparatus Stimulus configuration was similar to that employed in the pilot study; as in the pilot study, there was no cue. Location (left/right), color (red/green), and orientation of the target (vertically/horizontally elongated) were all randomized across trials (see fig. 23.1).

The stimuli were presented on the CRT display, controlled by a personal computer (Commodore Amiga 500). Target size was 0.5 degree × 0.4 degree, and its luminance was 6.4 cd/m^2 (hue: red (.555, .344); green (.320, .555)). The fixation point's size was 0.4° × 0.4°. Luminance of the background was 0.01 cd/m^2. The distance between the fixation point and the target was 6.0 degrees. Viewing distance was 114 cm. Subject's head was

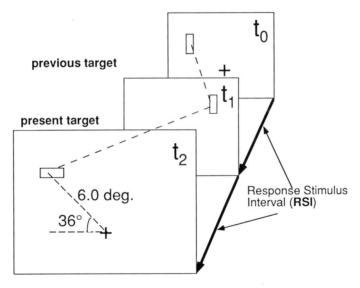

Figure 23.1 Stimulus configuration and sequence for RT experiment with single target (experiment 1.1).

fixed by the chin rest. Eye fixation was monitored in selected experiments using the *Ober2* system (Permobil Corp.; see the stimuli and apparatus section of experiment 1.3 for more details). The experiment was conducted in a completely dark room.

Procedure   The stimulus sequence is illustrated in figure 23.1. Subjects were asked to fixate on the fixation point all through the session, and to press a mouse button in response to each target presentation. Each of the subjects was engaged in four tasks in separate sessions: (1) simple detection; (2) location discrimination (left/right); (3) color discrimination (red/green); and (4) orientation discrimination (vertical/horizontal). The order of these sessions was randomized across subjects. RSI was also randomized (100/300/500/ 1,200 ms). Note that the stimuli and their sequence were identical across all the tasks. The subject made two-alternative forced-choice (2AFC) judgments by button pushing for all the tasks, except the simple detection task. Thus the only difference was the nature of the task.

Subjects performed a practice session (100 trials) before each session of the experiment; the total number of trials was 300 in each experimental session. We analyzed data based on the positional relationship between the previous and the present trials. RTs in error trials were eliminated from the data analysis. Sessions where the error rate for discrimination exceeded 10 percent were considered unreliable and eliminated.

Results   The results were fairly straightforward. IOR was obvious, that is, RT at the *same* location was *longer*, in the simple detection and the location discrimination tasks (see fig. 23.2, top). The opposite pattern of results, however, was found in the color and the orientation discrimination tasks; RT at the *same* location as in the previous trials was *shorter* than that at the different location (see fig. 23.2, bottom). We call this effect "facilitation of return" (FOR). The consistency of results across six subjects is obvious in table 23.1. We also pooled the data across the subjects and applied a four-way repeated-measures ANOVA (RSI × location × color × orientation). The results can be summarized as follows: (1) for the detection task, location ($p < .01$), orientation ($p < .01$), RSI ($p < .01$) and location × RSI ($p < .05$) factors were statistically significant; (2) for the location discrimination task, location and color × orientation factors were significant (both $p < .01$); (3) for the color discrimination task, location, color, location × color, and color × orientation factors were significant (all $p < .01$); and (4) for the orientation discrimination task, location ($p < .05$), location × orientation ($p < .01$), and color × RSI ($p < .05$) factors were significant.

Discussion   The opposite polarity of results between the two groups of tasks should be attributed to the task difference per se because the stimulus parameters and the responses were identical. However, it was not the distinc-

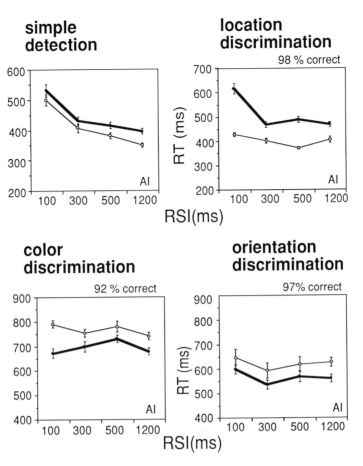

Figure 23.2 RT as function of RSI in single-target experiment (experiment 1.1). Results in four different tasks are shown separately in separate panels. Bold line indicates RT at same location, and thin line indicates RT at different location. Vertical bars show standard errors.

tion between detection and discrimination, but rather what information is necessary to perform the task, that seemed to be critical. On one hand, there were tasks that essentially require, or at least trigger, spatial orienting (detection and location discrimination), where we consistently found inhibition of return. On the other hand, there were tasks that require feature analysis (color and orientation discrimination), where we consistently found facilitation of return. The FOR is no doubt reminiscent of the benefits usually obtained with valid cues (e.g., Posner 1980). The critical difference, however, is that in our experiment there is no cue/target distinction, and no valid/invalid distinction either. That is, the kind of facilitation reported here is nothing to do with "informative" cues. The relationship of our findings to the facilitatory repetition effects reported by Pashler and Baylis (1991) and Maljkovic and Nakayama (1994) should be investigated in future.

Table 23.1 Summary of Results in Single-Target Experiment (Experiment 1.1)

Subjects	Orienting tasks		Feature tasks	
	Simple Detection	Location Discrim.	Color Discrim.	Orientation Discrim.
YT	$-$**	$-$**	$+$**	$+$**
SS	$-$**	$-$**	$+$**	$+$**
KS	$-$**	$-$**	$+$**	$+$**
AM	$-$**	$-$**	$+$**	ns
AI	$-$**	$-$**	$+$**	$+$**
SP	$-$**	$-$**	$+$**	$+$*

Note: Subjects YT and SS were nonnavie, while the others were naive. The data were analyzed by ANOVA. The IOR is indicated by $-$, whereas the FOR is indicated by $+$ symbols. Data were analyzed by ANOVA for statistical significance, as indicated by * and **.

23.4 GLOBAL ORIENTING VERSUS LOCAL FEATURE: THE CASE OF VERNIER TASK

The dichotomy is still ambiguous because spatial information could be used both for global orienting and elaborate analysis of object features. The question is whether the *global* spatial information is critical, or whatever is *spatial* is critical even at the finest scale, for IOR to occur. To answer this question, we next employed a vernier discrimination task.

Experiment 1.2: Vernier Task

Subjects Four subjects participated in the experiment: two naive and two nonnaive (the authors).

Stimuli and Apparatus The stimulus configuration and sequence and the apparatus were similar to those employed in experiment 1.1, except that this time the target consisted of two horizontal line segments and one dot located either above or below these reference lines (see fig. 23.3). The size of each line was 0.22 degree × 0.10 degree, and the dot size was 0.07 degree × 0.10 degree. The distance of the two lines was 0.22 degree, and the distance between the dot and the reference line was 0.10 degree. The distance between the two possible target locations was 20.2 degrees, and the distance between the fixation point and the target was 12.5 degrees. The viewing distance was 57 cm. The experiment was conducted in a completely dark room.

Procedure Subjects were asked to fixate on the fixation point all through the experimental session, and to make a 2AFC judgment as to whether the target dot was above or below the reference lines (We found this task particularly revealing because it required spatial information just as in the location discrimination, yet it was a typical task of elaborate feature analysis just as the color/orientation discrimination.) The stimulus (above/below), its location, and RSI were all randomized across trials. The data were analyzed primarily in terms of the positional relationship of the targets between the previous and the present trials.

Results and Discussion   The results showed a clear facilitation of return (see fig. 23.3B), supporting the notion that fine shape discriminations lead to FOR, whereas global spatial orienting is necessary for IOR. A three-way repeated-measures ANOVA (RSI × location × feature) revealed only the main effect of location as significant ($p < .01$).

We have recently conducted several other fine feature discrimination tasks, such as luminance discrimination and length discrimination of bar segment (Tanaka and Shimojo 1995). These tasks all lead to FOR, thus supporting the idea that the key feature for the FOR-type tasks is the necessity of fine details of object.

23.5   GENERALITY OF IOR ACROSS VARIOUS MOTOR RESPONSES

There was still a question about the nature of the response. So far we had only used button pushing as a response. Could the IOR be generalized to other types of motor response? To investigate the robustness and generality of IOR, we employed a more typical visually guided orienting, saccade eye movement task.

Experiment 1.3: Saccadic Eye Movement Task

Subjects   Four subjects participated in the experiment: two naive and two nonnaive (authors).

Stimuli and Apparatus   The stimulus set was identical with experiment 1.1, thus target's location, color, and orientation were again randomized across trials. The *Ober2* system (Permobil Inc.) was used for the eye movement recording. The temporal resolution of the measurement was set at 120 Hz, and the spatial resolution on the given condition was at, or better than, 0.3 degree. The subject's head was stabilized by a chin rest and a biting board. The observation distance was set at 40 cm; thus the distance between the fixation point and the target was 17.1 degrees.

Procedure   Subjects had to fixate on the fixation point initially and then to move their eyes as quickly as possible to the target when it was presented. Saccade reaction time (SRT) was measured as the delay between the target appearance and the initiation of the eye movement. Two hundred trials were

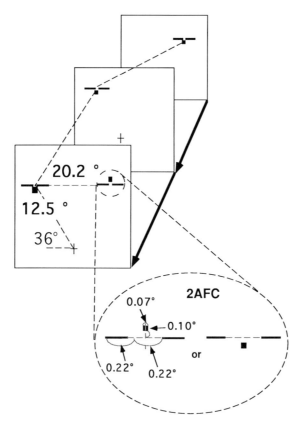

Figure 23.3 A. Vernier discrimination task, in which subject had to make 2AFC judgment as to whether target dot was above or below reference lines (experiment 1.2). B (next page). RT as function of RSI in vernier discrimination experiment. Bold line indicates RT at same location, and thin line indicates RT at different location. Vertical bars show standard error.

obtained from each subject. There were also 50 catch trials, where only the fixation point was presented and subjects were *not* supposed to move their eyes. This procedure was employed just to make sure that the subjects' saccades were really a response to the appearance of the visual target. SRTs below 50 ms and above 1,000 ms were eliminated from the analysis. The data were analyzed primarily in terms of the positional relationship of the targets between the previous and the present trials.

Results and Discussion The results show a strong IOR (see fig. 23.4). A four-way repeated measures ANOVA (RSI × location × color × shape) revealed the main effects of RSI and location as significant ($p < .01$). The results suggest that IOR reflects a common process among spatial orienting tasks (Posner 1980); they are also consistent with a more specific hypothesis that the necessary and sufficient condition for IOR to occur is that a saccade be programmed, but not necessarily executed (Rafal et al. 1989). The RTs were somewhat slower than in the previous studies, presumably because of

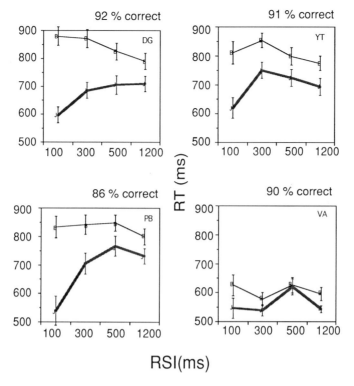

Figure 23.3 (cont.)

the randomization of location, the relatively low luminance, the large distance between the fixation and the target, and the existence of intermingled catch trials (20 percent of the total number of trials).

We also tried an arm-reaching task, in which the subject had to control the cursor on the CRT display by moving a mouse so that the cursor would reach the target as fast as possible. Here, we obtained the same, but somewhat exaggerated, IOR (Tanaka and Shimojo 1995).

23.6 FURTHER TESTS WITH THE POPOUT DISPLAY

To summarize thus far, all of our results indicate a clear dissociation between two types of visual task. One is the spatial orienting task that requires information about presence and global location of the target; this is where the IOR is commonly observed. The other is the feature-analyzing task that requires information about fine features of objects; this is where the FOR is commonly observed.

We would like to jump ahead and ask, Is there a limitation in terms of stimulus complexity for the IOR? It has been commonly believed that the sensory-guided spatial orienting heavily involves some subcortical loci such as the superior colliculus in its underlying neural circuit (Weiskranz et al. 1974; Robinson 1981; Hikosaka and Wurtz 1983; Schiller, Sandell, and

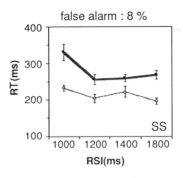

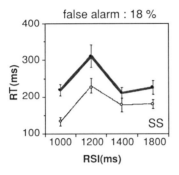

Figure 23.4 RT as function of RSI in saccade eye movement experiment (experiment 1.3). Bold line indicates RT at same location, and thin line indicates RT at different location. Vertical bars show standard error.

Maunsell 1984). Moreover, there seems to be a temporal hemifield dominance for IOR (Rafal et al. 1989). Together with some neuropsychological findings (Rafal et al. 1990), it has been taken as evidence for involvement of the retinotectal pathway in the underlying mechanism. Following this tradition, it might seem reasonable to assume that the neural mechanism underlying the IOR is mostly subcortical. Yet this assumption is far from convincing; most of the currently available studies only considered the simplest situation, where the target was the only visible besides the fixation point.

This raises the question of whether the IOR mechanism could extract global location of the target when there are many visible distractors (Treisman and Gelade 1980). To illustrate, see figure 23.5. In this popout display, the target is defined by a color different from that of distractors around it. According to the latest theory (Duncan and Humphreys 1989), the difficulty of search increases with two factors: increased similarity of targets to nontargets and decreased similarity between nontargets. This is an intriguing case because the location of the "odd-ball" target cannot be obtained unless vigorous, parallel feature analyses and interactions among the analyzers are done. This is presumably impossible to deal with in the subcortical loci such as the superior colliculus (Schiller, Sandall, and Maunsell 1984). Rather, it requires feature analysis, allegedly a part of early cortical processing (Karni and Sagi 1991, 1993; Lamme 1994; Zipser et al. 1994). In other words, the

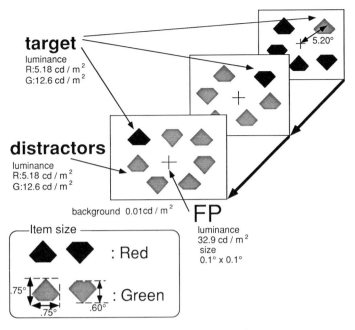

target
luminance
R:5.18 cd / m^2
G:12.6 cd / m^2

5.20°

distractors
luminance
R:5.18 cd / m^2
G:12.6 cd / m^2

background 0.01cd / m^2

FP
luminance
32.9 cd / m^2
size
0.1° x 0.1°

Item size

: Red

.75° : Green
.75° .60°

Figure 23.5 Stimulus configuration and sequence for popout experiments (Experiment 1.4).

information abstracted and used for the task is still *global-spatial*, yet it could be obtained only through massively parallel *feature* analysis. Thus, in theory, either the IOR or the FOR would be possible as a prediction, and the results would have an implication about the neural loci of IOR and FOR.

Employing this type of color popout display, we simply duplicated the four tasks (detection; location, color, and shape discrimination) in experiment 1.4.

Experiment 1.4: Popout Displays

Subjects   Four subjects participated in the experiment: two naive and two nonnaive (authors).

Stimuli and Apparatus   The target was defined by a color different from that of distractors around it, as in the typical experiment of single-feature visual search. The location, color, and shape of the popout target were again randomized. As shown in figure 23.5, the target and each of the distractors were diamond-shaped and were chopped off either at the top or the bottom (stimuli similar to that employed by Maljkovic and Nakayama 1994). The location of the target was randomized between left and right across trials. The locations of the distractors were randomized, and the color of the target were also randomized between red and green across trials. The RSI was randomized among 100, 300, 500 and 1,200 ms. The number of distractors were fixed at fifteen. The viewing distance was 114 cm. The experiment was conducted in a completely dark room.

Procedures Subjects were asked to fixate on the fixation point through the experimental sessions, while performing either a simple detection or a two-alternative, forced-choice discrimination task on the target and responding by mouse buttons. As in experiment 1.1 (single target), the following four tasks were employed in separate sessions: (1) simple detection; (2) location discrimination; (3) color discrimination; and (4) shape discrimination. In the case of color discrimination, subjects had to judge the color of target, and to press one of the mouse buttons accordingly. In the case of shape discrimination, subjects had to judge whether the top or the bottom corner of the diamond-shaped target was chopped off, and to press one of the buttons. This shape discrimination task was similar to that employed by Maljkovic and Nakayama (1994). Note that the target was defined always by color difference from the distractors, even in the shape discrimination.

Subjects initially performed a practice session up to 200 trials to get used to the task, and then an experimental session for each task. The experimental session consisted of 380 trials, including 20 percent of catch trials, where red and green distractors were spatially mixed and no target popped out. The purpose of this procedure was again to make sure that subjects were really responding to the popout stimuli. The data were analyzed primarily in terms of the positional relationship of the targets between the previous and the present trials.

Results and Discussion The results are shown in figure 23.6. Once again, we found IOR in the simple detection and the location discrimination tasks, and FOR in the color and shape discrimination tasks, in all of the four subjects. Moreover, there was a surprising tendency toward exaggerated difference both in IOR and FOR, even taking it into account that the RTs were generally longer with the popout displays than with the single-target displays. A four-way repeated-measures ANOVA (RSI × location × color × shape) was applied to each of the four tasks. The results can be summarized as follows: (1) for the detection and the location discrimination tasks, only the main effect of location reached the significant level ($p < .05$ and $p < .01$, respectively); and (2) for the color discrimination task, the main effects of location ($p < .01$), shape ($p < .05$), and RSI ($p < .01$) were all significant, as were all the interactions of location × shape ($p < .05$), location × RSI ($p < .01$), color × shape ($p < .05$), color × RSI ($p < .05$), shape × RSI ($p < .05$), location × shape × RSI ($p < .05$), and color × shape × RSI ($p < .05$).

We also tried another type of popout display, where the target was defined by orientations of the bar stimuli to obtain basically the same results (Tanaka and Shimojo 1994, 1995). These results further confirmed our initial hypothesis about the distinction between two visual functions. They also indicate the availability of output from the global texture analysis for the IOR mechanism, suggesting significant involvement of cortical areas such as V1 and V2 (Sagi and Julesz 1985; see Tanaka and Shimojo 1995 for more details of Experiment 1).

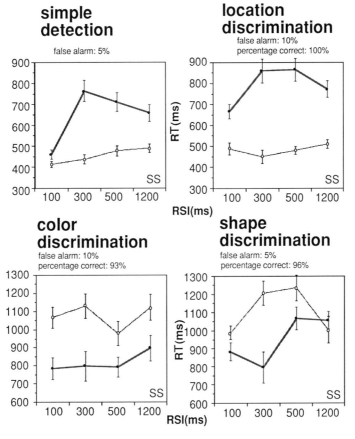

Figure 23.6 RT as function of RSI in color-based popout experiment (experiment 1.4). Results in four different tasks are shown separately in separate panels. Bold line indicates RT at same location, and thin line indicates RT at different location. Vertical bars show standard errors.

23.7 RELATION TO THE DISSOCIATION BETWEEN TWO VISUAL PATHWAYS: A SPECULATION

Our results are at least partly consistent with the well-known neurophysiological distinction between two visual pathways, the ventral-parietal and the dorsal-temporal pathways. They have been characterized as "where" versus "what" (Schneider 1969; Ungeleider and Mishikin 1982; Sagi and Julesz 1985; Duncan 1993; Livingstone and Hubel 1988), or as "action" versus "recognition" (Goodale and Milner 1992).[3] We demonstrated a clear dissociation between the two visual functions in RTs. Moreover, we eliminated the nature of the task (detection/discrimination) and of motor responses (button pressing, saccade eye movement, and arm reaching) as a decisive factor for IOR. Thus we identified the type of information the task demands (global location rather than fine characteristics of objects) as a more specific factor for IOR.

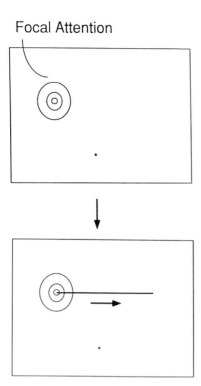

Focal Attention

Illusory line motion from
the attended side.

Figure 23.7 Line motion effect. Line probe, presented physically at once, could be seen to unfold from attended side.

Finally, does the dissociation we discovered have any value from the biological or ecological viewpoint? We think it does. Accept the assumption, for the time being, that there are indeed two functional pathways. The "where" or "orienting" pathway is allegedly for orienting to a new stimulus or event in the visual field. Its main purpose is to get ready for an unexpected and unpredictable event elsewhere than the currently attended object, and to respond to it as quickly as possible. This feature would be also very useful to facilitate visual search of any kind because avoiding repeated examinations of the same location would be desirable for finding a target. Thus it would make a lot of sense if this pathway increased sensitivity at new locations while sacrificing sensitivity at the same location.

On the other hand, the "what" or "feature" pathway is allegedly for identifying finer details of the concerned object. Its main purpose is to do feature analysis as much and as deeply as possible for the currently attended object. Thus it would make a biological sense if it increased efficiency at the same location while sacrificing it at different locations. The role of the former (orienting) mechanism is to bring the latter (analysis) mechanism to a new

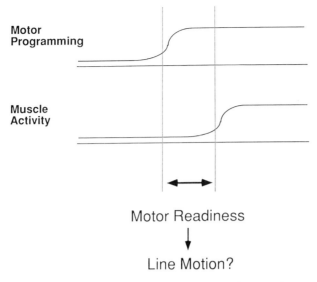

Motor
Programming

Muscle
Activity

Motor Readiness

↓

Line Motion?

Figure 23.8   Motor readiness, defined as internal process during period from onset of motor programming to onset of actual muscle activity.

location rather quickly. The former may correspond to the mechanism for the transient attention shift, that is, the disengagement/engagement of attention (Posner et al. 1984; Fischer and Breitmeyer 1987), while the latter presumably has a sustained characteristic (Hikosaka, Miyauchi, and Shimojo 1993a). This expectation is consistent with our data in that RTs were in general faster when IOR was observed, while RTs were in general slower when FOR was observed (see figs. 23.2–23.4 and 23.6; also see Tanaka and Shimojo 1995).

23.8   FROM SENSORY TO MOTOR LEVELS: MOTOR PERFORMANCE LEADS TO A LINE MOTION

As noted above, the reaction time task involves many different levels of information processing, from the sensory encoding to the motor programming. Thus it is unclear at what stage the IOR and the FOR occur.

In this regard, it would be intriguing to compare the reaction time paradigm with the line motion paradigm, which we describe elsewhere (see Hikosaka et al., chap. 10, this volume; also see Hikosaka, Miyauchi, and Shimojo, 1993b, c; Shimojo, Miyauchi, and Hikosaka 1992). The line motion is basically an illusory motion illusion, presumably induced by attentional gradient across the visual field (fig. 23.7). It can be induced by a visual cue, a nonvisual (auditory/somatosensory) cue, or voluntary effort; it is object-bound, rather than retinotopic. Because the line motion is a purely visual illusion that does not require any particular kind of motor response, it is reasonable to assume that the neural mechanism underlying this illusion is at a sensory/perceptual level. Thus it would be revealing to compare effects of

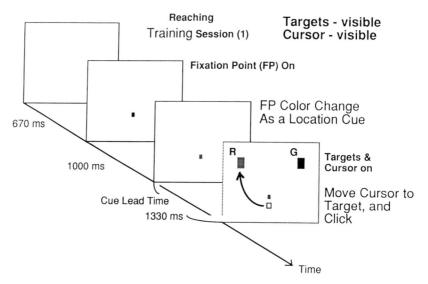

Figure 23.9 A. Stimulus configuration and sequence for arm-reaching training. Two targets were presented, red at left top, and green at right top. Subject's task was to move cursor to target indicated by color change of fixation point, and to click mouse button as quickly as possible. B (next page). Stimulus parameters for arm-reaching task. Stimulus configuration for saccade task, described later in the test, is also shown at bottom.

stimulus parameters on the line motion and various motor tasks, including the reaction time tasks, particularly because IOR indicates a facilitation at the opposite location to the previous stimulus, whereas the line motion indicates a facilitation at the same location.

Shimojo, Miyauchi, and Hikosaka (1993) conducted a series of experiments in which they examined whether motor readiness alone could lead to line motion. (Here we tentatively define *motor readiness* as the internal process for motor response during the period from the onset of motor programming to the onset of actual muscle activity; see fig. 23.8). We report these experiments in some detail below.

Experiment 2.1: Line Motion from the Goal Location of Prepared Arm Reaching

Because there were quite a few training sessions and test sessions, we first describe the subjects, stimuli, and apparatus, which were the same for all sessions, and then describe the procedures and results of these sessions separately.

Subjects Four subjects participated in all training and test sessions: one naive and three nonnaive (authors).

Stimuli and Apparatus Figure 23.9A illustrates the typical stimulus sequence for the initial training. Initially, the fixation point was presented for

Stimulus Parameters

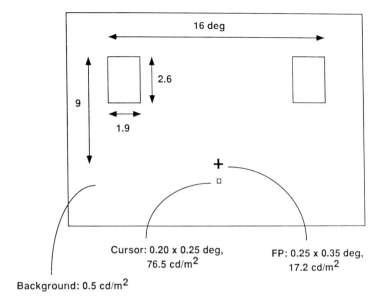

Figure 23.9 (cont.)

1,000 ms; then it changed its color, either to red or to green, as a location cue. After a cue lead time (1,330 ms), two targets were presented in the periphery. The top panel in figure 23.9B shows the spatial relationship among the fixation point, the targets, the cursor, and their luminances. The stimuli were presented on a CRT display, controlled by a personal computer (Commodore Amiga 3000). The observation distance was 57 cm.

Procedure   Subjects participated in two different training sessions before undertaking the test session.

Training session 1: Targets and cursor visible   The first training session employed a simple reaching task. Subjects had to move a mouse on a flat surface while monitoring its position on the CRT display so that it reached

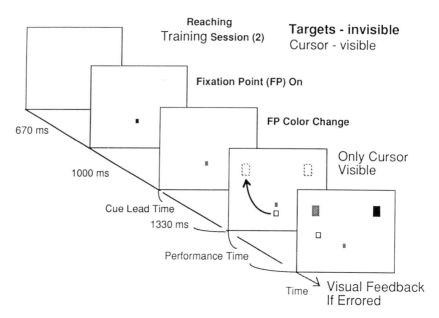

Figure 23.10 Stimulus configuration and sequence for memory-guided arm-reaching task 1. In training session 2, targets were made invisible, while cursor was visible.

the target location as fast as possible; they then had to click the mouse button. In the initial training, the fixation point, the cursor, and the target were all visible (see fig. 23.9A–B for the stimulus sequence and configuration). The red target was always presented at the top left, whereas the green target was at the top right corners of the CRT display. Initially, the subject had to stare at the gray fixation point. The fixation point then changed its color, to either red or green, as a signal for the target location (the colors were randomized across trials). Thus subjects had to move to cursor to the left target if the fixation point turned into red, and to the right target if the fixation point turned into green. Subjects had to fixate on the fixation point all through the trial. This was a relatively easy task, and all the subjects improved rather quickly within 200 trials.

Training session 2: Targets invisible, cursor visible In the second session of training, the targets (and then the cursor) were made invisible, so that subjects had to perform the reaching task based on their memory about the target's location (see fig. 23.10). Subjects initially stared at the fixation point and waited for its color change; they then decoded the meaning of it (red as to the left, green as to the right), moved the cursor to the invisible target, and clicked the mouse button. If subjects clicked the button outside of the target area, then the colored targets were visually presented as a feedback. The target area was made a little larger (about 150 percent of the original size) so that the task was still easy and all the subjects could become accurate within 200 trials.

Shimojo et al.

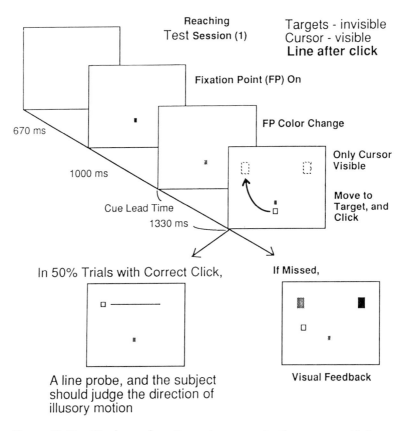

Figure 23.11 Stimulus configuration and sequence for the memory-guided arm-reaching task in test session with line motion (test session 1). Cursor was still visible, and line probe was presented only after the subject's button click response in this case. Line probe was presented in 50 percent of trials, which were randomly mixed with reaching trials.

Test session 1: Targets invisible, cursor visible, and line probe after button click After sufficient amount of training, a line probe was presented in 50 percent of trials, which were randomized and unpredictable (see fig. 23.11). Subjects were asked to judge direction of the perceptual unfolding of line, and it was scored in terms of its relation to the goal position of reaching.

Results and Discussion The line probe was almost always appeared to unfold from the target side, even though it was presented physically at once, as indicated by dark bars in figure 23.12. This was not at all surprising to us because of the visibility of the cursor. That is, the cursor was always visible in the target area when the line was presented, and the line motion could well be induced solely by the visual presence of the cursor. We knew already that a visible cue lead to line motion from the cued side (see Hikosaka et al., chap. 10, this volume).

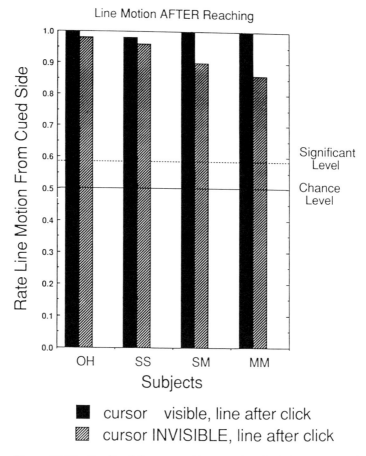

Figure 23.12 Results of the arm-reaching experiments (test session 1 and 2). Rate of line motion from target side is plotted in cursor-visible (filled) and cursor-invisible (shaded) conditions for each subject. In both conditions, line was always presented when subject moved cursor to target's location and clicked mouse button.

23.9 MOTOR PERFORMANCE WITHOUT VISUAL CUE LEADS TO LINE MOTION

To see if the visible cue is the only cause of the line motion, we further conducted the following training and test sessions.

Procedure

Training session 3: Targets invisible, cursor invisible   The cursor as well as the targets were now made invisible so that subjects had to rely completely on their memory (see fig. 23.13). Initially, subjects stared at the gray fixation point, whose color changed either to red or to green after 1,000 ms, as in the previous two training sessions. But this time, subjects had to wait until the fixation point blinked as a GO sign. The cue lead time (from the

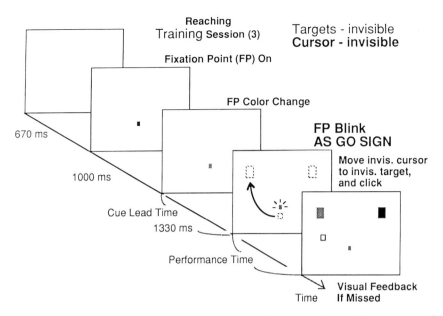

Figure 23.13 Stimulus configuration for memory-guided arm-reaching task 2. Targets and the cursor were both invisible, and subject had to wait for blink of fixation point before moving invisible cursor to invisible target and clicking the mouse button.

color change of fixation point to its blink) was fixed at 1,330 ms in this training session and the following test session. Once the FP blinked, then the subject had to move the invisible cursor quickly to the invisible target, whose location had been indicated by the color change of fixation point. Thus, during the period between the color change of fixation point and its blink, subjects were allowed to get ready but not allowed to actually start the reaching response. Subjects were explicitly instructed to "move the cursor as quickly and as accurately as possible, when the fixation point blinks" so that they were forced to develop specific motor readiness during the waiting period.

This task was more challenging, as would be easily suspected, but turned out not to be impossible, particularly when the target zone was made much larger and sufficient number of trials were given. In fact, the "correct" target zone was enlarged (× 2, both horizontally and vertically) to make this memory-guided task feasible. Training sessions were repeated until the success rate reached about 95 percent of trials. As a result, the subjects performed from 100 to 400 trials. When subjects reached the criterion, the second test session was given.

Test session 2: Targets invisible, cursor invisible, and line probe after button click A line probe was presented in 50 percent of trials, which were randomized and unpredictable. The line probe presented when subjects thought they reached the invisible target with the invisible cursor and thus

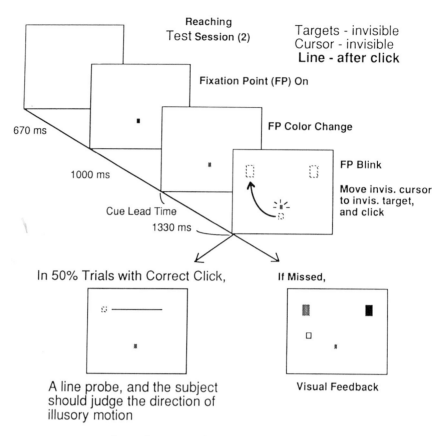

Figure 23.14 Stimulus configuration and sequence for memory-guided arm-reaching task 2 in test session with line motion (test session 2). Targets and cursor were both invisible, and line probe was presented at (and thus only after) subject's button click response. Line was presented in 50 percent of trials, which were randomly mixed with arm-reaching trials. Results are shown as shaded bars in figure 23.12.

clicked the mouse button (see fig. 23.14). Subjects had to judge from which side the line appeared to be drawn.

Results and Discussion The probe line consistently appeared to unfold from the target side for all of the four subjects, as indicated by shaded bars in figure 23.12. This was a new finding because nothing occurs anywhere in the visual field, except for the fixation point, which stayed in the middle, when the line probe was presented. Thus the line motion effect should be attributed to the motor response.

However, there was still an ambiguity in interpreting these results. There was a possibility that the line motion could be induced by nonvisual sensory feedback, that is, by somatosensory and kinesthetic feedback from the reaching movement. This was possible because Shimojo, Miyauchi, and Hikosaka (1992) had already shown that nonvisual cues, such a somatosensory or auditory cues, could also lead to line motion.

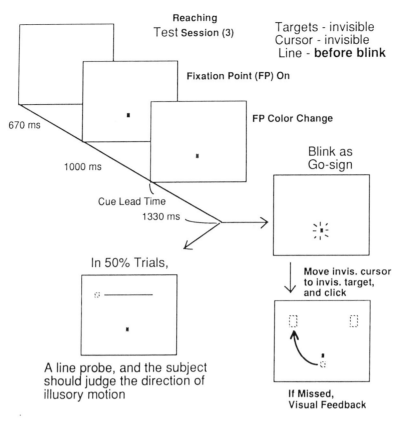

Figure 23.15   Stimulus configuration and sequence for memory-guided arm-reaching task 2 in test session with line motion (test session 3). Targets and cursor were both invisible, and this time, line probe was presented *after* color change but *before* blink of fixation point (GO sign). Line was presented in 50 percent of trials, which were randomly mixed with arm-reaching trials.

23.10   SENSORY FEEDBACK, OR MOTOR READINESS?

Procedure

Test session 3: Targets invisible, cursor invisible, and line probe before arm movement button click   So in the third test session, we presented a line probe *after* the color change but *before* the disappearance of the fixation point. This was done in 50 percent of the trials, which were randomly mixed with the ordinary invisible reaching trials (see fig. 23.15). Note that during the period between the color change and the blink of the fixation point, motor preprogramming or internal readiness would develop, but there was no muscle response and no kinesthetic or somatosensory feedback either. We reasoned that if the line motion was still observed, then it should be attributed to motor readiness per se, which was isolated from sensory feedback such as visual, kinesthetic or somatosensory.

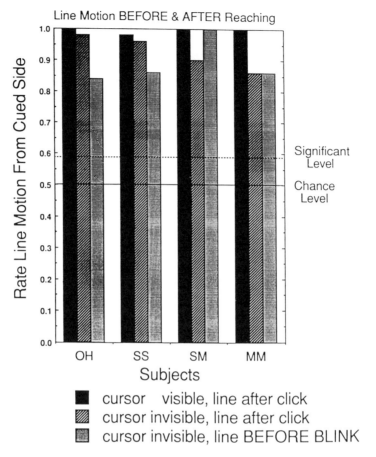

Line Motion BEFORE & AFTER Reaching

■ cursor   visible, line after click
▨ cursor invisible, line after click
▨ cursor invisible, line BEFORE BLINK

Figure 23.16 Results of "line before GO sign" condition (test session 3). Rate of line motion from target side is plotted for "line before GO sign" condition (gray, rightmost bar for each subject). Results for previous two conditions (cursor visible, line after click—black, leftmost bars; and cursor invisible, line after click—shaded, middle bars) are shown again for comparison.

Results and Discussion The results were indicated by light gray bars in figure 23.16. Even though the rate of line motion from the cued (motor readiness) side was slightly less than the other two conditions in all of the subjects, it was still well beyond the statistically significant level of $p = 0.5$.

Thus we found that internal readiness for the orienting response was sufficient to yield the line motion effect. This suggests that motor preprogramming facilitates visual information processing locally near the goal location, which in turn yields the illusion of line motion (the "prior entry" hypothesis; Hikosaka, Miyauchi, and Shimojo 1993a, b, c). It seems likely that the kind of attention that is triggered by memory-guided motor programming is related at least partly to the kind of attention that has been tapped by the line motion paradigm.

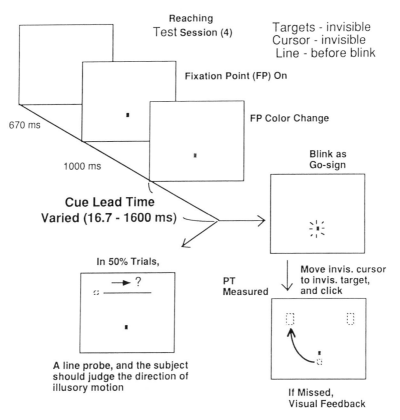

Figure 23.17 Stimulus configuration and sequence for the memory-guided arm-reaching task 2 in test session with line motion (test session 4). Conditions were same as those illustrated in figure 23.15, except that cue lead time was randomized (16.7–1,600 ms) across trials to assess rising time course of line motion effect.

By randomly manipulating the cue lead time (from the color change of fixation point to its blink as GO sign) among the trials, we could even assess the rising time course of motor readiness. This was what we tried in the last test session.

Procedure

Test session 4: Targets invisible, cursor invisible, and line probe before arm movement with cue lead time varied The stimuli and the procedure were the same as those in test session 3, except that the cue lead time was randomized in eight steps (16.7–1,600 ms) across trials (see fig. 23.17), and the results were analyzed in relation to the cue lead time.

Results and Discussion For an example of results, see figure 23.18, where we plotted the rate of line motion from the cued (motor readiness) side as a function of cue lead time (the solid curve in the figure). Also plotted is the

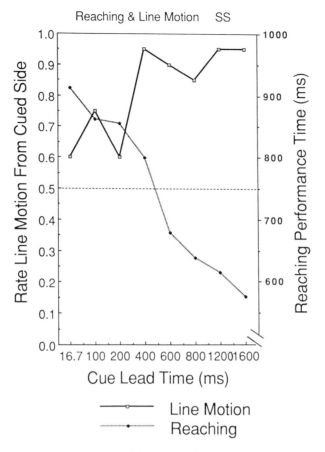

Figure 23.18 Results of the arm-reaching line motion experiment, with the cue lead time randomized (test session 4). Rate of line motion from cued (target) side is plotted against cue lead time for one subject as example (solid curve). Mean performance time of arm-reaching at each cue lead time was also calculated from arm-reaching trials and plotted in same panel (dotted curve).

performance time of reaching, which has been calculated from the reaching trials in the same test session (the dotted curve in the figure). As obvious in the figure, the rising time course of line motion was inversely correlated with the performance time of reaching, as the waiting time increased. The results were similar in this regard, though somewhat noisier, for the other subjects. This suggests that the attentional mechanism reflected in the line motion might in fact be related to the motor readiness for reaching.

23.11 SACCADE READINESS WITH THE LINE MOTION

To see if the finding could be generalized to another kind of motor response, we employed a saccadic eye movement task.

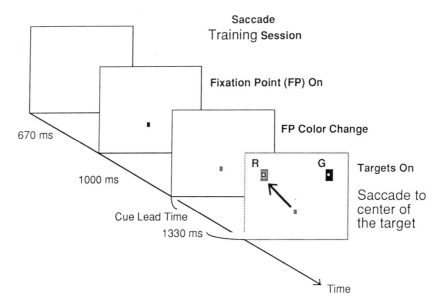

Figure 23.19 Stimulus configuration and sequence for saccade training (experiment 2.2). Stimulus parameters were very similar to those in arm-reaching experiments. Subject's task was to move eyes as quickly as possible to relevant target, which was indicated by color change of fixation.

Experiment 2.2: Line Motion from the Goal Location of Saccadic Eye Movement

Subjects Three of the authors participated in the experiment as the subjects.

Stimuli, apparatus and procedure All the details of experimental design were virtually identical to those in experiment 2.1 (see fig. 23.9B for the stimulus configuration), except for the nature of the task, which was to make a saccadic eye movement to the target as fast as possible. The saccade recording was done by the *Ober2* system. Subjects first participated in a training session (up to 200 trials; see fig. 23.19), and then a test session in which 50 percent of line probe trials were randomly mixed with the saccade trials (see fig. 23.20). The cue lead time was randomized in the same way as in the arm-reaching/line motion experiment (experiment 2.1, test session 4).

Results and Discussion We obtained essentially the same results. When the line probe was presented during the saccade readiness period (after the color change and before the blink of the fixation point), then the line appeared to unfold from the prepared goal location of the saccade. The rising time course of line motion in the saccade session (the thick curve in fig. 23.21) was quite comparable with that in the arm-reaching session (the thin curve in the figure). This was so for two other subjects as well.

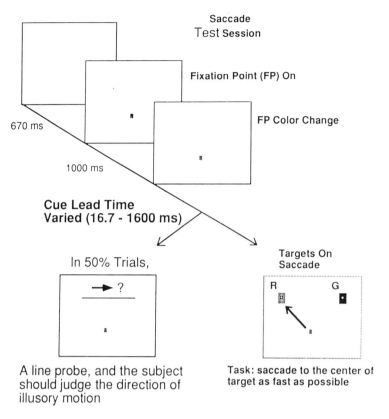

Figure 23.20 Stimulus configuration and sequence for saccade task, with line motion (experiment 2.2). Just as in arm-reaching experiment (2.1; see fig. 23.17), line probe was presented with varying cue lead time *before* blink of fixation point as GO sign. These line probe trials were 50 percent of total trials, and were again randomized with the saccade trials.

Thus the rising time courses of focal attention indicated by the line motion were very similar between two types of motor responses, saccadic eye movement and arm reaching. It is consistent with the idea that readiness or preprogramming for response to a particular target location is alone sufficient to yield a local facilitation strong enough to induce an illusory line motion. Some previous studies also have provided similar data (e.g., Rizzolatti et al. 1987; Klein 1980), though without the line motion as a measure.

23.12 A COMMON ATTENTION MECHANISM?

On the other hand, this does not necessarily mean that the line motion, which is a visual effect, and the motor programming, which is by definition nonvisual, could not be dissociable in terms of the relevant attention mechanism. We have several reasons for this skepticism. First, our subjects had been trained *visually* in the first training sessions; that is, their motor performance was guided by *visual* input and feedback. And even in the later training and

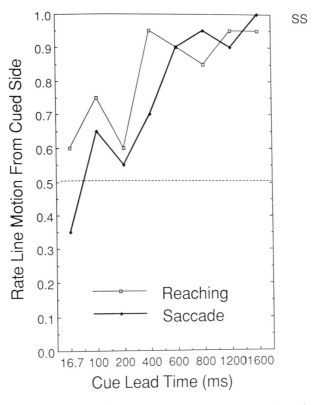

Figure 23.21 Results of saccade line motion experiment, with cue lead time randomized (experiment 2.2). Rate of line motion from the cued (target) side is plotted against cue lead time for one subject as an example (thick curve). Rate of line motion for same subject in previous arm-reaching experiment (2.1; see fig. 23.18) is replotted for comparison (thin curve).

tests, their performance was heavily based on *visual* memory. This could potentially explain why motor readiness inevitably triggered local facilitation at the target location in the *visual* field, which in turn led to a line motion.

Second, we actually conducted another subexperiment, where stimulus configuration and sequence were similar to the previous experiments. The only differences were that top half or the bottom half of the target was randomly chosen and made slightly brighter than the other half, and that subjects had to indicate which of the halves was brighter by a button-pressing response (a two-alternative, forced-choice task). Thus subjects still had to decode the meaning of color change of the fixation point to decide which target would be task-relevant, but also to constantly fixate on the fixation point and simply to do a visual discrimination task as fast as possible when the GO sign (= the blink of the fixation point) was given. Thus in order for the fastest response, subjects had to develop a visual expectation as to which location the relevant target would be at, and mentally "wait right there." We then randomized 50 percent of line probe trials with the rest of visual discrimination trials by varying the cue lead time, just as we did in the previous experiments. That is, the line probe was presented without the target in 50 percent of trials. As a result, we obtained a rising time course of line motion, which turned out to be highly similar to that obtained in the arm-reaching or the saccade experiments. This result could lead in two directions, however. On one hand, it could suggest the commonality of attentional mechanism between the motor and the visual tasks. That is, a single attentional mechanism could underly the motor programming and the line motion. But by the same token, it could also suggest that the attentional mechanism underlying the line motion during the motor readiness might still be *visual* in nature, owing to the heavily visual feedback/memory in the training.

Third and finally, there have been some studies in the literature that have failed to find evidence for attentional shift to the target prior to a particular motor response such as a saccade (Jon Driver, personal communication; Stelmach, Campsall, and Herdman 1993), while other studies have confirmed this possibility (Posner 1980; Klein 1980); it is still highly controversial (Remington and Pierce 1984).

For these reasons, it seems premature to conclude that a single attentional mechanism is underlying the memory-guided motor programming and the line motion. To be conservative, we could only conclude that motor readiness leads to a visual attentional effect at least under some conditions.

23.13 SUMMARY, CONCLUSIONS AND FUTURE DIRECTIONS

We found that *inhibition of return* occurred when the task required global spatial information, regardless of the nature of task, whether it was detection or discrimination. Inhibition of return also occurred in different kinds of motor tasks, such as the saccade eye movement or the arm-reaching tasks.

We found a opposite tendency, namely, *facilitation of return*, when the task required detailed feature of the target, such as color, shape, or vernier offset, even when the stimulus parameters were identical as before. This dichotomy seemed to be consistent with the neurophysiological dichotomy between the "where" and the "what" pathways.

Somewhat surprisingly, we also found the same kind of task-dependent dichotomy when the popout display was employed. This indicates that even when the task-demanded information of global location is based on parallel feature analysis, it still leads to *inhibition*, rather than facilitation. Thus it seems likely that the neural pathway underlying the inhibition of return significantly involves early cortical levels.

In the second half of the chapter, we raise the question of whether motor readiness alone can lead to purely visual attentional effect, that is, the line motion. The answer was yes both for the arm-reaching and the saccade tasks; the observed line motion effect could not be attributed to any kind of visual cue or nonvisual sensory feedback.

This does not necessarily indicate that the same attention mechanism is shared in the two cases, the motor readiness and the line motion. It could simply mean that motor readiness alone is sufficient to yield local facilitation of visual processing, which is responsible for the line motion, particularly when the subjects have been trained to perform the motor task based upon visual memory.

Also, our data have not yet addressed the original issue, namely, at which level the inhibition and facilitation of return occur, whether sensory, sensory-motor, or motor. In this regard, it would be interesting to compare the reaction time paradigm with the line motion paradigm, holding stimulus parameters as close as possible. This seems to be a promising way to resolve the prickly issue in the field: that is, of how many "attention mechanisms" we have to deal with.

ACKNOWLEDGMENT

The research projects reported here have been supported partly by Grant-in-Aid for Creative Basic Research from the Ministry of Education, Science, and Culture of Japan, the Human Frontier Science Program, and Nissan Cambridge Basic Research.

NOTES

1. It is believed that IOR occurs only when the peripheral cue is not informative, that is, when it does not predict the location of the target (Posner 1980; Posner and Cohen 1984). However, Tanaka and Shimojo (1993) systematically manipulated the probability that the target was presented at the same location as the previous target, successfully isolating the IOR from the predictability effect. For example, they compared two independent sessions: one in which the target was presented at the same location with $p = .8$ (the opposite location with $p = .2$), and the other in which it was presented at the opposite location with $p = .8$ (the same location with $p = .8$). They found that the RTs at the same locations in the former session tended to be larger than the RTs at the opposite locations in the latter session, even though the predictabilities were the same ($p = .8$). Thus the "location priming" (i.e., IOR) could be isolated from the "probability priming."

2. In fact, recent studies suggest that there might be two types of IOR, one related to eye movements and the other related to stimulus detection (Abrams and Dobkin, 1994; Tipper et al. 1994).

3. Goodale and Milner (1992) considered both the "action" and the "recognition" functions related to the "what" function in Ungeleider and Mishkin's (1982) terminology, so these two distinctions were not identical. To understand our data, we prefer "orienting" versus "feature analyses" as the best characterization.

REFERENCES

Abrams, R. A., and Dobkin, R. S. (1994). Object- and environment-based inhibition of return of visual attention. *Journal of Experimental Psychology: Human Perception and Performance, 20,* 467–477.

Broadbent, D. E. (1958). *Perception and communication*. Boston: Pergamon Press.

Duncan, J. (1993). Coordination of what and where in visual attention. *Perception, 22*, 1261–1270.

Duncan, J., and Humphreys, G. W. (1989) Visual search and stimulus similarity. *Psychological Review, 96*, 433–458.

Fischer, B., and Breitmeyer, B. (1987). Mechanisms of visual attention revealed by saccadic eye movements. *Neuropsychologia, 25*, 73–83.

Gibson, B., and Egeth, H. (1994). Inhibition of return to object-based and environment-based locations. *Perception and Psychophysics, 55*, 323–339.

Goodale, M. A., and Milner, A. D. (1992). Separate visual pathways for perception and action. *Trends in Neuroscience, 15*, 20–25.

Helmholtz, H. (1909/10). *Handbuch der Physiologischen Optik*. Hamburg: Verlag von Leopold Voss (Reprinted in Southall, J. P. C. (Ed.), New York: Dover, 1962).

Hikosaka, O., Miyauchi, S., and Shimojo, S. (1993a). Voluntary and stimulus-induced attention detected as motion sensation. *Perception, 22*, 517–526.

Hikosaka, O., Miyauchi, S., and Shimojo, S. (1993b). Focal visual attention produces illusory temporal order and motion sensation. *Vision Research, 33*, 1219–1240.

Hikosaka, O., Miyauchi, S., and Shimojo, S. (1993c). Visual attention revealed by an illusion of motion. *Neuroscience Research, 18*, 11–18.

Hikosaka, O., and Wurtz, R. H. (1983). Effects on eye movements of a GABA agonist and antagonist injected into monkey superior colliculus. *Brain Research, 272*, 368–372.

James, W. (1890). *The principles of psychology*. New York: Dover.

Karni, A., and Sagi, D. (1991). Where practice makes perfect in texture discrimination: Evidence for primary visual cortex plasticity. *Proceedings of the National Academy of Sciences, 88*, 4966–4970.

Karni, A., and Sagi, D. (1993). The time course of learning a visual skill. *Nature, 365*, 250–252.

Klein, R. (1980). Does oculomotor readiness mediate cognitive control of visual attention? In R. Nickerson (Ed.), *Attention and performance VIII*, 259–276. Hillsdale, NJ: Lawrence Erlbaum.

Kwak, H. W., and Egeth, H. (1992). Consequences of allocating attention to locations and to other attributes. *Perception and Psychophysics, 51*, 455–464.

Lamme, V. (1994). Neural correlates of figure-ground segregation in primary visual cortex. *Investigative Ophthalmology and Visual Science, 35*, 1489. Abstract.

Livingstone, M., and Hubel, D. (1988). Segregation of form, color, movement, and depth: Anatomy, physiology and perception. *Science, 240*, 740–749.

Maljkovic, V., and Nakayama, K. (1994). Priming of popout. I. Role of features. *Memory and Cognition, 22*, 657–672.

Maylor, E. (1985). Facilitatory and inhibitory components of orienting in visual space. *Attention and Performance, 11*, 189–194.

Nissen, J. M. (1985). Accessing features and objects: Is location special? *Attention and Performance, 11*, 205–218.

Pashler, H., and Baylis, G. (1991) Procedural learning. II. Intertrial repetition effects in speed-choice tasks. *Journal of Experimental Psychology: Learning, Memory, and Cognition, 17*, 33–48.

Posner, M. I. (1980). Orienting of attention. *Quarterly Journal of Experimental Psychology, 32,* 3–25.

Posner, M. I., and Cohen, Y. (1984). Components of visual orienting. *Attention and Performance, 10,* 531–556.

Posner, M. L, Walker, J. A., Friedrich, F. J., and Rafal, R. D. (1984). Effects of parietal injury on covert orienting of attention. *Journal of Neuroscience, 4,* 1863–1874.

Rafal, R. D., Calabresi, P. A., Brennan, C. W., and Scioltio, T. K. (1989). Saccade preparation inhibits reorienting to recently attended locations. *Journal of Experimental Psychology: Human Perception and Performance, 15,* 673–685.

Rafal, R. D., Smith, J., Krantz, J., Cohen, A., and Brennan, C. (1990). Extrageniculate vision in hemianopic humans: Saccade inhibition by signals in the blind field. *Science, 250,* 118–121.

Remington, R., and Pierce, L. (1984). Moving attention: Evidence for time-invariant shifts of visual selective attention. *Perception and Psychophysics, 35,* 393–399.

Rizzolatti, G., Riggio, L., Dascolo, I., and Umiltà, C. (1987) Reorienting attention across the horizontal and vertical meridians: Evidence for favor of a premotor theory of attention. *Neuropsychologia, 25,* 31–40.

Robinson, D. A. (1981). Control of eye movements. In Brooks, V. B. (Ed.), *Handbook of physiology,* vol. 2 pt. 2, 1275–1320, Bethesda, MD: American Physiological Society.

Sagi, D., and Julesz, B. (1985). "Where'" and "what" in vision. *Science, 228,* 1217–1219.

Schneider, G. E. (1969). Two visual systems. *Science, 164,* 895–902.

Schiller, P. H., Sandall, J. H., and Maunsell, J. H. R. (1984). The effect of superior colliculus and frontal eye field lesions on saccadic latency in the monkey. *Neuroscience Abstract, 10,* 60.

Shimojo, S., Miyauchi, S., and Hikosaka, O. (1992). Visual motion sensation yielded by non-visually driven attention. *Investigative Ophthalmology and Visual Science, 33,* 1262. Abstract.

Shimojo, S., Miyauchi, S., and Hikosaka, O. (1993). Line motion can be induced by visual expectation and memory, guided motor readiness. *Investigative Ophthalmology and Visual Science, 34,* 1290. Abstract.

Stelmach, L. B., Campsall, J. M., and Herdman, C. M. (1993). Allocation of attention prior to a saccade. *Investigative Ophthalmology and Visual Science, 34,* 1233. Abstract.

Tanaka, Y., and Shimojo, S. (1993). Location priming and probability priming are isolatable in detection and discrimination. *Investigative Ophthalmology and Visual Science, 34,* 1234. Abstract.

Tanaka, Y., and Shimojo, S. (1994). Location versus feature: Two visual functions separated by reaction time in the popout display. *Investigative Ophthalmology and Visual Science, 35,* 1619. Abstract.

Tanaka, Y., and Shimojo, S. (1995). Location vs. feature: reaction time reveals dissociation between two visual functions. *Vision Research,* in press.

Tassinari, G., Aglioti, S., Chelazzi, L., Marzi, C. A., and Berlucchi, G. (1987). Distribution in the visual field of the costs of voluntarily allocated attention and of the inhibitory aftereffects of covert orienting. *Neuropsychologia, 25,* 55–71.

Tassinari, G., Aglioti, S., Chelazzi, L., Peru, A., and Berlucchi, G. (1994). Do peripheral non-informative cues induce early facilitation of target detection? *Vision Research, 34,* 179–189.

Terry, K. M., Valdes, L. A., and Neill, T. (1994). Does "inhibition of return" occur in discrimination tasks? *Perception and Psychophysics, 55,* 279–286.

Tipper, S. P., Weaver, B., Jerreat, L. M., and Burak, A. L. (1994). Object- and environment-based inhibition of return of visual attention. *Journal of Experimental Psychology. Human Perception and Performance, 20,* 478–499.

Treisman, A. M., and Gelade, G. (1980). A feature-integration theory of attention. *Cognitive Psychology, 12,* 97–136.

Ungeleider, L. G., and Mishkin, M. (1982). Two cortical visual systems. In D. J. G. Ingle and J. W. Mansfield (Eds.), *Analysis of visual behavior,* 549–586. Cambridge, MA: MIT Press.

van der Heijden, A. H. C. (1991). *Selective attention in vision.* London: Routledge.

Weisklanz, L., Warrington, E. E., Sanders, M. D., and Marshall, J. (1974). Visual capacity in the hemianomic field following a restricted occipital ablation. *Brain, 97,* 704–728.

Zipser, K., Lee, T. S., Lamme, V. A. F., and Schiller, P. H. (1994). Invariance of figure-ground mechanisms in V1 for depth, orientation, luminance and chrominance cues. *Invest. Ophthalmol. Vis. Sci. 35:* 4.

IX Discussion

24   Integration of Information: Reflections on the Theme of Attention and Performance XVI

James L. McClelland

24.1 ANALYSIS AND SYNTHESIS

In the early 1980s the idea that key aspects of cognition arise from the independent activity of autonomous modules was popular in several areas of the cognitive and neural sciences. This divide-and-conquer approach was represented by Chomsky's (1980) position on the autonomy of language in general and syntax in particular, by Marr's (1982) emphasis on independent computation of surface properties from each of several distinct visual cues, and by Fodor's (1983) advocacy of modularity as a general principle of brain organization.

These ideas were advances over earlier approaches that attempted to encompass all of cognition or behavior in terms of a few very general principles. Paradigms like Gestalt psychology, genetic epistemology, and behaviorism were all radically different, but they each offered a broad framework intended to encompass a wide range of diverse phenomena. All of these approaches ultimately proved unsatisfying, and more modular approaches may have arisen in part because of the perception that one of the problems with these approaches lay in the very attempt to generalize so broadly. Chomsky certainly taught us a great deal more about language than Skinner, and Marr certainly took us beyond the vague holism of the Gestaltists toward a much more explicit computational understanding of the extraction of shape from visual cues. Focus on a specific domain and attention to its details, as if it were autonomous, has led to insights that have sharpened our understanding of language and perception. But now that these advances have been achieved, it may be time to go beyond modularity and consider integration again.

The sciences of mind and brain have seen an alternation between global approaches and more modular approaches before. In the nineteenth century, and into the twentieth, ideas about the organization of function in the brain alternated between varieties of equipotentialism and much more localist treatments. In my own scientific education, the history of this alternation was used to make two distinct and equally important points. Teitelbaum (1967), an important physiological psychologist of the 1960s, emphasized the importance of analysis *and* synthesis. First, we must carve the bird at its joints, he argued, and analyze the structure and functional contributions of each of its parts. But if we are to understand how it can fly we must reconnect these parts, and see how they work together. And Luria (1966, 1973), who is of course still widely known for his many contributions to cognitive neurology, stressed the idea of dynamic functional systems. He used the findings of the localizationists to show that each part has its own special role. But he noted the poverty of considering these parts in isolation and insisted that they must be seen as working in concert to achieve system-level functions such as perception, communication, and action.

In view of these points, it is encouraging to see just how much contemporary research builds on the contributions of the modularists in an effort to understand how the parts of the cognitive system work together. The present volume brings together a collection of such researchers, who consider the problem of integration from multiple perspectives and in multiple contexts. What they share—nearly all of them—is a commitment to the effort to understand how complex, intelligent functions are synthesized from simpler parts. Their efforts build on the analytic insights that arise from the modular approaches mentioned above, as well as on continuing work that combines analysis with an effort to understand the behavior of the parts in context.

24.2 INTEGRATION IN PERCEPTION, COMMUNICATION, ATTENTION, AND ACTION

When Toshio Inui proposed the theme of Attention and Performance XVI, he certainly touched a responsive chord in me, and in many other members of the executive committee. The theme of information integration turned out to provide a touchstone for a number of excellent contributions that fit together in many different ways. The goal of these remarks is to bring out some of the threads that link the chapters—and, in a few places, to touch on relevant work not presented in the symposium. While the exact shape of a full account of information integration in perception, communication, and action is not yet clearly in view, I hope these comments will help the reader weave some of the threads together and envision something of the fabric of this ultimate synthesis. At the least, I hope they will provide pointers to some of the main findings and ideas presented by the participants in this meeting.

The five broad questions Inui raised in his introduction form an excellent framework for my discussion, since they cut across the various specific topics covered in the conference and provide a structure in which the crucial points of nearly all the papers fit very neatly. However, I will order the questions differently for expository convenience, and I will add one more question at the end of the list:

• What are the limitations on the integration of information? Are there impenetrable modules in the cognitive system and, if so, what are their boundaries?

• Are there common principles of integration that span domains in which integration is necessary?

• How do constraints propagate efficiently for integration of information?

• Are there supramodal representations for integration across modalities, or is integration merely mutual constraint between modality or dimension specific representations?

• Are there dimensions that provide a strong organizing frame for integration? Are time and space examples of such dimensions?

• What role does attention play in the integration of information?

Limits on Integration

What are the limitations on the integration of information? Are there impenetrable modules in the cognitive system and, if so, what are their boundaries?

In the literature spawned by the emphasis on modularity in the late 1970s and 1980s, many findings were taken as evidence for the impenetrability of modules of various kinds. A great deal of this work focused on the study of language comprehension as it unfolds on-line during reading and listening. Leading this wave, Swinney (1979) explored the effect of context on the resolution of lexical ambiguity:

Rumor had it that, for years, the government building had been plagued with problems. The man was not surprised when he found several spiders, roaches, and other bugs in the corner of the room.

He probed for activations of appropriate and inappropriate meanings of the ambiguous word ("bugs") using a lexical decision probe related to the appropriate meaning (e.g., "ant") the inappropriate meaning (e.g., "spy") or unrelated to either meaning (e.g., "table"). When the probe occurred immediately after the ambiguous word, lexical decision times were faster to both spy and ant compared to the unrelated condition, and the difference between the priming effects in the two cases was not significant. This null finding was then taken to support the claim that immediate lexical access during language comprehension was unaffected by context. Lexical access then became one of the impenetrable submodules of the language processing system.

Swinney's (1979) experiment exemplifies a common research approach taken during this period: (1) manipulate a possible source of constraining influence on some process; (2) when a null effect is found, declare the process impenetrable to the source of constraining influence. Similar studies were carried out by other investigators, examining possible effects of varibables such as animacy and semantic plausibility on the assignment of syntactic constituent structure during sentence processing (Clifton and Ferreira 1989). As in the Swinney experiment, when null effects were found, the process was declared impenetrable to the manipulated variable. The net effect of these studies and others with similar logic was to suggest that lexical access, syntactic parsing, and several other processes were essentially autonomous modules impervious to contextual influences.

Yet even at the peak of this modularist wave, them were some indications that the processes in question might not be so impenetrable after all. In particular, Simpson (1981) found that context did influence initial activation of meanings of ambiguous words, if other factors (particularly, the relative frequency of the two alternative readings of the ambiguous word) were relatively balanced. Similarly, Taraban and McClelland (1988) found that plausibility affected initial syntactic parsing decisions in cases where other factors (syntactic cues favoring one or the other alternative parse) were relatively balanced. Reviewing this evidence, I suggested in a paper presented at Attention and Performance XII (McClelland 1987) that both lexical ambiguity resolution and syntactic ambiguity resolution might in fact be sensitive to contextual as well as intrinsic factors.

Several other groups of investigators have explored the possibility that lexical and syntactic aspects of language processing might exploit contextual as well as intrinsic factors. This tradition goes back at least to Miller (1962), and can he traced through the work of Bever (1970), Rumelhart (1977) and Marslen-Wilson (1987). Recent proponents include many of the participants in this symposium. MacDonald (chap. 17) provides a definitive statement of the current state of development of this approach. She characterizes lexical access and syntactic structure assignment as constraint satisfaction processes that exploit multiple sources of graded information. On this view, influences from various sources may differ in strength, but no one source is necessarily decisive—all sources contribute to the accumulation of evidence for each of the available alternatives (see below). She indicates how syntactic structure assignment may hinge on lexical ambiguity resolution and explains why contextual effects only emerge when other sources of constraint are in relative balance (see also Massaro, chap. 16).

In summary, a considerable body of recent literature on lexical and syntactic ambiguity resolution is consistent with the view that two of the processes prominently discussed as examples of autonomous processes impervious to contextual influences may not in fact be autonomous or impenetrable after all. While there still may be room for skepticism about the exact nature and timing of the influences of context on these processes, the current evidence certainly appears consistent with a constraint satisfaction view.

Of course lexical access and syntactic structure assignment are only two among many candidate processes, and there have certainly been claims of impenetrability in other domains besides these. Since the contributors to the present volume have nearly all been concerned with exploring the integration of information, it will probably come as no surprise that the emphasis is on instances in which a process does appear to be susceptible to multiple sources of information. Several of these cases may be surprising to those who adopt modular views of the architecture of cognition. Here are several of the most striking instances of information integration reported in the chapters of this volume:

1. Acoustic and visual cues are combined to determine the outcome of the process of phoneme identification (Massaro, chap. 16).

2. Visual, auditory, and tactile cues all contribute to the specification of the target of attention and the contents of the spotlight of attention (Driver and Grossenbacher, chap. 9; Hikosaka et al., chap. 10; Shimojo et al., chap. 23).

3. Proprioceptive information from multiple relevant joints ranging from the ankle to the neck is integrated with visual information in the specification of the location of objects in external space (Roll et al., chap. 12) and in the specification of the location of objects with respect to the body (Colby, chap. 7; Graziano and Gross, chap. 8).

4. Visual and spoken language inputs are integrated in determining the intended referent in a task involving instructed action in context (Tanenhaus et al., chap. 18).

In the face of the first three points a modularist might suggest that there are modules but these are defined not so much in terms of traditional sense modalities like proprioception, audition, vision, and so on, as in terms of broad functional systems, dedicated to language comprehension or action coordinated with objects in external space. But the work of Tanenhaus et al. (chap. 18) makes it clear that there is integration between the spatial and the linguistic modalities: language directs attention in space in real time, and spoken input and space work together to constrain linguistic interpretation. Altmann (chap. 19) extends this point further, drawing of the work of Sopena (1991) and his own recent simulations of artificial language learning to argue that a constraint called the "late closure constraint," which has often been taken to be a purely syntactic constraint, might well arise because language use and language acquisition occur in situations where interpretation of language and interpretation of the environment are mutually constraining. In particular, Altmann suggests that late closure may arise from an effect of language on directing attention to objects, together with a tendency to remain focused on one object until directed elsewhere. The general point is that language guides interpretation of the environment as much as the environment guides interpretation of language.

Along with all these indications that the functional systems underlying verbal and spatial cognition integrate many different sources of information, some of the papers in this volume do suggest some limits on the integration of information. Treisman and DeSchepper (chap. 2) show that there is enough perceptual integration even of unattended objects to produce long-lasting, object-specific aftereffects, but there is nevertheless a limit to the sophistication of the object-specific representations that are formed outside of attention; these representations seem to be simple representations of an enclosing contour rather than full structural descriptions. Hummel and Stankiewicz (chap. 5) suggest that the formation of full structural descriptions, providing an integrated representation of the object that could be recognizable across a transformation like mirror reversal, requires focal attention to the object for an extended period of time.

Another example of limits on integration is provided by studies reviewed by MacDonald (chap. 17), showing that exploitation of context may vary dramatically with individual differences in comprehension skill. While skilled readers often show robust context effects in both lexical and syntactic ambiguity resolution, poor readers often show little or no effect of context (Just and Carpenter 1992). The exact interpretation of the source of these individual differences is not entirely clear; Just and Carpenter suggest that maintaining context and processing current input impose competing demands, and that better comprehenders are better able to cope with these competing demands, and so are better able to maintain a representation of the context. Indeed, one possible reason for the strong contextual influences reported by Tanenhaus et al. (chap. 18) is that the context is available visually in their experiments, making reliance on maintaining it in memory unnecessary.

A final example of limits on integration is provided by Marks and Armstrong (chap. 11). They consider the visual and haptic perception of length and report two findings relevant to information integration. First, they find that although both visual and haptic perception of length exhibit distortions, these distortions are not strictly homologous; and second, they find that adaptation within one modality, which modulates these distortions, does not transfer to the other modality. These findings appear to suggest that visual and haptic cues are carried by separate input systems, each subject to independent adaptation, even if the results are ultimately combined to constrain representations of the shape and layout of objects in space.

Principles of Integration

Are there common principles of integration that span domains in which integration is necessary?

To address this question, it is useful to have some sort of common framework for thinking about different examples of information integration. One way to frame the issue of integration that encompasses integration in perception, comprehension, attention, and planning of action is to think of each of these processes as leading to the construction or selection of something we will call a "specification." We can view perception as the construction of a specification of a perceptual interpretation of a distal stimulus; we can view comprehension as the construction of a specification of a conceptual interpretation of a linguistic expression; we can view attention as the construction of a specification of an object of attention; and we can view planning as the construction of a specification of one action (or action sequence) out of the many possible actions that might be taken.

In many models specification is treated as a matter of selection of one of N enumerable alternatives. I will begin by considering this simpler case and then comment briefly on a generalization of the concept. For the case of integration for selection, there appears to be broad consensus among the participants in Attention and Performance XVI on three basic points:

1. Integration for selection depends on accumulation of support for each alternative from a range of different sources, including prior knowledge, current expectations, and one or more sources of input information.

2. The support contributed to each alternative by each source is a matter of degree, and the total support for each alternative that results from the combination of all of the sources is itself a continuous function of the support provided by all of the sources.

3. Selection occurs through a competition among the alternatives, where the outcome depends upon the relative amount of total support for each alternative, compared to all of the other alternatives.

These points are explicit (to varying degrees) in Massaro's fuzzy logical model of perception (chap. 16), in Bülthoff and Yuille's concept of competitive priors (chap. 3), in Rosenbaum et al.'s model of posture selection (chap. 13), in MacDonald's constraint satisfaction model of syntactic ambiguity resolution (chap. 17), and in Duncan's integrated competition model of selective attention (chap. 21), and they are implicit in several other places. Indeed, versions of these ideas can be found in many earlier works where integration of different sorts of information is considered, including Treisman (1964), Morton (1969), Rumelhart (1977), and even Marcus (1980). Of these, Marcus's 1980 book is especially interesting historically, in that it is generally regarded as a classic example of an effort to develop a highly autonomous syntactic parser in the context of the Chomskian view of syntax. Yet Marcus argues forcefully for the need to consider both semantic and syntactic constraints in parsing decisions and provides a very convincing argument in favor of a set of principles that are basically equivalent to the three points just listed. He notes that both syntactic constraints and semantic constraints must be matters of degree because neither is dominant in every case; and he suggests that selection in cases of conflict depends on the total amount of support for each alternative, whether it comes from syntax, semantics, or a combination of the two.

Of course, points 1–3 provide a very general framework that leaves room for important differences in details. Massaro (chap. 16) emphasizes that the contributions of various sources of support are generally treated as independent, while Bülthoff and Yuille (chap. 3) explicitly question this assumption. This contrast will be considered in more detail below.

It should also be noted that the exact formulation of the process of selection varies as well. The candidate selection schemes are (1) choose the best alternative (i.e., the one with the greatest total support) or (2) choose an alternative probabilistically, setting the probability of choosing a particular alternative proportional to its total support. These different proposals are discussed by Bülthoff and Yuille (chap. 3) and Massaro (chap. 16), respectively. These ideas are not very easy to distinguish empirically. The second scheme is naturally probabilistic, while the first gives rise to probabilistic performance if there is any noise in the inputs or the process that accumulates the total support. Rosenbaum et al. (chap. 13) introduce another possibility: construct a blended alternative by taking a weighted average of the alternatives, where the weights are proportional to the total support for each. This proposal goes beyond the mere selection of a single alternative, and provides a useful way of allowing some degree of generalization to novel cases. It is particularly useful when the alternatives are particular values of continuous parameters (such as the muscle length targets as in Rosenbaum et al. (chap. 13)), and the candidates with appreciable amounts of support are sufficiently close together in the space encompassing all possible alternatives.

As already suggested, the idea of selection of an existing alternative, or even of averaging similar alternatives, is unlikely to prove fully adequate to capture the creativity and flexibility of human perception, comprehension, and planning processes. What is needed is a more general framework. Classically (Fodor and Pylyshyn 1988), cognitive scientists have supposed that what is specified is a structural description—a structure consisting of a hierarchical arrangement of items assigned to roles. Each item in the structural description is either an embedded structural description or an atom. While this framework is surely vastly more powerful than the selection of one alternative out of N, it has not proven to be very tractable for capturing the integration of graded constraints. An alternative approach is to think of the specification as a pattern of activation over an ensemble of processing units. The settling of a network into an attractor state, consisting of a pattern of selected (active) elements, can then be seen as an implementation of such a selection process. This settling process can be regarded as a process of hill climbing in some ensemble measure of the goodness of the entire state (Hopfield 1982). While each element may participate in many patterns, the overall pattern can represent a novel configuration; the selection of the particular pattern that ends up being specified clearly depends on a graded synthesis and competition process that accords with the three points enumerated above (Rumelhart et al. 1986). Several methods for capturing complex hierarchical structure in such patterns of activation have been proposed (see the papers in Hinton 1991). A third approach is to view the object of specification as a sequence of states. While the item selected at a given point in a sequence may not be novel at all, the concatenation of several individually selected items can give rise to novel sequences. Given that sequences may be unbounded in length, productivity is thereby assured. Although many traditional sequential models do not provide for the graded synthesis of multiple constraints, there are now many sequential architectures that do (Jordan 1986; St. John and McClelland 1990; Jordan and Rumelhart 1992). In this volume,

Kawato's model of the specification of a sequence of motor commands (chap. 14) is a good example of a specification process in which the selection of the motor command at each time point depends on a graded synthesis of multiple constraints, including the motor commands programmed for adjacent time points. It seems likely that the future study of information integration will come to focus more and more sharply on specifications that involve patterns and/or sequences rather than simple selections of one out of N alternatives.

Constraint Propagation for Integration

How do constraints propagate efficiently for integration of information?

This is one of the central questions addressed by Attention and Performance XVI and gives rise to two more specific questions:

1. What is the time grain of constraint propagation?
2. How is the integration of constraints organized computationally?

There seems to be a degree of consensus on the first question, and a good deal of debate about the second.

Regarding the time grain, it appears that the propagation of constraints takes place *continuously*, so that the total support for each alternative in a selection task is continuously updated. Propagation is also apparently very rapid, so that selection and action become possible very shortly after sufficient support from a combination of sources is available. These points seem to be reasonably well established for auditory and visual on-line comprehension tasks, where they are supported through a large body of research by Marslen-Wilson and his colleagues (e.g., Marslen-Wilson 1987), and many models of language perception and comprehension incorporate these assumptions. Tanenhaus et al. (chap. 18) provide a very nice illustration of these points. When a subject must select a target for action from a combination of visual and auditory inputs, selection can occur very shortly after the auditory input is sufficient to rule out all but one of the alternatives consistent with the visual information. This shows that information from the auditory and the visual modalities is integrated in real time in the on-line comprehension process. The on-line character of the integration process is also reflected in the N400 component of the evoked potential, which reflects the combination of syntactic, semantic, lexical, and even episodic factors that influence the identification of words in context (see Kutas and King, chap. 20).

A further point relevant to the time course of integration is presented by MacDonald (chap. 17). She notes that when an ambiguity is encountered in language, the contextual information necessary to resolve the ambiguity often comes afterward, not before. In keeping with her claim that a particular source of information only has an effect when the alternatives for selection are at relatively balanced and intermediate levels of activation, she finds that subsequent context can influence ambiguity resolution, but only if it arrives close enough in time so that the alternatives that it affects are still in balance. As time passes, whichever alternative is stronger tends to dominate, and subsequent sources of constraint become ineffective.

Regarding the organization of the computations that lead to integration, several chapters in *Attention and Performance XVI* take explicit stands on this question. There appear to be essentially three kinds of views:

1. The feedforward view. According to the feedforward view, processing propagates in one direction—either from input to some central decision-making system for perceptual and comprehension tasks or from some internal specification of the desired action to a specification of the overt response, for motor control tasks. In this approach integration occurs bottom-up, and constraints from multiple sources are integrated only at central levels.

2. The interactive view. According to the interactive approach, constraints are propagated bidirectionally through a multilayered processing system. In this view integration occurs at every level of processing, based on constraints propagated top-down and bottom-up.

3. The intrinsic integration view. According to this approach, many if not all of the levels of processing envisioned in the first two approaches are seen as descriptive conveniences rather than actual separate parts of the mechanism. Instead, a pattern of activation over an ensemble of units is taken to encompass several levels of representation simultaneously.

Visual word recognition models provide examples of each of these three views. Feedforward models (e.g., Paap et al. 1982) propagate information from features to letters to words; and interactive models (e.g., McClelland and Rumelhart 1981) propagate information in both directions. Golden (1986) provides an example of an intrinsic integration model, in that his model has a single layer of units. Each unit corresponds to a visual feature of the letter in a particular position within the word; thus, to process four-letter words, there must be four sets of visual feature units. A letter, in this model, is a particular pattern over the feature units in one of these sets, and a word is a pattern over all of these sets. The network is trained with a connectionist learning rule to settle into states corresponding to particular words. In this model, integration across levels is intrinsic, in that the same pattern specifies at once the features, the letters, and the whole word.[1]

In my own scientific career I have explored all three of these alternatives (McClelland 1976, 1979; McClelland and Rumelhart 1981, 1985). This is not the place to attempt an extensive discussion of the merits of these alternatives. However, a few remarks may be in order to clarify the current state of play in the debate.

The *feedforward view* can be seen as consistent with many modular approaches to cognitive functions: Stimulus-driven processes provide separate sources of support for various alternatives in a selection task, and these sources are then combined with contextual influences and/or constraints imposed by task instructions to determine the outcome. A version of the feedforward view, put forward by Massaro (chap. 16), has been justified by the adequacy of his fuzzy logical model of perception (FLMP) and similar models to account for a large body of data from a wide range of experiments on integration of information. These studies show that subjects often choose among responses based on the combination of two or more separately manipulated sources of information in a way that suggests that the subjects treat each source of information as though it provides independent evidence for each of the possible alternatives. Massaro takes this independence as support for the view that each source of information is analyzed separately from all the others, and the results of these analyses are then simply multiplied together to yield the total support for each alternative. Responses are then chosen probabilistically, with the probability of choosing a particular response equal to the total support for that response, divided by the sum over all alternatives of the total support for each.

Two issues related to this proposal can be noted. First, as Bülthoff and Yuille argue in chapter 3, and as Frisby, Buckley and Freeman illustrate with experimental data (chap. 4), it is often the case that the interpretation of one source of information depends on the status of other sources. For example, Frisby et al. find that in estimating surface orientation, subjects may rely heavily on global linear perspective cues provided by the surface as a whole, when other cues indicate the surface is planar; when other cues indicate that the surface has local curvature, the global linear perspective cue is not used. (In fact this is quite sensible because the global surface orientation is not predictive of local surface orientation if the surface has local curvature.) Bülthoff and Yuille suggest that cases of violation of independence might reflect "incorrect modularization." They point to the existence of numerous cases where the interpretation of one set of cues depends critically on the state of other cues; they argue that these constraints can only be properly captured by considering them jointly rather than independently.

Second, it should be noted that what counts as an independent source of constraint is quite flexible in Massaro's model (chap. 16). Consider, for example, the sources of constraint on the identification of a target letter when it occurs in the context of other letters. Specifically, consider the identification of a target display element as a *c* or an *e* when it is followed by the letters _*oin*. In the FLMP the visual features of the target display element itself constitute one source of information, and the context, taken as a whole, constitutes another. In this case, if the target display element were a *c* it would form a word with the context, so the context is taken as providing more support for the *c* alternative than for the *e* alternative. While this is clearly a correct statement of the facts of the matter, something is lacking: namely, a specification of the computations performed on the visual inputs arising in the other letter positions that result in this support. This aspect of the FLMP has always made me feel that we should view it as characterizing the influence of different sources of information on the *outcome* of processing—when these are in fact independent—but we should continue to ask mechanistic questions about how the computation is actually performed.

The *interactive view* of the integration of information is proposed by Inui in his introductory chapter. It is explicitly adopted by Kawato (chap. 14) for integrating constraints in motor control, and by Duncan (chap. 21) for integrating multiple influences on the allocation of attention. The interactive activation approach to perception and language processing (Rumelhart 1977; McClelland and Rumelhart 1981; McClelland 1987, 1991) is part of the background of this Attention and Performance meeting; Inui, Kawato, and Duncan provide complementary motivations for selecting an interactive approach.

Inui (chap. 1) notes the arrangement of the brain into separate areas, each apparently specialized for the representation of a particular type of information in a particular format, and points to the bidirectional connections between these areas as support for the idea that integration occurs through the bidirectional propagation of influences.

Kawato (chap. 14) is concerned with integration of constraints arising from the specification of a reaching task (e.g., move the tip of your finger from point A to point B in external space) and constraints arising from the motor system (e.g., make a movement that minimizes the total amount of change of the commands to the muscles). He argues that the computation of a movement sequence that jointly satisfies both sets of constraints is only possible if the different constraints are imposed on representations of the movement in different frames of references. The constraint to move from A to B must be imposed and evaluated in a frame of reference where the dimensions are the axes of external three-dimensional space, while the constraint to minimize the total amount of change in the commands to the muscles must be imposed on a representation of the movement in a frame of reference where the dimensions correspond to the motor commands to each of the muscles. Kawato argues that a computation that propagates constraints bidirectionally between these two frames of reference is the most efficient way to settle on a sequence of motor commands conforming to both sets of constraints. A similar argument for aspects of vision is alluded to by Inui (chap. 1).

Duncan's suggestion in chapter 21 that attention is an emergent property of an activation and competition process relies heavily on the idea that the propagation of influences on attention is bidirectional. One of the great attractions of this approach (and the precursor offered by Phaf, van der Heijden, and Hudson 1990) is that the architecture used for perceptual processing also provides the mechanism for the propagation of attentional influences. This proposal can be seen as a contemporary—and much more physiologically based—version of Neisser's (1967) suggestion that what is attended is essentially what is incorporated into the percept by the constructive process of perceptual interpretation.

Duncan's proposal seems to presuppose acceptance of an interactive account of constraint propagation. After reading chapter 16, however, we certainly cannot say that an interactive account is universally accepted; Massaro provides an extensive critique of the particular version of the interactive approach represented by the stochastic interactive activation model (McClelland 1991). Some of his particular points are addressed elsewhere (Movellan and McClelland 1995). Here I will just make one key observation.

It was shown in McClelland (1991) that the stochastic interactive activation model implements exactly the computations specified by Massaro's FLMP. McClelland's 1991 model differs from the original version (McClelland and Rumelhart 1981) in two ways. First, it assumes that the outcome of the interactive activation process is variable, either due to variability in the inputs to the interactive activation process or to inherent randomness in the processing itself, or both. Second, it assumes that response selection occurs by simply selecting the processing unit corresponding to the most active alternative—the one receiving the most support from the overall interactive activation process. The fact that the stochastic interactive activation model implements the computation prescribed by FLMP may seem surprising; it certainly contradicts the claim of Massaro (1989) that bidirectional propagation of activation cannot capture the independent influences of different sources of information. However, this result follows from well-known facts about the probability distributions over the possible states of stochastic, bidirectionally connected networks (e.g., Boltzmann machines), and from the limits imposed on these probability distributions by the architectural constraints built into the interactive activation model.

The architectural constraint that leads the interactive activation model to conform to the FLMP is worth understanding because it relates to questions about what sorts of brain architecture would be expected to lead to independence as captured by FLMP and what sorts of brain architecture would lead to strong interactions of different sources of constraint. The crucial variable is not a matter of whether there are bidirectional influences; it is instead a matter of whether the influences that act at a particular level are *structurally independent*. Two sources of influence are said to be structurally independent if there are no direct connections between the channels that carry these influences to the processing units representing the alternatives. Bidirectional connections into and out of the units representing the alternatives may allow the sources to influence each other, but only indirectly, via the units representing the alternatives. Structural independence is violated only if there are other ways in which the two sources of influence on the alternatives can influence each other. We can illustrate this notion of structural independence using the interactive activation model (fig. 24.1 depicts the model more completely and accurately than the more familiar figure from McClelland and Rumelhart 1981). Consider again the situation in which an observer has to make a choice between *e* and *c* as the interpretation of a particular target display character presented as the first element of a four-character display, where the remaining elements are _oin. In the interactive activation model, the target display

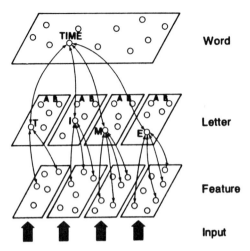

Figure 24.1 Interactive activation model of McClelland and Rumelhart (1981), showing four letter-processing channels each consisting of feature- and letter-level units, together with overarching word level. Units within rectangle are mutually inhibitory. Connections shown illustrate presence of bidirectional excitatory connections between mutually consistent features and letters, and between mutually consistent letters and words; only connections relevant to processing of single word "TIME" are shown. There is one unit for each letter-feature and each letter in each letter processing channel, and there is one unit for each word at word level. From McClelland (1985).

character and the context exert structurally independent influences on the units representing the letter alternatives in the first letter position: the units that carry information about the contents of the first display position to the alternatives have no direct connections with the units that carry information about the context. Interestingly, this independence is simultaneously true for all four letter positions. For each, the direct featural information and the contextual influences are structurally independent. It is also simultaneously true that at the word level, the contents of each letter position exert independent influences on each word alternative. Contextual influences arising from other sources that have structurally independent projections to the word level would likewise exert effects on word identification independent of those arising from the letter level.

What this argument shows, then, is that stochastic interactive activation implements an integration process simultaneously at different levels, and at different positions within a given level, and that the different sources of information exert their influences independently at all these different points in the processing system at the same time so long as these different sources are carried by structurally independent processing channels. Thus, it would appear that the stochastic interactive activation process, operating through bidirectional connections among units in networks that conform to the structural independence assumption, could represent the desired implementation of Massaro's FLMP.[2]

With this result in hand, we can now ask, why should the perceptual processing system ever adhere to the principle of structural independence? If processing is interactive, why should the interactions ever be constrained in this way? Is this, in fact, a residual form of imposed architectural modularity? Even though activation can propagate bidirectionally, so that higher-level influences can affect lower levels, the computation is nevertheless still tightly disciplined. Perhaps this limited form of interactive propagation of activation is structurally imposed by the brain to control the complexity of neural computation?

Structurally imposed constraints on interactive activation are certainly apparent in the brain; indeed, the topographic organization of many areas of the brain, and the fact that the propagation of information between maps maintains independence between moderately separated locations within each map, seem to suggest that there is some imposed modularity. However, it is worth noting that the topographic organization is refined and maintained by adaptive synaptic modification processes. Even if one begins with much fuller connectivity, adaptive synaptic modification processes will lead to structural independence where this reflects an actual statistical independence in the environment (Linsker 1986; Miller, Keller, and Stryker 1989). Structural independence may thus arise through adaptive connection modification processes in cases where the sources of constraint actually are conditionally independent. In this view, the ultimate basis for independence lies in the structure of the environment.

We finally turn to *the intrinsic integration view* with these considerations as context. This view was not discussed by any of the participants at Attention and Performance XVI, but it has become a force in connectionist circles since the advent of powerful learning algorithms such as backpropagation. As previously noted, the key insight to emerge from this connectionist work is the realization that standard cognitive units (letters, words, phrases, schemata, etc.) may be only descriptive conveniences, applied to characterize emergent properties of processing systems rather than reified directly within them. This idea is represented in connectionist models that span a range of specific applications (Elman 1990; Elman and Zipser 1987; Golden 1986; Rumelhart et al. 1986; St. John and McClelland 1990; Van Orden, Pennington, and Stone 1990). The burden of the simulations is to show how behavior thought to indicate the existence of various sorts of cognitive units can arise from a network with minimal prior structural commitments through an adaptive learning process. In this view, letters, words, and phrases do not exist on separate levels but are simply the coherent and relatively independent subpatterns of larger, more coherent whole patterns. Likewise, conceptually distinct types of constraints, such as syntactic versus semantic constraints on sentence structure or lexical versus phonotactic constraints on phoneme identity, are not reified in architectural distinctions in such models. Several models of this type (Golden 1986; Shillcock et al. 1992; St. John and Gernsbacher 1995) have been able to account for a number of findings previously accounted for by more structured interactive networks that honor the units and levels of the classicists.

Evidence from physiology might help determine to what extent different levels of description of structure offered by psychologists and linguists are represented separately in the brain, and to what extent they communicate bidirectionally. This evidence may be available for constraints on perception and action, which can be studied in primates but is more limited where the function in question only exists in humans, as in the case of language. There is a vast literature on the neuropsychology of language, together with a growing body of studies of language in the brain based on the use of non-invasive techniques, but the limitations of these methods leave considerable room for uncertainty about the representations used. One of the findings reported by Kutas and King (chap. 20) using event-related potentials (ERPs) illustrates some of the difficulties. Kutas and King found that variations in syntactic complexity lead to differences in brain activity recorded at frontal cites. But these findings do not tell us whether the actual computation of complex constructions occurs in frontal areas, or whether they indicate a generalized frontal response to variations in task difficulty. The authors are therefore cautious in their interpretation of the meaning of their findings for the functional organization of language processing.

In any case, as already suggested, the organization of the visual and somatosensory areas of the brain appears to suggest a great deal of discipline to the interactions among processing units. It is clearly not the case that the brain is, as Touretzky (personal communication) once put it, an "undifferenti-ated mass of connectoplasm," nor did it start that way at birth, to be shaped only by the structure present in experience. At the same time, however, evidence of sensitivity to structure in the behavior of a system should not necessarily be taken to mean that descriptive constructs such as phonemes and words will necessarily be reflected in hard-wired processing structures of the sort suggested by the interactive activation models.

Representations for Integration

Are there supramodal representations for integration across modalities, or is integration merely mutual constraint between modality- or dimension-specific representations?

Some of the most exciting ideas and findings reported at Attention and Performance XVI relate to this question. Introspection suggests to many people that we maintain a single, stable representation of the external world across fixations. Auditory, tactile, and visual inputs all contribute to the contents of this representation and so it seems to be supramodal in some sense, and it seems plausible that many of the examples of information integration reviewed in the chapters in this volume could arise from conver-gence of influences on this stable representation from different sources. Yet several of the papers presented at Attention and Performance XVI suggest a rather different conception of what may be happening in the brain. Instead of maintaining a supramodal representation for the integration of multiple sources of information, the brain may instead maintain many separate representations, each with its own frame of references that interactively constrain each other.

Both Colby (chap. 7) and Graziano and Gross (chap. 8) propose versions of this multiple coordinated reference frames view. A key aspect of this view is the notion that as each body part moves relative to other parts, and as the body moves relative to external space, the brain continually adjusts the mapping between these reference frames, and continually updates each representation to track the locations of objects in each. While the remapping process may seem complex, it has one beautiful result—it allows us to know where external objects are with respect to different parts of our body. If this information is given, the computation of the movement that must be made to bring an object into contact with a particular body part is greatly simplified.

Striking evidence of the remapping process is reported by Graziano and Gross (chap. 8), who recorded from neurons that represent the presence of an object in a receptive field defined with respect to one of the monkey's limbs. As the limb moves, stationary objects in the environment may come in and out of this receptive field. Likewise, as the eye moves, the region of retinocentric space that corresponds to the receptive field of the neuron continually changes. Thus locations in both allocentric and retinocentric space are continually remapped to locations in the limb-centered frame of reference. Graziano and Gross and Colby (chap. 7) both suggest that there may be neurons that code positions of objects with respect to many different body parts— amounting perhaps to scores of parallel and coordinated frames of reference!

A further, crucial finding described by Colby in chapter 7 is the observation that as the animal gets ready to initiate a movement of the body part in question, remapping can occur in anticipation of the effect of the movement—and neurons begin to fire in anticipation of targets that will be in their receptive field after the movement, Thus far, this demonstration has only been made with neurons that encode the locations of target stimuli with respect to the direction of gaze of the eyes. It will be interesting to see if such anticipatory remapping also occurs in other coordinate systems.

What signals enable the remapping process? The finding of Roll et al. (chap. 12) that movement illusions (apparent motion of a body part or of stimuli in extrapersonal space) can be induced by proprioceptive stimulation suggests that proprioception contributes to the remapping process; another source or remapping is "efference copy," recurrent feedback of the motor command. However, anticipatory remappings cannot reflect proprioception. Even efference copy is suspect an a source, though it could provide the relevant information if "intention" is coded neurally in terms of low-rate, anticipatory firing of the same neurons that will ultimately trigger the movement.

Exactly how coordination is maintained between effector-specific references frames remains somewhat obscure. Graziano and Gross (chap. 8) do not
deny there may be brain areas that maintain a representation of the observer's
place within an allocentric reference frame, but it plays no privileged or
crucial role for them in mediating between other frames of reference; rather, it
is just one of the many representations that is continually remapped like all of
the others. The authors do note that there are areas in the parietal lobes
where vision, touch, and proprioception come together, but they do not
identify them with specific frames of reference. One possibility is that these
areas capture conjunctions of inputs that are useful for mapping between
frames of reference, much as hidden units would in a connectionist network.

Dimensions for Integration

Are there dimensions that provide a strong organizing frame for integration?
Are time and space examples of such dimensions?

Findings relevant to these questions come from a number of the papers
presented at Attention and Performance XVI. I will consider the use of time
together with the role of attention in the next section. The use of space as
an organizing frame for integration is partially addressed by the answer to
the previous question. It appears that there may be many spatial frames of
reference all in use at one time, and constraints may be integrated simultaneously within each (cf. the discussion of Kawato's ideas on the integration of
constraints in extrinsic and muscle command coordinate systems in section
24.2.3).

A perspective that at first may seem to contradict the idea that constraints
are integrated in spatial frames of reference emerges in chapter 6, by Irwin
and Andrews. Summarizing twenty years of research on integration of information over successive fixations in vision, Irwin and Andrews note that there
is considerable evidence of integration of information over successive fixations, but that this integration appears not to occur within a common spatial
frame of reference that survives across eye movements. As evidence of this,
they note that integration proceeds just as well, whether or not the stimuli
giving rise to the information in the first fixation maintain their spatial position after the eye movement. Integration is even unaffected by alteration of
the physical form of the stimulus carrying the constraining information. The
authors cite evidence that partial information obtained from a parafoveal
presentation of a word on one fixation can facilitate the identification of the
same word when it is fixated after an eye movement, whether or not the
parafoveal and target presentations maintain a fixed position in external
space, and whether or not the word switches from uppercase to lowercase
type between fixations. The implication is that integration takes place via the
accumulation over fixations of constraints on the abstract identity of items,

independent of details of the exact form and spatial location of the stimulus that is the source of these constraints.

Within the context of the proposals of Graziano and Gross (chap. 8), these findings suggest that integration for the specification of the identity of objects occurs within a representational system quite different from the representational systems used to maintain information about the locations of objects in space relative to the body. This suggestion is consistent with the notion that there are separate processing streams for "what" and "where" (as Ungerleider and Mishkin, 1982, put it) or for "what" and "how" (as Goodale, chap. 15, and others in this volume put it), and that integration of "what" information takes place in a representation specifically structured to combine constraints on object identity, just as other representations are specifically structured to combine different sources of constraint on the spatial locations of objects relative to a particular body part. It must be added, however, that considerable work remains to be done to understand how the brain maintains coordination of information in these different representations.

Attention and Integration

What role does attention play in the integration of information?

It may be fitting to end our consideration of a symposium of the Society for Attention and Performance that focused on the integration of information with a consideration of the role of attention in information integration. As Duncan (chap. 21) stresses, every act of attention is an act of selection of some information and suppression of other sources. What purpose does this selection serve? Several of the contributors to this volume have advanced our understanding of this issue.

In Treisman's (1988) feature integration theory (FIT), attention is necessary to select the attributes of a single object so that they may be joined together into a single percept, represented separately from the features of other objects. A key aspect of Treisman's idea is that feature integration requires the sequential allocation of attention to just one object at a time. Each sequential act of attention selects the features of a single object and binds them together, opening an "object file" for the object. The file becomes a basis for immediate report of the features of the object as well as a record of the object in long term memory.

In response to Inui's question on the role of time in information integration (chap. 1), we can observe that in FIT, the activation of two features at the same time causes both to be entered into the object file; the only thing that prevents false conjunctions is the allocation of attention to a single object at a time. Thus time becomes the basis for conjoining features together into object representations.

The idea that time and attention play a special role in forming object representations has now been extended considerably by Hummel and

Stankiewicz (chap. 5). According to their model, there are two forms of perceptual processing of an object: a fast, initial, parallel form of processing that is capable of serving as the basis of recognition if the object has been seen before from the very same viewpoint; and a much slower, inherently time-dependent process, in which a structural description of the object is built up over time by considering each part, and its relation to the object as a whole, in succession. Segmentation itself occurs through a constraint-satisfaction process, in which elements that go together to form a coherent part mutually reinforce each other's activation and suppress simultaneous activation of elements belonging to other parts. In this way, the time over which attention is directed toward an object as a whole comes to be divided into shorter intervals, with attention cycling over the objects' parts across these shorter intervals.

The two modes of processing in the Hummel and Stankiewicz theory have strong parallels to the two modes of processing attested in FIT, where it is assumed that parallel processing can be used to detect the presence of a target, as long as that target is defined as a single feature, rather than a specific conjunction of features that must co-occur together in the same location (see Cohen and Ivry, chap. 22, for an exploration of evidence relevant to these ideas from studies of visual search among orientations and directions of movement). Sequential attention is only necessary to establish the correct bindings of features together in the same object. Much the same applies to the theory of Hummel and Stankiewicz, but with one interesting and important difference. In their model, the parallel processing of an entire object gives rise to a representation that is scale- and translation-invariant, though not invariant with respect to rotation. The representation captures the global shape of the object as a whole and of the shapes and relative locations of its parts, as seen from the observer's viewpoint. This extends the power of the parallel processing mechanism considerably beyond its original conception in FIT, allowing it to provide a basis for accurate recognition of familiar objects seen from familiar viewpoints.

The notion that the initial parallel processing of an item may establish at least a primitive representation of the object is consistent with the findings from the new work reported in Treisman's Association Lecture (Treisman and DeSchepper, chap. 2). They find that just one presentation of an object, even when it is not the focus of attention, gives rise to object specific aftereffects that can persist for many weeks. Because these aftereffects dissociate completely from explicit recognition memory, we would not want to identify them with the formation of an explicit episodic memory for the unattended object. Instead, in keeping with other interpretations of implicit perceptual learning phenomena, we might view them as aftereffects within the perceptual processing system itself.

The suggestion that parallel processing of a display may be more powerful and structured than had previously been thought brings us back again to the question of the need for focal attention. Both Treisman and DeSchepper (chap. 2) and Hummel and Stankiewicz (chap. 5) discuss the possibility that the perceptual processing of unattended objects may be incomplete. The results of Treisman and DeSchepper indicate that focal attention may also be necessary to form an explicit episodic memory. Given that such memories involve the integration of the representation of an object with the situation in which it occurs as well as its relation to the subject as experiencer (Tulving 1983), it may be best to consider these representations constructed within the focus of attention, not as disembodied "object files," but as conjunctive representations of the object in association with other aspects of the external and internal context represented in the distributed pattern of activation that corresponds to whatever is within the span of the subject's attention at the time the object is experienced. It appears that such episodic memories are initially formed in the hippocampus, where the state of activation over all of the higher-level representation systems of the brain may be brought together and interassociated via rapid synaptic modification (see McClelland, McNaughton, and O'Reilly 1995 for a recent discussion of this possibility).

24.3 CONCLUSION

The theme of integration of information in perception, language, attention, and action is very broad, and any attempt to summarize the state of our knowledge about it is surely doomed to oversimplification. Suffice it to say in concluding these reflections that the study of information integration within and across domains suggests many common principles and many issues that deserve much fuller consideration. Attention and Performance XVI certainly did not settle all the issues. I think Toshio Inui would join me in the hope that the meeting and this volume have brought out what the most significant issues are, together with some of the most promising directions that are being pursued to address them.

NOTES

Preparation of this chapter was supported by grants MH00385 and MH47566 from the National Institute of Mental Health. I thank Toshio Inui and David Plaut for comments on the first draft. Correspondence concerning this article may be sent to the author at the Department of Psychology, Carnegie Mellon University, Pittsburgh, PA 15213, or via E-mail to mcclelland + @cmu.edu.

1. In general, hidden units—units that do not correspond directly to features—may be required if such a model is to be able to learn each word as a separate attractor in a way that successfully mimics the interactive models. However, it is not at all clear that these hidden units will correspond to letters or words per se, or that it would necessarily make sense to view them as constituting a separate level of representation, "above" the feature level.

2. In fact, the architecture of the interactive activation model specifically predicts that some sources of influence on the selection among certain alternatives will not be independent. Consider the influence of separate manipulation of the context letters in positions 2, 3, and 4 on forced-choice identification of the letter in position 1. Because the context letters all

interact with each other at the word level, their influences are not generally expected to be independent. Movellan and McClelland (1995) have confirmed that independence is violated in just these conditions.

REFERENCES

Bever, T. G. (1970). The cognitive basis for linguistic structure. In J. R. Hayes (Ed.), *Cognition and the development of language*, 279–362. New York: Wiley.

Chomsky, N. (1980). Rules and representations. *Behavioral and Brain Sciences, 3*, 1–61.

Clifton, C., and Ferreira, F. (1989). Ambiguity in context. *Language and Cognitive Processes, 4*(SI), 77–104.

Elman, J. L. (1990). Finding structure in time. *Cognitive Science, 14*, 179–211.

Elman, J. L., and Zipser, D. (1987). *Discovering the hidden structure of speech.* Technical report 8701. San Diego: University of California, Institute for Cognitive Science.

Fodor, J. A. (1983). *Modularity of mind: An essay on faculty psychology.* Cambridge, MA: MIT Press.

Fodor, J. A., and Pylyshyn, Z. W. (1988). Connectionism and cognitive architecture: A critical analysis. *Cognition, 28*, 3–71.

Golden, R. M. (1986). A developmental neural model of visual word recognition. *Cognitive Science, 10*, 241–276.

Hinton, G. E. (Ed.). (1991). *Connectionist symbol processing.* Cambridge, MA: MIT Press.

Hopfield, J. J. (1982). Neural networks and physical systems with emergent collective computational abilities. *Proceedings of the National Academy of Sciences, 79*, 2554–2558.

Jordan, M. I. (1986). Attractor dynamics and parallelism in a connectionist sequential machine. In *Proceedings of the 8th Annual Conference of the Cognitive Science Society*, 531–546. Hillsdale, NJ: Erlbaum.

Jordan, M. I., and Rumelhart, D. E. (1992). Forward models: Supervised learning with a distal teacher. *Cognitive Science, 16*(3), 307–354.

Just, M. A., and Carpenter, R. A. (1992). A capacity theory of comprehension: Individual differences in working memory. *Psychological Review, 99*, 122–149.

Linsker, R. (1986). From basic network principles to neural architecture: Emergence of spatial-opponent cells. *Proceedings of the National Academy of Sciences, 83*, 7508–7512.

Luria, A. R. (1966). *Higher cortical functions in man.* New York: Basic Books.

Luria, A. R. (1973). *The working brain.* New York: Penguin.

Marcus, M. P. (1980). *A theory of syntactic recognition for natural language.* Cambridge, MA: MIT Press.

Marr, D. (1982). *Vision.* San Francisco: W. H. Freeman.

Marslen-Wilson, W. D. (1987). Functional parallelism in spoken word recognition. *Cognition, 25*, 71–102.

Massaro, D. W. (1989). Testing between the TRACE model and the fuzzy logical model of speech perception. *Cognitive Psychology, 21*, 398–421.

McClelland, J. L. (1976). Preliminary letter identification in the perception of words and nonwords. *Journal of Experimental Psychology: Human Perception and Performance, 2*, 80–91.

McClelland, J. L. (1979). On the time relations of mental processes: An examination of systems of processes in cascade. *Psychological Review, 86,* 287–330.

McClelland, J. L. (1985). Putting knowledge in its place: A scheme for programming parallel processing structures on the fly. *Cognitive Science, 9,* 113–146.

McClelland, J. L. (1987). The case for interactionism in language processing. In M. Coltheart (Ed.), *Attention and performance XII: The psychology of reading,* 1–36. London: Erlbaum.

McClelland, J. L. (1991). Stochastic interactive activation and the effect of context on perception. *Cognitive Psychology, 23,* 1–44.

McClelland, J. L., McNaughton, B. L., and O'Reilly, R. C. (1995). Why there are complementary learning systems in the hippocampus and neocortex: Insights from the successes and failures of connectionist models of teaming and memory. *Psychological Review, 102,* 419–457.

McClelland, J. L., and Rumelhart, D. E. (1981). An interactive activation model of context effects in letter perception. I. An account of basic findings. *Psychological Review, 88*(5), 375–407.

McClelland, J. L., and Rumelhart, D. E. (1985). Distributed memory and the representation of general and specific information. *Journal of Experimental Psychology: General, 114,* 159–188.

Miller, G. (1962). Some psychological studies of grammar. *American Psychologist, 17,* 748–762.

Miller, K. D., Keller, J. B., and Stryker, M. P. (1989). Ocular dominance column development: Analysis and simulation. *Science, 245,* 605–615.

Morton, J. (1969). The interaction of information in word recognition. *Psychological Review, 76,* 165–178.

Movellan, J. R., and McClelland, J. L. (1995). Stochastic interactive activation, Morton's Law, and optimal pattern recognition. Technical Report PDP.CNS.95.4. Pittsburgh: Department of Psychology, Carnegie Mellon University.

Neisser, U. (1967). *Cognitive psychology.* New York: Appleton, Century Croft.

Paap, K. R., Newsome, S. L., McDonald, J. E., and Schvaneveldt, R. W. (1982). An activation-verification model of letter and word recognition: The word superiority effect. *Psychological Review, 89,* 573–594.

Phaf, R. H., van der Heijden, A. H. C., and Hudson, P. T. W. (1990). SLAM: A connectionist model for attention in visual selection tasks. *Cognitive Psychology, 22,* 273–341.

Rumelhart, D. E. (1977). Toward an interactive model of reading. In S. Dornic (Ed.), *Attention and performance VI,* 573–603. Hillsdale, NJ: Erlbaum.

Rumelhart, D. E., Smolensky, P., McClelland, J. L., and Hinton, G. E. (1986). Schemata and sequential thought processes in PDP models. In J. L. McClelland, D. E. Rumelhart, and the PDP Research Group (Eds.), *Parallel distributed processing: Explorations in the microstructure of cognition.* Vol. 2, *Psychological and biological models,* 7–57. Cambridge, MA: MIT Press.

Shillcock, R., Lindsey, G., Levy, J., and Chater, N. (1992). A phonologically motivated input representation for modeling of auditory word perception in continuous speech. In *Proceedings of the Fourteenth Annual Conference of the Cognitive Science Society,* 408–413. Hillsdale, NJ: Erlbaum.

Simpson, G. B. (1981). Meaning dominance and semantic context in the processing of lexical ambiguity. *Journal of Verbal Learning and Verbal Behavior, 20,* 120–136.

Sopena, J. M. (1991). *ERSP: A distributed connectionist parser that uses embedded sequences to represent structure.* Technical report UB-PB-1-91. Barcelona: Department de Psicologia Basica, Universitat de Barcelona.

St. John, M. F., and Gernsbacher, M. A. (1995). Syntactic comprehension: Practice makes perfect and frequency makes fleet. In *Proceedings of the Seventeenth Annual Conference of the Cognitive Science Society*. Hillsdale, NJ: Erlbaum.

St. John, M. F., and McClelland, J. L. (1990). Learning and applying contextual constraints in sentence comprehension. *Artificial Intelligence, 46, 46*, 217–257.

Swinney, D. A. (1979). Lexical access during sentence comprehension: (Re)consideration of context effects. *Journal of Verbal Learning and Verbal Behavior, 18*, 645–659.

Taraban, R., and McClelland, J. L. (1988). Constituent attachment and thematic role assignment in sentence processing: Influences of content-based expectations. *Journal of Memory and Language, 27*, 597–632.

Teitelbaum, P. (1967). *Physiological psychology; Fundamental principles*. Englewood Cliffs, NJ: Prentice-Hall.

Treisman, A. M. (1964). Verbal cues, language, and meaning in selective attention. *American Journal of Psychology, 77*, 206–219.

Treisman, A. (1988). Features and Objects: The Fourteenth Bartlett Memorial Lecture. *Quarterly Journal of Experimental Psychology, 40A*, 201–237.

Tulving, E. (1983). *Elements of episodic memory*. New York: Oxford University Press.

Ungerleider, L. G., and Mishkin, M. (1982). Two cortical visual systems. In D. J. Ingli,. M. A. Goodale, and R. J. W. Mansfield (Eds.), *Analysis of sisual behavior*. Cambridge, MA: MIT Press.

Van Orden, G. C., Pennington, B. F., and Stone, G. O. (1990). Word identification in reading and the promise of subsymbolic psycholinguistics. *Psychological Review, 97*(4), 488–522.

Author Index

Oran, M. W., 380
O'Regan, J. K., 126, 127, 532, 534
O'Reilly, R. C., 653
O'Scalaidhe, S. P., 505
O'Seaghdha, P. G., 453n
Osterhout, L., 512
Osu, R., 357, 359
O'Toole, A., 67
Otto, T., 201

Paap, K. R., 399, 642
Palmer, J., 127
Palmer, S., 33
Palmer, S. E., 94, 127
Palumbo, C., 509
Pandya, D. N., 182, 200, 202, 353
Paquet, L., 113
Pareschi, R., 497
Parisi, G., 52
Parker, A. J., 80
Parker, S., 266, 283
Parkes, K. R., 23
Parthasarathy, H. B., 181
Pashler, H., 570, 580, 601
Paul, D., 67
Pavesi, G., 197
Payne, J. W., 80
Pearlmutter, N., 458, 476
Pearlmutter, N. J., 435, 436, 439, 440, 442,
   443, 444, 445, 446, 453n, 481
Peck, C. K., 196, 197
Pedotti, A., 190, 196, 197, 257
Pelisson, D., 382, 383
Penfield, W., 508
Pennington, B. F., 647
Pentland, A., 58, 60
Pentland, A. P., 3, 94
Perani, D., 562, 568
Perenin, M.-T., 372, 378
Perfetti, C. A., 442, 443, 481, 530
Perrett, D. I., 6, 97, 370, 380
Peru, A., 598, 599
Petersen, S. E., 242, 526, 527, 531, 549, 551,
   559
Peterson, M. A., 31
Pfaf, R. H., 644
Pfurtscheller, G., 509, 510
Phaf, R. H., 551, 552, 571
Phillips, R. J., 80
Picton, T. W., 511, 525
Pierce, L., 626
Pierson, J. M., 222
Pigarev, I. N., 158, 190, 197

Pinker, S., 6, 93, 95, 115, 485
Pisoni. D., 413
Pitt, M. A., 404, 405, 406, 408, 423, 424
Platt, J. R., 402
Plum, F., 502
Pocock, P. V., 513
Podotti, A., 158
Poeck, K., 509
Poggio, T., 3, 51, 54, 64, 95, 98, 114
Pola, J., 169
Polit, A., 328, 338
Pollack, J. B., 6
Pollard, S., 53
Pollatsek, A., 126, 128
Ponzoni-Maggi, S., 158, 159
Pook, P. K., 461
Popper, K., 402
Poranen, A., 157, 380
Porrill, J., 73
Posner, M. I., 172, 210, 242, 249, 250, 284,
   526, 531, 551, 558, 559, 562, 572, 598,
   601, 604, 607n, 611, 626, 627n
Potter, M. C., 97, 448
Potts, B. C., 264, 265, 266, 268, 274
Powell, T. P. S., 200, 202
Prablanc, C., 382, 383
Prakash, C., 398
Pribram, K. H., 380
Prinzmetal, W., 266
Pritchett, B. L., 482
Prud'homme, M., 307
Putz, P., 512
Pylyshyn, Z. W., 484, 640

Quest, D. O., 265
Quinlan, P. T., 95
Quinn, J. T., Jr., 329

Racicot, C. I., 373, 374, 378
Rafal, R., 210, 212–213
Rafal, R. D., 231, 558, 562, 604, 606, 611,
   626
Raichle, M. E., 526, 527
Rakowitz, S., 483, 484, 487, 494, 495
Ramachandran, V. S., 5
Rankin, K. M., 267, 283
Ratcliff, G., 202
Ratcliffe, R., 34
Rawlins, J. N. P., 201
Raymond, J. E., 569
Rayner, K., 125, 126, 128, 434, 438, 442,
   443, 444, 480, 481
Reber, A. S., 492

Terazzi, E., 370
Terry, K. M., 598, 599
Teuber, H. L., 212, 304, 308
Thomas, E. C., 283
Thomas, L., 562
Thomas, S., 380
Thommassen, A. J. W. M., 327
Thompson, H., 401
Thompson, L. W., 213, 222
Thorson, J., 239
Tipper, S. P., 18, 23, 31, 38, 42, 113, 114, 159, 598
Todd, J. T., 80
Tolls, E. T., 97, 109
Torre, V., 3, 51, 64
Toth, J. P., 27, 35
Tovee, M. J., 97, 109
Townsend, D. J., 539n
Townsend, J. T., 569
Townsend, V. M., 136
Trehub, A., 126
Treisman, A., 4, 15, 16, 17, 35, 39, 41, 42, 113, 125, 129, 130, 150, 210, 231, 232, 568, 639, 651
Treisman, A. M., 568–569, 579, 580, 581, 583, 585, 586, 591, 594n, 606, 639
Treves, A., 97, 109
Trueswell, J., 466, 481
Trueswell, J. C., 435, 436, 441, 442, 443, 444, 445, 456n, 457, 458, 481
Tsal, Y., 42
Tucker, D. M., 526
Tukmachi, E. S., 526
Tulving, E., 6, 653
Turvey, M. T., 321, 322
Tversky, B., 142
Tyler, L. K., 401, 413

Ullman, S., 95, 97, 98, 114, 581, 582, 583
Umiltà, C., 624
Ungeleider, L. G., 609, 627n
Ungerleider, I. G., 198
Ungerleider, L., 562
Ungerleider, L. G., 198, 240, 372, 373, 380, 549, 554, 559, 568, 651
Ungerleider, L. G., 159
Uno, Y., 322, 336, 337, 338, 341, 342, 344, 349, 356, 357, 359, 360, 362, 363, 364, 365
Urbano, A., 197
Uttal, W. R., 212

Valdes, L. A., 31, 598, 599
Vallar, G., 558, 562, 568

Vallbo, A. B., 305
van der Heijden, A. H. C., 551, 552, 571, 597, 644
van Doorn, A., 53
van Doorn, A. J., 75, 77, 82, 85
Van Doren, C. L., 283
Van Essen, D. C., 8, 114, 200, 242, 508, 590
Van Hoesen, G. W., 182, 200
Van Orden, G. C., 647
Van Petten, C., 511, 513, 514, 519, 526, 539n
Van Rensbergen, J., 127
Vatikiotis Bateson, E., 352
Vaughan, J., 318, 321, 323, 324, 325, 326, 328, 329
Vedel, J. P., 293, 296, 305
Velay, J. L., 293, 296, 308, 310–311
Vercher, J. L., 311
Verfaillie, K., 127
Vetter, T., 114
Videen, T. O., 526
Vighetto, A., 372, 378
Virzi, R. A., 579, 591
von der Malsburg, C., 95, 96, 97
von Grunau, M., 239
Von Helmholtz, H., 67
Vriezen, E., 34

Wada, Y., 350, 352, 353
Walker, J. A., 201, 558, 562, 611, 626
Walker, J. T., 267
Wall, S., 579
Wallace, M. T., 549
Walley, R. E., 552
Wallin, B. G., 293
Waltz, D. L., 6
Wang, J., 445
Ward, L. M., 210
Ward, P. B., 514
Ward, R., 569, 570
Wardell, J., 265
Warner, E., 264, 266–267, 280
Warren, P., 413, 414
Warrington, E. E., 605
Warrington, E. K., 17
Watanabe, F., 359
Watanabe, K., 186
Watanabe, T., 283
Waxman, A. M., 114
Weaver, B., 31, 159, 598
Weber, E. H., 265
Weber, J. T., 182, 200
Weiden, T. D., 552
Weinrich, M., 182, 197

Subject Index

Bidirectional neural network, 349
Bidirectional theory, 336
Bimodal cells, 182–197
Binding, 4, 95, 96, 101
Binocular convergence, 240
Body-part centered coordinates, 182, 190, 196–197
Bottom-up attention, 240, 241
Brain areas, 508, 526
　extrastriate visual, 508, 526
　language, 508
　size of, 508
　total number of, 508
Brain systems, 549–578
Broca's area, 507–508
Button pressing, as a response, 599

Capacity, limited, 597
Categorical structure, 51, 64
Cerebellum, 348
Cerebral cortex, 507–509
　Brodmann's parcellation of, 508
　and lack of association areas, 507
　occipitotemporal region, 526–528
　superior temporal gyrus, 527
　surface area of, 508
Clause boundaries, 531
Clauses, relative, 532–536
Coarticulation, 327, 417
Cohort, 462–466
Competitive priors, 60–64
Competitive processing, 549–578
Completion, amodal, 63–64
Comprehension, spoken language, 457–477
Computer vision, 65
Connectionist models, 484–486
Conscious processing, 16
Constraint models, 475–476
Constraint satisfaction, 481–482, 496, 652
Constraint-based models, 458, 460, 461, 466, 476
　lexicalist, 460, 476
Constraints, natural, 60
Construction, 640–641
Context, 52, 60–64
　and ambiguity, 458–461
　and language comprehension, 457–477
　and language processing, 458–461
　effects of, 514
　lexical, 403–404
　phonological, 408–409
　referential, 475–476, 481, 496
　sentence, 413–416

Contrastive focus, 471–472, 474
Contrastive stress, 472–474
Contrast set, 472, 474
Cooperative process, 58
Coordinate systems, multiple simultaneous, 649–650
Coordinate transformation, 171, 335
Coordinates, 243–258
　body-part centered, 182, 190, 196–197
　environmental, 246, 248, 250
　remap, 254, 255, 256, 258
　retinal, 243, 250
　retinotopic, 250, 251, 252, 256, 258
　spatial, and attention, 213, 230–232
　spatiotopic, 257
Corollary discharge, 171
Correlated constraints, 458, 461
Cortical processing, early, 606
Coupling, strong, 55
Coupling, weak, 55
Covert shift of attention, 172
Cross-modal attention, 252, 254
Cross-modal integration, 564
　and attention, 210, 230–232
Cross-modal spatial map, 255, 256, 258
Cross-modal transfer. See Transfer, cross-modal
Cue combination, 57
Cue integration, 49–70, 71–89
Cues, 252–258
　auditory, 252, 253, 255, 256
　non-visual, 252–258
　somatosensory, 252–258
Cue-target distinction, 598
Curved paths, 356

D.F., 370–380
Definiteness, 471
Definite noun phrases and reference, 468
Delay, 20–21
Detection, 597, 607
Dimensions, 579–594
　motion, 580–588, 590–594
　orientation, 580–581, 586–587, 589–592, 594
　velocity, 593
Discourse, 458
Discourse representation, 503
Discrimination, 597–607
Disengagement, of attention, 611
Dissociation of two visual functions, 597
Distributed code, 199
Distributed processing, 549–578